The **Rough**

D0558714

Nepal

written and researched by

James McConnachie and David Reed

with contributions from

Arnaud Galent, Emily Haslam-Jones and Shafik Meghji

ROUGH
GUIDES

www.roughguides.com

Contents

The people of Nepal
colour section
following p.240

The pace of change
colour section
following p.432

◄◄ Temple, Dakshinkali ◄ The Himalayas

Introduction to
Nepal

Nepal forms the very watershed of Asia. Landlocked between India and Tibet, it reaches from subtropical jungle to the icy Himalayas, and contains or shares eight of the world's ten highest mountains. Its cultural landscape is every bit as diverse: a dozen major ethnic groups, speaking as many as fifty languages and dialects, coexist in this narrow, jumbled buffer state, while two of the world's great religions, Hinduism and Buddhism, mingle with nature-worship and shamanic practices.

 Yet it's a testimony to Nepali tolerance and good humour that there's no tradition of ethnic or religious strife. Nepal was never colonized, a fact which comes through in fierce national pride and other, more idiosyncratic ways. Founded on trans-Himalayan trade, its dense, medieval cities display unique pagoda-style architecture, not to mention an astounding flair for festivals and pageantry. Above all, though, Nepal is a nation of unaffected villages and terraced countryside – some eighty percent of the population lives off the land – and whether you're trekking, biking or bouncing around in packed buses, sampling this rural lifestyle is perhaps the greatest pleasure of all.

But it would be misleading to portray Nepal as a fabled Shangri-la. Heavily reliant on its superpower neighbours, Nepal was, until 1990, one of the world's last remaining absolute monarchies, run by a regime that combined China's repressiveness and India's bureaucracy. Long politically and economically backward, it has developed at uncomfortable speed in some areas while stagnating in others, all the time undergoing bewilderingly rapid political change. Since 1990, it has passed from constitutional

monarchy to multi-party democracy and back. Following a wearying Maoist insurgency, which ended in 2006, it seems to have ended up as a federal republic – governed, for the time at least, by former Maoist rebels. Nepal seems always to be racing to catch up with history, and the sense of political excitement in the country is thrillingly palpable.

Travel within Nepal can be unpredictable. A handful of tourist areas are highly developed, even overdeveloped, but facilities elsewhere are rudimentary, and **getting around** is time-consuming and often uncomfortable. Nepalis are well used to shrugging off such inconveniences with the all-purpose, *Ke garne?* (What to do?) – a phrase and a mindset that many travellers quickly adopt.

Fact file

• With a land **area** of 147,000 square kilometres, Nepal is about the size of England and Wales combined. Usable land, however, is in short supply thanks to the precipitous terrain and a growing population of some 28 million, over a third of which is under 15 years old.

• Prior to 1951, only a few hundred outsiders had visited Nepal. Today, the country receives as many as 500,000 **tourists** annually, most of them from neighbouring India.

• Despite the fame of its Buddhist communities, Nepal was long the world's only Hindu kingdom, and Hindus still officially make up some eighty percent of the population – though many Nepalis combine Hindu, Buddhist, shamanic and animist practices.

• The decade-long **Maoist insurgency** ended in 2006, along with the career of the notorious King Gyanendra, but Nepal's politics remain volatile.

• With a per-capita annual **income** of US$470, Nepal ranked 145th out of 153 countries in the UN's 2008 Human Development Index. A quarter of the population lives on less than a dollar a day, and more than one in twenty children die before they reach their fifth birthday.

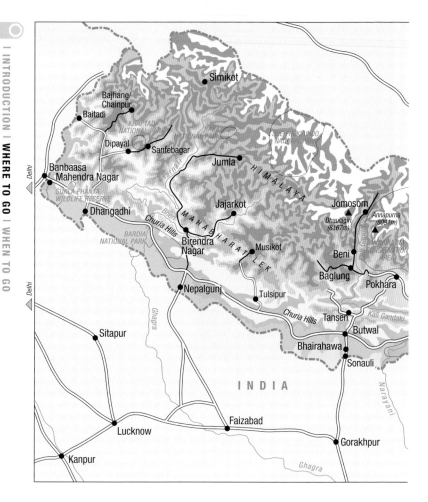

Where to go

Everyone touches down in **Kathmandu** at some point, but for all its exotic bustle, the capital is rather rough-going these days – logistically it makes a good base, but you won't want to spend lots of time here. Hindu temples, Buddhist stupas, rolling countryside and huddled brick villages provide incentives for touring the prosperous **Kathmandu Valley**, as do the historically independent city-states of **Patan** and **Bhaktapur**. The surrounding central hills are surprisingly undeveloped, apart from a couple of mountain view-points, while a few lesser routes, such as the road to the **Tibet border** and the

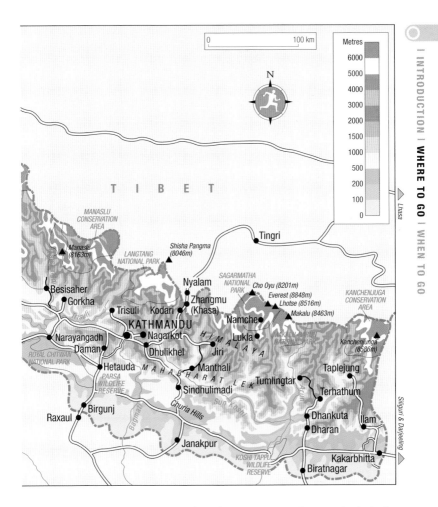

Tribhuwan Rajpath, make for adventurous travel – particularly by mountain bike or motorcycle.

The views get more dramatic, or at least more accessible, in the **Western hills**. **Pokhara**, set beside a lake and under a looming wall of peaks, is the closest you'll find to a resort in Nepal. Other hill towns – notably **Gorkha** with its impressive fortress, **Manakamana** with its wish-fulfilling temple, and laid-back **Tansen** – offer history and culture as well as scenery.

Nepal's diversity really becomes apparent in the ethnic villages and teeming jungle of the **Terai**. Most travellers venture no further than **Chitwan National Park**, where endangered Asian one-horned rhinos are easily viewable, but **Bardia National Park** and two other rarely visited wildlife reserves are out there for the more adventurous.

7

The lay of the land

Nepal's landscape divides neatly into three zones, running roughly west to east. The northernmost is the **Himalayan chain**, broken into a series of *himal* (permanently snow-covered mountain ranges) and alpine valleys, with pockets of high dry terrain lying in the rain shadow to the north, extensions of the great Tibetan plateau. The heartland of the country is the *pahar*, or Central Hills, a wide belt of muscular **foothills** and steep-sided, often terraced valleys; this zone includes two ranges (the Mahabharat Lek and the lower, southernmost Churia hills) as well as the miraculous bowl of the Kathmandu Valley. The southernmost strip is the **Terai**, a belt of hot, flat jungle and farmland. Culturally as well as geographically, it forms part of the Gangetic Plain of northern India.

Lumbini, Buddha's birthplace in the Western Terai, is a world-class pilgrimage site, as is **Janakpur**, a Hindu holy city in the east. Rolling tea plantations, weekly markets and a rich cultural mix figure prominently in the spectacular and little-visited **eastern hills**, most easily reached from the Terai.

And of course Nepal is probably the most famous destination in the world for a growing range of outdoor activities. **Trekking** from village to village through the hills and up into the high Himalayas is an unmiss-able experience. The scenery varies from cultivated terraces and lush rhododendron forests to glaciated valleys and absurdly lofty peaks, but the cultural interactions – sitting round a fire with local people, sharing tea with Buddhist monks – can be the most rewarding part of a trek. **Rafting** down Nepal's rivers offers not only adventure but also a different perspec-tive on the countryside and wildlife, while **mountain biking** brings you in contact with the land and its people at your own pace.

▲ Durbar Square, Kathmandu

When to go

t's hard to generalize about the climate of a country ranging from near sea level to the 8850m peak of Mount Everest. **Seasons** broadly prevail, centred around the summer monsoon, but each manifests itself very differently at different altitudes. Whenever you choose to go, you'll have to weigh other factors: most visitors want good mountain visibility, but don't forget about festivals and wildlife – or crowds and disease.

Around half of all tourists visit Nepal in the **autumn** (late Sept to late Nov). The weather is clear and dry, and temperatures are neither too cold in the high country nor too hot in the Terai. With the pollution and dust washed away by the monsoon rains, the mountains are at their most visible, making this the most popular time for trekking. Two major festivals, Dasain and Tihaar, also fall during this season. The downside is that the tourist quarters and trekking trails are heaving, prices are higher and it may be hard to find a decent room.

Winter (Dec & Jan) weather is mostly part clear and stable. It isn't especially cold at lower elevations – it never snows in Kathmandu, and afternoon temperatures are balmy – but the "mists of Indra" can make mornings dank and chilly (especially in unheated budget lodgings). Most travellers head down into India, leaving the tourist areas fairly quiet, and sometimes a bit lifeless, especially in trekking areas, where lodge-owners may shut up shop altogether. This is an excellent time to visit the Terai, where temperatures are relatively mild.

▼ Yak in Khumbu, the Everest region

The monsoon

A seasonal wind driven by extreme temperature fluctuations in Central Asia, the Asian monsoon is one of the world's great weather phenomena. As air over the Asian landmass warms in late spring and early summer, it rises, sucking in more air from the ocean periphery to take its place. The air drawn from the south, passing over the Indian Ocean, is laden with moisture; as soon as it's forced aloft and cooled (whether by updrafts over hot land, or by a barrier such as Nepal's hills and mountains), it reaches its saturation point and releases its moisture. With the approach of autumn, the flow reverses: cooling throughout the continent blows dry air outwards, bringing clear, stable conditions.

In Nepal, the monsoon generally advances from east to west, dropping more precipitation in the east. Terrain can affect rainfall considerably: areas lying in the "rain shadow" north of the Himalayas see very little monsoon moisture, while the south-facing ranges may receive precipitation long before the plains, even though they're further south. The latter effect is most dramatic where monsoon winds slam into high ranges with few intervening foothills, as they do around Pokhara.

Spring (Feb to mid-April) brings steadily warmer weather and longer days, plus weddings and more festivals. Rhododendrons are in bloom in the hills towards the end of this period, and as the Terai's long grasses have been cut, spring is the best time for viewing wildlife despite the increasing heat. All these pluses bring another tourist influx, albeit not as heavy as in the autumn. A disappointing haze can obscure the mountains from lower elevations, though it's usually possible to trek above it. Alongside the pre-monsoon, spring is also the season when you're more likely to pick up a stomach bug.

During the **pre-monsoon** (mid-April to early June) the heat grows progressively more stifling at lower elevations. Afternoon clouds and increasingly frequent showers help moderate temperatures a bit after mid- or late May, but this is offset by rising humidity. People get a little edgy with the heat; the pre-monsoon is known as the time for popular unrest, but also for the Kathmandu Valley's great rainmaking festival. Trek high, where the temperatures are more tolerable.

Nepalis welcome the **monsoon**, the timing of which may vary by a few weeks every year, but typically lasts from mid-June to mid-September. The rains break the enervating

monotony of the previous months, and the fields come alive with rushing water and green shoots. This can be a fascinating time to visit, when Nepal is at its most Nepali: the air is clean, flowers are in bloom, and fresh fruit and vegetables are particularly abundant. But there are also drawbacks: mountain views are rare, leeches come out in force along the mid-elevation trekking routes, roads may be blocked by landslides, and flights may be cancelled.

Average temperatures and rainfall

	Feb	Apr	Jun	Aug	Oct	Dec
Janakpur (70m), Terai plains						
Max/min (°C)	26/11	35/16	35/20	33/26	31/22	25/11
Max/min (°F)	79/52	95/15	96/68	91/79	88/72	77/52
Rain (mm)	20	40	40	310	70	10
Jomosom (2713m), Himalayan rainshadow						
Max/min (°C)	10/-2	19/4	23/12	23/13	18/6	12/-2
Max/min (°F)	50/28	66/39	73/53	73/55	64/43	54/28
Rain (mm)	10	20	20	30	30	10
Kathmandu (1300m), Central Hills						
Max/min (°C)	20/4	27/11	29/19	28/20	26/13	20/3
Max/min (°F)	68/39	81/52	84/66	82/68	79/55	68/37
Rain (mm)	20	60	260	320	60	150
Namche (3450m), high Himalayas						
Max/min (°C)	6/-6	12/1	15/6	16/8	12/2	7/-6
Max/min (°F)	43/21	54/34	59/43	61/46	54/36	45/21
Rain (mm)	20	30	140	240	80	40
Pokhara (800m), Western Hills						
Max/min (°C)	22/9	30/15	30/21	30/22	27/17	20/8
Max/min (°F)	71/48	86/59	86/70	86/72	81/62	68/46
Rain (mm)	30	120	700	850	170	20

things not to miss

It's not possible to see everything that Nepal has to offer in one trip – and we don't suggest you try. What follows is a selective and subjective taste of the country's highlights: outstanding national parks, spectacular wildlife, adventure sports, history and beautiful architecture. They're arranged in five colour-coded categories to help you find the very best things to see, do and experience. All entries have a page reference to take you straight into the guide, where you can find out more.

01 The Himalayas Page **378** • The world's greatest and most inspiring mountain range, with Everest as its wind-torn crown.

02 Daal bhaat Page **38** • Nepal's national dish, *daal bhaat* (rice and lentils) comes in countless variations.

03 Gorkha Page **228** • The ancestral home of Nepal's royal family is a quintessential hill town, albeit one with a fine temple and palace compound atop its spectacular ridgetop.

04 Janaki Mandir Page **326** • Worshippers come to Janakpur's Mughal-style Janaki Mandir in the name of legendary lovers Ram and Sita.

05 Phewa Tal Page **240** • Relax in a boat on Pokhara's placid lake and enjoy views of the Annapurna range.

06 Rafting Page **393** • A wonderful way to experience rural Nepal: running rapids, floating past jungle and villages, and camping on sandy beaches.

08 Momo Page **40** • These steamed meat or vegetable dumplings, resembling plump ravioli, are an addictive snack.

07 Chiya Page **41** • Leaving aside homebrew beer and raksi firewater, hot, sweet, milky, spiced *chiya* is Nepal's national drink.

09 Shivaraatri Page **43** • This winter festival brings tens of thousands of Shiva devotees to Pashupatinath, the holiest of river gorges.

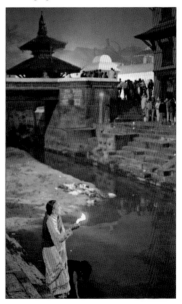

10 **Jungle wildlife** Pages **283** & **309** • Elephant rides get you close to the action in the national parks of the Terai.

12 **Bus journeys** Pages **34** & **176** • Chickens under the seats, sunbathers on the roof and spectacular hairpin bends: rides on a public bus may be uncomfortable, but they get you close to everyday life.

11 **Dasain** Page **44** • Dasain is the high point of the busy Nepali festival calendar – children celebrate by playing on bamboo swings.

13 **Trekking** Page **341** • The ultimate Thing Not To Miss in Nepal: an unequalled scenic and cultural experience.

14 **Yoga and meditation** Page **56** ● Long a spiritual "power place", the Kathmandu Valley now draws many Westerners seeking teachers in both the Hindu or Buddhist traditions.

15 **Boudha** Page **159** ● A proud Tibetan Buddhist community thrives in the shadow of the great stupa of Boudha, on the edge of Kathmandu.

16 **Old Kathmandu** Page **89** ● An intensely urban quarter of narrow alleys, bustling markets and countless temples and shrines.

17 **Bhaktapur** Page **181** ● The medieval Kathmandu Valley town of Bhaktapur is entirely built in dark carved wood and glowing pink brick.

Basics

Basics

Getting there

In the autumn and spring tourist high seasons (late Sept to mid-Nov, and late Feb to late March), flights to Kathmandu – Nepal's only international airport – often fill up months ahead, so book well in advance if you plan to travel at these times. As relatively few airlines serve Kathmandu, you may well find yourself making several hops with two or even three different carriers. Most people book tickets through to Kathmandu, but you can also make your own way to a major regional air hub such as Delhi or Bangkok, and arrange transport from there. These alternative gateways are popular mostly with travellers on longer trips, and those entering Nepal overland from neighbouring countries.

Airfares depend on the time of year, but timings of the high, low and shoulder seasons are calculated differently by each airline, and may not always coincide with tourist seasons. More important is where you're flying from; details are given in the relevant sections below. The price ranges quoted assume midweek travel, though flying at weekends may not add much to the fare, particularly if an airline only operates a couple of flights to Kathmandu each week, as is often the case.

You can sometimes cut costs by going through a **specialist flight agent** – either a consolidator, which buys up blocks of tickets from the airlines and sells them at a discount, or a **discount agent**, which in addition to dealing with discounted flights may also offer special student and youth fares and a range of other travel-related services – check out STA Travel (Ⓦstatravel.com/worldwide.htm) or Trailfinders (Ⓦwww.trailfinders.com).

You might want to consider buying a **Round-the-World** (RTW) ticket, but cheaper off-the-peg tickets don't generally allow you to fly both into and out of Kathmandu, meaning you'll have to make your way overland in at least one direction, book a separate connecting flight, or pay for a specialist, tailor-made RTW ticket. Figure on around £1500/US$2200 for a RTW ticket that includes Nepal, though you could spend less than £1000/US$1500 if you make your own way from Delhi or Bangkok.

Flights from the UK and Ireland

There are no nonstop **flights** from London to Kathmandu, and the half-dozen airlines that operate direct routes all make at least one stop en route, which means around twelve hours' total travel time. **Fares** are seasonal, with airlines generally charging full whack (£600–900, including taxes) for departures from late September to late November, and from early March to mid-April, as well as during the Christmas period. It's often possible, however, to find discounted fares (around £550), especially on less convenient routes, and prices drop in the low season, when you may be able to get a flight for £450 or so.

From London, Gulf Air, Jet Airways and Qatar Airways offer the most direct routings. At the time of writing, the Nepali national carrier, Nepal Airlines Corporation (NAC), had no flights to and from Europe.

Seats with the above airlines get booked early; there are alternatives, but they take longer. Biman Bangladesh's flights via Dhaka, for example, are worth considering for their prices, especially in Nepal's high season, but it's a long flight and you can face long waits in Dhaka for the connection to Kathmandu.

Many other airlines fly **from London to Delhi**, from where you can travel overland or catch a separate connecting flight to Kathmandu (see p.25). Flying to Delhi expands your options for getting a seat on the day of your choice, but it won't get you there any faster. Flights on Thai Airways and

Singapore Airlines aren't really worth considering from Europe because you'll have to double back from Bangkok or Singapore, and fares are similar or slightly higher than the more direct-routed flights.

From the British regions, it usually works out quickest and cheapest to make your way to London and fly from there, although Air France, British Airways and KLM fly to Delhi from numerous regional British airports via Paris, London and Amsterdam respectively.

There are no direct flights to Kathmandu from Ireland, so you'll have to fly via London. A fallback option, however, is to fly to India via another European hub, making a separate connection from Delhi to Kathmandu (see p.25). Air France, British Airways and KLM all fly from Dublin to Delhi via their respective capital cities.

Direct flights

Biman Bangladesh Airlines ☎020/7629 0252, ⊛www.bimanair.com. Daily flights during the high season between London and Kathmandu, via Dhaka: it's a long route but good deals are often available.

Gulf Air ☎0844/493 1717, ⊛www.gulfair.com. Reliable service to Kathmandu via Abu Dhabi or Bahrain, with up to five flights per week (though usually just three weekly in the tourist season). On the final leg, flights get booked up by Nepali migrant workers.

Jet Airways ☎0808/101 1199, ⊛www.jetairways.com. Efficient daily service from London to Kathmandu via Delhi.

Qatar Airways ☎0870/389 8090, ⊛www.qatarairways.com. Comfortable and relatively quick daily flights from London to Kathmandu, via Doha. The last leg is often booked up some time in advance by migrant workers.

Singapore Airlines ☎0844/800 2380, ⊛www.singaporeair.com. Flights from London to Kathmandu, via Bangkok – a very long way round. Uses subsidiary SilkAir for the last leg of the journey.

Thai Airways ☎0870/606 0911, ⊛www.thaiair.com. Long but reliable flights from London to Kathmandu, via Bangkok.

Specialist agents and tour operators

Classic Journeys ☎01773/873497, ⊛www.classicjourneys.co.uk. Operating for more than 25 years, this Nepal specialist offers the usual range of treks, plus wildlife expeditions.

Dragoman ☎01728/861133, ⊛www.dragoman.com. Extended overland journeys in purpose-built expedition vehicles.

Exodus ☎0845/863 9600, ⊛www.exodus.co.uk. Established company with trekking, cycling and sightseeing trips to Nepal and Tibet.

Explore Worldwide ☎0845/013 1539, ⊛www.explore.co.uk. Recommended operator offering Nepal and Tibet trips, featuring trekking and cultural activities. Good for single travellers.

Footprint Adventures ☎01522/804929, ⊛www.footprint-adventures.co.uk. Firm specializing in wildlife and bird-watching tours, plus trekking and rafting trips.

High Places ☎0845/257 7500, ⊛www.highplaces.co.uk. For the more serious trekker, specializing in high-altitude trekking and scaling peaks.

Himalayan Frontiers ☎01737/277190, ⊛www.himalayanfrontiers.co.uk. The pioneer of "parahawking" (where birds of prey fly with paragliders, searching out thermals) in Pokhara, and also runs more typical adventure trips.

Mountain Kingdoms ☎01453/844400, ⊛www.mountainkingdoms.com. Smallish, specialist UK-based company offering group treks across the Himalayas and beyond but with particular expertise on Nepal.

Jagged Globe ☎0845/345 8848, ⊛www.jagged-globe.co.uk. Trekking peaks and serious expeditions.

Muir's Tours ☎0118/950 2281, ⊛www.muirstours.org.uk. Renowned non-profit ethical tourism operator running small-group treks led by local guides, as well as cultural trips such as Buddhist study tours.

Naturetrek ☎01962/733051, ⊛www.naturetrek .co.uk. Leading specialist in birdwatching and wildlife tours, including treks.

Mongoose Travel ☎01271/850 224, ⊛www .mongoosetravel.co.uk. Small, committed UK company offering cultural tours and treks, with good ethical and environmental credentials.

Sherpa Expeditions ☎020/8577 2717, ⊛www .sherpaexpeditions.com. Runs Annapurna, Everest Base Camp and Dhaulagiri treks.

Terra Firma ☎01691/870321, ⊛www .terrafirmatravel.com. A wide range of treks, expeditions and wildlife/cultural tours, plus rafting and mountain-biking expeditions and tailor-made tours. Some options combine Tibet and Nepal.

Wildlife Worldwide ☎0845/130 6982, ⊛www .wildlifeworldwide.com. Trips for wildlife enthusiasts, focusing on the Western Terai parks, with side trips to Lumbini, Pokhara and North India available.

World Expeditions ☎020/8545 9030, ⊛www .worldexpeditions.co.uk. Australian-owned adventure company offering treks in Nepal, Tibet, India and beyond.

Flights from the US and Canada

Nepal is on the other side of the planet from the US and Canada. If you live on the east coast it's somewhat shorter to go via Europe (and, typically, then via the Middle East), and from the west coast it's shorter via the Far East; either way, it's a long haul involving one or more intermediate stops. Plenty of carriers fly to Delhi, Bangkok, Singapore and other Asian cities, from where you can catch a connecting flight to Kathmandu (see p.25).

Seasonal considerations may help determine your route; these seasons don't necessarily coincide with Nepal's autumn and spring tourist seasons. Most airlines consider high season to be summer and the period around Christmas; low season is winter (excluding Christmas), while spring and autumn may be considered low or shoulder season, depending on your route.

Prices quoted below assume midweek travel in low season, and exclude taxes. High season fares are up to $500 higher, and flying on weekends may add another $100 or so. Taxes and other surcharges can add $150 or more to the fare.

From east and central US

Flying eastwards, there are many route options, depending on where you want – or

don't want – to stop over. Figure on spending at least twenty hours in planes.

The best consolidator fares are invariably out of **New York**, and generally fall in the $1300–2000 range in low season, though you can occasionally find some for around $1000. Singapore Airlines usually comes in near the top of that range, but has excellent connections and the route avoids political hotspots. Somewhat cheaper tickets may be had on Gulf, Qatar Airways, Jet Airways or various others; these often have you crossing the Atlantic with one airline and then switching to another. The cheapest deals going tend to be on less appealing airlines and involve more numerous stopovers.

The story is similar from other eastern and midwestern cities, but fares will be a shade higher. In many cases the cheapest option will be to go via New York to take advantage of the rock-bottom consolidated fares from there. From the midwest, **flying west** via Los Angeles may not cost any more, in case you've got a Far Eastern stopover in mind.

From West Coast US

From the West Coast, flying takes about the same time eastwards or westwards – a minimum of 24 hours. **Westbound** routes are sometimes cheaper and often more peaceful, although unless you choose your flights carefully you could end up having to stay overnight en route, usually in Bangkok or Singapore. Low season consolidator **fares** are usually in the $1200–1800 range, though as from the east coast you can sometimes find deals for around $1000. Thai and Singapore fly direct to Kathmandu via their respective capitals; Thai has daily flights and better service, but Singapore has the advantage of flying out of San Francisco as well as LA. Many other airlines (such as Cathay Pacific, China Airlines and United) can take you as far as Hong Kong or Bangkok, where you'll switch to Thai.

From Canada

The cheapest discounted deals tend to be **from Toronto**, flying eastwards, and cost from around Can$2400, depending on the season. Consolidators can route you on any number of airlines through London (see p.19) or Frankfurt (to pick up a Singapore Airlines connection), or use various European carriers to fly via their respective capitals to Delhi, then hopping from there to Kathmandu. Westbound flights via southeast Asia on Thai or Singapore should cost a few hundred dollars more.

From Vancouver, flying west is the clear choice. Singapore has a direct service to Kathmandu (via Singapore), while China Airlines, Air Canada and a few others fly to Bangkok, from where you can pick up Thai Airways. Other options are to fly via Seattle (served by Northwest) or Los Angeles (Thai's US gateway).

From **other central and eastern cities**, you can go via Toronto, Vancouver or possibly New York or Los Angeles. The latter two are worth considering because of the cheap consolidator flights from there (see p.21). Most connecting flights to Toronto or Vancouver will add $300 or so to the fares.

Direct flights

Gulf Air ☎1-888/359 4853, ⓦwww.gulfairco .com. Regular services from New York to Kathmandu, via London and Bahrain.

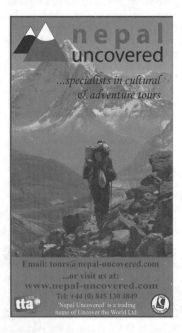

Jet Airways ☎1-877/853 9538, ⓦwww .jetairways.com. Daily from New York to Kathmandu, via Brussels and Delhi.

Singapore Airlines ☎1-800/742 3333, ⓦwww .singaporeair.com. Los Angeles, San Francisco and Vancouver to Kathmandu, via Tokyo and Singapore; New York or Chicago to Kathmandu, via Frankfurt and Singapore. Uses subsidiary SilkAir for the last leg of the journey.

Thai Airways ☎1-800/426 5204, ⓦwww.thaiair .com. Los Angeles to Kathmandu via Bangkok; also connections to Delhi and Kolkata (Calcutta).

Specialist agents and tour operators

Above the Clouds Trekking ☎1-802/482 4848, ⓦwww.aboveclouds.com. Family-run operator offering some unusual treks, for example in the Mustang areas; particularly good for family treks.

Adventure Center ☎1-800/228 8747, ⓦwww .adventurecenter.com. Large company offering wildlife, trekking and sightseeing tours throughout the region.

Canadian Himalayan Expeditions ☎1-800/563 8735, ⓦwww.himalayanexpeditions.com. Wide range of small-group treks and peak expeditions, with rafting and wildlife extensions.

Friends in High Places ☎1-781/354 9851, ⓦwww.fihp.com. Kathmandu-based company offering mostly customized itineraries, especially treks.

Journeys International ☎1-800/255 8735, ⓦwww.journeys.travel. Worldwide trekking agency covering the standard routes, plus a few off-the-beaten track options; family treks also arranged.

Mountain Travel Sobek ☎1-888/831 7526, ⓦwww.mtsobek.com. Lauded high-end trekking and rafting company, with easy to strenuous routes, plus wildlife and customised trips.

Trek Holidays ☎1-888/456 3522, ⓦwww .trekholidays.com. Canada's largest wholesale travel company, offering a large selection of overland, trekking, trekking peaks, rafting and wildlife trips.

Flights from Australia, New Zealand and South Africa

Flying to Nepal **from Australia** invariably means Thai Airways via Bangkok or Singapore Airlines via Singapore, with a stopover on the way on both routes. Flying **from New Zealand** generally means travelling via Sydney. Singapore Airlines, however, flies direct daily from Auckland to Singapore, from where you can pick up the Sydney flight to Kathmandu.

A cheaper option might be to fly to Bangkok and pick up an onward ticket to

Six steps to a better kind of travel

At Rough Guides we are passionately committed to travel. We feel strongly that only through travelling do we truly come to understand the world we live in and the people we share it with – plus tourism has brought a great deal of **benefit** to developing economies around the world over the last few decades. But the extraordinary growth in tourism has also damaged some places irreparably, and of course **climate change** is exacerbated by most forms of transport, especially flying. This means that now more than ever it's important to **travel thoughtfully** and **responsibly**, with respect for the cultures you're visiting – not only to derive the most benefit from your trip but also to preserve the best bits of the planet for everyone to enjoy. At Rough Guides we feel there are six main areas in which you can make a difference:

- Consider what you're contributing to the **local economy**, and how much the services you use do the same, whether it's through employing local workers and guides or sourcing locally grown produce and local services.
- Consider the **environment** on holiday as well as at home. Water is scarce in many developing destinations, and the biodiversity of local flora and fauna can be adversely affected by tourism. Try to patronize businesses that take account of this.
- Travel with a purpose, not just to tick off experiences. Consider **spending longer** in a place, and getting to know it and its people.
- Give thought to how often you **fly**. Try to avoid short hops by air and more harmful night flights.
- Consider **alternatives to flying**, travelling instead by bus, train, boat and even by bike or on foot where possible.
- Make your trips **"climate neutral"** via a reputable carbon offset scheme. All Rough Guide flights are offset, and every year we donate money to a variety of charities devoted to combating the effects of climate change.

Nepal (around US$350) from there, although obviously this option lacks the certainty of a through ticket. Fares to Delhi are about the same as to Kathmandu, so another possibility – although not the most economical one – is to fly into India and fly or travel overland into Nepal from there (see p.24). A final option is to fly via Hong Kong, from where occasional flights connect with Kathmandu.

As ever, **airfares** depend on the time of year (which doesn't always correspond to the autumn and spring tourist seasons in Nepal). Generally, low season runs from mid-January to late February, and from early October to the end of November; high season is from around mid-May to August, and early December to mid-January; shoulder season takes up the rest of the year. Low-season prices to Kathmandu via Singapore or Bangkok start at roughly A$1700 from Australia, and NZ$2300 from New Zealand,

and can be several hundred dollars (in either currency) higher in peak season. Fares out of Perth may be cheaper by A$100 or so, since the flying time is shorter.

Travelling from **South Africa**, Thai Airways and Singapore Airlines both have regular flights from Johannesburg to Kathmandu, via Bangkok and Singapore respectively.

Direct flights

Singapore Airlines Australia ☎ 131 011, New Zealand ☎ 09/379 3209, South Africa ☎ 011/880 8560; ☜ www.singaporeair.com. Three or four flights a week from Singapore to Kathmandu, and numerous connecting flights from cities in Australia and New Zealand. Uses subsidiary SilkAir for the last leg of the journey.
Thai Airways Australia ☎ 1300/651 960, New Zealand ☎ 09/377 3886, South Africa ☎ 011/268 2580; ☜ www.thaiair.com. Daily flights to Kathmandu from Sydney, Auckland and Perth, with a one-night stopover in Bangkok required.

Specialist agents and tour operators

Abercrombie and Kent Australia ☎1800/331 429, New Zealand ☎09/579 3369; ⓦwww .abercrombiekent.com. Upmarket tours of India and Nepal.

Intrepid Travel Australia ☎1300/364 512, ⓦwww.intrepidtravel.com.au. Small-group tours, mostly treks on standard routes, but also wildilfe, rafting and India trips, with an ethical emphasis.

Peregrine Adventures Australia ☎03/8601 4444, ⓦwww.peregrineadventures.com. Introductory-level tours of Nepal, some combining visits to India, Bhutan or Tibet.

Ultimate Descents International ☎03/543 2301, ⓦwww.ultimatedescents.com. Leading rafting operator.

Getting there from neighbouring countries

Many travellers combine Nepal with a trip to India, even if they're just making the connection with a budget flight to or from Delhi. There are numerous **border crossings** between the two countries, and overland routes can easily be planned to take in many of northern India's most renowned sights. Flying between Delhi and Kathmandu rewards you with Himalayan views and opens up a wider choice of international flights. Travel from Tibet is possible as long as you have the correct permit for travel in the country; entering Tibet from Nepal, however, is limited to group tours.

The classic **Asia overland** trip is just about alive and kicking, despite periodic political reroutings; leaving Europe behind at Istanbul, the usual approach from the west traverses Turkey, angles down through Iran, crosses Pakistan and enters India at Amritsar. Several expedition operators (see lists of tour companies on p.20 & p.22) run trips lasting up to twenty-five weeks in specially designed vehicles all the way through to Kathmandu.

Overland from India

Transport connections between **India** and Nepal are well developed, with travel agents in Delhi, Darjeeling and other major train junctions in the north selling bus packages to Kathmandu. However, these are often rip-offs, and in any case it's easy to ride to the

border and make your own way from there – you'll almost certainly end up on the same Nepali bus anyway.

Three **border crossings** see the vast majority of travellers: Sonauli/Belahiya, the most popular entry point, reachable from Delhi, Varanasi and most of North India (via Gorakhpur); Raxaul/Birgunj, accessible from Bodh Gaya and Kolkata via Patna; and Kakarbhitta, serving Darjeeling and Kolkata via Siliguri. A fourth, Banbaasa/ Mahendra Nagar, is handy for the Uttar Pradesh hill stations and (relatively speaking) for Delhi too; it's still a long way from Mahendra Nagar to Kathmandu, but it would be quite possible to plan a trip to Nepal based solely around the western national parks and Pokhara. All these border crossings are described in the relevant sections of the Guide.

Two **other border points** (near Nepalgunj and Dhangadhi) are also open to tourists, but they're rarely used. Other crossings near Janakpur, Biratnagar and Ilam rarely admit foreigners, though they may eventually become official entry points. Since you can't be sure ahead of time that you'll be allowed through, you should probably enter the country via one of the official crossings to avoid a wasted journey; then, if you're up for adventure on the way out, check with the Department of Immigration in Kathmandu before setting off to find out what else is open.

By private vehicle

Needless to say, bringing a **private vehicle** into Nepal is a big commitment, and requires nerves of steel to cope with local driving conditions (see p.32 for tips). The trade-off is that you don't have to deal with Nepali buses, and you get to go at your own pace, bring lots more gear and have your own personal space. You can enter Nepal – slowly – via any official border crossing.

If you're driving all the way from your home country, the best strategy is to obtain a **carnet de passage**, a document intended to ensure you don't illegally sell the vehicle while out of the country. A *carnet* is available from the AA or similar motoring organizations. It may also be possible to get one in India if the vehicle was purchased there. You'd also do well to come equipped with an **international driving licence**.

By bicycle

Entering Nepal by **bicycle** involves no special paperwork, and the main routes are summarized below. Cycling from India is best done in December and January, when the weather is coolest. If entering via one of the far-western or far-eastern crossings, be prepared to spend one or more nights in really basic accommodation (like the floor of a teashop).

Birgunj–Kathmandu A spectacular but extremely strenuous ride up and over the Tribhuwan Rajpath – the climb is so tough from the south that this is probably a better route for leaving Nepal than entering it. Unfortunately, Birgunj is the least pleasant of Nepal's border crossings. Distance 185km, elevations ranging from 90m above sea level to 2490m.

Kakarbhitta–Kathmandu An adventurous route from Darjeeling through little-visited plains country, though it requires a fair bit of hammering down long stretches of highway. The final leg can be along the Rajpath or an easier way via Chitwan. Distance 540km, elevations 80m–2490m.

Sonauli–Pokhara An excellent introduction to Nepal, this is a scenic, reasonably cycle-friendly route offering side trips to Lumbini and Tansen.

The road may deteriorate over short stretches. Distance 185km, elevations 90–1500m.

Mahendra Nagar–Pokhara The most rural way from Delhi, with some long, straight, dull stretches across the plains. Passes two great wildlife parks and then joins the Sonauli–Pokhara route. Distance 750km, elevations 80–1500m.

Kodari–Kathmandu The only route from Tibet (see below). The mostly downhill Nepal stretch will seem tame compared to the ride from Lhasa to the border, though it's exciting enough coming up it. Distance 230m, elevations 630–1640m.

From Tibet

Any advice on travelling in **Tibet** is liable to be out of date by the time it's printed, so seek current information before going there. At the time of writing, China was allowing individuals with the proper paperwork for Tibet travel to exit the country at Zhangmu (Kodari on the Nepali side) on the Lhasa–Kathmandu highway, but only groups were being permitted to enter Tibet there. If you've managed to **cycle** all the way from Lhasa, you ought to be fit and acclimatized enough to make it the rest of the way to Nepal – but this is an extremely arduous journey along a mostly unpaved road, crossing two passes of at least 5000m, and should only be attempted in good weather.

See box on p.145 for more details on getting to and from Tibet.

Asian connections by plane

Booking a separate flight between Kathmandu and any of the main **Asian air hubs** opens up a host of alternative international routes. You're unlikely to save much money by flying indirectly, particularly via India, but there may be a better choice of dates. Flying to Delhi and then on to Kathmandu is a popular route, and opens the possibility of seeing something of India, even if you can't stomach going overland. Coming from Australia, New Zealand or the western side of the US or Canada, it's easy to break your journey in Southeast Asia, and there's a fair chance of saving money by picking up a separate ticket once you're there. Kathmandu is also served by flights from a handful of major **Indian cities**, while services to smaller destinations in northern India come and go.

One-way **airfares** between most Asian cities and Kathmandu don't usually vary much, though it's still always worth shopping around for a discounted ticket, particularly if you're booking from within Asia. Note that NAC and Indian Airlines (IA) give a 25 percent discount to under-thirties on the Delhi flights.

The following approximate single fares between Asian cities and Kathmandu are likely to cost slightly more when booked from outside Asia. Airlines serving the routes are given in brackets.

Asian connections

Bangkok (Thai) – US$350
Delhi (Jet, NAC, IA) – US$85
Dhaka (Biman Bangladesh) – US$300
Hong Kong (Dragon) – US$500
Lhasa (Air China) – US$390
Paro (Druk Air) – US$190
Singapore (Singapore Airlines/SilkAir) – US$500
Shanghai (Air China) – US$500

Getting around

Getting around is one of the biggest challenges of travelling in Nepal. Distances aren't great, but the roads are poor and extremely slow, and public buses are uncomfortable. Tourist buses make the best of the most-travelled routes, however, and you can always hire a motorcycle, or club together with two or three others to charter a taxi or jeep on a daily rate. And don't rule out flying: you'll be rewarded with stunning mountain views.

Nepal has one of the least-developed **road networks** in the world. Highways are irregularly maintained, and each monsoon takes a toll on road surfaces, so in the space of one year a stretch of road can go from wonderful to hellish. Wherever you travel, the route will probably be new in parts, disintegrated in parts, and under construction in others. Blockades or general strikes (*bandh*) can make travel virtually impossible – see p.62. All this has an unfortunate effect on tourism: most travellers just aren't willing to endure the long and bumpy journeys it takes to get far afield in Nepal, so they stick to a circuit of a few easily accessible destinations in the middle of the country.

The **cost of transport** is trifling. Even the longest journeys on public buses will come to no more than Rs400, and the six-hour tourist bus from Kathmandu to Pokhara costs less than Rs400. If you have enough people to fill it, a hired taxi or jeep works out at good value, costing under US$12 a head per day.

Flights are much more expensive, with one-way fares in the region of US$50–120.

By bus

Public buses ply every paved road in Nepal. The bus network is completely and chaotically private but all fares are fixed for public services (not for tourist ones). For **express buses** it works out to about Rs20 per hour. Allowing for bad roads, overloaded buses, tea stops, meal stops, constant picking up and letting off of passengers, and the occasional flat tyre or worse, the average speed in the hills is barely 25km per hour, and on remote, unpaved roads it can be as little as 10kph. Along the Mahendra Highway, in the Terai, it's more like 50kph in an express bus.

Bus **frequencies** and approximate journey times are given throughout the guide. Inevitably, these figures should be taken with a pinch of salt: the bus network seems to grow every year, but political troubles or festivals

Nepali place names

Even though Devanaagari (the script of Nepali and Hindi) spellings are phonetic, **transliterating** them into the Roman alphabet is a disputed science. Some places will never shake off the erroneous spellings bestowed on them by early British colonialists – Kathmandu, for instance, looks more like Kaathmaadau when properly transliterated. Where place names are Sanskrit- or Hindi-based, the Nepali pronunciation sometimes differs from the accepted spelling – the names Vishnu (a Hindu god) and Vajra (a tantric symbol) sound like Bishnu and Bajra in Nepali. This book follows local pronunciations as consistently as possible, except in cases where this would be out of step with every map in print.

can dramatically reduce the number of buses, and some gravel or dirt roads are closed altogether during the monsoon.

Open-air **bus stations** (often known as a *bas park* or *bas island*) are typically located in the dustiest parts of town. Tickets are sold either from a small booth or through the barred window of the *ticket ophis*. Destinations may not be written in English, but people are usually happy to help you out if you ask.

In Kathmandu and Pokhara you may find it easier to make arrangements through a ticket agent (but heed the warnings given below), while in cities you can ask your hotel to buy a ticket for you.

Ticket agents

With their funfair signs advertising "Bus and Train to India" and "Exciting Jungle Safari", **ticket agents** are the used-car salesmen of Nepal, preying on travellers' faith in the apparently limitless possibilities of the Orient. Though they make themselves out to be budget travel agencies, many are inept, and some are downright dishonest. Naturally, they all mark up the price of the tickets they sell.

For a seat on a public bus, a ticket agent can save you the trouble of making an extra trip to the bus station. For tourist bus services, whose offices are often located just down the street, an agent doesn't provide much value for his fee. Ticket agents are also useful for hiring vehicles, but shop around.

Be wary when ticket agents try to sell you anything more complicated than the above. Don't book a **trek** or **river trip** through an agent – deal directly with the tour operator, who can give you straight information and

will be accountable if anything goes wrong. Wildlife packages (see p.271) and tickets to India (see p.145) booked through an agent have additional drawbacks. Finally, go to a recommended agency to arrange air tickets or anything involving computerized bookings.

Tourist buses

Regularly scheduled **tourist buses** connect Kathmandu with Pokhara, Chitwan National Park, Lumbini and Nagarkot, and Pokhara with Chitwan and Sonauli. Additional services may start up in time.

The vehicles are usually in good condition, making for a much safer ride than in a public bus. They aren't supposed to take more passengers than there are seats (though they may pick up a few anyway), so the journey should also be more comfortable and somewhat faster, too. There should be just two seats on either side of the aisle ("2x2"), making for a roomier ride than on public "2x3" buses, and the seats should be reasonably well padded.

A couple of companies operate more expensive buses with intermittent air-conditioning, but you don't get much for paying roughly triple the cost. Services billed as minibuses are somewhat faster than full-sized buses. **Luggage** is kept safely stowed under a tarpaulin on the roof or in a cargo compartment, but put a lock on your bag just to be sure, and keep valuables with you inside.

Tickets are widely touted in Kathmandu and Pokhara. Buses depart from the tourist quarters of those cities. Book seats at least one or two days in advance. Since tourist bus fares aren't regulated, and ticket agents often add an undisclosed commission onto the price, it's worth shopping around.

Public express buses

Long-distance public bus services generally operate on an express basis. Not that they don't make any stops: an "express" bus will stop as often as necessary on the way out of town until it's full and drop passengers off as it approaches its destination. Still, express services are a lot faster and more comfortable than a local bus.

Express buses fall into two categories. **Day buses** usually cover the medium-distance routes (approximately 6–12 hours) and set off in the morning to arrive at their destination before nightfall or not long after. Day buses may be 2x2s or 2x3s and can vary a lot in comfort level – some are fiendishly short on legroom.

Night buses, which operate on the longest routes (ten- to twenty-plus hours), depart in the afternoon or early evening to arrive the following morning. On these you're assured of 2x2 reclining seats with padding and adequate legroom. Between all the lurching, honking, tea stops and blaring music you won't get much sleep (bring earplugs and something to cover your eyes). Night journeys are also more dangerous, since it's not uncommon for drivers to fall asleep at the wheel.

Like tourist buses, and unlike local buses, express buses allow you to **reserve seats** in advance. Do this, or you could end up in one of the ejector seats along the back. Numbering begins from the front of the bus: the prized seats #1A and #2A, on the left by the front door, often have the most legroom. Check the seating chart to see what's available. Fortunately Nepalis don't tend to plan very far ahead, so you can usually get away with buying a ticket just a few hours beforehand; the exception is during the big autumn festivals, when buses are packed with people heading back to their villages and seats get booked up several days in advance. The ticket should indicate the vehicle number.

Every public bus has at least one **conductor**, often a young boy. Most know enough English to at least understand where you want to go, and are remarkably diligent in letting you know when you've got there. If a conductor seems to disappear with your five-hundred-rupee note, it'll be because he's waiting until he's collected enough tickets to give you the change.

Most express buses give you the choice of stowing your **baggage** on the roof or in a locked hold in the back. Having all your things with you is of course the best insurance policy against theft, but it's inconvenient. Putting bags in the hold is usually the next-safest option, especially on night buses; you may need to pay a small fee at the bus's point of origin. Baggage stowed on the roof is probably okay during the day, but you can never be completely sure – if possible, lock your bag to the roof rack, and keep an eye out during stops; you don't need to pay to store bags on the roof, but a small tip to the conductor may encourage him to keep his eyes open.

Local buses

Serving mainly shorter routes or slow, remote roads, **local buses** are ancient, battered contraptions with seats designed for midgets. The idea is to cram as many passengers in as possible – indeed, a bus isn't making money until it's nearly full to bursting, and it can get suffocating inside.

This can lead to infuriating false starts, as the driver inches forward and the conductor runs around trying to round up customers. Once on the road, the bus will stop any time it's flagged down.

Local buses often depart from a separate bus park or just a widening in the road, and tickets are bought on board. Since seats often can't be reserved, the only way to be sure of getting one is to board the bus early and wait. If you're just picking up a bus along the way you're likely to join the crush standing in the aisle, and low ceilings add to the discomfort.

Unless your **bag** is small, it will have to go on the roof; during daylight hours it should be safe there as long as it's locked, but again, keep all valuables on your person. **Riding on the roof** can actually be quite pleasant, but it's dangerous and illegal. Even if you've got a seat, safety is a concern: these buses are often overworked, overloaded and poorly maintained.

By jeep and truck

Almost every roadhead in the country is being extended, often on local initiative, by way of a dirt track making its painful way deeper into the countryside. And where the bus comes to the end of the road, you can rely on finding a **jeep** to take you further. In some parts of the country you'll find old Land Rovers, in others Indian Marutis or even Nepalese Sherpas, but they're almost always fairly battered, often with some ingenious modifications to allow them to take more passengers. Where the road is well-used, jeeps of this sort leave as soon as they're full. Roads of this sort are prone to being closed by landslides, fallen trees and other natural shocks, particularly in the monsoon season.

If no buses or jeeps are going your way, you may be able to get there by **truck**. Most trucks in Nepal are ungainly Indian-built Tatas ferrying fuel to Kathmandu or building materials to hill boomtowns, or "Public Carriers" – gaily decorated hauliers-for-hire operating on both sides of the Indian border. Many do a sideline in hauling passengers, and charge set fares comparable to what you'd pay on a bus. Fully laden, they go even slower than buses. The ride is comfortable enough if you get a seat in the cab, and certainly scenic if you have to sit or stand in the back – either way, the trip is bound to be eventful.

However, trucks aren't licensed as passenger vehicles, and so take little interest in passenger **safety** and are unaccountable for losses: watch your luggage. Women journeying by truck will probably prefer to join up with a companion. Jeeps and trucks generally wait at major junctions until full – if you ask around it should be easy enough to **reserve** a space.

If you're really stuck, you could try **hitching**. There aren't many private vehicles in Nepal, though, and anyone you manage to flag down will expect money.

By plane and helicopter

There may be times when $80 spent on an **internal flight** seems a small price to pay to avoid 24 hours on a bus – and, of course, the views are thrown in free. An hour-long scenic loop out of Kathmandu, the so-called "**mountain flight**", is very popular among tourists who want to get an armchair view of Everest – see p.143. Internal flights are generally reliable and reasonably priced (usually $55–120, depending on the length), though try to steer clear of the government-owned Nepal Airlines Corporation (NAC), which has a deservedly poor reputation.

Given Nepal's mountainous terrain, aircraft play a vital role in the country's transport network. Of the thirty or so cities and towns with **airstrips** (see map below) almost half are two or more days' walk from a road. Most flights begin or end in Kathmandu, but

two other airports in the Terai – Nepalganj in the west, Biratnagar in the east – serve as secondary hubs. Popular destinations, such as Lukla in the Everest region, or a major Terai city like Nepalganj, get up to ten flights a day. Obscure airstrips, however, particularly those in the remoter hill areas, may receive only one flight a week in certain seasons. What's more, these less profitable routes tend to be served exclusively by NAC. For frequencies and flight times, see the "Travel details" section at the end of each chapter; and double-check locally.

Numerous **private airlines** compete fairly efficiently on the main domestic inter-city and tourist trekking routes. Their prices are around ten percent higher than NAC, but are well worth it for increased reliability and flexibility; for more on booking tickets with them, see p.143.

Three makes of **propeller planes** designed for mountain flying are commonly used in Nepal: 44-seat Avros, 18-seat Dornier 228s and 17-seat Twin Otters. Flying in one of these small craft is a splendid way to get clear views of the Himalayas and the incredible maze of Nepal's middle hills. Thermals can make the ride bumpy, and landings on mountain airstrips are always memorable.

Domestic airlines and routes

Agni Air Shantinagar ☎01/410 7812, ⓦwww .agniair.com. Janakpur, Jomosom, Phaplu, Pokhara, Lukla, Tumlingtar.

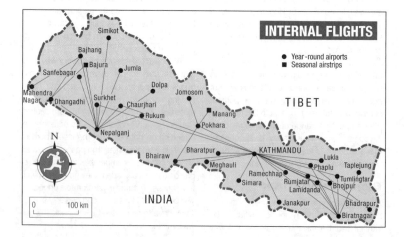

Buddha Air Hattisar ☎01/443 7025, ⓦwww
.buddhaair.com. Bhadrapur, Bhairahawa, Bharatpur,
Biratnagar, Dhangadhi, Janakpur, Nepalganj, Pokhara,
Simara.

Cosmic Air Kalimatidole ☎01/449 0146, ⓦwww
.cosmicair.com. Bharatpur, Bhairahawa, Biratnagar,
Nepalgunj, Pokhara, Tumlingtar.

Gorkha Airlines Hattisar ☎01/443 5121,
ⓦwww.gorkhaairlines.com/gorkha. Bhadrapur,
Bhairahawa, Bharatpur, Biratnagar, Janakpur,
Jomsom, Jumla, Lukla, Phaphlu, Pokhara, Simara,
Simikot, Tumlingtar.

Nepal Airlines (NAC) corner of New Rd and
Kantipath ☎01/424 4055, ⓦwww.royalnepal-airlines
.com.The tourist sales office handles flights to
Bharatpur, Lukla and Pokhara. The domestic sales
office, in the same building, handles all other internal
flights: Bajura, Bhajang, Bhojpur, Biratnagar, Chaurjhari,
Dhangadhi, Dolpa, Jumla, Lamidanda, Manang,
Nepalgunj, Ramechhap, Rukum, Rumjatar, Simara,
Surkhet, Taplejung, Tumlingtar.

Sita Air Sinamangal ☎01/448 7110, ⓦwww
.sitaair.com.np. Bajhang, Biratnagar, Chaurjhari,
Dang, Dhangadhi, Jomsom, Lukla, Nepalgunj,
Pokhara, Simikot, Tumlingtar.

Yeti Airlines Lazimpath ☎01/446 5495, ⓦwww
.yetiairlines.com.Bhadrapur, Bhairahawa, Bharatpur,
Biratnagar, Dolpa, Janakpur, Jumla, Lamidanda,
Lukla, Meghauli, Nepalgunj, Phaplu, Pokhara, Simara,
Simikot, Surkhet, Tumlingtar.

Sample one-way airfares

Kathmandu to: Biratnagar ($121); Lukla ($99);
Nepalgunj ($111); Pokhara ($69); Tumlingtar ($70).
Nepalgunj to: Jumla ($65); Simikot ($98).
Pokhara to: Jomosom ($55); Manang ($56).

Tickets

Tickets can be bought in hard currency
only, usually US dollars. You can **book**
tickets through a travel agent, who will have
a handle on who's flying where and when,
and may be able to offer a small discount off
the quoted fare. At the time of writing, all
domestic airlines were levying a $2
insurance surcharge on top of the prices
quoted in the guide.

At off-peak times you shouldn't have any
trouble getting a **seat**. However, during the
trekking season, flights out of airstrips along
the popular trails may be booked up months
in advance by trekking agencies. If you're
finding you can't get a seat, all is not lost.
Agencies frequently overbook, releasing their
unused tickets on the day of departure, so
you may be able to buy a returned ticket
from the airline on the morning you want to
travel. Otherwise, adjust your schedule and
go a week or two later, by which time the
agency peak should have tapered off.

Check in early for popular flights, which
are often overbooked by the airlines. Getting
there early will also improve your chances of
getting a seat on the side of the plane with
the best mountain views.

Safety and delays

Government scrutiny of the airline industry is
minimal, and while it's true that most aircraft
are leased from overseas companies that set
maintenance and pilot performance require-
ments, there are **crashes** every year. The
mountainous terrain is the main problem,
although baggage overloading is a contributing factor. Radar was installed at
Kathmandu airport after the Airbus crashes
of 1992, but for the most part you are relying
on pilot skill and experience. It's a close call
whether flying is more, or less, dangerous
than travelling by bus.

Another problem with flying in Nepal is
delays and cancellations, usually due to
weather. Few airstrips have even the simplest
landing beacons, and many of them are
surrounded by hills, so there must be good
visibility to land – if there's fog or the cloud
ceiling is too low, the plane won't fly. Since
clouds usually increase as the day wears on,
delays often turn into cancellations. If your
flight is cancelled, you may be placed at the
bottom of a waiting list, rather than being
given space on the next available flight; in
busy times or during extended periods of
bad weather, the wait can be several days.
Pad your schedule accordingly.

Helicopters

A half-dozen companies offer charter
helicopter services in Nepal. What they'd
like to sell you is a three- or four-hour sightseeing junket up to a mountain meadow and
back. At $100–200 per hour per person,
that's a pretty expensive picnic – the
mountain flight is a better deal (see p.30).
More commonly, though, these services are
used by trekking parties with more money

than time, who charter a chopper for upwards of $1000 to pick them up at a prearranged spot to save them several days' backtracking. Companies are supposed to charter only entire aircraft, but in practice if a helicopter is returning empty from a trekking landing strip to Kathmandu or Pokhara, the pilot will take on individual passengers for about the same price as a seat on a plane. You can arrange this informally yourself at airstrips, or go through local agents.

Driving and cycling

It's really liberating to have your **own wheels** in Nepal. Besides being faster and more comfortable than a bus, a car (or jeep) will enable you to get to places you'd never go by bus, and stop wherever and whenever you like. **Rented vehicles** always come with a driver in Nepal, which means you don't have to grapple with the country's chaotic roads. However, if you rent a motorcycle or bring your own vehicle to Nepal, you'll find that driving is sometimes fun, sometimes terrifying, and always challenging. Most advice can be summed up in two words: **drive defensively**.

The hairiest driving is in Kathmandu, where the roads are incredibly congested with vehicles, pedestrians, cyclists, cows, pushcarts and street vendors. Observance of traffic regulations is fairly lax, with drivers constantly jockeying for position irrespective of lane markings or traffic signals. On **round-abouts**, confusion arises (for visitors) because priority officially goes to vehicles *entering* the intersection, not those already going around it.

Follow local practice and use your horn liberally: to alert other vehicles and pedestrians that you're there, when rounding sharp corners, when overtaking. Most vehicles you want to overtake will want you to wait for their signal – a hand wave or – confusingly – a right-turning indicator.

Watch your speed on the **highways**, which are rarely free of unmarked hazards: potholes, landslides, washed-out bridges, speed bumps, grain spread out to dry, goats and the like. And watch out for those **cows**: the penalty for killing one is up to twelve years in prison, the same as for killing a person.

Finally, **filling stations** can be found on main roads at the outskirts of all major towns. Fuel is *tel*; some sell only diesel (*dizel*), but will show you where you can get petrol (*giyas*) – in smaller towns it's dispensed unofficially by small shops. At the time of writing, the cost of petrol was around Rs90 per litre.

Cars and jeeps

In Kathmandu and Pokhara, chartering a **taxi** by the day is the cheapest option for short or medium-distance journeys. The going rate for trips within the Kathmandu or Pokhara valleys is about $20–25 a day, including petrol. Most taxis aren't roadworthy for long distances, and usually aren't permitted to travel beyond certain checkpoints anyway. If you do take a taxi on a longer trip, petrol becomes a more significant expense, so the driver will probably prefer to quote a price for a particular destination or itinerary, plus an extra $8 or so for every night he's away from home to cover meals and accommodation.

Jeeps (or Land Rovers) are better for longer journeys and larger parties, and also for carrying kayaks or bikes. They can be rented through some travel agents in Kathmandu, Pokhara and the bigger Terai cities, and cost proportionately more than cars. Prices for all vehicle rentals are by negotiation, so it's a good idea to have your lodge owner help. Avis and Hertz have representatives in Kathmandu, but renting a vehicle through them is much more expensive (about $50 a day).

Motorcycles and scooters

A **motorcycle** requires more nerve than a car, but it's also more versatile. You'll want to have had plenty of riding experience and you should of course have a licence, though it's unlikely to be checked. You may be expected to leave an air ticket, passport or large sum of money as a deposit. Check brakes, oil and fuel level, horn, lights and indicators before setting off, and make sure to get a helmet.

Indian-made **street bikes** can be rented in Kathmandu and Pokhara; you'll pay about $6 a day, and petrol is extra. These small

(100cc or 135cc) two-stroke models aren't suitable for covering hundreds of kilometres a day, but are quite sufficient for day-trips or even touring the country at a leisurely pace. Top speed is about 70kph, which is faster than you really want to be going on Nepali highways anyway. Two people can share a bike – you'll see three or even four Nepalis riding together – but doubling up can be rather nerve-racking over long distances and on rough roads. Riding solo, you can handle just about anything a four-wheel-drive vehicle can.

Quite a few travellers bring 350cc or 500cc Enfields into Nepal from India, where they can easily be purchased and later resold to other travellers. These bikes have a lot more heft for long-distance cruising, and can easily carry two riders and gear, but are heavy and hard to handle off-road.

Motorcycling carries some risk. Also note that rented bikes carry no insurance – if you break anything, you pay for it. Stick to back roads (they're more pleasant anyway), and take care on wet dirt roads, which can be extremely slippery.

By bicycle

A rented **bicycle** (*saikal*) is the logical choice for most day-to-day getting around. One-speeders (usually Indian-made Hero models) are good enough for most around-town cycling, and cost Rs150–200 per day, though you may be able to negotiate a deal for a longer period. They're incredibly heavy and their brakes are poor, but they're sturdy and have built-in locks.

For more money, a **mountain bike** will get you there in greater comfort, and is essential for longer distances or anything steep – a few shops in Kathmandu and Pokhara rent top-quality models. More tips on mountain-biking and bike rental are given in Chapter Nine.

Bike rental shops are rare outside of Kathmandu, Pokhara and Chitwan, but you can often strike a deal with a lodge owner or cycle repairman. Check brakes, spokes, tyres and chain carefully before setting off. A bell is pretty well essential. Repair shops are everywhere, but they won't have mountain bike parts. Theft is a concern, especially with a flashier bike – be sure to take it inside your guesthouse compound at night.

City transport

Taxis, identified by black number plates, are confined mainly to Kathmandu and Pokhara, and you'll find details on their idiosyncrasies in the relevant sections of the guide. A metered ride will cost about Rs24 per kilometre, with the meter starting at Rs10. You can also hire a taxi by the day (see p.32).

Fixed-route "Vikram" **tempos**, three wheeled, passenger-carrying scooters, fit eight or ten. They set off when they're full, stop at designated points, and usually charge only a few rupees per head. They are noisy and put out noxious fumes, although battery-powered *safaa* ("clean") tempos make a more pleasant alternative in Kathmandu.

Pedal-powered cycle **rikshaws** are slow and bumpy, but may come in handy for short distances through Kathmandu's narrow, crowded streets. In Terai cities they're an invaluable way to get around. Be sure to establish the fare before setting off (Rs10–30 per kilometre, depending on how touristy the place is).

Few cities in Nepal are so large that you're dependent on public transport. Where available, **city buses**, minibuses and micro-buses are usually too crowded, slow or infrequent to be worthwhile, but you may find yourself using them to visit certain sights in the Kathmandu Valley. Fares are just a few rupees.

Accommodation

Finding a place to sleep is hardly ever a problem in Nepal, although only the established tourist centres offer much of a choice. Friendly and well-managed guesthouses are found almost anywhere that attracts tourists. If you go trekking or visit a wildlife park, you'll find a greater variety of accommodation, from rude lodges along the trail to luxurious tented camps in the jungle. A handful of village-stay schemes allow you to taste traditional rural life.

Prices vary considerably, depending on where you stay and when. You can pay anything from a couple of dollars per night in a trekking lodge to over $200 in a wildlife-viewing resort, but guesthouses, where most travellers stay, typically charge between $5 and $25. Outside the October to December high season, or if things are unusually quiet, prices can drop by up to fifty percent: the simple question *discount paunchha?* (any discount?) will often do the trick. Nearly all guesthouses have a wide spread of rooms, from budget, shared-bath boxes to rooms with televisions and an attached bathroom. In the Terai, prices depend on whether the room has a fan or air-conditioning (a/c).

Apart from at the cheapest places, you can usually pay in **dollars** as well as rupees. Many mid- and top-range give their prices in dollars, but rupees are accepted.

Hotels and guesthouses take **bookings**, and reservations are worth considering in the busy seasons, during local festivals or if you expect to arrive late in the day. In Kathmandu particularly, booking ahead often gets you a free airport pick-up. Otherwise it's rarely worth the bother, especially in the cheapest places, which may have a hazy notion of how to take bookings. Nevertheless, listings in the guide give phone numbers and websites for all lodgings that have them. **Single rooms** are usually doubles offered at between half and two-thirds of the price.

Lodges

Off the beaten track, **lodges** are aimed at Nepali travellers, and are usually known as "hotel and lodge" (confusingly, the "hotel" bit means there's a diner). Some are luxurious – in bigger Terai cities there will usually be at least one upmarket place with creature comforts (such as a/c or a generator for the inevitable power cuts) – but for the most part Nepalis are more concerned about the quality of the rice than the cleanliness of the bathrooms, so you may have to settle for something less salubrious. Stark concrete floors, cold-water showers and smelly squat toilets are the rule, though you'll rarely pay more than Rs300, frequently half that. Often not much English is spoken. Sheets and cotton quilts are usually provided, but it's a good idea to bring your own sleeping sheet to protect against bedbugs and lice. Noise is always a problem: earplugs can block out the worst of it. In the Terai, mosquito netting (or mosquito coils) and a ceiling fan that works are crucial.

This is not to say that Nepali lodges are to be avoided. Often the most primitive places – the ones with no electricity, where you sit on the mud floor by a smoky fire and eat with your hosts – are the most rewarding. **Trekking lodges** can take this form (though there are some remarkably comfortable lodges out there too), and are described in Chapter Seven.

Guesthouses

Most tourist-oriented places to stay in Nepal call themselves **guesthouses**. This category covers everything from primitive flophouses to well-appointed small hotels. Many places offer a spread of rooms at different prices, and inexpensive dorm beds are sometimes available too. By and large, those that cater to foreigners do so very efficiently: most innkeepers speak excellent English, and can arrange anything for you from laundry to bus tickets to trekking/porter hire. Those that

Accommodation price codes

All accommodation listed in this guide has been graded according to the **price codes** below, which are based on the cost of the least expensive double room in the October/November high season, and include government and service taxes (which can add up to 23 percent) where applicable. At other times, proprietors are usually more amenable to bargaining, and you may be able to negotiate a drop of as much as fifty percent. It's worth bargaining at any time, however: you can often get a discount simply by asking for one. In budget places, the code may relate to rooms with a "common" (shared) bathroom; expect to pay a bit more – say in the ❸ range instead of ❷ – for a room with an attached bathroom. Where a real spread of rooms are available in different classes and at very different prices, we've given prices as a range, such as ❷–❺.

❶ Rs300 and under
❷ Rs301–500
❸ Rs501–750

❹ US$10–15
❺ US$16–25
❻ US$26–40

❼ US$41–80
❽ US$81–150
❾ US$151 and over

serve a mainly Nepali clientele are usually more basic, and less attuned to the particular needs of Westerners.

Despite assurances to the contrary, you can't necessarily count on constant **hot water** (many places rely on solar panels) nor uninterrupted electricity (power cuts are a daily occurrence, though some establishments have generators). If constant hot water is important to you, ask what kind of water-heating system the guesthouse has – best of all is "geyser" (pronounced "geezer"), which means an electric immersion heater or backup.

All but the really cheap guesthouses will have a safe for **valuables**, and more upmarket places have lock-boxes in each room. It's a good idea to leave your passport and most of your money there; a photocopy of the relevant pages of your passport will suffice for moneychanging (but not for getting visas or trekking permits).

Budget guesthouses

Kathmandu and Pokhara have their own tourist quarters where fierce competition among **budget guesthouses** ensures great value. In these enclaves, all but the very cheapest places provide hot running water (though perhaps only sporadically), flush toilets, foam mattresses and (usually) clean sheets and quilts – a sleeping bag should not be necessary. Elsewhere in Nepal, expect rooms to be plainer and maybe scruffier, and the innkeepers to be less savvy

about what you might want. In the Terai, a room fan is normally provided. Most guesthouses also offer some sort of roof-terrace or garden, a supply of (supposedly) boiled and filtered water, a phone and TV. They're never heated, however, which makes them rather cold in winter.

Rooms in most budget places **cost** Rs300–750 (❷–❸), and standards can vary considerably. It's well worth remembering that there's usually a choice of **shared bathroom** or en suite. Rooms that cost less than about Rs400 are likely to be "common bath"; pay more and you can be fairly sure of "attached". The advantages of attached baths are obvious: you don't have to lock up your valuables, walk up and down halls in partial undress, or wait until the bathroom becomes free (a disaster if you've got the runs). In cheaper places, however, attached bathrooms aren't necessarily an asset, as they can make the room damp and smelly.

Mid-range guesthouses

Mid-range guesthouses (for lack of a better term) are becoming increasingly popular. These tend to be more spacious buildings where there's a lobby of sorts, the rooms have carpeting, nicer furniture, a fan and often a phone and TV, toilet paper is provided in the bathrooms, the hot water is more reliable and daily maid service is available. The better ones will provide a portable electric heater in winter. Most quote their prices in dollars, though you can pay in rupees. Some may add up to 23 percent in service and government taxes, and many even accept payment by credit card.

Figure on **paying** $10–25 (**④**–**⑤**) for a double room of this sort. Even if everything is listed as attached bath, there may be a couple of cheaper rooms with common bath, so it's well worth asking what's on offer; this is a good way to open up price negotiations, too.

Hotels and resorts

It's hard to generalize about the more expensive **hotels and resorts**. Some charge a hefty premium to insulate you from the Nepal you came to see, while others offer unique experiences of the country. Prices for international-type features begin around the $50 mark (**⑦**) but expect to pay more like $85 a night (**⑧**) or more for a genuinely classy experience.

This guide also recommends several smaller resort hotels that offer something unique, like a breathtaking view or the only hot shower for miles around. After a trek or a long spell of roughing it, a night or two in one of these places can be just what the doctor ordered.

Jungle lodges and **tented camps** inside the Terai wildlife parks are typically the most expensive options of all. A stay in one is indeed the experience of a lifetime, but if $200 or more per night is beyond your reach, there are plenty of more affordable outfits just outside Chitwan and Bardia national parks.

Camping

Perhaps surprisingly, **camping** doesn't come high on the agenda in Nepal. Much of the country is well settled, every flat patch of ground is farmed, and rooms are so cheap that camping offers little saving. The only campground is in Pokhara.

It's a different story, of course, if you're **rafting or trekking**, and camping is also possible in certain jungle areas near or even inside the Terai wildlife parks. Long-distance cyclists might find it useful to bring a tent along to avoid spending nights in roadside fleapits en route to more interesting places. Between October and May, many terraces in the hills are left fallow, and you can pitch a tent if you ask permission and keep out of the owner's way. Set up well away from villages, unless you want to be the locals' entertainment for the evening. Don't burn wood – the locals need it more than you do. An unattended tent will probably be safe if zipped shut, but anything left outside is liable to disappear.

Village stays and homestays

Nepal is a predominantly rural society, and its rich culture and ethnic diversity are best experienced in its villages. A growing number of programmes enable visitors to stay overnight in private homes in traditional villages far from the tourist trails. **Village stays** (also called village tourism or homestays) offer a unique opportunity for comfortable cultural immersion, and could become a good way to disperse visitors and spread the economic benefits of tourism into rural areas. The idea is that a tour operator contracts with a whole village to accommodate and entertain guests; rooms in local

---

Sustainable tourism

While tourism is a key part of Nepal's economy, it doesn't always have a positive impact on the country. The **Responsible Travel Nepal** initiative provides Nepali tourism companies – hotels and resorts, trekking and adventure companies, travel agencies and so on – with training and support to encourage them to ensure their activities and management practices follow sustainable tourism principles. Crucially, it emphasises the business benefits of adopting these principles, helping the companies to build links with operators and travellers around the world, improve their marketing work and expand their businesses. Responsible Travel Nepal's website (ⓦ www.responsibletravelnepal.com) provides information about the companies participating, and is a useful first port of call when planning activities in Nepal.

houses are fitted with bathrooms and a few tourist-style comforts, host families are trained to prepare meals that won't disturb delicate Western constitutions, and a guide accompanies the guests to interpret, if necessary. Participating villages tend to be located a couple of hours' walk from the nearest road – close enough to be easily accessible for less-than-fit visitors, yet far enough to receive less outside influence than even the smallest village on a trekking route.

There are numerous **village tourism programmes**, including one in Chispani, southeast of Pokhara near Rup Tal, run by the Pokhara-based Child Welfare Scheme (contact *Nature's Grace Lodge* in Pokhara for details ☏061/207177); another operator,

Lama Adventure Treks and Expeditions, runs programmes in Tamang villages southeast of Kathmandu; details of it and Kathmandu-based schemes can be found on p.87. Most village tourism schemes prefer groups of at least three or four people, so if you're an individual or couple you should contact the companies well in advance and adjust your schedule to co-ordinate with already-scheduled departures.

A few language institutes and other organizations in Kathmandu also organize **informal homestays** with individual families in and around the valley. Most of these are intended specifically to provide Nepali language immersion, but it's a great way to make local friends, whatever the official motive.

Eating and drinking

Nepal – specifically Kathmandu – is renowned as the budget eating capital of Asia. Sadly, its reputation is based not on Nepali but pseudo-Western food: pizza, chips (fries), "sizzling" steaks and apple pie are the staples of tourist restaurants. Outside the popular areas, the chief complaint of travellers is lack of variety in the diet, though with a little extra willingness to experiment, a range of dishes can be found.

Indeed, a vast range of flavours can be found just in **daal bhaat**, the national dish of rice, lentils, lightly curried vegetables and pickles; though it can also be disappointingly bland. In the Kathmandu Valley, the indigenous Newars have their own unique cuisine of spicy meat and vegetable dishes, while *roti* (bread) and the vast range of Indian curries, snacks and sweets comes into play in the Terai; in the high mountains, the traditional diet consists of noodle soups, potatoes and toasted flour. *Chow-chow* packet noodles, cooked up as a spicy soup snack, are ubiquitous.

Cheap as it is, food tends to be the biggest daily **cost** for budget travellers. A tourist dinner will cost Rs150–300 per person; double or more in a posh place. *Daal bhaat* costs roughly Rs50 anywhere except in

tourist areas (where it'll cost double to ten times that), and you can fill up on road snacks like noodles or *momo* dumplings for under Rs100.

Where to eat

Tourist restaurants in Kathmandu, Pokhara and a few other well-visited places show a knack for sensing what travellers want and simulating it with basic ingredients. Some specialize in particular cuisines, but the majority attempt a little of everything. Display cases full of extravagant cakes and pies are a standard come-on.

Local **Nepali diners** (*bhojanalaya* or, confusingly enough, *hotel*) are traditionally humble affairs, offering a limited choice of dishes or just *daal bhaat*. Menus don't exist, but the food will normally be on display or cooking in full view, so all you have to do is point. Utensils should be available on request, but if not, try doing as Nepalis do and eat with your right hand – see p.53 for more on social taboos relating to eating. In towns and cities, eateries tend to be dark, almost conspiratorial places, unmarked and hidden behind curtains. On the highways they're bustlingly public and spill outdoors in an effort to win business. Terai cities always have a fancy (by Nepali standards) restaurant or two, patronized by businessmen and Indian tourists.

Teahouses (*chiyapasal*) really only sell tea and basic snacks, while the simple **taverns** (*bhatti*) of the Kathmandu Valley and the western hills put the emphasis on alcoholic drinks and meat snacks, but may serve Nepali meals. Trailside, both *chiyapasal* and *bhatti* are typically modest operations run out of family kitchens. **Sweet shops** (*mithai-pasal*), identified by their shiny display cases, are intended to fill the gap between the traditional mid-morning and early evening meals; besides sweets and tea, they also do South Indian and Nepali savoury snacks.

Street vendors sell fruit, nuts, roasted corn, fried bread and various fried specialities. As often as not, food will come to you when you're travelling – at every bus stop, vendors will clamber aboard or hawk their wares through the window.

Vegetarians will feel at home in Nepal, since meat is considered a luxury. Tourist menus invariably include veggie items.

Nepali food

Daal bhaat tarkaari (*daal* means lentil, *bhaat* rice and *tarkaari* vegetable), usually just known as **daal bhaat**, isn't just the most popular meal in Nepal. For many Nepalis it's the only meal they ever eat, twice a day, every day of their lives, and they don't feel they've eaten properly without it. Indeed, in much of Nepal, *bhaat* is a synonym for food and *khaanaa* (food) is a synonym for rice. The *daal bhaat* served in restaurants ranges from excellent to derisory – it's a meal that's really meant to be eaten at home – so if you spend much time trekking or travelling off the beaten track you'll probably quickly tire of it. It's worth looking out for establishments sporting the name Thakali – Nepalis believe

this ethnic group (originating in the hills around Annapurna) produces a good *daal bhaat,* and they are usually right.

That said, a good **achhaar** (a sort of relish or pickle made with tomato, radish or whatever's in season) can liven up a *daal bhaat* tremendously. Once you've entered the world of *daal bhaat*, you'll learn that there are endless subtle variations in the flavours and grades of rice and in the idea of good *daal* from the buttery, yellow gunge of *raharkodaal* to the king of winter lentils, *maaskodaal*, cooked in an iron pot until it turns from green to black. Among the vegetable accompaniments, look out for *gundruk*, a tangy staple of fermented vegetables. Salty spinach and cauliflower with potatoes are other standards.

Daal bhaat is often served on a gleaming steel platter divided into compartments; add the *daal* and other condiments to the rice, knead the resulting mixture into mouth-sized balls with the right hand, then push it off the fingers into your mouth with the thumb. One price covers unlimited refills, except in tourist-savvy establishments.

Most Nepalis begin the day with a cup of tea and little else, eating *daal bhaat* some time in the **mid-morning** (often around nine or ten o'clock) and again in the **evening**, with just a snack of potatoes, *makkai* (popcorn) or noodles in between. *Daal bhaat* times in Kathmandu are pushing later and later towards lunchtime but, outside the city, it's worth remembering that if you turn up for your *khaanaa* at noon it'll either be cold or take hours to cook from scratch.

You'll usually be able to supplement a plate of *daal bhaat* with small side dishes of *maasu* (meat) – chicken, goat or, in riverside bazaars, fish – marinated in spices and fried in oil or **ghiu** (clarified butter). In Indian-influenced Terai towns you can often get *taarekodaal*, fried with *ghiu* and spices, and *roti* instead of rice. **Sukuti** (dried, spiced meat fried in oil) is popular everywhere. You could make a meal out of rice or *chiura* (beaten, dried rice) and **sekuwa** (kebabs of spicy marinated meat chunks) or **taareko maachhaa** (fried fish), common in the Terai. If you're invited into a peasant home in the high hills you might be served **dhedo** (a dough made from water mixed with toasted corn, millet or wheat flour) instead of rice. Some say *dhedo* with *gundruk*, not *daal bhaat*, is the real national food of Nepal, though it's only just started to appear on the menu of Thakali restaurants.

Nepali **desserts** include *khir* (rice pudding), *sikarni* (thick, creamy yogurt with cinnamon, raisins and nuts) and versions of Indian sweets.

Newari food

Like many aspects of Newari culture (see p.180), **Newari food** is all too often regarded as exotic but too weird for outsiders. It's complex, subtle, delicious and devilishly hard to make: most dishes require absolutely fresh ingredients and/or very long preparation times.

Most specialities are quite spicy, and based around four mainstays: buffalo, rice, pulses and vegetables (especially radish). The Newars use every part of the buffalo, or "buff": **momocha** (meat-filled steamed dumplings), **choyila** (buff cubes fried with spices and greens), **palula** (spicy buff with ginger sauce) and **kachila** (a paté of minced raw buff, mixed with ginger and mustard oil) are some of the more accessible dishes; others are made from tongue, stomach, lung, blood, bone marrow and so on. Because of caste restrictions, Newars rarely eat boiled rice outside the home. Newari restaurants therefore serve it in the form of **baji** (*chiura* in Nepali) – rice that's been partially cooked and then rolled flat and dried, looking something like rolled oats – or **chataamari** (a sort of pizza made with rice flour, usually topped with minced buff). Pulses and beans play a role in several other preparations, notably **woh** (fried lentil-flour patties, also known as *baara* in Nepali), **kwati** (a soup made with several varieties of sprouted beans), **musyapalu** (a dry mix of roasted soya beans and ginger) and **bhuti** (boiled soya beans with spices and herbs). Various vegetable mixtures are available seasonally, including **pancha kol** (a curry made with five vegetables) and **alu achhaar** (boiled potato in a spicy sauce). The best veggie option to try is *alutama*, a sour soup made with bamboo shoots and potatoes. Radish

turns up in myriad forms of *achhaar*. Order two or three of these dishes per person, together with *baji*, and share them around.

International food

Kathmandu and Pokhara are the poles of a free-market free-for-all of tourist restaurants offering a taste of every cuisine under the sun. There's no denying that this **international food** is tasty, but the sheer range of choice (when some people struggle to eat rice twice a day) can seem fairly grotesque, and has the unfortunate side effect of isolating many visitors from Nepalese cooking.

Sizzling steaks (usually buffalo meat), lasagne and pizza have been the mainstay for years, but restaurants have moved upmarket into dedicated cuisines, notably Chinese, French, Italian, Japanese, Korean, Mexican and Thai. Monosodium glutamate is often used, tending to make all tourist food taste the same; it can also cause allergic reactions (try asking for food without "tasting powder").

Most tourist restaurants do deals of eggs, hash browns and toast for **breakfast**. Porridge or muesli make healthy alternatives. Out in the sticks, you'll have to adjust your eating schedule to mid-morning *daal bhaat*, or down greasy omelettes and packet-noodles.

Indian food

The dishes you're most likely to encounter in Nepal are from **northern India**: thick, rich **curries** and **tandoori**. **Roti** (bread) is the accompaniment: *chapati* (round, flat unleavened bread) are widely available, *naan* (bigger, chewier versions), *paratha* (layered shallow-fried bread) and *puri* (puffy fried *bread*) less common.

In Kathmandu you'll also run across South Indian canteens, which serve a predominantly vegetarian cuisine that employs the same ingredients in very different ways. The staple dish here is the **masala dosa**, a rice-flour pancake rolled around curried potatoes, served with **sambhar** (a savoury daal flavoured with tamarind) and coconut chutney.

There are an incredible array of Indian **sweets**, including *laddu*, yellow-and-orange speckled semolina balls; *jalebi*, orange pretzel-shaped tubes of deep-fried, syrup-soaked treacle; *barphi*, silver leafed fudgy diamonds; *gulabjamun*, spongy balls in super-sweet syrup; and *ras malai*, cream cheese balls in a milky, perfumed syrup.

Tibetan food

Strictly speaking, "Tibetan" refers to nationals of Tibet, but the people of several other highland ethnic groups eat what could be called Tibetan food.

Momo, arguably the most famous and popular of Tibetan dishes, are available throughout upland Nepal. Distant cousins to ravioli, the half-moon-shapes are filled with meat, vegetables and ginger, steamed, and served with hot tomato salsa and a bowl of broth. Fried *momo* are called *kothe*. *Shyaphagle*, made from the same ingredients, are Tibetan-style pasties. Tibetan cuisine is also full of hearty soups called **thukpa** or **thenthuk**, consisting of noodles, meat and vegetables in broth.

For a group feast, try the huge **gyakok** (chicken, pork, prawns, fish, tofu, eggs and vegetables), which gets its name from the brass container it's served in; *gyakok* is found in tourist restaurants and has to be ordered several hours ahead. In trekking lodges you'll encounter pitta-like Tibetan **bread**.

The average peasant seldom eats any of the above: the most common standbys in the high country are **potatoes** and **tsampa** (toasted barley flour) mixed with milk or tea to make a porridge paste.

Road food

Snacks are available at every stop. Common fare includes **pakora** (vegetables dipped in chickpea-flour batter, deep fried), and **bean curry** served with *puris* or *roti*. Another possibility is **dahi chiura**, a mixture of yogurt and beaten rice. If you're in a hurry, you can grab a handful of **samosas** (curried vegetables in fried pastry triangles), *baara* (fried lentil patties), or other titbits on a leaf plate.

In the hill towns and around Kathmandu, huge aluminium steamers placed by the restaurant door advertise **momo**. Hugely popular as a lunchtime snack, these meat-filled dumplings are served with a tomato or chilli sauce.

If nothing else, there will always be packet **noodles** (*chow-chow*). They can either be boiled as a soup, stir-fried as chow mein, or eaten straight from the packet, the method favoured by children in Nepal.

Other snacks

Imported **chocolates** are sold in tourist areas, and waxy Indian substitutes can be found in most towns. **Biscuits** and cheap boiled **sweets** (confusingly enough, called *chocolet* in Nepali) are sold everywhere. **Ice cream** brands such as Kwality and Vadilal are safe, but steer well clear of unbranded varieties of ice-lollies. **Cheese**, produced from cow, buffalo and occasionally yak milk (nak milk in fact – the yak is the male and the nak the female), comes in several styles and is sold in tourist areas along trekking routes. Watch out for *churpi*, a native cheese made from dried buttermilk – it's inedibly hard.

Fruit

Which fruits are available depends on the season, but there's usually a good choice imported from India. Lovely **mandarin oranges**, which ripen throughout the late autumn and winter, grow from the Terai up to around 1200m and are sweetest near the upper end of their range. Autumn and winter also bring **papaya** in the Terai and lower hills, **Asian pears**, **apples** and **sugar cane**. **Mangoes** from the Terai start ripening in May and are available throughout most of the summer, as are **lychees**, **watermelons**, **pineapples** and **guavas**. **Bananas**, harvested year-round at the lower elevations, are sold from bicycles everywhere.

Drinks

Water (*paani*) is automatically served with food in Nepali restaurants – but verification is difficult, so it's best to pass. Brands of bottled water are widely available and usually safe, although some tests have found germs in supposedly sterilized water; check that the seal is intact. You can always purify your own water (see p.49).

Soft drinks (*chiso*) are sold just about everywhere for around Rs20, but prices rise as you move into roadless areas. Lemon soda, made with soda water and a squeeze of lime juice, makes a good sugarless alternative.

Tea (*chiya*), something of a national beverage, is traditionally brewed by boiling tea

Tobacco and paan

Nepalis love their **cigarettes** (*churot*). The cheaper packeted cigarettes like Yak and Khukuri are harsh and strong for most Western tastes. Marlboro are widely available, while the most similar luxury domestic brand is Surya. After the evening meal, old men may be seen smoking tobacco in a hookah (hubble-bubble), or occasionally passing around a chilam (clay pipe).

Many Nepali men make quite a production of preparing **chewing tobacco** (*surti*), slapping and rubbing it in the palm of the hand before placing behind the lower lip. *Surti* comes in little foil packets hung outside most general stores.

At least as popular, particularly near India, is the digestive and mild stimulant paan. A paan seller starts with a betel leaf, upon which he spreads various ingredients, the most common being jharda (tobacco) or mitha (sweet). Paan-wallahs also sell foil packets of paan parag, a simple, ready-made mix.

dust with milk (*dudh*) and water, with heaps of sugar (*chini*) and a bit of ginger, cardamom or pepper. In tourist restaurants you'll be offered "black" or "milk" tea with a teabag – you have to specify "Nepali" or "*masala*" tea if you want it made the traditional way. You can also ask for lemon tea or "hot lemon". Tibetans take their tea with salt and yak butter, which is definitely an acquired taste.

Locally produced **coffee** and fancy espresso machines are increasingly available in Nepal, though most restaurants just do a very milky instant.

Roadside stalls serve freshly squeezed **fruit juices** and **lassis**, but the practice of adding water and sugar is widespread – if the water comes from the tap, as is usually the case, your chances of catching something are high. Fruit juice in cartons is sold in many shops.

Alcohol

Beer (*biyar*) makes a fine accompaniment to Nepali and Indian food. Foreign brands brewed by local ventures – notably San Miguel, Carlsberg and Tuborg, all taste much the same as each other and the domestic lagers. They come in 650ml bottles and cost a fairly standard Rs110. Non-recyclable aluminium cans are becoming more common.

An amazing and amusing selection of **spirits** is bottled in Nepal, ranging from the classic Khukuri Rum (dark and raisiny) to a myriad of cheap whiskies. They're cheap and rough, but tolerable when mixed. Look out for regional specialities like the apricot and apple brandies of Marpha, north of Pokhara. Imported spirits and **wine** are available in supermarkets and convenience stores at imported prices; many tourist restaurants and bars serve wine by the glass, and make cocktails.

Nepalis are avid **home brewers** and distillers. Home-brewed beer often made from rice or millet is commonly referred to by the Tibetan or hill word, *chhang*. *Raksi*, which is ubiquitous in hill Nepal, is a distilled version of the same and bears a heady resemblance to tequila or grappa. Harder to find, but perhaps the most pleasant drink of all, is a highland homebrew called **tongba**. The ingredients are a jug or tankard of fermented millet, a straw and a flask of hot water: you pour the water in, let it steep, and suck the mildly alcoholic brew through the straw until you reach the bottom; you repeat the process until the flavour and the alcohol run out and it can easily lubricate an entire evening.

Thanks to recent **legislation**, pubs and bars must now stop serving at 11pm.

Festivals, holidays and entertainment

Stumbling onto a local festival may prove to be the highlight of your travels in Nepal – and given the sheer number of them, you'd be unlucky not to. Though most are religious in nature, merrymaking, not solemnity, is the order of the day, and onlookers are always welcome. You're even more likely to come across Nepali music and dance, which are passions for many Nepalis, and form an integral part of most festivals. The language barrier means that few tourists seek out Nepali cinema, for all its popularity among Nepali urban youth.

Festivals

Festivals may be Hindu, Buddhist, animist or a hybrid of all three. **Hindu events** can take the form of huge pilgrimages and fairs (*mela*), or more introspective gatherings such as ritual bathings at sacred confluences (*tribeni*) or special acts of worship (*puja*) at temples. Many see animal sacrifices followed by jolly family feasts, with priests and musicians usually on hand. Parades and processions (*jaatra*) are common, especially in the Kathmandu Valley, where idols are periodically ferried around on great, swaying chariots.

Buddhist festivals are no less colourful, typically bringing together maroon-robed clergy and lay pilgrims to walk and prostrate themselves around stupas (dome-shaped monuments, usually repainted specially for the occasion), and sometimes featuring elaborately costumed dances.

Many of Nepal's **animist** peoples follow the Hindu calendar, but local nature-worshipping rites take place across the hills throughout the year, many of them unrecorded by the outside world. **Shamanic rites** usually take place at home, at the request of a particular family, although shamans themselves have their own calendar of fairs (*mela*) at which they converge on a particular holy spot, often high in the mountains. You'll have to travel widely and sensitively to have the chance to witness a shaman in action.

Jubilant (and public), Nepali **weddings** are always scheduled on astrologically auspicious days, which fall in the greatest numbers during the months of Magh, Phaagun and Baisaakh (see opposite). The approach of a wedding party is often heralded by a hired *band baajaa* or brass band – sounding like a Dixieland sextet playing in a pentatonic scale – and open-air feasts go on until the early hours. The bride usually wears red, and for the rest of her married life she will colour the parting of her hair with red *sindur*.

Funeral processions are understandably sombre and should be left in peace. The body is normally carried to the cremation site within hours of death by white-shrouded friends and relatives; white is the colour of mourning for Hindus, and the eldest son is expected to shave his head and wear white for a year following the death of a parent. Many of the hill tribes conduct special shamanic rites to guide the deceased's soul to the land of the dead.

Festival dates

Knowing when and where festivals are to be held will not only enliven your time in Nepal, but should also help you avoid annoyances such as closed offices and booked-up buses. Unfortunately, as most are governed by the lunar calendar, **festival dates** vary annually, and determining them more than a year in advance is a highly complicated business best left to astrologers. Each lunar cycle is divided into "bright" (waning) and "dark" (waxing) halves, which are in turn divided into fourteen lunar "days". Each of these days has a name – *purnima* is the full moon, *astami* the eighth day, *aunshi* the new moon, and so on. Thus lunar festivals are always observed on a given day of either the bright or dark half of a given Nepali month. The following list details Nepal's most widely observed festivals, plus a few notable smaller events. Many other local ones are described in the relevant chapters. Few festivals fall in the months of Jeth (May–June), Asaar (June–July) and Poush (Dec–Jan). For a full discussion of the Nepali calendar, with a list of months, see p.68. For upcoming festival dates, check one of the Nepali calendars on the **web** (try ⓦwww.visitnepal.com or www.nepalhomepage.com).

Magh (Jan–Feb)

Magh (or **Makar**) **Sankranti** Marking a rare solar (rather than lunar) event in the Nepali calendar – the day the sun is farthest from the earth – the first day of Magh (Jan 14 or 15) is an occasion for ritual bathing at all sacred river confluences, especially at Devghat and Sankhu. The day also begins a month-long period during which families do daily readings of the *Swasthani*, a uniquely Nepali compilation of Hindu myths, and many women emulate Parvati's fast for Shiva, one of the *Swasthani* stories.

Basanta Panchami This one-day spring festival is celebrated on the fifth day after the new moon in most Hindu hill areas. The day is also known as Saraswati Puja, after the goddess of learning, and Shri Panchami, after the Buddhist saint Manjushri. School playgrounds are decorated with streamers and children have their books and pens blessed; high-caste boys may undergo a special rite of passage.

Phaagun (Feb–March)

Losar Tibetan New Year falls on the new moon of either Magh or Phaagun, and is preceded by three days of drinking, dancing and feasting. The day itself is celebrated most avidly at Boudha, where morning rituals culminate with horn blasts and the hurling of *tsampa*. Losar is a time for families to be together, and is the highlight of the calendar in Buddhist highland areas, as well as in Tibetan settlements near Kathmandu and Pokhara.

Shivaraatri Falling on the new moon of Phaagun, "Shiva's Night" is marked by bonfires and evening vigils in all Hindu areas, but most spectacularly at Pashupatinath, where tens of thousands of pilgrims and sadhus from all over the subcontinent gather for Nepal's best-known *mela* (religious fair). Fervent worship and bizarre yogic demonstrations can be seen throughout the day throughout the Pashupatinath complex. Children collect firewood money by holding pieces of string across the road to block passersby – foreigners are considered easy prey. Nepalis say the festival is usually followed by a final few days of winter weather, which is Shiva's way of encouraging the Indian sadhus to go home.

Holi Nepal's version of the springtime water festival, common to many Asian countries, is an impish affair lasting about a week, and commemorates a myth in which the god Krishna, when still a boy, outsmarted the demoness Holika. During this period, anyone – bus passengers included – is a fair target for water balloons and coloured powder (usually red, the colour of rejoicing). It culminates in a general free-for-all on Phaagun Purnima, the full-moon day of Phaagun.

Chait (March–April)

Chait Dasain Like its autumn namesake, the "little Dasain", observed on the eighth day after the new moon, involves lots of animal sacrifices. The goriest action takes place at goddess temples, such as the one at Gorkha, and in the Kot courtyard near Kathmandu's Durbar Square, where the army's top brass come to witness the beheading of numerous buffalo and goats.

Ram Nawami The birthday of Lord Ram is observed on the ninth day after the full moon at all temples dedicated to Vishnu in his incarnation as the hero of the Ramayana, one of the great Hindu epics. By far the biggest and most colourful celebrations take place in Janakpur, where thousands of pilgrims flock to the Ram temple.

Seto Machhendranath Jaatra Kathmandu's answer to Patan's Raato Machhendranath Jaatra (see below), this sees a lumbering wooden chariot containing the white mask of the god Machhendranath pulled through the narrow lanes of the old city for four days, starting on Chait Dasain.

Baisaakh (April–May)

Nawa Barsa Nepali New Year, which always falls on the first day of Baisaakh (April 13 or 14), is observed with localized parades. Culminating on Nawa Barsa, Bhaktapur's five-day celebration, known as Bisket or Biska, is the most colourful, combining religious processions with a rowdy tug-of-war (see p.188); the nearby settlements of Thimi and Bode host similarly wild scenes.

Raato Machhendranath Jaatra Nepal's most spectacular festival: thousands gather to watch as the image of Machhendranath, the Kathmandu Valley's rain-bringing deity, is pulled around the streets of Patan in a swaying, sixty-foot-high chariot. It moves only on astrologically auspicious days, taking four weeks or more to complete its journey. For more detail, see p.120.

Buddha Jayanti The anniversary of the Buddha's birth, enlightenment and death is celebrated on the full-moon day of Baisaakh at all Buddhist temples, but most visibly at Swayambhu, where the freshly repainted stupa is decorated with thousands of lights the night before; on the day, ritual dances are performed here by priests dressed as the five aspects of Buddhahood. Processions are also held at the Boudha stupa and in Patan. Observances at the Buddha's birthplace, Lumbini, are rather sparse.

Saaun (July–Aug)

Janai Purnima The annual changing of the sacred thread (*janai*) worn by high-caste Hindu men takes place at holy bathing sites throughout the country on the full-moon day of Saaun. Men and women of any caste may also receive a yellow-and-orange "protective band" (*raksha bandhan*) around one wrist, which is then worn until Tihaar, when it's supposed to be tied onto the tail of a cow. Mass observances are held at Gosainkund, a holy lake high in the mountains north of Kathmandu; Pashupatinath, outside Kathmandu; and most prominently at Patan's Kumbeshwar temple, where priests sit cross-legged tying strings and bestowing *tikas*, and *jhankri* (hill shamans) perform sacred dances.

Gaai Jaatra Newari tradition has it that Yamraj, the god of death, opens the gates of judgement on the day of the full moon, allowing departed souls to enter. Falling on the day after the full moon, Gaai Jaatra honours cows (*gaai*), who are supposed to lead departed souls to Yamraj's abode. Processions in Kathmandu, Bhaktapur and other Newari towns are both solemn and whimsical: an occasion for families to honour loved ones who have died in the past year, but also for young boys to dress up in fanciful cow costumes or masquerade as sadhus. In Bhaktapur, where the festival is known as Gunhi Punhi and starts a day earlier (coinciding with Janai Purnima), men parade around town in humorous costumes. Satirical street performances are less common nowadays than they once were, but newspapers and magazines publish caustic Gaai Jaatra specials.

Nag Panchami On the fifth day after the new moon, Kathmandu Valley residents quietly propitiate the *nag* (snake spirits), who are traditionally held to control the monsoon rains and earthquakes, by pasting pictures of *nag* over their doorways with cow dung and offering milk, rice and other favourite *nag* foods to the images. Wells are cleaned only on this day, when the *nag* are believed to be away worshipping their ancestral deities.

Ghanta Karna On the fourteenth day after the full moon, residents of Kathmandu Valley towns celebrate the victory of the gods over the demon Ghanta Karna ("Bell Ears") by erecting effigies and then burning or tearing them down, to childrens' delight.

Bhadau (Aug–Sept)

Krishna Astami (also called **Krishna Jayanti** or **Krishna Janmastahmi**). Krishna temples such as Patan's Krishna Mandir throng with thousands of worshippers celebrating the god's birth on the seventh day after the full moon. Vigils are also held the night before.

Tij The three-day "Women's Festival", which starts on the third day after the new moon, sees groups of women clad in red (the colour of rejoicing and domestic harmony) singing and dancing through the streets. Letting their families fend for themselves for once, they start with a girls' night out, feasting until midnight when they begin a day-long fast. On the second day they queue up to worship Shiva at the Pashupatinath temple outside of Kathmandu, and break the fast and ritually bathe to remove their sins on the final day.

Indra Jaatra A wild week of chariot processions and masked-dance performances in Kathmandu, held around the full moon of Bhadau. On the last day, which is also known as Kumari Jaatra, beer flows from the mouth of an idol in Durbar Square.

Yartung A swashbuckling fair held at Muktinath, in the Annapurna trekking region, centred around the full-moon day and featuring horse-racing, dancing, drinking and gambling.

Asoj (Sept–Oct)

Dasain (known as **Dashera** near India). Although Hindu in origin, Nepal's longest and greatest festival is enthusiastically embraced by members of almost all religious and ethnic groups. It stretches over fifteen days, from the new moon to the full moon of Asoj, with the liveliest action taking place on the seventh, ninth and tenth days. Normally falling just after the summer rice harvest is in, Dasain is a time for families to gather (buses get extremely crowded with homeward-bound passengers), children to be indulged (with kites, makeshift swings and miniature ferris wheels), and animals to be sacrificed (the markets are filled with doomed goats). On the first day, known as Ghatasthapana, people plant *jamura* (barley) in a *kalash* (sanctified vessel), representing Durga, Dasain's honoured goddess; the seedlings will be picked and worn in the hair on the tenth day. Devotees congregate at local goddess temples throughout the next nine nights. A separate festival, **Panchali Bhairab Jaatra**, features late-night processions between the Bhairab's shrine and the Kumari Ghar in Kathmandu, and coincides with the fourth and fifth days of Dasain. On the seventh day, Fulpati, a bouquet of sacred flowers (*fulpati*) is carried in a procession from Rani Pokhari to the Hanuman Dhoka Palace in Kathmandu, with many VIPs in attendance. The ninth day, Navami, begins at midnight with tantric buffalo sacrifices inside the forbidden Taleju (a form of Durga) temples of the Kathmandu Valley; throughout the day, animals are ritually beheaded publicly in the Kot Courtyard near Kathmandu's Durbar Square, and in every village and city of Nepal; their blood is sprinkled on tools, vehicles and even aircraft to impart Durga's *shakti* (power). These rituals commemorate Durga's slaying of the demon Mahisasur, and more generally, the triumph of good over evil. Bijaya Dasami, the "Victorious Tenth Day", celebrates Ram's victory over the demon Ravana – with Durga's help. Various processions and masked dance troupes ply the streets and families visit their elders to receive blessings and *tika*.

Kaattik (Oct–Nov)

Tihaar (Diwali near India). Lasting for five days, starting two days before the new moon, the "Festival of Lights" is associated with Yamraj, the god of death, and Lakshmi, the goddess of wealth and good fortune. On the first day, Nepalis set out food on leaf plates for crows, regarded as Yamraj's messengers; on the second, they honour dogs as Yamraj's gatekeepers, giving them *tika*, flower garlands and special foods; and on the third they garland cows both as the symbol of Lakshmi and as the soul's guide to Yamarj's underworld. The festival's most picturesque event, Lakshmi Puja, comes on the evening of the third day, when families throughout Nepal ring their homes with oil lamps, candles or electric lights to guide Lakshmi to their homes so she can bless them with prosperity for the year. Trusting in her, many Nepalis gamble on street corners, and student groups make the rounds singing "Diusire", a form of musical fundraising. Firecrackers have also become a big part of the fun for kids. To Newars, the fourth day is known as Mha Puja ("Self-Worship"), an occasion for private rituals, and also their New Year's Day, marked by banners, well-wishing and motorcycle parades in the Kathmandu Valley's three main cities. On the fifth day, Bhaai Tika, sisters recall the myth of Jamuna, who tricked Yamraj into postponing her brother's death indefinitely, by blessing their younger brothers and giving them flower garlands, *tika* and sweetmeats.
Chhath Coinciding with the third day of Tihaar, this festival honours Surya, the sun god, and is one of the most important for the Maithili-speaking people of the eastern Terai. Chhath is celebrated most ardently in Janakpur, where women gather by ponds and rivers to greet the sun's first rays with prayers, offerings and ritual baths.

Mangsir (Nov–Dec)

Ram-Sita Biwaha Panchami As many as 100,000 pilgrims converge on Janakpur for this five-day gathering, beginning on the new moon of Mangsir. The highlight is the re-enactment of the wedding of Ram and Sita, the divine, star-crossed lovers of the Ramayana, one of the great Hindu epics. Janakpur's stature as a holy city rests on its having been the location of the original wedding.
Mani Rimdu Held at Tengboche and Chiwong monasteries in the Everest region around the full moon of the ninth Tibetan month (usually Oct/Nov), this colourful Sherpa masked dance dramatizes Buddhism's victory over the ancient Bon religion in eighth-century Tibet. A similar event is held in May or June at Thami.

Music and dance

Music is as common as conversation in Nepal. In the hills, travelling minstrels (*gaaine*) make their living singing ballads and accompanying themselves on the *sarangi*, a hand-carved, four-stringed fiddle. Teenagers of ethnic groups from the hills traditionally attract the attention of the opposite sex by exchanging teasing verses. After-dinner singalongs are popular, even in

Kathmandu, and of course music is indispensable in all festivals.

Traditional Nepali music is often drowned out by the rising tide of **Indian film music**, with its surging strings and hysterically shrill vocals, yet the mercifully calm and villagey **Nepali folk music** still gets a good airing, and there's a burgeoning **Nepali pop** scene that adds varying degrees of local flavour to a broadly rock sound. Restaurants and bars in the tourist quarters of Kathmandu and Pokhara host free performances by local folk groups, and weekend-night gigs by Nepali rock and reggae cover bands.

Nepali music is inseparable from **dance**, especially at festivals. Nepali dance is an unaffected folk art – neither wildly athletic nor subtle, it depicts everyday activities such as work and courtship. Each region and ethnic group has its own distinct traditions, and during your travels you should get a chance to join a local hoedown or two, if not a full-blown festival extravaganza. Look out, too, for the stick dance of the lowland Tharus, performed regularly at lodges around Chitwan National Park.

Staged **culture shows** in Kathmandu and Pokhara are a long way from the real thing, but they do provide a taste of folk and religious dances, and hint at the incredible cultural diversity contained in such a small country. Most troupes perform such standards as the dance of the *jhankri*

(shaman-exorcists still consulted by many hill-dwelling Nepalis); the sleeve-twirling dance of the Sherpas; the flirting dance of the hill-dwelling Tamangs; the Tharus' fanciful peacock dance; perhaps a formal priestly dance, to the accompaniment of a classical *raga* (musical piece); and at least one of the dances of the Kathmandu Valley's holiday-loving Newars.

For more information on Nepali folk music, see the box on p.206.

Cinema

Nepal's love–hate relationship with India is perhaps best illustrated by its **cinema**: Nepalis might grouse about cultural imperialism, but that doesn't stop them rushing to see the latest schmaltz and pyrotechnics from Bollywood. Though Nepali films are still the exception, and are less slick than Indian productions, they're much more popular when they're on. You won't, of course, find English subtitles, but an expedition to a Nepali screening (cinemas are found in every major town) makes a lively antidote to the usual impressions of Nepali culture given by festivals, folk-dances and the like. **DVD** rental shops are commonplace in the main cities. Some tourist restaurants screen Hollywood flicks on DVD, many of them amazingly current – bootleg DVDs often hit the streets in Kathmandu long before their official release.

Health

Hygiene is not one of Nepal's strong points. Sanitation is poor, and lots of bugs make the rounds, especially during spring and monsoon. But don't panic – by coming prepared and looking after yourself while there, you're unlikely to come down with anything worse than a cold or the local version of "Delhi belly".

This section deals with health matters mainly in the context of Western-style medicine. Traditional ayurvedic and Tibetan practices are discussed later on p.56. For more detailed advice, refer to the books recommended on p.466, or the websites listed on p.51.

Before you go

No **inoculations** are required for Nepal, but hepatitis A, typhoid and meningitis jabs are recommended, and it's worth being up to date with tetanus, polio, mumps and measles boosters. Malaria tablets, injections for Japanese B encephalitis and rabies are also worth considering. All of these can be obtained in Kathmandu, but it's better to get nasty things like injections done before, especially as it takes **some weeks** for certain inoculation courses.

If you have any medical conditions or concerns about your health, don't set off without seeing a **doctor** first. Medicines are sold over the counter everywhere, but it's best to bring your prescribed medications. Consider having a dental check-up before you go. If you wear glasses, bring an extra pair; if you wear contacts bring a backup pair of glasses as a precaution against dust and pollution.

Recommended inoculations

Most travellers decide to inoculate themselves against the following diseases, which are on the whole fairly ghastly but not fatal. Deciding which to protect yourself against is a matter of risk management.

Hepatitis A is an infection or inflammation of the liver that causes mild fever, nausea/vomiting, loss of appetite and jaundice. It's fairly common in Nepal, and while it won't kill you, it'll put a swift end to your travels and lay you up for several months. It's transmitted through contaminated food and water, so sensible hygiene will reduce the risk of catching it, but you can't count on fastidiousness alone. The **Havrix** or **Vaqta** vaccines afford the best protection for a year, or for ten years if followed up by a booster. Note that children under the age of about ten don't need to be vaccinated against hepatitis A; the disease is very mild in childhood and getting it confers lifelong immunity.

Typhoid and paratyphoid are common in Nepal, and are also spread through contaminated food and water. These nearly identical diseases produce a persistent high fever, headaches, abdominal pains and diarrhoea, but are treatable with antibiotics and are rarely fatal. Paratyphoid usually occurs in epidemics and is less severe. The best inoculation against typhoid is **TyphimVi**, which doesn't protect against paratyphoid but is effective and has few side effects. Boosters are needed every three years. **The Whole Cell Killed** typhoid vaccine is slightly

less effective against typhoid, and causes slight fever, but it does offer protection against paratyphoid.

You should have a **tetanus booster** every ten years, whether you travel or not – and within five years of acquiring a dirty wound. Assuming you were vaccinated for **polio** in childhood, only one booster is necessary during your adult life. Immunizations against **mumps** and **measles** are recommended for anyone who wasn't vaccinated as a child and hasn't already had these diseases.

Flu is no more prevalent in Nepal than elsewhere, but you might consider getting a flu shot before you leave just to reduce the risk of spending several days sick during your holiday.

Optional inoculations

The following diseases are all rare, but potentially fatal.

Meningicoccal meningitis, spread by airborne bacteria (through coughs and sneezes, for example), is a very serious disease that attacks the lining of the brain, and can cause death in as little as a day. While localized cases are occasionally reported in Nepal, and there was an epidemic in the early 1980s, the chances of catching meningitis are remote. That said, the injection is very effective, causes few side effects, and lasts for three to five years. For advice on altitude sickness and other trekking hazards, plus a first-aid checklist, see p.356.

Although **rabies** is a problem in Nepal, the best advice is to give dogs and monkeys a wide berth. It can be cured by five post-exposure injections, administered over a month, that are 100 percent effective if given in reasonable time. This is available in Kathmandu, although it costs upwards of $600. The *pre*-exposure vaccine involves three injections over four weeks, which gives some protection for three years; if you get bitten, you'll still have to get two more boosters. It's probably not worth it except for long-stays and children, who may not report every contact with animals to their parents. See p.51 for advice on dealing with animal bites.

Japanese B encephalitis, though potentially fatal, is mostly confined to the more jungly portions of the Terai around monsoon time. Visitors to Kathmandu and the Terai who are staying for a long period between April and October should certainly consider vaccinating against it. Rural areas where pigs are kept are most risky. The inoculation is in the form of three injections given over a month.

Hepatitis B is a more serious version of Hepatitis A, but (like AIDS) is passed on through blood and sexual contact. The vaccine is recommended for those working in a medical environment or who engage in unprotected sex. Long-term travellers are sometimes vaccinated as they might have an accident and need to receive blood. The Twinrix vaccine combines Hepatitis A and B protection.

Don't bother with the **cholera inoculation** – few authorities believe it's worthwhile, and the risk in Nepal is minimal.

Malaria prophylaxis

Most visitors won't need to take **malaria** tablets. The disease hasn't been eradicated in Nepal, but it is unknown above 1000m, and rare outside the monsoon months. The risk to short-term travellers is very low indeed but it's well worth taking the **anti-mosquito** measures described below, especially during the rainy season.

Prophylaxis (regular doses of tablets) *is* worth considering if you plan to visit the **Terai** (which includes Chitwan and Bardia national parks) between June and September. Longer-term visitors and anyone visiting India should seek expert advice, and rafters should remember that valleys in the hills can be lower than 1000m. The new anti-malarial drug **Malarone** is, by all reports, a good option; note that tablets are much cheaper in Kathmandu than at home.

Precautions

The lack of **sanitation** in Nepal is sometimes overhyped – it's not worth getting too uptight about it or you'll never enjoy anything, and you'll run the risk of rebuffing Nepalese hospitality. The best advice is to follow the guidelines below when you can.

Given that most travellers are careful about drinking dirty water, **food** is thought to be the worst culprit, and it's usually tourist restaurants and "Western" dishes that bring the most grief: more people get sick in Kathmandu than anywhere else in Nepal. Be particularly wary of anything reheated, and food that's been sitting where flies can land on it. Nepali food is usually fine and you can probably trust anything that's been boiled or fried in your presence, although meat can sometimes be dodgy, particularly lightly fried snack dishes. Raw, unpeeled fruit and vegetables – including pickles – should always be viewed with **suspicion** in local places, though all but the cheapest tourist restaurants usually have acceptable salads, fruit juices and *lassis* these days.

Kathmandu's **polluted air** gives many people respiratory infections within a few days of arrival; asthmatics and others with breathing problems are particularly affected. Minimize your exposure by staying off the main boulevards, wearing a face mask if necessary. You can also help your immune system by keeping warm, dry and well rested (especially if jetlagged). Most importantly, get out of the valley to where the air is fresh as quickly as possible.

You need to be particularly vigilant about **personal hygiene** while travelling in Nepal. That means, above all, washing your hands often – waterless antibacterial soap comes in handy. Keep any cuts clean and disinfected. If you're staying in cheap guesthouses, bring a **sleeping sheet** to keep fleas and lice at bay. Scabies and hookworm can be picked up through bare feet, so it's best to always wear **shoes**, flip-flops (sandals, or *chappal* in Nepali) can be bought anywhere in Nepal, and provide reasonable protection in bathrooms.

When travelling in the Terai, don't give **mosquitoes** the opportunity to bite you. They're hungriest from dusk to dawn, when you need to wear repellent and/or long-sleeved clothes (watch for ankles), sleep under netting and use plug-in mosquito killing/deterring devices or smokey coils. Remember that very few mosquitoes carry malaria, so you don't need to worry over every bite. Try not to scratch bites as infection may result – tiger balm or dry soap can relieve the itching.

Travellers in rural areas of the eastern Terai should protect against **sandflies** in the same way as they transmit the disease **visceral leishmaniasis**, also called **kala-azar**, which causes fever and potentially fatal enlargement of the spleen – though it hasn't affected any tourists to date.

Take the usual precautions to avoid **sunburn** and **dehydration**. Obviously, susceptibility to sunburn varies, but you'll probably want at least medium protection, and high protection will be necessary while trekking. Sunscreen is available, though sometimes fake.

Water

Untreated **water** should be **avoided** when possible and you may not always notice the risk. Water, clean or dirty, is regarded as a purifying agent in Nepal, and plates and glasses are customarily rinsed just before use: if you're handed wet utensils it's a good idea to give them a discreet wipe. Use bottled water when brushing your teeth, and keep your mouth closed in the shower (no singing). Thamel restaurants are likely to use clean water for **ice**, but while its consumption isn't the game of Russian roulette it once was, it's probably still worth steering clear. Similarly, many guesthouses provide filter water, but you can't guarantee it was boiled first, or that the filters are clean. **Tea** and **bottled drinks** are generally safe.

Mineral water is widely available in Nepal, but to avoid leaving behind a trail of plastic, you may prefer to purify your own. If boiling and filtering isn't an option, adding tablets that can be bought in outdoor-sports shops or, more cheaply, in tourist areas of Kathmandu is easy. Cheaper still is **Lugol's Solution**, sold by pharmacies all over Nepal with a free plastic dropper. Use one tablet or four drops per litre (more if the water's cloudy), wait twenty minutes (thirty if it's cold), and drink. The medicinal taste can be counteracted by adding a little vitamin C powder (available in Nepalese pharmacies), but only **after** the water is purified.

To **store** your purified water, you can recycle an old mineral water bottle and hang it in a natty string carry-bag, sold in tourist areas. Sturdier bottles are available in trekking shops. Outdoors stores in Europe and the US stock a bewildering range of portable water-treatment devices, and bottles.

AIDS

Nepal's isolation gave it a decade's grace from the **AIDS** epidemic, but now the disease is a significant problem that no one wants to talk about. Almost **ninety percent** of transmissions in Nepal are thought to be through heterosexual contact, especially in the context of migrant workers and prostitution. Indian brothels, where many Nepali women work (see p.450), are full of HIV-positive sex workers.

Carry **condoms** with you (locally available but it's best to bring some) and **insist** on using them. Condoms also protect you from other sexually transmitted diseases such as hepatitis B. Trekking guides can be considered a relatively high-risk group, so sexual relationships should probably be treated with appropriate **caution**.

If you get a shave from a barber, make sure he uses a clean blade, and don't go for ear-piercing, acupuncture or tattooing unless you're satisfied the equipment is sterile. Should you need an injection, make sure that new, **sterile equipment** is used. If you need a blood transfusion, bear in mind that the Nepalese blood supply isn't **adequately screened**; any blood you receive should be from voluntary rather than commercial donor banks.

Common ailments

Chances are that at some point during your travels in Nepal you'll feel ill. In the majority of cases, it won't be something you need a doctor for but sod's law says it will happen somewhere remote and inconvenient. The following information should help with **self-diagnosis**, although it is *not* a substitute for professional medical advice. If you're unable to get to a clinic – a strong possibility when trekking – you might choose to self-medicate, and dosages are given below.

Antibiotics shouldn't be taken lightly: they pre-empt the body's ability to develop its own immunity to disease, and can increase susceptibility to other problems by killing off all organisms in the digestive system (yogurt or curd can replenish them to some extent, as can acidophilus tablets – also good for thrush and fungal infections). Some may cause allergic reactions or unpleasant side effects, and the more a particular antibiotic is used, the sooner organisms become resistant to it. It's not a bad idea to travel with a course of the drugs mentioned here, but make sure you have the dosage explained to you. In the case of serious or persistent intestinal problems, you're strongly urged to have a **stool test** done at a clinic (see p.52), where the doctor can make a diagnosis and prescription.

Some of the illnesses and parasites you can pick up in Nepal may not show themselves immediately. If you become ill within a year of **returning home,** tell the doctor where you've been.

Intestinal troubles

Diarrhoea is the most common bane of travellers. If it's mild and not accompanied by other major symptoms, it should pass of its own accord within a few days without treatment. However, it's essential to replace the fluids and salts you're losing – JeevanJal, sold in packets everywhere, is a cheap and effective oral **rehydration** formula. Bananas and fizzy drinks are also good for replacing electrolytes. "Starving the bug to death" is an old wives' tale, though you're unlikely to be hungry. Diarrhoea tablets like **Imodium** will plug you up if you have to travel.

If the diarrhoea comes on suddenly and is accompanied by cramps and vomiting, there's a good chance it's **food poisoning**, brought on by toxins secreted by foreign bacteria. There's nothing you can do other than keep replacing fluids, but it should run its course within 24 to 48 hours. If you're feverish, have severe diarrhoea that lasts more than three days or if you see blood or mucus in your stools, seek treatment.

Bacterial diarrhoea, which causes 85 percent of identifiable cases, is recognizable by its sudden onset, accompanied by nausea and vomiting, stomach cramps and sometimes fever. The treatment is one 400mg tablet of the antibiotic Norfloxacin/ Norbactin every twelve hours for five days, or one 500mg tablet of ciprofloxacin every twelve hours for three days.

About five percent of diarrhoea cases in Nepal are giardiasis (**giardia**), which produces three or four loose stools a day, and is often recognizable by copious, foul-smelling belches and farts. The cure is a single dose of 2g of tinidazole (four 500mg tablets of locally available "tiniba"), which can make you tired and nauseous for 24 hours, and absolutely shouldn't be mixed with alcohol.

Amoebic dysentery is relatively rare. Setting in gradually, it manifests itself in frequent, small, watery bowel movements, often accompanied by fever. To self-medicate, take one 500mg tablet of Tinidazole four times a day for three days. This must be followed by taking one 500mg Diloxaride Furoate (Furamide) tablet every eight hours for ten days, in order to kill amoebic cysts that can infect the liver.

If the diarrhoea is associated with fatigue and appetite loss over many days, and occurs between April and November, it may be the result of **cyclospora** (sometimes called blue-green algae). Another water-borne condition, it's treated with the antibiotic trimethoprim sulfamethoxazole (Bactrim or Septra). Again, be sure to keep rehydrating. Iodine and chlorine do not kill cyclospora, so drink **boiled water** if you can during the peak months of June and July.

Finally, bear in mind that oral drugs, such as malaria pills or the contraceptive pill, are rendered **less effective** or completely **ineffective** if taken while suffering from diarrhoea.

Flu and fever

Flu-like symptoms – fever, headache, runny nose, fatigue, aching muscles – may mean nothing more than the latest virus. Rest and aspirin/paracetamol should do the trick. However, strep throat, bronchial or sinus infections will require an antibiotic course such as erythromycin or amoxycillin. Flu symptoms and jaundice (yellowing of the eyes) point to hepatitis, which is best treated with rest and a plane ticket home.

A **serious fever** or delirium is cause for real concern. Diagnosis is tricky; it's safe to say the sufferer needs to be taken to a doctor as quickly as possible. To begin with, try bringing the fever down with aspirin/paracetamol. If the fever rises and falls dramatically every few hours, it may be **malaria**, which, in the absence of medical help, can be zapped with three tablets of pyralfin (Fansidar). If the fever is consistently high for four or more days, it may be **typhoid** – again, only if no doctor is available, treat with ciprofloxacin/norfloxacin or chloramphenicol.

Minor symptoms

Minor **muscle cramps**, experienced after exercise or sweating, may indicate you're low on sodium – a teaspoon of salt will bring rapid relief. Likewise, a simple **headache** may just mean you're dehydrated. (However, a severe headache, accompanied by eye pain, neck stiffness and a temperature, could mean meningitis – in which case get to a doctor pronto.)

Itchy skin is often traced to mosquito bites, but can also be fleas, lice or scabies picked up from dirty bedclothes. The latter, a burrowing mite, generally goes for the spaces between fingers and toes. Shampoos and lotions are available in Nepal. Air out your bedding and wash your clothes thoroughly.

Worms may enter your body through the skin (especially the soles of the feet), or through food. An itchy anus is a common symptom, and you may even see them in your stools. They are easy to treat with worming tablets, available locally.

Animal bites and leeches

For **animal bites** or scratches, *immediately* wash the wound with soap and water for at least five minutes then rinse with Providone iodine (found in Nepal); if this isn't available, use 40–70 percent alcohol – local *raksi* could do the trick. This should kill any rabies virus on the spot but anyone bitten by an animal should hightail it to a Kathmandu clinic for expensive post-exposure rabies shots (see p.141). The disease's incubation period is ten to ninety days – ideally, you're supposed to capture the animal alive for observation.

Thickly vegetated country, such as the Terai national parks or low-lying trekking areas, can come alive with **leeches** during the monsoon. Protect yourself by wearing **insect repellent** and long clothing – though the little tykes can even work their way through the eyelets of your boots. There's probably little harm in letting them have their fill and dropping off, but there is a small risk of **infection**, particularly if you pick them off

and the mouth parts get left behind in the wound. Salt, iodine or heat from a lighter or match can be applied to make them drop off – or try breaking the leech's suction by gently sliding a fingernail around first the thinner, then the thicker end of the animal.

Getting medical help

In a non-emergency situation, make for one of the traveller-oriented **clinics** in Kathmandu. Run to Western standards, these can diagnose most common ailments, write prescriptions and give inoculations. In other cities and towns, local clinics (often attached to pharmacies) can usually provide adequate care. An array of Indian-manufactured medicines are available without prescription in the **pharmacies** of all major towns, but check the **sell-by date**.

In the event of serious injury or illness, contact your **embassy** for a list of recommended **doctors**. The majority are in Kathmandu and speak English. It's a good idea to register with your embassy or consulate on arrival; it's especially important if you go trekking or rafting to ensure prompt evacuation if necessary. There's a list of Kathmandu contacts on p.141.

Hospitals are listed in the Kathmandu and Pokhara sections of the guide; other are located in Dhulikhel, Tansen and the bigger Terai cities. Most are poorly equipped and should you be unlucky enough to have to stay in hospital, note that nursing staff do not perform many routine functions: relatives are expected to feed patients, change bedpans and monitor IVs.

Online medical resources for travellers

ⓦ **www.cdc.gov** The Centers for Disease Control and Prevention: outbreak warnings, inoculations, precautions and other background information.
ⓦ **www.ciwec-clinic.com** The Kathmandu-based clinic that is the authoritative source of information on Nepal-related medicine; its website contains excellent articles on relevant health matters.
ⓦ **www.sentex.net/~iamat** The International Association for Medical Assistance to Travellers can provide a list of English-speaking doctors in Nepal plus information on diseases and inoculations.
ⓦ **www.tripprep.com** Travel Health Online provides a comprehensive database of necessary

vaccinations for most destinations, and medical service provider information.

UK and Ireland

Hospital for Tropical Diseases Travel Clinic ☎0845/155 5000 or 020/7387 4411, Ⓦwww .thehtd.org.
MASTA (Medical Advisory Service for Travellers Abroad) Ⓦwww.masta-travel-health .com. Lists travel health clinics.
Tropical Medical Bureau Republic of Ireland ☎1850/487 674, Ⓦwww.tmb.ie.

US and Canada

CDC ☎1-800/311-3435, or Ⓦwww.cdc.gov /travel. Official US government travel health site.

International Society for Travel Medicine
☎1-770/736-7060, Ⓦwww.istm.org. Has a full list of travel health clinics.
Canadian Society for International Health
☎613/241-5785, Ⓦwww.csih.org. Extensive list of travel health centres.

Australia, New Zealand and South Africa

Travellers' Medical and Vaccination Centre ☎1300/658 844, Ⓦwww.tmvc.com.au. Lists travel clinics in Australia, New Zealand and South Africa.

Culture and etiquette

Customs and traditions run deep in Nepal. As few Nepalis get the chance to travel abroad, the majority's exposure to the outside world is through visitors. This puts a great responsibility on the traveller to be sensitive to Nepali ways and values, though in tourist enclaves – Kathmandu's Thamel and Pokhara's Lakeside – they've seen it all before.

Many different **ethnic groups** coexist in Nepal, each with their own complex customs, as detailed in the *People of Nepal* colour section. In the Kathmandu Valley, where they mix the most, there's a necessarily high degree of tolerance toward different clothes and lifestyles – a fact that travellers sense, and often abuse. Away from the tourist areas, however, ethnic groups are quite parochial, and foreign ways may cause offence. That said, many taboos relax the further and higher you head into the mountains, as Hindu rules of behaviour are only partially shared by Buddhist and animist ethnic groups.

The **do's and don'ts** listed here are more flexible than they sound. You'll make gaffes all the time and Nepalis will rarely say anything. The list is hardly exhaustive, either: when in doubt, do as you see Nepalis doing.

Common courtesies

Nepalis grow up surrounded by other people; they like to be with others, and will assume you do too. As a foreigner, you're likely to be an **object of curiosity** to anyone who rarely has the chance to travel far, and you may be joined in the street or on the trail by someone who just wants to chat. Nepalis will constantly be befriending you, wanting to exchange addresses, take photos and extracting solemn promises that you will write to them.

Giving the Nepali **greeting**, *namaste* ("I salute the god within you"), your palms held together as if praying, is one of the most attractive and addictive of Nepalese customs. It isn't used freely or casually: think of it as "how do you do?" rather than "hello!" If you want to show great respect, *namaskar* is a more formal or subservient variant.

Another delightful aspect of Nepali culture is the familiar ways Nepalis address each other: it's well worth learning *didi* ("older sister"), *bahini* ("younger sister"), *daai* ("older brother"), *bhaai* ("younger brother"), *buwa* ("father") and *aamaa* ("mother") for the warm reaction they'll usually provoke. To be more formal or respectful, just add *ji* to the end of someone's name, as in *"namaste*, John-*ji"*.

The word *dhanyabaad* is usually translated as thank you but you'll rarely hear it, except in urban or tourist areas. It is normally reserved for an act beyond the call of duty – so if you feel you have to say something, "thank you" in English is widely understood.

The gestures for "**yes**" and "**no**" are also confusing. To indicate agreement, tilt your head slightly to one side and then back the other way. To tell a tout or a seller "no", hold one hand in up front of you, palm forwards, and swivel your wrist subtly, as if you were adjusting a bracelet; shaking the head in the Western fashion looks too much like "yes". To point use the chin, rather than the finger.

Caste and status

In Nepal, where Hinduism is tempered by Buddhist and other influences, **caste** doesn't seem to dominate social interactions to quite the extent that it does in India. Nevertheless, caste *is* deeply ingrained in the national psyche, as even non-Hindus were historically assigned places in the hierarchy. Following India's lead, Nepal "abolished" the caste system in 1963, but millennia-old habits cannot be dismantled overnight; the Maoists may be virulently opposed to the system, but many of their leaders come from a high caste background. Though professions are changing and "love marriage" is more popular, for most Nepalis, caste and status still determine what they do for a living, whom they may (or must) marry, where they can live and who they can associate with.

In a Hindu society, foreigners are technically casteless, but they can be considered **polluting** to orthodox, high-caste Hindus. In Nepal, this is really only a big deal in the remote far western hills, but wherever you travel you should be sensitive to minor caste restrictions: for example, you may not be allowed into the kitchen of a high-caste Hindu home.

Status (*ijat*) is an equally important factor in Nepalese society. Meeting for the first time, Nepalis observe a ritual of asking each other's name, hometown, and profession, all to determine relative status and therefore the correct level of deference. As a Westerner you have a lot of status, and relatively speaking you're fabulously wealthy – be prepared for questions.

Eating

Probably the greatest number of Nepali taboos – to an outsider's way of thinking – have to do with **food**. One underlying principle is that once you've touched something to your lips, it's polluted (*jutho*) for everyone else. If you take a sip from someone else's water bottle, try not to let it touch your lips (and the same applies if it's your own – you're expected to share). Don't eat off someone else's plate or offer anyone food you've taken a bite of, and don't touch cooked food until you've bought it.

Another all-important point of etiquette is, if eating with your **hands** – use the right one only. In most Asian countries, the left hand is reserved for washing after defecating; you can use it to hold a glass or utensil while you eat, but don't wipe your mouth, or pass food with it. It's considered good manners to give and receive everything with the right hand. In order to convey respect, offer money, food or gifts with both hands, or with the right hand while the left touches the wrist.

Clothing and the body

Nepalis are innately conservative in their attitudes to **clothing**. Clearly, you're not Nepali, but it's worth knowing how you may come across. The following hints apply especially in temples and monasteries.

Men should always wear a shirt in public, and long trousers if possible (shorts are for low caste or home, but OK in tourist areas). For **women** in villages, a sari or skirt that hangs to mid-calf level is traditional, though trousers are acceptable these days. Girls in Kathmandu and Pokhara do wear shorts or a short skirt, but this is new and you still run the risk of being seen as sexually available, so be prepared for what it brings. More surprisingly, perhaps, shoulders should also be covered up – a T-shirt is much more appropriate than a vest. Looking **clean** shows respect – ungroomed travellers are distasteful and confusing to Nepalis, who will wear the best they can afford.

Nudity is a sensitive issue. Only women with babies or small children bare their breasts. When Nepali men bathe in public, they do it in their underwear, and women bathe underneath a *lungi* (sarong). Foreigners are expected to do likewise. In Nepal, the forehead is regarded as the most sacred part of the body and it's impolite to touch an adult Nepali's head. The feet are the most unclean part, so don't put yours on chairs or tables, and when sitting, try not to point the soles of your feet at anyone. It's bad manners to step over the legs of someone seated: in a crowded space Nepalis will wait for you to draw in your feet so they can pass.

Nepali views about **displays of affection** may seem counterintuitive. It's considered acceptable for friends of the same sex to hold hands in public, but not for lovers of the opposite sex. Couples who cuddle or kiss in public will at best draw unwelcome attention. At worst, you've offended everyone around you and reinforced the dangerous notion that foreign women are sex objects. Handshaking has increased with the Maoists' popularity, but not all women will feel comfortable to shake a man's hand.

Temples and homes

Major **Hindu temples** or their innermost sanctums are usually off-limits to nonbelievers, who are a possible cause of ritual pollution. It may feel like unfair discrimination, but respect the rule; it's a small part of a highly complex set of beliefs.

Where you are allowed in, be respectful, take your shoes off before entering (it's worth wearing slip-ons if you're doing a lot of temple-visiting), don't take photos unless you've asked permission, and leave a few rupees in the donation box. Try not to touch offerings or shrines. Leather is usually not allowed in temple precincts.

Similar sensitivity is due at Buddhist temples and monasteries. If you're granted an audience with a lama, it's traditional to present him with a *kata* (a ceremonial white scarf, usually sold nearby). Walk around Buddhist stupas and monuments clockwise – that is, keep the monument on your right.

If invited for a meal in a **private home**, you can bring fruit or sweets (your hosts may not drink alcohol), but don't expect thanks as gifts tend to be received without any fuss. Take your shoes off when entering, or follow the example of your host. When the food is served you may be expected to eat first, so you won't be able to follow your host's lead. Take less than you can eat – asking for seconds is the best compliment you can give. The meal is typically served at the end of a gathering; when the eating is done, everyone leaves.

Sherpas and some other highland groups regard the **family hearth** as sacred, so don't throw rubbish or scraps into it.

Hustle and hassle

Indian-style **hustle** is on the rise in Nepal. You'll get a major dose of it at the airport or

---

Hiring a guide

Even if you're not going on a trek, hiring a **guide** is a great way to get under the skin of Nepal – you may even be invited home to meet the family. Most people only think of hiring a guide for a **trek** (see p.347), but they're even more essential when tracking **wildlife** in the Terai parks. If you find a good guide, stick with him (guides are usually male); a day guide in Chitwan, for instance, might well be willing to accompany you to Bardia National Park. In town, would-be guides, often masquerading as friendly students, position themselves strategically at temples and palaces, but you'll probably do better to find one through an innkeeper or travel agent. An inexperienced guide hired informally will usually charge about Rs750 a day; otherwise guides command upwards of Rs1000 a day; paying up to double that amount (Rs2000/$25) for an experienced and knowledgeable guide would be fair. Generally, you get what you pay for.

any major bus station, where touts bearing guesthouse cards lie in wait to accost arriving tourists. They also cruise the tourist strips of Kathmandu, offering drugs. For the most part, though, Nepali touts aren't as parasitic as their Indian brethren, and if you're entering Nepal from North India, where aggressive touts have to be dealt with firmly, adjust your attitude. Ignore them entirely – try to look occupied with something else – and they're likely to ignore you. If that doesn't work, most touts will leave you alone if asked nicely, whereas they'll take a rude brush-off personally.

The tourist zones are full of other lone entrepreneurs and middlemen – **touts** by any other name. Ticket agents (see p.27), rikshaw-wallahs, innkeepers and guides are ever-anxious to broker services and information. Naturally they take a cut, but as with touts, they usually get their commission from the seller; your price is bumped up correspondingly. If you don't know where to spend the night or change money, a tout's services are certainly worth a few rupees, but in general, cutting out the middleman gives you more control over the transaction. You should find, without being too mercenary about it, that a few rupees (and smiles) given to people whose services you may require again will smooth the way and make your stay much more pleasant.

Beggars

As in most developing countries, dealing with **beggars** is part and parcel of travelling in Nepal. The pathos might initially get to you, as well it should, but you will probably adjust to it fairly quickly. A thornier dilemma is how to cope with panhandling kids.

A small number of bona fide beggars make an honest living from *bakshish* (alms). Hindus and Buddhists have a long and honourable tradition of giving to lepers, the disabled, sadhus and monks. It's terrifyingly easy for a **Nepali woman** to find herself destitute and on the street, either widowed or divorced – perhaps for failing to bear a son or from a dowry dispute. There are no **unemployment benefits** in Nepal, and the state pension is just Rs100 a year; anyone who can't work and has no family support generally turns to begging (or prostitution). Few would do so if they had an alternative.

In the hills, ailing locals will occasionally approach foreigners for **medicine**: it's probably best not to make any prescriptions unless you're qualified to diagnose the illness. However, before leaving the country you can donate unused medicines to the destitute through the dispensary at Kathmandu's Bir Hospital, or to the Himalayan Buddhist Meditation Centre in Kathmandu, which gives them to monks.

Children

Throughout Nepal – but principally along the tourist trails – **children** will hound you. Repeatedly shouting "*namaste*" or "hello" at the weird-looking stranger is universal and often kids will ask you for "one rupee", "chocolate" or "pen". Sometimes they're cute, sometimes a pain. They're not orphans or beggars, just ordinary school-kids who've seen too many well-meaning but thoughtless tourists handing out little gifts wherever they go.

A laugh and a firm-but-gentle *hoinaholaa!* ("I don't think so!") is usually enough. Few children would ever ask a Nepali for money, so reacting like one will quickly embarrass them into leaving you alone. Sometimes they will tag along for hours, giving you the Chinese water-torture treatment, but the best defence is a sense of humour: better that they laugh with you than at you.

Street children are another matter. They're begging for real, but you should still think twice before giving to them – see p.101.

Spiritual pursuits and alternative therapies

Nepal has a multitude of traditional and progressive disciplines, and though the country can seem something of a spiritual supermarket, its tolerant atmosphere makes it a great place to challenge your assumptions and study other systems of thought.

The past twenty years have seen an explosion of outfits teaching yoga and meditation to both foreigners and locals. The allied health fields of ayurvedic and Tibetan medicine are also an attraction for many travellers to Nepal. Many programmes don't require a lengthy commitment, although any **residential courses** are worth booking well in advance – contact details are given in the guide where possible. For more detailed background on Hinduism and Buddhism, which provide the spiritual bases for many practices, see "Religion", p.429.

Yoga

Yoga is more than just exercises – it's a system of spiritual, mental and physical self-discipline, designed to unify the individual's consciousness with the universe. Techniques include **Karma yoga** (basically altruism), **Bhakti yoga** (devotion, recognisable by the chanting) and **Jnana yoga** (deep meditation, best practised only after mastering one of the other kinds).

What most westerners would recognise as yoga springs from **Raja yoga**, probably formulated around 600 BC. It has eight *astanga*, or limbs (not to be confused with the yoga style with the same name), each a step to realisation. Three of these have a physical emphasis, and it is from this root that yoga's reputation for pretzel poses and headstands comes. Whatever the name of a particular variation, be it Bikram, Kundalini, Ashtanga, all types of yoga that that use *asanas* (or positions) as an aid to developing the self, are generally referred to as Hatha yoga.

Most practices also include **Pranayam** – breathing exercises. You'll find several kinds in Nepal, including the **Sivanand** school (a slow style with *asanas* and lots of spiritual guidance), **Iyengar** (a very exacting school that uses some props and focuses on alignment) and practices that follow particular gurus from India, usually including elements of Raja, Bhakti and Karma yoga.

Yoga centres around Kathmandu and Pokhara are rounded up on p.139 & p.248.

Buddhist meditation and study

Meditation is closely related to yoga, and the two often overlap: much of yoga (Kundalini for example) involves meditation, and Buddhist meditation draws on many Hindu yogic practices. However, meditation centres in Nepal generally follow the Tibetan Buddhist tradition.

Buddhist meditation is a science of mind. To Buddhists, mind is the cause of confusion and ego, and the aim of meditation is to transcend these. *vipassana* ("insight") is the kernel of all forms of Buddhist meditation; related to Hatha yoga, it emphasizes the minute observation of physical sensations and mental processes to achieve a clear understanding of mind. Another basic practice common to most schools of Buddhism, *shamatha* ("calm abiding") attunes and sharpens the mind by means of coming back again and again to a meditative discipline (breathing, visualization, etc). Several centres in the Kathmandu Valley run rigorous residential courses in this practice – see p.138 for details of one that caters to foreigners.

Tibetan Buddhist centres start students out with *vipassana* and *shamatha* as the foundation for a large armoury of meditation practices. An adept (novice) will cultivate Buddha-like qualities through visualization techniques – meditating on the deity that manifests a particular quality, while chanting the *mantra* and performing the *mudra* (hand gesture) associated with that deity. The Tibetan Buddhist path also involves numerous rituals, such as prayer, offerings, circumambulation and other meritorious acts; committed followers will take vows, too. Kathmandu has several centres offering introductory courses (see p.138).

A big part of Tibetan Buddhism is the **teacher–disciple relationship**. More advanced students of the *dharma* will want to study under one of the lamas at Boudha (see p.162), some of whom give discourses in English.

Ayurveda

Ayurveda (often spelled "ayurved") is the oldest school of medicine still practised. It is a holistic system that assumes the fundamental sameness of self and nature. Unlike the allopathic medicine of the West, which identifies what ails you and then kills it, ayurveda looks at the whole patient: disease is regarded as a symptom of imbalance, so it's the imbalance that's treated, not the disease.

Ayurvedic theory holds that the body is controlled by **three forces** (*tridosha*), which are a reflection of the forces within the self: *pitta*, the hot force of the sun, rules the digestive processes and metabolism; *kapha*, the moon, the creator of tides and rhythms, is cooling and governs the body's organs, fluids and lubricants; while *vata*, wind, relates to movement and the nervous system. A healthy body has the three forces in balance. To diagnose an imbalance, the ayurvedic doctor investigates the physical complaint but also family background, daily habits and emotional traits.

Treatment of an imbalance is typically with inexpensive herbal remedies designed to alter whichever of the three forces is out of whack. In addition, the doctor may prescribe some yogic cleansing to rid the body of waste substances. To the uninitiated, these techniques will sound rather off-putting – such as swallowing a long strip of cloth, a short section at a time, and then pulling it back up again to remove mucus from the stomach.

You'll find ayurvedic **doctors and clinics** throughout the Hindu parts of Nepal, but those who are able to deal with foreigners are confined mainly to Kathmandu (see p.139).

Tibetan medicine

Medicine is one of the traditional branches of study for Tibetan Buddhist monks. Like ayurveda, from which it derives, **Tibetan medicine** promotes health by maintaining the correct balance of three humours: *beken*, phlegm, which when out of balance is responsible for disorders of the upper body; *tiba*, heat or bile, associated with intestinal diseases; and *lung*, meaning wind, which may produce nervousness or depression.

Tibetan medicine is as much a **spiritual discipline** as a physical one. Tibetan doctors regularly meditate on the "medicine Buddha", a manifestation of the Buddha's compassion and healing power. The physician diagnoses imbalance by examining the tongue, pulse and urine, and by determining the patient's psychological state through questioning. He'll then prescribe a treatment to counteract the imbalance, which initially may only be a change of diet or behaviour (for instance, "cold" disorders – those to do with wind – are treated with "hot" foods and activities). For quicker relief, he'll prescribe one of a range of herbal–mineral tablets, which have been empowered by special rites.

Recommended **clinics** specializing in Tibetan medicine are listed in the Kathmandu (p.140) and Boudha (p.164) sections.

Massage and therapies

Nepal, like many Asian countries, has its own indigenous form of **massage**. Nepali massage is a deep treatment that works mainly on the joints. It's not all that relaxing, but it can be just the job after a trek. Nepalis themselves rarely receive massages after the age of about three, and would find it hard to conceive of paying for one, but numerous masseurs ply their services to foreigners. Most practitioners also offer shiatsu, Swedish or Thai massage.

Dubious-looking signs in the tourist areas frequently advertise "Yoga & Massage", which has become a sort of shorthand for a long menu of un-Nepali services: steam baths (usually a makeshift box with a hole in the top for your head to stick out), reflexology, herbal treatments and the like. Some of these serve as fronts for prostitution (see p.140).

Women's Nepal

In most parts of the country, women will be of interest mainly as foreigners rather than for their gender, but a few specific tips are given below.

Life as a **Nepali woman** can mean years of unrelenting toil with little recognition. For women travellers, however, most parts of Nepal are relatively easy: the atmosphere is tolerant and inquisitive rather than threatening or dangerous. Nepali society is on the whole chaste, almost prudish; men are mostly respectful to, and perhaps a little in awe of, foreign women. **Sexual harassment** is unlikely to upset your travels: you might get staring and catcalling or a rare attempt to cop a feel in a crowd, but it's not as bad as in India, or indeed most of the world, and seldom goes any further than words. Your chief danger comes from the rare predatory trekking guide (see p.348).

However, wearing **revealing clothes** will up the chances of receiving unwelcome advances. It's easy for Nepali men to get the idea that foreign women are wanton – relatively speaking, they are. Wearing a short dress, shorts or thin, revealing material may reinforce this stereotype. That doesn't mean you have to wear Nepali clothes, it just means that you ought to wear modest things that don't reveal thighs or breasts. In tourist areas you can buy cheap garments that fit the bill. If you trek on one of the popular routes and see how many trekkers wear skimpy clothes, you might wonder whether this is obsolete advice. It isn't. Nepalis along the main routes have seen everything by now, and are too polite to say anything, but you can pretty much forget about any rewarding cross-cultural interactions. In classy urban nightspots miniskirts are becoming more common, but not cleavage.

A woman **travelling or trekking alone** won't be hassled so much as pitied. Going alone (*eklai*) is most un-Nepali behaviour. Locals (of both sexes) will ask if you haven't got a husband – usually out of genuine concern, not as a come-on. Teaming up with another female stops the comments as effectively as being with a man. If you find yourself on a public bus, you can make your way to the front compartment, where preference is usually given to women and children.

Terai cities and **border towns** are another matter, unfortunately: avoid wearing tight clothes. As in northern India, misconceptions about Western women mean men could try for a surreptitious grope or even expose themselves. Travelling with a man generally shields you from this sort of behaviour. Don't be afraid to make a public scene in the event of an untoward advance – that's what a Nepali woman would do. Though he'll pretend it wasn't him, all eyes will be upon him and he won't try it again.

Of course, you may find you want to strike up a relationship with a **Nepali man**. If so, you should have no trouble finding eligible candidates in the tourist bars. Quite a few women travellers fall for trekking or rafting guides and Kathmandu has a small but growing community of women who have married and settled. However, Nepali men are not without their own agendas: exotic romance, conquest, perhaps even a ticket out of Nepal. If you suspect ulterior motives, let him down gently but firmly and he'll usually retreat gracefully. Be aware also that AIDS is a growing and largely concealed problem.

Meeting women

A frustrating aspect of travelling in Nepal is the difficulty of making contact with **Nepali women**. Tourism is still controlled by men; women are expected to spend their time in the home, get fewer educational opportunities and speak much less English. If you're lucky enough to be invited to a Nepali home for a meal, chances are the women of the house will remain in the kitchen while you eat, only emerging to clear the plates and eat the leftovers. Upper class women, who may even work with foreigners, are often well educated and free of these restrictions, but they have few encounters with travellers.

Sexual politics are different among **highland ethnic groups**, which is as good a reason as any for going trekking. Along trekking routes, many women run teahouses single-handedly while their husbands are off guiding or portering. Proud, enterprising and flamboyant, these "*didis*" are some of the most wonderful people you're likely to meet anywhere. Language may be a problem off the popular trails, but that doesn't rule out all communication. Anywhere you go, having a child with you will always open doors. For more on women's issues, see p.449.

Living and working in Nepal

Working or studying while in Nepal can add a satisfying focus to your trip, and deepen your understanding of another way of life. It's certainly the best way to meet and get to know Nepalis.

Unfortunately, you can't stay longer than 150 days in any calendar year on a **tourist visa** without special permission (though that means you can stay almost a year if your trip straddles two calendar years). To stay longer, you have to get a **longer-term visa** (such as the business, residential or study visas), but they're more expensive and require an application from an accredited organization to the relevant Nepalese government ministry.

Working

If you feel you've received a lot from Nepal, **volunteering** is a good way to give something back. You can volunteer on a less formal, shorter-term basis through a couple of organizations in Kathmandu that match willing foreigners with projects (p.80). The old people's hospices in Pashupatinath and Chabahil run by Mother Teresa's Sisters of Charity welcome walk-in help on a day-to-day basis. The Kathmandu Environmental Education Project, Himalayan Explorers Connection and Himalayan Rescue Association offices in Kathmandu can always use workers.

Postings with the Peace Corps, VSO and other **voluntary agencies** abound, providing you've got the relevant skills and the determination to stay two or more years. People with experience in education, health, nutrition, agriculture, forestry and other areas are preferred. Many other aid agencies (such as Action Aid, Save the Children, CARE and Oxfam) operate in Nepal and occasionally take on specialists. See p.443 for an idea of what to expect.

If you just want an open-ended arrangement for a few weeks or so, teaching English is a good option. Language schools in Kathmandu and Pokhara occasionally take people on, although the pay is negligible. A certificate or even experience isn't always necessary. Numerous organizations run longer, more formal teaching programmes (see p.60), often aimed at young people, but you'll pay for the privilege, once you've factored in training and support fees.

Paid work is almost impossible to find locally, and it's against the law to work on a tourist visa. Some people find jobs as guides, but as more locals become trained, you may want to question the ethics of taking a job that could be done by a Nepali who can't leave the country to find alternatives. Qualified masseurs and yoga/meditation instructors may be able to find work in Kathmandu or Pokhara – try contacting the places listed in those sections.

If you can persuade the Department of Industry that you've got a good idea, you may qualify for a business visa. If you've got upwards of $100,000 dollars to invest, you may even qualify for a residential visa.

Studying

A few **language schools** in Kathmandu offer intensive courses in Nepali, Newari or Tibetan (see p.141). Opportunities to study yoga and Tibetan Buddhism are summarized on p.56. Several American universities run study programmes in Nepal; see the list below.

For anything longer-term or more formal you'll need to apply in writing to Tribhuwan University (Campus of International Languages, PO Box 4339, Exhibition Rd, Kathmandu, Nepal ☎01/422 8916 or 422 6713), which runs courses in Nepali, Tibetan, Sanskrit and Newari. Nepali courses are usually offered for either three years (six semesters) or six weeks (sixty hours), but tailored courses can be offered to groups of students, and the campus has run one-year courses in the past.

Study and work programmes

Campus of International Languages Tribhuwan University ☎01/422 8916, ⊛www.bishwobhasa .edu.np. Kathmandu's first and most highly regarded university.

Educate the Children ⊛www.etc-nepal.org. Three-month teaching stints.

Global Action Nepal⊛www.gannepal.org. Small, friendly Nepal-based organization offering structured six-month English-language teaching placements in schools across Nepal. Mostly aimed at UK-based young people.

Himalayan Explorers Connection ⊛www.hec .org. Information on more than fifty programmes and

opportunities. The club also runs its own volunteer programme for teachers in the Khumbu region.

Himalayan Rescue Association ⊛www .himalayanrescue.org. Accepts four doctors each autumn and spring to staff its high-altitude aid posts; the waiting list is two or three years long, but it can't hurt to write.

Naropa Institute ⊛www.naropa.edu /studyabroad/. Colorado institution that runs a thirteen-week course on Tibetan Buddhism each autumn at Boudha.

Peace Corps ☎1-800/424-8580, ⊛www .peacecorps.gov. Places US citizens with specialist qualifications or skills in two-year postings.

School for International Training ⊛www.sit .edu.Based in Brattleboro, Vermont, the School has its own campus in Kathmandu.

School of South Asian Studies ⊛www.wisc .edu/. Full-year study programmes with the University of Wisconsin–Madison.

Students Partnership Worldwide ⊛www .spwnepal.org.np. Six-month schoolteaching placements and environmental education programmes. Foreign volunteers are paired with Nepalis. Relatively expensive, but the training is thorough.

Study Abroad.com ⊛www.studyabroad.com. Good list of contacts and programmes for study and volunteer opportunities in Nepal.

VSO (Voluntary Service Overseas) ⊛www.vso .org.uk. Highly respected charity that sends qualified professionals from the UK, US and EU (in the fields of education, health, community and social work, forestry, engineering, information technology, law and media) to spend two years or more working for local wages on projects beneficial to developing countries. There are special programmes for young people and the over-60s, too.

Travel essentials

Children and babies

Kids always help break the ice with strangers, and in Nepal they unleash even more than the usual hospitality. Nepal can be a magical place for a child to visit. Elephant-headed gods, a living goddess who gets to

play the coolest kind of dress-up, snake charmers, elephant rides, cows, chickens and goats in the streets, festivals and pageantry and amazing sights on every corner: it's like being right inside a fairy tale or adventure story, and kids drink it up.

Arranging **childcare** is no problem, since labour is cheap and Nepalis generally love kids. Often you don't need to make arrangements – your offspring will be taken in hand by the nearest adult or older child. Some children (especially those with fair skin and blond hair) may be uncomfortable with the unaccustomed attention, however.

Parents will of course have to take extra **precautions** in the light of Nepal's poor sanitation, dogs, crowds, traffic, pollution, bright sun, rooftops and steep slopes. It may be hard to keep hands clean and yucky stuff out of mouths. You'll have to keep a firm grip on small children while out and about; drum home the necessity of keeping away from dogs and only drinking clean water. If your child comes down with diarrhoea, it's extremely important to keep him or her hydrated and topped up on salts – have oral rehydration formula on hand.

Naturally you'll want to plan a more modest itinerary and travel in greater comfort with children than you might on your own. Nepal's winding, bumpy roads are likely to make kids travel-sick, so take bus journeys in very small doses, or rent a car. Most cheap lodgings will be out of the question on account of their bathroom arrangements. In tourist areas it should be no problem finding food that kids will eat, but elsewhere they're bound to turn their noses up at "spicy" food and anything too unfamiliar. Few restaurants have high chairs. Baby food and disposable nappies/diapers are available in Kathmandu and Pokhara, but are hard to come by elsewhere. Some toys and books can be purchased in Nepal, but bring a supply of your own. Carry small tots in a backpack or papoose – a stroller or pushchair will be virtually useless.

Trekking with children is generally a wonderful experience (see p.359), though it can be logistically awkward if they're too old to ride in a backpack and too young to hike on their own (though mules or horses can often be arranged on many routes). You'll need one or more porters for all the kiddie paraphernalia; porters can also carry young ones in modified *doko* (wicker baskets). Trekking with an agency can alleviate some of the hassles – ask what special facilities they provide for children.

Costs

Your money goes a long way in Nepal. Off the tourist routes, it can actually be hard to spend **$20 a day**, including food, transport and accommodation. On the other hand, Kathmandu and some of the other tourist traps can burn a hole in your pocket rather faster than you might expect. Even so, it's still possible for a frugal traveller to keep to **$15 a day** in the capital, although the figure can effortlessly balloon to $30 or more simply by choosing slightly nicer hotels and restaurants. If you like to travel in greater luxury, you should expect to spend **$60 or more per day**, depending mainly on standard of accommodation.

You'll inevitably **pay over the odds** for things at first, and it may even feel as if people are charging you as much as they think they can get away with, but that's hardly a market principle exclusive to Nepal. Bargain where appropriate, but don't begrudge a few rupees to someone who's worked hard for them and who, all too often, needs them very badly. Youth/student **ID cards** are of practically no use.

Many hotels (particularly the more expensive ones) and some restaurants quote their prices exclusive of the thirteen percent "government" **tax** (essentially a value-added tax) and charge another ten percent service charge. Price codes given in this book are always inclusive of tax.

No matter how tight your budget, it would be foolish not to splurge now and then on some of the things that make Nepal unique: trekking on your own costs almost nothing, but you might prefer to hire a porter or guide or pay for a fully catered trek. Rafting, biking and wildlife trips also work out to be relatively expensive, but are well worth it. And few visitors will be able to resist buying at least something from Nepal's rich range of handicrafts.

One expense that you might not expect is having to pay a **fee** to enter some of the major monumental zones in the Kathmandu Valley. There have always been hefty fees to trek or view wildlife in the national parks and conservation areas, and of course you expect to pay to visit museums and certain buildings, but tourists are now charged admission to enter entire historic districts.

And where Nepalis must pay a fee to enter, foreigners inevitably pay a much higher one. To some extent, these fees have been prompted by international pressure on Nepal to protect and clean up its UNESCO-designated World Heritage Sites. Local officials argue that users of the sites should fund their upkeep, and they don't see anything wrong with putting the main burden on foreigners – they cause impacts that locals don't, and it's their governments that are making a stink about cleaning up the sites.

You also have to pay a steep extra fee to bring a **video camera** into certain parks and sights.

Crime

Nepal is one of the most crime-free countries in the world, which is all the more remarkable when you consider the huge gulf between rich and poor. However, it would be foolish not to take a few simple precautions.

The main concern is **petty theft**. Store valuables that you're not using in your hotel or guesthouse safe, and carry the rest in a money belt or pouch around your neck. In a dormitory, keep your bag locked and any expensive items with you. A padlock can be purchased cheaply in Nepal; it doesn't have to be big, as deterrence is the main thing. Some public bus routes have reputations for baggage theft – see p.28 for advice. **Pickpockets** (who are often street children) operate in crowded urban areas, especially during festivals, and tend to home in on unprotected tourist wallets and handbags; best advice is to keep vigilant.

If you're robbed, report it as soon as possible to the **police** headquarters of the district in which the robbery occurred. Policemen are apt to be friendly and consoling, if not much help. For **insurance** purposes, go to the Interpol Section of the police headquarters in Durbar Square, Kathmandu, to fill in a report; you'll need a copy of it to claim from your insurer once back home. Bring a photocopy of the pages in your passport containing your photo and your Nepali visa, together with two passport photos. Dress smartly and expect an uphill battle – they're jaded by stolen travellers' cheque scams.

Violent crime is rare. An occasional concern is a certain amount of hooliganism or sexual aggression in the Kathmandu tourist bars, though Thamel is well policed and the Maoist government's hostility to late-night venues has made it less likely that problems will arise. Women, by and large, are treated with great respect. Over the years, there have been a couple of well-publicized sex murders in the national parks on the edge of the Kathmandu Valley, and a few Western women have been raped, but most problems come about within relationships with Nepali men – trekking or rafting guides, for instance (see p.348) – not due to attack by strangers. The countryside, for the most part, is very safe. There has always been a small risk of violent attack by bandits on remote trekking trails, however, and this risk has been somewhat higher since the Maoist insurrection. Trekkers encountering Maoist (or pretend-Maoist) groups have generally been treated with courteousness. In the past, many were approached at gunpoint for "donations", but the Maoists in government have mostly managed to curtail these kinds of operations. In the Terai, there are a number of armed Madhesi groups that continue to attack state institutions, but tourists are not targets and you are unlikely to be affected much beyond the odd delayed bus, roadblock or *bandh* (see opposite).

There are several ways to get on the wrong side of the law, none of them worth it. **Smuggling** is the usual cause of serious trouble – drugs and gold are the big no-no's, and if you get caught with commercial quantities of either you'll be looking at a more or less automatic five to twenty years in prison.

In Nepal, where government servants are poorly paid, a little **bakshish** sometimes greases the wheels. Nepali police don't bust tourists simply in order to get bribes, but if you're accused of something it might not hurt to make an offer, in an extremely careful, euphemistic and deniable way. This shouldn't be necessary if you're the victim of a crime, although you may feel like offering a "reward".

The worst trouble you're likely to run into is one of Nepal's all-too-common **civil disturbances**. Political parties (in particular their militant youth wings), student organizations and anyone else with a gripe may call a *chakka jam* (traffic halt) or *bandh* (general strike). In either case, most shops pull down their shutters as well, and all motorized vehicles stay off the roads after about 8am to avoid having their windows smashed – you'll have great difficulty making any travel connections, but on the plus side the lack of traffic means the streets are less polluted and more pleasant to wander around. Demonstrations sometimes involve rock-throwing, tear gas and *lathis* (Asian-style police batons), but you'd have to go out of your way to get mixed up in this.

Drugs

Drugs are of course illegal in Nepal, but it is difficult to walk through Thamel or any of the other major tourist destinations without being sidled up to by a whispering dealer and offered **hash** (and, less frequently, **opium** and **heroin** from the Golden Triangle). Cannabis grows wild throughout hill Nepal; old folks sometimes smoke it as an evening tonic and it is used in a few religious rituals. It would be incredibly stupid to go through customs with drugs, but discreet possession inside the country carries virtually no risk; flash dope around, though, and you could conceivably get shopped by an innkeeper. While the drug dealers are often shady characters, they are not generally informants.

Electricity

Power comes at 220 volts/50 cycles per second, when you can get it: virtually all electricity in Nepal is generated by hydro-electric projects, so lengthy power cuts ("load shedding") are a daily occurrence, especially in spring when water levels get low. Most places tourists go are now electri-fied, and smarter hotels and restaurants often have back-up generators.

Emergencies

Dial ☎100 for the police. Hospitals and other organisations have their own telephone numbers for an ambulance, but get a Nepali-speaker to do the talking. Registering with your embassy can speed things up in the event of an emergency.

Entry regulations

All foreign nationals except Indians need a **visa** to enter Nepal. These are free (for 30 days) for nationals of other South Asian Area Regional Cooperation (SAARC) countries: Pakistan, Bhutan and Bangladesh. All other nationals have to pay for them (see p.145). Tourist visas are issued on arrival at Kathmandu airport and official overland entry points. At the former, queues can be painfully long, so you may prefer to get one in advance from a Nepali embassy or consulate in your own country. Have a passport-size photo at the ready, and if possible bring exact change for the visa fee. At the airport, you can pay in US dollars, euros, pounds sterling or other major foreign currencies. At overland entry points, officials tend to demand US dollars or Nepali rupees, though other major foreign currencies should be accepted too.

The **fee structure** at the time of writing was $15 for 15 days, $40 for 30 days and $100 for 90 days; all are multiple entry visas. Fees may change without warning, however, so double-check at Ⓦwww.immi.gov.np before setting out. Tourist visas can be extended up to a maximum of 150 days in a calendar year: an extension of 15 days or less costs $30; for more than 15 days, it costs $2 per day. Extensions are granted only at the Kathmandu or Pokhara Depart-ment of Immigration offices – a somewhat tedious procedure, especially in high season, when queues can run to two hours or more. Submit your passport and one passport-size photo with your application. A transit visa, valid for 24 hours and non-extendable, costs $5.

Don't overstay more than a couple of days, and for heaven's sake *don't* tamper with your visa – tourists have been fined and even jailed for these seemingly minor infractions.

It is no longer necessary to have a **trekking permit** to visit the most popular trekking regions. You'll have to pay **national park entry fees**, however, which cover the Annapurna, Everest and Langtang areas, while there is an entry fee to enter some parts of the Kathmandu Valley (see p.183). A handful of very remote regions, such as Upper Dolpo and Mustang, are still restricted, and require permits to enter. For more detailed discussion, see Chapter Seven.

Customs officers are fairly lax on entry, but they might note fancy electronic gear in your passport so you can't sell it in Nepal. Checks are more thorough on departure, and it is illegal to export objects over 100 years old. To take out antiques, you need a special certificate from the Department of Archeology on Ram Shah Path in Kathmandu.

Selected Nepali embassies and consulates

A complete list of Nepali embassies and consulates abroad can be found at ⓦwww .welcomenepal.com.

Australia Suite 2.02, 24 Marcus Clarke St, Canberra City ☏02/6162 1554, ⓦwww.necan.gov.np.
India Barakhamba Rd, New Delhi 110001 ☏11/ 2332 7361.
New Zealand 278 A Remuera Rd, Auckland 5 ☏09/520 3169.
UK 12a Kensington Palace Gardens, London W8 4QU ☏020/7229 1594, ⓦwww.nepembassy.org.uk.
US 2131 Leroy Place NW, Washington, DC 20008 ☏202/667 4550, ⓦwww.nepalembassyusa.org.

Gay and lesbian Nepal

Nepalis will often tell you gays and lesbians don't exist in their country – and openly it can appear that they don't. While the **gay scene** in Kathmandu is growing slowly, and there are tentative signs that the government may be taking a more progressive line than in the past, homosexuality is still very much frowned upon. (In true Victorian fashion, lesbianism is barely even considered a possibility.)

In a society where men routinely hold hands and often share beds, gay **couples** may feel a certain freedom in being able to be close in public, but otherwise the same advice on sexual behaviour in public applies as for heterosexual couples (see p.54). The only approach a gay traveller is likely to get is from touts who might offer, at the end of a long inventory of drugs, "nice Nepali girls", and if that doesn't work, boys. But it's nothing like the scene in, say, Thailand. For more information, contact the Blue Diamond Society (☏01/444 3350, ⓦwww.bds.org .np), a Kathmandu-based gay rights pressure group.

Information and websites

The handful of **Nepal Tourism Board** offices inside the country are generally friendly, if not necessarily full of information. Staff usually speak good English and can help with festival dates, local bus schedules and the like, and supply a growing range of printed materials if they're not out of stock. But for the most part, you're left to find your own way through a confusing thicket of advertising and signboards.

You'll get the most useful information from other travellers. Check the informal **notice boards** in restaurants and guesthouses around the tourist quarters for news of upcoming events or to find travelling or trekking companions. In the capital, the offices of the **Kathmandu Environmental Education Project** and the **Himalayan Rescue Association** (see p.80) can help out with information on trekking routes and conditions. Despite its shameless advertiser bias, the magazine *Nepal Traveller* has some useful articles – reading it online (ⓦwww .nepal-traveller.com) is much easier than finding a hard copy.

Nepal is well provided for **online**, though some sites are pretty self-serving, and others frankly bizarre. You only have to find one Nepal site to find the rest, since they're well linked. More trekking websites are recommended in the trekking chapter, while other specific sites are listed throughout the main guide text.

Useful websites

ⓦ**www.catmando.com** Comprehensive (if rarely updated) lists of Nepal-based businesses, including hotels, travel and trekking agencies.
ⓦ**www.fco.gov.uk/travel** This British Foreign and Commonwealth Office site is usually the most detailed government advisory service on travel to Nepal.
ⓦ**www.himalayanrescue.org** Useful resource for trekkers, run by non-profit organisation the Himalayan Rescue Association.
ⓦ**www.keepnepal.org** Homepage of the Kathmandu Environmental Education Project (KEEP) - particularly good for environmental, cultural and trekking information.
ⓦ**www.mapmandu.com** Online Kathmandu map and location finder.

ⓦ **www.nepalhomepage.com** Helpful Nepal gateway, with extensive FAQs on travel in Nepal, local yellow pages, directories of trekking agencies and embassies, and photos. Information is not always up-to-date though.

ⓦ **www.nepalnews.com** Superb news service with links to just about every Nepali media outlet, including English-language newspapers and magazines. Start with the *Kathmandu Post* or *Nepali Times*.

ⓦ **www.pilgrimsbooks.com** The online branch of Kathmandu's largest bookstore, with hundreds of Nepal-related titles available.

ⓦ **http://travel.state.gov** The US Department of State's website details the dangers of travelling to most countries in the world.

ⓦ **www.welcomenepal.com** The useful website of the Nepal Tourism Board.

ⓦ **www.yetizone.com** Online guide to trekking in the Himalayas.

Insurance

It's worth taking out **insurance** before travelling, to cover against theft, loss and illness or injury. Before paying for a new policy, however, it's worth checking whether you're already covered: some all-risks home insurance policies may cover your possessions when overseas, and many medical schemes include cover when abroad.

After exhausting the possibilities above, you might want to contact a **specialist travel insurance** company. A typical policy usually provides cover for the loss of baggage, tickets and – up to a certain limit – cash, as well as cancellation or curtailment of your journey. Most of them exclude so-called dangerous sports unless an extra premium is paid: in Nepal this can mean whitewater rafting, trekking and climbing, though probably not kayaking or jeep safaris. Many policies can be chopped and changed – for example, sickness and accident benefits can often be excluded or included at will. If you do take medical coverage, ascertain whether benefits will be paid as treatment proceeds or only after return home, and whether there is a 24-hour medical emergency number. When securing baggage cover, make sure that the per-article limit – typically under £500 – will cover your most valuable possession. If you need to make a claim, you should keep **receipts** for medicines and medical treatment, and in the event you have

anything stolen, you must obtain an official statement from the police.

Internet

It is easy to get online in Nepal: **internet cafés** are abundant in tourist areas, and even out-of-the-way towns have one or two. Outside of Kathmandu and Pokhara, however, connections can be painfully slow. Expect to pay around Rs60/hr. To avoid frustration later, it's also worth finding out whether a power cut is due before going online, as only a few Thamel-based cyber cafés have back-up generators.

Laundry

Most hotels and guesthouses provide laundry services, generally charging around Rs5–50 per item. In Thamel and other tourist areas, there are numerous laundries charging around Rs50 per kilogram, some with a turnaround time of just a few hours. If you're doing your own, detergent is sold in inexpensive packets in cities, or you can buy a cheap cube of local laundry soap almost anywhere.

The media

Nepal's news traditionally came in the form of the *gaine* minstrel, but in modern Nepal radio is the most powerful media, reaching even the most remote areas. Television is spreading rapidly in the wake of electricity, newspapers are widely read in urban areas and, where there are phone lines, the internet provides a point of contact with the outside world for a few rupees an hour.

Newspapers and magazines

Despite a literacy rate of less than thirty percent, Nepal boasts more than a thousand **newspapers** – an outgrowth of two noble Brahmanic traditions: punditry and gossip. Several are published in English, the most readable and incisive being the weekly *Nepali Times*. Of the dailies, the *Kathmandu Post* remains the frontrunner, overshadowing *The Himalayan Times* and *Rising Nepal*. All are hard to find outside big cities, but they are available online at ⓦ www.nepalnews.com.

A number of **magazines** are published in English, the most interesting and easy to find being *Himal*, a bimonthly current affairs journal covering South Asia. A wide range of international publications such as the *International Herald Tribune*, *Time* and *Newsweek* are available from bookshops in Kathmandu and Pokhara, as is glossy expat mag *ECS* and the occasional few-days-old foreign newspaper.

TV and radio

Only a decade ago Nepali **TV** amounted to six hours a day of amateurish domestic news focused on royal engagements sandwiched between a few songs. These days there are more than a dozen channels with current affairs, serials, pop videos and programmes in local dialects. The rapid spread of **cable and satellite TV** – Indian serials, pop videos, Hollywood movies and all the advertising broadcast with them – is challenging attitudes to traditional values. More and more hotel rooms have TVs, and you can catch CNN, BBC World and movies and sitcoms in both English and Hindi.

The government-run **Radio Nepal** (Ⓦwww .radio-nepal.com), on 103 FM, is probably still the most influential of the nation's media, catering to the illiterate majority of Nepalis and reaching villages well beyond the circulation of any newspaper. With a daily format of music, news, English-language lessons, dramas and development messages, it has been a powerful force for cultural and linguistic unity. The station carries English-language news bulletins daily at 8pm.

Local **FM stations** are sprouting like mushrooms and increasingly using ethnic languages and local dialects. There are a couple of English-language ones in the Kathmandu Valley; the trendiest is Kantipur 96.1 FM. If you're travelling with a short-wave radio, you can pick up the BBC World Service: Ⓦwww.bbc.co.uk/worldservice lists the frequencies.

Money and banks

Nepal's unit of currency is the **rupee** (*rupiya*), which is divided into 100 *paisa*. At the time of writing, the **exchange rate** was around Rs81 to the US dollar, Rs117 to £1 and Rs107 to the euro. Most Nepali money is paper (coins are relatively rare). **Notes** come in denominations of Rs1, 2, 5, 10, 20, 25, 50, 100, 250, 500 and 1000.

More upmarket tourist businesses will usually quote prices in US dollars, and may even expect payment in that currency. This guide reflects the situation on the ground: the dollar price is listed if that's what the business quotes. A fistful of rupees will rarely be refused, but if you're planning to stay in classy hotels, or book flights or rafting trips, it's worth bringing some US currency. A selection of denominations is useful; make sure the bills are relatively new, too.

One minor annoyance of travelling in Nepal is **getting change**. Even in tourist areas, business people will hum and haw about breaking a large note. Trying to pass even a Rs500 note to a trekking lodge owner or a rikshaw driver is sure to invite delays, since few Nepalis can afford to keep much spare change lying around. It gets to be a game of bluff between buyer and seller, both hoarding a wad of small notes for occasions when exact change is vital. It pays to carry a range of smaller bills.

ATMs are increasingly common in Nepali towns, and most travellers rely on them for funds.

Credit and debit cards

Travel agents, luxury hotels and some of the mid-range guesthouses accept major **credit cards**, but budget outfits don't, and while an increasing number of retailers take plastic, they typically add a three to five percent processing fee onto the amount, which you may be able to get waived during the bargaining process. Manual transactions (those not submitted by an electronic swipe device) may take months to appear on your bill. All but a very few traders are honest, but be wary if a proprietor insists on taking your card out of sight for processing.

ATMs are numerous in Kathmandu, and most decent-sized towns have at least one: almost all accept foreign debit and credit cards (though you may face a few problems if you have a Cirrus card) and have instructions in English, and many are open 24 hours. It is worth letting your bank or credit card company know you intend to use your card in Nepal before leaving home, as they sometimes stop cards used abroad for fear that they have been cloned or stolen. Some banks also issue credit card cash advances, and American Express cardholders can similarly draw money at the Amex office in Kathmandu (see p.140).

Traveller's cheques

Traveller's cheques are of course more secure than cash, and in Nepal they sometimes bring a slightly higher official exchange rate, just about offsetting the commission you pay when buying them. Any major brand will do. **US dollar** cheques are widely accepted in tourist areas, and cheques denominated in other major currencies are usually accepted as well. If you're travelling off the beaten track, however, it's wiser to stick to cash.

Banks and moneychangers

Using **banks** in Nepal is, by south Asian standards, surprisingly hassle-free. Numerous private banks and the quasi-government Nepal Bank vie for tourist business, as do a horde of government-registered **money-changers**. Banks tend to give slightly better rates than moneychangers, though the latter are often more convenient.

Moneychangers can be found wherever there are significant numbers of tourists. Private bank branches are located mainly in larger cities, with government banks typically providing the only service in smaller, untouristed places. **Hours** for foreign exchange vary: at least one Kathmandu airport moneychanger operates around the clock, Nepal Bank's central Kathmandu (New Road) branch stays open seven days a week, and some private banks keep extended hours, but lesser branches generally change money only 9am–3pm Mon–Fri, often closing early on Fridays. Moneychangers keep generous hours – usually 9am–8pm, seven days a week.

Hold onto all exchange receipts, as you'll need them for **changing money back** when you leave. Some private banks in Kathmandu will buy rupees back, as will banks at the Kathmandu airport and at official border crossings. However, they may have trouble giving the exact change equivalent in foreign currency, and may be able to give it only in US dollars. If you're entering India, changing Nepali currency into Indian currency is no problem.

The only reason to change money on the **black market** would be if all official outlets were closed. If you do it, know the official rate, haggle hard and be on your guard.

Opening hours

In the Kathmandu Valley, **government offices** and **post offices** are open Mon–Fri 9am–5pm (sometimes closing at 4pm mid-Nov to mid-Feb); outside the Valley, they often open Sunday as well.

Museum closing days vary, although they are usually closed at least one day a week; opening times are fairly similar to office hours. **Shops** keep long hours, usually from 9–10am to 7–8pm, and in tourist areas usually stay open seven days a week. Some **banks** in tourist areas and Kathmandu are also generous with their hours, but elsewhere you'll generally have to do your transactions Mon–Fri 9am–3pm. Money-changers keep longer hours.

Travel agents tend to work from around 9am to the early evening; **airline offices** are open roughly the same hours as government offices, and may well be closed for lunch between 1pm and 2pm. **Embassy** and consulate hours are all over the place, so it's impossible to generalize.

Nepal's hectic calendar of **national holidays** can shut down offices for up to a week at a time. Dates vary from year to year – Nepal has its own calendar, the Vikram Sambat, which began in 57 BC. The year starts in mid-April and consists of twelve months that are a fortnight or so out of step with the Western ones. Complicating matters further are religious **festivals**, which are calculated according to the lunar calendar, while Tibetan and Newari festivals follow calendars of their own (see p.42).

Phones

Nepal's telecommunications network has improved in recent years, and it could hardly be easier for visitors to make calls. All tourist areas and major towns have **telephone/internet shops** that offer a variety of ways to make cheap international calls. Many accept payment by credit card, too. Simpler telephone-only outfits, which advertise themselves with the acronyms ISD/STD/IDD (international subscriber dialling/standard

The Nepali year

Nepal's calendar has three major differences from the Western one: it is 57 (or, for three months of the year, 56) years ahead of the Western calendar; its months start and finish approximately two weeks out of kilter with their international equivalents; and the New Year officially begins with the month of Baisaakh, in mid-April. This "Bikram Sambat" calendar was established by the legendary Indian emperor Vikramaditya; India long since went over to the European model but Nepal, which resisted colonization, has maintained tradition. Inevitably, there are calls for change. Some want to return to use the "Nepal Sambat" of the Kathmandu Valley's indigenous Newari people; others prefer to modernize.

For now, the only likely change is the **skipping of an entire Nepali month** in 2066 BS, or AD 2010. The idea is to compensate for the Nepali calendar's lack of a leap year (and thus return the festivals to their original seasons) by deleting the last month of the year, Chait, which would normally begin on March 14, 2010. The calendar would thus jump straight from the last day of Phaagun 2066 BS (13 March 2010) to the first day of the new year, 1 Baisaakh 2067 BS. If the proposal goes ahead, festival dates for that year will all fall one month earlier than listed in this book. That said, the decision of astrologers, on whom festival dates depend, are notoriously unpredictable, as they are based around the phases of the moon. (For a full discussion of festival dates, see p.42.) The common **names** of the Nepali months are listed below; alternative spellings, sometimes based on classical Sanskrit, are often seen.

Baisaakh (April–May)	Kaattik (Oct–Nov)
Jeth (May–June)	Mangsir (Nov–Dec)
Asaar (June–July)	Poush (Dec–Jan)
Saaun (July–Aug)	Magh (Jan–Feb)
Bhadau (Aug–Sept)	Phaagun (Feb–March)
Asoj (Sept–Oct)	Chait (March–April)

trunk dialling/international direct dialling), can be found almost everywhere there's a phone line. Most district headquarters have government-operated telephone offices, which are slightly cheaper but considerably less user-friendly.

Nepali numbers are always eight digits long: in the Kathmandu Valley the ☏01 area code is followed by a seven-digit number; elsewhere, a three-digit area code is followed by a six-digit number; mobile phone numbers are ten digits long. You don't need to dial the area code when you're calling landlines from within that area. Numbers in the Kathmandu chapter of this guide are listed with codes, but note that you'll need to remove ☏01 when dialling from within the Valley.

International calls

Most telecommunications shops offer a choice between conventional and internet phone services. Conventional **international**

calls are expensive from Nepal: about Rs80–160 per minute from Kathmandu. Calls to North America are usually the cheapest, followed by Europe and Australia/ New Zealand.

You can save money using the "**callback**" system, however, for which you pay the full whack for the initial call to tell your party the number where you can be reached, but then only a fee rupees per minute for the incoming call – some places will allow you to receive calls for free. You can also call **collect** to many countries, but the per-minute charge to you is the same as with a callback, and much higher for the person at the other end.

Internet calls (generally Skype) are much cheaper options, and typically cost Rs5/ min, though it's better to make them from a cyber café with a fast connection. It's also worth checking whether there's a power cut due before making a call. Internet connections aren't yet fast enough for video calls.

Mobile phones

Mobile phones have really taken off in Nepal over the last few years and coverage is now generally pretty good within the Kathmandu Valley, Pokhara and much of the Terai (though more patchy in rural and hilly areas) and should continue to improve over the next few years. You can generally use foreign sim cards in Nepal, but it is much cheaper to buy a local sim card: Mera is the best network for coverage (you can even call from Poon Hill on it); the CDMA-based Sky phone also has great coverage, but is pricey; and NTC is the cheapest network.

Calling home from Nepal

US and Canada: 00 + 1+ city code
Australia: 00 + 61 + city code
New Zealand: 00 + 64 + city code
UK and Northern Ireland: 00 + 44 + city code
Republic of Ireland: 00 + 353 + city code
South Africa: 00 + 27 + city code

Post

Post generally takes at least ten days to get to or from Nepal – if it arrives at all. Postcards go through fine, but envelopes or parcels that look like they might contain anything of value sometimes go astray; even sending things registered offers no guarantees. Letters can be sent to a hotel or a friend's home, or care of **poste restante** in Kathmandu and, less reliably, Pokhara (see p.141 & p.249). Mail should be addressed: Name, Poste Restante, GPO, Kathmandu (or Pokhara), Nepal. Print your name clearly with the surname underlined or capitalized. Mail is held for about two months, and can be redirected on request.

In Kathmandu, American Express handles mail for cardholders and those carrying Amex cheques, and US citizens can receive mail c/o the Consular Section of the American Embassy.

When **sending mail** in Nepal, there's rarely a need to deal directly with the postal system; most hotels will take it to the post office for you. Book and postcard shops in tourist areas sell stamps for a nominal extra fee, and many also have their own, largely reliable, mail drop-off boxes. Where no such services exist, take your letters or cards to the post office yourself and have the stamps franked before your eyes, or wait to send them from Kathmandu, where they've got a higher probability of reaching their destination. Never use a public letterbox: the stamps will be removed and resold, and your correspondence used to wrap peanuts.

Parcels can be sent by air or sea. Sea mail is cheaper but takes a lot longer (three months or more) and, as it first has to go by land to Kolkata, there are more opportunities for it to go missing. Again, the private sector is much easier to deal with than the official postal service. **Shipping agents** and **air freight services** in Kathmandu will shield you from much of the frustration and red tape, and provide packing materials to boot, but for this they charge almost twice as much as the post office. Be sure you're dealing with a reputable company – a few are recommended on p.141. Don't entrust shipping to a handicrafts shop.

Time zones

Nepal is 5 hours 45 minutes ahead of GMT. That makes it 5 hours 45 minutes ahead of

---

Domestic calls

The international code for Nepal is 977. When dialling a number in Nepal from abroad, drop the "0" at the beginning of the area code. Private phone shops charge from around Rs10-20 for **trunk** (domestic long-distance) calls, depending on the distance. Your hotel or guesthouse, and any shop with a phone on the counter, will let you make **local calls** for a few rupees. Public phones in Nepal are practically nonexistent. While this guide gives local **phone numbers** where they exist, be aware that numbers in Nepal change frequently. (Nepalis, accustomed to this, often start conversations with the phrase *Kaahaa pariyo?* – "Where have I reached?"). If the number has changed, **directory enquiries** (☏197 from a landline or ☏1414 or 1498 from a mobile) might be able to help, but have a Nepali translate for you.

London, 10 hours 45 minutes ahead of New York, 13 hours 45 minutes ahead of Los Angeles, and 4 hours 15 minutes behind Sydney. Nepal doesn't observe daylight saving time, so daylight saving time elsewhere reduces/increases the time difference by one hour.

Tipping

Tipping isn't compulsory, but a reward to be bestowed for good service or withheld for bad. Remember to check if the new ten percent service charge has been added, and only tip on top, for exceptional service. If not, Rs30 or so should be sufficient in all but the fanciest places. Don't tip taxi drivers, except maybe to round up the fare to the nearest Rs5 or Rs10. Trekking porters and guides have their own expectations – see Chapter Seven. Don't tip anyone until full completion of the service.

Toilets and rubbish

You may be dismayed by the amount of **rubbish** in the streets. People throw their litter on the ground, where it may, or may not be swept up or burnt; bins are rare. The best policy is to find a big pile that's already there, and add yours to it.

Where they exist, **toilets** range from "Western" (sit-down) flush jobs to a shed over a hole. In lodges – tourist ones aside – the norm is a squat toilet. When travelling by bus, there will almost always be a bathroom available at stops, but sometimes there is nothing but a designated field. When in doubt, ask *Toilet kahaachha?* ("Where is the toilet?"). Don't flush toilet paper: put it in the basket provided. It's not provided in more basic places, so buy your own. Nepalis use a jug of water and the left hand.

As many villages have no covered **toilets**, it's deemed okay to defecate in the open – but out of sight of others, in the early morning or after dark. Men may urinate in public away from buildings – discreetly – but women have to find a sheltered spot.

Travellers with disabilities

Although **disability** is common here, Nepal is a poor country without the means to cater for disabled travellers. If you walk with difficulty, you'll find the steep slopes, stairs and uneven pavements hard going. Open sewers, potholes, crowds and a lack of proper street crossings will all make it hard for a blind traveller to get around. That said, guides and porters are readily available and should be prepared to provide whatever assistance you need. Nepalis are also likely to be very helpful.

With a companion, there's no reason why you can't enjoy many of Nepal's activities, including elephant rides, scenic mountain flights and sightseeing by private car. If you rent a taxi for the day, the driver is certain to help you in and out, and perhaps around the sites you visit. A safari in one of the Terai wildlife parks should be feasible, and even a trek, catered to your needs by an agency, with a bit of notice, might not be out of the question – mules or horses can be used on a number of trekking routes, for example.

Basic **wheelchairs** are available in the Kathmandu airport, and smaller airports, including Pokhara, are mostly at ground level. Generally, however, facilities for the disabled are nonexistent, so you should bring your own wheelchair or other necessary walking aids or equipment. Hotels aren't geared up for disabled guests, though the most expensive ones have lifts and (sometimes) ramps.

Guide

Guide

1

Kathmandu and Patan

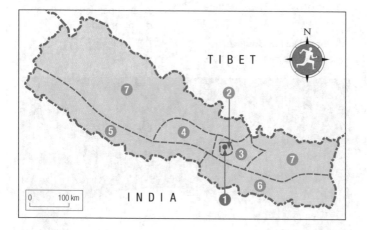

CHAPTER 1 # Highlights

* **Kathmandu Durbar Square**
An old royal palace, a living
goddess, temples, statues,
vegetable sellers and curio
hawkers come together in this
touristy yet vibrant hub.
See p.91

* **The Bagmati ghats** Little-
visited relics and cremation
platforms dot these neglected
riverside embankments.
See p.102 & p.118

* **Swayambhu** This hilltop
temple complex is a profound
microcosm of Nepali culture.
See p.105

* **Patan Durbar Square** The
apex of Newari architecture,

crowned by the classy Patan
Museum. See p.114

* **The Golden Temple** Nepal's
most opulent little temple,
and the spiritual hub of old
Patan. See p.117

* **Eating out** The city's
restaurants serve a
bewildering array of cuisines,
from fine French dining to
Tibetan street food.
See p.121

* **Meditation and yoga
courses** Kathmandu's
spiritual supermarket caters
to dabblers and serious
seekers alike. See p.138

▲ Swayambhu temple

Kathmandu and Patan

How to describe **KATHMANDU**? A medieval time capsule? An environmental disaster? A tourist trap? A holy city? A dump? All of the above. There are a thousand Kathmandus, all layered together in an extravagant morass of chaos and sophistication. With a population well over 700,000, Nepal's capital is far and away the country's biggest and most cosmopolitan city: a melting pot of a dozen ethnic groups, and home town of the Newars – master craftsmen and traders extraordinaire (see p.180). Trade, indeed, created Kathmandu – for at least a thousand years it controlled the most important caravan route between Tibet and India – and trade has always funded its Newari artisans. Little wonder, perhaps, that the city has so deftly embraced the tourist business.

The Kathmandu most travellers experience, **Thamel**, is like a thumping, developing-world theme park, filled with hotels and lodges, restaurants serving a mish-mash of international dishes, souvenir shops, second-hand book stores, imitation trekking gear, pirated DVDs, and touts flogging tiger balm and hashish. The **old city**, though squeezed by traffic and a growing population, is still studded with timeless temples and splendid architecture. Its narrow lanes seethe with an incredible crush of humanity, echoing with the din of bicycle bells, motorbike engines, religious music, construction and car horns, and reeking of incense, spices, sewage and exhaust fumes. Sacred cows roam the streets, as do holy men, beggars and street urchins.

To the south, the separate municipality of **Patan** was once the capital of an independent kingdom; though now subsumed into the greater Kathmandu conurbation, it has its own quieter and better-preserved historic district, marked by numerous Buddhist *bahal* (monastery compounds, some still active), proud artistry, and a conspicuous community of foreign residents, predominantly the staff of international NGOs and charities.

These quarters represent only part of a complex and eccentric city, which also encompasses squatter shantytowns, decrepit ministry buildings, swanky shopping streets, sequestered suburbs and heaving bazaars. Perhaps the predominant images of contemporary Kathmandu are those that pass for progress: hellish traffic jams and pollution; a jostling skyline of rooftop water-storage tanks and obsolete satellite dishes; suburban sprawl, cybercafés, nightclubs and rubbish heaps; crippling daily power cuts (sometimes up to ten hours a day) and backup

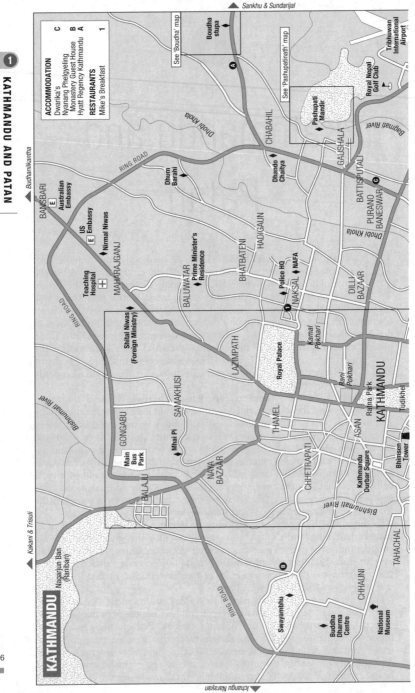

KATHMANDU

ACCOMMODATION
Dwarika's   C
Nyatang Phelgyeling
Monastery Guest House   B
Hyatt Regency Kathmandu   A

RESTAURANTS
Mike's Breakfast   1

Sankhu & Sundarijal

Boudha stupa

See 'Boudha' map

Tribhuvan International Airport

See 'Pashupatinath' map

Buchanilkantha

Royal Nepal Golf Club

Pashupati Mandir

CHABAHIL

Dhobi Khola

RING ROAD

Dhando Chaitya

GAUSHALA

Bagmati River

BANSBARI

Dhum Barahi

Australian Embassy

US Embassy

Nirmal Niwas

MAHARAJGANJ

Teaching Hospital

RING ROAD

Shital Niwas (Foreign Ministry)

Prime Minister's Residence

BALUWATAR

HADIGAUN

BHATBATENI

Police HQ

NAFA

NAKSAL

BATTISPUTALI

PURANO BANESWAR

DILLI BAZAAR

Dhobi Khola

LAZIMPATH

Kamal Pokhari

Royal Palace

Rani Pokhari

Ratna Park

KATHMANDU

Bishnumati River

GONGABU

SAMAKHUSI

Mhai Pi

Main Bus Park

THAMEL

NAYA BAZAAR

CHHETRAPATI

ASAN

Kathmandu Durbar Square

Bhimsen Tower

Tudikhel

BALAJU

Bishnumati River

Kakani & Trisuli

Nagarjun Ban (Raniban)

RING ROAD

CHHAUNI

Swayambhu

Buddha Dharma Centre

National Museum

TAHACHAL

Ichangu Narayan

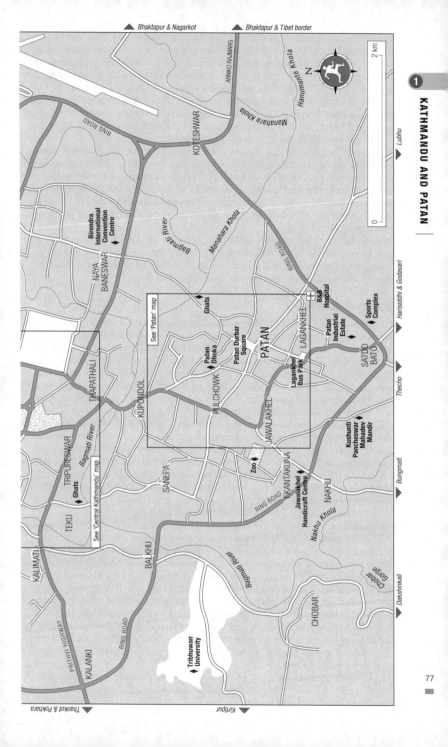

Bhaktapur & Nagarkot

Bhaktapur & Tibet border

ARNIKO RAJMARG

KOTESHWAR

Hanumante Khola

Manahara Khola

N

2 km

0

Birendra
International
Convention
Centre

Bagmati River

Manahara Khola

RING ROAD

RING ROAD

NAYA
BANESWAR

Lubhu

See 'Patan' map

Ghats

B&B
Hospital

Harisiddhi & Godavari

PATAN

Sports
Complex

Patan
Dhoka

Patan Durbar
Square

Patan
Industrial
Estate

LAGANKHEL

THAPATHALI

KUPONDOL

PILCHOWK

Lagankhel
Bus Park

SATDO
BATO

TRIPURESWAR

Bagmati River

JAWALAKHEL

Thecho

TEKU

Ghats

SANEPA

Zoo

EKANTAKUNA

Kushunti
Pancheswar
Mahadev
Mandir

See 'Central Kathmandu' map

Jawalakhel
Handicraft Centre

NAKHU

Bungmati

KALIMATI

Bagmati River

RING ROAD

BALKHU

Nakhu Khola

Chobar
Gorge

Dakshinkali

PRITHVI HIGHWAY

RING ROAD

KALANKI

Tribhuwan
University

CHOBAR

Thankot & Pokhara

Kirtipur

generators; chauffeured SUVs and families on motorbikes. The city hasn't abandoned its traditional identity, but the rapid pace of change has produced an intense, often overwhelming, urban environment. New buildings are thrown up in a haphazard manner, with little concern for aesthetics or safety (according to a sobering 2008 Nepal Red Cross Society report, an earthquake measuring 7-8 on the Richter scale could destroy sixty percent of Kathmandu's buildings, including most hospitals, and kill tens of thousands). Anyone visiting Nepal for its natural beauty is likely to be disillusioned by Kathmandu.

Nevertheless, Kathmandu is likely to be your first port of call – all overseas flights land in the capital, and most roads lead to it – and you probably won't be able to avoid spending at least a couple of days here. It has all the **embassies** and airline offices, Nepal's best-developed **communications facilities**, and a welter of **trekking and travel agencies**. At least as important, in the minds of long-haul travellers anyway, are the capital's **restaurants and bars**, and an easy **social scene**, all of which makes Kathmandu the natural place to get your bearings in Nepal.

Nevertheless, you'd be well advised to get your business here over with as quickly as possible. If you're intending to do any sightseeing around the valley, consider basing yourself in the healthier surroundings of Bhaktapur or Boudha (see Chapter Two), avoiding the city as much as possible.

Some history

People must have occupied what is now Kathmandu for thousands of years, but chroniclers attribute the city's founding to Gunakamadev, who reigned in the late ninth century – by which time sophisticated urban centres had already been established by the **Lichhavi** kings at Pashupatinath and other sites in the surrounding valley. Kathmandu, originally known as Kantipur, took its present name from the Kasthamandap (Pavilion of Wood) that was constructed as a rest-house along the main Tibet–India trade route in the late twelfth century, and which still stands in the city centre.

The city rose to prominence under the **Malla** kings, who took control of the valley in the thirteenth century, ushering in a golden age of art and architecture lasting more than five hundred years. Kathmandu's finest buildings and monuments, including those of its spectacular Durbar Square, date from this period. At the start of the Malla era, Kathmandu ranked as a sovereign state alongside the valley's other two major cities, Bhaktapur and Patan, but soon fell under the rule of the former. The cities were again divided in the fifteenth century, and a long period of intrigue and rivalry followed.

Malla rule ended abruptly in 1769, when Prithvi Narayan Shah of Gorkha, a previously undistinguished hill state to the west, captured the valley as the first conquest in his historic unification of Nepal. Kathmandu fared well in defeat, being made capital of the new nation and seat of the new **Shah** dynasty.

Although politically outmanoeuvred from 1846 to 1951 by the powerful **Rana** family, who ruled as hereditary prime ministers and left Kathmandu with a legacy of enormous whitewashed Neoclassical palaces, the Shahs were essentially in power until April 2006, with the final decade consumed by a debilitating civil war with Maoist forces. A peace deal was struck later that year and in early 2007 the Maoists joined an interim government. A general election in April 2008 left the Maoists as the biggest party in parliament, and a month later Nepal's monarchy was abolished.

Kathmandu remains the focus of all national political power – and, frequently, political protest – while its industrial and financial activities continue to fuel a round-the-clock building boom.

Orientation and arrival

Despite chaotic first appearances, Kathmandu is surprisingly easy to get to grips with. The following, along with the map on p.77, should help with **orientation**.

Tradition has it that old Kathmandu (1290m) was laid out in the shape of a *khukuri* knife. Positioned at what would be the hilt of the knife is **Durbar Square**, while the oldest neighbourhoods stretch northeast and (to a lesser extent) southwest. **New Road**, the city's main shopping street, runs east from the square. The minaret-like **Bhimsen Tower** provides a useful landmark south of New Road. Kathmandu's budget hotels are concentrated in **Thamel**, north of Durbar Square in a newer part of town, with a handful still left in **Jhochhe**, better known to tourists as **Freak Street** (which refers back to when it was an essential stop on the hippie trail across Asia) immediately south of the square.

Suburban Kathmandu sprawls mainly east of **Kantipath**, the main north–south thoroughfare, and is dominated by two landmarks, the **Royal Palace** and the **Tudikhel** (parade ground). Many of Kathmandu's expensive hotels, restaurants and boutiques, as well as many of the airline offices, are located along **Durbar Marg**, the broad boulevard running south from the main palace gate. West of the Bishnumati River is the hilltop temple of **Swayambhu**.

The separate municipality of **Patan** lies just across the Bagmati River to the south. It also has a **Durbar Square**, with most of its important temples to the north and south of the square. **Patan Dhoka** – the old city gate – lies northwest of the square, while **Mangal Bazaar**, an important crosstown route, skirts its southern edge. Broader, more conventional boulevards running from the Bagmati bridge to the big roundabout of **Jawalakhel Chowk** and from there to the Lagankhel bus park effectively divide the old city from its suburbs to the west and south.

Kathmandu and Patan are encircled by an ugly **ring road**, which effectively defines the boundaries of this chapter.

Arriving by air

All international flights land at **Tribhuwan International Airport**, 5km east of the city centre. Tourist visas (see p.63) are issued on arrival, and baggage claim is downstairs, where you should be able to grab a trolley. These are free to use; ignore anyone who tries to charge a fee for them. There's an **exchange counter** in the immigration hall with surprisingly decent rates. Nearby is a **tourist information** desk, open for all arriving flights, and a hotel association booking service, mostly for the more expensive hotels. If you've booked a room in advance, many hotels offer a **free pick-up**, but there's also a pre-paid **taxi** booth with fixed prices: Rs500 to Thamel, Rs550 to Boudha and Rs750 to Bhaktapur. You have to walk quite a way from the arrivals gate to find an unofficial taxi; the Rs100–150 saving is probably not worthwhile. Even after apparently agreeing to take you to your stated destination, a driver may try to deliver you to a guesthouse offering an especially handsome commission. Be firm.

Accommodation touts – who, together with a motley assortment of hangers-on, congregate outside – may offer a "free" ride if you stay at their lodge, but the fare and the tout's commission will just get added to your room charge.

Local **buses** offer a cheap but inconvenient alternative, departing from the main intersection at the end of the airport drive – a 200m walk – and terminating at the City Bus Park, nearly 2km from most guesthouses. Forget it.

Where are the mountains?

They're there – behind the smog. In the 1990s, peaks such as Ganesh I, Langtang Lirung and Dorje Lakpa could be seen most mornings from Kathmandu. Now they're rarely visible from the metropolitan area except on clear mornings after a soaking rain, or on *bandh* (general strike) days when all traffic is banned.

Kathmandu ranks among the world's most polluted cities, and the **traffic and fumes** on its main streets are appalling. The ever-increasing number of cars, motorbikes, buses and lorries, fuel adulteration (a sizeable amount of kerosene illegally finds its way into fuel tanks), lax emissions tests, poorly surfaced roads, rapid urbanisation, rubbish dumping and high levels of general pollution, means air quality frequently reaches "unhealthy" levels, according to official measurements. This toxic brew irritates lungs and eyes, weakens immune systems and increases the long-term risk of various health problems (see p.452).

If you can help it, don't stay more than a couple of days in Kathmandu at the start of your trip. If you do, you're likely to come down with a chest or sinus infection that will dog you for days and may be hard to shake if you go trekking.

An unpleasant wrinkle to the airport arrival experience is the leech-like young men who crowd around and render all sorts of unasked-for assistance then demand a tip. If you don't want their help, say so upfront and make it clear you will be giving them no money.

Arriving by bus

Tourist buses from Pokhara, Chitwan and (less frequently) other destinations depart and arrive from Kantipath near Tridevi Marg in Thamel. Coming from the Indian border or Pokhara by public bus, you'll arrive at the New (Naya) Bus Park, located at Gongabu at the extreme north end of the city; taxis (see opposite) charge around Rs350 to most tourist destinations. Buses from the Tibet border, Jiri and towns along those roads generally terminate at the City Bus Park, also known as the Old (Purano) Bus Park, east of the city centre and a Rs150–300 taxi ride to most lodgings.

Information and maps

The **Tourist Service Center** (Mon–Fri 10am–5pm; ☎01/425 6909, ⓦwww .welcomenepal.com) has free maps and leaflets, but it's inconveniently located in Bhrikuti Mandap, the public exhibition ground east of the Tudikhel. You can get **trekking permits** (see p.136) and **Trekkers' Information Management System** (TIMS) cards here (see p.136), and there is a small ethnographic museum (Rs25). Alternatively there's a much smaller, little-visited tourist office in **Thamel** (Mon–Fri 10am–5pm, no ☎) opposite *Tasi Dhargey Inn*. Both offices have tourist police booths.

Nepal Traveller (ⓦwww.nepal-traveller.com), a free **magazine**, has some useful articles, but hard copies are difficult to track down so read it online instead. Far more readily available are local English-language **newspapers** like the *Kathmandu Post* and the *Himala yan Times*. For current travel information, check the **noticeboards** in guesthouses and restaurants.

The **Kathmandu Environmental Education Project**, or KEEP (Sun–Fri, 10am–5pm; ☎01/421 6775, ⓦwww.keepnepal.org) near Jyatha Thamel, offers advice, mainly on trekking, homestays and volunteering, and has an eco shop and a **simple** café, which is a good place for meeting other trekkers. Another helpful nonprofit organisation is the **Himalayan Rescue Association** (Sun–Fri 10am-5pm; ☎01/444 0292, ⓦwww.himalayanrescue .org), north of the Royal Palace. Both have useful trekking-related noticeboards.

The advertiser-supported city **maps** given away by the tourist offices are less detailed than the ones in this book. Bookshops sell better versions, including quality Mapple/Karto Atelier maps; Nepa's modestly priced pocket map of Kathmandu and Patan is decent value. Mapmandu (ⓦwww.mapmandu.com) is a useful online map and location finder. Maps of trekking routes and other areas are recommended, where relevant, elsewhere in the guide.

Getting around

You'll probably find you do most of your exploration of the old city on foot, but here's a rundown of transport options for sights further afield.

Taxis, tempos and rikshaws

Taxis are fairly cheap and the most comfortable way to travel longer distances in Kathmandu – though they don't work well in the crowded old city. A couple of companies operate fleet taxis (☎01/422 4374 or 426 6642); have your guest-house make the call. Freelance cabs tend to wait in designated areas such as Tridevi Marg, the main Thamel intersection, along Dharma Path, at the Jamal end of Durbar Marg, at the Mangal Bazaar side of Patan Durbar Square, and Jawalakhel Chowk. Both types have meters, and drivers are supposed to use them. However, it's standard practice to negotiate a flat rate for most destinations. If you can't find a driver willing to use the meter, try surprising them with a bit of Nepali (*Meter-maa januhunchha?* – "Will you go by the meter?"). Fares are generally a bit higher after dark.

Fixed-route tempos ply routes throughout the city; many originate from two locations along Kantipath, just north of Rani Pokhari and just north of the GPO, but you can get on at any of their frequent stopping points.

Cycle **rikshaws** are really only worthwhile for short distances on narrow, crowded streets. Establish a price before setting off.

Local buses, minibuses and microbuses

Local **buses** and **minibuses** cover some of the same city routes as fixed-route tempos, but they're really meant for longer journeys around the valley. They're cheap (prices fluctuate, but expect to pay around Rs20), but slow and extremely crowded, particularly at rush hour, so they're easiest to cope with if you get on at the starting point. The newer **microbuses** are more comfortable passenger vans, although the ones that run on bottled propane tend to stink of gas inside.

Bicycles

Cycling is a good way to get to many sights in the surrounding valley, but traffic and pollution make it miserable work in central Kathmandu. There are a couple of cheap rental places just south of Chhetrapati Chowk and a few others scattered around Thamel, but for better-quality cycles, head to one of the Thamel mountain bike operators (see p.137). Basic, **one-speed bikes** rent for around Rs250 per day, **mountain bikes** with helmets (and sometimes handy repair kits) from Rs500–1000. The lane south of the National Theatre, just west of Kantipath, is the place to buy a **new bike**. Consider wearing a mask (sold in pharmacies) or a dampened handkerchief to block out fumes.

Motorcycles and vehicles

Riding a **motorcycle** is a great way to explore the Kathmandu Valley and beyond (though not much fun inside the ring road). Several Thamel operators rent 125–250cc motorcycles from Rs500 a day, excluding petrol. You generally need to leave a plane ticket or passport as security, and you're supposed to show a driving licence. Himalayan Enfielders (☎01/444 0462), next to the Israeli embassy in Lazimpath, is a good place to start; it offers rentals, repairs, spares, tours and instruction. Singh Motorbike Centre, near *Thamel House* restaurant, also does rentals. Refer to the driving tips on p.32.

To **hire a car** and driver, try a travel agent (see p.142) or your hotel; how much you pay depends on your haggling skills, but around Rs4000 per day is the current going rate. It's often cheaper to negotiate a deal with a taxi driver.

Accommodation

Kathmandu has myriad **accommodation** options, with something for every budget. The most popular budget lodges fill up early in the high season (especially in Oct). Book ahead if you can, but if that's not possible, just show up: Thamel and Jhochhe guesthouses are all cheek by jowl, so if one's full, just try the next.

See p.34 for a rundown of the sort of **facilities** to expect for your money. During the winter, when Kathmandu can be chilly, even cheap guesthouses will provide cotton quilts, but you'll probably have to pay at least $20 a night to get a portable heater; only the more expensive hotels have central heating. Try to get a room that doesn't overlook the street: Kathmandu's barking dogs, banging pots and traffic noise can wake the dead. Note that price code spreads (ie 5–6) denote rooms with varying degrees of luxury.

You don't have to stay in Kathmandu or Patan, as Boudha (p.159), Bhaktapur (p.181), Dakshinkali (p.175) or Godavari (p.178) are all easily accessible.

Thamel

Tourist ghettos like **Thamel** follow a circular logic: most people stay there because, well, most people stay there. And the more people stay there, the more Thamel turns itself into what it thinks foreigners want it to be, which increases its popularity. Especially in the high season, there's so much hype, and so little that has anything to do with Nepal, that you may wonder why it remains as popular as it does.

"Thamel" nowadays refers to a large area containing a ridiculous number of guesthouses. The listings below are split into three geographical groupings. **Central Thamel** comprises the strips immediately north, south and east of the *Kathmandu Guest House,* where tourist development began and has now reached its unholy zenith. **North Thamel** includes Paknajol, Bhagwan Bahal and

▲ Nepal's frenetic traveller hub, Thamel

Kaisher Mahal – neighbourhoods that are no longer distinct from Thamel proper, but are at least a bit less circusy. **South Thamel** spans the areas of Chhetrapati, Thahiti and Jyatha, which while similarly in thrall to tourism manage to preserve more of the architecture and culture of the old city.

For locations, see the Thamel map (p.84) unless otherwise indicated.

Central Thamel

Hotel Garuda Thamel Northwest ☎01/470 0340, ⓦwww.garuda-hotel.com. Popular with the mountaineering fraternity – signed photos of noted climbers adorn the walls – the Garuda has straightforward rooms with private baths; the more expensive also have TVs, phones and balconies. Some are a bit murky, however. ④–⑤

Kathmandu Guest House Thamel Northwest ☎01/470 0800, ⓦwww.ktmgh.com. Thamel's original and best-known guesthouse is set well back from the noisy street, with a pleasant garden. There are nine classes of rooms from "ultra basic" boxes (③) to "super deluxe" en-suites (⑦), though the hotel's reputation means all are overpriced. There are also innumerable services including a barber, beauty salon, several bars and eateries, souvenir shops and a travel agency as well as a useful notice board.

Hotel Potala Narsingh Camp ☎01/470 0680, ⓦwww.potalahotel.com. Run by an incredibly friendly Tibetan family, this centrally located place has rooms which are good value but cramped and a little dark. Some have private facilities and there's also a roof terrace. ②

North Thamel

Hotel Courtyard Zed St ☎01/470 0476, ⓔhotel@courtyard.wlink.com.np. Cross the bridges over the water feature to reach this charming, sheltered hotel, which has large, swish en-suites, Newari architectural touches, a funky bar with cosy sofas and a range of massage options. ⑦

Hotel Encounter Nepal Lekhnath Marg ☎01/444 0534, ⓦwww.encounternepal.com. Well-run hotel, though close to a traffic-choked road. The "standard" rooms with private bath and TV are the best option, but you can pay more for a balcony and a/c. The cheapest rooms, in a different building, are a little gloomy, but not bad. ④–⑤

Holy Lodge Saat Ghumti ☎01/470 0265. The carpets are a little grubby, but otherwise the rooms – set around a central courtyard – are decent enough for travellers on a budget; those with shared bathrooms offer the best value. ②–④

International Guest House Paknajol (see map, p.90) ☎01/425 2299, ⓦwww.ighouse.com. This hotel, popular with Japanese travellers, feels far away from the Thamel bustle, and while the stuffed animal heads and horns on the walls are a bit

83

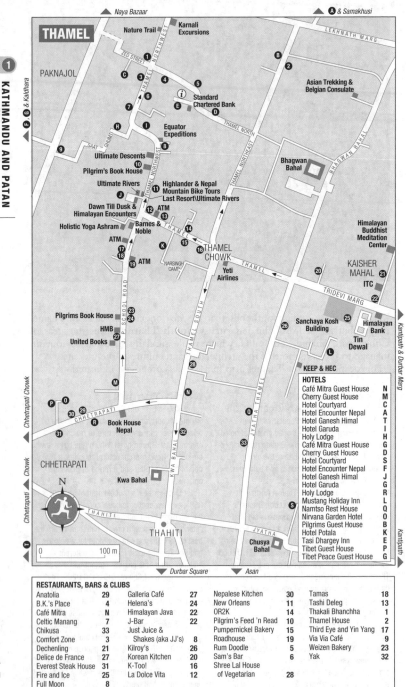

THAMEL

Naya Bazaar

A & Samakhusi

LEKHNATH MARG

Nature Trail

Karnali Excursions

PAKNAJOL

ZED STREET

THAMEL NORTHWEST

Asian Trekking & Belgian Consulate

Standard Chartered Bank

THAMEL NORTH

Equator Expeditions

SAAT GHUMTI

Ultimate Descents

Pilgrim's Book House

Ultimate Rivers

Highlander & Nepal Mountain Bike Tours
Last Resort\Ultimate Rivers

THAMEL NORTHEAST

Bhagwan Bahal

BHAGWAN BAHAL

Dawn Till Dusk & Himalayan Encounters

ATM

Holistic Yoga Ashram

Barnes & Noble

Himalayan Buddhist Meditation Center

ATM

THAMEL CHOWK

NARSINGH CAMP

THAMEL

KAISHER MAHAL

ITC

ATM

Yeti Airlines

J.P. SCHOOL ROAD

TRIDEVI MARG

Kantipath & Durbar Marg

Pilgrims Book House

HMB

THAMEL SOUTH

Sanchaya Kosh Building

Himalayan Bank

United Books

Tin Dewal

KEEP & HEC

Kantipath

HOTELS

Café Mitra Guest House	N
Cherry Guest House	M
Hotel Courtyard	C
Hotel Encounter Nepal	A
Hotel Ganesh Himal	T
Hotel Garuda	I
Holy Lodge	H
Café Mitra Guest House	G
Cherry Guest House	D
Hotel Courtyard	S
Hotel Encounter Nepal	F
Hotel Ganesh Himal	J
Hotel Garuda	G
Holy Lodge	R
Mustang Holiday Inn	L
Namtso Rest House	Q
Nirvana Garden Hotel	O
Pilgrims Guest House	B
Hotel Potala	K
Tasi Dhargey Inn	E
Tibet Guest House	P
Tibet Peace Guest House	G

JYATHA THAMEL

CHHETRAPATI

Book House Nepal

Kwa Bahal

KWA BAHAL

N

THAHITI

JYATHA

THAHITI

Chusya Bahal

0 — 100 m

Durbar Square

Asan

RESTAURANTS, BARS & CLUBS

Anatolia	29	Galleria Café	27	Nepalese Kitchen	30	Tamas	18
B.K.'s Place	4	Helena's	24	New Orleans	11	Tashi Deleg	13
Café Mitra	N	Himalayan Java	22	OR2K	14	Thakali Bhanchha	1
Celtic Manang	7	J-Bar	22	Pilgrim's Feed 'n Read	10	Thamel House	2
Chikusa	33	Just Juice &		Pumpernickel Bakery	15	Third Eye and Yin Yang	17
Comfort Zone	3	Shakes (aka JJ's)	8	Roadhouse	19	Via Via Café	9
Dechenling	21	Kilroy's	26	Rum Doodle	5	Weizen Bakery	23
Delice de France	27	Korean Kitchen	20	Sam's Bar	6	Yak	32
Everest Steak House	31	K-Too!	16	Shree Lal House			
Fire and Ice	25	La Dolce Vita	12	of Vegetarian	28		
Full Moon	8						

& Kaldhara

Chhetrapati Chowk

Chhetrapati Chowk

CHHETRAPATI

CHHETRAPATI

incongruous, the garden is immaculate and the rooms neat and tidy. Rates include breakfast. **⑤–⑥**

Hotel Karma Thamel North ☎01/441 7897, ⓦwww.hotelkarma.com. This economical hotel does the basics well: rooms all have private bath and are clean and well-tended, while the staff are welcoming and helpful. **④**

Kathmandu Garden House Paknajol (see map, p.90) ☎01/438 1239, ⓔktmghouse@wlink.com.np. One of a string of cheapies along a fairly quiet lane; the no-frills rooms come with miniscule attached baths, and there's a flower-filled garden and a book exchange. **③–④**

Kathmandu Peace Guest House Paknajol (see map, p.90) ☎01/438 0369, ⓦwww.ktmpeaceguesthouse.com. Close to *Kathmandu Garden House*, this secluded, laid-back place has clean and simple rooms, with either shared or private facilities (the latter are a better bet), a garden and excellent views from the rooftop. **④–⑤**

Pilgrims Guest House Bhagwan Bahal ☎01/444 0565, ⓔpilgrimsghouse@yahoo.com. A busy place, well-attuned to the needs of travellers, with a range of very clean rooms. There's a restaurant-bar in the garden and an informative notice board. **③–⑤**

Tasi Dhargey Inn Thamel North ☎01/470 0030, ⓦwww.hoteltasidhargey.com. Bustling, efficient hotel, right in the heart of things. The top floor rooms (with private bath, TV and dated decor) are the pick of the bunch, but all are fine. **③–④**

Tibet Peace Guest House Paknajol (see Central Kathmandu map, p.90) ☎01/438 1026, ⓦwww.tibetpeace.com. Something of a haven, offering twee but serviceable rooms with either private or shared bath, and nice touches like security boxes, a garden and an in-house Reiki practitioner. **④–⑤**

South Thamel

Café Mitra Guest House Thamel South ☎01/425 9015, ⓦwww.cafemitra.com. Behind the restaurant of the same name, this excellent-value boutique guesthouse has only four rooms, each looking out onto a garden courtyard. The exemplary en suites have been decorated with flair and attention – features include wood-effect floors and stylish sinks. **⑦**

Cherry Guest House J.P. School Rd. Alongside a pink interior, warm welcome and loyal Korean following, *Cherry Guest House* has clean but decidedly Spartan rooms with shared or private baths at absolutely rock bottom prices. **①–②**

Hotel Ganesh Himal South of Chhetrapati ☎01/426 3598, ⓦwww.ganeshhimal.com. Away from the tourist scrum of central Thamel, and with its own garden, *Ganesh Himal* is a very popular – if occasionally a little chaotic – hotel with clean, turquoise-coloured rooms with private baths, free filtered water and internet access. **⑤**

Kantipur Temple House Jyatha ☎01/425 0131, ⓦwww.kantipurtemplehouse.com. An architecturally appealing tower-like building with attractive en suites – views vary, so look at a few – a "no plastic" purchasing policy, great service and a lawn garden featuring a meditating Buddha statue. **⑦**

Khangsar Guest House Chhetrapati ☎01/426 0788, ⓔkhangsar@wlink.com.np. While the beds sag and the decor could do with a freshen-up, rooms at this tall, multi-storey hotel are clean and decent value, and the roof terrace offers good mountain views. **④**

Mustang Holiday Inn Off Jyatha Thamel ☎01/424 9041, ⓦwww.mustangholidayinn.com.np. Owned by the Mustang royal family, this hotel has worn but acceptable rooms with private bath and TV (some also have snooker table-green carpets). There's little difference between standard and deluxe rooms. **④**

Namtso Rest House Jyatha Thamel ☎01/425 1238, ⓔnamtsorh@wlink.com.np. Follow a marble staircase up to this superior low-cost hotel, which has plain, forensically clean rooms with modern attached baths, phones and TVs. Go for one that catches the afternoon sun. **④**

Nirvana Garden Hotel Chhetrapati ☎01/425 6200, ⓦwww.nirvanagarden.com. The carefully-tended garden gives the hotel a serene air, despite the central position, though it may be a little low-key for some. The reasonably priced en suites have marble bathrooms and little seating areas. **⑦**

Tibet Guest House Chhetrapati ☎01/426 0383, ⓦwww.tibetguesthouse.com. Big, professional hotel straddling the budget and mid-range brackets: those in the latter category are comfortable and come with TV and private baths; if you're paying less, however, there are better cheapies nearby. Good online discounts. **④–⑥**

Jhochhe (Freak Street)

Jhochhe (aka **Freak Street**) is quieter and less touristy than Thamel, much more authentically Nepali, closer to the old city sights (it's actually part of the old city), and noticeably cheaper. However, it also has considerably fewer of the restaurants and other facilities that make Thamel so convenient, comprised mainly of older traditional buildings and somewhat poky family-run businesses.

But, of course, that's precisely what makes it an interesting place to stay. For locations, see map below.

Annapurna Lodge Jhochhe ☎01/424 7684. You'll have to crouch as you go up the stairs, but the rooms, with either private or shared baths, are clean and simple. There's also a pleasant outdoor restaurant. ❶–❷

Century Lodge Jhochhe ☎01/424 7641, ✉centurylodge1972@yahoo.com. Despite the gloomy entrance, the rooms are cheerful and the ones with shared facilities (squat toilets) often have small balconies. The low ceilings, however, rule it out for any six-footers. ❷

Himalaya's Guest House Between Jhochhe and Chikamugal ☎01/425 8444, ✉himalgst @hotmail.com. Hidden at the end of a narrow alley (follow the signs from the square), this welcoming family home has a sizeable library, roof garden and spick and span rooms, which get better the higher up the building you go (some even have TVs). ❷

Monumental Paradise Jhochhe ☎01/424 0876, ✉mparadise52@hotmail.com. A garish, luminous Ganesh wall hanging greets you in the lobby, while rooms are a tad more comfortable than others in the area. There's also a roof terrace and bar. ❸

Hotel Sugat Basantapur ☎01/424 5824, ✉maryman@mos.com.np. Dusty old place with a faint hippie air, relying on its prime Basantapur Square location. The threadbare rooms are generally clean enough, and some of those with shared baths have great views (as has the roof terrace). ❷

Durbar Marg and Lazimpath

Accommodation elsewhere in the city is more spread out. Running south from the Royal Palace, **Durbar Marg** holds a handful of Kathmandu's poshest hotels (all with a/c en suites), as well as many upscale restaurants and shops. Running north from the Royal Palace, **Lazimpath** boasts a selection of mid- and top-end hotels, and some interesting restaurants and bars.

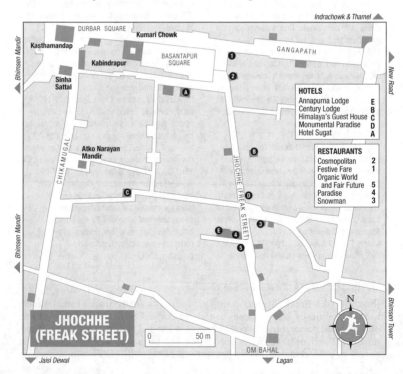

Indrachowk & Thamel ▲

DURBAR SQUARE

Kumari Chowk

Kasthamandap

BASANTAPUR SQUARE

GANGAPATH

Kabindrapur

Sinha Sattal

New Road ▶

HOTELS
Annapurna Lodge	E
Century Lodge	B
Himalaya's Guest House	C
Monumental Paradise	D
Hotel Sugat	A

CHIKAMUGAL

Atko Narayan Mandir

RESTAURANTS
Cosmopolitan	2
Festive Fare	1
Organic World and Fair Future	5
Paradise	4
Snowman	3

JHOCHHE (FREAK STREET)

Bhimsen Mandir

Bhimsen Mandir

Bhimsen Tower ▶

N

JHOCHHE (FREAK STREET)

0   50 m

▼ Jaisi Dewal

OM BAHAL

▼ Lagan

Village tourism and homestays

A great way to connect directly with local culture, and learn a bit of Nepali, is to take part in a **village tourism** or **homestay** programme (see p.36), in which participants stay in a private home, living and eating with the family. Alongside the Kathmandu-based organisations listed below, staff at the Tourist Service Centre can also advise about placements.

ITC Thamel ☎01/441 4490, www.itcnepal.com. Offers homestays, volunteer placements and language courses.

Lama Adventure Treks and Expeditions Thamel ☎01/441 0925, Ⓦwww.lama adventure.com. Provides homestays in a number of villages, including Timal Thulo, Parsel and Arubot.

Durbar Marg hotels are shown on the Kantipath and Durbar Marg map (p.88). For Lazimpath hotels, see the Central Kathmandu map (p.90). Both areas are a short walk from Thamel.

Hotel Ambassador Lazimpath ☎01/441 4432, Ⓦwww.nepalshotel.com. Solid mid-range hotel on a busy junction with bright rooms, the best of which overlook the garden and have tubs and a/c. ⑥

Hotel de l'Annapurna Durbar Marg ☎01/422 1711, Ⓦwww.annapurna-hotel.com. Long-running and well-located, with a big pool, sauna, tennis courts and casino, but now past its prime (something particularly evident in the less expensive rooms). ⑧

Hotel Manaslu Lazimpath ☎01/441 0071, Ⓦwww.hotelmanaslu.com. In the shadow of the *Radisson*, this hotel boasts well-appointed rooms, (some overlooking the garden), with traditional carved windows, a pseudo-American bar and a pool complete with water-spouting statues. ⑦

Radisson Kathmandu Lazimpath ☎01/441 1818, Ⓦwww.radisson.com. Giant, reliable and very comfortable hotel, but with a bland international chain feel. Highlights include the eye-catching rooftop pool and one of the city's best equipped fitness centres. ⑧–⑨

Hotel Shangri-la Lazimpath ☎01/441 2999, Ⓦwww.hotelshangrila.com. Tucked away in embassyland, with restful flower gardens, pool, gym, children's play area and rooms in soothing colours. ⑧–⑨

Hotel Shanker Lazimpath ☎01/441 0151, Ⓦwww.shankerhotel.com.np. A refurbished palace with a sprinkling of French architectural influences and elegant en suites, including very appealing split-level "double decker" rooms. ⑧

Hotel Yak & Yeti Durbar Marg ☎01/248 999, Ⓦwww.yakandyeti.com. One of Kathmandu's most prestigious hotels, in a 100-year-old former Rana palace, with opulent rooms, excellent restaurants, manicured grounds, two pools, tennis courts, health club and casino. ⑨

West of the Bishnumati and eastern neighbourhoods

There's only one real reason to stay **west of the Bishnumati**, and that's to be near the popular Swayambhu stupa. There aren't many hotels and guesthouses here though. The city's best hotel, *Dwarika's*, is close to the Pashupatinath temple complex in **Battisputali**.

For locations, see the Kathmandu map (p.77) unless otherwise stated.

Dwarika's Battisputali ☎01/447 9488, Ⓦwww.dwarikas.com. If money is no object, this is the place to stay. Easily the most traditional of the five-stars, with woodwork salvaged from temple and house renovations, many rooms (around $300) have their own courtyards and four-poster king-size beds. The restaurant and service are also excellent. ⑨

Gokarna Forest Resort ☎01/445 1212, Ⓦwww .gokarna.com. Luxurious "country club" resort, with traditional Nepali-style architecture and a wonderfully peaceful location within the pristine (apart

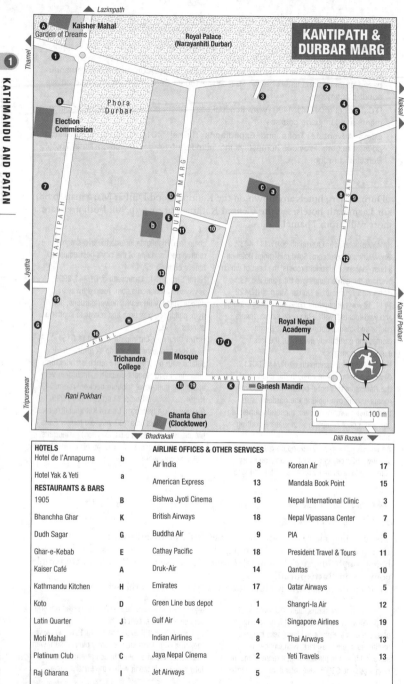

KANTIPATH & DURBAR MARG

HOTELS		AIRLINE OFFICES & OTHER SERVICES			
Hotel de l'Annapurna	b	Air India	8	Korean Air	17
Hotel Yak & Yeti	a	American Express	13	Mandala Book Point	15
RESTAURANTS & BARS		Bishwa Jyoti Cinema	16	Nepal International Clinic	3
1905	B	British Airways	18	Nepal Vipassana Center	7
Bhanchha Ghar	K	Buddha Air	9	PIA	6
Dudh Sagar	G	Cathay Pacific	18	President Travel & Tours	11
Ghar-e-Kebab	E	Druk-Air	14	Qantas	10
Kaiser Café	A	Emirates	17	Qatar Airways	5
Kathmandu Kitchen	H	Green Line bus depot	1	Shangri-la Air	12
Koto	D	Gulf Air	4	Singapore Airlines	19
Latin Quarter	J	Indian Airlines	8	Thai Airways	13
Moti Mahal	F	Jaya Nepal Cinema	2	Yeti Travels	13
Platinum Club	C	Jet Airways	5		
Raj Gharana	I				

from the golf course) Gokarna forest, 14km from the city centre. There's an indoor pool, forest trails, a spa, and, of course, golf. ❽

Hyatt Regency Kathmandu ☎ 01/491 1234, ⓦ www.hyatt.com. Nepal's biggest five-star hotel dominates the skyline 1km west of the stupa. Offers everything you'd expect for the money (upwards of $250) including plentiful "heritage" detailing, a fashionable restaurant-bar and a casino. ❾

Nyanang Phelgyeling Monastery Guest House Swayambhu ☎ 01/427 9576, ⓔ nya@phel.wlink .com.np. Recently renovated, this monastery-run

establishment is right at Swayambhu and has long marble hallways and austere but spotless rooms with attached bath, some with stupa views. ❷

🏃 **Hotel Vajra** Bijeshwari (about 1km east of Swayambhu; see Central Kathmandu Map) ☎ 01/427 1545, ⓦ www.hotelvajra.com. Resembling a pagoda, *Vajra* has an elaborate Tibetan fresco in the hall, a library, beautiful carvings and a theatre. Some rooms have shared facilities, others are en suite (a few of the latter have their own balconies, at no extra cost). The views of Swayambhu from the roof terrace are the icing on the cake. ❺–❼

Patan

Patan, south of Kathmandu, offers a pleasant alternative to the Kathmandu scene. Its culture is more intact, yet it has sufficient restaurants and facilities, and easy enough access to Kathmandu. There's a distinct lack of accommodation in the old part of Patan and what there is fills up early, so book ahead.

For locations, see the Patan map (p.113) unless otherwise noted.

Café de Patan Guest House Mangal Bazaar ☎ 01/553 7599, ⓦ www.cafedepatan.com. Small, very popular lodge attached to the eponymous eatery, with simple, bright and clean rooms (shared or private bath). Service and the location on the edge of the square are both excellent. ❸–❹

Mahabuddha Guest House Uku Bahal, opposite the Mahabuddha temple ☎ 01/554 0575, ⓔ mhg @mos.com.np. Rooms, each named after a Nepali mountain, are homely with attached bathrooms, but some are lacking in natural light. There's an apartment for longer stays and an internet café. ❸

🏃 **New Chen** Near Durbar Square ☎ 01/553 3532, ⓦ www.newachen.com. Traditional Newari house refurbished via a UNESCO loan and turned into an outstanding, intimate and great value eight-room boutique hotel. Carved wood, brickwork, low ceilings and excellent service

ensure a memorable stay. At the time of writing a nearby café was being renovated under the same UNESCO project. ❻–❼

Summit Hotel Kupondol Heights ☎ 01/552 1810, ⓦ www.summit-nepal.com. The more expensive, tasteful en suites, some with mountain views, are a great choice, though some of the cheaper rooms fail to reach the same heights. There's also an outdoor pool, a relaxing garden and a good restaurant-bar. ❼–❽

Third World Guest House Durbar Square (see map, p.115) ☎ 01/552 2187, ⓔ thirdworld.patan @gmail.com. Unbeatable location, but the management has rested on its laurels: rooms look directly out onto the square, but are a bit rough around the edges, while the views from the attached restaurant are unsurpassed (though the food is only so-so). ❹–❺

The old city

The Kathmandu most travellers come to see is the **old city**, a tangle of narrow alleys and temples immediately north and south of the central Durbar Square. It's a bustling, intensely urban quarter, where tall extended-family dwellings block out the sun, dark, open-fronted shops crowd the lanes and vegetable sellers clog the intersections. The fundamental building block of the old city is the *bahal* (or *baha*) – a set of buildings joined at right angles around a central courtyard. Kathmandu is honeycombed with *bahal*, many of which were originally Buddhist monasteries, but have since reverted to residential use.

Though the city goes to bed early, there's always something happening from before dawn to around 10pm, including early morning religious rites (*puja*) and

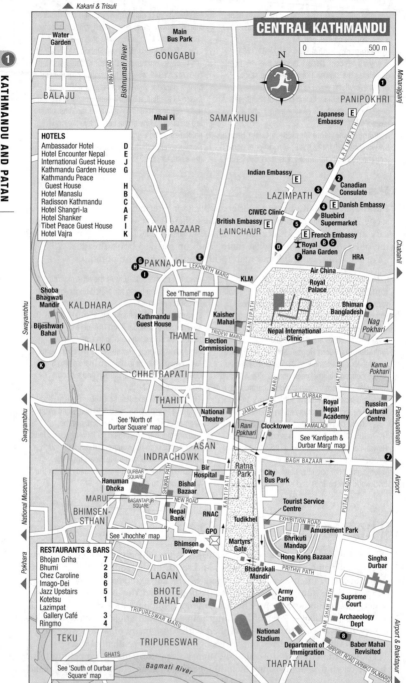

CENTRAL KATHMANDU

0 — 500 m

N

HOTELS

Ambassador Hotel	D
Hotel Encounter Nepal	E
International Guest House	J
Kathmandu Garden House	G
Kathmandu Peace Guest House	H
Hotel Manaslu	B
Radisson Kathmandu	C
Hotel Shangri-la	A
Hotel Shanker	F
Tibet Peace Guest House	I
Hotel Vajra	K

RESTAURANTS & BARS

Bhojan Griha	7
Bhumi	2
Chez Caroline	8
Imago-Dei	6
Jazz Upstairs	5
Kotetsu	1
Lazimpat Gallery Café	3
Ringmo	4

Kakani & Trisuli

Water Garden

Main Bus Park

GONGABU

BALAJU

RING ROAD

Bishnumati River

PANIPOKHRI

Maharajganj

Mhai Pi

SAMAKHUSI

Japanese Embassy E

Indian Embassy E

Canadian Consulate

LAZIMPATH

Danish Embassy E

CIWEC Clinic

British Embassy E

LAINCHAUR

NAYA BAZAAR

Bluebird Supermarket

French Embassy E

Royal Hana Garden

HRA

Air China

Royal Palace

Bhiman Bangladesh

Nag Pokhari

Chabahil

Shoba Bhagwati Mandir

KALDHARA

PAKNAJOL

LEKHNATH MARG

KLM

See 'Thamel' map

Kaisher Mahal

Nepal International Clinic

Kamal Pokhari

Bijeshwari Bahal

DHALKO

Swayambhu

Kathmandu Guest House

THAMEL

TRIDEVI MARG

Election Commission

Kamal Pokhari

CHHETRAPATI

THAHITI

National Theatre

JAMAL

DURBAR MARG

LAL DURBAR

Royal Nepal Academy

Russian Cultural Centre

Pashupatinath

See 'North of Durbar Square' map

Rani Pokhari

Clocktower

KAMALADI

See 'Kantipath & Durbar Marg' map

ASAN

INDRACHOWK

BAGH BAZAAR

Bir Hospital

DURBAR SQUARE

SHUKRA PATH

Bishal Bazaar

Ratna Park

City Bus Park

Airport

HATTISAR

Hanuman Dhoka

BASANTAPUR SQUARE

MARU

NEW ROAD

Nepal Bank

RNAC

KANTIPATH

Tudikhel

Tourist Service Centre

EXHIBITION ROAD

Amusement Park

PUTALI SADAK

National Museum

BHIMSEN-STHAN

See 'Jhochhe' map

GPO

Bhimsen Tower

Martyrs' Gate

Bhrikuti Mandap

Hong Kong Bazaar

PRITHVI PATH

Singha Durbar

Pokhara

LAGAN

BHOTE BAHAL

Bhadrakali Mandir

Supreme Court

Jails

Army Camp

RAM SHAH PATH

Archaeology Dept

TRIPURESHWAR MARG

See 'South of Durbar Square' map

TEKU

GHATS

LAGAN

National Stadium

Department of Immigration

THAPATHALI

Baber Mahal Revisited

Airport Road / Arniko Rajmarg

Airport & Bhaktapur

Bagmati River

Kirtipur

Patan

Patan

after-dinner devotional hymn-singing (*bhajan*) in the neighbourhoods of Indra-chowk, Asan or Chhetrapati.

Durbar Square

Teeming, touristy **Durbar Square** is the natural place to begin sightseeing. The fascinating old royal palace (*durbar*), running along the eastern edge of the square, takes up more space than all the other monuments combined. Kumari Chowk, home of Kathmandu's "living goddess", overlooks from the south. The square itself is squeezed by the palace into two parts: at the south-western end is the Kasthamandap, the ancient building that probably gave Kathmandu its name, while the northern part is taken up by a varied procession of statues and temples.

A Rs200 **entrance fee** is collected at checkposts guarding the square's main approaches. The ticket is valid for one day, but you can get a free extension for anything up to the length of your visa by taking your ticket and passport to the site office; for longer than three days, you (officially) also need to take a passport photo.

Hanuman Dhoka (Old Royal Palace)

The rambling **Old Royal Palace** (Tues–Sun: Feb–Oct 10.30am–4pm; Nov–Jan 10.30am–3pm; Rs250, in addition to Durbar Square entry fee) is usually called **Hanuman Dhoka**.

Its oldest, eastern wings date from the mid-sixteenth century, but there was probably a palace here before then. Malla kings built most of the rest by the late seventeenth century, and after capturing Kathmandu in 1768, Prithvi Narayan Shah added four lookout towers at the southeastern corner. Finally, the Ranas left their mark with the garish Neoclassical facade along the southwestern flank. Nepal's former royal family last lived here in 1886, before moving to the northern end of town. Only a fraction of the five-acre palace and grounds is open to the public.

The entrance

Entrance to the palace is through the Hanuman Dhoka (Hanuman Gate), a brightly decorated doorway at the east side of the northern part of Durbar Square, named after the monkey god **Hanuman**, whose statue stands outside. Installed by the seventeenth-century king Pratap Malla to drive away evil spirits, the figure is veiled to render its gaze safe to mortals, and smothered in *abhir* (red paste). Ram's right-hand man in the Hindu Ramayana epic, Hanuman was revered by Nepali kings, who, like Ram, were held to be incarnations of the god Vishnu. On the left as you enter stands a masterful sculpture of another Vishnu incarnation, the man-lion **Narasingh**, tearing apart a demon. Pratap Malla supposedly commissioned the statue to appease Vishnu, whom he feared he had offended by dancing in a Narasingh costume.

Interior courtyards

The entrance opens to **Nassal Chowk**, the large central courtyard that provided the setting for King Birendra's coronation in 1975. The brick wings that form its southern and eastern flanks date from the sixteenth century and boast painstakingly carved wooden doorways, windows and struts. At the north-eastern corner of the square, the five-tiered pagoda-like turret, notable for its round roofs, is the **Panch Mukhi Hanuman Mandir**: "Five-Faced Hanuman" is supposed to have the faces of an ass, man-bird, man-lion, boar and monkey. Along the northern side of the courtyard is the Malla kings' audience hall.

Although the palace boasts ten courtyards, visitors are allowed to enter only Nassal Chowk and **Lohan Chowk**. **Mul Chowk**, which can be glimpsed through a doorway off Nassal Chowk, contains a temple to Taleju Bhawani, the ancestral deity of the Malla kings, and sacrifices are made to her in the courtyard during the Dasain festival. To the north, but not visible, **Mohan Chowk** is supposed to have a sunken royal bath with a golden waterspout.

The museums and Basantapur Tower

Housed in the west and south wings overlooking Nassal Chowk, the **Tribhuwan Museum** (same opening times as Hanuman Dhoka, but closes at 2pm on Sun; leave bags and cameras in lockers at the entrance) features a collection of memorabilia from the reign of Tribhuwan, though there's little in the way of English-language explanation. Often referred to as *rashtrapita* ("father of the nation"), Tribhuwan is fondly remembered for his pivotal role in restoring the monarchy in 1951 and opening up Nepal to the outside world. Looking at the displayed photos and newspaper clippings, you get a sense of the high drama of 1950–51, when the king sought asylum in India and then, having served as the figurehead for resistance efforts against the crumbling Rana regime, returned triumphantly to power. Also on display are thrones, jewel-studded coronation ornaments, royal furniture, guns, trophies and even a casket.

The museum leads to the massive nine-storey **Basantapur Tower**, the biggest of the four raised by Prithvi Narayan Shah in honour of the four main cities of the Kathmandu Valley. (Basantapur means "place of spring" and refers to Kathmandu itself. The tower is also referred to as Nautele Durbar, or Nine-Storey Palace.) You can ascend to a kind of crow's nest enclosed by pitched wooden screens to get fine views in four directions.

From the tower you can descend directly to Nassal Chowk, or carry on through labyrinthine corridors to the **Mahendra Museum**. Like the Tribhuwan exhibit, this one marches chronologically through the life and times of a monarch. The displays include a tally card of the animals Mahendra shot around the world, and recreations of his office and cabinet room. The museum exits onto Lohan Chowk. The adjoining **King Birendra Museum**, dedicated to Mahendra's successor, remains closed following his assassination in 2001 (see p.426).

Kumari Chowk

At the southern end of the square stands **Kumari Chowk**, the gilded cage of Kathmandu's Raj Kumari, the pre-eminent of a dozen or more "living goddesses" in the valley. No other temple better illustrates the living, breathing and endlessly adaptable nature of religion in Nepal, with its freewheeling blend of Hindu, Buddhist and indigenous elements.

The cult of the **Kumari** – a prepubescent girl worshipped as a living incarnation of the goddess Taleju – probably goes back to the early Middle Ages. Jaya Prakash, the last Malla king of Kathmandu, institutionalized the practice when he built the Kumari Chowk in 1757. According to legend, Jaya Prakash, a particularly paranoid and weak king, offended Taleju by lusting after her, and to atone for his sin she ordered him to select a virgin girl in whom the goddess could dwell. He also established the tradition – which ended in 2008 – that each year during the Indra Jaatra festival, the Kumari should bestow a *tika* (auspicious mark) on the forehead of the king who was to reign for the coming year.

Although the Kumari is considered a Hindu goddess, she is chosen from the Buddhist Shakya clan of goldsmiths, and the traditional selection process is reminiscent of the Tibetan Buddhist method of finding reincarnated lamas. Elders interview Shakya girls aged between three and five, ideally shortlisting

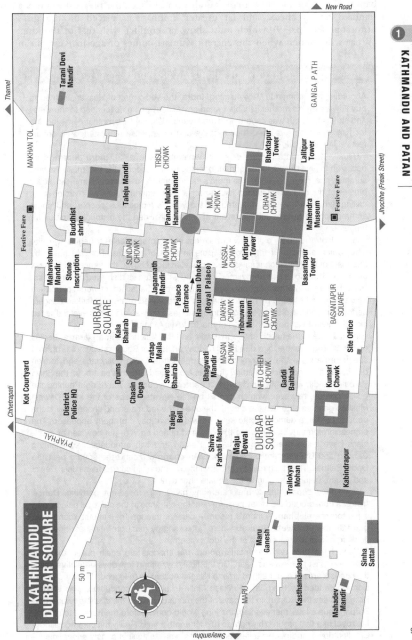

KATHMANDU DURBAR SQUARE

New Road ▲

GANGA PATH

Jhochhe (Freak Street) ▶

Festive Fare

Bhaktapur Tower

Lalitpur Tower

Mahendra Museum

LOHAN CHOWK

MUL CHOWK

Basantapur Tower

Kirtipur Tower

NASSAL CHOWK

BASANTAPUR SQUARE

Site Office

Kumari Chowk

Kabindrapur

Sinha Sattal

Mahadev Mandir

Kasthamandap

Maru Ganesh

Trailokya Mohan

DURBAR SQUARE

Gaddi Baithak

NHU CHHEN CHOWK

LAMO CHOWK

Tribhuwan Museum

DAKHA CHOWK

MASAN CHOWK

Bhagwati Mandir

Maju Dewal

Shiva Parbati Mandir

Taleju Bell

Chasin Dega

Drums

Sweta Bhairab

Pratap Malla

Kala Bhairab

DURBAR SQUARE

Hanuman Dhoka (Royal Palace)

Palace Entrance

Jagannath Mandir

MOHAN CHOWK

SUNDARI CHOWK

Stone Inscription

Mahavishnu Mandir

Panch Mukhti Hanuman Mandir

Buddhist shrine

Taleju Mandir

TRISUL CHOWK

Tarani Devi Mandir

Festive Fare

MAKHAN TOL

Thamel ▲

District Police HQ

Kot Courtyard

Chhetrapati ▲

PYAPHAL

MARU

Swayambhu ▼

N

0   50 m

those who exhibit 32 auspicious signs: a neck like a conch shell, body like a banyan tree, eyelashes like a cow's and so on. In fact, the physical exam is a standard health check, and far greater emphasis is placed on the girl's horoscope (see p.439), which must show no conflict with that of the king. (What will happen when the current Kumari comes of age in Republican

Indra Jaatra: eight days of pomp and partying

According to Kathmandu Valley legend, **Indra**, the Vedic King of Heaven, wanted to buy flowers for his mother. Unable to find any in heaven, he descended to the valley and stole some, but was caught and imprisoned. When Indra's mother came looking for him, the people realized their mistake and to appease him, started an annual festival in his honour.

Usually held in late August or early September (see p.42), **Indra Jaatra** is an occasion to give thanks to the god for bringing the monsoon rains that make the vital summer rice crop possible. Yet Indra's humiliation is a parallel theme, as straw effigies of the god are placed in jails. Another local legend claims an invading king, calling himself Indra, was defeated by the valley's indigenous people, and some anthropologists believe such an event may have provided the historical impetus for the festival.

Indra Jaatra features eight days of almost nonstop spectacle. It begins with the ceremonial raising of a fifty-foot-tall **pole** in front of the Kala Bhairab statue by members of the Manandhar (oil-presser) caste. In Indrachowk, the famous blue mask of **Akash Bhairab**, a god sometimes identified with Indra, is displayed, as are lesser Bhairab images in other neighbourhoods. Locals do *puja* (an act of worship) to them by day, and light lamps by night in memory of deceased relatives. Masked dancers perform around the old city, and one group stages a tableau of the *das avatar* (the ten incarnations of Vishnu) at the base of the Trailokya Mohan.

Indra Jaatra is the fusion of two festivals, and the second, **Kumari Jaatra**, begins on the afternoon of the third day. From midday on, Durbar Square steadily fills up with spectators and, in the balcony of the Gaddi Baithak, with politicians and foreign dignitaries dressed in formal attire. (Tourists are herded into an area around the Shiva Parbati Mandir, where it's hard to get a decent view unless you're right behind the police cordon; however, women can sit on the elevated steps of the Maju Dewal.) Masked dancers entertain the crowd: the one in the red mask and shaggy hair is the popular **Lakhe**, a demon said to keep other spirits at bay if properly appeased. The procession formerly began when the king and queen arrived, but now senior politicians have taken over their roles. The Kumari and two attendants, representing Ganesh and Bhairab, are pulled in wooden **chariots** around the square past the Gaddi Baithak. They then make a circuit of the southern old city, as far as Jaisi Dewal and Lagan, before returning to the square after dark.

When they depart, the formal ceremony gives way to all-out partying. **Dance troupes** from around the valley perform near the entrance to the old royal palace, and a pantomime **elephant** – Indra's mount – careers through the streets. Young men gravitate toward **Sweta Bhairab** where, after lengthy ritual preliminaries, rice beer flows from a pipe sticking out of the idol's mouth.

Without the VIPs and ceremonial pomp, the chariots are again pulled the next afternoon, past Nardevi and Asan. On the final day, after a few days of relative calm, the chariots are pulled for a third time to Kilagal. According to legend, this last procession was added by King Jaya Prakash Malla to allow his concubine, who lived in Kilagal, to see the Kumari. In the days of the monarchy, when the chariots returned to Durbar Square later that evening, the king would come before the Kumari to receive the **royal tika** that assured his right to rule for another year. Finally the ceremonial pole is pulled down, and people take pieces of it as amulets against ghosts and spirits.

Nepal is uncertain.) The young goddess lives a cloistered life inside the Kumari Chowk and is only carried outside on her throne during Indra Jaatra and a handful of other festivals; her feet are never allowed to touch the ground. The goddess's spirit leaves her when she menstruates or otherwise bleeds, whereupon she's retired with a modest pension. The transition to life as an ordinary mortal can be hard, and she may have difficulty finding a husband, since legend has it that the man who marries an ex-Kumari will die young. The present Kumari was installed in October 2008, when she was three years old.

Non-Hindus aren't allowed past the Kumari Chowk's *bahal*-style **courtyard**, which is decorated with exquisitely carved (if weathered) windows, pillars and doorways. When someone slips enough cash to her handlers, the Kumari, dressed in auspicious red and wearing heavy silver jewellery, her forehead painted red with an elaborate "third eye" in the middle, shows herself at one of the first-floor windows. (Your chances of a sighting are higher in the morning or late afternoon.) She's believed to answer her visitors' unspoken questions with the look on her face. Cameras are okay inside the courtyard, but photographing the Kumari is strictly forbidden.

The chariot that carries the Kumari around during the Indra Jaatra festival is garaged next door to the Kumari Chowk. The big wooden chariot-yokes from past processions, which according to tradition may not be destroyed, are laid out nearby. The broad, bricked area to the east is **Basantapur Square**, once the site of royal elephant stables, where souvenir sellers now spread their wares.

Other temples and monuments

Dozens of temples (*mandir*), *dewal* (stepped platforms) and statues litter Durbar Square. The following are highlights.

The Kasthamandap

According to legend, the **Kasthamandap**, standing at the southwestern end of the square, is Kathmandu's oldest building, and one of the oldest wooden buildings in the world. It's said to have been constructed from the wood of a single tree in the late twelfth century (**Sinha Sattal**, the smaller version to the south, was made from the leftovers), but what you see today is mostly the result of several renovations since 1630. An open, pagoda-roofed pavilion (*mandap*), it served for several centuries as a rest-house (*sattal*) along the Tibet trade route, and probably formed the nucleus of early Kathmandu. This corner of the square, called Maru Tol, still has the look of a crossroads, with vendors hawking fruit, vegetables and flowers. Many of the city's homeless sleep in the Kasthamandap at night.

The Shah kings converted the Kasthamandap into a temple to their lineage deity (see box, p.97), **Gorakhnath**, whose statue stands in the middle of the pavilion. A Brahman priest usually sets up shop here to dispense instruction and conduct rituals. In four niches set around are shrines to Ganesh, the god of good fortune, which supposedly represent the celebrated Ganesh temples of the Kathmandu Valley (at Chabahil, Bhaktapur, Chobar and Bungmati), thus enabling Kathmandu residents to pay tribute to all four at once.

The building to the southeast of the Kasthamandap is **Kabindrapur**, a temple built in the seventeenth century for the staging of dance performances. Also known as Dhansa, it's dedicated to Shiva in his role as Nasa-dyo ("Lord of the Dance" in Newari), and is mostly patronized by musicians and dancers. Opposite Kabindrapur, occupying its own side square, is a brick *shikra* (Indian-style, corncob-shaped temple) to Mahadev (Shiva).

Maru Ganesh and Trailokya Mohan

Immediately north of the Kasthamandap stands yet another Ganesh shrine, **Maru Ganesh**. A ring on his bell is usually the preliminary act of any *puja*, and this shrine is the first stop for people intending to worship at the other temples on Durbar Square. Ganesh's trusty "vehicle", a rat, is perched on a plinth of the Kasthamandap, across the way. The lane heading west from here used to be called Pie Alley – in its 1970s heyday it boasted many pie shops, but most have now gone the way of hash shops and hippies.

The three-roofed pagoda between the Kasthamandap and the Kumari Chowk is the seventeenth-century **Trailokya Mohan**, dedicated to Narayan (a Nepali name for Vishnu). A much-photographed statue of the angelic Garud, Vishnu's man-bird vehicle, kneels in his customary palms-together *namaste* position in front of the temple.

Gaddi Baithak

The part of the Royal Palace facing the Trailokya Mohan is the **Gaddi Baithak**, a ponderous early twentieth-century addition that pretty much sums up Rana-era architecture. Some purists bemoan the Neoclassical building's distorting effect on Durbar Square's proportions, but it adds a bit of spice to the mix. The west-facing balcony serves as the VIP viewing stand during Indra Jaatra (see box, p.94).

The antiquity of the Durbar Square area was confirmed during the construction of the Gaddi Baithak, when workers uncovered what is believed to be remnants of a Lichhavi-era temple. The find spot is enclosed by a small grate in the middle of the road near the southwest corner of the Gaddi Baithak.

Maju Dewal and Shiva Parbati Mandir

North of the Trailokya Mohan, the huge seventeenth-century **Maju Dewal** sits high atop a pyramid of nine stepped levels. Climb to the top for a god's-eye view of the square. From this height you can look straight across at the rectangular **Shiva Parbati Mandir**, erected in the eighteenth century by one of the early Shah kings. Painted figures of Shiva and his consort Parbati lean out of the first-floor window, looking like they're about to toss the bouquet and dash off to the honeymoon suite. Despite the temple's popular name, the actual objects of worship inside are nine images of the mother goddesses associated with the nine planets.

Around the Taleju Bell

North of the Shiva Parbati temple, the square narrows and then opens out to another temple-clogged area. Ranged along the left (western) side are the eighteenth-century **Taleju Bell**; the octagonal, seventeenth-century **Chasin Dega**, dedicated to Krishna the flute player; and a pair of ceremonial **drums** from the eighteenth century. The bell and drums were historically sounded as an alarm or call to congregate, but are now used only during the festival of Dasain.

Next to the palace opposite the bell, a small bas-relief depicts **Jambhuwan**, the legendary teacher of Hanuman. Just to the north of this, look up to see the **Kun Jhyal**, a gold-plated window frame flanked by two ivory ones, once used by Malla kings to watch processions in the square below.

Sweta and Kala Bhairabs

Just beyond, set against the palace wall but not very visible behind a wooden screen, is the snarling ten-foot-high gilded head of **Sweta Bhairab** (White Bhairab), a terrifying, blood-swilling aspect of Shiva. The screen comes down

A word about the confusing matter of royal deities: Gorakhnath, a mythologized Indian guru, was revered as a kind of guardian angel by all the Shah kings, and Taleju Bhawani, to whom many temples and bells are dedicated in the Kathmandu, Patan and Bhaktapur Durbar squares, played a similar role for the Malla kings. The kings of both dynasties worshipped the Kumari, but mainly as a public gesture to secure her *tika*, which lent credibility to their divine right to rule.

during Indra Jaatra (see box, p.94). The column nearby supports a gilded statue of **King Pratap Malla** and family, a self-congratulatory art form that was all the rage among the Malla kings of the late seventeenth century.

North of this, on the other side of the small Degu Taleju Mandir, the massive, roly-poly image of **Kala Bhairab** (Black Bhairab) dances on the corpse of a demon. Carved from a single twelve-foot slab of stone, it was found in a field north of Kathmandu during the reign of Pratap Malla, but probably dates to Lichhavi times. It used to be said that anyone who told a lie in front of it would vomit blood and die. One story has it that when the chief justice's office stood across the way, so many witnesses died while testifying that a temple had to be erected to shield the court from Kala Bhairab's wide-eyed stare.

The Jagannath Mandir and erotic carvings

East of Pratap Malla's column stands the sixteenth-century pagoda-style **Jagannath Mandir**, dedicated to the god whose runaway-chariot festival in India gave us the word "juggernaut". The struts supporting the lower roof of this temple contain Kathmandu's most tittered-about **erotic carvings**, although such images are actually quite common in Nepali temples.

Scholars disagree over the significance of these little vignettes, which often feature outrageous athletics, threesomes and bestiality. Some suggest sex in this context is being offered as a tantric path to enlightenment, but a more popular belief is that the goddess of lightning is a chaste virgin who wouldn't dare strike a temple so decorated.

Nearby, along the palace outer wall, is a **stone inscription** in fifteen languages, carved in 1664 by King Pratap Malla, the prime architect of Durbar Square's temples, and something of a linguist. The inscription is a poem to the goddess Kali, and the story goes that if anyone can read the whole thing, milk will gush from the tap. There are two words in French and one in English.

The Taleju Mandir

Set atop a twelve-tiered plinth and rising forty metres above the northeast end of the square, the magnificent **Taleju Mandir** looks down on you with haughty grandeur. Kathmandu's biggest temple, it was erected in the mid-sixteenth century by King Mahendra Malla, who decreed no building should exceed it in height – a ban that remained in force until the middle of the twentieth century. It's open only on the ninth day of Dasain, and then only to Nepalis.

Taleju Bhawani, a South Indian goddess imported in the fourteenth century by the Mallas, is considered by Hindus to be a form of the mother goddess Durga, while Buddhist Newars count her as one of the Taras, tantric female deities. Behind the Taleju Mandir, reached by a doorway from Makhan Tol, sits the brick god-house of **Tarani Devi**, Taleju's "older sister".

North of Durbar Square

Kathmandu's oldest, liveliest streets lie north and northeast of Durbar Square. You could make a more or less circular swing through the area (as this section does), but you'll almost certainly be diverted somewhere along the way. The sights described here are only a backdrop for the old city's fascinating street life.

Indrachowk

The old trade route to Tibet passes through Durbar Square and becomes a narrow lane after it rounds the Taleju Mandir. Passing through **Makhan Tol** – the name harks back to a time when butter (*makhan*) was sold here – it runs a gauntlet of *thangka* (Buddhist scroll painting) sellers and then takes a northeasterly bearing towards Kathmandu's traditional goldsmiths' neighbourhood.

The first big intersection you reach is **Indrachowk**, named in honour of the Vedic (early Hindu) king of the gods. A sort of Asian Zeus, complete with thunderbolt, Indra fell from grace in India centuries ago, but in the Kathmandu Valley he still rates his own festival (see p.94). The newly renovated house-like temple on the west side of the crossroads is that of **Akash Bhairab** (Sky, or Blue, Bhairab), considered the equivalent of Indra and represented by a large snarling blue head. Newars also call this deity Aju-dyo, claiming the idol is what's left of a native king who was beheaded in the Mahabharata epic. The upstairs temple is out-of-bounds to non-Hindus, while the downstairs is rented out to shopkeepers to fund the temple's upkeep.

Kel Tol and Seto Machhendranath

The tumultuous street heading north from Indrachowk is the direct route to Thamel, but the old Tibet road continues to the small square of **Kel Tol** and the seventeenth-century temple of **Seto** (or Sweta) **Machhendranath**, one of

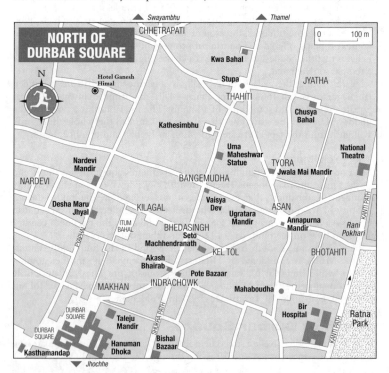

two main shrines to the protector god of the Kathmandu Valley. Like his "Red" cousin in Patan (see p.120), "White" Machhendranath is feted in a great chariot festival during the month of Chaitra (March–April).

Newars know this god as Karunamaya Lokeshwar, the *bodhisattva* of compassion, while Tibetans consider him Jowo Dzamling Karmo, White Lord of the World. Yet another name, **Jama-dyo**, traces back to a legend in which the white mask of Machhendranath was stolen by marauders from the west during ancient times. The invading king's family is said to have been afflicted with incurable diseases for six generations, until one of them took the idol back to Kathmandu and buried it in a field in Jamal, near what is now Durbar Marg. When a farmer rediscovered the image in the fifteenth century, it was immediately hailed as Jama-dyo – God of Jamal – and installed in this location, which is accordingly known as **Jamal** (or Jana) **Bahal**.

The entrance to the well-concealed courtyard is a gate at the west side of Kel Tol. Among the many votive *chaityas* and figures is a weathered old stone figure of Amitabha (one of the *panchabuddha*, the five personifications of Buddhahood), a Victorian bronze statue converted into an incense holder, three Tara figures on pillars, and the Kanaka Chaitya, a Lichhavi-era stone hemisphere that was the original centrepiece of this *bahal* before Machhendranath stole the show. The main temple features some beautiful gilt-copper repoussé work on the outside, but an iron grille, installed to thwart temple thieves, robs it of its aesthetic appeal. This kind of precaution is still unusual in Nepal, a country whose artistic riches are all the more remarkable for being so public. Unfortunately, the risk of theft, driven by demand from Western collectors, has made it necessary here.

To Asan
Beyond Kel Tol, the street is known mainly for its brass, copper and stainless steel wares: you'll see a bewildering array of incense holders, *thaal* (trays), water jugs, and vessels designed to hold sanctified water or cow's urine for *puja*. On the left, **Tilang Ghar**, a former Rana general's residence, is decorated with a stucco frieze of marching soldiers. The three-tiered octagonal **Krishna Mandir**, no longer active, is half obscured by the encroachments of surrounding buildings.

The last and most exuberant intersection along this route is **Asan**, the ancestral home of many of the wealthiest Newari families in the old trading economy. Asan used to be the main fruit and vegetable market north of Durbar Square, and produce is still sold in the streets leading east and north from here, while the trade in spices, homemade balls of soap, candles, oil, incense and other household wares has shifted to Kel Tol and Indrachowk.

The gilt-roofed pagoda at the south side of the square is the temple of **Annapurna**, the goddess of grain and abundance, and a manifestation of Lakshmi, the popular goddess of wealth. A lavish little affair, the pagoda bristles with icons and imagery, and in festival seasons its roof is strung with electric bulbs like a Christmas tree.

Mahaboudha and Bangemudha
From Asan, the trade route angles up to Kantipath and the modern city, while an alley heading south leads to **Mahaboudha**. Stuck in a rather unattractive square and said to date back to the sixth-century king Basantdev, this plain white stupa takes its name from the big statue of the Buddha in an adjacent brick shelter.

Walk westwards from Asan and you'll first pass the small three-tiered pagoda of **Ugratara**, a goddess believed to cure eyesight problems, before returning to the main Indrachowk–Thamel lane at **Bangemudha**. Just south of this square is a somewhat odd shrine to **Vaisya Dev**, the Newari toothache god. Commonly billed as the "Toothache Tree", it's actually the butt end of a log, embedded in the side of a building, and it used to be common practice to seek the god's help with dental problems by banging a nail into the log. (Bangemudha – "Crooked Stick" – refers to the legendary tree from which the log was cut.) Nowadays, many dentists advertise their services with grinning signs nearby.

At the north end of Bangemudha, a priceless fifth-century **Buddha figure** stands neglected in a tacky, tiled niche. Continuing north another one hundred metres, a lattice doorway on the right opens to a small recess housing a ninth-century **Uma Maheshwar**, a standard motif depicting Shiva and Parbati as a cosy couple atop Mount Kailas.

Kathesimbhu and Thahiti

Central Kathmandu's biggest stupa, **Kathesimbhu** stands in a square off to the left about two hundred metres north of Bangemudha. The temple is only a modest replica of the more impressive Swayambhu stupa (its name is a contraction of "Kathmandu Swayambhu"), but for those too old or infirm to climb to Swayambhu (see p.105), rites performed here earn the same merit. According to legend, it was built with earth left over after Swayambhu's construction; Lichhavi-era sculptures hereabouts attest to the antiquity of the site, but the stupa itself probably dates from the late seventeenth century. Like its namesake, Kathesimbhu has an associated shrine to the smallpox goddess Harati, located in the northwestern corner of the square.

Traffic circulates around another stupa at **Thahiti**, the next square north on the way to Thamel. Because they're continually replastered, stupas never look very old and are hard to date, but this one probably goes back to the fifteenth century. One of Kathmandu's finest old *bahal*, the seventeenth-century **Chusya Bahal** stands about two blocks east of Thahiti. It's recognizable by the two stone lions out in front and a meticulously carved wooden *torana* (decorative shield) above the doorway.

Thamel

In the **Thamel** tourist zone north of Thahiti, old buildings are scarce and about the only sights are the goodies in the restaurant windows. **Kwa Bahal**, a traditional courtyard tucked away just off the touristy main drag, is one of several *bahal* in Kathmandu and Patan that have their own Kumaris. **Bhagwan Bahal**, which lends its name to an area north of Thamel Chowk, is home to a little-used pagoda whose most notable feature is a collection of kitchen pans and utensils nailed to the front wall as offerings to the deity. ("Bikrama Sila Mahabihar", the name on the sign in front, refers to a moribund monastery contained within the complex.) During the spring festival of Holi, a portrait of the *bahal*'s eleventh-century founder is displayed to celebrate his slaying of demons on his return from a trade delegation to Lhasa.

Chhetrapati and Nardevi

At the southwestern fringe of Thamel lies boisterous **Chhetrapati**, a six-way intersection of almost perpetual motion. Though the neighbourhood lacks any ancient monuments, it supports a central *pati* (open shelter) resembling an Edwardian bandstand, around which religious processions and impromptu musical jamborees are frequent occurrences. During Shiva Raatri in February, sadhus build fires on the platform and light up their chilams, and during Tihaar the iron railings are decorated with oil lamps.

Kathmandu's street children

The plight of **street children** is a relatively modern phenomenon. Ground down by rural poverty and domestic violence, many children run away to the capital in search of a better life. Some are lured by often-false promises of high-paying jobs in tourism. The children are frequently referred to as *khate*, a derogatory term referring to scrap plastic collectors. International organisation Child Protection Centres and Services (CPES) estimates that there are between 1200 and 1500 street children in Kathmandu, predominantly boys.

The conditions street children endure are arguably more debilitating than rural poverty. Homeless, they sleep in doorways, *pati* (open shelters) or unfinished buildings. Weakened and malnourished by a poor diet and contaminated water, few are without disease. Many sniff glue or become addicted to harder drugs. They're regularly beaten by the police, and vulnerable to sexual violence and abuse (including from tourists).

Your alms will do more good if given to a charity working with beggars, rather than to the beggars themselves. For more information, contact CPES (℡01/421 5426, ⓦwww.cpes-int.org), or the charities Child Workers in Nepal (℡01/428 2255, ⓦwww.cwin.org.np) and Voice of Children (℡01/421 5426, ⓦwww.voiceofchildren.org.np).

From Chhetrapati it's a straight run south to the Kasthamandap; this street is favoured as an assembly point for protest marches, since the police can't easily secure it. On the right if you're walking south, the **Nardevi Mandir** is believed to have been established by the ninth-century founder of Kathmandu, Gunakamadev, though the present structure is merely medieval. The temple's deity, known as Sweta (White) Kali or Neta Ajima, is said to have received human sacrifice in ancient times; visible inside the temple are three silver images of Kali. The area to the west of the temple has a reputation as an important centre of ayurvedic medicine, with a college, hospital and many doctors' practices and pharmacies.

South of Durbar Square

The old city **south of Durbar Square** is home mainly to working-class castes and, increasingly, immigrant squatters from other parts of Nepal. With fewer traders, it's less touristy than the quarters north of the square, although New Road, which bristles and throbs with consumerism, is as lively a street as any in Kathmandu.

Bhimsensthan

A small square southwest of the Kasthamandap, down a lane leading to the Bishnumati River, **Bhimsensthan** is named after one of Nepal's favourite gods. Bhimsen, the strongman son of Vayu the wind god, is one of the famous five brothers of the Hindu epic Mahabharata who has been adopted as the patron saint of Newari merchants: you'll see pictures of him in shops everywhere.

The Bhimsen temple here was founded in the twelfth century. The current structure was built in the eighteenth, but is frequently renovated to look much newer. The shrine on the upper floor is open only to Hindus, while the ground floor is, fittingly, occupied by shops.

Pachali Bhairab

The most interesting part of south Kathmandu begins with **Pachali Bhairab**, an open-air shrine marooned among the city's maintenance facilities. To find it, head west on Tripureswar Marg and then south on the back road to Patan; finally, bear left at a fork marked by a small park.

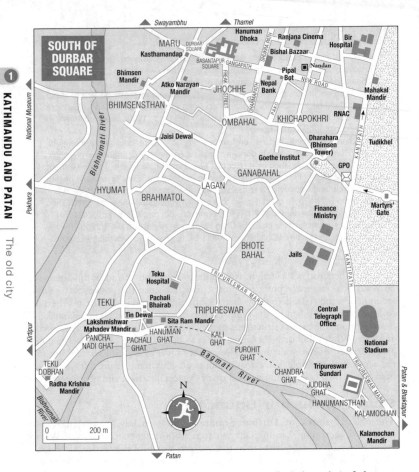

Compared to the uninspiring area you've just walked through it feels very peaceful here. The tiny gilded idol of Bhairab stands in a sunken sanctuary, dwarfed by a huge pipal tree and a life-sized human figure laid out like a pharaoh's casket. The repoussé figure is a **betal**, Bhairab's vehicle and a likeness of death which, in Nepali Hinduism, is believed to protect against death (the old principle of fighting fire with fire). *Betal* normally take the form of miniature skulls or skeletons at temple entrances, so this one is unusual for being so large.

According to legend this shrine was established by Kathmandu's founder, the ninth-century King Gunakamadev, to protect the city's southern gate. For many centuries, all treaties were signed with Pachali Bhairab as witness, in the belief that the god would strike dead anyone who broke the agreement. A procession starts here on the fourth and fifth nights of Dasain before moving on to Durbar Square.

The Bagmati ghats

A path from Pachali Bhairab leads to the Bagmati River **ghats**, stretching as far as the eye can see in either direction. Statues, temples and all manner of artefacts are jumbled along these stone-paved embankments – especially to the west, where the Bishnumati joins the Bagmati – and you could easily spend several hours here. The area has been the subject of a proposed restoration project for many years, so perhaps someday it will enjoy a much-deserved renaissance. For the time being, though, it's in a pretty sorry state of neglect.

Pachali Ghat

The path forks before reaching the river, but both ways lead to **Pachali Ghat** and its remarkable collection of Hindu and Buddhist statuary. If you take the right fork, you'll enter an area that serves as a neat introduction to the Newari pantheon of gods. Statues in niches along the right-hand wall depict (from right to left) Hanuman, Saraswati, the green and white Taras, Bhairab, Ganesh, a *linga/yoni*, a standing Vishnu, the Buddha, Ram, Shiva as sadhu, and a flute-playing Krishna. On the left are many more, concluding with depictions of the ten incarnations (*das avatar*) of Vishnu: fish, tortoise, the boar Baraha, the man-lion Narasingh, the dwarf Vaman, the Brahman Parasuram, the mythical heroes Ram and Krishna, the Buddha, and finally Kalki, the saviour yet to come.

Off to the right, the three-tiered **Lakshmishwar Mahadev Mandir** occupies a crumbling *bahal* that's been taken over by a school. The temple's construction was sponsored by the late-eighteenth-century queen Rajendra Laskhmi Devi Shah.

Pancha Nadi Ghat

Continuing downstream (westwards), you pass under an old footbridge and a modern motorable one, both leading to Patan's northern suburb of Sanepa. Beyond, **Pancha Nadi Ghat** used to be one of Kathmandu's most important sites for ritual bathing, but no longer, as the Bagmati has receded from the embankment: the river is literally shrinking as its water is siphoned off for ever-growing industrial and domestic needs. The several pilgrims' shelters (*sattal*) and rest-houses (*dharmsala*) along here have been taken over by squatters.

A small **sleeping Vishnu** in this area recalls, in miniature, the great statue at Budhanilkantha (see p.166). Cremations are infrequently held at the nearby **burning ghats** and butchers slaughter animals down by the river in the early morning – the buffalo you see here today could turn up in your *momo* tomorrow.

The confluence area

The embankment ends just short of **Teku Dobhan**, the confluence (*dobhan*) of Kathmandu's two main rivers, the Bagmati and the Bishnumati. The spot is also known as Chintamani Tirtha – a *tirtha* is a sacred place associated with *nag* (snake spirits).

The confluence area is ancient, though none of the temples or buildings is more than a century old. The most prominent is the **Radha Krishna Mandir**, a brick *shikra* built in the 1930s; flute-playing Krishna is the middle of three figures inside. The rest-house behind the temple, **Manandhar Sattal**, is named after a wealthy nineteenth-century trader who was forced to retire here after his property was confiscated by the prime minister. The next-door building is an unused electric crematorium built in the 1970s. The riverbank from here downstream to the ring road has been used as a landfill: this dumping site, like an earlier one further upstream near the Pashupatinath temple complex, will leach toxins into the river for decades to come.

Tin Dewal

Returning to Pachali Ghat and heading upstream (eastwards), you reach the atmospheric **Tin Dewal** ("Three Temples") by an entrance from the riverside.

The temple's popular name refers to its three brick *shikra* sharing a common base and ground floor – an unusual combination of Indian and Nepali styles, with some fine brick detailing.

A sign identifies the site by its official name, which is transliterated into English as Bomveer Vikalashora Shibalaya. The complex was erected in 1850 by Bom Bahadur Kunwar, brother of Jang Bahadur Rana, who'd seized power in a bloody coup four years earlier. A *shivalaya* (a shrine containing a *linga*) can be seen behind each of the temple's three lattice doors.

Further east there's a 300-metre break in the embankment, as a path makes its way through a semi-permanent **shantytown**. Its residents – landless rubbish-pickers, day labourers and street vendors – have moved in as the river has receded, and take their chances each monsoon.

Tripureswar Sundari and Kalamochan Mandir

From Hanumansthan a path leads away from the river to Tripureswar Marg via the **Tripureswar Sundari**, a derelict quadrangle squatted by a collective of low-caste families. The square's central temple, a massive three-tiered pagoda dedicated to Mahadev (Shiva), was erected in the early nineteenth century by Queen Lalit Tripura Sundari in memory of her husband Rana Bahadur Shah, who was assassinated in one of the period's many episodes of court intrigue.

Continuing north on this path brings you back to the buzzing, sputtering crosstown traffic of Tripureswar Marg. To the southeast lies the marvellously hideous **Kalamochan Mandir**, a study in Rana excess, resembling a grotesque white wedding cake, with gargoyles snarling at its four corners.

New Road, Jhochhe and Bhimsen Tower

Rebuilt after a disastrous 1934 earthquake, **New Road** cuts a swath of modernity through the old city east of Basantapur Square. Wealthy Nepalis and Indian tourists swarm its shops for perfume, jewellery, kitchen appliances, consumer electronics and myriad other imported goods.

The statue at the west end of New Road commemorates Prime Minister Juddha Shamsher Rana, who is credited with rebuilding the road (and much of Kathmandu) after the 1934 earthquake. **Pipal Bot**, a venerable old tree about midway along the road's south side, provides a natural canopy for shoeshiners and newspaper and magazine vendors, and is a favourite gathering place for Kathmandu's intelligentsia and gossipmongers.

Immediately south of Basantapur Square, **Jhochhe** (**Freak Street**) isn't prime sightseeing territory, but it does have unique historical associations. For a few foggy years in the late 1960s and early 1970s, this was an important stop on the hippy trail through Asia. In those days, before the invention of Thamel, Jhochhe was the place to hang out. Grass and hash were legal, and "freaks" had the freedom of the city. It all ended suddenly in 1974, with a series of stricter immigration and drug laws. To catch a whiff of that halcyon time, look out for the faded "Mr Kool's Munchies and Drinks Store" sign, before heading to the *Snowman*; the Freak Street pie shop in which Cat Stevens is said to have written his classic (and now all but forgotten) song *Kathmandu* was probably much like this one.

A lane heading east from Jhochhe leads to Kathmandu's main fish market and on to **Dharahara**, the tall minaret-like tower overlooking the GPO. Commonly known as **Bhimsen Tower**, it was built in 1832 by the prime minister, Bhimsen Thapa, possibly in imitation of Kolkata's Ochterlony Monument, erected four years earlier. The nearby **Sun Dhara** (Golden Water Tap), a *mandala*-shaped sunken bathing area, was created by Thapa in 1821.

West of the Bishnumati

Most of Kathmandu **west of the Bishnumati River** was settled relatively recently, with much of the development focused on the ugly Kalimati–Kalanki corridor and the suburbs either side. The only real antiquities are the famous **Swayambhu** stupa and a few shrines and temples that can be visited en route, plus the exhibits preserved in the **National Museum**. All of these sights are within fairly easy walking distance of central Kathmandu or Thamel, but to make a circuit of all of them it's more pleasant to hire a bike or taxi for the day (taxis wait at Swayambhu, but are hard to find near the museum).

Swayambhu and around

Swayambhu (or Swayambhunath), magnificently set atop a conical hill 2km west of Thamel, is a great place to get your bearings, geographically and culturally, in your first few days in Nepal: the hill commands a sweeping view of the Kathmandu Valley, and the temple complex is overrun with pilgrims and monkeys.

The ancient stupa is the most profound expression of Buddhist symbolism in Nepal (many *bahal* in the valley contain a replica of it), and the source of the valley's creation myth. Inscriptions date the stupa to the fifth century, and there's reason to believe the hill was used for animist rites even before Buddhism arrived in the valley two thousand years ago. Tantric Buddhists consider it the chief "power point" of the Kathmandu Valley; one chronicle states an act of worship here carries thirteen billion times more merit than anywhere else. To call it the "Monkey Temple" (its tourist nickname) is to trivialize it.

Since the Chinese invasion of Tibet in 1959, the surrounding area has become home to many exiled Tibetans. You'll see them and many other Buddhist pilgrims making a full circumambulation (*kora*) of the hill, queuing up to spin the gigantic fixed prayer wheels and the six thousand smaller ones that encircle the perimeter, and frequently twirling their own hand-held ones. The place is so steeped in lore and pregnant with detail you'll never absorb it all in a single

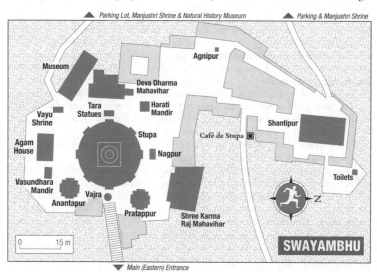

visit. Try going early in the morning at *puja* time, or at night when the red-robed monks pad softly around the dome, murmuring mantras.

Swayambhu's main **festivals** are Buddha Jayanti (April or May) and Losar (Feb or March), when pilgrims throng around the stupa and monks splash arcs of saffron paint over it in a lotus-flower pattern. Many also flock here each morning during the month-long Gunla festivities (Aug or Sept) to mark the "rain's retreat" with music and offerings to the monks.

A visit to Swayambhu can be turned into a longer hike or bike trip by continuing on to Ichangu Narayan (see p.169).

Getting there

The main entrance is at the eastern foot of the hill, and **getting there** is simple on foot or cycle. From Thamel, the easiest way is via Chhetrapati, from where a small road heads straight towards Swayambhu, passing *Hotel Vajra* en route. From Jhochhe or Durbar Square, take the lane running northwest from the Maru Ganesh shrine. Either way, it should take about twenty minutes to walk it. If you're cycling, the local kids will expect you to cough up a few rupees' protection money for your bike. Buses run irregularly between the City Bus Park and the eastern entrance. A taxi can take you up to a small car park near the top, just west of the stupa. **Admission**, paid at booths at the main entrances, is Rs100.

A paved road circles the base of the hill. Although there are several other ways up, the steep main path from the **eastern entrance**, with its three-hundred-odd centuries-smoothed steps, is the most dramatic. The **Buddha statues** near the bottom are from the seventeenth century, while a second group further up was donated in the early part of the twentieth century. The chiselled slates sold by entrepreneurs along the path are *mani* stones, inscribed, in Tibetan script, with the ubiquitous Buddhist mantra *Om mani padme hum* ("Hail to the jewel in the lotus").

You can get **food** at a few snack places near the eastern entrance, at the far (northwestern) side of the stupa precinct (*Café de Stupa* has good views) and at the southern base of the hill. If you eat in the open, beware of the monkeys: they'll snatch at anything that even looks like food.

The stupa

According to Buddhist scriptures, the Kathmandu Valley was once a snake-infested lake (geologists agree about the lake: see p.420). Ninety-one aeons ago, a perfect, radiant lotus flower appeared on the surface of the lake, which the gods proclaimed to be Swayambhu ("self-created"), the abstract essence of Buddhahood. **Manjushri**, the *bodhisattva* of knowledge, drew his sword and cut a gorge at Chobar, south of Kathmandu, to drain the lake and allow humans to worship Swayambhu. As the water receded, the lotus settled on top of a hill and Manjushri established a shrine to it, before turning his attention to ridding the valley of snakes (see p.440) and establishing its first civilization. Another legend tells how, when Manjushri cut his hair at Swayambhu, the strands that fell on the ground grew into trees, and the lice turned into monkeys.

The apparently simple structure of the **stupa** belies an immensely complex physical representation of Buddhist cosmology, and the purpose of walking round it is to meditate on this. The solid, whitewashed dome (*garbha*) symbolizes the womb or creation. Set in niches at the cardinal points, statues of **dhyani** (meditating) **Buddhas** correspond to the four elements (earth, air, fire and water) and a fifth, placed at an angle, to the sky or space. Each represents a different aspect of Buddhahood: the hand positions, colours and "vehicles" (the animal statues below) of each are significant. The *dhyani* Buddhas are the same

▲ Swayambhu temple

characters who appear on virtually every *chaitya* around the Kathmandu Valley. At each of the sub-cardinal points sit **female counterparts**, who in tantric Buddhism represent the wisdom aspect that must be united – figuratively speaking – with the compassionate male force to achieve enlightenment.

The gilded **cube** (*harmika*) surmounting the stupa surrounds a thick wooden pillar, which may be considered the phallic complement to the female dome. The **eyes** painted on it are those of the all-seeing Adi-Buddha (primordial Buddha), staring in all four directions. Between the eyes is a curl of hair (*urna*), one of the identifying features of a Buddha, and the thing that looks like a nose is a miraculous light emanating from the *urna* (it can also be interpreted as the Nepali figure "one", conveying the unity of all things). A **spire** of gold disks stacked above the pillar represents the thirteen steps to enlightenment, while the *torana*, or gold plaques above the painted eyes, also show the five *dhyani* Buddhas, known collectively as the *panchabuddha*. Finally, the umbrella at the top symbolizes the attainment of enlightenment: some say it contains a bowl filled with precious gems.

Shrines around the stupa

The stupa is surrounded by an incredible array of shrines and votive items, most of which have been donated over the past four centuries by merit-seeking kings and nobles. The bronze sceptre-like object at the top of the steps is a vastly oversized **vajra**, a tantric symbol of power and indestructibility; its pedestal is carved with the twelve animals of the Tibetan zodiac. The twin bullet-shaped *shikra* on either side of this, known as **Pratappur** and **Anantapur**, were installed by King Pratap Malla during a seventeenth-century dispute with Tibet, on the advice of an Indian guru. The story of the king's gift, and his subsequent victory over the Tibetans, is engraved on the twin bells in front of the *shikra*.

Moving around clockwise, as is the custom at all stupas, the brick hut to the south of Anantapur is **Vasundhara Mandir**, dedicated to the earth goddess Vasundhara, who's more or less synonymous with Annapurna and Lakshmi, the goddesses of grain and wealth respectively. Further on – past the priests' quarters and a number of *chaitya* – is a small marble-faced shrine to **Vayu**, the Vedic god of wind and storms.

The tiny **museum** behind the shrine contains bas-relief statues of gods, Buddhist and Hindu, which are beautiful to look at, but only tersely identified. Next door and up a flight of steps, the **Deva Dharma Mahavihar** is a small, uneventful monastery, open to the public. In front of this, close to the stupa behind protective caging, stand two acclaimed bronze statues of the **White and Green Taras**, deified princess wives of an eighth-century Tibetan king.

A few paces further on squats a gilt-roofed temple built to appease **Harati** (also known as **Ajima**), traditionally the goddess of smallpox but now regarded as governing all childhood diseases. Like many Newari deities, Harati/Ajima is both feared (as a bringer of disease) and revered (as a protectress, if properly appeased). Harati/Ajima's shrine is extremely popular, and you'll see queues of mothers with kids in tow, waiting to make offerings. The nineteenth-century idol was carved to replace an earlier one smashed by King Rana Bahadur Shah after his wife died of smallpox.

Agnipur, an insignificant-looking lump on the pavement in the extreme northwest corner of the complex, marked by two tiny lions in front, is a seldom-visited shrine to the Vedic fire god Agni, the relayer of burnt offerings to heaven. **Nagpur**, a bathtub-sized tank at the north point of the stupa, propitiates the valley's snake spirits, and when it's not filled with water you can see the idol at the bottom. Finally, the **Shree Karma Raj Mahavihar**, an active monastery at the northeast corner of the compound, contains a big Buddha and numerous butter candles, which Tibetan Buddhists light in much the same way Catholics do. You can catch the sonorous chanting of the monks at around 3 or 4pm every day.

Shantipur

A 1500-year-old mystery surrounds **Shantipur**, the otherwise plain, box-like building northwest of the stupa. Shanti Shri, a fifth-century holy man, is supposed to have sealed himself in a vault beneath the temple to meditate, vowing not to emerge until the valley needed him. Commentators write that he subsequently attained a mystic state of immortality, and according to devout believers he's still in there.

King Pratap Malla, who entered the chamber in 1658 to seek magical help in ending a drought, experienced adventures worthy of Indiana Jones. According to scholar Keith Dowman, the king recounted how he entered alone and descended to the second subterranean level. In the first room "bats as large as kites or hawks came to kill the light", while in the second room "ghosts, flesh-eating spirits and hungry ghosts came to beg", clutching at anyone who failed to pacify them. Of the third room he said, "If you cannot pacify the snakes by pouring out milk, they chase and bind you. Having pacified them you can walk on their bodies". Finally, Pratap Malla found the saint in an almost skeletal form, and was rewarded with a *nag* rain-making emblem.

Faded frescoes on the walls of the outer sanctum show scenes from the Swayambhu Purana, a seventeenth-century scripture recounting the story of Manjushri's sword act and other creation myths. Shantipur, also known as Akashpur ("Sky-place"), completes a cycle of shrines to the five elemental spirits: earth, air, fire, water (snakes) and sky.

The Manjushri Shrine

The **Manjushri Shrine**, located on a prayer-flag-capped spur of the hilltop to the west, comes second only to the main stupa in antiquity – the canopied *chaitya* is reckoned to be 1500 years old. Manjushri, the Buddhist god of wisdom and founder of civilization in the valley, is traditionally depicted by an empty niche in the *chaitya*, but an image of Saraswati, the Hindu goddess of learning, was placed in the niche three hundred years ago, and so the shrine is now on the pilgrimage circuit for Hindus as well. Schoolchildren make a special trip here on Saraswati Puja, in late January or early February, to have their books and pencils blessed.

The Natural History Museum

The morbidly amusing **Natural History Museum** (Sun–Fri 10am–4pm; Rs50, camera Rs40) is on your right as you follow the road from the car park down the south side of Swayambhu hill. Its jumbled collection of stuffed birds and shrivelled animals in old-fashioned display cases looks like it was cobbled together from the trophy rooms of hoary old Rana hunters. The weirdness is fun for its own sake though and the specimens might give you an idea of what to look for when you get to the mountains or jungle.

Bijeshwari and Shoba Bhagwati

Bijeshwari, along the west bank of the Bishnumati on the way to Swayambhu, used to be Kathmandu's execution ground. While Tibetans and other immigrants broke the taboo against settling near the cursed ground a generation ago, a fear of ghosts still endures, as do two important but little-visited temples.

Bijeshwari Bahal, perched at the top of a flight of steps above the river, is the centre of worship of an esoteric Buddhist goddess, Bijeshwari (Lord of Victory), who is also known as Akash (Sky) Yogini and sometimes counted as the fifth of the valley's Bajra Yoginis, the wrathful aspects of the tantric Tara goddesses.

Just upstream stands a cremation pavilion, and beyond that, the Hindu **Shobha Bhagwati Mandir**. Bhagwati is a common Nepali name for the mother goddess, and this idol of her is considered to be among the most powerful manifestations in the valley: early in the morning you might see political candidates, students preparing for exams, or anyone requiring quiet strength coming here to do *puja* to her. According to legend, the sculptor of the Shobha Bhagwati image here carved it with his feet, his hands having been cut off by a jealous king to prevent him from reproducing an earlier master-work in the king's collection.

The National Museum

The **National Museum**, based in an old Rana armoury 1km south of Swayambhu (daily except Thurs: 10.30am–3pm, Mon closes 2pm; Rs100, camera Rs50; leave bags in lockers at entrance) is no curatorial coup, but you'll come away with a better appreciation of the intertwining of religion, art, myth and history in Nepal.

The art building

Count on spending most of your time in the **art building**. The collection of **stone sculptures** showcases an amazing artistic consistency spanning almost two thousand years, from the Lichhavi period (second to ninth centuries) through to the tantric-influenced Malla dynasties (thirteenth to eighteenth centuries). The oldest is a life-size statue of King Jaya Varma from 184 AD.

The **metalwork** exhibit pays tribute to a later art form which blossomed under patronage from Tibet. A trio of stunning fourteenth-century bronzes of tantric deities form the centrepieces.

Other exhibits include exceptional images, window frames and *torana* (ornate shields mounted over the doors of temples) carved from **wood**. On the ground floor are a couple of dozen rare **poubha** (Nepali scroll paintings) from the sixteenth century and later.

The Buddhist Art Gallery

The red-brick building at the back of the compound houses the **Buddhist Art Gallery**, which gives a patchy overview of artistic traditions from three distinct parts of the country. The **Terai section** represents the most ancient and archeologically important area in Nepal: the environs of Lumbini, the Buddha's birthplace. The **Kathmandu Valley section** surveys the valley's considerable artistic contributions in brass, stone and painting from a Buddhist perspective. Finally, the small **Northern Himalayan section** contains *thangka*, bronzes and ritual objects.

The history building

A Rana-style mansion on the right as you enter the compound, the **history building** is aimed mainly at school groups, with a hotchpotch of animal carcasses, bones, dolls, a moon rock, and weaponry. The top floor houses the **National Numismatic Museum**, displaying coins representing the reign of every Nepali king from the Malla and Shah dynasties.

East of Kantipath

Old photographs of Kathmandu show the area **east of Kantipath** dominated by the palaces and residences of the ruling Rana family, with villages – Hadigaun, Dilli Bazaar, Baneswar – surrounded by farmland beyond. Today, the palaces have mostly been taken over by government ministries, while the boulevards around the old Royal Palace are lined with airline offices and high-end hotels; the old villages have become congested bazaars, and the farmland subdivided into walled suburban compounds.

For Pashupatinath, which lies just east of the ring road, see p.153.

Kaisher Mahal

On the corner of Tridevi Marg and Kantipath, **Kaisher Mahal**, former residence of Field Marshal Kaisher Shamsher Rana (1891–1964), now serves as a government building. Inside, the **Kaisher Library** (daily: summer Mon 10am–3pm, Tues–Sun 10am–5pm; winter Mon 10am–3pm, Tues–Sun 10am–4pm) has long shelves of European books, cabinets of Sanskrit manuscripts, a suit of armour, a stuffed tiger and portraits of famous acquaintances.

Kaisher Shamsher Rana is said to have laid out the grounds of his mansion as a **"Garden of Dreams"** (daily 9am–10pm; Rs160), with areas devoted to each of the six seasons. Trees were planted to ensure that different fruits ripened year-round. A $1m renovation was completed in 2007, and this idyllic spot provides a wonderful respite from the nearby Thamel chaos, with an excellent restaurant, photo gallery and regular cultural events. Keep an eye out for the giant fruit bats in the trees.

Another sort of colonial landmark, **Fora Durbar**, the swish R&R compound for American expats, hides behind high brick walls at the southeastern corner of the Tridevi Marg–Kantipath roundabout. Across Kantipath is the former palace of Prince Basundhara, now the vastly oversized office of Nepal's Election Commission.

To the north, just beyond the British Embassy in Lainchaur, is the nineteenth-century **British Cemetery**, a relic of the 1816 Treaty of Segauli (see p.422), under which Nepal was obliged to accept a British "resident". Ask at the embassy if you want to have a look around the cemetery.

The Royal Palace (Narayanhiti Durbar)

An architectural travesty from the 1960s, the Royal Palace looks like something out of Buck Rogers, with echoes of the Mormon Tabernacle. Built in front of an earlier palace dating from around 1900, it was inaugurated in 1970 for then Crown Prince Birendra's wedding. Its Nepali name, Narayanhiti-Durbar, refers to a water tap (*hiti*) east of the main entrance. Much of the property is now used by the foreign office and various security services.

Many Nepalis avert their eyes when they walk past the palace, or avoid passing it altogether, for it evokes painful memories as the scene of the inexplicable royal massacre of June 1, 2001, when Crown Prince Dipendra killed his entire immediate family and five other relatives before apparently turning the gun on himself (see p.426). In early 2009, the government opened up part of the Royal Palace as a museum (Thurs–Mon 11am–3pm; Rs500), with Tribhuvan Sadan, where the massacre took place, among the areas accessible to visitors.

Around Rani Pokhari

Rani Pokhari (Queen's Pool), the large square tank east of Asan, was built in the seventeenth century by King Pratap Malla to console his queen after the death of their favourite son; the shrine in the middle, opened one day a year during the Tihaar festival, is more recent. The pavements around the pool and nearby **Ratna Park** (officially renamed Shankhadhar Park) are active centres for small-time trade, including prostitution.

East of Rani Pokhari rises the c.1900 **Ghanta Ghar** (clock tower) – like Bhimsen Tower, a landmark only in the functional sense – and Kathmandu's two **mosques**. Muslims first settled in Kathmandu as traders five centuries ago, and now represent only a tiny fraction of Nepal's half-million "Musalmans".

Around the Tudikhel

Kathmandu's **Tudikhel** is the biggest military parade ground in Nepal. Percival Landon, an early-twentieth-century traveller, proclaimed it "level as Lord's", as in London's famous cricket ground. An institution rooted in Nepal's warring past, the *tudikhel* is a feature of every town of consequence throughout the hills. Unfortunately, although Kathmandu's Tudikhel provides a sizeable chunk of open space in the middle of the city, it's no green lung: it has few trees and actually adds to the city's pollution problem by forcing traffic to bottleneck around it.

On the Kantipath side of the Tudikhel stands the **Mahakal Mandir**, whose modern surroundings have in no way diminished the reverence of its worshippers: pedestrians and motorists commonly touch a hand to the forehead as they pass.

East of the Tudikhel, **Bhrikuti Mandap** serves as an amusement park and part-time exhibition ground. The nearby **Martyrs' Gate** commemorates the four ringleaders of a failed 1940 attempt to overthrow the Rana regime.

Singha Durbar and Baber Mahal Revisited

Undoubtedly the most impressive structure ever raised by the Ranas, **Singha Durbar** dominates the governmental quarter in the southeastern part of the city. Once the biggest building in Asia, the prime ministers' palace of a thousand rooms was built in 1901 by Chandra Shamsher Rana, who employed workers round the clock for two years to complete it and fill it with European extravagances, all for the then unconscionable sum of Rs2.5 million. It's said the entire population of Kathmandu abstained from *daal*, an ingredient in traditional mortar, during the construction.

The palace was mostly destroyed by fire in 1973, and only the main wing was restored for use as parliamentary offices. Numerous governmental ministries, departments and the Gallery Baithak (home of Nepal's parliament) now occupy new buildings and original outbuildings elsewhere in the vast complex. You can peek at the main wing's colonnaded facade through the sweeping front (western) gate.

If you're down this way, call in at **Baber Mahal Revisited**, off a tree-lined street south of Singha Durbar. A restored Rana palace with shops, restaurants and peaceful courtyards, it's a heavenly retreat (daily; 9am–10.30/11pm).

Eastern neighbourhoods

While Kathmandu's eastern and northeastern neighbourhoods have little of scenic interest, they do provide insights into contemporary life in the capital.

Crowded **Bagh Bazaar** and **Dilli Bazaar** pretty much sum up one end of the spectrum, with their computer institutes, lawyers' cubbyholes, and shops selling office furniture and "suitings and shirtings". Dilli Bazaar is also the home of Nepal's stock exchange. The other extreme is found further north in the shady lanes of **Bhatbateni**, **Baluwatar** and **Maharajganj**, where old, new and foreign money hides in walled compounds, along with embassies, aid organizations and corporate mansions.

Between the two lie the hopeful settlements of a burgeoning middle class, who build their houses one floor at a time, and send their children off in uniforms to "English boarding schools" with names such as "Bright Future" and "Radiant Readers".

Hadigaun and Dhum Barahi

Like most ancient cities, Kathmandu was formed by the gradual merging of once-separate villages. Excavations suggest **Hadigaun**, now a northeastern suburb, is one of the oldest of Kathmandu's original settlements. Evidence of Hadigaun's age comes from the overgrown fifth-century Vishnu shrine, **Dhum Barahi**, in a schoolyard a further 1km northeast where, inside the small brick shelter a whimsical fifth-century image illustrates the tale of Barahi (Vishnu in his incarnation as a boar) rescuing the earth goddess Prithvi from the bottom of the sea.

To get here, head north out of Hadigaun and when in doubt always take the right fork.

Patan (Lalitpur)

Now largely absorbed by greater Kathmandu, **Patan** was once the capital of a powerful independent kingdom, and still maintains a defiantly distinct identity. Compared to Kathmandu it's quieter, less frenetic and more Buddhist. Patan is sophisticated and, in a Nepali sort of way, bohemian: while Kathmanduites are busy amassing power and wealth, Patan's residents appreciate the finer things of life, which perhaps explains the area's alternate name, **Lalitpur** ("City of Beauty"). Above all, it remains a proud city of **artisans**.

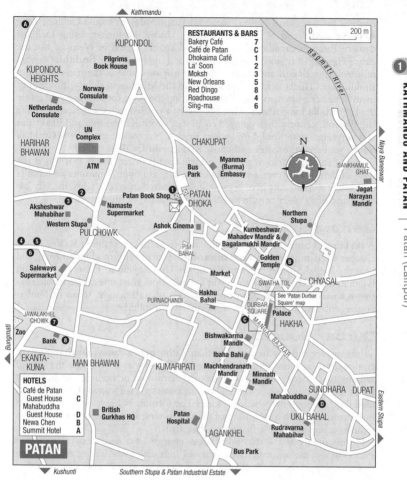

Patan produces much of Nepal's fine metalwork, and its craftspeople have created some of the most extraordinarily lavish temples, *hiti* and *bahal* in the country. *Bahal* – their doorways here always guarded by cuddly stone lions with overbites – are a particular feature of Patan, and a few still function as active monasteries. In the past two decades, Patan has also emerged as the de facto **foreign aid** capital of Nepal: the UN offices and diverse smaller organizations are scattered around the western suburbs, as are many expat residences.

In legend and in fact, Patan is the oldest city in the Kathmandu Valley. **Manjushri**, the great lake-drainer, is supposed to have founded Manjupatan, the forerunner of Patan, right after he enshrined Swayambhu, while the so-called Ashokan stupas, earthen mounds standing at four cardinal points around Patan, seem to support the legend that the Indian emperor **Ashoka** visited the valley in the third century BC (historians are sceptical). More reliable legend ascribes Patan's founding to **Yalambar**, second-century king of the Kirats, an ancient tribe that provided the original stock for the valley's Newari population (which explains the traditional Newari name for Patan, **Yala**), or to the Lichhavi King **Arideva** at the end of the third century. Under the long-running Lichhavi dynasty, Patan emerged as the cultural and artistic capital of Nepal, if not the entire Himalayan region. It maintained strong links with the **Buddhist** centres of learning in Bengal and Bihar – thereby playing a role in the transmission of Buddhism to Tibet – and when these fell to the Muslims in the twelfth century, many scholars and artists fled to Patan, setting the stage for a renaissance under the later **Malla** kings. Patan existed as part of a unified valley kingdom until the late fifteenth century, then enjoyed equal status with Kathmandu and Bhaktapur as a sovereign state until 1769, when Prithvi Narayan Shah and his Gorkhali band conquered the valley and chose Kathmandu for their capital.

One of Patan's charms is that its historic core is frozen much as it was at the time of defeat. However, see it while you can: although a number of temples and public monuments have been skilfully restored in recent years, the city has lost many of its older private buildings in the name of modernisation.

Getting there

A **taxi** from Thamel or central Kathmandu to Patan costs around Rs300. Much cheaper fixed-route **tempo** and **microbus** services run from Durbar Marg and near the Nepal Airlines office in Kantipath. Don't **cycle** to Patan via the main Bagmati bridge and Kupondol – you'll expire from the fumes. A better alternative is to cross the river from the Teku area of Kathmandu, south of Durbar Square, entering Patan through its northwestern suburbs.

Durbar Square

While smaller and less monumental than Kathmandu's, Patan's **Durbar Square** comes across as more refined and less touristy. Maybe it's because the city of artisans has a better eye for architectural harmony; or because Patan, which hasn't been a capital since the eighteenth century, has escaped the continuous meddling of monument-building kings. The formula is, however, similar to that in Kathmandu, with a solemn royal palace looming along one side and assorted temples grouped in the remaining public areas.

Tourists must pay a Rs200 **admission charge** (at a desk next to the Royal Palace) to visit the square between 7am and 7pm. Otherwise it's free. Ask for a free extension (up to the length of your visa) if you want to visit more than once.

The Royal Palace

Patan's richly decorated **Royal Palace** was largely constructed during the second half of the seventeenth century, but substantially rebuilt after both the Gorkhali invasion of 1769 and the 1934 earthquake. It consists of three main wings, each enclosing a central courtyard and reached by a separate entrance.

The courtyard of the small, southernmost wing, **Sundari Chowk**, contains what must surely be one of the world's grandest bathtubs, the seventeenth-century **Tusha Hiti**. This sunken royal bath, decorated with Hindu gods and goddesses, is shaped like a *yoni*, the symbol of female sexuality, and ringed with serpents. The courtyard surrounding it is covered in ornate woodwork, including many fabulous carved doorways, windows, *torana*, and images of deities individually set into niches.

Mul Chowk, the next wing to the north, served as the royal family residence until Patan's fall in 1769. A sadly deteriorated gilt door in the right-hand wall of the courtyard, leading to the private Taleju Mandir, is flanked by statues of the Indian river goddesses **Ganga** and **Jamuna**, the latter riding a *makana* – a mythical cross between a crocodile and an elephant, whose curling snout decorates almost every public water spout in Nepal. Behind and to the left of Mul Chowk rises the octagonal, three-tiered **Taleju Bhawani Mandir**.

Yet another Taleju temple, the monolithic **Degu Talle**, towers just north of Mul Chowk. Seven storeys high and the tallest building on the block, it was erected in 1640 by Siddhi Narsingh Malla, during whose reign much of the palace and square were built, but had to be completely rebuilt after being razed in the 1934 earthquake.

The Patan Museum

The palace's northernmost wing, Mani Keshab Narayan Chowk, once served as the palace of another noted seventeenth-century king, Yoganarendra Malla. It too suffered in the 1934 earthquake and at the time was only clumsily rebuilt.

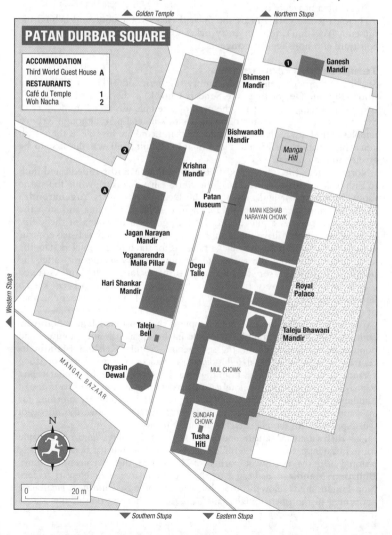

▲ Golden Temple   ▲ Northern Stupa

PATAN DURBAR SQUARE

ACCOMMODATION
Third World Guest House **A**
RESTAURANTS
Café du Temple   **1**
Woh Nacha   **2**

Bhimsen Mandir

Ganesh Mandir

Bishwanath Mandir

Manga Hiti

Krishna Mandir

Patan Museum

MANI KESHAB NARAYAN CHOWK

Jagan Narayan Mandir

Yoganarendra Malla Pillar

Degu Talle

Royal Palace

Hari Shankar Mandir

Taleju Bhawani Mandir

Taleju Bell

MANGAL BAZAAR

Chyasin Dewal

MUL CHOWK

Western Stupa

SUNDARI CHOWK

Tusha Hiti

N

0   20 m

▼ Southern Stupa   ▼ Eastern Stupa

With assistance from the Austrian government, however, it has been restored to house the splendid **Patan Museum** (daily 10.30am–5.30pm; Rs250).

The museum displays a well-curated **permanent collection** of important bronzes, stone sculptures and woodcarvings, a gilded Malla throne and archival photographs. The exhibits are arranged thematically to lead you through Hindu, Buddhist and Tantric iconography, temple construction, ritual objects and metallurgical processes, all supported by excellent explanatory text. Moreover, the building itself, with its newly stuccoed walls and artful lighting, suggests the royal palace Yoganarendra Malla might have built had he reigned at the beginning of the twenty-first century. From the interior balconies you can look out onto the courtyard below and its central Lakshmi shrine, and watch the *kinkinimali*, leaf-shaped tin cut-outs hanging from the eaves, fluttering in the breeze. A stunning gold window above the exterior main entrance depicts Vishnu and a heavenly host.

There's a sedate **café**, run by the *Summit Hotel*, in the courtyard behind the museum (you don't need an entry ticket to eat here), and a **gift shop**. The courtyard also hosts regular **concerts**.

Temples and monuments

Starting at the newer, eighteenth-century southern end of Durbar Square, the stone **Chyasin Dewal** (opposite Sundari Chowk) is the lesser of the square's two Krishna temples. Some say the octagonal temple was raised in memory of the eight wives that committed *sati* on a king's funeral pyre, although Krishna temples almost always have eight sides to commemorate his role as the eighth *avatar* (incarnation) of Vishnu. The cast-iron **Taleju Bell** was the first to be erected in the valley, in 1736.

North of here, the finely carved **Hari Shankar Mandir** is dedicated both to Vishnu (sometimes called Hari) and Shiva (alias Shankar), while the statue mounted on a pillar and praying to the Degu Talle depicts **Yoganarendra Malla**. An angry cobra rears up like a halo behind the king, and atop the cobra's head perches a gilded bird. Like all god-fearing rulers of the valley, Yoganarendra would have made sure to appease the *nag*, animist snake spirits who deliver or withhold the valley's rains. As for the bird, chroniclers state the king, upon abdicating the throne to become a *sunyasan* (hermit) after the untimely death of his son, told his subjects that as long as the bird remained they would know he was still alive. To this day, many people in Patan keep a light burning and a bed is kept ready for the absent king in an upper chamber of the palace.

Continuing northwards, the next temple is the two-tiered **Jagan Narayan**, built in 1565; if this is the oldest temple in the square, the most unusual and popular one is its neighbour, the seventeenth-century **Krishna Mandir**. Its central structure, a Mughal-style *shikra*, is girdled by three levels of stone verandas, with detailed scenes from the great Hindu epics, the Mahabharata and Ramayana, carved along the lintels. An incarnation of Vishnu, Krishna is one of Hinduism's best-loved characters. Worshippers gather here every morning for *puja* and on Krishna's birthday, in August or early September, the queue of worshippers at this temple stretches around the block.

The **Bishwanath Mandir** contains a copy of the Shiva *linga* of the same name in Varanasi, India. The temple collapsed in 1990, but has been seamlessly restored. On the northwest corner of the square, the seventeenth-century **Bhimsen Mandir** is dedicated to the ever-popular god of Newari traders. Non-Hindus aren't allowed inside, but you can often see and hear *puja* being performed in the open upstairs sanctuary. Across the way, one of the valley's largest sunken public bathing tanks, **Manga Hiti**, has been operational since the sixth century.

North and west of Durbar Square

Some of Patan's most interesting sights – the Golden and Kumbeshwar temples and the ghats – lie **north of Durbar Square**, but there's also plenty of seren-dipitous exploring to be done among the back alleys **west of the square**. For more detail on this area, pick up a copy of *Patan Walkabout*, an informative booklet available from the bookshop at Patan Dhoka (Rs75).

Hiranyavarna Mahavihara (The Golden Temple)

The **Hiranyavarna Mahavihara** – Sanskrit for "Golden Monastery", but all the tour guides call it the **Golden Temple** – is the most opulent little temple in Nepal. The three-tiered pagoda occupies one side of the cramped courtyard of Kwa Bahal, a still-active twelfth-century Buddhist Newari monastery and the spiritual hub of old Patan. During early-morning *puja*, the *bahal* is a fascinating theatre of Nepali religion in all its perplexing glory. **Admission** is Rs50 (no set hours); nothing leather is allowed inside.

The temple's gilt facade, embossed with images of Buddhas and Taras, is regarded as the pre-eminent example of large-scale repoussé **metalwork** in Nepal, while in the middle of the courtyard, a small, lavishly ornamented shrine contains a priceless silver and gold Swayambhu *chaitya*. Both the shrine and the main temple are further decorated with what look like long metallic neckties: these *pataka* are supposed to provide a slide for the gods when they descend to answer worshippers' prayers. The *bahal* is so crammed with images, ornaments and fine details that a full account of all its wonders would fill a book.

Sakyamuni Buddha is the temple's *kwapadya* (main image). According to **legend**, it was made homeless in the twelfth century when the temple it formerly resided in collapsed. When King Bhaskardev built it a new temple, the image informed him in a dream it wished to move to a new place where mice chased cats. One day the king saw a golden mouse chasing a cat here at Kwa Bahal, and so he set about building a new, golden temple on the spot. Rats are thus allowed to run free here, as are tortoises, for in legend the universe rests on the back of a tortoise.

Though no longer a residential monastery, the Mahavihara is an important centre of lay worship, following well-established Buddhist rituals and iconography that draw from both the Newari and the Tibetan traditions. Its principal priest, a boy no older than twelve, tends the main shrine. A Tibetan-style *gompa* upstairs on the northeastern side of the courtyard, which you can visit, is evidence of the spiritual ties forged between Patan and Tibet through centuries of trade.

Swatha Tol

Swatha Tol, an attractive intersection one block east of the Golden Temple, lies poised between Durbar Square and the more traditional neighbourhoods to the north, and seems to combine the best of both worlds. The square's centrepiece, the three-tiered **Radha Krishna Mandir**, has been restored, and the lovers Krishna and **Radha**, to whom this temple is dedicated, are a favourite subject for Indian sandalwood carvers.

The Kumbeshwar Mahadev and Bagalamukhi temples

Patan's oldest temple, and one of only two freestanding five-tiered pagodas in Nepal (the other is in Bhaktapur), the **Kumbeshwar Mahadev Mandir** was built as a two-roofed structure in 1392, and despite the addition of three more levels in the seventeenth century, it remains well proportioned. Shiva is the honoured deity here: inside you can see a stone *linga* and a brass one with four faces; Nandi, Shiva's patient mount, waits outside. The temple owes its name to an episode in which a pilgrim at Gosainkund, the sacred lake high in the mountains north of Kathmandu, dropped a pot (*kumbha*) into the water there. Much later, the same pot appeared in the water tank here, giving rise to the belief that the tank is fed by an underground channel from Gosainkund, and adding to Shiva's roll of titles that of Kumbeshwar – Lord of the Pots.

Thanks to this connection, Kumbeshwar's water tank is regarded as an alternative venue during Gosainkund's great annual **festival, Janai Purnima**, which takes place on the day of the late July or early August full moon, and sees Brahmans and Chhetris formally changing the sacred thread (*janai*) that distinguishes them as members of the "twice-born" castes. Thousands come to have their threads renewed and pay respect to a *linga* erected in the middle of the tank, while Tamang *jhankri* (shamans) perform ritual dances and young boys dive and splash in the water.

Though smaller and less to look at, the **Bagalamukhi Mandir**, occupying the southern end of the same compound, inspires far more day-to-day devotion. Considered a powerful wish-fulfilling manifestation of the goddess Kali, Bagalamukhi traditionally appeals to women seeking domestic harmony and anyone requiring strength to overcome adversity.

Just north of the compound, the **Kumbeshwar Technical School** provides vocational and literacy training for poor women, orphans and other disadvantaged people, supported in part by sales from its shop.

The Northern Stupa and on to the ghats

Just northeast of the Kumbeshwar Mahadev, the **Northern Stupa** is the smallest and most central of the Ashokan mounds, and the only one that's been sealed over with plaster. Although it doesn't look wildly interesting for a supposedly 2200-year-old monument, you can let your imagination dwell on what treasures or relics Ashoka might have buried here – the contents are unlikely ever to see the light of day, since archeological digs are prohibited in the valley.

The stupa stands at the edge of the city. From here the road south plunges back between brick tenements and neglected temples to Durbar Square. Northwards, it wends through receding farmland towards Patan's **Sankhamul Ghat**, a half-kilometre-long embankment near the junction of the Manohara and Bagmati rivers and Patan's main cremation site.

East of the footbridge, flanked by sagging pilgrims' shelters and statues of Hanuman and Ganesh, a path leads under an arch and up to the exotic **Jagat Narayan** temple complex, named after its builder, nineteenth-century prime minister Jagat Shamsher.

West to Pulchowk

From **Mangal Bazaar**, central Patan's main drag heads out towards the Western Stupa. One of Patan's less-touristed former monasteries, **Hakhu Bahal** (also known as Ratnakar Mahabihar), rises on the left after 300m and is the seat of Patan's Kumari. The **Western Stupa** comes alive one day a year when the great chariot procession of Raato Machhendranath (see box, p.120) gets started just to the south.

Northwest to Patan Dhoka

The northwestern quarter of old Patan is a jumble of *bahal* – the lane leading from the Golden Temple west takes you past quite a few. Another few blocks to the north is **Patan Dhoka**, a small bazaar area and bus park surrounding an unremarkable city gate.

South and east of the square

South of Durbar Square, you essentially have two choices. The southbound street passes the **Machhendranath temple** and other sights en route to the Lagankhel bus park, while the continuation of Mangal Bazaar leads southeast to **Mahabuddha**. The area directly east of Durbar Square, though short on specific sights, is an active **artisans' quarter**.

Bishwakarma Mandir and Ibaha Bahi

One of Patan's most charming streets runs parallel to Mangal Bazaar, a block to the south. This is an area of metalworkers and sellers of household wares, which perhaps accounts for the **Bishwakarma Mandir**'s facade of hammered gilt-copper and froggy copper lions standing guard. Unfortunately the facade is now unphotographable due to a railing installed to deter thieves. The name Bishwakarma refers both to the god of artisans and members of the blacksmiths caste. Patan's second-oldest monastery, **Ibaha Bahi**, stands one block further to the south. Founded in 1427, the *bahal* was restored with assistance from the Nippon Institute of Technology.

Machhendranath Mandir

Outwardly, Patan's **Machhendranath Mandir** resembles many others: a huge seventeenth-century brick pagoda adorned with beautifully carved, gaudily painted struts and *torana*. It stands in an extra-large compound called Ta Bahal, about 300m south of Durbar Square.

What makes this temple extraordinary is its idol, **Raato Machhendranath** ("Red Machhendranath"), a painted shingle of sandalwood which, for several weeks beginning in late April, is the object of one of Nepal's most extraordinary festivals (see box, p.120). Older than his white counterpart in Kathmandu, Raato Machhendranath is a god of many guises. To Newars he is Bunga Dyo, the androgynous god of agricultural prosperity and a manifestation of the great cult figure Karunamaya. To Buddhists of other ethnic groups he is Avalok-iteshwara or Lokeshwar, the *bodhisattva* of compassion. As Machhendranath, the progenitor of the *nath* (lord) cult, he's the spirit of a seventh-century Hindu guru who once taught the Shah kings' beloved saint, Gorakhnath. Legend has it that Gorakhnath once visited the valley and, offended that he wasn't accorded a full reception, caused a drought by rounding up all the rain-bringing snakes. The locals sent a posse to Assam to fetch Machhendranath, who came to their rescue in the form of a bee. Wishing to pay tribute to his guru, Gorakhnath had to release the snakes, whereupon the rains returned and Machhendranath came to be revered as a rain-maker.

Minnath and on to the Southern Stupa

Set behind a *hiti* (sunken bathing tank) across the street from the Machhen-dranath Mandir entrance, the smaller sixteenth-century **Minnath Mandir** is dedicated to another mythologized Indian saint. South of here, the main road widens to include a busy open-air bazaar and the chaotic **Lagankhel** minibus park. It's not really worth travelling another kilometre south to visit the grassy **Southern Stupa**, though if you're going to the Patan Industrial Estate (see the "Shopping" section), you'll pass by it.

Raato Machhendranath's big ride

The Kathmandu Valley's oldest, longest and most exciting festival, the **Machhendra-nath Raath Jaatra** begins the day after the full moon of Baisaakh (April/May), when priests ritually bathe Raato Machhendranath's sandalwood idol in Patan's Lagankhel square. Moved back to its temple at Ta Bahal, the idol spends the next ten days undergoing the life-cycle rituals of Buddhist Newars. Meanwhile, just south of the Western Stupa at Pulchowk, Machhendranath's chariot (*raath*) – more like a mobile temple – is assembled and its sixty-foot-high tower of poles and vegetation constructed. A smaller chariot to carry Minnath is also built.

The idols are eventually installed in their chariots and the great **procession** begins. Scores of men heave at the ropes; Machhendranath's unwieldy vehicle rocks, teeters and suddenly lurches forward, its spire swaying and grazing buildings as it passes. The crowd roars, people leap out of the way, and the chariot comes to a stubborn stop until the pullers regroup and try to budge it again. Separately, local children pull Minnath's chariot. It goes on like this, in stages, for four or more weeks, until the chariots reach Jawalakhel Chowk, a journey of about 4km.

At Jawalakhel, the stage is set for the dramatic **Bhoto Jaatra**. A huge crowd begins assembling before noon on a day ordained by the astrologers – usually the fourth day after the chariots' arrival at the chowk. At around 4 or 5pm, Patan's Kumari is carried in by palanquin. Local VIPs climb aboard Machhendranath's chariot and take turns holding aloft the god's magical jewelled vest. Since the procession culminates during the showery pre-monsoon, Machhendranath usually obliges with rain: bring an umbrella.

Machhendranath's idol is then carried to Bungmati, 6km to the south (see p.176) where it is welcomed home with great fanfare; the cult of Raato Machhendranath being believed to have originated in Bungmati, accounting for the god's Newari name, Bunga Dyo ("God of Bunga"). The idol spends the summer months in Bungmati before being transported back to Ta Bahal, but once every twelve years it's kept in Bungmati all winter and the chariot procession begins and ends there. That will next happen in 2015.

Southeast to Mahabuddha

Mangal Bazaar gets quieter and better as you walk east of Durbar Square. After 300m it reaches **Sundhara**, a sunken bathing area with four golden (*sun*) spouts (*dhara*). East of here is **Dupat**, whose close, dark alleys are brimming with atmosphere. To the south is **Uku Bahal**, Patan's main metalsmithing area and home of the famed Mahabuddha temple.

Nicknamed "Temple of a Thousand Buddhas", **Mahabuddha** is constructed entirely of terracotta tiles – each one bearing the Buddha's image. This remarkable Rococo structure mimics the famous Mahabodhi Temple of Bodhgaya, India, where its builder, an enthusiastic seventeenth-century Patan architect, had previously meditated for several years. Although the likeness is only approximate, the temple introduced the Indian *shikra* form to Nepal, which to this day remains prevalent around Patan. Reduced to rubble during the 1934 earthquake, it was put back together again and the smaller temple beside it was built from the spare parts. The structure is so tightly hemmed-in by residences you'll need to go up into one of the surrounding metal handicrafts sellers' buildings to get a decent view.

The name of this neighbourhood, Uku (or Oku) Bahal, comes from the now-defunct Buddhist monastery at the next intersection to the south, which also goes by the handle **Rudravarna Mahabihar** ("Red Monastery"). Though it's undergone a renovation, it's believed to be Patan's oldest – the wooden struts on the north side of the courtyard date from the thirteenth century.

Jawalakhel and around

The name **Jawalakhel** (pronounced *Jowl*-akel) applies to a wide area around the Jawalakhel Chowk roundabout and south from there down to the ring road. The southern part – often referred to as **Ekantakuna** ("Lonely Corner") – is Patan's Tibetan ghetto.

Ekantakuna

The former Tibetan refugee camp at **Ekantakuna** is arguably the best place in the valley to watch carpets being made (see p.133). There's no big temple here, only one small monastery, and – except for the carpet-weaving centre and nearby carpet shops – not a lot of commercial vitality.

Tibetans started pouring into the Kathmandu Valley immediately after the Chinese annexation of Tibet and the flight of the Dalai Lama in 1959. By 1960 their plight prompted the International Red Cross to set up a transit camp at Jawalakhel, later assigned to the Swiss Red Cross, which in turn formed the Swiss Association for Technical Assistance (SATA) to help Tibetans on a long-term basis. SATA encouraged carpet-making and other cottage industries, and by 1964 the Jawalakhel "transit camp" was a registered company. A generation and a half on, Jawalakhel's Tibetans are prospering from the booming **carpet industry**, and many have left the centre to establish businesses and live closer to Buddhist holy places.

The zoo

Nepal's only **zoo** (daily 10am–5pm; Rs150) – often rendered "jew" by Nepali-speakers – occupies a former Rana estate just southwest of Jawalakhel Chowk. It's probably the best attraction for young children in the Kathmandu Valley: besides looking at the animals, they can take elephant and pedalo rides. **Food** is available and there are picnic spots. Most of the species kept here are indigenous to Nepal, (rhinos, elephants, deer, monkeys) but conditions aren't great. For background on Nepal's wildlife, see Contexts.

Eating

Scores of **restaurants** and **cafés** line the lanes of Kathmandu's tourist quarters, and more spring up after each monsoon. While a few carry on in a funky 1970s style, a growing number have gone upmarket, emulating French bistros, Italian trattorias and English pubs.

While **Tibetan**, **Chinese** and **Indian** dishes have long been widespread, **Japanese**, **Thai** and **Korean** restaurants are increasingly common – and generally of a very high standard. You can also find a few more unusual choices – it's possible to eat, for example, Russian, Middle Eastern, Australian and Bhutanese food. There are also innumerable restaurants catering to travellers with all-purpose "**continental**" menus; they're all pretty samey, featuring "buff" steaks, variable attempts at pasta and pizza, and a few pseudo-Mexican and Greek dishes. Bakeries producing the ever-popular **pastries and cakes** are similarly ubiquitous.

The best news of all is that fine **Nepali** and **Newari** food – not just *daal bhaat*, but also special dishes traditionally only served in homes or during festivals – are increasingly available in tourist restaurants as well as in local eateries, and are slowly taking their place among the other distinguished South Asian cuisines.

Not many tourist restaurants are all-**vegetarian**, but quite a few of the Indian ones are and every Nepali restaurant does *daal bhaat* (which is vegetarian unless you specifically request meat). Almost every restaurant serves at least a few meatless dishes, and even Tibetan places usually do vegetable *momo*.

It's all too easy to overemphasize food in Kathmandu, however – it can also be the greatest peril of staying here. More travellers get **sick** in the capital than anywhere else, more often than not as a result of placing too much trust in the hygiene of tourist restaurants. Indeed, Nepali restaurants are arguably safer, since chefs know what they're doing when they prepare Nepali food. The places listed here are generally reliable, but heed the words of caution in Basics (p.49).

Prices are reasonable and, unless you're on a really tight budget, have at least one special meal at one of the posh restaurants to get the full maharaja experience. Phone numbers are given for restaurants where it's advisable to book ahead for dinner.

For picnic ingredients and other **provisions**, stores in Thamel sell just about everything you could want – chocolate, bread, cheese, biscuits, fruit, beer and so

Nepali, Newari and Tibetan restaurants in Kathmandu and Patan

A good way to experience a culture is through its cuisine. Here's a quick index of restaurants that specialize in the **ethnic cuisines** of Nepal. For more information on a given restaurant, go to the section indicated after its name.

Nepali and Newari

Several of the restaurants recommended here are geared towards tour groups and consequently are on the expensive side, but worth it. At the other extreme are the many dirt-cheap menuless *bhojanalaya* (diners) and *bhatti* (taverns), which advertise themselves with a curtain hung over the entrance and are impossible to recommend by name. Most are Newari equivalents of a greasy spoon, but the best ones are fantastic. Ask around for suggestions, or try your luck in the area north of Asan or north and west of Patan's Durbar Square. Many tourist restaurants advertise "special Nepali meals", which usually turn out to be rather ordinary *daal bhaat*. There are loads of inexpensive *sekuwa* joints on Putali Sadak Road, north of Singha Durbar, frequented by a predominantly male crowd from late afternoon. They're great with a beer. See p.38 for a rundown of Nepali and Newari dishes.

Bhanchha Ghar, Kamaladi see p.125

Bhumi, Lazimpath see p.125

Bhojan Griha, Dilli Bazaar see p.125

Festive Fare, Jhochhe and New Road see p.125

Krishnarpan, Battisputali see p.124

Nepalese Kitchen, Chhetrapati, South Thamel see p.124

Thakali Bhanchha, corner of Thamel Northwest and Zed Street see p.123

Thamel House, Thamel Northeast see p.124

Woh Nacha, Patan Durbar Square see p.126

Tibetan

Tibetan restaurants offer some of the cheapest tourist food in Kathmandu, and you pay even less at the many *momo* kitchens throughout the old city – just look for the big aluminium steamers, or listen for the roar of the propane cookers. Again, see Basics for descriptions of popular Tibetan dishes.

Dechenling, North of Trivedi Marg, North Thamel see p.123

Tashi Deleg, Central Thamel see p.123

Yak, Kwa Bahal, South Thamel see p.125

on. For a wider selection of imported goods, go to the the Bluebird supermarket in Lazimpath, or Namaste Supermarket or Saleways in Patan.

Thamel

As with lodgings, **Thamel** has all the newest, trendiest and most professional budget restaurants. Though many have become so stylish, they've priced themselves out of the budget category, sampling them is one of the great pleasures of staying in the district.

Unless otherwise noted, the restaurants below are marked on the Thamel map (see p.84).

Central Thamel

Just Juice & Shakes (aka JJ's) Thamel Northwest. Grab one of the handful of stools and order a fresh juice, shake or smoothie (all around Rs50): there are some unusual combos, like carrot and papaya, plus breakfast items.

K-Too! Thamel. An offshoot of *Kilroys*, with a pub atmosphere, sandwiches, burgers and steaks (including a chateaubriand), live sport on the TV, board games and good beers. Mains Rs250–700.

La Dolce Vita Thamel. The pizzas and pastas are pretty close to the mark (though the tiramisu has rum in it) and the red and white checked table clothes and Italian posters help to give it a trattoria look. Mains Rs250–400.

New Orleans Thamel Northwest. One of the few Thamel restaurants expats still visit, *New Orleans* is set in the courtyard of a Newari house and has a tasty menu (from Indian to Cajun) and often live jazz. It rents out apartments, and has another branch in Patan. Mains around Rs300–600.

OR2K Thamel. Perch on cushions, enjoy the chilled, candle-lit vibe, swap stories with the next table and tuck into generous portions of falafel, hummus and other Middle Eastern treats. Rs250 for a big main meal.

Pilgrim's Feed 'n Read Thamel Northwest, behind the main Pilgrim's Book House. This soothing garden café, lulled by tabla and sitar music, has good south Indian vegetarian options and is perfect for idling away a few hours with the paper or a good book. Mains around Rs250.

Pumpernickel Bakery Thamel. Long-running, always-busy café with a garden out back and quality baked goods, which are probably worth the few extra rupees they charge. Cakes Rs75–150 per slice.

Roadhouse J.P. School Rd. Draws an older crowd with play-it-safe, well-prepared dishes like wood-oven pizzas, lasagne, tiramisu and Baskin Robbins ice cream. The goat's cheese salad is a highlight, and there's another branch in Patan. Mains Rs300–500.

Tashi Deleg Thamel. One of Thamel's best budget eateries, with Mexican, Italian and continental

staples and better Tibetan food like *rhichossi* (*momo* soup). Staff are friendly without being sycophantic. Mains Rs85–150.

Third Eye and Yin Yang J.P. School Rd. Two neighbouring restaurants under the same management: the former features mainly North Indian cuisine, while the latter specialises in Thai food (the seafood stands out). Mains Rs300–700 at both.

North Thamel

B.K.'s Place Thamel North. Open-air snack bar serving what they – and more importantly many others – claim to be Kathmandu's best "finger-chips" (fries). Less than Rs100.

Comfort Zone Thamel Northwest. Although it sounds like a massage parlour, *Comfort Zone* is actually a modish roof terrace restaurant-bar, specialising in Korean BBQ (try the spicy pork) and frozen cocktails. Mains Rs250 upwards.

Dechenling North of Trivedi Marg. Unique in Kathmandu, *Dechenling* serves dishes like *kewa dhatsi* (a fiery Bhutanese potato and cheese curry) and *shabrel* (Tibetan meatballs) in a pleasant garden with colonial-style cane chairs. Mains Rs250–400.

Himalayan Java Tridevi Marg. Hip US-style coffee house, with Nepali and organic options, all manner of syrups and toppings, cookies and brownies. Ideal for brunch or a mid-afternoon refresher. Coffee less than Rs100.

Korean Kitchen North of Tridevi Marg. Sit cross-legged at one of three low tables at this family-run place and enjoy authentic Korean cuisine: go for a chicken, pork, fish or beef "lunchbox", also available for take-out. "Lunchboxes" Rs200–250.

Rum Doodle Thamel North. Signed paper "footprints" of Everest summiteers are tacked up on the wall of this famous, long-running restaurant-bar, which offers pizzas, steaks and chicken in a basket. Mains Rs300–450.

Thakali Bhanchha corner of Thamel Northwest and Zed St. A mainly local crowd comes to this unpretentious Nepali-Tibetan restaurant, which has dishes of the Thakali people of the Annapurna

Five-star dining

If you can't afford to stay in one of Kathmandu's five-star hotels, the next best thing is to have dinner in one: for not much more than the cost of a meal at a good Thamel restaurant, you'll have an experience unavailable back home at almost any price. The best of the **hotel restaurants** offer sumptuous food, unusual specialities, opulent decor, over-the-top service and music and/or dance performances. For peace of mind, it's worth booking and dressing up a bit if you plan to visit these restaurants, though neither is essential.

The *Yak & Yeti's* (☏01/424 8999) **Chimney** was founded by Boris Lissanevitch, the legendary Russian adventurer who opened Kathmandu's first hotel in the 1950s, and preserves his memory with dishes like chicken Kiev and baked Alaska. At the *Soaltee Crowne Plaza* (☏01/427 3999), once the palace of Prince Basundhara, **Kakori** self-consciously apes the style and cuisine of the Nawabs of Lucknow in North India. At *Hotel de l'Annapurna's* (☏01/422 1711) **Ghar-e-Kebab** the kitchen is partially open, so you can watch the chefs prepare your North Indian meal first-hand. *Dwarika's* (☏01/447 9488) goes the whole hog with **Krishnarpan**: the tables are made of antique latticework, and the excellent Nepali food (some meals run to 22 courses) is served on traditional tableware. Finally, the *Everest Hotel's* (☏01/478 0100) **Far Pavilions** serves Mughal food with fine views of the city from its seventh-floor windows. Expect to pay around Rs900 upwards for a meal at any of these.

region, bargain set meals and a *sekuwa* joint on the roof. Set meals Rs95–145.

Thamel House Thamel Northeast. Exemplary Nepali and Newari food – including unusual items like wild boar – served in the covered patio garden of an evocative old townhouse. Mains Rs250 upwards; huge thalis Rs550–650.

South Thamel

Anatolia Chhetrapati. Drawing a Muslim crowd from across Kathmandu, this halal restaurant specialises in sizzling kebabs from India, Turkey and China. Just try to block out the sickly pink walls. Mains Rs225–400.

Chikusa Jyatha Thamel. Tiny café, popular with French-speakers, both from Nepal and abroad, serving proper coffee, lassis (including green tea flavour), economical breakfasts (around Rs150) with thick wedges of toast and Japanese set meals (around Rs220). Closes at 2pm on Sun.

Café Mitra Thamel South. Seductive restaurant in a quaint old house, with exposed beams, smartly laid tables and steeply priced mains like grilled mackerel. Don't miss the perfectly-risen chocolate souffle. Mains Rs400–900.

Delice de France J.P. School Road. Refined second-floor restaurant decked out with black and white photos and curious triangular-backed seats. It has French (and some Nepali) dishes – think blue cheese crepes, chicken liver terrine and tarte tartin. Mains Rs400–750.

Everest Steak House Chhetrapati. A regular stop-off for returning trekkers, with steaks in a range of

sauces: from the traditional (pepper) to the exotic (Hawaiian). Mains Rs300–500.

Fire and Ice Tridevi Marg. With a name inspired by a Robert Frost poem, *Fire and Ice* has the best thinnish crust pizzas in town, as well as risottos and ice cream. Mains Rs300–400.

Galleria Café J.P. School Rd. Just below *Delice de France*, this suave café has a stripped-back feel, Illy coffee, sandwiches, salads and cakes, as well as, sadly, a cloying playlist of 80s ballads. Sandwiches around Rs200.

Helena's J.P. School Rd. One of Thamel's oldest establishments, with great views from its sun-trap of a roof terrace, although the menu holds no surprises and service is slow. Mains Rs300–400.

Kilroy's of Kathmandu Jyatha Thamel. Run by a highly credentialled (and self-promoting) Irish chef, with a smart dining area, kitsch garden, slightly overbearing staff and a predominantly European and Indian menu. The desserts, especially the light-as-air bread and butter pudding, are the highlights. Mains Rs300–700.

Nepalese Kitchen Chhetrapati. A shaded, plant-filled courtyard restaurant with a good line in thali-style Nepali food and breakfast items. Thalis Rs185.

Shree Lal House of Vegetarian Thamel South. Excellent meat-free Indian food, including many vegan options, at this first-floor restaurant, which has faux wrought-iron chairs and marble tables. Mains Rs100–150.

Weizen Bakery J.P. School Rd. Cheaper, but not quite as good as the *Pumpernickel*, *Weizen* has

pineapple pastries, bagels, brown rolls, brownies and much more. Pastries from Rs60.
Yak Kwa Bahal. Join the Buddhist monks who come to this dimly-lit eatery for traditional Tibetan fare, such as *guma* (sausages) and the four-person *gyakok* (a brass container of meat, vegetables, tofu and vermicelli), which you can wash down with hot tungba beer. Mains Rs60–90.

Jhochhe (Freak Street) and New Road

Jhochhe is noticeably cheaper than Thamel, but has a smaller and less interesting selection of restaurants. Nearby, just off **New Road**, is a good Indian establishment. Unless otherwise noted, see the Jhochhe map (p.86) for locations.

Cosmopolitan Jhochhe. Score a window seat and gaze out over the square from this cramped, smoky joint, haunted by the ghosts of travellers past. Low-cost breakfasts and mains like moussaka and stroganoff are on offer. Mains from Rs150.
Festive Fare Corner of Jhochhe and Ganga Path (with another branch at Makhan Tol – see the Durbar Square map). The food is nothing special at this Seventies concrete monolith, but the views from the rooftop tables are superb. Mains from Rs250.
Nandan Off New Rd (see map, p.102). You may have to queue for a table at lunchtime, but this vegetarian restaurant, patronized by Kathmandu's Indian residents, is worth the wait. Go for a thali and finish up with a to-die-for *ras malai*. Mains Rs200–300.

Organic World and Fair Future Jhochhe. A recent addition to Freak St, and perhaps a sign of things to come, with unusual offerings such as goat's cheese sandwiches, lemon grass tea and various "prebiotic" concoctions. Grab a stool or straw cushion and watch the world go by. Sandwiches and snacks around Rs100.
Paradise Jhochhe. A venerable Freak St institution, though perhaps more popular than it deserves, serving decent vegetarian food. Mains around Rs100.
Snowman Jhochhe. Operating continuously since 1968, this is the only original Freak St pie shop still going, and it's got a kind of cool that doesn't go out of fashion. The apple crumble and chocolate cakes are great, but the atmosphere's the real attraction. Cakes Rs50–60 per slice.

Kantipath, Durbar Marg, Lazimpath and beyond

Durbar Marg is famous for its fine restaurants, especially Nepali and Indian ones, while **Lazimpath** has a growing selection of better-value places, popular with foreign residents and Kathmandu's middle classes. **Kantipath** has less choice, but still a couple of places worth checking out. Of the many restaurants scattered around the city **east and north** of these streets, those mentioned are of the upscale variety.

Unless otherwise noted, see the Central Kathmandu map (p.76) for locations.

1905 Kantipath ☏01/422 5272 (see map, p.88). Cross a bridge over a sunken lily pond to reach this beautiful colonial-style building (the menu tells you about its interesting history). Dishes are predominantly Asian (including a few from Burma), though you can also get a top Philly cheese steak. Bizarrely, there's a bowling alley next door. Mains Rs450–825.
Bhanchha Ghar Kamaladi ☏01/422 5172 (see map, p.88). Nepali nouvelle cuisine, featuring delicacies such as wild mushroom curry and buckwheat chapatis, served in a beautifully converted Newari house. Nightly culture show. Mains Rs450 upwards.
Bhojan Griha Dilli Bazaar ☏01/441 1603. The "house of food", a fabulous 150-year-old restored Rana priest's mansion, provides a culture show with dinner: while the Nepali cuisine is unexceptional, the dance and music, from across the country, is entertaining. Mains Rs500 upwards.

Bhumi Lazimpath. A pub area near the entrance, filled with posters of Liverpool footballers and boasting an extensive drinks menu, gives way to a stylish, contemporary Nepali-Newari restaurant with Mithila artwork. Mains Rs100–250.
Chez Caroline Baber Mahal Revisited, off Airport Rd ☏01/426 3070. Classy French restaurant with terrace seating and a patisserie. The menu is generally high quality, and suitably pricey, though there are some less expensive lunch options. Mains Rs500–1200.
Dudh Sagar Kantipath (see map, p.88). Unpretentious, bustling canteen serving speedy South Indian dosas and other vegetarian dishes, as well as toothsome sweets. Meals less than Rs100.
Imago-Dei East of the Royal Palace. An airy, modern cafe, with leather sofas, attached art gallery and appealing sandwiches and wraps, such as a meatball sub. The desserts – peanut butter

brownies and baked cheesecake among them – are equally inviting. Sandwiches from Rs200.

Kaiser Café Garden of Dreams ☏01/442 5340. Run by *Dwarika's*, this tranquil place has seating in a romantic, vaguely Edwardian pavilion; all white pillars and arches. The menu ranges from coffee and sandwiches to delicious main meals like prawn kebabs. Mains Rs500 upwards.

Kotetsu Lazimpath. Widely considered to be the best Japanese restaurant in town; if you manage to get a seat at the counter of this little place, you could find yourself eating next to the Japanese ambassador, a regular visitor. Mains Rs400 upwards.

Koto Durbar Marg ☏01/226025 (see map, p.88). Above Hot Breads, this lauded Japanese restaurant, with plain tiled floors and wooden tables, has its focus firmly on the food: the teriyaki, onigiri (rice balls cooked in seaweed), tempura and sushi all hit the spot. Mains Rs140–450.

Mike's Breakfast Naksal (see map, p.76). The eponymous founder sadly passed away in 2008, but his restaurant is still going strong, and remains the place to beat for vast, spot-on US breakfasts like *huevos rancheros* and waffles. Friday is pizza night. The attached Indigo Gallery is also well worth a look. Breakfasts Rs280–430.

Moti Mahal Durbar Marg (see map, p.88). Ignore the location right next to a choked roundabout and concentrate on the authentic, reasonably-priced Indian food: the tandoori items and thalis, in particular, compare favourably with the more expensive Indian restaurants nearby. Mains Rs100–200.

Ringmo Lazimpath. Still going strong after more than 36 years, this is an excellent place for a budget breakfast and superlative, thick US-style buckwheat pancakes (try the apple, or chocolate and banana varieties). The joint next door does great samosas. Breakfast from around Rs100.

Patan

Several restaurants and cafés cluster around **Patan Durbar Square** targeting day-trippers. They're often packed at lunchtime, but at night you'll feel like you've got them to yourself. The restaurants in the **west side** of Patan are patronized mainly by expats and well-heeled locals. Alongside those listed below, reliable Thamel restaurants *New Orleans* and *Roadhouse* both have branches in Patan; the former has a lovely garden and regular live jazz performances.

Unless otherwise noted, see the Patan Durbar Square map (p.115) for locations of places in the "Durbar Square and around" listings; see the main Patan map (p.113) for places in the "Patan: west side" listings.

Durbar Square and around

Café du Temple North side of Durbar Square. The sunny roof terrace has great views, and the piped Nepali classical music aids relaxation. The Indian food is pretty good too. Mains from Rs150.

Woh Nacha Immediately west of the Krishna Mandir (there's no sign). Foreign customers inevitably attract interest at this dark, smoke-stained *woh* eatery, but you get an unbeatable insight into traditional local life. Meals around Rs50.

Patan west side

Bakery Café Jawalakhel Chowk. One of a chain of semi-fast-food restaurants serving burgers, pizza, hot dogs and so on. Employs hearing-impaired staff (just point at the menu). Snacks less than Rs100.

Café de Patan Café de Patan Guest House, Mangal Bazaar. A traveller's favourite for more than 25 years, with courtyard and roof-terrace seating. It has well-prepared Nepali thalis (around Rs300) and refreshing lassis.

Dhokaima Café Patan Dhoka. Beyond a less-than-promising entrance close to the

bus stand, *Dhokaima* proves a sophisticated place: sit at a glass table and have a cocktail or glass of organic wine and something from the inviting menu – dishes include shrimp scampi and shitake mushrooms on garlic toast. Ask about the regular art and cultural events in the adjoining building. Mains from around Rs250.

La' Soon Pulchowk. Probably the only place in Kathmandu you can get West African peanut soup, *La' Soon* has a restful tree-filled garden and draws a crowd from the nearby NGO offices. Mains Rs250–350.

Red Dingo Jawalakhel Chowk. Chic, contemporary Australian restaurant with excellent service, nice touches like free mineral water and hearty tucker such as meat pie, chips and salad. Just ask them to turn off the Robbie Williams. Mains around Rs300.

Sing-ma North of Jawalakhel Chowk. Cheerful Chinese joint with speedy service, a few Malaysian options like beef *rendang* alongside more numerous Cantonese dishes, and yummy cheesecakes. Closed on Sat. Mains Rs125–200.

Nightlife and entertainment

In October 2008 the government declared all restaurants, bars and clubs must close by 11pm in Kathmandu, and 10pm in Patan, claiming many were "illegal" and encouraged prostitution. As a result of this generally unpopular decision, the capital's nightlife scene is pretty subdued. However, while most venues adhere to the law, some stay open later, and it seems probable the regulation will be relaxed as time passes.

Even if you're not able to have a really late night, there's plenty to keep you entertained: what follows is an overview of **permanent attractions**, from bars and clubs to cultural shows and cinemas – check the notice boards to find out about special events in high season.

Bars and nightclubs

As with the tourist restaurants, Thamel's **bars and nightclubs** are more like a Nepali's imagined idea of what they must be like than the real thing, but on the whole they're fine for meeting, mixing and prolonging an otherwise short evening. The Thamel bars attract mainly backpackers, and a few young Nepali men hoping to hook up with Western women – some can be pretty seedy. A handful of fancier **nightclubs** elsewhere in the city attract a more diverse clientele; they're often cheesy and typically have a cover charge. Keep an eye out when you're heading home after 10pm, as **muggings** do sometimes occur.

Unless otherwise noted, see the Thamel map (p.84) for locations.

Bars and nightclubs

Celtic Manang Thamel Northwest. Underlit joint with orange, patterned walls, cushions to lounge on, regular video nights and an Irish owner who ensures you can get a can of Guinness.

Full Moon Thamel Northwest. A cool little place with bamboo walls, low seats and an eclectic range of music.

Jazz Upstairs Lazimpath (see map, p.90). On a narrow lane, diagonally opposite the French embassy, this welcoming bar is not to be missed: it has a great vibe, live jazz performances (Wed and Sat), top *momos* and a mixed crowd, which has on occasion included Sting.

J-Bar Tridevi Marg. Behind *Himalayan Java*, J-Bar – all white and chrome décor – is a step above the typical Thamel venue. Two things to watch out for: the dancefloor can be slippery and the barman often sets the bar top alight to impress guests.

Moksh Patan (see map, p.113). The garden and roof terrace play host to quality bands every Tues and Fri evening, drawing a healthy sprinkling of expats.

Platinum Club Hotel Yak & Yeti (see map, p.88). Often stages parties and DJ sets, though entry fees can be steep (around Rs700, usually with a free drink). In the hotel's lobby, there are regular salsa classes and dances (also try the *Latin Quarter* bar, near Kamaladi).

Sam's Bar Thamel Northwest. A mix of travellers and locals attend this lively, welcoming place, which has a reggae night on Sat, with a more diverse playlist than the standard Bob Marley classics.

Tamas J.P. School Rd. The white lounge chairs, fabric drapes and translucent bar ooze style, while drinks such as a guava and mint martini show a great deal more imagination than the norm. It's popular with well-heeled Nepalis, and there are plans to add a spa.

Via Via Café Saat Ghumti. With sister outposts as far away as Zanzibar and Buenos Aires, and specialising in raksi cocktails, this lively bar may encourage you to take part in the Friday open mic night, or dance to Afro-Latin beats on Saturdays.

Culture shows

Music and dance are essential parts of Nepali life, and perhaps nowhere more so than in Kathmandu, where neighbourhood festivals, parades and weddings are an almost daily occurrence. In other regions, you'll encounter markedly

Kathmandu's festivals

Your chances of coinciding with a **festival** while in Kathmandu are good, since the capital spends about a month out of every year partying. Those listed here are just the main events; there are many others centred around local temples and neighbourhoods. See p.42 for dates and longer descriptions of the major festivals.

Magh (Jan–Feb)
Basanta Panchami The spring festival is marked by a VIP ceremony in Durbar Square on the fifth day after the full moon. Children celebrate Saraswati Puja on the same day at Swayambhu.

Phaagun (Feb–March)
Losar Tibetan New Year, observed at Swayambhu on the full moon of February, but more significantly at Boudha (see p.159).

Shiva Raatri "Shiva's Night" is celebrated with bonfires in Kathmandu on the new moon of Phaagun, but the most interesting observances are at Pashupatinath (see p.153).

Phaagun Purnima (Holi) Youths bombard each other and passers-by with coloured powder and water. The festival lasts a week, but peaks on the day of the full moon.

Chait (March–April)
Chait Dasain On the morning of the eighth day after the new moon, the army's top-ranking officers gather at the Kot compound, at the northwestern end of Durbar Square, for the beheading of dozens of buffalo and goats and to troop their regimental colours.

Seto Machhendranath Jaatra A flamboyant chariot procession in which the white idol of Machhendranath is placed in a towering chariot and pulled from Jamal to an area south of Jhochhe in at least three daily stages. The festival starts on Chait Dasain.

Ghora Jaatra Equestrian and gymnastics displays, plus military demonstrations at the Tudikhel on the afternoon before the full moon.

Baisaakh (April–May)
Nawa Barsa On Nepali New Year (April 13 or 14), there are parades in Kathmandu, but Bhaktapur's festivities are more exciting (see p.181).

Raato Machhendranath Jaatra An amazing, uniquely Newari extravaganza in which an immense chariot is pulled through old Patan over a period of several weeks (see box, p.120).

different styles of music and dance, and while it's more fun to see these performances in their native context, it might be worth checking out a **culture show** before you leave the capital to get a sampler of Nepal's folk and performing arts.

Several Thamel restaurants host free folk music performances, and most of the deluxe hotels do pricey dinner shows. You can catch the unusual "kumari dance", as well as classical Nepali music, at *Kathmandu Kitchen* on Jamal. Infrequent cultural evenings are held at the Royal Nepal Academy, off Kamaladi, and other venues such as the Patan Museum. Alternatively try either of the following.

Hotel Vajra Bijeshwari ℡01/427 1695, ⓦwww .hotelvajra.com. The *Vajra's* resident ensemble does a superb classical Nepali dance, music and drama programme. Private dance, vocal and instrumental instruction is also available.

New Himalchuli Cultural Group Nursery Marg in Lazimpath ℡01/441 5280, ⓔhimalchuli@enet .com.np. Nightly folk performances in the high season.

Buddha Jayanti The anniversary of the Buddha's birth, enlightenment and death, celebrated on the morning of the full moon at Swayambhu: thousands come to do *puja*, and priests dressed as the *panchabuddha* perform ritual dances.

Saaun (July–Aug)
Janai Purnima The annual changing of the sacred thread worn by high-caste Hindu men (and of temporary wrist bands that may be worn by men and women of any caste), on the day of the full moon, at Patan's Kumbeshwar Mandir and other temples.

Ghanta Karna Demon effigies are burned throughout the city on the fourteenth day after the full moon of Saaun.

Gaai Jaatra Held the day after the full moon, the Cow Festival is marked by processions through the old city, led by garlanded boys dressed as cows. A good place to watch is in front of the former Royal Palace's entrance in Durbar Square.

Bhadau (Aug–Sept)
Krishna Astami (Krishna Jayanti) Krishna's birthday, in which thousands of women queue for *puja* at Patan's Krishna Mandir.

Tij A three-day Women's Festival, starting on the third day after the full moon: the most public aspects take place at Pashupatinath (see p.153), but women may be seen singing and dancing anywhere.

Indra Jaatra A wild week of chariot processions and masked-dance performances held around the full moon of Bhadau (see box, p.94).

Asoj (Sept–Oct)
Dasain A mammoth ten-day festival celebrated in most parts of Nepal, concluding on the full moon of Asoj. In Kathmandu, mass sacrifices are held at the Kot courtyard near Durbar Square on the ninth day, Durga Puja, with *tikas* bestowed on all and sundry on the last day.

Kaattik (Oct–Nov)
Tihaar The Festival of Lights, celebrated with masses of oil lamps throughout the city and five days of special observances. Lakshmi Puja, falling on the full moon of Kaattik, is the highlight. Newars celebrate the fourth day as their new year.

Ghazal and "dance"

As with so many other cultural imports from south of the border, Kathmandu has been quick to embrace **ghazal** (an Indian style of popular music). Troupes tend to work the better Indian restaurants, where they provide dinnertime accompaniment from a platform over to the side somewhere. A typical ensemble consists of an amplified tabla, guitar, harmonium and/or synthesizer. The singer, who gets top billing, croons in a plaintive voice. Love is the theme, and the sentimental lyrics – typically in Urdu or Hindi, but often in Nepali – draw on a long tradition going back to the great Persian poets.

To catch a *ghazal* act, try *Ghar-e-Kebab* or *Moti Mahal* in Durbar Marg, or *Raj Gharana* at the top of the Kathmandu Plaza Building on the corner of Lal Durbar and Kamaladi.

Another curious trend in Kathmandu is the popularity of so-called **dance** bars, which involve (generally) fully-clothed women dancing under lights on a makeshift stage to loud Nepali pop music. The dancing is more traditional than suggestive, but the customers are almost always men and some arrange for private services after hours.

Theatre, cinema and other performances

Outside the tourist arena, scheduled arts performances are relatively rare. However, the *Hotel Vajra's* resident **theatre** group (☎01/427 1695) stages frequent performances, often in English, including adaptations of everything from Shakespeare to Hindu epics.

Several **cinemas** show the latest Bollywood blockbusters (and the odd Hollywood hit). Try the Bishwa Jyoti on Jamal or the Ranjana north of New Road.

The Russian Cultural Center (☎01/441 5453, ⓦwww.russiancultureinnepal.org), Kamal Pokhari, screens films from across South Asia, and hosts several film festivals, including the Kathmandu International Mountain Film Festival in December (in even years). The Film South Asian festival (ⓦwww.himalassociation.org/fsa), in October, in odd years, is also worth looking out for. The Alliance Française (☎01/424 1163, ⓦwww.alliancefrancaise.org.np), in Thapathali, and the Goethe Institute (☎01/425 0871, ⓦwww.goethe-kathmandu.com.np), in Khichapokhari, show films in their respective languages. The British Council (☎01/441 0789, ⓦwww.britishcouncil.org/nepal) in Lainchaur has (less frequent) screenings and events.

Some restaurants and bars show pirated **DVDs**; try *Lazimpat Gallery Café*, near *Ringmo*, or *Celtic Manang*. In the high season, the *Kathmandu Guest House* hosts **screenings, slide shows** and **talks**. The Indigo Gallery (☎01/442 4303, ⓔIndigo@wlink.com.np) at *Mike's Breakfast* also does impromptu slide shows.

Casinos

A night at one of Kathmandu's **casinos** (ⓦwww.casinosnepal.com) is a weirdly memorable experience. They're frequented mainly by avid Indians and bored Westerners staying at the affiliated deluxe hotels (some Nepalis also play, even though they're legally barred from entering). Admission is free, but you generally have to purchase a minimum amount of chips. *Soaltee Crowne Plaza, Hotel de l'Annapurna, Yak & Yeti* and *Everest Hotel* - among others - all have casinos.

Shopping

Kathmandu and Patan are obvious places to do some serious **shopping**. The sheer volume of stuff on sale in Kathmandu, and the fierce competition among sellers, makes it possible to get some very good deals, especially if you're adept at bargaining. Many items sold in Kathmandu are actually made in Patan however, so shopping there will enable you to watch pieces being made and (maybe) get a lower price.

Thamel offers Nepal's largest gathering of shops selling handicrafts and other tourist paraphernalia. **Durbar Marg** specializes in high-end crafts, antiques, jewellery and fashions. Other more modest handicraft shopping areas include **Jhochhe**; the area north of **Patan Durbar Square**; and the Tibetan-influenced **Ekantakuna** (Jawalakhel) section of Patan. The busy boulevards of **Kupondol** and **Lazimpath** boast several designer clothing boutiques and nonprofit outlets selling Nepali-styled home furnishings and contemporary crafts.

If you want to shop where Nepalis do, check out the **old city** around **Asan** and **Indrachowk**, **New Road** and the lanes north and south of it, Patan's

Mangal Bazaar and the street running south to Lagankhel, and the so-called **Hong Kong Bazaar**, a canopied flea market encircling the Bhrikuti Mandap exhibition ground. Kathmandu **Durbar Square's night market** is also a good place for a bargain.

By contrast, **Baber Mahal Revisited** is an upmarket shopping complex set in a beautifully restored former Rana Prime Minister's palace. The shops are Aladdin's caves of fine and unusual crafts, though prices are relatively high. Many taxi drivers are unfamiliar with the complex, and will assume you mean Baber Mahal, a ministry building off the Airport Road, just to the south. Fortunately, it's only a short walk around.

The **Patan Industrial Estate**, just beyond the Southern Stupa, has a dozen or so handicraft factory showrooms, where you can learn about Nepali handicrafts and the processes used to make them, as well as make purchases. The estate is within walking distance of old Patan, but along a dreadful corridor, so consider taking a taxi. Most shops here are open daily except Sun 10am–6pm.

Bargain everywhere, even when prices are supposedly "fixed". There's no firm guide to what to expect to have knocked off, and the initial price could be anything from ten to one thousand percent over the going rate.

The government is hypervigilant about the export of **antiques** more than one hundred years old. Not being experts, customs officials tend to err on the side of caution and reject any item that looks like it might be old. To avoid difficulties, take any suspect items to the Department of Archaeology on Ram Shah Path and have them tag it as okay for a small fee.

Metal and jewellery

Patan has always been renowned for its metalsmiths, who produce religious (mainly Buddhist) **statues**. Uku Bahal is their traditional neighbourhood, and you'll find dozens of retail outlets-cum-workshops there. Pieces run from crude little statuettes to magnificent large-scale works of art. Simple statuettes, bells, singing bowls, bracelets and other metal items are sold throughout the city.

▲ Buddhist statues for sale in Kathmandu

Khukuri knives are widely sold wherever there are tourists, though you may have problems taking them into your home country. Brass sets of **bagh chal**, Nepal's "tigers and goats" game, are also common.

Gold and silversmiths in the old city (mainly north and west of Indrachowk) produce fine traditional **jewellery**; tourist shops sell cheaper but perhaps more wearable ornaments. **Gem** sellers are grouped mainly at the east end of New Road, but watch out for scams.

Three good jewellers are: Maizan, with branches in *Hotel Ambassador*, *Dwarika's* and *New Orleans* in Patan, who are particularly good at designing personalised items; the less expensive Masala Beads, also in *New Orleans*, as well as Patan and Thamel North; and Millennium Crafts on Thamel Jyatha, which specializes in silverwork.

Wood and paper

Many Nepali carved-**wood** crafts – picture frames based on Newari window designs, statues of deities and animals – are best bought in Bhaktapur (see p.192), although several shops around Patan Durbar Square also deal in these items. For exquisite (and expensive) non-traditional Nepali-style furniture, mirror frames and windows, visit the **Woodcarving Studio** (T974/102 8053, W www .leebirch.com) in Patan, just west and north of the main Ekantakuna intersection, up the hill from the Tibetan area.

Numerous shops in Thamel sell beautiful **paper** products, many made from *lokta*, handmade paper produced from the bark of an indigenous shrub. You can buy colourful **papier-mâché masks** and **puppets** all over the place, but these are produced – and better represented – in Bhaktapur and Thimi (see p.192 & p.195).

Thangka, poubha and other fine art

It's hard to say where to look for **thangka** (or **poubha**, a similar ritual scroll painting in the Newari, rather than Tibetan, style) bargains, as there are so many standard depictions and levels of quality.

A good **thangka** is the product of hundreds – or even thousands – of hours of painstaking work. A cotton canvas is first stretched across a frame and burnished to a smooth surface that will take the finest detail. The design is next drawn or traced in pencil; there is little room for deviation from accepted styles, for a *thangka* is an expression of religious truths, not an opportunity for artistic licence. Large areas of colour are then blocked in, often by an apprentice, and finally the master painter will take over, breathing life into the figure with lining, stippling, facial features, shading and, finally, the eyes of the main figure.

Thangka can be grouped into four main genres. The **Wheel of Life**, perhaps the most common, places life and all its delusions inside a circle held firmly in the clutches of red-faced Yama, god of death. A second standard image is the **Buddha's life story**. Many *thangka* feature tantric **deities**, either benign or menacing; such an image serves as a meditation tool in visualization techniques. **Mandala** (mystical diagrams) are also used in meditation. That's just the tip of the iceberg. A full exposition of *thangka* iconography would fill volumes – ask a dealer or artist to lead you through a few images step by step.

There are many *thangka* shops at the north end of Kathmandu Durbar Square, around Thamel and north of Patan Durbar Square. Some also sell paintings based on traditional Tibetan medical texts, and a few in Patan display *thangka*-influenced naive **landscape paintings** – they're mass-produced for the tourist market, but still make nice souvenirs. Some Kathmandu artists are starting to produce more individualistic works, usually **watercolours**.

Kathmandu also has a growing number of **fine art galleries**, including Indigo Gallery, Naksal (inside *Mike's Breakfast*); Siddhartha Gallery, Baber Mahal Revisited; and Park Gallery, Pulchowk, Patan.

Carpets

The Tibetan-style handwoven **carpet** industry, once a modest income-generator for Tibetan refugees, has evolved into one of Nepal's biggest export earners. Typically Tibetan wool – from sheep bred for their unusually long, high-tensile wool – is blended with foreign (generally New Zealand) processed wool. Once spun into yarn, much of the spinning is still done by hand, producing a distinctive, slightly irregular look. It is then dyed and rolled into balls.

Tibetan-style carpets are produced by the **cut-loop** method, which bears little relation to the process employed by Middle Eastern and Chinese artisans. Rather than tying thousands of individual knots, the weaver loops the yarn in and out of the vertical warp threads and around a horizontally placed rod; when the row is finished, the weaver draws a knife across the loops, freeing the rod.

Once the weaving is finished, the carpets are trimmed to give an even finish, in some cases embossed and then washed, an industrial process which **pollutes local streams** with chemicals linked with birth defects. Most carpets are made-to-order for the export market, with distribution controlled by a small collection of traders. Prices vary widely: at the bottom end expect to pay around $50 per square metre; top-of-the-range carpets can be three times this, or even more. (Many Nepali producers are now also producing Afghan, Middle Eastern and Kashmiri-style carpets, though these are rarely as fine as the originals.)

The easiest place to see carpets being **made** is in the Jawalakhel Handicraft Center (Sun–Fri 9am–6pm, Sat 10am–5pm; ☎01/552 5237, ⓦwww.jhcnepal .com) at the former Tibetan refugee camp in the Ekantakuna section of Patan, Nepal's oldest and most famous carpet-weaving centre. The complex includes a fixed-price sales showroom, where profits benefit elderly and poor Tibetans, and a couple of souvenir shops. Prices are by and large cheaper at many other private shops on the road leading back to Patan.

The carpet industry in Nepal – and throughout Asia – remains plagued by a serious **child-labour** problem. The Nepal Rugmark Foundation (☎01/411 2047, ⓦwww.nepalrugmark.org) is an NGO that operates a certification scheme for responsible carpets producers and outlets.

Other souvenirs and curios

Vendors in Basantapur Square and Thamel flog a vast array of **Tibetan-style curios**, while a few Thamel and Durbar Marg boutiques sell genuine antique Tibetan chests and dressers. Countless shops in the tourist areas carry identical ranges of **Kashmiri**, **Rajasthani** and **Afghan** handicrafts; others sell Nepali **tea**, **incense**, **essential oils**, and relatively inexpensive saffron and other **spices**.

Small shops in Thamel, Chhetrapati and Khichapokhari (south of New Rd) stock Nepali **musical instruments**, while hack minstrels doggedly peddle *sarangi* (traditional fiddles).

Nepali artisans turn out an ever-expanding range of **contemporary crafts** that adapt traditional materials or motifs to foreign tastes. The impetus for many of these innovations has come from a few income-generation projects supported by aid organizations, which operate their own sales outlets (see box, p.134), although many products are now widely imitated.

Amrita Craft on J.P. School Road has a wide range of crafts, gifts and clothes; it wholesales to a number of other shops in Thamel, so prices are keen.

Clothing and fashion

Thamel and Jhochhe are full of shops selling **wool** sweaters, jackets, mittens and socks, which are among Nepal's best bargains. **Cotton** garments are particularly cheap, in both senses of the word, but might be just the ticket for short-term travel needs. Tailors, usually found inside the T-shirt shops, are skilled at machine-**embroidering** designs on clothing.

Pashminas and much cheaper yak wool equivalents are sold everywhere (try the Kwa Bahal end of Thamel, and Navadurga Pashmina and Black Pashmina, both in Thamel), and there are some very good deals to be had. **Topi**, the caps Nepali men wear, are sold around Asan. You'll find **sari material** in New Road and around Indrachowk, and you can have items made to order from shops east of Asan. Wonderfabs, with outlets in Baber Mahal Revisited and on New Road, specializes in quality fabrics and clothes. Other textiles are sold in the nonprofit shops (see box below). **Leather** jackets and bags can be found at Zebra Rose, near the *Radisson* in Lazimpath.

A number of boutiques on Durbar Marg, Lazimpath, Patan and in Baber Mahal Revisited sell **designer fashions** with a Nepali flavour, usually in silk or other natural materials. Tailors can also make **men's suits** to order; ask in fabric shop Linen Club, Durbar Marg, for suggestions.

For more contemporary fashions, try U.F.O, Kumaripati, Patan; the World Trade Centre mall near the National Stadium and the Bluebird mall in Thapathali. Eve, with several branches in Thamel and Le Petit Prince, near *Yin Yang* restaurant, is also worth a look.

Ethical shopping

In many of Kathmandu's shops, only a fraction (often less than five percent) of a shopkeeper's profit on any given item actually finds its way back to the person who produced it in the first place. Meanwhile a growing number of outlets in tourist areas spuriously claim to be fair trade or to support, for example, women's skills development programmes. The following shops, however, genuinely exist to fund charitable causes or sell crafts made by income-generation projects.

Dhankuta Sisters Kupondol. Representing village women in the eastern hills, selling mainly *dhaka* clothes.

Dhukuti Kupondol, north of *Hotel Himalaya*. One of Nepal's biggest nonprofit shops, run by a village and low-income project marketing association, stocking a wide variety of cotton items, sweaters, dolls, copper vessels, basketry and leather.

Kumbeshwar Technical School north of Kumbeshwar Mandir, Patan. One of the few places to buy one-hundred-percent Tibetan-wool carpets, plus other woollen garments and wooden products made by the nonprofit school's students.

Mahaguthi branches in Kupondol and Lazimpath. This supports a home for destitute women, and sells a good selection of textiles, crafts, jewellery and home furnishings.

Maheela Thamel Northwest. Small shop in aid of the Women's Foundation of Nepal, which helps women get a fair wage for their weaving work, selling *dhaka* clothing and crafts.

Sana Hastakala branches in Kupondol and Lazimpath. Good selection and display of woollens, *dhaka*, pashmina, dresses, ceramics, paper, Mithila art, toys and general gift items. Supports projects mainly run by and for women producers.

Other bargains

With close trading links to the Far East, Kathmandu has relatively cheap prices on consumer gadgets. **Cameras**, **MP3 players** and other **electronic devices** can be found on New Road, though the selection is patchy and models may be a year or two out of date. You'll pay more for equipment with an international warranty. **Sunglasses** and **glasses frames** are also a good deal here. Charges are very reasonable for **prescription lenses**, too, but leave plenty of time for your order to be filled in case of mistakes.

Books and maps

Kathmandu has one of Asia's greatest concentrations of English-language **bookshops**. Almost all will buy back books for half the price you originally paid.

Barnes and Noble J.P. School Rd. Not the range of the US chain it pinched the name from, but still pretty good.

Book House Nepal Chhetrapati. Good selection of fiction, both new and used, and friendly staff.

Mandala Book Point Kantipath. Comprehensive range, particularly good for French and German language texts.

The Map Shop J.P. School Rd and Jyatha Thamel. An outlet for Nepa/Himalayan Map House, with an extensive selection of their products.

Pilgrim's Book House Two branches in Thamel and one In Kupondol, Patan. Extensive reference sections on all things Nepali, Indian and Tibetan including religion, mysticism, health, travel, language and development. There are also maps, postcards, paper, CDs, DVDs and incense.

United Books J.P. School Rd. Strong on fiction, current affairs, travel writing and second-hand books.

Music and DVDs

Many shops in Thamel sell cheap pirated rock/pop **CDs**, as well as East–West mood music, contemporary releases and folk compilations from Nepal, Tibet and India. Some will also download them to your MP3 player. Countless shops and stalls throughout the city sell Nepali folk and pop, and Indian pop and movie soundtracks. Prices at these stalls will be less than half what the tourist places charge. Pirated **DVDs** of Western movies and TV shows are similarly common. See p.206 for more on Nepali music.

Outdoor equipment

You can buy or rent almost any sort of **outdoor equipment** in Kathmandu. Most of the **new gear** is locally produced and low quality. You'll also find some legitimate name-brand stuff made in the Far East, but it's not necessarily up to export standards. Go to the tailors in Jyatha if you want something made or copied in nylon.

A few shops specialize in quality **secondhand** stuff – generally expedition cast-offs and stuff sold by other trekkers: climbing hardware, gas stoves, water bottles, glacier glasses, plastic boots, authentic name-brand clothing, packs and so on. Except for the climbing hardware, it will cost at least as much as in your home country.

For genuine branded trekking gear, head to The North Face shop on Tridevi Marg, near *Himalayan Java*. Gear can also be **rented**; try Shona's in Jyatha Thamel.

For a full trekking equipment checklist, see p.355.

Trekking, rafting and other activities

Most people book organized outdoor activities like trekking, rafting and mountain-biking in Kathmandu because that's where most of the operators and agents are.

If you want to do, say, a mix of rafting and trekking, you don't necessarily have to book through two different outfits: most can organize **multiactivity adventures** in partnership with other specialists. Consolidation has been a recent trend, and a few companies – such as Adventure Centre Asia (which includes Ultimate Descents Nepal and Himalayan Mountain Bikes), Equator Expeditions, Himalayan Encounters and Ultimate Rivers – now offer one-stop shopping for a variety of outdoor experiences.

You should be aware that the confusing similarity between two prominent companies is not accidental. Ultimate Descents Nepal and its sister operation, Borderland Resort, pioneered slickly marketed multiactivity packages, and had the field pretty much to themselves until a nasty management bust-up a few years ago. Since then, one of the former partners has continued to run Ultimate Descents Nepal and Borderland, while the other has founded two competing operations, Ultimate Rivers and The Last Resort. Thoroughly confusing matters, Ultimate Rivers markets trips overseas under the name Ultimate Descents.

Trekking companies

For a full discussion of the pros and cons of trekking with a group versus doing it independently, see Chapter Seven. As explained there, individual budget trekking companies can't be recommended because the quality of their service can vary so much from trip to trip. The following are more expensive outfits which have reputations for high standards.

Asian Trekking Bhagwan Bahal ℡01/442 4249, ⊛www.astrek.com/asiantrekking. Established company offering a wide range of treks on both standard and more remote routes. It also has a climbing wall outside its office.

Highlander Thamel Northwest ℡01/470 0563, ⊛www.highlandernepal.com. Another well-respected operator, Highlander offers off-the-beaten-track treks in Nepal, Tibet, Bhutan and India.

Nature Trail Thamel Northwest ℡01/470 1925, ⊛www.naturetrailnepal.com. Experienced agency, used by VSO staff, organising tours and treks throughout Nepal.

River operators

Because of the extra safety considerations (see Chapter Eight), it's even riskier to recommend budget **river operators**. The ones listed here are reputable and more expensive. All raft the most popular rivers (scheduled departures in season) and can organize trips on other rivers on demand.

Trekking red tape in Kathmandu

Trekking permits are now only required for a few sensitive areas, and are obtainable only through a trekking agency (for more detail see Chapter Seven). However, if your trek passes through any of Nepal's national parks or conservation areas, it's advisable to buy your **entrance ticket** before departure. In the Tourist Service Centre, in Bhrikuti Mandap, are counters for the National Trust for Nature Conservation (winter daily 9am–4pm; summer Sun–Fri 9am–3pm), where you can get permits for the Annapurna and Manaslu regions, and the Department of National Parks and Wildlife (Sun–Fri 9am–2pm), for essentially everywhere else, as well as an office providing **Trekkers' Information Management System** (TIMS) cards.

Equator, Ultimate Descents and Ultimate Rivers have **kayaks** available on their trips. These companies, among others, also run **kayak schools** on the Seti River, near Pokhara (see p.247), and can hire out equipment.

Equator Expeditions Thamel Northwest ☎01/470 0854, ⓦwww.equatorexpeditionsnepal.com. Covers all the major rivers, provides courses for rafting and kayak guides, and offers treks. Affiliated with *Sukute Beach Adventure Resort*.
Himalayan Encounters Thamel Northwest, in the forecourt of the *Kathmandu Guest House* ☎01/470 0426, ⓦwww.himalayanencounters .com. Nepal's longest-serving rafting operator, with experienced guides.

The Last Resort/Ultimate Rivers Thamel Northwest ☎01/470 0525, ⓦwww.thelastresort .com.np. A spinoff from Ultimate Descents, with a wide range of rafting, kayaking and canyoning trips, plus one of the world's highest bungy jumps.
Ultimate Descents Nepal Thamel Northwest ☎01/470 1295, ⓦwww.udnepal.com. One of Nepal's biggest river operators, with good equipment, safety record and guides. Affiliated with *Borderland Resort* and Himalayan Mountain Bikes.

Mountain bike tours

The following companies operate **mountain bike tours**. Advice on tours, independent biking, equipment and routes is given in Chapter Nine. For information on renting bikes in Kathmandu, see p.81.

Dawn Till Dusk Thamel Northwest, in the forecourt of the *Kathmandu Guest House* ☎01/470 0286, ⓦwww.nepalbiking.com. A seasoned operator offering short and long trips, including customized off-road itineraries. Good bikes and repair facilities.
Himalayan Mountain Bikes Just off J.P. School Rd ☎01/4212860, ⓦwww.bikeasia.info. Nepal's original mountain bike operator, with the most highly

developed range of itineraries: from day-trips in the Kathmandu Valley to extended tours throughout the region. Quality equipment and repair shop.
Nepal Mountain Bike Tours Thamel Northwest, opposite The Last Resort office ☎01/470 1701, ⓦwww.bikehimalayas.com. Popular company, which organises the annual Nepal Mountain Bike Race and runs tours, including the classic Nagarkot–Dhulikhel–Namobuddha circuit.

Wildlife package tours

Although most of the **budget lodges** near Chitwan and Bardia national parks are represented by agents in Kathmandu, their packages are not recommended as Nepal's major wildlife parks are easily accessible by public transport. Also, their packages are more expensive than doing it yourself (a straightforward process) and many are rather rushed. See the Chitwan and Bardia sections (p.269 & p.302) for full details on doing it yourself.

For **luxury jungle lodges** and **tented camps**, you do need to book ahead. See the relevant listings for Chitwan National Park (p.277), Bardia National Park (p.306), Sukla Phanta Wildlife Reserve (p.312) and Koshi Tappu Wildlife Reserve (p.329).

Other outdoor activities

The Last Resort (☎01/470 0525, ⓦwww.thelastresort.com.np) offers **bungy jumps** off a 160-metre-high suspension bridge over the Bhote Koshi, a three-hour drive northeast of Kathmandu near the Tibet border. Packages, including transportation and food, start at €65.

Both The Last Resort and the nearby Borderland Resort (☎01/470 1295, ⓦwww.udnepal.com) also run **canyoning** programmes from around €60.

Balloon Sunrise Nepal (☎01/443 1078) offers hot-air balloon flights (around $200) from points in the Kathmandu Valley.

Sports and recreation

The National Stadium, at the southern end of Kantipath, hosts frequent **football** (soccer) matches, and is also the headquarters for various martial arts clubs. **Cricket** is played at the Institute of Engineering campus in Patan and other venues. The *Soaltee*, *l'Annapurna* and *Yak & Yeti* hotels have **tennis** courts, open to nonresidents for a fee. For **golf**, there's the Royal Nepal Golf Club (℡01/447 2836; temporary memberships available), a nine-hole course near the airport, where hazards include monkeys from nearby Pashupatinath. For an international-standard eighteen-hole course, head to Gokarna (p.163).

The *Hotel de l'Annapurna* and *Yak & Yeti* both allow nonguests to use their **pools** for a modest charge. The *Royal Hana Garden* (℡01/441 6200), a Japanese restaurant near the French embassy in Lazimpath, offers **hot-spring baths** in a green secluded grotto (Rs340, including soap, shampoo, sarong and green tea). The food's not bad either.

Meditation, yoga and astrology

Not surprisingly, Kathmandu is an important centre for **spiritual pursuits**. This section sketches out the general possibilities, concentrating on established outfits that cater specifically for Westerners; a scan through the posters in the popular lodges and restaurants will turn up others. See also the organizations listed in the next section on alternative therapies, as there's a lot of overlap between these disciplines. You'll find brief introductions to meditation and yoga on p.56.

Meditation

The **Himalayan Buddhist Meditation Centre** (℡01/441 0402, ⓦwww .fpmt-hbmc.org) in Thamel, north of Tridevi Marg, provides free hour-long meditation sessions (Mon–Fri 8.30am & 5.30pm), as well as more advanced courses, and instruction in Buddhist ritual dance and Reiki. HBMC is affiliated with Kopan Monastery, north of Boudha (p.162), and another monastery in Pokhara (p.248).

Nepal Vipassana Centre (℡01/425 0581, ⓦwww.dhamma.org) runs ten-day residential courses at its Budhanilkantha centre. These aren't for the frivolous: daily meditation begins at 4.30am, and silence is kept for the duration. To register or find out more, visit the centre's Kathmandu office (Sun–Fri 10am–5pm) in the courtyard of Jyoti Bhawan, behind Nabil Bank on Kantipath. All courses are funded by donations.

For those interested in residential study of Tibetan Buddhism, the **Buddha Dharma Center** (℡01/428 2744), located on a high point south of Swayambhu, offers instruction under the direction of Lopon Tsechu Rinpoche. Many more opportunities exist in Boudha.

Kathmandu supports a thriving Osho industry which includes a travel agency (Osho World Travel in Thamel; ℡01/470 0073), a bi-monthly magazine and three meditation centres. The **Asheesh Osho Meditation Centre** (℡01/427 1385) in Tahachal conducts one-hour dynamic meditation sessions every morning; these are open to all and the fee is a donation. It has a second centre in Lazimpath (℡01/441 4502). The third venue, **Osho Tapoban Forest Retreat Centre** (℡01/435 3762, ⓦwww.tapoban.com), located in a beautiful setting north of Nagarjun Ban, hosts occasional retreats as well as daily meditations and discourses, and can provide accommodation (❸–❺) and meals.

Yoga

Patanjali Yoga Center (T01/427 8437, Wwww.yogakathmandu.com), in Tahachal, next to *Shrestha Guest House*, offers daily drop-in classes, private tuition and five-day intensive courses in pure astanga yoga. Contact the centre for information on residential study and its teacher training programme in Pokhara. Patanjali staff also lead daily introductory yoga sessions at the **Healing Hands Center** (see "Massage", p.140).

The Yoga Studio (T01/441 7900, Echrissieg@wlink.com.np) teaches hatha yoga in the Iyengar method. The resident instructors teach a regular schedule of classes, as well as occasional longer courses. The studio is in Tangal, about a ten-minute bike ride east of Thamel, but it's hard to find – call ahead for directions. It also offers beginner classes at Patan's *Summit Hotel*.

Of the many outfits in Thamel, the **Holistic Yoga Ashrama** (T01/470 1334, Wwww.holisticyoga.com.np), off J.P. School Road on the lane leading to *Pheasant Lodge*, is one that gets positive reviews; it also offers meditation, massage and Reiki sessions. The **Kamma Healing Centre** (T01/425 6618) in Babar Mahal Revisited is another good choice.

Astrology

It's best not to single out individual **astrologers** in the Kathmandu area, partly because few of them speak English, but mostly because they all have their own flocks to look after and it wouldn't be fair to rain hordes of foreign horoscope-seekers down on them. Try offering your innkeeper or a guide a commission to take you to their astrologer and translate for you – you'll get a fascinating glimpse into an extremely important but behind-the-scenes aspect of Newari life (see p.439).

To have a **horoscope** prepared you'll need to provide the exact time and place of birth (if you don't know the time, the astrologer may be able to improvise by reading your palm). It'll then take up to a week to produce an annual chart, longer for a full span-of-life chart. In a separate session, the astrologer will interpret it for you. The fee for the entire service may run to Rs1000. If nothing else, you'll come away with a beautiful and unique work of art, hand-calligraphed and painted on a parchment scroll.

Alternative therapies

Many of what we in the West call **alternative therapies** are, of course, established practice in Nepal. The full range of remedies is quite a bit greater than what you see in this section, which focuses on what's accessible to the average visitor. See p.57 for a bit of background on these practices.

Ayurvedic medicine

For private consultations, contact **Dr R.R. Koirala** at the Ayurveda Health House (Sun–Fri 9am-6pm; T01/435 8761, Wwww.ayurveda.com.np) a group practice in Dhapsi, near *Hotel Shahanshah*, or **Dr Mana Bajracharya** (T01/422 3960), a world-famous practioner based behind the Bir Hospital in central Kathmandu.

To fill ayurvedic prescriptions, visit the **Gorkha Ayurved Company**, south of Chhetrapati Chowk, or if your Nepali is up to it, any of the ayurvedic *pharmas* lining the lane running west from the Nardevi Mandir.

Tibetan medicine

Kunphen Tibetan Medical Clinic (℡01/425 1920; Mon–Fri 10am–5pm), north of Chhetrapati Chowk, is basically a front office for a Tibetan medicine company, whose products it sells, but its diagnostic services are recommended. **Kailash Medical and Astro Society** (℡01/448 4869), with outlets in Dhobichaur (the road leading northwest from Chhetrapati Chowk) and Boudha, offers a comparable range of treatments and keeps similar hours. Another good option is **Sechen Clinic** in Boudha (see p.164).

Massage

A few legitimate **masseurs** practise in Thamel and other tourist/expat areas, though they come and go – again, check the notice boards. Also ask to see credentials. A Nepali massage should cost around Rs500 per hour; other types of massage cost more.

A highly-recommended organisation is **Himalayan Healers** (ⓦ www.himalay anhealers.org), based at *Hotel Ambassador* (℡01/441 4432) in Lazimpath, and in several other hotels across Nepal: the organisation trains members of "untouchable" castes in massage and spa techniques. The **Healing Hands Center** near the Russian embassy in Maharajganj (℡985/103 8447, ⓦ www.ancientmassage.com) provides Thai massage, as well as t'ai chi, yoga and meditation sessions. **Sotai** (℡01/554 3045), near the Herman Bakery in Patan, specialises in Japanese body balancing techniques. Many deluxe hotels have their own in-house masseurs.

Most of the "Yoga and Massage" signs around Thamel have been put there by charlatans attracted by the princely sums tourists will pay to have their bodies rubbed. Some offer "special" massages. **Prostitution** isn't always very obvious in places like Thamel, but it happens; some estimates suggest there are as many as five thousand sex workers in Kathmandu. While most prostitutes are women, a significant number are men, often targeting female travellers.

Listings

Airlines, domestic Buddha Air, Hattisar ℡01/443 7025; Gorkha Airlines, Maharajganj ℡01/443 5121; Nepal Airlines (NAC), corner of New Rd and Kantipath ℡01/424 4055 (tourist sales office handles flights to Bharatpur, Jomosom, Lukla, mountain flights and Pokhara; domestic sales office, located down the lane running along the west side of the building, handles all other internal flights); Sita Air, Sinamangal ℡01/448 7110; Yeti Airlines, Thamel Chowk ℡01/421 3012.

Airlines, international Air China, north side of Royal Palace ℡01/444 0650; Air India/Indian Airlines, Hattisar ℡01/441 6721; Biman Bangladesh Airlines, east side of Royal Palace ℡01/443 4740; British Airways, Kamaladi ℡01/422 6611; Cathay Pacific, Kamaladi 01/424 8944; Druk-Air, Durbar Marg ℡01/441 0089; Emirates, north of Kamaladi ℡01/425 2048; Gulf Air, Hattisar ℡01/443 5322; Jet Airways, Hattisar ℡01/422 2121; KLM, Lekhnath Marg ℡01/441 0089; Korean Air, north of Kamaladi ℡01/425 2048;

Nepal Airlines (NAC), corner of Kantipath and New Rd ℡01/424 4055; Pakistan International Airways (PIA), Hattisar ℡01/443 9324; Qantas, Durbar Marg ℡01/422 0245; Qatar Airways, Hattisar ℡01/425 7712; SAS, Kupondol, Patan ℡01/552 4232; Singapore Airlines, Kamaladi ℡01/422 2908; Thai Airways, Durbar Marg ℡01/422 3565.

American Express The local agent is Yeti Travels and Tours, Durbar Marg (Mon–Fri 10am–1pm & 2–5pm). You can receive mail at the office if you can produce an Amex card or traveller's cheques.

Banks and money There are moneychangers all over Thamel, and scattered about Jhochhe, Durbar Marg and Patan Durbar Square; they typically open daily 9am–8pm. Nepal Bank on New Rd has longer opening hours than most other banks (daily 7am–7pm) and offers good exchange rates. Standard Chartered Bank has a convenient branch on Thamel North. There are numerous ATMs in Thamel – all accept foreign cards and several operate 24hr a day – and many more throughout the city.

Communications Most hotels provide internet access for guests; the more expensive ones often have decent business centres with a wider range of equipment, including fax machines and photocopiers. Cyber cafés are easy to find in Thamel and Jhochhe, and virtually every commercial street has one; most charge around Rs60 per hour, Rs20 for printouts. MSN Cyber Café, near Hotel Potala in Thamel, is one of the best, offering quicker than average access, Skype (Rs5 per min), international phone calls, CD/DVD burning, plenty of computers and a generator in case of power cuts. Mobile phone coverage is generally pretty good within the Kathmandu Valley; buying a local sim card (widely available) works out much cheaper than using one from your home country; Mera has the best coverage, NTC is the cheapest. For landline calls, head to one of the many ISD/STD/IDD centres or internet cafés; local calls cost only a few rupees, while international calls start at around Rs50 per minute; Skype calls (typically Rs5 per min) are a much better bet.

Embassies and consulates Australia, Bansbari ☎01/437 1678; Belgium, off Thamel Northeast ☎01/441 3732; Canada, Lazimpath ☎01/441 5193; Denmark, Lazimpath ☎01/441 3010; Finland, Lazimpath ☎01/441 7221; France, Lazimpath ☎01/441 8034; Germany, Gyaneswar ☎01/441 6832; Israel, Lazimpath ☎01/441 1811; Italy, Baluwatar ☎01/441 2280; Japan, Panipokhari ☎01/442 6680; Mexico, Baluwatar ☎01/442 0018; Netherlands, Kupondol Heights, Patan ☎01/552 3444; New Zealand, Dilli Bazaar ☎01/441 2436; Norway, Kupondol Heights, Patan ☎01/554 5307; Poland, Ganabahal ☎01/424 9114; Russia, Baluwatar ☎01/441 2155; South Korea, Tahachal ☎01/427 0172; Spain, Battisputali ☎01/447 0770; Sweden, Khichapokhari ☎01/422 0939; Switzerland, Jawalakhel, Patan ☎01/553 8488; UK, Lainchaur ☎01/441 1590; US, Maharajganj ☎01/400 7200. For India, Tibet (China) and other countries in the region, see "Moving on", p.146.

Emergencies Several organisations provide ambulances (including the Red Cross ☎01/422 8094; Nepal Chamber of Commerce ☎01/423 0213; and Norvic International Hospital ☎01/425 8554), but taking a taxi is generally quicker. See also "Police".

Hospitals, clinics and pharmacies The best Western-standard clinic is CIWEC, near the British Embassy in Lainchaur (daily 24hr for emergencies; clinic hours Mon–Fri 9am–5pm; ☎01/442 4111, ⓦwww.ciwec-clinic.com), which has very proficient Western and Nepali staff, and is a great source of information, though charges are high by Nepali

standards. The Nepal International Clinic (NIC), a block east of the Royal Palace entrance (daily 9am–1pm & 2–5pm; ☎01/443 5357, ⓦwww.nepalinternationalclinic.com), is also good, and a bit cheaper. Several clinics in Thamel offer more hit-or-miss care and can't be recommended. Medicines can be purchased at *pharma* (pharmacies) everywhere, with or without prescription. CIWEC and NIC can refer you to a specialist physician if need be. A number of small private hospitals operate in the valley; two with good reputations among expats and NGO staff are B&B Hospital (☎01/553 1930) in Patan and Norvic International Hospital (☎01/425 8554) in Thapathali. Of the public facilities, Patan Hospital (☎01/552 2295) is reasonably modern, while Bir Hospital (☎01/422 1119) is central but very basic and best avoided. If you're in really bad shape, you'll be sent to Bangkok.

Language courses ITC (☎01/441 4490, ⓦwww.itcnepal.com) off Tridevi Marg, Thamel, provides beginner, refresher and advanced courses. The Kathmandu Institute of Nepali Language on Bhagwan Bahal in Thamel (☎01/443 2652, ⓦwww.ktmnepalilanguage.com) is a good alternative. For long-term study opportunities, see p.59.

Newspapers and magazines Tourist bookshops stock a wide variety of international newspapers and magazines, including *Time*, *Newsweek*, *International Herald Tribune* and *Le Monde Diplomatique*. British papers are harder to find; try the small news stand near the *Fire and Ice* restaurant on Tridevi Marg, Thamel. The local English-language dailies are sold at the main bookstores, supermarkets and from pavement vendors on New Rd.

Police If you're the victim of a crime, first contact the Tourist Police (☎01/422 0818), in the Tourist Service Center in Bhrikuti Mandap, which is supposed to have an English-speaking officer on duty 10am–5pm. They also have officers at the Thamel tourist office (☎01/442 9750) and at booths in Durbar Square and other tourist areas. Outside regular hours, have a Nepali-speaker call ☎01/100. Report thefts to a tourist police officer or the district police headquarters, which in Kathmandu is on the west side of Durbar Square and in Patan at Jawalakhel Chowk. Ask for the Interpol section. The national police HQ and Interpol office is in Naksal.

Post and shipping The GPO (General Post Office) in Kantipath is open Mon–Fri 9am–5pm and has a poste restante section. Letters are filed alphabetically in self-serve pigeonholes; check under both your first and last initial. Bookshops and other stores sell stamps, and will generally (for a small charge) take mail for franking; hotels and many guesthouses will also do this. Shipping agents can take the headache out of sending parcels home: try Atlas de Cargo, Hattisar ☎01/444 5666, ⓦ www .atlascargo.com; or Sharmasons Movers, Kantipath ☎01/424 7907. Air-freight services include DHL, Naya Baneswore ☎01/478 2427, ⓦ www.dhl.com; United Parcel Service, care of local agent Shangri La Tours, Kantipath ☎01/423 2219, ⓦ www.ups .com; and Federal Express, care of Everest De Cargo, Kantipath ☎01/426 9248, ⓦ www.fedex .com. Parcels can also be sent from the Foreign Post Office (Mon–Fri 9am–5pm) next door to the GPO, but although cheaper, the experience is completely exasperating – set aside the whole morning.

Radio and TV Numerous FM radio stations operate in the Kathmandu Valley, with programmes in Nepali and English, including Kantipur FM on 96.1, Sagarmatha 102.4 and FM Kathmandu on 100. Radio Nepal, heard on several medium-wave frequencies, reads English-language news bulletins at 8am and 8pm. The BBC World Service is on 103 FM. Cable TV services carry CNN, BBC World Service, and English-language movie and sports channels, as well as Nepal TV and plenty of Indian programming. Programme schedules are given in the daily papers.

Tours Greenline Tours (☎01/425 7544, ⓦ www .greenline.com.np), Tridevi Marg, runs half- and full-day guided tours of various sites around the Kathmandu Valley from Rs500–1000.

Travel agents Ample Travels, in front of *Hotel Vaishali* in Thamel ☎01/442 3148, ⓦ www .ampletravels.com; Natraj Tours and Travels, in the forecourt of the *Kathmandu Guest House* ☎01/422 2906, ⓦ www.natrajtours.com; President Travel and Tours, Durbar Marg ☎01/422 0245, ⓦ www .president-travels.com; Wayfarers, J.P. School Rd ☎01/426 6010, ⓦ www.wayfarers.com.np.

Visa extensions Apply at the Department of Immigration (Mon–Fri: mid-Nov to mid-Feb 9am–2pm, rest of year 9am–3pm ☎01/422 1996), on a lane off the corner of Airport Road and Ram Shah Path (though there are tentative plans to relocate it over the next couple of years). You should be able to collect your passport later the same day. See p.63 for general information on visa extensions.

Moving on

What follows is a full rundown on buying tickets, arranging transport and trips, and getting visas.

Travel within Nepal

Most people make Kathmandu their base for **travels within Nepal**. The country is so centralized, with Kathmandu its transport hub, that a grand tour easily becomes a series of trips out from the capital and back again. This has its advantages: you can make good use of the tourist bus services and choose from the most reputable trekking, rafting and cycle-touring companies. It's also easy to leave luggage with your guesthouse in Kathmandu, allowing you to travel lightly around the country.

Buses

Various companies operate regular **tourist buses** or minibuses to Pokhara and Sauraha (for Chitwan National Park), and less frequently to Nagarkot and Lumbini. The Pokhara and Chitwan services are worth considering if your destination lies anywhere along the routes to those places. Even though tickets cost as much as double the public bus fare, they're still cheap (Rs250–1500, depending on destination and level of comfort). Some buses are operated by guesthouses, so price and availability may depend on whether you're willing to commit to staying in that establishment. Minibuses cost more because they're a bit faster and more comfortable. Tickets for tourist services are available through any agent (although not every agent will be able to sell tickets for every bus). Most buses depart from Kantipath near Tridevi Marg, usually in the early morning.

   Greenline Tours (☎01/425 7544, ⓦ www.greenline.com.np) runs some of the most comfortable (and expensive) tourist services, with daily departures to

Internal flights from Kathmandu

The following is a list of the most common direct flights from Kathmandu; indirect flights to Dolpa, Jumla and Simikot (via Nepalgunj), Taplejung (via Biratnagar) and Jomosom (via Pokhara) are also available. For a map showing all domestic routes, see p.30. Fares will vary slightly by airline, with Nepal Airlines generally cheaper but far less reliable than the private carriers; the prices below are generally based on Yeti Airlines and Buddha Air tariffs. Note services are subject to cancellation and change, particularly those in the high mountain areas, which sometimes even leave early.

	Frequency	Time	One-way fare (US$)
Bhadrapur	5 daily	45min	156
Bhairahawa	5 daily	35min	120
Bharatpur	4 daily	25min	86
Biratnagar	10–15 daily	40min	125
Dhangadhi	2 daily	1hr 20min	187
Janakpur	4 daily	25min	110
Lamidanda	4 weekly	35min	120
Lukla	up to 19 daily	35min	119
Meghauli	1 daily	30min	109
Mountain flight	up to 16 daily	1hr	166
Nepalgunj	5-6 daily	50min	155
Phaplu	6 weekly	35min	113
Pokhara	16-17 daily	25min	96
Simara	6 daily	15min	80
Tumlingtar	1-2 daily	45min	115

Pokhara ($18) and Sauraha ($15); the service to Lumbini was suspended at the time of writing. Buses depart at 7.30am from Greenline's office on Tridevi Marg, and lunch is included.

Most privately operated **express and night buses** depart from the Naya (New) Bus Park in Gongabu, 3km north of Thamel on the Ring Road. Those serving destinations along the Arniko Highway (such as Dhulikhel, Barhabise, Tatopani and Jiri) leave from the City Bus Park (also known as Purano "Old" Bus Park) on the east side of the Tudikhel. You'd have to be a real do-it-yourselfer to go to the bus park to buy your own ticket – book through an agent, and consider his commission as money well spent. See the box above for approximate frequencies and journey times.

Local buses (including buses to all destinations in the Kathmandu Valley) originate at the City Bus Park, and generally leave when full, so get there early if you want a seat.

Internal flights
Internal flight schedules are seasonal and fairly volatile, so you're better off making bookings through one of the travel agents listed on p.142. Local contact information for airlines is given on p.140. The box above gives details on services to the airstrips that can be reached directly from Kathmandu (others require plane changes and layovers, often overnight). For the most out-of-the-way destinations, your only choice will be Nepal Airlines, the unreliable state-owned carrier.

Note that there's an airport departure tax of Rs170 for domestic flights.

Leaving Nepal

Overland **connections from Nepal** to India and Tibet are well developed. Kathmandu is the usual setting-off point, since it's the only place in Nepal to get Indian visas and join Tibet tours. For other countries you'll almost certainly have to fly: see p.140 & p.142 for details of recommended travel agents and international airline offices. It's worth shopping around, as even supposedly standard airfares may vary from one agent to the next.

Bus services from Kathmandu

Tourist buses

	Frequency (per day)	Time (minimum)
Lumbini	0–1*	9–10hr
Nagarkot	0–1*	2hr 30min
Pokhara	up to 12*	6–7hr
Sauraha/Chitwan	0–3*	4hr 30min–6hr

*Frequencies vary from low to high season, and depending on demand.

Express buses

	Day service		Night service	
	Daily frequency	Time	Daily frequency	Time
Barhabise	every 30min	4–5hr	–	–
Besisahar	7	7–8hr	–	–
Bhairahawa	every 10min	8–9hr	every 30min	10–11hr
Biratnagar	12	12–13hr		
Birgunj	8	8hr	12	12hr
Butwal	every 10min	6–7hr	every 30min	9-10hr
Dhangadhi	–	–	3	15hr
Dhankuta	–	–	1	17hr
Dharan	10	14hr	16	15hr
Dhunche	3	10hr	–	–
Dipayal	–	–	1	22hr
Gorkha	6	4hr	–	–
Hetauda (via Daman)	6	5hr	–	–
Hetauda (via Narayangadh)	every 30min	6hr	–	–
Hile	–	–	1	18hr
Ilam	–	–	1	19hr
Janakpur	3	9hr	3	10hr
Jiri	7	10–12hr	–	–
Kakarbhitta	10	15–16hr	25	15–16hr
Lumbini	4	9–11hr	1	10–11hr
Mahendra Nagar	1	16–17hr	5	16–17hr
Meghauli	7	6–8hr	–	–
Narayangadh	every 20min	4–5hr	–	–
Nepalgunj	4	13hr	16	13hr
Pokhara	27	5–7hr	5	6–7hr
Sauraha (Chitwan)	2	5–6hr	–	–
Tadi Bazaar (Chitwan)	every 20min	5–6hr	–	–
Tansen (Palpa)	1	11–12hr	1	11–12hr
Tatopani	every 30min	4–5hr	–	–
Taulihawa	1	11hr	1	11hr
Trisuli	every 15min	3–4hr	–	–

By air

If you're flying out of Nepal, **reconfirm** your flight at least 72 hours prior to departure or you may lose your seat. You can usually do it by phone (airline contacts are given on p.140). A travel agent will reconfirm for you for a small fee.

When checking in at Tribhuwan Airport (☎01/447 1933), first join the queue to pay your **passenger service charge** (departure tax) – it's an astronomical Rs1695 (Rs1356 if you're flying to a South Asian Area Regional Cooperation, or SAARC, country - India, Pakistan, Bangladesh and Bhutan).

Overland to India

If you're travelling on to **India**, you can buy a bus ticket to the border and then make your own onward arrangements from there or book a package deal from a ticket agent that takes you all the way to your first Indian destination.

The first way is cheaper, more reliable and usually no more difficult. Seven **border crossings** between Nepal and India are open to foreigners. The most popular are Sonauli and Birgunj, served by day buses from Kathmandu. Other border crossings can be reached by night buses, but unless you're in a big hurry you'll probably want to stop off en route. See the relevant sections in Chapters Five and Six for details on the various border crossings. **Indian Railways tickets** (🌐www.irctc.co.in) can be booked online, and the e-tickets printed out.

The second way has been known to cause a lot of heartache, especially where reserved train tickets are involved. Given that a typical **bus–train package** to India involves three different tickets and as many as six companies or agents, the chances of something going wrong are high.

If you need the assurance of an advance booking, be sure to make arrangements at least a week ahead of time to allow for delays and mistakes, and if the agent tells you your ticket is being held at the border, demand your money back. Be particularly careful when booking first-class sleepers, as there's a racket in replacing them with second-class sleepers or first-class seats. Never surrender your receipt to anyone – without it you've got no proof of what you paid for.

There is also a daily **direct bus** to Delhi via Sonauli (at least 36hr; $50), but this is a truly horrendous journey. To organise any of these packages, try **travel agents** Wayfarers (☎01/426 6010, 🌐www.wayfarers.com.np) or Shikhar Nepal Tours and Travels (☎01/424 1669), both on J.P. School Road in Thamel.

The Indian visa two-step

Applying for an Indian **tourist visa** in Kathmandu is a hugely convoluted processes – allow one week. All costs are given in Nepali rupees.

Apply in person at the **Indian Embassy** (☎01/441 4990), just off Lazimpath. Application hours are Mon–Fri 9.30am–noon (with lots of holidays). Bring your passport, two passport-sized photos and a black pen. Read the signboard instructions first. The time-consuming part is obtaining "clearance" from your home country (so try to do this before you leave home) which is needed before your visa application can even be considered. Just getting your hands on a clearance form, filling it in and paying the fee will kill the better part of a morning. After waiting a week for the clearance, you must come back to pay for the visa, which you'll finally be able to collect later that day. A six-month tourist visa costs Rs3050 for most nationalities, plus Rs300 for the clearance telex or fax.

A fifteen-day **transit visa** (Rs800) takes a day or so, but is not extendable, and its validity starts on the date of issue (not the date you enter India).

Travelling to Tibet

China's official policy is that foreigners wanting to enter **Tibet** from Nepal must join a **tour** - a policy strictly enforced, particularly following the wave of Tibetan protests against Chinese rule in 2008. The Chinese embassy on Hattisar only issues group visas through official tour agents, and doesn't deal with individuals. Visas are for fifteen to twenty days ($45 for most nationalities, $128 for Americans), and officially non-extendable, although in practice it may be possible in Lhasa. If you already have a Chinese visa in your passport, it will be deleted when you are given a Tibetan visa. Regulations are notoriously prone to change, and the Tibetan border has occasionally been closed in the past, so it's important to ask around about the current situation.

The standard eight-day, seven-night tour costs around $900; you travel up by road and fly back, and the price includes the visa, all transport, accommodation (typically a couple of nights in dorm rooms followed by stays in more comfortable mid-range hotels), breakfast and an English-speaking Tibetan guide. Including side trips to Rongbuk (base camp for Everest on the Tibet side) or other sights in central Tibet will bump up the cost further. More adventurous itineraries, such as trekking around holy Mount Kailash or cycling from Lhasa to Nepal, take at least two weeks and start at around $1500. These are fixed-departure prices – small custom groups cost significantly more.

You have to stay with the group for the duration of the tour, but can – in theory – head off on your own afterwards for as long as your visa allows, and then make your own way back to Nepal or head into China; an outgoing ticket from Lhasa is a prerequisite. A one-way flight between Kathmandu and Lhasa costs around $390.

The Tibet **high season** is April to September; monsoon landslides make the overland route more difficult in the latter part of that period, but there's almost always a way to get through. Tours aren't generally run between the middle of December and early March – the roads are usually okay, but the operators don't want to risk groups getting stranded in a snowstorm.

Travelling by road between Kathmandu and Lhasa is an exciting but gruelling four- or five-day trip, so most people fly at least one way. Flying to Lhasa and overlanding back is preferable because it allows you to acclimatize to Lhasa's 3700m elevation before going over the 5000m passes, and flights back can be heavily booked. See p.215 for advice on crossing the border.

Nepali travel agencies subcontract most arrangements in Tibet, and when things go wrong or facilities don't match what was promised, many simply pass the buck. The following agencies have reasonably good reputations to uphold. Some trekking companies and mountain-bike tour operators (see p.136 & p.137) also run trips.

Arniko Travel Baluwatar ☎01/443 9906, ⓦwww
.arnikotravel.com.
Green Hill Tours Thamel Northwest, just north of
the Kathmandu Guest House ☎01/442 2467,
ⓦwww.greenhill-tours.com.

Wayfarers J.P. School Rd ☎01/426 6010, ⓦwww
.wayfarers.com.np.

Visas for other Asian countries

If you're moving on to other parts of Asia, the following embassies and consulates in Kathmandu issue **visas**. Call ahead to find out application times and procedures, as they change from time to time.

Bangladesh Maharajganj, on the ring road
☎01/437 0438.
Myanmar (Burma) Chakupat, Patan ☎01/553 4766.

Pakistan Tangal ☎01/437 4024.
Thailand Bansbari, north of the ring road on the
way to Budhanilkantha ☎01/437 1410.

The Kathmandu Valley

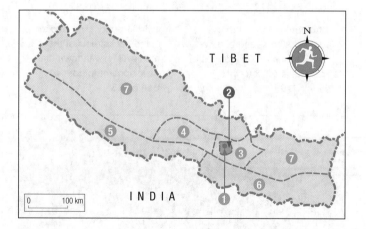

CHAPTER 2 # Highlights

✳ **Pashupatinath** The most sacred of Nepal's Hindu temple complexes is veiled by the smoke of funeral pyres. See p.153

✳ **Boudha** Before dawn and dusk, Buddhist monks, nuns and pilgrims flock to the vast white dome of the stupa. See p.159

✳ **Dakshinkali road** The bloodiest and strangest of Tantric shrines lies at the end of the Valley's most interesting road. See p.172

✳ **Phulchoki** Hike or bike through shrine- and bird-rich forest to the 2762m summit of the "Place of Flowers". See p.179

✳ **Bishanku Narayan** This peaceful Hindu shrine is modestly hidden in a still-rural fold of the Valley. See p.179

✳ **Bhaktapur** The most immaculately preserved of the valley's ancient cities is no museum: Newari life continues here as it has for centuries. See p.181

✳ **Changu Narayan** Exquisitely carved ancient sculptures and a rural, ridgetop setting make this the finest of the Valley's temples. See p.192

✳ **Thimi** Pottery kilns smoke in the backstreets of the medieval Newari town that development forgot. See p.195

▲ Kathmandu Valley

2

The Kathmandu Valley

Within the relentlessly steep terrain of midland Nepal, the **Kathmandu Valley** is something of a geographical freak: a bowl of gently undulating, richly fertile land, lifted up towards the sky like some kind of sacrifice. It may only be some 25km across, but it is densely packed with sacred sites. So much so, in fact, that it was long referred to as "Nepal mandala ", implying that the entire valley acted as a gigantic spiritual diagram, or circle. "The valley consists of as many temples as there are houses", enthused William Kirkpatrick, the first Englishman to reach Kathmandu, and as many idols as there are men."

Although the valley's sacred geography remains largely unchanged, the number of houses – and people – has soared since Kirkpatrick's day. It is the country's economic engine, and pulls young Nepalis in from the hills with an irresistible force. Thanks also to refugees fleeing the Maoist insurrection of the early 2000s, the valley's population has doubled in the last ten or fifteen years, to close on two million. In the 1980s, two-thirds of the valley was farmland: it's now a third. What was once a rural paradise is fast becoming a giant conurbation, with the concrete spreading almost to the valley rim on the north and western sides, and smog obscuring the view of distant mountains on all but the clearest of days.

Despite rampant development, the valley's underlying traditions have proved remarkably resilient. It was long the stage for the quarrels of three rival city-states, Kathmandu, Patan and Bhaktapur, and these divisions remain ingrained in valley society. Kathmandu and Patan have now grown together within the confines of the Ring Road (and are covered together therefore, in Chapter 1), but **Bhaktapur**, on the east side of the Bagmati River, remains proudly separate. Like the other, smaller Newari towns of the valley – **Kirtipur**, **Thimi**, **Sankhu**, **Bungamati** – it preserves a distinctly medieval air, its wood and brick-built houses tightly clustered together around alleyways and temple plazas, and the lives of its residents still bound up with the paddy fields outside the city walls. On the edges of the valley, meanwhile, in the lush side-valleys and on the steep slopes of the rim, the countryside continues to shimmer in an undulating patchwork of paddy fields – brown, golden or brilliant green, depending on the season.

In the heart of the valley, the sheer density of sights is phenomenal. Just beyond the Ring Road beat the twin hearts of Nepali religion: the Shiva temple

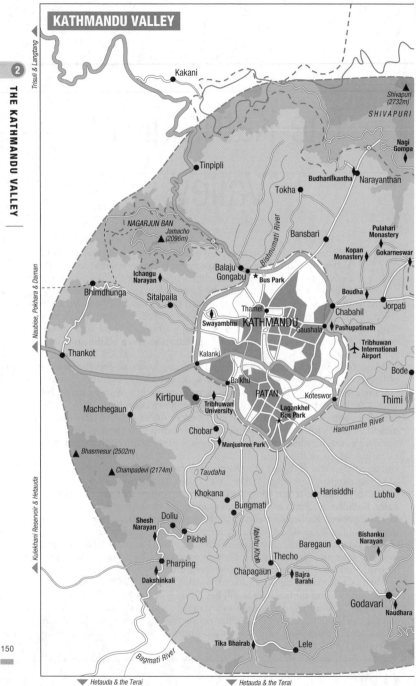

KATHMANDU VALLEY

Trisuli & Langtang

Naubise, Pokhara & Daman

Kulekhani Reservoir & Hetauda

Kakani

Shivapuri (2732m)

SHIVAPURI

Nagi Gompa

Tinpipli

Budhanilkantha
Narayanthan

Tokha

Bishmumati River

NAGARJUN BAN
Jamacho (2096m)

Bansbari

Pulahari Monastery

Kopan Monastery
Gokarneswar

Balaju
Gongabu
★ Bus Park

Bhimdhunga

Ichangu Narayan

Sitalpaila

Boudha

Jorpati

Thamel
KATHMANDU
Swayambhu

Chabahil

Gaushala
Pashupatinath

Thankot

Kalanki

Tribhuwan International Airport

Bode

Balkhu

PATAN

Koteswor

Thimi

Kirtipur

Tribhuwan University

Lagankhel Bus Park ★

Machhegaun

Chobar

Hanumante River

Manjushree Park

Bhasmesur (2502m)

Champadevi (2174m)

O Taudaha

Khokana

Bungmati

Harisiddhi

Lubhu

Shesh Narayan

Dollu

Pikhel

Makhu Khola

Baregaun

Bishanku Narayan

Pharping

Thecho

Dakshinkali

Chapagaun

Bajra Barahi

Godavari

Naudhara

Tika Bhairab

Lele

Bagmati River

▼ Hetauda & the Terai   ▼ Hetauda & the Terai

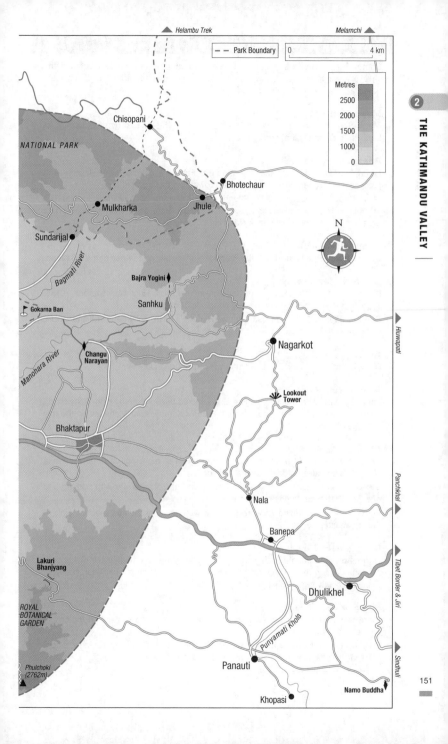

Kathmandu Valley's major festivals

Some of the festivals listed in the Kathmandu chapter are also celebrated in the valley. Again, most are reckoned by the lunar calendar, so check locally for exact dates.

Magh (Jan–Feb)
Magh Sankranti The first day of Magh (Jan 14 or 15), marked by ritual bathing at Patan's Sankhamul Ghat and at Sankhu.

Phaagun (Feb–March)
Losar Tibetan New Year, the new moon of February, celebrated at Boudha with processions, horn-blowing and *tsampa*-throwing on the big third day.
Shiva Raatri On the full moon of Phaagun, the Pashupatinath *mela* (fair) attracts tens of thousands of ganja-smoking pilgrims and holy men, while children everywhere collect money for bonfires on "Shiva's Night".

Chait (March–April)
Balaju Jaatra Ritual bathing at the Balaju Water Garden on the day of the full moon.

Baisaakh (April–May)
Bisket Bhaktapur's celebration of Nepali New Year (April 13 or 14) – see box, p.188. Thimi and Bode have their own idiosyncratic festivities.
Buddha Jayanti The anniversary of the Buddha's birth, enlightenment and death, celebrated at Boudha.

Asaar (June–July)
Dalai Lama's Birthday Observed informally at Boudha (July 6).

Saaun (July–Aug)
Janai Purnima The annual changing of the sacred thread worn by high-caste Hindu men, involving bathing and splashing at Patan's Kumbeshwar Mahadev on the day of the full moon.

Bhadau (Aug–Sept)
Krishna Jayanti Krishna's birthday, marked by an all-night vigil at Patan's Krishna Mandir on the seventh day after the full moon.
Gokarna Aunsi Nepali "Father's Day", observed at Gokarneswar with bathing and offerings on the day of the new moon.
Tij A day of ritual bathing for women on the third day after the new moon, mainly at Pashupatinath.

Kaattik (Oct–Nov)
Haribondhini Ekadashi Bathing and *puja* on the eleventh day after the new moon. The main action takes place at the Vishnu sites of Budhanilkantha, Sesh Narayan, Bishanku Narayan and Changu Narayan.

Mangsir (Nov–Dec)
Indrayani Jaatra Deities are paraded through Kirtipur on palanquins on the day of the new moon.
Bala Chaturdashi All-night vigil at Pashupatinath on the night of the new moon, involving candles and ritual seed-offerings to dead relatives.

and sombre cremation ghats at **Pashupatinath**, the sacred centre of Nepali Hinduism; and the vast, white stupa at **Boudha**, the hub of Tibetan Buddhism's small renaissance. Other Hindu holy places provide moving reminders of the sacred geography that lies behind the brick and concrete: the sleeping Vishnu statues at **Budhanilkantha** and **Balaju**, the sacrificial pit of **Dakshinkali** and the hilltop temple of **Changu Narayan** are the most outstanding.

Hiking and cycling are best in the valley fringe. Trails lead beyond the botanical gardens at **Godavari** to the shrine of **Bishanku Narayan**, and up through rich forests to **Phulchoki**, the highest point on the valley rim. For more woodland solitude and views, hike up **Shivapuri**, Nagarjun Ban's **Jamacho**, or any high point on the valley rim.

All of the places described in this chapter are within day-tripping range of Kathmandu, although in several cases you're urged to stay overnight, perhaps before continuing on to the destinations described in Chapter 3, The Central Hills (see p.197).

Getting around the valley

Taxis are the quickest way to travel, and you can negotiate surprisingly reasonable rates for a return trip – just make sure you specify ample waiting time. **Buses** and microbuses bring you into (very) close contact with real Nepal. Most destinations in the Valley are served by buses running at fifteen-minute intervals or less, so you'll rarely wait long; around the Ring Road, you can jump on and off buses pretty much at will. And buses are cheap: inside the valley, only the longest bus journeys cost more than Rs25 or so. A **bike** or **motorcycle** is best if you're touring around the rural parts of the valley and you want maximum flexibility to stop and go. However, getting out of Kathmandu is not part of the fun, so if you're cycling, consider loading the bike on top of a taxi or bus at least to get beyond the Ring Road.

The Kathmandu city/valley **maps** sold in tourist areas will probably suffice for general sightseeing. Nepa Maps 1:50,000 *Around Kathmandu Valley* is pretty accurate, even if not all the trails on the edge of the valley are adequately marked.

Pashupatinath

Nepal's holiest Hindu pilgrimage site, **PASHUPATINATH** (pronounced Posh-*patty*-nat) is an amazing enclave of temples, statues, pilgrims and half-naked holy men, crammed up against the mouth of a ravine, and straddling a *tirtha*, or sacred crossroads. For all the vibrant sacred activity, it is the sombre sight of public cremation that, for many, proves the most lasting image. The complex lies just beyond the Ring Road, 4km east of Kathmandu. Perhaps more than anywhere else in Nepal, this is a place to modestly cover legs and arms – for women especially. It's also important to respect the privacy of bathers, worshippers and the grieving families at cremation pyres, particularly if taking photographs.

The entire complex overflows with pilgrims from all over the subcontinent during the wild **festival** of Shiva Raatri (held on the full moon of Feb–March), which commemorates Shiva's *tandava* dance of destruction, according to some, or his drinking of blue poison to save the gods (see p.167), according to others. Devout locals also come for special services on full moon days and on the eleventh lunar day (*ekadashi*) after each full and new moon.

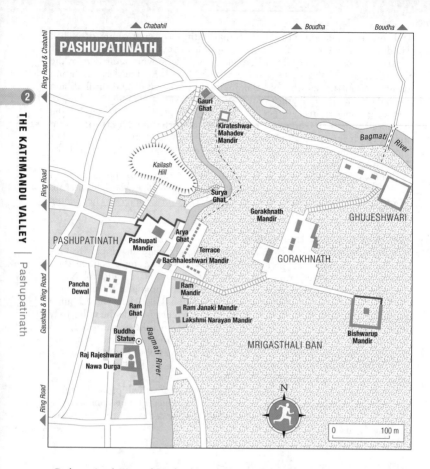

PASHUPATINATH

Gauri
Ghat

Kirateshwar
Mahadev
Mandir

Bagmati River

Kailash
Hill

Surya
Ghat

Gorakhnath
Mandir

GHUJESHWARI

PASHUPATINATH

Pashupati
Mandir

Arya
Ghat

Terrace

Bachhaleshwari Mandir

GORAKHNATH

Pancha
Dewal

Ram
Ghat

Ram
Mandir

Ram Janaki Mandir

Lakshmi Narayan Mandir

MRIGASTHALI BAN

Bishwarup
Mandir

Buddha
Statue

Bagmati River

Raj Rajeshwari
Nawa Durga

N

0   100 m

Pashupatinath is a relatively short **taxi** ride from central Kathmandu (about Rs200). It's a **cyclable** distance (past the Royal Palace, then via Kamal Pokhari to Gaushala, a busy, intersection on the Ring Road close to the main gate) but the traffic is pretty horrendous. Safaa **tempos** originate next to RNAC on Kantipath, while **microbuses** leave from Shahid Gate and Ratna Park; all are numbered 2, and will drop you at Gaushala or Chabahil (see p.163), before continuing on to Boudha. Approaching from the Gaushala crossroads on the Ring Road, take the eastward, downward-sloping road, then turn almost immediately left down a lane that leads through a scrubby park and past flower and trinket stalls for 500m; it arrives one block west of Pancha Dewal.

Visitors are usually approached by **guides**, who sometimes ease the introduction by presenting themselves initially as friendly "students". Some are knowledgeable and friendly, others ill-informed and out for what they can get; most ask to be paid what you think the tour was worth. Otherwise, there are few concessions to Western visitors. For **food**, there's a small snack stall beside the Gorakhnath temple, and various *daal bhaat* and sweet shops in Pashupatinath village and around Gaushala. If you're looking for an authentic **souvenir**, check out the things Nepalis buy: cheap votive icons, statuettes, *linga* replicas, conch shells, *shaligram* (fossil-bearing stones), offertory vessels, *motimala* (pearl necklaces, supposed to be good for the health of the mind) and bangles. The *rudraksha* or "tears of Shiva " necklaces, made from the seeds of the Ultrasum tree, make an interesting buy – you'll see strings of them around the necks of the sadhus.

Pashupati Mandir

The **Pashupati Mandir** is the holy of holies for Nepali Shaivas, followers of Shiva. As in many temples in Nepal, admission is for Hindus only (which in practice means anyone who looks South Asian). From the outside, though, you can glimpse the two familiar symbols of Shiva, found here in gargantuan scale: a two-storey-high *trisul* (trident), and the enormous golden backside of Nandi, Shiva's faithful bull.

The gold–clad pagoda dates from the late seventeenth century, but inscriptions indicate that a temple has stood here since at least the fifth century, and some historians suspect that the origin of the site as a sacred place dates back to the third century BC, and probably to a pre–Hindu animistic cult. Certainly,

Sadhus

Sadhus, the dreadlocked holy men usually seen lurking around Hindu temples, are essentially an Indian phenomenon. However, Nepal, being the setting for many of the amorous and ascetic exploits of sadhus' favourite deity, Shiva, is a favourite stomping ground for them. Sadhus are especially common at Pashupatinath, which is rated as one of the subcontinent's four most important Shaiva pilgrimage sites. During the festival of Shiva Raatri, Pashupatinath hosts a full-scale sadhu convention, with the government laying on free firewood for the festival.

Shaiva sadhus follow Shiva in one of his best-loved and most enigmatic guises: the wild, dishevelled **yogin**, the master of yoga, who sits motionless atop a Himalayan peak for aeons at a time and whose hair is the source of the mighty Ganga (Ganges) river. Traditionally, sadhus live solitary lives, always on the move, subsisting on alms and owning nothing but what they carry. They bear Shiva's emblems: the *trisul* (trident), *damaru* (two-sided drum), a necklace of furrowed *rudraksha* seeds, and perhaps a conch shell for blowing haunting calls across the cosmic ocean. Some smear themselves with ashes, symbolizing Shiva's role as the destroyer, who reduces all things to ash so that creation can begin anew. The trident-shaped *tika* of Shiva is often painted on their foreheads, although they may employ scores of other *tika* patterns, each with its own cult affiliation and symbolism.

Sadhus have a strange role model in Shiva, who is both a mountaintop ascetic and the omnipotent god of the phallus. Some, such as the members of the Gorakhnath cult (which has a strong presence at Pashupatinath), follow the tantric **"left-hand" path**, employing deliberately transgressive practices to free themselves of sensual passions and transcend the illusory physical world. The most notorious of these spiritual exercises is the tying of a heavy stone to the penis, thus destroying the erectile tissues and helping to tame the distractions of sexual desire. **Aghoris**, the most extreme of the left-hand practitioners, are famed for their cult of death, embracing the forbidden in order to destroy it. Cremation grounds like Pashupatinath are effectively their temples, and they are even rumoured to ingest human flesh – all in pursuit of the liberation of the soul.

Like Shiva, sadhus also make liberal use of **intoxicants** as a path to spiritual insight. It was Shiva, in fact, who supposedly discovered the transcendental powers of *ganja* (cannabis), which grows wild throughout hill Nepal. Sadhus usually consume the weed in the form of *bhang* (a liquid preparation) or *charas* (hashish, smoked in a vertical clay pipe known as a chilam). With each toke, the holy man intones "*Bam Shankar*": "I am Shiva".

the benign **Pashupati, Lord of the Animals,** is not Shiva in his ordinary guise. This mild god has been progressively incorporated into Hindu culture, however, and adopted as a kind of national tutelary deity. Nepali schoolchildren are taught that Shiva, to escape his heavenly obligations, assumed the guise of a one-horned stag and fled to the forest here. The other gods pursued him and, laying hold of him, broke off his horn, which was transformed into the powerful Pashupati *linga*. The *linga* was later lost, only to be rediscovered at its present site by a cow who magically began sprinkling the spot with her milk.

Hidden inside, the famed, fourteenth-century **Pashupati linga** displays four carved faces of Shiva, plus a fifth, invisible one on the top (Buddhists claim one of the faces is that of the Buddha). Hindus associate this *linga* with the story of how Shiva transformed his phallus into an infinite pillar of light and challenged Brahma and Vishnu – the other members of the Hindu trinity – to find its ends. Brahma flew heavenward, while Vishnu plumbed the depths of hell. Both were forced to abandon the search, but Brahma falsely boasted of success, only to be caught out by Shiva. Shaivas say that's why Brahma is seldom worshipped, Vishnu gets his fair share, and Shiva is revered above all.

The temple emerged as a hotbed of tantric practices in the eleventh century and remained so for four hundred years, until King Yaksha Malla reined things in by importing conventional Brahman **priests** from South India, although the *bhandaris* (temple assistants) are always Newars born in the immediate area. Wearing the ceremonial orange robes of the Pashupata sect, the priests array the *linga* in brocade silk and bathe it with curd, ghee, honey, sugar and milk. (This arrangement continued undisturbed until 2009, when the Maoist government tried to expel the Indians from the temple; popular outrage prevented them from succeeding.) Hindu pilgrims are expected to distribute offerings to the priests and then make a circuit of the temple and the 365 *shivalinga* and other secondary shrines scattered about the precinct. Most also distribute alms to beggars lined along some of the nearby lanes. If you choose to give, arm yourself with a sufficient stockpile of small change (*saano paisa*), available from nearby vendors.

The ghats and riverbank

Hindus exit the temple via a back way leading down to the west bank of the Bagmati, while tourists approach the river just to the south, where a Rs250 **entry fee** is levied at the gate by the twin footbridges – which afford the best view of the action. On each side, the river is lined with stone embankments and studded with temples – an indication of the site's sanctity. To die and be cremated here is the pinnacle of religious achievement, virtually guaranteeing release from the cycle of rebirths. Wives used to commit *sati* on their husbands' funeral pyres here, and although the practice was outlawed early in the twentieth century, it's still widely believed that husbands and wives who bathe here together will be remarried in the next life.

Bathing is second only to cremation, and considered especially meritorious on full-moon days, on Magh Sankranti (usually Jan 14) and Bala Chaturdashi (late Nov or early Dec), and, for women, during the festival of Tij (late Aug or early Sept). Most days you'll just see children splashing about in the water, seemingly oblivious to the pollution – both ritual and actual.

Arya Ghat

From the bridge, you get the best view of **Arya Ghat**, on the upstream side, the cremation area reserved for the higher castes. The platform furthest upstream (so placed for obvious reasons) was once exclusively dedicated to the royal family; next down, just above the bridge, is the ghat for "VVIPs" – prominent politicians, minor royals and, these days, anyone else who can afford it. After the palace massacre in June 2001 (see p.426), the army had to build a temporary ghat between the two to accommodate all the royal bodies.

Even if there's no cremation in progress, you may see people lying prone on stretchers with their feet in the Bagmati. Many of the buildings around the main temple, including the tall, whitewashed ones overlooking the river, are *dharmsala* (pilgrims' rest houses), set aside here for devout Hindus approaching death. In their final hour, they are laid by the river and given a last drink of the holy water – which probably finishes them off.

Housed in a small stone reliquary beside the royal ghat (which unfortunately means you can't get up close to it) is a famed seventh-century statue of **Virupaksha**, the "Three-Eyed Shiva ", whose Mongoloid features are said to betray the figure's pre-Hindu origins. The image is also associated with Kalki, the tenth and final incarnation of Vishnu, a sort of messiah figure who will bring the present Kali Yuga (Age of Kali) to a close and usher in a new, virtuous cycle of history. The statue is half-submerged in the Bagmati: some claim that the idol is gradually sinking, and its final disappearance will mark the end of the age; others say that Virupaksha will be released from the waters when he has earned enough merit from visiting pilgrims.

Bacchaleshwari Mandir and Ram Ghat

The small pagoda between the bridges is the **Bachhaleshwari Mandir**, dedicated to Shiva's consort Parbati in one of her mother-goddess roles. Cremations are held almost continuously at the next embankment downstream, **Ram Ghat**, which is used by all castes. You're usually allowed access to the terrace immediately behind. It goes without saying that photography is discouraged; you might also want to avoid the smoke from the pyres, with its disquieting barbecue tang.

Towards the southern end of Ram Ghat, a small eleventh-century (some say fifth-century) **Buddha statue** sticks out of the paving. Just beyond, a bumper-sized, tipped-over *linga* ensconced in a round brick battlement is believed to date from the fifth century. The southernmost building shelters two temples in its open courtyard. The oval **Raj Rajeshwari** is named after a powerful, nineteenth-century queen who was forced to commit *sati* after her husband's death, while the gilded pagoda of **Nawa Durga** is devoted to the nine fierce manifestations of the goddess Durga.

The east bank

The east bank of the river has a palpably restful atmosphere thanks to **Mrigasthali Ban**, the woods in which Shiva is supposed to have cavorted as a stag. Deer are

---

Volunteering at Pancha Dewal

Pashupatinath is more than just a place of cremation: it's also a centre for the old, sick and infirm. The massive Pancha Dewal, which stands a few yards short of the main ticket gate behind Ram Ghat (you may glimpse its five Mughal-style cupolas peeking over the walls) is an important **old people's home**. One wing is operated by Mother Teresa's Missionaries of Charity (the government runs the rest), and it's an excellent place to experience a different side of Nepal. The sisters need help each morning changing and cleaning sheets, helping residents to wash, clipping nails, scrubbing pots and so on – humble work, but that's the whole idea. Arrive in the morning if you're interested; look for the sisters (who speak English) in their trademark white saris with blue trim.

still kept here, safe behind a protective fence, ready for the god's enjoyment. Upstream of the twin bridges, the stone terraces are studded with fifteen great **shivalaya** (boxy *linga* shelters). Erected in the mid-nineteenth century by the Ranas and the royal family, they honour women who committed *sati* on the pyres opposite; photo-me sadhus stake out lucrative perches around them.

Above the terraces, it's possible to pick your way northwards along the top of the cliff heading towards the **Kirateshwar Mahadev temple** (see opposite). The path teeters somewhat between the forest fence and the gorge below, but offers good views of the river. You can peer down to **Surya Ghat**, the site of several meditation caves hewn out of the cliffs, and still used by sadhus today.

To the south of the chief stone staircase ascending the hill stands a wide, paved enclosure, which during Shiva Raatri is chock-a-block with sadhus and other spiritual exhibitionists. There are three rather undistinguished, Indian-donated temples which seem a bit out of place in this Nepali, Shaivite power-place: one is dedicated to **Ram**, Vishnu's incarnation as a mortal in the Ramayana epic; another to **Lakshmi Narayan**, in honour of Vishnu (Narayan) and his wealth-bringing wife Lakshmi; and a third to **Ram Janaki**, referring to the family of Ram's beloved wife Sita. The fenced-off forested area to the right belongs to a more indigenous tradition: it is a **cemetery** set aside for Nepal's few "burying" groups, which include Rais and Limbus of the eastern hills.

Gorakhnath

The main stairway up the east bank heads up past troupes of light-fingered and occasionally aggressive monkeys towards the mellow **Gorakhnath Mandir** at the top of the hill. The temple itself, a medium-sized *shikra* structure dedicated to the patron deity of the Shah kings, is less interesting than the adjoining resthouses, home to resident and passing sadhus. Most astonishing still is the sight of scores of **shivalaya** arranged in crumbling rows in the forest, mottled by shade and shafts of sunlight. The place has the romantic, ruined feel of an overgrown cemetery, with broken statuary lying undisturbed and stone inscriptions recording long-forgotten decrees. You could easily mistake the *shivalaya* for tombs, but their iconography – the *trisul*, statues of Nandi and Shiva (always with an erection), the *linga* atop the *yoni* – proclaims them to be Shiva shrines. It would be a fine spot for a picnic if it weren't for the monkeys.

The onion dome rising above the trees to the southeast of Gorakhnath is the **Bishwarup Mandir** (entrance only to Hindus), dedicated to Vishnu in his many-limbed "universal form". Dominating the sanctum is a six-metre-tall statue of Shiva and Parbati in the state of *yab-yum* (sexual union).

Ghujeshwari and back

The **Ghujeshwari** (or Ghuyeshwari) **Mandir** sits at the bottom of the path that continues downhill from Gorakhnath, overlooking a giant sacred fig tree. Here, too, non-Hindus can only peek from outside. The story goes that Shiva's first wife, Sati, offended by some insult, threw herself onto a fire (giving rise to the term *sati*, or *suttee*). Shiva retrieved her corpse and, blinded by grief, flew to and fro across the subcontinent, scattering parts of the body in 51 sacred places. Ghujeshwari is where Sati's vagina fell. As a consequence, the temple here represents the female counterpart to the Pashupati *linga* and is held to be every bit as sacred, its chief focus being a *kalash* (vessel) kept in a sunken pit and containing an "odiferous liquid". Buddhists consider Ghujeshwari to be one of the valley's four mystic Bajra Yoginis – powerful tantric goddesses – and the site to be the seed from which the Swayambhu lotus grew.

Just across the river from Ghujeshwari stands a controversial **sewage treatment centre**, the construction of which was delayed after arguments between the secular authorities, who planned to clean up the effluents entering the river from settlements upstream, and the *mul bhatta* of the temple, who objected to the treated water being reintroduced above the complex on the grounds that it wasn't holy.

From Ghujeshwari a lane follows the river downstream past the **Kirateshwar Mahadev Mandir**, which serves the Kirati ethnic groups of the hills – chiefly Rais and Limbus. You can often hear worshippers singing *bhajan* here, especially on full-moon evenings. Below lies **Gauri Ghat**, a peaceful spot where the river enters the Pashupatinath ravine; you can cross the river here and circle back around over the grassy knoll of **Kailash Hill**. From the eastern edge of Kailash, a steep staircase leads down to Surya Ghat (see p.158), or you can continue on to the Pashupati Mandir's main gate.

Boudha

To ancient travellers along the Kathmandu–Tibet trade route, the ten-kilometre corridor from Pashupatinath to Sankhu was known as the zone of *siddhi* (supernatural powers), where guardian deities dwelt and all wishes were granted. The biggest, most auspicious landmark along this route was – and still is – the great stupa at **BOUDHA** (or **BOUDHANATH**), about 5km northeast of downtown Kathmandu.

One of the world's largest stupas, Boudha is also the most important Tibetan Buddhist monument outside Tibet. Tibetans simply call it Chorten Chempo – "Great Stupa" – and since 1959 it has become the Mecca of **Tibetan exiles** in Nepal. Tibetans now run most of the businesses along the main road and around the stupa, while the construction of monasteries has spawned a regular suburban sprawl to the north. Despite the tour groups and souvenir sellers, Boudha gives you a thorough dunking in Tibetan culture, past and present. Early morning and dusk are the best times to be here, when the resonant chanting of monks and the otherworldly cacophony of their music drifts from the upper rooms of the houses that ring the stupa, and pilgrims perform *kora*, shuffling and prostrating their way around the dome.

If you want an extra helping of Tibetan culture, go during the **festival** of Losar in February or March, when Boudha hosts the biggest Tibetan New Year celebration in Nepal. Other busy times are Buddha Jayanti (the Buddha's birthday), held on the full moon of April–May, when an image of the Buddha is paraded around the stupa aboard an elephant, and the full moon of March–April, when ethnic Tamangs – the original guardians of the stupa – converge here to arrange marriages, and hundreds of eligible brides are sat around the stupa for inspection. Full moon and new moon days in general attract more pilgrims, since acts of worship earn more merit on these days.

From Kathmandu, crowded **minibuses** and **buses** depart the City Bus Park frequently for Boudha, **tempos** from Kantipath near RNAC, and **microbuses** from Shahid Gate, but you're better off going by **taxi** (about Rs250). However you travel, you'll be dropped off close to the main gate, where a Rs100 charge is levied on tourists. Boudha is not a place to cycle to: the main road along here is one of the valley's busiest and most polluted.

The site

Assigning a reliable age to Boudha is impossible, and historians are left at the mercy of legends, which seem to fix its origins around the fifth century AD.

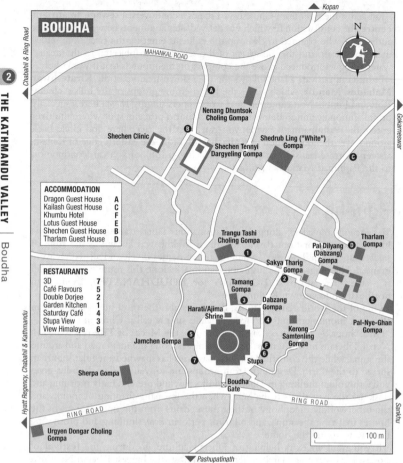

BOUDHA

N

Kopan

Chabahil & Ring Road

MAHANKAL ROAD

Gokarneswar

Nenang Dhuntsok
Choling Gompa

Shechen Clinic

Shechen Tennyi
Dargyeling Gompa

Shedrub Ling ("White")
Gompa

ACCOMMODATION
Dragon Guest House	A
Kailash Guest House	C
Khumbu Hotel	F
Lotus Guest House	E
Shechen Guest House	B
Tharlam Guest House	D

Trangu Tashi
Choling Gompa

Tharlam
Gompa

Pal Dilyang
(Dabzang)
Gompa

Sakya Tharig
Gompa

RESTAURANTS
3D	7
Café Flavours	5
Double Dorjee	2
Garden Kitchen	1
Saturday Café	4
Stupa View	3
View Himalaya	6

Tamang
Gompa

Dabzang
Gompa

Harati/Ajima
Shrine

Kerong
Samtenling
Gompa

Pal-Nye-Ghan
Gompa

Jamchen Gompa

Stupa

Sherpa Gompa

Boudha
Gate

Hyatt Regency, Chabahil & Kathmandu

RING ROAD

RING ROAD

Sankhu

Urgyen Dongar Choling
Gompa

0   100 m

Pashupatinath

A **Tibetan text** relates how a daughter of Indra stole flowers from heaven and was reassigned to earth as a lowly poultryman's daughter, yet prospered and decided to use some of her wealth to build a stupa to honour a mythical Buddha of a previous age. She petitioned the king, who cynically granted her only as much land as could be covered by a buffalo hide. Undaunted, the woman cut the hide into thread-thin strips and joined them end to end to enclose a gigantic area.

The **Newari legend** has a firmer historical grounding, involving a drought that struck Kathmandu during the reign of the early Lichhavi king, Vrisadev. When court astrologers advised that only the sacrifice of a virtuous man would bring rain, Vrisadev commanded his son Mandev to go to the royal well on a moonless night and decapitate the shrouded body he would find there. Mandev obeyed, only to find to his horror that he had sacrificed his own father. When he asked the goddess Bajra Yogini of Sankhu how to expiate his guilt, she let fly a bird and told him to build a stupa at the spot where it landed, which was Boudha.

Whatever its legendary origins, it's almost certain that the stupa encloses **holy relics**, perhaps parts of the Buddha's body (bones, hair, teeth) and objects touched or used by him, along with sacred texts and other ritual objects. The stupa has been sealed for centuries, of course, so no one knows exactly what lies within, but the undoubted presence of these relics is in no small degree responsible for the stupa's power, and its ability to command veneration.

Around the stupa

While less embellished than Swayambhu, Boudha is in its own way more interactive: you can climb up onto the stupa's base from its northern end, and kids sometimes even fly kites from it. The dome is elevated on three twenty-cornered plinths of decreasing size, which reinforce the notion of the stupa as a *mandala*, or meditation tool. As usual, the primordial Buddha's searching blue eyes are painted on the four sides of the central spire, and above them rise the thirteen golden steps to *nirvana*. Instead of five *dhyani* Buddhas, however, 108 (an auspicious number) much smaller images are set in niches around the dome, describing a broad pantheon of Buddhas, lamas and protector deities. Prayer wheels are mounted around the perimeter wall – it's said that each spin of a prayer wheel here is the equivalent of reciting the mantra embossed on it eleven thousand times.

The small **Ajima shrine** at the far side of the stupa shelters the ghoulish image of the goddess Ajima literally sucking the guts out of a corpse, reflecting her malevolent aspect as the bringer of disease. More popularly known as Harati, she was a much-feared abductor of children until, it is said, the Buddha taught her a lesson by stealing one of her own brood. Buddhist Newars take care to propitiate her suitably, however, in which case she acts as the revered protectress of their children. Next door is a room-sized prayer wheel – all are welcome to spin it – and on the other side of the shrine you'll see the tanks where whitewash is mixed during festivals. Behind lies the newly built **Tamang gompa**, whose balcony makes a good vantage point.

Boudha's **pilgrims** are arguably its greatest attraction, as the stupa is famed throughout the Himalayan region for its powers of wish-fulfilment and blessing. You'll see pilgrims repeatedly circumambulating the stupa, and doing endless sequences of prostrations in a secluded area on one of the upper terraces. Prayer wheels, heavy silver jewellery and rainbow-striped aprons are better indicators of a pilgrim's Tibetan origins than facial features, as Nepali Bhotiyas, people of Tibetan ethnicity and Tamangs from the central hills also visit Boudha in force.

The monasteries and back lanes

Where Swayambhu (see p.105) was traditionally sacred to Newar Buddhists, Boudha has always been essentially **Tibetan** in culture. Since the Chinese invasion, what was once a pilgrimage site has become the second pole of Tibetan religion, alongside Dharamsala in India. Over the last thirty-odd years, Western donations and canny business ventures have laid down the foundations of considerable wealth in the Tibetan community, and much of it has piously appeared above ground in the shape of *gompa*, or **monasteries**. There are some twenty scattered around the neighbourhood (a complete map is painted on a wall near the Ajima shrine). Most are named after *gompa* in Tibet that were destroyed by the Chinese, and preserve the same lineages of teachers and reincarnate lamas. While all four of the major Tibetan Buddhist sects are represented (see p.437), the majority belong to the Nyingma-pa, the oldest order of Tibetan Buddhism – and that of Nepal's ethnic Tamangs, who still own much of the land around Boudha.

Only a few **monasteries** keep their doors open throughout the day, but most welcome spectators during their cacophonous morning and dusk *puja,* or prayer ritual (see p.432). The interior of the main *lhakang* (assembly hall) is typically

Boudha's dharma scene

Boudha's **Western community** is well established, though to become a part of it you need either an introduction or a lot of time, since serious Western students of *dharma* tend to regard tourists as spiritual interference. But as those in the know say, if you're ready you will find a teacher here. Some will go on to warn enthusiastic newcomers that there are good teachers and bad, and Buddhism is big business in Boudha. Still, many Westerners rate Boudha as the best place in the world to **study** Tibetan Buddhism, for although **Dharamsala** in India is better known, thanks to the presence of the Dalai Lama, the Tibetan government-in-exile creates a politically rather than spiritually charged atmosphere there. Moreover, Dharamsala is heavily dominated by the Dalai Lama's Gelug-pa order, whereas at Boudha all four sects are well represented, making it easier to sample the different traditions.

Western monks and **nuns** wear the same maroon robes and have taken the same monastic vows as ordained Tibetans but aren't expected to make the same commitment to a monastery. Most cram as much personal instruction as possible into their time, and then try to maintain a long-distance teacher-disciple relationship from home.

Other Westerners come to Boudha for a season of **individual study**. Some are trying Buddhism on for size, others earnestly shopping around for a teacher. Most Rinpoches (or "respected teachers ") at Boudha give occasional open talks – with or without English translation – and normally agree to one-on-one meetings with anyone who shows a keen interest. Perennially popular among the *dharma* set is **Chökyi Nyima Rinpoche**, the English-speaking abbot of Ka Nying Shedrub Ling. Known as the "White Monastery" (Ⓦwww.shedrub.org), it is quite heavily oriented towards Westerners; it holds open bilingual teachings most Saturday mornings, runs meditation courses and seminars during the tourist season, and is affiliated to Kathmandu University for longer degree programmes (Ⓦwww.shedra.com).

The death in 1991 of **Dilgo Khyentse** of Shechen Tennyi Dargyeling, the "Bhutanese Monastery", has left a large gap, but it is being filled by his grandson, the current abbott, **Shechen Rabjam Rinpoche**, who teaches courses in English (Ⓦwww.shechen.org). He also acts as tutor to Dilgo Khyentse's *yangsi* (reincarnated successor), Urgen Tenzin Jigme Lhundrup, who was enthroned at the monastery in 1997 at the age of four and is now studying in Bhutan. The Sakya school is represented

dominated by gilded statues of Buddhas and Bodhisattvas and decorated with silk brocade hangings and polychrome murals depicting fearsome guardians of the faith, symbolic deities and cosmological patterns (see Contexts, p.435).

If you follow either of the two lanes heading **north of the stupa**, the romance evaporates in short order: this is Boudha the boomtown, an unplanned quagmire of garbage-strewn lanes, unlovely new buildings, schools and carpet factories – the latter contributing to serious pollution and awful road congestion, as well as to the bank balances of their owners.

Further afield

Boomtown aside, Boudha makes a good springboard for several walks and bike rides in this part of the valley. **Kopan Monastery**, occupying a ridge about 3km due north of the stupa, is an easy target, and is something of a pilgrimage destination for its astoundingly richly decorated "1000-Buddha stupa", so named for the inordinate number of holy relics it contains. You can take a taxi all the way, but it's a pleasant walk.

Half an hour's walk further to the east (beyond the giant, brand-new temple of the Amitabha Foundation), **Pulahari Monastery** sits atop the

at Boudha by the Jamchen Lhakhang Monastery, headed by the English-speaking Shabdrung Ngawang Kyenrab Rinchen Paljor. The monastery also sponsors the Boudha-based International Buddhist Academy (@www.sakyaiba.edu.np), which offers an annual ten-day retreat and four- and eight-week Buddhist philosophy and Tibetan language courses. Lama Tsering Wangdu Rinpoche, of Shelkar Chode Monastery (@www.lamawangdu.org), holds open sessions most mornings from 9–11am; visitors can also attend the remarkable Chöd ritual, a Tantric, symbolic sacrificing of the flesh performed on the 10th and 25th of the Tibetan month.

Outside Boudha, **Kopan Monastery**, 3km north of Boudha (@www.kopan-monastery .com), is one of the most open to interested Westerners, with daily guided meditations in the peak season and a well-regarded month-long intensive course in November. Its renowned rinpoche, **Lama Yeshe,** passed away in 1986, but a Spanish boy was recognized as his reincarnation and, under its energetic abbot, **Lama Zopa Rinpoche**, the monastery remains as busy as ever with a full schedule of courses and teachings, including many aimed at beginners or simply the spiritually curious. Pulahari Monastery, further along the ridge from Kopan (@www.jamgonkongtrul.org), is another major centre for long-term Western Buddhists, despite the death in 1994 of its abbot **Jamgon Kongtrul Rinpoche** and the subsequent installation of his young *yangsi* who is now being schooled at the monastery. **Thrangu Rinpoche's** grand-scale temple and teaching complex at Namobuddha (see p.210), **Thrangu Tashi Yangtse Monastery**, attracts many Western students.

To find out about upcoming teachings, check out the restaurant noticeboards around Boudha, or try asking at one of the monasteries mentioned above – or consulting their websites. You could also enrol on the **courses** run by the Himalayan Buddhist Meditation Centre, at Keshar Mahal Marg, in Thamel (☎01/441 0402, @fpmt-hbmc.org); their weekend "Buddhism in a nutshell " course is popular.

One of the simplest ways of spending time in Boudha without committing to full-time study is to volunteer with one of the many **charities** sponsored by monasteries or individual Rinpoches. One of the biggest is **Karuna Shechen** (@karuna-shechen.org), run by French author and monk Mathieu Ricard and based at Shechen monastery, which operates clinics and schools in Tibet and Nepal. Another, **Rokpa** (@www.rokpa .org), runs a winter soup kitchen and a home for street children.

ridge like the superstructure of an enormous container ship; its huge new prayer hall is perhaps the most richly and exquisitely decorated in Nepal. Both monasteries are usually open to visitors in daylight hours, unless there's a ceremony on.

From either Kopan or Pulahari, it's a strenuous two- or three-hour hike north up a wooded ridge to **Nagi Gompa** (see p.168), though you probably shouldn't go without help finding the way. From Pulahari, it's less than 2km downhill on a paved road to **Gokarneswar**, where an imposing Shiva temple gazes across the Bagmati River to the peaceful Gokarna Forest – which encloses the luxury *Gokarna Forest Resort*, golf club and spa (see p.87). Frequent mini- and microbuses run from here back to Boudha and Kathmandu, along the main road from Sundarijal, the trailhead for Helambu treks (see p.362).

Pashupatinath (see p.153) is only about a half-hour's walk southwest of Boudha. A lane leads away from the main road almost opposite the entrance to the stupa, running through fields increasingly colonized by spreading urbanization. Sankhu (see p.165) and Gokarneswar can easily be reached by bike or bus.

Straddling the Ring Road west of Boudha, the ancient settlement of **Chabahil** is unfortunately now blighted by traffic and characterless construction. However,

Tibetans have long been drawn to its stupa (known locally as **Dhando Chaitya**), which despite its newish appearance dates to Lichhavi times. One chronicle states that it was constructed by Dharmadev, a fifth-century king, although legend attributes it to Charumati, who settled here and married a local prince after accompanying her father Ashoka on his apocryphal pilgrimage to the Kathmandu Valley in the third century BC. The prince, Devapala, is credited with founding Deopatan, one of the valley's ancient capitals and now the site of Pashupatinath. In a brick shelter at the south end of the compound stands a sixth-century statue of Padmapani Lokeshwar, carved in black stone. Chabahil's Nepalis rally round the **Chandra Binayak Mandir**, one of the valley's four principal Ganesh temples, located in the reasonably atmospheric bazaar west of the main Chabahil intersection.

Boudha practicalities

Most tourist facilities – a moneychanger, a **bank,** and photo, phone and internet shops – can be found in the vicinity of the stupa. The nearest **ATM** (24hr) is just outside the main gate, on the left as you exit. There are lots of **Tibetan medicine clinics**, but the Shechen Clinic (℡01/448 7924; Mon–Fri & Sun 9am–4.30pm), opposite the Shechen monastery, is perhaps the most useful place to go: as well as Tibetan treatments, it offers homeopathy and Western/drug-based medicine – and uses some of the Rs500 consultation fee to subsidize healthcare for local people.

Accommodation

There's a good range of moderately priced **accommodation** in Boudha, so it's well worth staying overnight to enjoy the place after the day-trippers are gone – and before they arrive. Most lodgings are within easy walking distance of the stupa. The ones attached to monasteries are perhaps the most colourful, but expect early morning wake-up calls courtesy of horns, drums and chanting monks. It's generally worth calling ahead, as popular places fill up, especially around the time of festivals, enthronements of lamas and the like.

Dragon Guest House ℡01/447 9562, ℮dragon@ntc.net.np. A comfortable little establishment run by a family from Mustang in a quiet area. Decently furnished rooms are stacked up in a tall tower – upper rooms are airier. Has a friendly atmosphere, with lots of returnees, so it's a good place to meet people. At least a 5min walk from the stupa. ❸

Kailash Guest House ℡01/448 0741. Something of a dive, but if budget is the priority it's decent enough. Overlooks the noisy main lane leading north from the stupa, but the back rooms are quieter. ❶

Khumbu Hotel ℡01/446 5241, ⓦwww .khumbuhotel.com.np. Friendly and professional boutique hotel right on the stupa plaza. Rooms are smart, with wood panelling, parquet floors, TVs and gleaming bathrooms. Tibetan murals and mannequins in the common areas give it character, and there's a terrace restaurant. ❺

Lotus Guest House ℡01/447 2320. Clean, quiet and spacious, with minimalist low-rise buildings arranged around a pleasant garden. Operated by the next-door monastery. If it's full, the adjacent *Pema Guest House* (❷) isn't dissimilar. ❷

Shechen Guest House ℡01/447 9009, ⓦwww.shechenguesthouse.com.np. Tucked away in a quiet area, with simple but pleasant rooms livened up by oddments of Tibetan fabrics. Owned by the adjacent Shechen monastery, so there are often visiting monks taking tea in the well-tended gardens and restaurant. Good breakfasts, with home-made bread. ❹

Tharlam Guest House ℡01/449 6878, ℮tharlamgh@yahoo.com. Fairly new three-storey building, with good-value, spotless rooms set among distinctly grand surroundings. These belong to the monastery behind, for which it acts as a kind of gatehouse – which means an early-morning *puja* call. ❸

Eating

A handful of **restaurants** around the stupa plaza target day-trippers, with rooftop seating and standard tourist menus. Most are lacklustre, but stick to Tibetan food and enjoy the view and you can't go wrong. Other, more authentic Tibetan places – with trademark curtained doors and windows, dim lighting and white cotton seat covers – are tucked away in the back lanes and on the main road.

3D Restaurant The basement cafeteria setting isn't particularly appealing, but the *Triple Dorjee*, or "3D", has a solid local reputation for inexpensive and authentic Tibetan food.

Café Flavours Sophisticated establishment which has a vaguely Manhattanish basement with people on laptops sucking on cappuccinos and brownies. Also has a back terrace and offers a full menu.

Double Dorjee A cosy Tibetan den that's long been popular with insiders. Good Tibetan food and some inexpensive Western choices.

Garden Kitchen Restaurant A gate in a back alley leads to a real oasis: a spacious terracotta-floored courtyard surrounded by greenery and thronging with the *dharma* crowd working up a spiritual appetite over coffee, cakes, and reasonably priced Western and Tibetan food.

Saturday Café Has the obligatory rooftop with stupa view, and also offers organic produce (delicious curd), good cakes, wi-fi and an attached bookshop.

Stupa View Boudha's premier restaurant, with prices to match. Vegetarian, with fairly imaginative dishes (good pasta and tofu), plus there's a full bar and roof terrace.

View Himalaya Restaurant Unexceptional if wide-ranging menu, with a rooftop perfectly positioned to catch the evening sun and, sometimes, views of Ganesh Himal.

Shopping

Run-of-the-mill **souvenirs** at Boudha are notoriously overpriced, but this is the place to come if you're seeking genuinely obscure or antique items. Keep an eye out for tea tables, jewellery, flasks, butter-tea churns and prayer-flag printing blocks. For **thangka**, Tushita Heaven Handicraft, on the main stupa plaza in Boudha, is a co-operative of *thangka* artists, some of whom can be seen at work in the shop. More Buddhist art can be found at the Tsering Art School, an offshoot of the adjacent Shechen Monastery; most of its business is with local monasteries so it's an excellent place to learn about what you're buying. The Tibet Musical Cultural Center, on the northwest side of the stupa plaza, sells traditional **musical instruments** and provides instruction.

Boudha is also a good place to buy prayer flags, brocade banners, Tibetan incense, *chuba* (Tibetan wraparound dresses) and maroon monks' garb, as well as specialist books on Tibetan Buddhism – not to mention traditional wood-block printed texts and meditation CDs. Boudha Book Store, just to the south of *View Himalaya Restaurant*, on the main stupa plaza, has a good book selection.

Sankhu Bajra Yogini

The paved road past Boudha – one of the old trade routes to Tibet – rolls eastwards as far as **SANKHU**. It's still one of the Valley's larger Newari towns, but the situation in a rural corner, hard up against the forested hills, gives it a pleasant backwater feel. There's a old bazaar area to the east of the main north–south road, but the town is worth visiting mainly for its temple to **Bajra Yogini**, whose gilded roof glints from a grove of trees on the wooded hillside north of town. To make the two-kilometre hike, follow the main road through the arch at the north end of town, then bear left after 400m on a cobbled path. If you're on wheels, continue on the road for another 1km to where it peters out (a taxi can take you this far). The last half-hour or so is a stiff climb up steep stone steps, but pleasantly shaded by the forest.

Bajra Yogini is the eldest of a ferocious foursome of tantric goddesses specially venerated in the Kathmandu Valley. To Buddhist Newars – her main devotees – she is identified with Ugratara, the wrathful, corpse-trampling emanation of Tara, one of the female aspects of Buddhahood. Hindus identify her as Durga (Kali), the most terrifying of the eight mother goddesses. She's also known as Khadga Yogini, for the sword (*khadga*) held in her right hand. The current **temple** dates from the seventeenth century, though the smaller building next to it is more ancient: indeed, its natural stone dome may well be the original seventh-century object of worship at this site. The stone just to the right of the temple door is a *nag* (snake) shrine. In the back wall of the compound, a small square opening indicates a meditation **cave**. Another cave just behind the *pati* west of the compound (recognizable by the faint Tibetan inscription of the Avalokitesvara mantra over the door) is known as Dharma Pap Gupha: those who can squeeze through the opening into the inner chamber demonstrate their virtue (*dharma*); those who can't, their vice (*pap*).

Steps lead up, past scurrying troupes of monkeys, to a picturesque, Rana-era **pilgrim's rest house**, set around a courtyard. The wing nearest the temple houses a subsidiary shrine to Bajra Yogini, tucked away on the first floor. Touching the goddess herself is forbidden, so this gilt copper copy was created for the annual **jatra** procession down to Sankhu (held for nine days from the full to the new moon of March–April); as a mother goddess, she is flanked by her two children. On the ground floor, below, a seventh-century **Buddha head** and an enormous overturned **frying pan** are displayed. These belong respectively to Vrisadev, whose decapitation led to the founding of Boudha (see p.160) and to an ancient king who offered his own body as a daily sacrificial fry-up to Bajra Yogini. According to legend, the goddess would restore him to life and endow him with supernatural powers; when a rival tried to copy the trick, the goddess accepted his flesh, with no resurrection, and then turned over the frying pan to indicate that she would require no more sacrifices. Blood sacrifices are now performed only in front of the triangular stone of **Bhairab**, Bajra Yogini's consort, which guards the path some hundred-odd steps below the temple; on the average day it gleams darkly with fresh blood.

Practicalities

After the March–April *jatra*, Sankhu's other main **festival** is Magh Sankranti (Jan 14 or 15), observed with bathing just upstream of the town. Snack **food** can be found in the bazaar but there's nothing oriented towards tourists.

Buses run from Kathmandu's City Bus Park every ten minutes or so. Cycling is possible, though there's heavy industrial traffic around Jorpati (just east of Boudha). With a mountain bike, you can continue on to Nagarkot (see p.199): head north from the old bazaar area on the main road. Other, rougher trails ascend the ridge to Changu Narayan (see p.192).

Budhanilkantha and Shivapuri

A paved road leads 8km north from Kathmandu to **Narayanthan**, a roadside village centred on **BUDHANILKANTHA** (pronounced *Bu*da-nil-*kan*ta), the site of a monolithic and hugely impressive sleeping Vishnu statue. A visit can be combined with a **hike** or **mountain bike** ride up to the thickly forested peak of **Shivapuri**, from which there are some of the finest Himalayan views anywhere in the Valley. The road from Kathmandu to Budhanilkantha is busy at first, but a quieter route heads north to Tokha then cuts across east.

Buses to Budhanilkantha leave from the City Bus Park every fifteen minutes or so, while **microbuses** leave from Ratna Park. Roughly eight buses a day continue as far as the Shivapuri park gate, a journey of some 45 minutes. There's not much **accommodation** in these parts. The luxury *Park Village Resort* (☎01/437 3935, ⊛ktmgh.com/parkvillage; ❼), just off the main road about 200m short of the gate to the Budhanilkantha shrine, is a pleasant, sunny compound set around lawns and a pool, but it's hard to think of a reason to stay out here – conferences aside. More tempting is *Shivapuri Heights Cottage* (☎984/137 1927, ⊛www.shivapuricottage.com, ❻), a pair of attractive, traditionally designed cottages five minutes' walk off the road, on the edge of the Shivapuri forest; it has great views of the valley and is a popular weekend retreat for expats. Staying here would also enable an early start for the dawn hike to the summit.

The Sleeping Vishnu

The valley's largest stone sculpture, the five-metre-long **Sleeping Vishnu** (Jalakshayan Narayan) at Budhanilkantha, reclines in a recessed water tank like an oversized astronaut in suspended animation. Carved from a type of basalt found miles away in the southern hills, it was apparently dragged here by forced labour during the reign of the seventh-century monarch Vishnugupta, who controlled the Valley under the Licchavi king Bhimarjunadev, much as the Ranas ruled in the name of the Shah dynasty in the early twentieth century. According to legend the image was lost and buried for centuries, only to be rediscovered by a farmer tilling his fields.

Hindus may enter the sanctum area to do *puja* before the Sleeping Vishnu; others may only view it from between concrete railings. Priests and novices continually tend, bathe and anoint the image but the bustle of religious activity is at its height at morning and evening *puja* (9–10am and 6–7pm).

Budhanilkantha's name has been a source of endless confusion. It has nothing to do with the Buddha (*budha* means "old ", though that doesn't stop Buddhist Newars from worshipping the image). The real puzzler is why Budhanilkantha (literally, "Old Blue-Throat"), a title which unquestionably refers to Shiva, has been attached here to Vishnu. The myth of **Shiva's blue throat**, a favourite in Nepal, relates how the gods churned the ocean of existence and inadvertently unleashed a poison that threatened to destroy the world. They begged Shiva to save them from their blunder and he obliged by drinking the poison. His throat burning, the great god flew up to the range north of Kathmandu, struck the mountainside with his trident to create a lake, Gosainkund, and quenched his thirst – suffering no lasting ill effect except for a blue patch on his throat. The water in the Sleeping Vishnu's tank is popularly believed to originate in Gosain-kund, and Shaivas claim a reclining image of Shiva can be seen under the waters of the lake during the annual Shiva festival there in August, which perhaps explains the association. Local legend maintains that a mirror-image statue of Shiva lies on the statue's underside.

Nonetheless, the Budhanilkantha sculpture bears all the hallmarks of Vishnu or, as he's often called in Nepal, **Narayan**. It depicts Vishnu floating in the ocean of existence upon the endless snake Shesh; from his navel will grow Brahma and the rest of creation. Each year the god is said to "awaken" from his summer slumber during the Haribondhini Ekadashi **festival** in late October or early November, an event that draws thousands of worshippers.

Historically, one person who would never put in an appearance here was the king of Nepal. Some attribute this absence to a seventeenth-century curse; others to the fact that the monarchs were held to be reincarnations of Vishnu and should never gaze upon their own image.

The surrounding **bazaar** supports a lively trade in religious paraphernalia, sweets and tea.

Up to Shivapuri

At 2732m, **Shivapuri** (or Sheopuri) is the second-highest point on the valley rim. It lies within the forested **Shivapuri National Park**, designed to protect the valley's water supply. The gate (Rs250 admission) stands 2km north of Budhanilkantha. The most appealing ascent trail takes you past **Nagi Gompa**, a former Tamang monastery gifted to the renowned lama Urgyen Rinpoche, and now occupied by nuns – along with the odd Western *dharma* student sent up from Boudha for a few days' meditation. It is sometimes possible to persuade a motorbike or even a taxi along the dirt road from the gate to Nagi Gompa, but it's a pleasant walk of an hour or so, climbing and contouring eastward through the forest.

From Nagi Gompa, a trail continues more steeply up the ridge to the **peak of Shivapuri**. It takes anything from two to three hours from the nunnery (when in doubt, bear left) and the vertical gain, nearly 1200m, shouldn't be taken lightly: pack food and sufficient water. Towards the top of the walk you'll pass **Baghdwar**, where the holy Bagmati River gushes forth from the mouth of a silver tiger's head, and a Hindu hermitage. Clouds tend to move in by lunchtime but if you're up early enough you should have superb views of the Himalayas, from Jugal and Ganesh Himal out to Himalchuli, and eastwards from Langtang Lirung to Dorje Lakpa. To be sure of the views, you can camp on the flat, grassy summit (Rs100 per tent is charged at the park gate).

It's also possible to hike to Shivapuri from Gokarna or by a more direct route from Budhanilkantha, and some good, longer routes are possible on a mountain bike (see p.412).

Nagarjun Ban, Balaju and Ichangu

The Valley's northwestern fringe is its most congested. Kathmandu sprawls right to the very edge of the basin, while the main road to Trisuli (see p.414) heaves itself smokily out of the valley. **Nagarjun Ban**, which is part of the Shivapuri–Nagarjun National Park, provides a pleasant swathe of green, however, and under its wooded slopes lie the curious Sleeping Vishnu at **Balaju** and the rustic temple of **Ichangu Narayan**. It's true that the forest is no match for Shivapuri (see p.166), the Vishnu plays second fiddle to the one at Budhanilkantha (see p.167) and the temple is distinctly ordinary compared to the similarly-named Changu Narayan (see p.192), but they're all at least located handily close to the city centre.

Frequent **buses** from the City Bus Park and **microbuses** from Ratna Park (via Lekhnath Marg, in north Thamel) run to **Balaju** and almost as far as the Nagarjun Ban gate, but both of these destinations are within easy **cycling** distance of Kathmandu – and a mountain bike will stand you in good stead once you get to Nagarjun Ban.

Simple snack **food** is available in Balaju. If you're cycling or walking to Nagarjun Ban, you can eat in more pleasant surroundings at a few outdoor cafés along the main road beyond the forest entrance.

Balaju

BALAJU's Water Garden (daily 7am–7pm; Rs5) is really a suburban picnic park just beyond the Ring Road and Balaju Industrial Estate. It lies some 2km northwest of Thamel along the road to Trisuli. The name comes from **Baais dhara**, an open water tank feeding twenty-two (*baais*) stone spouts (*dhara*). It heaves with bathing worshippers during the **festival** of Lhuti Punhi, observed on the day of the full moon of March–April. The park's chief attraction, however, is a **Sleeping Vishnu** statue which was once thought to be a copy of the more famous and much larger seventh-century image at Budhanilkantha (see p.167), but may actually antedate it. The iconography is obscure, but the god appears to be holding a conch and mace in his two left hands, and ashes and a rosary in his right (attributes of Vishnu and Shiva respectively), making the figure a Shankar-Narayan or half-Vishnu, half-Shiva. If so, the compromise may reflect the balancing act of the early Gupta rulers, who introduced Vaishnavism but continued to honour the more ancient, popular worship of Shiva.

Nagarjun Ban and Jamacho

Two kilometres up the road from Balaju stands the park gate to **Nagarjun Ban** (also known as Rani Ban), a large and surprisingly wild forest reserve (daily 6am–6pm; pedestrians and cyclists Rs10, motorcyclists Rs30, cars and elephants Rs100). An unpaved road winds from the gate to the *chaitya*-topped summit of 2096m **Jamacho**, but you can hike more directly up the ridge along a five-kilometre trail (allow at least two hours on foot). You'll pass numerous limestone **caves** with Buddhist legends attached.

The gate is the only official entrance to the reserve but various **trails** thread through the forest and exit at a number of points around the perimeter. Perhaps the most useful route cuts down from the main Jamacho road due south towards Ichangu Narayan, but at the time of writing it was blocked off by a police checkpost. **Mountain-bike** routes are described on p.413.

Ichangu Narayan

According to tradition, a Narayan temple occupies each of the four cardinal points of Kathmandu Valley. The western one, **Ichangu Narayan**, is rustic rather than distinguished, but it nestles in a surprisingly pleasant rural side valley at the southern base of Jamacho. A roughish road leaves the Ring Road immediately opposite Swayambhunath's western tip (4km south of Balaju); there's no bus, but taxis wait at this junction, or you can hike or bike up through the suburb of Halchok towards a small notch in the ridge behind a big Buddhist monastery; from here an increasingly rough road descends into the Ichangu valley to reach the temple after about 3km.

Just after the saddle, another road breaks off to the south beside a quarry; from here you can **mountain bike** westwards to Bhimdhunga and on to Thankot, astride the west bound Prithvi Highway.

Kirtipur

Once-proud **KIRTIPUR** (City of Glory) occupies a long, low battleship of a ridge 5km southwest of Kathmandu. Commanding a panoramic – not to mention strategic – view of the valley, the well-preserved old town is vehicle-free and great for a morning or afternoon's wandering.

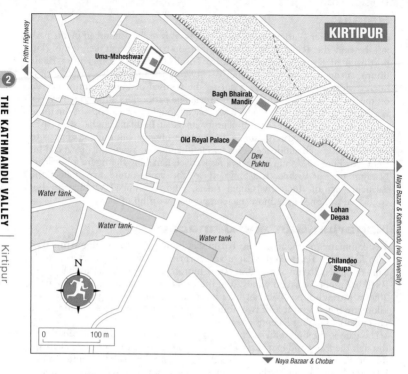

Prithvi Highway

KIRTIPUR

Uma-Maheshwar

Bagh Bhairab
Mandir

Old Royal Palace

*Dev
Pukhu*

Water tank

Lohan
Degaa

Water tank

Water tank

Chilandeo
Stupa

N

0   100 m

Naya Bazaar & Kathmandu (via University)

▼ *Naya Bazaar & Chobar*

Established as a western outpost of Patan in the twelfth century, Kirtipur had gained nominal independence by the time Prithvi Narayan Shah began his final conquest of the Kathmandu Valley in 1767. The Gorkha king considered the town to be the **military linchpin** of the valley and made its capture his first priority. After two separate attacks and a six-month siege, with no help forthcoming from Patan, Kirtipur surrendered on the understanding it would receive a total amnesty. Instead, in an **atrocity** intended to demoralize the remaining opposition in the valley, Prithvi Shah ordered his troops to cut off the noses and lips of every man and boy in Kirtipur. Supposedly, only men skilled in the playing of wind instruments were spared. The rest of the valley fell within a year.

In modern times, Kirtipur's hilltop position has proved more of a handicap than an asset. The commerce all takes place at the foot of the hill, in **Naya Bazaar**, the "New Market" (with its Thai-style Theravada Buddhist temple). It's here, too, that you'll notice the throngs of resident students from the adjacent **Tribhuwan University** – Nepal's chief centre of higher education, and a hotbed of political activism in recent years. The upper town is splendidly preserved, having recently completed a conservation and beautification project which furnished the streets with fine stone paving and restored many – but not yet all – of its temples. Despite the clean-up, it preserves an authentically old-world atmosphere, too: many residents of the old town are Jyapus, from the Newari farming subcaste, and they still work the fields surrounding town. In spring and autumn, the streets are full of sheaves being threshed and grain being stored.

Microbuses and **minibuses** (every 5–10min) run from the City Bus Park to Naya Bazaar, from where it's a ten-minute walk up to the village. **Cycling** to Kirtipur is relatively enjoyable – once you're free of Kathmandu – and a bike is useful for exploring the countryside beyond, towards Chobar and Dakshinkali, perhaps (see p.175). The main way there is via Tribhuwan University, off the Dakshinkali road (turn right at the red-brick gate and take the left fork 1km later). Other paths lead to Kirtipur from the Prithvi (Kathmandu–Pokhara) Highway, the Ring Road and Chobar. For **food**, you can't expect much more than samosas or chow mein in Naya Bazaar.

Bagh Bhairab Mandir

The road from the university switchbacks to the saddle of Kirtipur's twin-humped ridge and deposits you in a square outside the prodigious **Bagh Bhairab Mandir**, which serves double duty as a war memorial and a cathedral to Bhairab in his tiger (*bagh*) form. Dating from the early sixteenth century, it's one of the oldest and best-preserved Newari pagodas in the valley. Mounted on the outside of the temple is a collection of rusty **weapons** captured during the siege of Kirtipur, and faded murals depicting scenes from the Mahabharat can be seen on the upper walls of the ground floor.

Local legend relates that a shepherd, to pass the time, fashioned a tiger image out of burrs. The shepherd went off in search of a poinsettia leaf for the tongue, but when he returned he found his sheep gone – and the tiger's mouth dripping with blood. To honour the miraculously bloodthirsty Bhairab, the people enshrined in this temple a clay tiger, its face is covered with a silver, tongueless **Bhairab mask** which is remade every twenty or thirty years. The mask is hidden, but a tiny porthole on the eastern side of the temple – positioned so as to catch the dawn sun – may allow you to sneak a glimpse.

Local musicians perform *bhajan* early in the morning and around dinnertime near the shrine, and on Tuesdays and Saturdays people sacrifice animals in front of it. In an upper chamber is kept a separate image of Indrayani, one of the Kathmandu Valley's eight mother goddesses (*ashta matrika*), who, according to one Cinderella-like legend, was bossed around by the other goddesses until she miraculously turned a pumpkin into gold. Kirtipur's biggest **festival, Indrayani Jatra,** is in late November or early December, when Indrayani and Ganesh are paraded through town on palanquins and a pair of pigeons are ceremonially released.

From the north side of the compound there are fantastic views across Kathmandu. At the opposite, southern end, between the two entrances, a small pagoda shrine dedicated to Ganesh houses an ancient – possibly pre-Lichhavi (pre-fourth century) – statue of a standing **Shiva**, armless but equipped with a potently erect penis. Along the back wall sit five tiny mother-goddess statues associated with five sheep that escaped the tiger; they're thought to date from the fifth century. Under a metallic umbrella in the northeast (far right) corner is a small statue of **Dhartimata**, an earth goddess, shown in a graphic state of giving birth – to what, no one seems to know. Women do *puja* to this statue to aid against problems during pregnancy and childbirth.

Uma-Maheshwar Mandir and Chilandeo Stupa

Kirtipur is a pleasantly confusing maze of stony alleys, but navigating isn't hard so long as you stick to the ridgeline. The northwestern end of town is predominantly Hindu, the southeastern Buddhist.

At the top of the northern, Hindu hump stands the elephant-guarded **Uma-Maheshwar Mandir**, whose temple bell is a copy, cast in the unlikely setting of Croydon, England. The original bell tolled the hours in the old Kathmandu clock tower for many years before the structure collapsed in the earthquake of 1934. Long unfinished, the wooden struts under the lowest pagoda roof were finally adorned with the traditional carvings in 2008. The erotic scenes on the lowest level are supposed to have less to do with *Kamasutra*-style sexual gymnastics and more with local Tantric and fertility traditions; that said, the artist does seem to have let his imagination off the leash.

Heading southeastwards from the Bagh Bhairab temple first brings you to the Lohan Degaa, a stone *shikra* shared by both Hindu and Buddhist worshippers. Beyond, the atmospheric **Chilandeo Stupa** crowns the southern hill, its exposed brickwork lending a hoary antiquity generally lacking in better-maintained stupas. Chilandeo (also known as Chilancho Bahal) is popularly supposed to have been erected by Ashoka. The ridge that rears up so impressively to the southwest is Champadevi (see box below), one of the high points along the valley rim.

The Dakshinkali road

The longest and most varied of the valley's roads begins at the busy Balkhu junction of the Ring Road, at the southwest corner of Kathmandu, just short of Kirtipur. From Balkhu the road snakes its way along a fold in the valley rim towards the famous sacrificial shrine of Dakshinkali. En route it passes several temples and Buddhist monasteries. Beyond Dakshinkali, it's now possible to hop over the hills in a jeep, descending to the Terai at Hetauda (see box, p.174).

Buses for Dakshinkali depart from Kathmandu's City Bus Park as soon as they are filled – roughly every fifteen minutes. Kathmandu travel agents offer guided **tours** on Tuesday and Saturday mornings (about Rs300), or you could hire your own **taxi** (about Rs1000 return to Dakshinkali for a half-day). For real independence, go by **mountain bike**; the outward (upward) leg takes at least two hours, but you can put your bike on the roof of the bus for the price of a small tip.

Chobar village

The village of **CHOBAR**, 3km south of the Ring Road, caps the top of a deceptively tall hill overlooking the main road and Bagmati River winding

---

Hikes to Champadevi and Bhasmesur

The southwestern rim of the Valley rears up in a prominent fishtail of twin peaks. Trails to the eastern summit, **Champadevi,** start from near Taudaha, Pikhel and Pharping. A hike up one trail and down another will take four to six hours (bring plenty of food and water), though you can cut into the time considerably if you have a 4WD. The first trail begins where the road makes an abrupt bend beyond Taudaha, climbing steeply southwestwards to gain the ridge and then more gradually along it to the stupa-marked summit (2278m). From Pikhel, a dirt road heads north to the ridge, entering a splendid pine forest and passing the *Haatiban Resort* (see p.174), then tracks northwest to join the first trail. The Pharping route follows a dirt road up a valley south of the ridge as far as a small pond, from where the trail veers northwards straight up to the ridge.

Bhasmesur (2502m) is another hour's walk along the ridge from Champadevi, separated from it by a saddle. It can also be reached from Kirtipur: start by following the dirt road southwest from Naya Bazaar and then west to Machhegaun, from where a trail switchbacks up to a saddle on the ridge just north of the summit.

below. From the bus stop, an apparently endless stone stairway leads up through the forest to the huddle of old-fashioned houses and hilltop **Adinath Mandir**. (Cyclists should take the paved road which breaks right from the main road a little further south.) The temple's front is festooned with kitchen utensils, offered to Lokeshwar, the temple's deity. Explanations for this curious custom are various: newlyweds say it ensures a happy union, others claim it's a rite for the departed. Lokeshwar is worshipped here in the form of a red mask, which bears a close resemblance to Patan's Rato Machhendranath.

There's only one **place to stay**, and with its peaceful terraced gardens and wonderful views, *Chobar Le Village Resort* (T01/441 8151, Wwww.nepal villageresort.com; ❺) makes a lovely weekend retreat. Its three rooms – one of them a large, open-plan loft apartment – have exposed stone walls and beams, and are filled with sculptures and idiosyncratic bits of woodcarving.

Chobar gorge and cave

When Manjushri drained the Kathmandu Valley of its legendary lake, **Chobar Gorge** was one of the places he smote with his sword to release the waters. As the Bagmati River slices through a wrinkle in the valley floor, 1km south of Chobar and just beside the Dakshinkali road, it really does look like the work of a neat sword stroke. To see it, you can get off the bus either beside the sign for **Manjushree Park** at the top of the hill and walk down, or at the cluster of shacks at the bottom and walk back up.

Manjushree Park itself is a kind of rockery garden spread out over the hillside, with an entrance fee of Rs50 (daylight hours) that allows you to wander its concrete stairways and descend part way into the gorge itself. The gorge is impressively sheer but the stench of the foaming Bagmati as it vomits forth from the Valley rather detracts from the experience. More promisingly, the park ticket offices can sell you a guided tour (15min tour $3; 1hr tour $10) of **Chobar Gupha**, a cave system which is theoretically the third-largest in South Asia – although blasting at the now-defunct Himal Cement Factory has reduced the extent of the navigable passageways. Still, there are plenty of tight corners to squeeze through and holes to scramble down: wear old clothes; guides have some spare torches.

The best gorge vantage point, at the upstream end, is free-to-view. The twitchy suspension **footbridge**, custom-cast by a Scottish foundry and assembled here in 1907, stands beside a new road bridge which cuts through towards Patan and the Bungamati road. Immediately upstream stands the seventeenth-century **Jal Binayak** temple. The tip of its rocky outcrop is worshipped as Ganesh, and women sell leaf-plates of the god's favourite foods – meat, milk, soybeans, banana, ginger, pickles – to offer as *puja*.

Two kilometres beyond Chobar, the road passes the **Taudaha** pond, a watering hole for winter migrant birds, including many different duck species and nationally threatened birds such as the oriental darter, falcated duck and Baillon's crane. According to legend, when Manjushri drained the Kathmandu Valley he left Taudaha as a home for the snakes, and the serpent king Karkatnag still lives at the bottom, coiled around a heap of treasure.

Shesh Narayan (Yanglesho)

From Taudaha the road ascends steadily for another 6km to its highest point, a little beyond Pikhel. Two **resort hotels** perch in the hills above: the chalet-style *Dakshinkali Hill Resort* sits in the peaceful Dollu side-valley, 2km off the road (T01/471 0072, Wwww.dakhillresort.com; ❹); it has a pool and caters for conferences. The more isolated, but distinctly swish, *Haatiban Resort* sits astride a pine-clad ridge above Pikhel, beside the rough road heading up towards Champadevi (℡01/471 0122; ❽); it offers great views and guided hikes.

Two kilometres beyond the high point, the quiet and shady **pools** of **Shesh Narayan** crouch under a wooded hillside. Hindus worship Vishnu here as the mighty creator who formed the universe out of the cosmic ocean; the snake Shesh (or Ananta), the "remainder" of the cosmic waters after Vishnu's creation, is symbolized by the four pools. A sculpture depicting Surya riding his twelve-horse chariot stands half-submerged in the semicircular pool. Steps from here lead to Narayan's **temple** at the base of a limestone overhang, whose serpentine stalactites are said by Vaishnavas to be the "milk", or blessing, of Shesh. To the left of the temple is another hunk of eroded limestone known as Chaumunda – you're supposed to put your ear to it to hear the sound of running water.

To the right of the temple, a half-height wood latticed doorway conceals a cave that Buddhists call **Yanglesho**, where Guru Padma Sambhava, the eighth-century founder of the Nyingma-pa sect of Tibetan Buddhism, is supposed to have wrestled with a horde of *nag* and turned them to stone. The story probably refers to the saint's struggle to introduce his brand of tantric Buddhism from India.

Pharping

A few hundred metres beyond Shesh Narayan, **PHARPING** is unexpectedly large and lively for this distant corner of the valley. The original Newari village is now overshadowed by a Tibetan Buddhist boomtown, with upwards of a dozen monasteries and retreat centres taking advantage of the clean air. The wooded ridge above is festooned with strings of brightly coloured prayer flags.

The best way to see Pharping is to make like a Buddhist pilgrim – of which there are many – and walk the sacred circuit. It can be done in a leisurely hour. Turning off the ever-more-noxious junction with the main road, you walk up past a 3.5-metre golden **statue of Guru Rinpoche** in a giant glass case – a sign of things to come. Passing a cluster of cafés and houses, and the ornate, white-and-gold, bell-like *chorten* of the Sakya Tharik Gompa, you come to a set of steps, just before the road rises and turns to the right. These lead up to a cluster of monastery buildings and a small **shrine room** where butter lamps burn in honour of a "self-arisen" image of the Buddhist deity **Green Tara**, who protects from danger. The miraculous image turns out to be a hand-sized figurine standing out from the naked rock in bas-relief. A Hindu Ganesh statue sits incongruously alongside, while other rocky pimples to the right are supposed to be further Taras in the process of emanation. A duty monk recites the Green Tara *puja* at all hours of the day and night.

Steps continue upwards to the **Asura Cave**, a narrow fissure filled with votive offerings to the irrepressible Padma Sambhava, aka Guru Rinpoche, who is said to have achieved enlightenment here. His two footprints and (less obvious) clawing hand-marks are apparently signs of the cosmic power he realized at that moment. From here, the trail turns back towards the main road, passing through other monastery buildings then, after about ten minutes, starts descending towards the golden-roofed **Pharping Bajra Yogini temple**, one of the valley's four tantric temples dedicated to the angry female aspect of Buddhahood. The first-floor sanctum conceals two prancing images of Bajra Yogini, each holding a skull-cup and knife. Steps lead down from here directly to the main Pharping road, just above the Guru Rinpoche statue.

The best of the homely, Tibetan-oriented **restaurants** is the *Snowland*, 200m up from the Dakshinkali road junction. The simple *Family Guesthouse* (☏ 01/471 0412, ✉ familyguesthouse@yahoo.com; ❸) is conveniently set just back from the main road. However the only reason to stay at Pharping is to study at a monastery – and most have their own inexpensive guesthouses. Rigdzin Phodrang Gompa, under the respected Ralo Rinpoche, is perhaps the most open to the uninitiated seeking shorter-term retreats.

Dakshinkali

The best and worst aspect of **DAKSHINKALI** is that everything happens out in the open. The famous sacrificial pit of Southern Kali – the last stop for hundreds of chickens, goats and pigs every week – lies at the bottom of a steep, forested ravine, affording an intimate view of Nepali religious rituals. The spectacle makes many people feel uncomfortable – if it's not squeamishness, it'll

▲ Life happens on the street in Dakshinkali

be the sense of prying. That said, the public bloodbath is quite a sight, and attracts busloads at the holiest times: Saturday and Tuesday mornings. Asthami, the eighth day after a new or full moon, draws the largest crowds of all.

From the bus stop, a path leads through a small bazaar of stalls selling food, drinks and sacrificial accessories. The **shrine** is directly below the bazaar, positioned at the auspicious confluence of two streams. Tiled like an abattoir (for easy hosing down) and covered with a gilt canopy, the sacred area consists of little more than a row of short statuettes, Kali being the heavily decorated one under the canopy. From the back of the shrine, stone steps lead up through a pine wood to a small promontory where there's a subsidiary shrine to Mata, Kali's mother, and good views across to Pharping.

Dakshinkali is as much a picnic area as a holy spot. The sacrifice done, families make for the pavilions that surround the shrine and merrily cook up the remains of their offerings. If you didn't sacrifice anything, you can get fried snacks from the "fast-food" stalls near the gate to the shrine. For a good, sit-down **meal,** make for the *Dakshinkali Village Inn* (☎01/471 0053, ⓦwww .dakchhinkali.com; ⑥), set just back from the Dakshinkali gate. It's a pleasant resort-in-miniature with balconied brick bungalows set around gardens, and would make a pleasant overnight stop if you want to get to the action early. If you're on a bicycle, you can make a great downhill descent from here into the valley of the lower Bagmati.

Bungmati and around

Two paved roads run due south from Patan, on either side of the Nakhkhu River. The western road runs straight to **BUNGMATI**, 5km south of the Ring Road. As a brick huddle atop a hillock, centred on a sunny central square, Bungmati could almost be a Tuscan village. It is in fact one of the better-preserved Newari towns in the valley. Bungmati is also a renowned centre for woodcarving: open workshops show artisans at work, and it's always possible to buy direct.

Buses stop on the eastern edge of town. Plunge down any of the narrow, brick alleys leading downhill to the west, and you'll soon find your way to the broad, teeming central plaza, dominated by the whitewashed *shikra* of **Machhen-dranath**, whose more ancient Newari name is Bunga Dyo ("God of Bunga"). According to legend, Bungmati marks the spot where Machhendranath, having

A note on Hindu animal sacrifices

If orthodox Indian Hindus are very much of the "pure veg", non-violent persuasion, their Tantrically-inclined Nepali cousins have a more bloodthirsty bent. At least, the thirst is on the part of **Kali**, Nepal's fearsome – yet strangely popular – mother goddess who demands blood sacrifice in return for her favours. Nepalis are curiously gentle in their worship: they lead their offerings to the slaughter tenderly, often whispering prayers in the animal's ear and sprinkling its head with water to encourage it to shrug in assent; they believe that the death of this "unfortunate brother" will give it the chance to be reborn as a higher life form. Only uncastrated males, preferably dark in colour, are used. At Dakshinkali, men of a special caste slit the animals' throats and let the blood spray over the idols. Brahman priests oversee the butchering and instruct worshippers in all the complex rituals that follow. However, you don't need to speak Nepali to get the gist of the explanations.

Agriculture in the Valley

Even as the capital's swelling population threatens to fill the Kathmandu Valley in lot after lot of detached, blockhouse, commuter concrete, the Jyapus, indigenous Newari farmers, continue to live in huddled-up, brick-built towns, digging their fields by hand in the time-honoured fashion: with a distinctive two-handed spade called *kodaalo* (*ku* in Newari). The Valley's soil repays such labour-intensive care: it is endowed with a fertile, black clay called *kalimati*, a by-product of sediment from the prehistoric lake, and is low enough in elevation to support two or even three main crops a year. **Rice** is seeded in special irrigated beds shortly before the first monsoon rains in June, and seedlings are transplanted into flooded terraces no later than the end of July. Normally women do this job, using their toes to bed each shoot in the mud. The stalks grow green and bushy during the summer, turning a golden brown and producing mature grain by October.

Harvest time is lazily anarchic: sheaves are spread out on paved roads for cars to loosen the kernels, and then run through portable hand-cranked threshers or bashed against rocks. The grain is gathered in bamboo trays (*nanglo*) and tossed in the wind to winnow away the chaff, or, if there's no wind, *nanglo* can be used to fan away the chaff. Some sheaves are left in stacks to ferment for up to two weeks, producing a sort of baby food called *hakuja*, or "black" rice. The rice dealt with, terraces are then planted with **winter wheat**. Sadly, the period of planting, when the soil looks bare and brown, coincides with the peak tourist season. The wheat is harvested in April or May, after which a third crop of pulses or maize can often be squeezed in. Vegetables are raised year-round at the edges of plots or, in the case of squashes, festooned along fences and on top of shrubs and low trees.

Most Kathmandu Valley farmers are tenants, and have to pay huge proportions of their harvests in rent. But their lot has improved in the past generation: **land reform** in the 1950s and 1960s was relatively diligently implemented near the capital, helping to get landlords and moneylenders off the backs of small farmers, and the Maoist government has also forced landowners to break up and sell off larger holdings. However, the traditional Newari system of **inheritance**, in which family property is divided up among the sons, means that landholdings actually get smaller with each generation. That presents a contrasting problem: farms that are too small to make mechanical equipment worthwhile, necessitating labour-intensive methods and keeping productivity low.

arrived in the valley in the form of a bee to save it from drought, was "born" as the valley's protector-rainmaker. Each summer at the end of Patan's Rato Machhendranath festival, the god's red mask is brought to the Bungmati temple for a six-month residency, but every twelfth year it is kept here through the winter and then pulled by lumbering chariot all the way to Patan (see p.112).

In the southeast corner of the square, a smaller, more traditional temple is dedicated to **Bhairab** in his angry form. This god demands blood sacrifices, and is rarely disappointed. You can climb the steps to peek through the door at his extravagantly fierce gold repoussé mask, and the large skull bowl on the floor where he receives sacrifices.

One kilometre to the north, **Khokana** resembles Bungmati in many ways, but somehow lacks the character and magnetism of its neighbour. It's locally renowned for its mustard oil, and in season the presses run full tilt. Khokana's pagoda-style **Shekali Mai Mandir**, a massive three-tiered job, honours a local nature goddess. Midway between Khokana and Bungmati stands the poorly maintained **Karya Binayak**, another of the valley's four Ganesh temples.

The Chapagaun road

The road due south of Patan's Lagankhel bus park serves two traditional, brick-built Newari towns: **Thecho**, 8km south of Patan, and **Chapagaun**, 1km further south. More attractive than either is the seventeenth-century **Bajra Barahi Mandir**, secreted in a small wood 500m east along a track from Chapagaun, and dedicated to the goddess Kali. The main road continues south for another 4km to **Tika Bhairab**, an abstract mural of the god Bhairab, painted on a wall at the junction of two small streams. If you're on a mountain bike, however, the more picturesque route from Chapagaun to Tika Bhairab takes you east then south, via the Lele Valley (see p.413); it's also possible to cut through to the Godavari road (see p.413), and the hardy can even continue right through to Hetauda and the Terai (see p.415).

Godavari and Phulchoki

The greenest, most pristine part of the valley lies at its southeastern edge, around **Godavari** (pronounced Go-*dao*-ri). Nestling at the foot of forested Phulchoki, the highest peak of the valley rim, are the pleasant Royal Botanical Garden, the temple at Naudhara and the rustic shrine of Bishanku Narayan. From Patan's Lagankhel bus park **microbuses** depart every ten or fifteen minutes for Godavari.

The only **accommodation** in these parts is the pricey *Godavari Village Resort* (T 01/556 0675, W www.godavariresort.com.np; 9), located about 2km north of Godavari. It has a pleasantly landscaped rural setting and sympathetic Newari-style cottages, plus a pool and health club, and is chiefly oriented towards conferences and wealthy weekenders. Beyond the resort, a quiet unpaved road leads westwards through farm country to the Bajra Barahi Mandir and Chapagaun.

Harisiddhi and Godavari

Four kilometres south of Patan, the Godavari road passes through **HARIS-IDDHI**, a traditional Newari town with a sinister legend. Its pagoda-style **Bal Kumari Mandir** – reached by walking straight up a stepped path where the main road jinks left – was once said to have been the centre of a child-sacrifice cult.

Beyond Harisiddhi, the road quietens as it climbs, ending at **GODAVARI**, beautifully situated up against the heavily wooded valley slopes. The **Royal Botanical Garden** (daily: mid-Feb to mid-Nov 10am–5pm; mid-Nov to mid-Feb 10am–4pm; Rs100) lies 1km beyond a sleepy little bus park. (Some buses from Patan go all the way to the park gate, but you'll usually have to walk the last kilometre: turn left down a paved road at the top end of the bus park and left again just before a clump of local restaurants to reach the main gate.) Kipling wrote that "the wildest dreams of Kew/Are the facts of Kathmandu", and this might seem to be the obvious place to put his theory to the test. The garden is in fact more a peaceful picnic-spot than anything else (as well as a popular location for local pop videos), but there is a resplendent orchid house and of course some fine trees. The labelling is inadequate, but the book *Enjoy Trees*, sold in most Kathmandu bookshops, makes a good stand-in.

A little short of the park gate, just off the road, the otherwise inconspicuous spring-fed water tank of **Godavari Kunda** hosts a big *mela* every twelve years during July and August (the next will be in 2011). The adjacent **Buddhist retreat centre**, which must have one of the most fabulous back gardens in the world, is an offshoot of Than *gompa*, in Pharping, and only for the serious seeker of enlightenment: the minimum stay is three years.

Naudhara

The road bearing straight ahead from the bus park passes the renowned St Xavier School and the entrance to the local Community Forest, whose User's Group exacts a modest **toll** (Rs10) on all travellers. Immediately beyond, to the left of the road and opposite an unsightly marble quarry, lies the temple complex of **Naudhara**. The name means "nine spouts" and that's exactly what you'll find, along with worshippers and local women washing clothes. The site is especially holy to the Silwar caste, who come here in huge numbers to worship their ancestral god in the full moon of the month of Bhadau (Aug–Sept). Just left of the spouts stands a small temple, said to represent the feet of the local mother goddess **Phulchoki Mai**. The shrine is kept locked to protect the sacred (but withered) tree-stump inside from Buddhist relic-hunters who were chipping away at the holy wood.

Phulchoki

Pilgrims eager to ascend to Phulchoki Mai's "head", or principal shrine, can take the trail that starts directly behind Nau Dhara. Getting to the top of **Phulchoki** (2762m) involves a stiff walk of at least four hours and 1200m of ascent; it shouldn't be undertaken alone. The whole mountain is covered by luxuriant **forest**, and as you climb from subtropical base to temperate summit you pass through mixed stands of *chilaune* (*Schima wallichii*), *katus* (*Castanopsis indica* or Nepal chestnut) and holly, with Nepali alder in the ravines; higher up there are evergreen oaks, laurel and, of course, rhododendron. The forest is one of the best places in Nepal for **birdwatching** – a trained eye is supposed to be able to spot a hundred or more species in a day – and is also superb for flowers and their attendant butterflies. Phulchoki means "flower-covered" and you'll see orchids, morning glories, corydalis and, in spring, endless rhododendrons.

If the **summit** isn't wreathed in clouds, you'll have a magnificent view of a wide range of the Himalayas and practically the entire Kathmandu Valley (smog permitting). The effect is only slightly marred by the presence of an army base and microwave relay station, not to mention the switchbacking **summit road** which allows a less energetic ascent – assuming you can find a taxi driver willing to commit his car to the only partially paved surface.

Bishanku Narayan

The lovely, sheltered side-valley of **Bishanku** is one of the Kathmandu Valley's most idyllic and unspoilt corners. From the Godavari bus park, follow the dirt road that turns sharply left, almost breaking back on the motor road; you can also get there from the western (back) entrance of the botanical garden. Either way, it's roughly an hour on foot to the shrine of **Bishanku Narayan**, situated in a notch in the ridge on the far northwest side of the little valley, overlooking the paddy and mustard fields that line the valley floor.

One of the valley's four main Narayan (Vishnu) sites, Bishanku is not a temple – rather, it's a small **cave** reached by a set of precarious steps. A chain-mail curtain protects the god's image inside the cave. If you're thin enough, you can descend through another narrow fissure; according to popular belief, those who manage to squeeze through it will be absolved of past sins.

179

The Newars

The **Newars** are a special case. Their stronghold is a valley – the Kathmandu Valley – which, while geographically located within Nepal's hill region, has its own distinct climate and history. Newars themselves are careful to distinguish themselves from other hill peoples, and although they're an ethnic minority nationally, their majority presence in the pivotal Kathmandu Valley has enabled them to exert a cultural influence far beyond their numbers. An outsider could easily make the mistake of thinking that Newari culture is Nepali culture.

Many anthropologists believe that the root stock of the Newars is the **Kirats**, a clan who legendarily ruled the Kathmandu Valley between the seventh century BC and the second century AD. However, Newari culture has been in the making for millennia, as waves of immigrants, overlords, traders and usurpers have mingled in the melting pot of the valley. These arrivals contributed new customs, beliefs and skills to the overall stew, but they weren't completely assimilated – rather, they found their own niches in society, maintaining internal social structures and traditions and fulfilling unique spiritual and professional roles. In time, these *thars* (clans) were formally organized into a Newari caste system that mirrored that of the Baahun–Chhetris and, still later, became nested within it. Thus Newari society is a microcosm of Nepali society, with many shared cultural traits and a common language (Newari), but also with an enormous amount of diversity among its members.

Newari **religion** is so complex that it must be described separately elsewhere (see p.438); suffice to say that individual Newars may identify themselves as either Hindu or Buddhist, depending on their *thar*'s historical origin, but this makes little difference to their fundamental doctrines or practices. **Kinship** roles are extremely important to Newars, and are reinforced by elaborate life-cycle rituals and annual feasts; likewise, each *thar* has its role to play in festivals and other public events. A uniquely Newar social invention is the *guthi*, a kind of kinship-based Rotary club which maintains temples and resthouses, organizes festivals and, indirectly, ensures the transmission of Newar culture from one generation to the next. *Guthi* have been in serious decline since the 1960s, however, when land reform deprived them of much of their income from holdings around the valley.

With so great an emphasis placed on **social relationships**, it's little wonder that Newars like to live so close together. Unlike other hill peoples, they're urbanites at heart. Their cities are masterpieces of density, with tall tenements pressing against narrow alleys and shopfronts opening directly onto streets. In the past couple of centuries, Newar traders have colonized lucrative crossroads and recreated their bustling bazaars throughout Nepal. Even Newari farmers build their villages in compact, urban nuclei (partly to conserve the fertile farmland of the valley).

Centuries of domination by foreign rulers have, if anything, only accentuated the uniqueness of Newari art and architecture. For 1500 years the Newars have sustained an almost continuous artistic flowering in stone, wood, metal and brick. They're believed to have invented the pagoda, and it was a Newari architect, Arniko, who led a Nepali delegation in the thirteenth century to introduce the technique to the Chinese. The pagoda style of stacked, strut-supported roofs finds unique expression in Nepali (read Newari) temples, and is echoed in the overhanging eaves of Newari houses.

Newars are easily recognized. Traditionally they carry heavy loads in baskets suspended at either end of a shoulder pole (*nol*), in contrast with Nepali hill people who carry things on their backs supported by a tumpline from the forehead. As for clothing, you can usually tell a Newari woman by the fanned pleats at the front of her sari; men have mostly abandoned traditional dress, but some still wear the customary *daura suruwal* and waistcoat.

Bhaktapur

In the soft, dusty light of evening the old city of Bhaktapur, with its pagoda roofs and its harmonious blend of wood, mud-brick and copper, looked extraordinarily beautiful. It was as though a faded medieval tapestry were tacked on to the pale tea-rose sky. In the foreground a farmhouse was on fire, and orange flames licked like liquescent dragon's tongues across the thatched roof. One thought of Chaucer's England and Rabelais's France; of a world of intense, violent passions and brilliant colour, where sin was plentiful but so were grace and forgiveness...

Charlie Pye-Smith, *Travels in Nepal*

Kathmandu's field of gravity weakens somewhere east of the airport; beyond, you fall into the rich atmosphere of **BHAKTAPUR** (also known as **BHADGAUN**). Rising in a tight mass of warm brick out of the fertile fields of the valley, the city looks something like Kathmandu must have been before the arrival of the modern world. In among Bhaktapur's herringbone-paved streets and narrow alleys, the atmosphere is no less medieval: women wash at public taps, men in traditional dress lounge in the many *sattal*, or covered loggias, peasants squat by the road selling meagre baskets of vegetables and worshippers assiduously attend neighbourhood shrines. And everywhere the burnt-peach hue of bricks is offset by the deep brown of intensely carved wood – the essential media of the Newari architects.

Even today, well over half of Bhaktapur's population is from the agricultural Jyapu caste of the Newars, and it may well be the city's tightly-knit, inward-looking nature that has saved it from the free-for-all expansion that overwhelms Kathmandu. Thanks to a long-term German-funded restoration and sanitation programme, and to the policies of its independent-minded municipal council, much of the city is **pedestrianized**. Temples and public shelters have been restored with the money raised from the entrance fee, and new buildings are now required to follow traditional architectural styles. This is one Nepali city that has got its act together, and it wears its status as a UNESCO World Heritage site proudly.

It's hardly surprising therefore that some relatively **upmarket** travellers head to Bhaktapur straight from Kathmandu airport. During the day, tour groups and persistent "student" guides mill about enthusiastically in the beguiling main squares, but after hours, or in among the maze of backstreets, it would be hard not to feel the pulse of this quintessential Newari city.

Some history

The "City of Devotees" was probably founded in the ninth century, and by 1200 it was ruling Nepal. In that year Bhaktapur witnessed the launch of the **Malla era** when, according to the Nepali chronicles, King Aridev, upon being called out of a wrestling bout to hear of the birth of a son, bestowed on the prince the hereditary title Malla ("wrestler"). To this day, beefy carved wrestlers are the city's trademark temple guardians. Bhaktapur ruled the valley until 1482, when Yaksha Malla divided the kingdom among his three sons, setting in train three centuries of continuous squabbling.

It was a Bhaktapur king who helped to bring the Malla era to a close in 1766 by inviting **Prithvi Narayan Shah**, the Gorkha leader, to aid him in a quarrel against Kathmandu. Seizing on this pretext, Prithvi Narayan conquered the valley within three years, Bhaktapur being the last of the three capitals to surrender.

Arrival, orientation and information

Bhaktapur drapes across an east–west fold in the valley, its southern fringe sliding down towards the sluggish Hanumante River. Owing to a gradual westward drift,

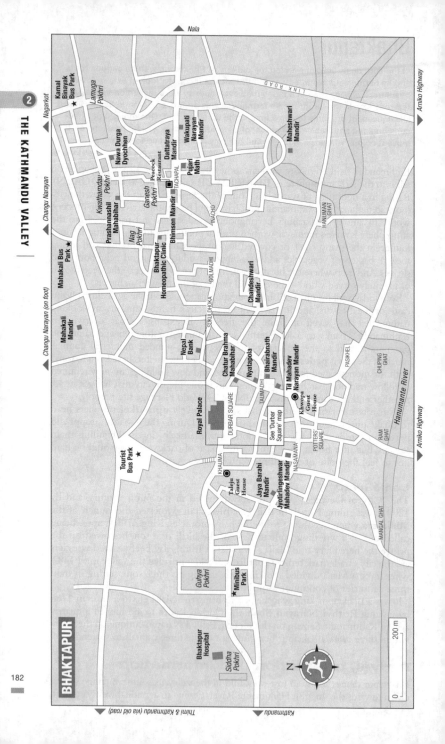

BHAKTAPUR

Nala

Amiko Highway

Link Road

Nagarkot

Kamal Binayak Bus Park
Lamuga Pokhri

Changu Narayan

Nawa Durga Dyochhen

Kwathamdau Pokhri

Prashannashil Mahabihar

Ganesh Pokhri
Peacock Restaurant
Dattatraya Mandir
TACHAPAL
Wakupati Narayan Mandir
Pujari Math

Maheshwari Mandir

Mahakali Bus Park

Nag Pokhri
Bhaktapur Homeopathic Clinic
Bhimsen Mandir
INACHO

Changu Narayan (on foot)

Mahakali Mandir

GOLMADHI

Chandeshwari Mandir

HANUMAN GHAT

Nepal Bank

SUKULDHOKA

Chatur Brahma Mahabihar
Nyatapola
Bhairabnath Mandir

Til Mahadev Narayan Mandir

PASKHEL

CHUPING GHAT

Royal Palace

DURBAR SQUARE

TAUMADHI

Khwopa Guest House

Hanumante River

See 'Durbar Square' map

Tourist Bus Park

KHAUMA

NASAMANA

POTTERS' SQUARE

RAM GHAT

Amiko Highway

Taleju Guest House

Jaya Barahi Mandir

Jyotirlingeshwar Mahadev Mandir

Guhya Pokhri
Minibus Park

MANGAL GHAT

Bhaktapur Hospital

Siddha Pokhri

N

200 m

0

Thimi & Kathmandu (via old road)

Kathmandu

the city has two centres (residents of the two halves stage a boisterous tug-of-war during the city's annual Bisket festival) and three main squares. In the west, **Durbar Square** and **Taumadhi Tol** dominate the post-fifteenth-century city, while **Tachapal Tol** (**Dattatreya Square**) presides over the older east end.

Handiest of the **buses** to Bhaktapur is the "Express" minibus service from Kathmandu's City Bus Park, arriving at the bus park next to Siddha Pokhri, a five-minute walk west of Durbar Square. The route follows the main Arniko Highway which is one of the most choked and choking roads in Nepal, although there are plans to upgrade it to a terrifying six lanes. Frequent Banepa-, Dhulikhel- and Barhabise-bound buses from the City Bus Park drop you on the Arniko Highway about ten minutes' walk south of town. Local buses from Nagarkot terminate at Kamal Binayak, five minutes northeast of Tachapal. If you come on a private tour bus you'll be deposited at the Tourist Bus Park, just north of Durbar Square. **Taxis** (Rs500 or more from Kathmandu; Rs800 or so from Nagarkot) will take you only to the nearest city gate. Only a masochist would **cycle** to Bhaktapur on the main road from Kathmandu. Once beyond the airport, however, it's possible to turn off the busy trunk road (either just before or just after the Manchara River) and head up to join the old road which leads past Thimi (see p.195) to Bhaktapur.

Bhaktapur is compact enough to be explored on foot. There's an ATM on Durbar Square itself, and a **bank** with an ATM in the Mini Mart at Surya Binayak. Plenty of places offer international **telephone** and internet services. Most guesthouses can make bookings on tourist **buses** and even on domestic flights, saving you a trip to Kathmandu, and may be able to find you a rental bike if you want to explore the environs. Bhaktapur's **hospital** would not be a great place to have to go in an emergency. However, the **Bhaktapur Homeo-pathic Clinic**, at Nagh Pokhari (℡01/661 3197), is well-regarded; hours vary depending on individual staff schedules.

Accommodation

Most **guesthouses** in Bhaktapur are small and exceptionally well located in the area around Taumadhi and Durbar Square (though this means that early morning *puja* bells may prevent a lie-in). As a rule prices are somewhat higher than for comparable lodgings in Kathmandu, but Bhaktapur is worth it. The city doesn't have that many beds, so book ahead in busy times, or arrive as early as possible in the day.

Bhadgaon Guest House ℡01/661 0488, ⊛www .bhadgaon.com.np. It's on the pricey side, but the rooms are comfortably appointed and the uniformed staff give the place a professional feel. Just eleven rooms – one of them deluxe, with its own terrace –

plus a relatively drab annexe. There's a calm central garden area and a good rooftop restaurant. ⑥
Golden Gate Guest House ℡01/661 0534, ⓔgoldengatge@mail.com.np. Relatively large concrete block with faded rooms, but it's clean,

friendly, pleasantly secluded and has good views from the roof and upper (more expensive) rooms. ❷
Khwopa Guest House ☎01/661 4661, ⓦwww .khwopa-guesthouse.com.np. Homely place with ten cosy (if rather dark), low-ceilinged rooms piled up over three floors. Furnishings are simple but the communal parts are attractive, with wooden fittings and terracotta tiles. ❸
Kumari Guest House ☎01/661 8266, ⓔkumari @craftcoll.wlink.com.np. Bright, spacious rooms, with comfortable, carved-wood beds, in a new guesthouse between Taumadhi Tol and Durbar Square. ❹
Pagoda Guest House ☎01/661 3248, ⓦwww .pagodaguesthouse.com.np. Friendly, family-run place with creeper-festooned balconies overlooking a small front court and the Nyatapola. Only the more expensive rooms have views, but they're all clean and well-furnished. ❹
Newa Guest House ☎01/691 6335. The newest and poshest hotel in town, done up in 2007 in a smart version of classic Newari style, with terra-cotta floor tiles, bamboo furniture, carved-wood

windows and lots of cream linen fabrics. Two deluxe rooms share a private terrace. ❻
Shiva Guest House ☎01/661 3912, ⓦwww .shivaguesthouse.com. This was the first guest-house in Bhaktapur, and it has a classic location overlooking the Pashupati Mandir. Unexceptional but reasonably cheerful inside, with helpful management. Good food, too. There's a range of rooms, from simple ones with shared bathrooms (❸) to en suites with views of the square (❺).
Siddhi Laxmi Guest House ☎01/661 2500, ⓔsiddhilaxmi.guesthouse@gmail.com. The seven rooms are rather squeezed into this ancient building, but it has bags of character for the price, with oddments of Newari interior décor more than offsetting the slightly tired bathrooms. The more expensive rooms are larger and have balconies. ❸
Taleju Guest House ☎01/661 3020, ⓔtaleju_ghr @hotmail.com. Occupying a modern block just outside the western entrance gate, this is not really why you come to Bhaktapur, but the rooms are large, clean and well-furnished. ❸

Durbar Square

Bhaktapur's **Durbar Square** hasn't got quite the same gusto as its namesakes in Kathmandu and Patan. Isolated near the old city's edge, it's neither a commercial nor a social focal point, and it has lacked a certain architectural harmony ever since the 1934 earthquake claimed several of its temples. Despite all that, it boasts one of Nepal's proudest artistic achievements – the **Golden Gate** – plus the National Art Gallery.

The square enjoyed one brief, magnificent renaissance during the shooting of the 1995 film **Little Buddha**, when it was used as the location for many of the ancient flashback scenes. Director Bernardo Bertolucci transformed the area beyond recognition: high, simulated brick walls were erected to block modern sightlines and the palace front was extended with false balconies and columns. Residents won't soon forget that Hollywood facelift – nor the handsome fees Bertolucci paid them for the use of their houses and shopfronts.

The Royal Palace

Bhaktapur's **Royal Palace** originally stood further east, near Tachapal Tol, but was shifted westwards (like the city) in the fifteenth century, and may have lost various wings along the way. It is said to have once had 99 *chowks* (courtyards), and while this number is almost certainly fanciful, there would have been many more than the five which are all that remain since the renovation and demolition works of 1934. Further structural works are planned in order to rescue the palace from serious subsidence problems, so some areas may be closed off. Worst affected is the palace's superbly carved eastern wing, known as the **Pancha-panna Jhyale Durbar** ("Palace of Fifty-Five Windows "), which was raised around 1700 by Bupalendra Malla, Bhaktapur's great builder-king, whose *namaste*-ing figure kneels on a stone **pillar** opposite.

The Golden Gate and Mul Chowk

While the **Golden Gate** (Sun Dhoka) probably wouldn't be so famous if it were made of wood or stone – it is, in fact, gilt copper repoussé – its detail and

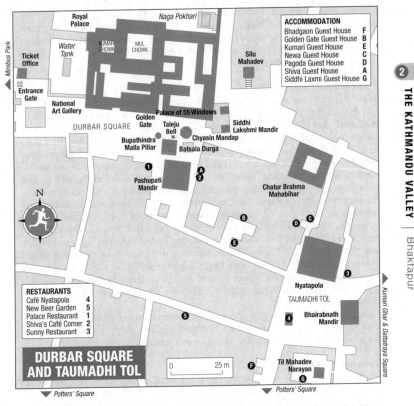

Within the map image: Royal Palace · Naga Pokhari · Water Tank · KUMARI CHOWK · MUL CHOWK · Silu Mahadev · Ticket Office · Entrance Gate · National Art Gallery · DURBAR SQUARE · Golden Gate · Taleju Bell · Palace of 55 Windows · Siddhi Lakshmi Mandir · Bupathindra Malla Pillar · Chyasin Mandap · Batsala Durga · Pashupati Mandir · Chatur Brahma Mahabihar · Nyatapola · TAUMADHI TOL · Bhairabnath Mandir · Til Mahadev Narayan · Potters' Square · Minibus Park · Kumari Ghar & Dattatraya Square

ACCOMMODATION
Bhadgaon Guest House	F
Golden Gate Guest House	B
Kumari Guest House	E
Newa Guest House	C
Pagoda Guest House	D
Shiva Guest House	A
Siddhi Laxmi Guest House	G

RESTAURANTS
Café Nyatapola	4
New Beer Garden	5
Palace Restaurant	1
Shiva's Café Corner	2
Sunny Restaurant	3

DURBAR SQUARE AND TAUMADHI TOL

0   25 m

sheer exuberance have ensured its current renown. The *torana* above the door features a squat Garud and a ten-armed, four-headed Taleju, the Mallas' guardian deity, but to locals the most powerful figures are those of Bhairab and Kali, situated chest-high on either side of the gate. These alone among the statues are covered in red *abhir* and yellow *keshori* powder, showing that they are still worshipped today.

Upon entry, you follow an outdoor passage around to another impressive doorway, depicting the goddess Taleju and her heavenly host in wood. Beyond it lies the ornate, polychrome **Mul Chowk**, which is probably the oldest surviving part of the complex, and is regarded by art historians as one of the most exquisite palace courtyards in the whole of the Valley. You can peer in through the door to catch tantalizing glimpses of the riotously elaborate metalwork, carvings and wallpaintings, but photographs are forbidden, and only Hindus can enter to see the metal *kalash* (vessel) representing the goddess. The actual Taleju idol hidden in the sanctum in the south wing – said to be a *yantra*, or mystical diagram – may be seen by initiates only. South Indian in origin, Taleju was brought here by the fourteenth-century king Harisinghadev, and was also adopted by the royal houses of Kathmandu and Patan. She was never much worshipped by commoners, however, and the dynasties that patronized her are long gone. Those who worship her today equate her with Bhagwati or Durga.

The door facing you across the courtyard leads into the fabled **Kumari Chowk**, said by the few who know it to be as old and as beautiful as Mul

Chowk, though smaller. Turning back towards the Golden Gate, a doorway on the left leads through to **Naga Pokhari** ("Snake Pond "), a regal bathing tank dating from the early sixteenth century. The extraordinary waterspout writhes with images of thirsty animals in gilt copper, overlooked by two sinister gilt *nag* figures standing clear of the water.

The National Art Gallery

Stone friezes at the entrance of the palace's western wing portray Vishnu Varahi and Narasimha, Vishnu's boar and man-lion avatar. They guard the excellent **National Art Gallery** (mid-Jan to mid-Oct Mon 10.30am–2pm, Tues–Sat 10.30am–4pm; mid-Oct to mid-Jan Mon 10.30am–2pm, Tues–Sat 10.30am–3pm; Rs100), which is chiefly devoted to tantric *poubha* and *thangka* paintings of the fierce local gods Bhairab and Kali. The latter is seen in many of his 64 blood-curdling forms, including White Bhairab, Lion-faced and Fire-breathing. The collection also includes illuminated pages of religious texts going back as far as the eleventh century, a few erotic miniatures, some wonderful stone images and inscriptions from the Malla dynasty and a series of royal portraits ending, pointedly, with Dipendra. The high-ceilinged main hall, upstairs, houses a fine depiction of Nritaswor, the dancing, copulating Tantric union of Shiva and Shakti, and the curious *Sata Chakra Darsan*, showing the location of the seven power points (*chakra*) of the human body. In the adjacent gallery, an eighteenth-century *paubha* labelled "Gorkha Palace " acts as a wonderful botanical-zoological-topographical map of Nepal, stretching from the Terai to cranes soaring over the Himalayas.

English-speaking **guides** may be available for private tours, which are well worth joining; the price and length would be negotiable. The **entry ticket** is also good for admission to the two smaller museums in Dattatreya Square (see p.190).

The square

Durbar Square itself won't detain you for long; in any case, as a parade of regal set-pieces it never had much connection with the religious life of the town. Near the main gate at the west end you can admire a pair of multiple-armed statues of **Bhairab** and **Ugrachandi**, whose sculptor reportedly had his hands cut off by order of the Bhaktapur king to ensure that he wouldn't reproduce the images in Kathmandu or Patan. Among the clutch of minor temples opposite, a Shiva *shikra* showcases the often overlooked Newar art of brickwork.

In the entire square, only the fifteenth-century **Pashupati Mandir** at the busier, more touristy eastern end receives much in the way of reverence. The oldest structure extant here, the temple houses a copy of the exalted Pashupati-nath *linga*, and its roof struts sport some wildly deviant erotic carvings. Next door stands the mid-eighteenth-century stone *shikra* of **Batsala Durga** and the obligatory **Taleju Bell**, plus a smaller replica known generally as the "**Bell of Barking Dogs**", so called because its toll evidently inflicts ultrasonic agony on local canines.

Behind the bell rises the **Chyasin Mandap**, the Pavilion of the Eight Corners, erected in 1990 as an exact replica of an eighteenth-century structure destroyed in the 1934 earthquake. German architects did a first-rate job of relocating original pillars and lintels and integrating them into a new, steel-reinforced structure, but they had to do without the original carved roof-struts, which have adorned the entrance archway leading into Kathmandu's New Road since 1934. East of here are another fine stone *shikra* to Durga and the platforms of other demolished and half-heartedly rebuilt temples. This end of

▲ Bhaktapur: a medieval jewel and a living, working Newar city

the square is slated for renovation, and in the long term may even see the construction of new temples.

Rare for predominantly Hindu Bhaktapur, the well-preserved **Chatur Brahma Mahabihar**, east of the square, attracts Buddhist as well as Hindu worshippers, and is a gathering place for neighbourhood metalsmiths in the evening; you might hear *bhajan* hymn singing, with its languorous accompaniment on harmonium and tabla.

Taumadhi Tol

One hundred metres southeast of Durbar Square, **Taumadhi Tol** is the nerve centre of Bhaktapur's Newari culture. It's a lively place to linger, even at night, when men sing *bhajan* hymns (especially on full moon nights) and street vendors sell *momos* and other snacks from their mobile stalls. In mid-April this square serves as the assembly point for Bisket, Nepal's foremost New Year celebration (see box, p.188).

Dominating Taumadhi and all of Bhaktapur, the graceful, five-tiered **Nyatapola** is Nepal's tallest and most classically proportioned pagoda. So obscure is its deity, a tantric goddess named Siddhi Lakshmi, that she apparently has no devotees, and the sanctuary has been barred to all but priests ever since its completion in 1702. Perhaps that's why the temple is named not for a deity but, uniquely, for its architectural dimensions: in Newari, *nyata* means "five-stepped" and *pola* means "roof". The Nyatapola's five pairs of temple guardians – Malla wrestlers, elephants, lions, griffins and two minor goddesses, Baghini (Tigress) and Singhini (Lioness) – are as famous as the temple itself. Each pair is supposed to be ten times as strong as the pair below. Bisket chariot components, including the solid wooden wheels, can be seen stacked up behind the temple.

The heavy, thick-set **Bhairabnath Mandir** is as different from the slender Nyatapola as one pagoda could possibly be from another. The most peculiar thing about this heavy-set building, in fact, is the tiny Bhairab idol mounted on a sort of mantel on the front of the temple (several other figures are kept inside, including the larger mask that leads the Bisket parade). A story is told that Bhairab, travelling incognito, once came to Bhaktapur to watch the Bisket festivities. Divining the god's presence and hoping to extract a boon, the priests bound him with tantric spells, and when he tried to escape by sinking into the ground they chopped off his head. Now Bhairab, or at least his head, gets to ride in the Bisket parade every year – inside a locked box on board the chariot. The *kinkinimalla*, or golden metal fringe at the very top of the temple, is held to be particularly fine.

Hidden away on the southeast side of the square, the seventeenth-century **Til Mahadev Narayan Mandir** displays all the iconography of a Vishnu (Narayan) temple: a gilded *sankha* (conch), *chakra* (wheel) and Garud are all hoisted on pillars out in front. The temple's name, it's said, derives from an incident involving a trader from Thimi who, upon unfolding his wares here, magically discovered the image of Narayan in a consignment of sesame seeds (*til*).

A block northeast of the Bhairabnath Mandir stands Bhaktapur's **Kumari Ghar**. An image of the goddess is kept upstairs and is only displayed publicly during Bisket. The living goddess herself resides in another building north of Tachapal Tol.

Bisket: New Year, Bhaktapur style

While many Nepali festivals have their origins in religious myth, Bhaktapur's high-spirited **Bisket** festival is based on a fairy tale. Similar fables appear in Zoroastrian myth and in the biblical Apocrypha's Book of Tobit. According to the local version, a Bhaktapur king wanted to marry off his daughter, but each time he made a match, the groom would turn up dead in the marital bed the next morning. Eligible bachelors were soon thin on the ground, and the people prayed for deliverance from the curse. One day a stranger came to town and learned of the situation from his host, whose son was due to be the next groom, and offered to take the son's place. Forcing himself to stay awake after doing the act with the princess, the stranger watched as two deadly serpents slithered out of her nostrils. The hero slew the snakes, broke the spell and won the undying gratitude of the people, who now celebrate his deed with an annual festival. The festival's Newari name, Biska, is a contraction of two words meaning "snake " and "death ".

Bisket also differs from most Nepali festivals in that its date is reckoned by the solar calendar, not the lunar one, which means it always starts on April 9 or 10. It kicks off with a raucous **tug-of-war** in Taumadhi Tol, in which residents of the upper and lower halves of the city try to pull a creaky, three-storied chariot containing the image of Bhairab to their respective sides; you can usually see the chariot's wheels lying beside the Bhairab temple. On the fourth day – the day before Nawa Barsa (Nepali New Year) – Bhairab and another smaller chariot are pulled to the sloping open area above Chuping Ghat. When they're in place, men of the city struggle to raise a 25-metre-high **ceremonial pole** with a crossbeam to which are attached two banners representing the two slain snakes – an exciting and sometimes dangerous operation.

The pole stays up until the next afternoon, when residents again take up a tug-of-war, this time trying to pull the mighty pole down to their side. (This is an even more dangerous performance: on one or two occasions people have been killed by the falling pole.) The pole's plunge marks the official beginning of the **new year**. Bisket continues for another four days, with a wild parade of *khats*, or gorgeous palanquins for deities, in the eastern part of the city, a candlelight procession to Dattatreya Square, an all-city display of temple deities, and a final tug-of-war over Bhairab's chariot.

West to the Potters' Square

Like a brick canyon, Bhaktapur's main commercial thoroughfare runs from Taumadhi west to the city gate. Roughly 150m along, you'll reach a kind of playground of sculptures and shrines, and a *shikra* that rejoices in the name of **Jyotirlingeshwar Mahadev**, freely translatable as "Great God of the Resplendent Phallus" – a reference to a myth in which Shiva challenges Brahma and Vishnu to find the end of his organ (they never do). Further west, where the street's brick cobbles temporarily give way to flagstones, the **Jaya Barahi Mandir** – one of many whose recent face-lift was paid for by the tourist entrance fee – commemorates the *shakti* (consort) of Vishnu the boar; you have to stand well back from this broad edifice to see its pagoda roofs.

Dark, damp alleys beckon on either side of the main road – north towards Durbar Square and south to the river. An obligatory destination in this area is Kumale Tol, the **Potters' Square**, a sloping open space southwest of Taumadhi Tol. Until recently, Bhaktapur's potters (*kumal*) worked here fairly anonymously, cranking out simple water vessels, stovepipes, disposable yogurt pots and the like. Nowadays the square has blossomed into quite a little tourist attraction, and as its output has shifted to tourist knick-knacks, workaday pottery is increasingly being produced in other, smaller squares in the eastern part of the city, or in neighbouring Thimi. Ironically, the tourist market gives these potters an incentive to stick to mostly traditional methods. You'll see them kneading their clay by hand, and a few still form their vessels on hand-powered wheels. The finished creations are set out in soldierly rows to dry in the sun for a day or two before firing, which turns them from grey to brick red.

Tachapal Tol (Dattatreya Square)

From Taumadhi, the eastern segment of Bhaktapur's main artery snakes its way to the original and still-beating heart of the city, **Tachapal Tol** (or **Dattatreya Square**). Here again a pair of temples loom over the square, older than those of Taumadhi if not as eye-catching. More notably, though, Tachapal conceals Nepal's most celebrated masterpiece of woodcarving, the Pujari Math's Peacock Window, and a superb woodcarving museum. You'll also find the finest woodwork studios in Nepal here, which are well worth a browse, even if you haven't got room in your rucksack for an eight-foot, Rs100,000 peacock-window reproduction.

Just north of Tachapal, a second open space around Ganesh Pokhri is equally busy with *pasal* (shops) and street vendors. South of the square is also good for exploring, as Bhaktapur's medieval backstreets spill down the steep slope to the river-like tributaries.

Dattatreya and Bhimsen temples

Rearing up behind an angelic pillar-statue of Garud, the **Dattatreya Mandir** is Bhaktapur's oldest structure. The temple was raised in 1427 during the reign of Yaksha Malla, the last king to rule the valley from Bhaktapur. Like the Kastha-mandap of Kathmandu, which it resembles, it was once a *sattal*, a three-storey loggia and public meeting place, and is similarly reputed to have been built from the wood of a single tree. Dattatreya, a sort of one-size-fits-all deity imported from southern India, epitomizes the religious syncretism that Nepal is famous for: to Vaishnavas, Dattatreya is an incarnation of Vishnu, while Shaivas hail him as Shiva's guru and Buddhists even fit him into their pantheon as a *bodhisattva*.

The oblong temple at the opposite end of the square belongs to **Bhimsen**, the patron saint of Newari merchants, whose territory Tachapal is. As usual for a Bhimsen temple, the ground floor is open – making a popular meeting place – and the shrine is hidden upstairs.

The Pujari Math

Behind and to the right of the Dattatreya temple stands the sumptuous eighteenth-century **Pujari Math**, one of a dozen priests' quarters (*math*) that once ringed Tachapal Tol. Similar to Buddhist *bahal*, these *math* typically sheltered communities of Hindu devotees loyal to a single leader or sect. Like *bahal*, most have now also been converted to other, secular uses. Given the nature of the caste system, it's not surprising that the grandest houses in the city traditionally belonged to priests. The Pujari Math's awesome windows can be seen on two sides; the often-imitated **Peacock Window**, overlooking a narrow lane on the building's far (east) side, has for two centuries been acclaimed as the zenith of Nepali window-lattice carving.

The woodcarving and brass museums

Don't miss the small **Woodcarving Museum** (same hours and ticket as National Art Gallery, see p.186) on the upper floors of the Pujari Math, which enables you to get closer to exquisite temple carvings than is normally possible. Highlights of the collection are an alluring fifteenth-century Nartaki Devi, a large, waist-up Bhairava (Bhairab) of the seventeenth century, several magnificent *steles* and *torana*, and various abstractly weathered temple struts. The tiny **courtyard** is a lavish, almost oppressive, concentration of woodcarving virtuosity, and possibly the finest in the country.

The **Brass and Bronze Museum** (same hours and ticket as the National Art Gallery) consists of domestic and ritual vessels and implements, their esoteric uses giving a good insight into just how complex traditional Nepali culture can be.

Nawa Durga Dyochhen and points east

North of Tachapal, the **Nawa Durga Dyochhen** honours the nine manifestations of Durga. According to legend, they used to eat solitary travellers, turning the area east of Bhaktapur into a Bermuda triangle until a priest managed to cast a tantric spell on them. The Nawa Durga occupy a special place in Bhaktapur's spiritual landscape: the city is said to be delimited by symbolic Nawa Durga stones (*pith*), and most *tol* (neighbourhoods) have adopted one of the nine as their protector goddess.

Most famous of all are the **Nawa Durga dancers**, a troupe whose members are drawn from the caste of flower sellers. Each wears a painted clay mask which, empowered by tantric incantations, enables the wearer to become the very embodiment of the deity. Every September a new set of masks is moulded and painted, each with its own iconography – there are actually thirteen in all: the Nawa Durga plus four attendant deities. On Bijaya Dasami, the "victorious tenth day" of Dasain (usually early Oct), the dancers and accompanying musicians gather at Brahmayani Pith, about one kilometre east of town, and dance all the way to the Golden Gate, where they re-enact the legend of Durga's victory over a buffalo demon. The troupe continues to perform at designated places on days determined by the lunar calendar throughout the winter and spring wedding and festival seasons. In the month of Bhadau (Aug–Sept) their masks are formally retired and burned. You can buy miniature reproductions all over town.

West of the Nawa Durga Dyochhen, the **Prashannashil Mahabihar**, distinguished by its pagoda-style cupola, is another of Bhaktapur's few Buddhist institutions. East along the main road from Tachapal, the **Wakupati Narayan Mandir**, where local Jyapus worship Vishnu as a harvest god, displays no fewer than five Garuds mounted on pillars in a line.

Along the Hanumante Khola

The **Hanumante Khola** is Bhaktapur's humble tributary of the River Ganga, its name deriving from the monkey god Hanuman who, locals like to think, stopped here for a drink on his way back from the Himalayas after gathering medicinal herbs to heal Ram's brother in an episode of the Ramayana. Like all rivers in the valley, it's pretty disgusting, but **Hanuman Ghat**, located straight downhill from Tachapal Tol where two tributaries join, manages to transcend the stink. Morning *puja* and ablutions are a daily routine for many, while old-timers come here just to hang out. The area is reached by passing between two jumbo *shivalinga* hoisted on octagonal plinths. Behind the left-hand one is the Ram temple that gives the ghat its Hanuman association: a statue of the monkey god outside the sanctum pays tribute to his master sheltered within. Another Hanuman, painted orange, keeps watch over a clutter of small Shiva *linga* scattered around the confluence area.

Downhill from Taumadhi Tol, **Chuping Ghat's** temple complex has been partially restored and taken over by Kathmandu University's Department of Music, and sometimes offers short courses in Nepali music. If it's open you can go in – there's a lovely garden, and students may be heard practising their instruments. The long, sloping area above the ghat is the focal point on New Year's Day (Nawa Barsa) in April, when a 25-metre *linga* pole is ceremonially toppled by the throng. This area is inhabited mainly by members of the sweeper caste, so much of Bhaktapur's rubbish ends up nearby.

Ram Ghat, below Potters' Square, has little to offer beyond a run-of-the-mill Ram temple. **Mangal Ghat**, further downstream, boasts a more atmospheric selection of neglected artefacts, and by following the trail of *linga* across the river you'll end up at a forbidding Kali temple in one of Bhaktapur's satellite villages.

Eating

Most of the guesthouses have their own **restaurants** with standard tourist menus. Meanwhile, several cafés overlooking the various squares cater mainly to day-trippers: they're pricey but great places for soaking up the atmosphere, and maybe the sun.

For something more authentically Nepali, there are plenty of cheap *bhojanalaya* west of Durbar Square and around the bus park, and Newari *bhatti* are found throughout the old city. If nothing else, you can always load up on thick, presweetened yogurt (Bhaktapur's famed *juju dhau* – "king of curds"), available from local stalls at a fraction of the price charged in tourist restaurants.

Café Nyatapola Inflated prices, but the location, in a former temple in Taumadhi Tol, is irresistible, and the atmosphere is fairly smart. Apart from the luxurious three-course *daal bhat*, the food is mostly snacky, with omelettes, chips and Newari meat and egg side dishes. Usually closed in the evening.

New Beer Garden Tucked down a back alley, this really is like a pub with an attached garden. Popular with locals for beer and Newari snacks, which are excellent: try the Newari

set meal. Also offers sizzlers, Tibetan dishes and pizzas at fair prices.

Palace Restaurant The long and atmospheric dining room is the main attraction, hidden behind ancient windows and feeling almost like a train carriage. The menu is on the pricey side, but covers all the bases from Italian to Indian and Nepali to Chinese.

Peacock Restaurant You can't beat the surroundings – the restaurant occupies a former *math* overlooking Dattatreya Square – but the food is somewhat uninspiring for the price.

Shiva's Café Corner One of the better guesthouse restaurants, with the interior made cosy by a big wooden bar and beams above, and views through the window onto Durbar Square. The food is surprisingly good for a menu which runs the gamut from Chinese to Mexican via pasta and curry dishes. Prices are fairly reasonable.

Sunny Restaurant The food is only competent, but the location is the thing, with a south-facing terrace right next to the Nyatapola – and relatively uninflated prices.

Shopping

Bhaktapur offers a relatively modest selection of most of the tourist-oriented goods you can buy in Kathmandu, usually at similar prices. The best buys are perhaps **wood** (see p.132) and the renowned Nawa Durga **puppets** and papier-mâché **masks** (see p.132). And of course you can pick up cheap **pottery** at the Potters' Square: animal figures, planters, candlestick holders, ashtrays, piggy banks (onomatopoeically called *kutrukke*) and so on. Nepalis recognize Bhaktapur for its traditional **textiles**, such as black-and-red *pataasi* material and the formal *Bhadgaonle topi* headgear. There are plentiful woollens and pashmina shawls for sale, too. Several shops around Taumadhi sell quality **thangka** and **watercolours** of local scenes, painted locally, while **metal** pieces such as incense holders and traditional ritual objects are also produced here.

Changu Narayan

The beautiful, tranquil site of **CHANGU NARAYAN** is a must. Perched at the abrupt end of the ridge north of Bhaktapur, the ancient temple complex commands a fine view of the valley in three directions. "One remembers all the wealth of carving of the rest of the Valley," wrote Percival Landon in 1928, "but when all is recalled it is probably to the shrine of Changu Narayan that one offers the palm. Perhaps one drives back home from Bhatgaon more full of thought than from any other expedition to the many outlying places of this crowded centre of holiness and history and art." Despite the competing attractions of the local souvenir industry, the site retains its pensive, palpably ancient atmosphere – not to mention the finest collection of statues outside the National Museum.

An **entrance fee** of Rs100 is charged at the main gate by the small bus park. From Bhaktapur, **minibuses** leave every thirty minutes from the Mahakali bus park – little more than a turning where the main tarmac road passes the north side of the city. **Taxis** from Bhaktapur cost upwards of Rs500. If you're **cycling** you'll need a mountain bike because the last two kilometres or so are very steep. On foot from Bhaktapur, it's better to take one of the other two roads which set off from the north side of town; these soon converge and become a pleasant trail that passes through rural villages before a steep ascent to reach the temple after 5km, or roughly 1hr 30min on foot.

Time permitting, a good ten-kilometre **hike** is Nagarkot to Bhaktapur via Changu Narayan (see p.203). It's also possible to walk or mountain bike to Sankhu (see p.165), 5km to the northeast. This trail begins along the dirt road heading northeast from the Changu bus park (take the first fork on the left), though without a guide you may need to ask local help finding the way, and you'll have to cross the Manohara River on foot – easy in the dry season, impassable after rain. A quicker, more reliable route cuts down directly from the west end of the temple, then heads 1km north across the fields (make for the

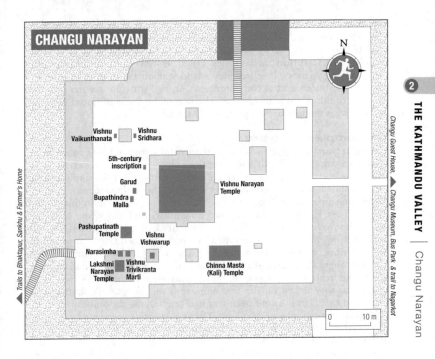

mobile phone mast) to the Sankhu road, via a footbridge over the river; frequent buses run along this road between Kathmandu and Sankhu.

Up to the temple

From the miniature bus park, steps lead up the single main street along the top of the ridge towards the temple at its apex. On the way up you'll pass plentiful souvenir shops and the small and eccentric **Changu Museum** (daily 8am–6pm; Rs140), set in an old-fashioned Newari townhouse and offering up a beguiling display of traditional utensils. The owner leads you up and down narrow wooden staircases, from the family kitchen and prayer room on the top floor to the rice storage cupboard and *raksi* still at ground level. Also on show are a collection of Nepali coins – including a medieval one claimed to be the world's smallest – a bowl of 220-year-old rice, a holy, hairy cow's gallstone and other curiosities.

A few steps further up the hill stands the **temple**, set in a quiet quadrangle of rest houses and pilgrims' shelters. It is the valley's oldest Vaishnava site, with a documented history running back to the fifth century AD – the same date as the original stone image of Vishnu, covered in a seventh-century gilt sheath, which is kept hidden inside the sanctuary from profane view. From time to time, the statue is said to sweat miraculously, indicating that Vishnu is battling with the *nag* spirits, and the cloth used to wipe the god's brow is considered a charm against snake bites.

The temple building itself was reconstructed around 1700. The repoussé work on the front of the building is as intricate as any you'll find in Nepal, as are the carved, painted struts supporting the roofs. A measure of the temple's ritual importance, meanwhile, is the exaggerated size of the four traditional emblems of Vishnu – the wheel (*chakra*), conch (*sankha*), lotus (*padma*) and mace (*gada*) – mounted on two pillars at its western corners. The base of the *chakra* pillar bears the **oldest inscription** in the valley. Dated 454 AD and attributed to the Lichhavi king Mandev, it relates how Mandev, upon the death of his father, dissuaded his mother from committing *sati*, saying "what use are the joys and pleasures of this world without you?" The face of the statue of Garud opposite (see below) is thought to be a portrait of Mandev.

The temple courtyard

The **courtyard** of Changu Narayan is an exhilarating outdoor museum of priceless works of art. With few exceptions almost all the statues pertain to Vishnu or his faithful carrier, Garud. Probably dating from the sixth century, the celebrated statue of **Garud** kneels before the main doorway, looking human but for a pair of wings and a cobra scarf – a representation found only in Nepali art. He used to be mounted on a pillar, the broken base of which is lying just to his right. Garud's association with snakes is legendary. It is said that when his mother was kidnapped by his stepmother, Garud appealed to his serpentine stepbrothers to free her, which they did on condition that Garud brought them ambrosia from Indra's heaven. Although Indra later flew down and reclaimed his pot of nectar (leaving the snakes to split their tongues as they licked up the few drops spilt on the grass), Vishnu was so impressed that Garud hadn't been tempted to consume the ambrosia that he immediately hired him as his mount. The statues inside a screened cage next to Garud commemorate **King Bupalendra Malla** of Bhaktapur and his queen Bubana Lakshmi, who ruled during the late seventeenth and early eighteenth centuries. The king's gold-plated image was stolen in September 2001, only to be discovered by a cowherd the next day, half buried in a nearby field.

The eighth-century image of **Vishnu Vishwarup** (Vishnu of the Universal Form) is an awesome composition, even if it has lost its top right corner. In its lower portion, it shows Vishnu reclining on the snake of infinity in the ocean of existence; above, he rises from the waters before a heavenly host, his thousand heads and arms symbolizing sheer omnipotence. The latter image is borrowed from an episode in the Mahabharat in which the warrior Arjuna loses his nerve and Krishna (an incarnation of Vishnu) appears in this universal form to dictate the entire Bhagavad Gita by way of encouragement.

Two notable statues rest on the platform of the adjacent Lakshmi Narayan temple. The eighth-century **Vishnu Trivikranta Murti**, Vishnu of the Three Strides, illustrates a much-loved story in which the god reclaimed the universe from the demon king Bali. Disguised as a dwarf (another of his ten incarnations), Vishnu petitioned Bali for a patch of ground where he could meditate, which need only be as far as the dwarf could cover in three strides; when Bali agreed, Vishnu grew to his full divine height and bounded over the earth, sky and heavens. An even older version of this statue is held in the National Museum. The adjacent eleventh- or twelfth-century image – also covered in red *abhir* powder, an indication that worship is very much alive – depicts Vishnu in yet another of his incarnations, that of the man-lion **Narasimha**.

At the northwest corner of the compound, the twelfth- or thirteenth-century **Vishnu Vaikunthanata** shows a purposeful Vishnu riding Garud like some sort of hip space traveller. Nearby stands a **Vishnu Sridhara** of the ninth or tenth century, an early example of what has since become the standard Nepali representation of Vishnu.

Smaller temples in the compound are dedicated to **Chinna Masta** (a local version of Kali), Lakshmi (the goddess of wealth, Vishnu's consort) and Shiva. Some scholars speculate that Chinna Masta is the mother goddess who was worshipped at this site in prehistoric times. Her cult endures: a Chinna Masta Mai chariot procession is held here in the Nepali month of Baisaakh (April–May).

Practicalities

Two friendly guesthouses make Changu an appealing place to overnight. The *Changu Guest House,* right next to the temple (℡01/661 6652, ✉saritabhatta @hotmail.com; ❸) has four simple little rooms with views across the valley towards Bhaktapur. Down below the temple, on the steep west side, the *Farmer's Home* (℡01/692 2210, ⓦwww.farmershome.info; ❸) has four big rooms done up in a traditional style, with rush mats, wicker lampshades and clay wallpaint; its restaurant has a fine terrace view and some good Newari specialities – you can even try goat's blood soup if you order in advance. There are a couple of cheaper guesthouses in and around the village as well, so you're unlikely to be stuck for a bed.

Thimi and around

THIMI, the valley's fourth-largest town, spreads across a minor eminence 4km west of Bhaktapur. The name is said to be a corruption of *chhemi,* meaning "capable people", a bit of flattery offered by Bhaktapur to make up for the fact that the town used to get mauled every time Bhaktapur picked a fight with Kathmandu or Patan. Little has changed: caught between Kathmandu's rampant development and Bhaktapur's careful spirit of conservation, Thimi has rather lost out. Recently the town has revived its ancient name of **MADHYAPUR** ("Middle Place") – which says it all.

Any **bus** to Bhaktapur or beyond will drop you off at the southern end of Thimi, but you'll get a far more favourable introduction by **cycling** in along the old road to Bhaktapur, which skirts the town to the north. **Minibuses** from Bhaktapur and Kathmandu also ply this back route. The high street runs due south from a small temple with two yellow roofs, reaching the main Kathmandu road after just over one kilometre.

Thimi's main attraction is its tradition of open-air **pottery** production. Some potters may have moved on to electric wheels and kerosene-fired kilns, but in the maze of the town's back-alleys and courtyards you can still see barrow-loads of raw clay and potters spinning their wheels by hand with long sticks. Most extraordinary are the open-air kilns: huge heaps of sand and charcoal belching smoke from carefully tended vents. The main pottery quarter lies in the smoky heart of town: turn west at Chapacho, the cluster of small temples halfway down the high street, opposite the Community Health Clinic.

Thimi is also known for **papier-mâché masks**, which originated with the local Chitrakar family, famed for generations as purveyors of fine festival masks. They still produce them in a range of sizes and styles, notably snarling Bhairab, kindly Kumari and elephant-headed Ganesh.

The town itself is grotty and oddly sullen. The main north–south lane is dotted with *chortens* and modest temples, but the only sight of note, the sixteenth-century pagoda temple of **Balkumari,** comes just short of its southern end. Childless couples come here to pray to the "Child Kumari" – represented by an

Full details for travelling beyond the Kathmandu Valley are given on pp.142–146.

unmistakable, vulva-like gilt slit – presenting her with coconuts as a symbol of fertility. The temple is bespattered with pigeon droppings and has been protected by a steel cage since its precious peacock statue was stolen in 2001; the current figure, atop its tall pillar, is a reproduction. The temple is the focus of the **Sindoor Jatra** festival for Nepali New Year (in April), when dozens of deities are ferried around on palanquins and red powder (red being the colour of rejoicing) is thrown like confetti.

Bode

A small, tight-knit Newari community, **BODE** is built on a bluff overlooking the Manohara River, 1km north of Thimi. The village's main shrine, the **Mahalakshmi Mandir**, stands at the northwest corner of the village, a modest and not particularly well-maintained two-tiered pagoda. The goddess of wealth, Maha (Great) Lakshmi is feted during a three-day festival beginning on New Year's Day (here called Baisaakh Sankranti, meaning the first day of Baisaakh – April 13 or 14). The highlight of the proceedings comes on the second day, when a volunteer has his tongue bored with a thin steel spike and, thus impaled and bearing a disc-shaped object with flaming torches mounted on it, accompanies the goddess as she's paraded around the village. Volunteers believe that they won't bleed if they've followed a prescribed three-day fast and have sufficient faith, and that by performing this act they'll go directly to heaven when they die.

The Central Hills

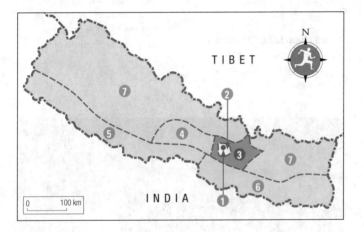

CHAPTER 3

Highlights

✳ **Nagarkot** An expansive view of the Himalayas, just two hours from Kathmandu. See p.199

✳ **Panauti** Perfect miniature pagoda complex at the holy confluence of two rivers. See p.204

✳ **Dhulikhel** See the sun rise over the Himalayas from the hilltop shrine above this friendly Newari town. See p.206

✳ **Namobuddha** One of the holiest Tibetian Buddhist pilgrimage sites in the Himalayas, a gentle day hike away from Dhulikhel See p.210

✳ **The Bhote Koshi** The whitest water of all, charging down from the Tibet border and offering some of the world's best rafting. See p.213

✳ **The Tribhuwan Rajpath** Nepal's first road, built in the 1950s, stretches from the Kathmandu Valley to the Terai and remains the best and toughest cycle route of all. See p.217

▲ Himalayan view

The Central Hills

t's only when you leave it that you appreciate just how extraordinary the Kathmandu Valley really is, surrounded by a 700km band of jumbled foothills, offering barely enough flat land to build a volleyball court. Only half a dozen roads fight their way out of the Valley, but they are enough to make the **Central Hills** the most accessible area in the largely roadless hill country – though not necessarily the most travelled. To the northeast, the **Arniko Highway** follows the old Kathmandu–Lhasa trade route through broad valleys and misty gorges to the Tibet border; northwestwards, the **Trisuli Road** snakes its way down into a subtropical valley nearly 1000m lower than Kathmandu; while west and then south, the **Tribhuwan Rajpath**, Nepal's first highway, takes a dramatically tortuous route on its way to the Terai. The scenery in this area is a shade less dramatic than you'll encounter further west, but the land is nonetheless varied, rugged and only partially tamed by defiant terraces.

Most places in this chapter are easy overnights from anywhere in the Kathmandu Valley. The most popular are those that involve mountain views: **Nagarkot** and **Dhulikhel**, with well-developed lodgings, are acknowledged classics. **Daman** has the most comprehensive views, but requires a little more effort to reach. These vantage points can't compare with what you'll see on a trek, but they provide a taste of the Himalayas and can also serve as springboards for hiking and mountain biking explorations. The **Tibet border** area, meanwhile, is developing into something of a magnet for extreme sports. Although cultural attractions are relatively few outside the Kathmandu Valley, **Panauti** is among Nepal's most intriguing small towns, and all the more so because it's so seldom visited.

To an extent, the boundaries of this chapter are dictated by travel formalities: towns and **day hikes** are described here, while longer backcountry **treks** are saved for Chapter Seven. Many of the places described in this and the previous chapters could even be strung together in one long quasi-trek or mountain-bike ride.

Despite a relative abundance of roads, **buses** in the central hills are slow and infrequent, and relatively few travellers brave them. However, the region does contain some of Nepal's most popular and rewarding **mountain bike** and **motorcycling** routes.

Nagarkot

Set on a ridge northeast of Bhaktapur, **NAGARKOT** (1950m) is no quaint hilltop village. The series of hotels is here for one reason only: the classic panorama of the Himalayas. While the view isn't as expansive as from Daman,

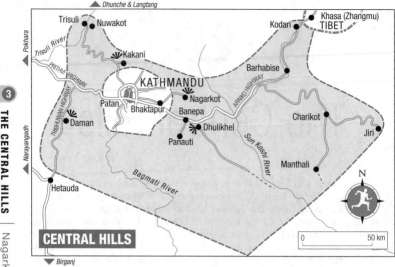

and the area not half as interesting as Dhulikhel, it's easy to get to from Kathmandu and you don't have to stay in an expensive hotel to get a fantastic view from your window.

The first tourists are thought to have been a troop of Punjabi mercenaries recruited to defend the Valley against Prithvi Narayan's troops. Stationed at the now-vanished ridgetop fort, they quickly succumbed to the "mountain air", proving drunkenly incapable when the Gurkha invaders finally arrived. Since those times, numerous guesthouses have sprouted along some two kilometres of ridge, but the main attractions haven't changed much. Taking in the sunrise view, either from your hotel or the view tower further back along the ridge, is the standard activity. Many take the chance to just chill out, but there's a wealth of **hiking** and **biking** opportunities too. Since Nagarkot is located at a high point and easily reached on a good road, many people get a lift up and then hike or bike back down.

Arrival and information

A daily tourist **bus** departs at 1pm (2hr 30min; Rs300) from near the *Malla* hotel, Lekhnath Marg, in Kathmandu to Nagarkot; the return service leaves at 3pm. Book tickets a day in advance from a Kathmandu travel agent, via your hotel or from the shop opposite *Hotel Galaxy View Tower* in Nagarkot (alternatively phone ☎84/160 4668 or 980/332 1730). Public buses to Nagarkot from Kathmandu go via Bhaktapur (if a direct service isn't available when you want to travel, just go to Bhaktapur, from where there are more frequent connections in both directions). A **taxi** to Kathmandu costs around Rs1800, to Dhulikhel around Rs2000 and to Bhaktapur Rs700-800. Free transport should be provided if you're booked into one of the more expensive hotels.

The easiest **cycle route** up is along the main road from Bhaktapur. It's consistently steep for the last 12km but is paved all the way and relatively free of traffic. Unpaved – and generally steeper – roads and tracks head up from Changu Narayan, Sankhu, Nala and other points – see Routes down from Nagarkot, p.203. It's also possible to walk up any of these routes.

Accommodation

Nagarkot's sobriquet of "Thamel-on-the-Hill" isn't quite deserved, but there has been a similar boom in hotel construction. Many hotels have offices or agents in Thamel, charging ridiculously inflated **prices** for prebooked rooms; while it may be advisable to book ahead in high season, you'll get a better rate if you call direct. The price will be even lower if you just show up – as much as fifty percent off the published rate in the more expensive places, sometimes more.

The **view** is the major selling point, but just a few hotels boast a complete panorama. Only the most deluxe places are heated, and although quilts are provided, it's worth bringing a sleeping bag in the colder months. A torch (flashlight) for walking between buildings after dark is also handy.

Inexpensive and mid-range

Hotel Chautari Keyman ☎01/668 0075. Popular with tour groups, with cavernous en suites boasting tubs, wood-effect floors and TVs. However, at the time of writing a new hotel was being built close by, which could compromise some rooms' views. **7**

Eco-Home ☎01/668 0180. The warmest welcome in town complete with nice touches such as hot water bottles at night. Delightful rooms have futons, prayer flags, masks, photos, lamps fashioned from mini tree trunks and pristine private baths, though no real views. There's an Internet café downstairs. **4**

Hotel at the End of the Universe ☎01/668 0011, ⊛www.endoftheuniverse.biz. Near the Mahankal Temple, offering simple rooms with attached hot water facilities, cottages suitable for families (not all have hot water) and more comfortable en suites with views. Staff can also arrange volunteering opportunities. **2**–**5**

Hotel Galaxy View Tower ☎01/668 0122, ⊛www.hotelgalaxyviewtower.com. No tower, and the views (from the terrace) aren't as special as the name suggests, but the sizeable rooms with private baths are clean and pretty comfortable. **4**

Hotel Green Valley ☎01/668 0078. The standard rooms, with attached baths, are plain, the "deluxe" ones a touch smarter, but the real selling point is the stunning panoramic views both have. Chocolate cake and apple pie are also on offer in the basic café. **3**–**4**

Nagarkot Farmhouse ☎01/622 8087, ⊛www.nagarkotfarmhouse.com. Nearly 2km north of the bus stop on the road to Sankhu. Under the same management as Kathmandu's excellent *Hotel Vajra*, this red-brick lodge has compact rooms, restful grounds and massage treatments. **6**–**7**

Peaceful Cottage ☎01/668 0077, ⊜peacefulcottage@hotmail.com. In a fairly secluded location, *Peaceful Cottage* feels as if it's about to be consumed by the forest. There's a rooftop view tower and a choice of cottages or rooms in the main building; most have great vistas and intricately carved wooden beds. **5**–**6**

Hotel Sunshine ☎01/426 2687, ⊛www.sunshinehotel.com.np. While some of the carpeting is a bit worn, the en-suites have modern bathrooms with tubs and their own balconies. Ask for a corner room (such as no. 206), with eye-catching views out of two windows. **4**–**5**

Unkai Resort ☎01/668 0178, ⊜anniett@mos.com.np. Wonderfully situated a 20min walk from the bus stand with some of Nagarkot's best views from the terrace and the more expensive en-suites, this tranquil place is frequented mainly by Japanese travellers. There's also a four-bed dorm (Rs200). **4**–**6**

Hotel View Point ☎01/668 0123, ⊛www.hotelviewpoint.com.np. The rooms are nothing special, and undoubtedly overpriced, but the hotel stakes its reputation on the killer views – both from the rooms themselves and from the top of its unmistakable tower. **6**–**7**

Expensive

Club Himalaya Resort ☎01/668 0080, ⊜club@mos.com.np. Much more attractive from the inside looking out than vice versa, *Club Himalaya*'s high-end en suites have superlative views from their balconies. There's also an indoor pool, sauna and Jacuzzi. **8**

Hotel Country Villa ☎01/668 0128, ⊛www.hotelcountryvilla.com. Large en-suites with high ceilings, colourful rugs, pine wood panelling and TVs. If you tire of the views, there are plenty of activities on offer, including pony trekking and tennis. **7**–**8**

The Fort Resort ☎01/668 0069, ⊛www.mountain-retreats.com. A well-run hotel, with traditional architecture, attractive en-suites and cottages, a lovely garden, a top restaurant and unbroken views. **8**

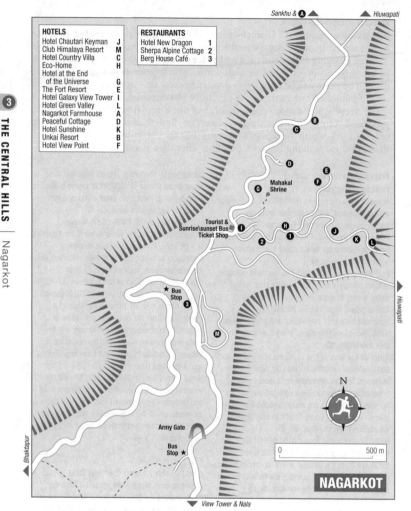

Sankhu & Ⓐ ▲ ▲ Hiuwapati

HOTELS
Hotel Chautari Keyman J
Club Himalaya Resort M
Hotel Country Villa C
Eco-Home H
Hotel at the End
  of the Universe G
The Fort Resort E
Hotel Galaxy View Tower I
Hotel Green Valley L
Nagarkot Farmhouse A
Peaceful Cottage D
Hotel Sunshine K
Unkai Resort B
Hotel View Point F

RESTAURANTS
Hotel New Dragon 1
Sherpa Alpine Cottage 2
Berg House Café 3

Mahakal
Shrine

Tourist &
Sunrise\sunset Bus
Ticket Shop

★ Bus
Stop

Army Gate

Bus
Stop ★

Bhaktapur ◀

Hiuwapati ▶

N

0   500 m

NAGARKOT

▼ View Tower & Nala

The view

Most guesthouses have good views, but you'll get even better ones from the **view tower** at the highest southern point of the ridge (2164m), an hour or more's walk from most hotels along a tarmac road. When you get here you'll understand why Nagarkot has been the site of a fort (*kot*) since Rana times: this hilltop controlled the eastern entrance to the Kathmandu Valley and the vital trade route to Tibet. There's still a large army training base in this area, though relations with the community in Nagarkot are understandably strained after a drunken soldier shot and killed eleven local people in 2005.

The view is dominated by the **Langtang range**, which on good days looms alarmingly close above a wall of dark rock. Haze usually obscures anything west of Ganesh Himal, though you can sometimes see Himchuli and even Annapurna. The view to the east is even more weather-dependent, and the mountains of

Khumbu rarely appear as more than a rose-tinted dawn haze. On a good day, Everest can be seen, but only from high up, near the view tower: it's the second peak left of the rounded m-shaped mountain.

A sunrise/sunset **bus** service (book through your hotel or at the shop opposite *Hotel View Tower*; Rs400) has turned the tower area into something of a circus, particularly on peak season mornings. For more peace, and equally good views, stop off at one of the grassy mounds just short of the tower. Nearer to the hotel area, there are good views from the tiny Mahakal shrine, from where the only obstructions are the ever-growing towers of Hotel View Point and Peaceful Cottage: good viewpoints themselves, they are accessible to non-guests, generally for free.

Eating

Food at the budget guesthouses usually doesn't live up to expectations, though some of the expensive hotels offer some pretty fine dining. *Hotel New Dragon*, opposite *Eco-Home*, has a decent, predominantly Indian and Chinese, menu to enjoy on its sun-filled terrace; as the evening draws in, a "Mustang coffee" (which is perked up with local Khukuri rum) may be more in order. Nearby *Sherpa Alpine Cottage* has thatched roof structures and Tibetan fare. There are several cheap, low-key eateries dotted around the bus stand, but the *Berg House Café* is a step ahead, with sugary breakfast items including chocolate porridge and French toast – and a sprinkling of Indian and Chinese dishes.

If you eat dinner out, take a **torch** as it will be a dark walk back to your hotel.

Routes down from Nagarkot

There are some excellent mountain biking, hiking and motorcycling opportunities around Nagarkot. Probably the most popular goes via **Changu Narayan** (see p.192) to Bhaktapur, three or four hours on foot, or half that on a mountain bike or motorcycle. The route follows the main road to Phedi, from where you take a dirt road to Changu Narayan. It's another 6km from Changu down to Bhaktapur.

The descent to **Sankhu** (p.165) is favoured by mountain-bikers. The route forks just beyond *Nagarkot Farmhouse*: the left-hand route is steep, rutted and good fun; the right-hand one is smoother and longer.

A longer two-day trek to **Shivapuri National Park** (p.166) initially follows the latter route, then bears north on a rough motorable road to the Watershed. Most hikers spend a night in Bhotechaur, near the Jhule entry point to the Watershed (Rs250 entry) for access to the national park (see p.166). There are several basic lodges here. It's then an easy day's walk to Sundarijal or Nagi Gompa (see p.168), and an optional hard third day up to the summit of Shivapuri and back to Kathmandu via Budhanilkantha. You can't ride up to the summit, but cyclists can make it from Nagarkot to Nagi Gompa or further in a day, and to Kakani in two days.

Heading to **Nala** (see p.204), continue south from the view tower, from where it's a stiff 700m descent along any of three different routes. The road that bears right around the tower is the easiest for biking. The other two trails, via the villages of Tukucha and Ghimiregaun, descend from a track heading left from the tower. Yet another option is to descend eastwards to **Hiuwapati**, deep down in the valley of the Indrawati River.

A decent **map** makes all of these excursions much easier, although they are possible without one. The best are the 1:25,000 sheets by HMG/FINNIDA, available in Kathmandu bookshops, but Himalayan Map House equivalents will suffice.

Banepa and Panauti

Leaving the Kathmandu Valley through a gap at its eastern edge, Nepal's only road to the Tibet border is the **Arniko Rajmarg** (**Arniko Highway**). Constructed by the Chinese in the mid-1960s – to long-standing rival India's great distress – the highway is a busy conduit for lorry-loads of Chinese goods by way of Lhasa. Appropriately, it's named after the thirteenth-century Nepali architect who led a delegation to Beijing and taught the Chinese how to build pagodas. The first stop along the highway is **Banepa**, which together with **Nala** and **Panauti** once comprised a short-lived independent kingdom east of the Kathmandu Valley.

Many **buses** ply the Arniko Highway as far as Banepa. However, it's much prettier and less stressful to enter this area by mountain **bike** or motorcycle from Bhaktapur (entering Nala from the west along a dirt road) or Patan (via Lubhu and the Lakuri Bhanjyang – see p.413).

Banepa

BANEPA, 26km east of Kathmandu, was for centuries an important staging post to Tibet, and now – such is progress – an unattractive pitstop for buses heading up the Arniko Highway. From the first roundabout north of the highway, a road leading northeastwards to Panchkhal (p.211) first passes by Scheer Memorial Hospital, and the **Chandeshwari Mandir**, overlooking a set of cremation ghats. The three-tiered temple, which is currently undergoing significant restoration, is best known for the psychedelic fresco of Bhairab decorating its exterior. It commemorates Bhagwati who, according to Hindu scripture, slew a giant called Chand here, earning her the title Chandeshwari ("Lord of Chand"). Chandeshwari's image is the object of a chariot festival here coinciding with Nepali New Year (April 13 or 14).

A second unpaved road heads 3km northwestwards to **NALA**, a parochial village near the head of the Punyamati Valley, with a seventeenth-century Bhagwati pagoda. From here you can continue west along a dirt road, passing a Lokeshwar temple on the outskirts of town, to reach Bhaktapur in 10km. Three lesser tracks branching off from it ascend to Nagarkot via different routes (see p.203).

Panauti

Built on a single stratum of rock, **PANAUTI** is said to be the best place in the Valley to be when the next earthquake hits. It's an enticing enough place at any time, leading a self-sufficient existence in its own small valley 7km south of Banepa. The best-preserved Newari town after Bhaktapur, the centre is a perfect nugget of extended-family dwellings, temples and public meeting houses, all built in the Newars' signature pink brick and carved wood. At the bottom end of the restored old centre, a cluster of riverside temples and ghats makes a delightfully sleepy alternative to Pashupatinath's gaudier treasures. Although most travellers pass through Panauti only briefly on their way between Namobuddha and Dhulikhel, it's an enchanting place to spend the night: wandering among the temples and bazaars in the half-light is quite special.

The most pleasant way of **getting here** is by bike, either from Lubhu (see p.413), Banepa (see above) or Dhulikhel (see p.206) and Namobuddha (see box, p.210). The latter route is also feasible on foot. Alternatively, walk from the summit of Phulchoki (see p.179) – you'll need a good topo map and the whole day. Frequent **buses** to Panauti depart from Kathmandu's City Bus Park, calling

▲ The Newari town of Khware Panauti

at Bhaktapur and Banepa en route. To get to Dhulikhel from Panauti, you have to change buses at Banepa.

The Town

Wedged between the Punyamati and Roshi streams, Panauti forms the shape of a triangle, with a serpent (*nag*) idol standing at each of its three corners to protect against floods. Buses pull up at the newer northwest corner, but the oldest and most interesting sights are concentrated at the streams' confluence at the east end of town, approached through a distinctive entry gate.

The shrine area at the sacred confluence, known as the **Khware** or **Tribeni Ghat**, is one of those tranquil spots that can waylay you for hours. The large *sattal* (pilgrims' house) here sports an eclectic range of frescoes depicting scenes from Hindu (and some Buddhist) mythology: Vishnu in cosmic sleep, Ram killing the ten-headed demon king Ravana, and even Krishna being chased up a tree by a pack of naked *gopi* (milkmaids). Krishna is the featured deity of the pagoda temple next door, too, where he's shown serenading his *gopi* groupies with a flute. Other small shrines dotted around the complex are dedicated to just about every deity known to Hinduism.

The Khware has been regarded as a *tirtha* (sacred power place) since ancient times, and on the first day of the month of Magh (usually Jan 14), it draws hundreds of people for ritual bathing. Beside the river, the tombstone-shaped ramps set into the ghats are where dying people are laid out, allowing their feet to be immersed in the water at the moment of death. Orthodox cremations are held at the actual confluence, but local Newars are cremated on the opposite bank, apparently to prevent their ghosts troubling the town. A footbridge crosses over to the recently restored seventeenth-century **Brahmayani Mandir**, from which the mythical Padmati Khola is said to flow during the town's *mela*, held every twelve years on the first day of Magh. The next occurrence will be in 2010. Brahmayani's *dyochhen* (god house) is located in Paumari Tol, in the heart of the old town.

Just west of the Khware, the massive, three-tiered **Indreshwar Mahadev Mandir** stands in the middle of a lovely walled quadrangle. The temple is

Folk music

Folk music (*git lok*) and dancing remains an important aspect of life in the Central Hills – and Nepal as a whole – particularly during festivals and holidays, when the men of a village or neighbourhood will typically gather for an evening session of singing and socializing. Women rarely perform on these occasions. The **maadal** (a horizontally-held two-sided drum) plays a central role, often accompanied by other drums, harmonium and *murali* (bamboo piccolo) or *bansuri* (flute). After some preliminary tapping on the *maadal*, a group member will strike up a familiar verse, and everyone joins in on the chorus. Young men and women of the hill tribes also sing improvised, flirtatious call-and-response duets known as **dohori**, and sing and dance at **rodi ghar**, originally a Gurung courtship event, now adopted by many other hill tribes.

Folk music traditions vary among the country's myriad ethnic groups, but the true sound of Nepal can be said to be the soft, melodic and rhythmically complex music of the hills. **Jhyaure**, the *maadal*-based music of the western hills, has emerged as the most popular. **Selo**, the music of the Tamangs, utilizing the *dhime* (big two-sided drum) has also been adopted by many other communities. Meanwhile, the music of the **Jyapu** (Newari farmers) has a lively rhythm, though the singing has a difficult to appreciate nasal quality.

While folk music is by definition an amateur pursuit, there are two traditional castes of **professional musicians**: wandering minstrels (*gaaine* or *gandarbha*), who were an important unifying force in the hills, relaying news, songs and musical styles from village to village; and *damai*, members of the tailor caste, who have for generations served as wedding musicians.

dedicated to Shiva, the "Lord of Indra" in several myths, who is represented by a magnificent brass four-faced *linga*. Some authorities believe this to be the original temple (albeit restored since a 1988 earthquake) that was raised here in 1294, which would make it the oldest surviving pagoda in Nepal. The graceful and sensuous roof struts have been dated to the fourteenth century, although they may have been recycled. Each carved from a single piece of wood, they predate the Malla style of carving the arms separately and then attaching them to the strut figures. Sharing the compound is the smaller, rectangular temple of Unmatta Bhairab, distinguished by three carved wooden figures occupying its upstairs windows. "Unmatta" refers to Bhairab's erotic form, in which he is depicted as a terrifying, red-bodied demon with a prominent hard-on.

Practicalities

The best **place to stay** is *Hotel Panauti* (☏01/166 1055; ❸), about 200m along the main road south from the bus park; fortunately it has decent, straight-forward **rooms** – private or shared facilities, with hot water – as there are few other alternatives. The hotel also has a pleasant garden and a reasonable rooftop **restaurant**. There are a few other simple eateries near the Indreshwar Mandir compound and by the entry gate down to Khware.

Dhulikhel

DHULIKHEL is justly famous as a well-preserved Newari town, mountain viewpoint, and hiking and biking hub, but its popularity is waning as moderni-zation takes its toll. Located 5km east of Banepa, just beyond the Kathmandu Valley rim, it sits in a saddle at the relatively low elevation of 1550m, making it warmer than Nagarkot. A number of hotels are positioned along the highway to catch the **mountain views**, but there are more pleasant places to stay in the woods above town, on the way to a small summit from which the full Himalayan vista can be seen.

These days, Dhulikhel is something of a boomtown – not necessarily a good thing for visitors in search of tranquillity. The municipality donated a large tract of land below town to **Kathmandu University**, Nepal's first private campus, which opened in 1991, and the Dhulikhel hospital, established five years later, has earned a reputation as one of the better public ones in Nepal.

However, the most significant development is yet to come, as a new 158km route to **Sindhulimadi** and the eastern Terai snaking out from the town's western and southern flanks is constructed. Donated by Japan, the road is expected to draw as much as half of the traffic between the Kathmandu Valley and India, all of which currently has to squeeze through Thankot. Work started in 1996, but progress has been slow, as a result of the conflict, a lack of funds and the difficulties posed by the terrain.

The 37km stretch between Bardibas and Sindhulimadi and the 50km between Dhulikhel and Nepalthok are both finished. When the rest of the road is eventually completed, Dhulikhel may become one of Nepal's principal transport junctions, with all the revving and tooting that entails.

Arrival and information

Local **buses** to Dhulikhel (every half an hour from Kathmandu's City Bus Park or, more frequently, from Bhaktapur) can be exasperatingly slow, taking around two hours from Kathmandu and one hour from Bhaktapur. You can ask to be dropped off at any of the hotels along the highway, but for most of the cheap lodgings you'll want to stay on until the small bus park, a short walk away from the main square, Mahendra Chowk. To get to Nagarkot by bus from here, you'll need to change at Bhaktapur. A **taxi** should cost around Rs1500 from Kathmandu. On a **bike**, it's better to come on one of the back ways: via Lubhu–Panauti, Bhaktapur–Nala or Nagarkot–Nala.

There's a small **tourist office** (daily except Tues 10am–5pm; no ☎), where you can get the locally produced booklet, *Ten Walks Around Dhulikhel*, which

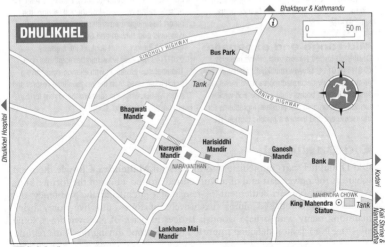

doesn't offer much beyond route descriptions but might be a good buy if you plan to stay a few days. The nearest **ATM** is in Banepa.

Accommodation

Dhulikhel used to get more independent travellers, but nowadays most of its **accommodation** is geared towards upmarket tour groups. Only a handful of the resort hotels ranged along the noisy highway ridge are worth considering; the older guesthouses along the route of the sunrise walk are much better located. More expensive places may offer substantial discounts to walk-in customers. An hours' drive east of Dhulikhel along the Sindhuli Highway is Apa Villa Phulbari (ⓦwww.apavilla.com; $50 per night per person, including breakfast; also cheaper dorm accommodation), which has stylish rooms, a beautiful garden, home-grown organic food and lovely views.

Budget

Nawaranga Guest House 300m east of Mahendra Chowk ☏01/166 1226. The last of Dhulikhel's original budget guesthouses is just about clinging on and still maintains a chilled hippie vibe. Dilapidated and ramshackle with threadbare but clean rooms with shared or private squat toilets, *Nawaranga* also has a small gallery, book exchange, and partial views from the roof. ❷–❸

Panorama View Lodge Near the Kali temple ☏01/168 0786, ⓦwww.panoramaviewlodge.com. Dynamite views, splendid isolation and faded rooms, with or without attached bath. However, it may be a bit uneventful for some and is a hassle to get to unless you have wheels. ❹

Snow View Guest House 1km east of Mahendra Chowk ☏984/148 2487. While it lacks the traveller buzz of *Nawaranga*, *Snow View* has slightly more comfortable – though still pretty basic – rooms and Western toilets. It's tucked away in the woods on the way up to the Kali shrine viewpoint. Views from the rooms are limited but lovely, framed by the hills. ❷–❸

Mid-range and expensive

Dhulikhel Lodge Resort Just off the highway ☏01/149 0114, ⓦwww.dhulikhellodgeresort.com. All the tastefully decorated rooms have views, as well as checked bedspreads, photos and wicker furniture. An organic plot provides ingredients for the restaurant and there's a bucolic garden. ❽

Dhulikhel Mountain Resort On the highway 4km east of Dhulikhel ☏01/442 0776, ⓦwww .dhulikhelmountainresort.com. Set in 20 acres of grounds, in a very scenic location, but nowhere near Dhulikhel. The en suites, in individual red brick bungalows with thatched roofs, feel a little bare, but there is range of massages on offer. ❽

🏃 **High View Resort** On a side road 600m off the highway ☏01/149 0048, ⓦwww .highviewresort.com. Along a winding path and up a steep flight of steps, *High View* has neat, good value en suites, with little private balconies, all with great views, even from the shower. The cheaper rooms are just smaller versions of the more expensive ones. ❻–❼

Himalayan Shangri-La Resort 1.5km east of Mahendra Chowk ☏01/149 0612, ⓦwww .dwarikasgroup.com. Run by the exemplary *Dwarika's* in Kathmandu, *Shangri-La* doesn't quite hit those heights yet remains a fine choice. Sumptuously peaceful location, spread across the hillside in the woods below the Kali shrine, the resort has elegant en suites ($180) with huge windows and Newari and Gurung flourishes. ❾

Mirabel Resort Hotel Just off the highway ☏01/149 0972, ⓦwww.mirabelresorthotel.com. The spacious en-suites with all mod-cons have a touch more class than the neighbouring resorts and super vistas, while the restaurant and roof terrace are equally appealing. ❽

Old Dhulikhel

Old Dhulikhel starts immediately to the west of **Mahendra Chowk**, the main square at the newer, east end of town, centred around a bust of the former king. A traditional Newari settlement of remarkable architectural consistency, old Dhulikhel is comprised almost exclusively of four- and five-storey brick mansions, many with ornate wooden lattices in place of glass windows, some affecting Neoclassical detailing imported from Europe during the Rana regime.

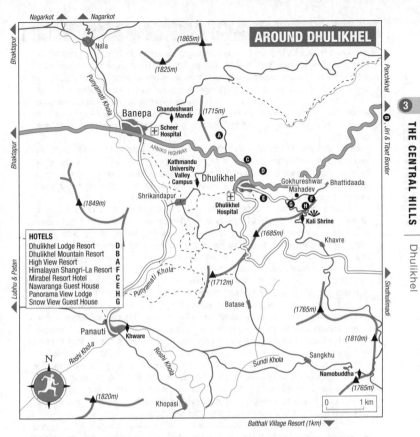

Balthali Village Resort (1km) ▼

These huge houses are extended-family dwellings; some Dhulikhel clans number fifty or more members. The older buildings, held together only by mud mortar, show some serious cracks from the infamous 1934 earthquake; Dhulikhel also experienced damage during the 1988 quake centred near Dharan in the eastern Terai.

Wandering around Dhulikhel is basically a matter of following your nose, but highlights include the central square of **Narayanthan**, containing a temple to Narayan and a smaller one to Harisiddhi (both emanations of Vishnu), and the **Bhagwati Mandir**, set at the high point of the village with partial mountain views. Members of the Bhagwati temple association often do *bhajan* in the next-door building.

The sunrise walk

The done thing in Dhulikhel is to hike to the high point southeast of town in time for sunrise over the peaks. To get to the top, take the road leading east from Mahendra Chowk for about 1km, passing a big recreation area on the left, and then go right at the next fork. Cyclists will have to stay on the graded road, but hikers can take a more direct, gullied path that branches left almost immediately. On foot, allow about 45 minutes from Dhulikhel to the top, plus any time spent gawking at the numerous birds and butterflies that have returned to the area

Hardened trekkers might sniff at the Namobuddha circuit, but it's a pleasant hike or bike ride. The scenery isn't spectacular, and the dusty, ungraded road gets some vehicle traffic, but the route takes you through mostly unspoiled countryside and there are some pleasant woods and interesting stops on the way. A **bike** will enable you to zip through the less interesting sections; if you **walk** you can get onto some lesser trails in the latter half of the circuit. A full loop could be done in four or five hours on foot, but with food stops and side trips on the way round, it'll take most of the day.

It's worth trying to combine Namobuddha with a sunrise walk to the Kali shrine (see p.209), although this requires a degree of organization that most people won't be able to manage first thing in the morning. Note, children along the circuit have been known to tease foreigners; it's a game you cannot win – just don't betray any exasperation.

The route follows the road beyond the Kali shrine, passing through the village of **Khavre**, crossing the Sindhuli Highway after 2.5km, and contouring close to the crest of a ridge for another 7km to an intersection at a small saddle. True off-the-beaten-path riding can be found down any of the tracks off to the left in this section, particularly the one at this last junction (see the HMG/FINNIDA map series for details). For Namobuddha, though, bear right.

Resting on a red-earth ledge near the top of a jungly ridge, **Namobuddha** (or **Namura**) is one of the three holiest Tibetan pilgrimage sites south of the Himalayas. Similar in spirit to Boudha, it's becoming something of a Tibetan Buddhist boomtown (or boom-village at least), particularly during the February/March pilgrimage season, when Tibetans and Bhotiyas arrive by the vanload to circumambulate it. The stupa celebrates the compassion of a young prince (in some versions, the Buddha himself) who encountered a starving tigress about to devour a small child, and offered his own flesh to her – a sacrifice that ensured his canonization as a Bodhisattva. The Tibetan name of the stupa, Takmo Lujin (Tiger Body Gift), links it explicitly to the well-known legend. According to one Tibetan scribe, the name Namobuddha (Hail to the Buddha) came into popular usage in the seventeenth century, when the superstition took hold that the site's real name should not be uttered.

Among the houses and teashops surrounding the stupa is a scruffy little Tamang *gompa*. Since the 1980s, however, the main Buddhist population at Namobuddha has been Tibetan. A steep path leads up to the ridge behind, which is festooned with *chaitya*, prayer flags and a collection of Tibetan monasteries, retreats and lesser stupas, many of which are satellites of the mothership at Boudha. In a small shelter near the top is a famous stone relief sculpture of the prince feeding his flesh to the tigress. A hole near the shelter's base is said to be the tiger's lair.

The road descends from Namobuddha to **Sangkhu**, where a right fork leads to Batase and eventually back to Dhulikhel along various roads or trails (refer to the Around Dhulikhel map on p.209). However, it's about the same distance (9km) to Panauti (see p.204), and this is a preferable alternative if you have the time to spend the night there. From Panauti you can return to Dhulikhel a number of different ways by foot or bike, or by bus with a change at Banepa.

If you decide to stay along the way, the Trangu Tashi Choling Monastery above Namobuddha has a small **guesthouse** but it's mainly for long-term retreat participants. Simple rooms (❷) can be found at the smaller monastery at the farther end of the ridge; you'll be expected to eat with the monks and costs are negligible. Down at Namobuddha itself, dorm beds (❶–❷) can be had at the teahouses opposite and alongside the Tamang *gompa*. A step up in class is *Balthali Village Resort* (⊕01/410 8210, ⓦwww.balthalivillageresort.com; ❼), about half an hour east of Namobuddha: a kind of village of cottages built in traditional style, with simple, cosy rooms, Himalayan views and the opportunity to view – and even participate in – Nepali rural life.

since local reforestation programmes came to maturity – two types of birds to look out for are racquet-tailed drongos and turtle doves. The **summit** (1715m) is marked by a small Kali shrine and, unfortunately, a small microwave tower. The peaks from Ganesh Himal to Everest are visible from here, and the sight of Dhulikhel's brick houses, salmon in the dawn light and perhaps wreathed in mist, is pretty wonderful, too.

On the way back down you can call in at a small, mossy temple complex, hidden down a flagstone path that angles off to the left just past the *Snow View Guest House*. The main temple, known as the **Gokureshwar Mahadev Mandir**, contains a large bronze *linga*. A couple of the adjacent Ram temple's marble statues have been lopped off at the ankles by temple-robbers – a persistent problem in Nepal, fuelled by demand from foreign collectors.

Eating

Dhulikhel has no tourist **restaurants**, other than those attached to guesthouses and hotels. Of the cheapies, *Nawaranga Guest House* has decent traveller food and various baked goods. Both it and the *Snow View* (where toast and eggs are on offer for breakfast and *daal bhaat* for the rest of the day) have convenience going for them if you're looking for breakfast or lunch after a hard morning's mountain-viewing. Any of the smarter hotel restaurants (particularly the *Mirabel* and *Himalayan Shangri-La Resort*) are worth a splurge, reckon on spending around Rs600-750 for a meal at either. For simple Nepali fast food, try the places around the bus park, or in the bazaar area east of the *Nawaranga Guest House*.

The road to Tibet

Tour groups bound for **Tibet** follow the Arniko Highway to **Kodari**, the only official border crossing from Nepal, and a few individual travellers make the trip up to the border just to see it. Rafting, canyoning and bungy-jumping parties also pass this way en route to rafting trips on the Sun Koshi, or to the adventure resorts on the Bhote Koshi river. Trekkers on their way to **Jiri**, the main trailhead for the Everest region, follow the Arniko Highway for most of its length before heading off on a spectacular side road.

There are no scheduled tourist **bus** services in this area, but regular (around every half an hour) public buses, including the odd express service, ply both the Arniko Highway and the Jiri road. These services depart from Kathmandu's City (Purano) Bus Park, not the main one at Gongabu; you can also get on at Bhaktapur or Dhulikhel, but don't expect to get a seat. Both these routes make excellent adventures on a **bike**.

To the border

Traffic drops off beyond Dhulikhel, but **buses** are relatively frequent: from Kathmandu to Barhabise they run every half an hour (more frequently in the morning), and some also carry on to the border.

Dhulikhel to Dolalghat

From Dhulikhel, the Arniko Highway descends 600m into the broad Panchkhal Valley, a lush, irrigated plain cultivated with rice paddy, sugar cane and tropical fruits. So-called Zero Kilometre, little more than a collection of snack stalls, just beyond the village of **Panchkhal**, is a minor gateway to the Helambu trekking region: an unpaved road, served by local buses, heads north

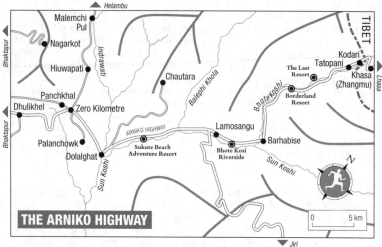

past **Hiuwapati** (see p.203) to the trailhead at Malemchi Pul. Near Zero
Kilometre another rough road to the south leads 9km to **PALANCHOWK**,
home of the famous black-stone Palanchowk Bhagwati, which draws pilgrims
seeking protection in time of need. *Sunkoshi Adventure Retreat* (℡01/622 4586,
Ⓦwww.theretreatnepal.com; ⑤–⑥), a few minutes' walk above the village, is
more of a plain old resort than a retreat, but it does offer horse riding, fishing
and a sauna, and is a good base for exploring the area on foot, mountain bike
or raft.

The highway reaches its lowest (and hottest) point 29km beyond Dhulikhel
at **Dolalghat** (634m), a small market town clumped at either end of the bridge
across the impressively vast and braided Indrawati River. This is the put-in point
for many rafting trips on the Sun Koshi, which joins the Indrawati just around
the corner. A paved side road forks left just beyond Dolalghat to reach **Chautara**
(1400m), a workaday Newari bazaar and an obscure trailhead for Helambu
treks, after 25km. The town is served by direct buses from Kathmandu, but has
only bare-bones Nepali inns; a Bhimsen temple at a high point of the ridge 3km
further up the road offers good views.

The Sun Koshi Valley

The scenery begins to change after Dolalghat, as the highway bends northeastwards up the deep, terraced **Sun Koshi Valley**. Nepal's terraces, while marvellous
feats of engineering, are a sign of agricultural desperation: with so little flat land
available and a growing number of mouths to feed, hill people have no choice but
to farm ever steeper and less productive slopes. Terraces make good farming and
environmental sense – they stabilize the topsoil and form a stopgap against erosion
on deforested slopes – but maintaining them is a tremendously labour-intensive
chore that detracts from the actual business of growing food, and building more
terraces inevitably brings about further deforestation.

Having built the Arniko Highway, China has poured much of its aid to Nepal
into infrastructure projects along the route. The first of these to come into view
is a hydroelectric diversion, whose spillway and powerhouse are located just
beyond the turning for Jiri. Human impact on the valley is much in evidence for
the next couple of kilometres to **Lamosangu** (740m), which is distinguished by
a defunct magnesite processing plant, a ropeway and a big pile of castings.

Up the Bhote Koshi

A few kilometres upstream of **Lamosangu**, the highway proceeds up the larger of two tributaries, the **Bhote Koshi**, or Tibet River, which it follows to its source in Tibet. Taking advantage of both the highway and the river is a series of **adventure resorts** (see box, p.214), which offer organized rafting, trekking and canyoning trips, and also make an attractive place to soak up the sunshine that penetrates the steep valley. **Barhabise**, just beyond Lamosangu, straddles the river on either side of a hefty bridge and is the last town of any size before the border. Its bazaar is little more than a line of open shopfronts selling *daal bhaat* and Chinese goods, but the area around it is still a traditional centre for the production of *lokta* paper, made from the bark of a type of shrub native to the hills above; you can visit any of the local operations, which are easily recognized by their rows of frames tilted to dry in the sun.

▲ rafting on the Bhote Koshi river

Buses to and from Kathmandu arrive and depart at least every half an hour from the south side of the bridge, while hourly buses bound for the border depart from the northern end of town, on the opposite bank – an arrangement that leaves the bazaar unusually peaceful. You're unlikely to be stranded here, but several **lodges** in Barhabise let cold-water rooms: *Bhotekoshi Guest House* (☎01/148 9085; ❶), right by the bridge on the east bank, is as run-down as the rest, but some rooms – and the terrace – overlook the river.

The road north from Barhabise is fine during the dry season, but can be difficult during the **monsoon**, though your journey is far more likely to be delayed rather than curtailed. The Chinese who engineered this highway put it in the most unstable zone near the bottom of the valley, which made it easier to build but harder to maintain – given the precipitous terrain between here and Tibet, they may not have had any other options. In the dry season, the

Adventure resorts on the Bhote Koshi

The raging Bhote Koshi's reputation as one of the most extreme **rafting** rivers in Nepal, and the fact that there's actually only about a day's worth of rafting to be done, attracts a young, fast-moving, thrill-seeking crowd. The big rafting operators have been quick to develop the trend and, as well as the classic rafting trip, now offer **mountain-biking**, **trekking** and **canyoning** expeditions, as well as one of the world's highest **bungy** jumps. Three major companies base their operations in attractive tented resort camps which – even if you're not intent on throwing yourself downriver on a raft, or off a bridge attached to an elastic rope – make excellent bases for exploring the valley or just chilling out for a few days. In season, the atmosphere is transient, as clients arrive in groups and are bussed up and down the river to the various put-in and pull-out points, but there are usually a few travellers arriving from Tibet and expats escaping Kathmandu to leaven the mix of international adrenalin junkies. At relatively balmy altitudes of between 900m and 1200m, the valley is nearly as warm as Pokhara.

Equator Expeditions' **Sukute Beach Adventure Resort** (☎01/435 6644, ⓦwww .equatorexpeditionsnepal.com) is the closest to Kathmandu, sitting alongside a wider, gentler stretch of the Sun Koshi between Dolalghat and the Balephi bridge. A mix of safari tents and more comfortable rooms with attached baths overlook a broad sandy stretch of the riverbank, and there's an attractive swimming pool, tandoori restaurant and pool table.

Ultimate Descents was first in the area with the now well-established **Borderland Resort** (☎01/470 1295, ⓦwww.borderlandresorts.com), set at the bottom of the gorge 9km north of Barhabise. It's a sedate, relaxing place, with three classes of tents, a pool and nice gardens.

Furthest north of the trio, Ultimate Rivers' 🌴 **The Last Resort** (☎01/470 0525, ⓦwww.thelastresort.com.np) has the most spectacular location, accessed by a footbridge suspended 160m above the gorge that also serves as the launching point for their bungy jump (€65 including transport and lunch), one of the world's highest and the only one in Nepal. If the bungy doesn't sate your appetite, you can always try the canyon swing (same price) as well. The resort itself is the funkiest of the three, with the smartest tents, beautifully landscaped grounds, sauna and plunge pool, massage and spa options from the excellent Himalayan Healers, and a sociable bar, though the river is some distance below. Ultimate Rivers also runs the more rudimentary **Bhote Kosi Riverside**, 2km beyond Lamosangu.

Prices for all of the above usually come as part of packages including activities, or at least meals, so it's worth shopping around for the best deal of the moment. Expect to pay around $40 per person for an overnight stay with full board (but no activities); $45 for a day's rafting and $65 for canyoning (both including transport and lunch, but not accommodation).

journey to the border should take around thirty minutes, during the monsoon it can take three times as long.

In the autumn, Nepal's famed **honey-hunters** can sometimes be seen clinging to the cliffs below the road in pursuit of hives. Afternoon rain is common up here, even in the dry season, and despite a general scarcity of trees near the river, everything is intensely green, with waterfalls splashing down cliff faces at every turn. As the road approaches **Tatopani** the scenery is interrupted by a series of hydroelectric plants, and more are in the offing. Just before Tatopani is a police checkpost, and from here up, the Bhote Koshi forms the **border** – Tibet is just across the river.

Tatopani to the border

Until the mid-1980s, **TATOPANI** (1530m) enjoyed a small following among Westerners, who came to gaze into forbidden Tibet and soak in the village's hot springs (*taato paani* means "hot water"). Now Tibet is open again, Tatopani has fallen out of fashion and is probably too dull for most, unless you're into offbeat locales.

The village stretches along the highway for almost a kilometre. Tamangs (see box, p.216) are in the majority at this altitude, and they maintain a small **gompa** a five-minute walk above the southern bazaar. The building is modest, but looks out on a fine view of the valley and, up at the head of it, the start of the Tibetan plateau. The **hot springs** (Rs10) are at the northern end of the village: the water splashes out of pipes into a concrete pool and is used strictly for washing. If you take the waters, remember that nudity offends in Nepal.

Western menus have disappeared from Tatopani, but a few **lodges** limp on from the good old days: *New Family Guest House* (☎01/169 0245; ❸) is slightly pricey for what it is, but clean and friendly enough, and the toilets even have river views. It also has a **restaurant** serving the usual Nepali fare with a few Chinese rice and noodle dishes thrown in for less than Rs100 per meal. Signs of China's proximity are everywhere: you'll see chopsticks and thermos flasks in every kitchen, and some places sell Chinese beer.

Just over a kilometre from Tatopani is the bustling, fly-bitten village of **KODARI** (1600-1640m), rising up to a scruffy agglomeration of shops, lodges and checkposts just short of the Tibetan border. You're unlikely to be stuck here, but if you need to stay try *Manakamana Guest House* (☎980/363 1973; ❷), which has austere rooms with shared squat toilets, and the marginally cheaper, similarly spartan, Tibetan-run *Lhasa* (no ☎; ❶). There are a number of **snack joints** in the town selling the usual mix of Nepali snacks, Tibetan fare (including *momos*), and a few Chinese-style noodle dishes.

Buses leave Kodari regularly for Kathmandu (up to 5hr) via Barhabise until around nightfall; there are two quicker express buses leaving at 6am and 1pm (in the opposite direction they leave at 7am and 2pm). A **taxi** to Kathmandu should cost around Rs3500, though you'll have to bargain. Ask around, as there's often someone willing to split the ride. This route is also great by mountain **bike**; ask at one of the Thamel operators if you're interested. Rather than heading straight for Kathmandu however, consider spending a night or two in the towns of Dhulikhel (see p.206) or Bhaktapur (see p.181), which are much pleasanter places to wind down after China.

The border

Disabuse yourself of any visions of high, snowy passes into Tibet. The border sits at the bottom of a deep valley, with nary a yak in sight. The lowest point along the Nepal–Tibet border, **Kodari** has always been the preferred crossing for traders between Kathmandu and Lhasa. Its low elevation isn't as extraordinary as it might seem, though: the main Himalayan chain, which the border generally follows, is breached in several places by rivers that are older than the mountains themselves. In the case of Kodari, the border was actually shifted further south after an ill-advised war with Tibet in 1792.

The actual frontier is marked by the so-called **Friendship Bridge**, which spans the Bhote Koshi at the top end of town, guarded at either end by Nepali and (very strict) Chinese soldiers. Up at the head of the valley, 600m higher than Kodari, the Chinese buildings of **Khasa** (or **Zhangmu**) cling to the side of a mountain – that's the extent of the view of Tibet from here. A steady stream of Nepalis and a few Chinese cross the bridge during daylight hours: Nepalis shop in the tax-free zone just over the border, while Chinese citizens travel down to Barhabise where Bollywood films and Indian fashions are popular purchases. Officially, Tibetans with Nepali citizenship cards are allowed over, but in practice they face serious difficulties. Be very careful about **taking photos** of Tibet: Chinese border guards (including plain clothes officers) are very sensitive and have snatched and broken cameras in the past.

If you are **crossing the border** you will have to get out of your vehicle and pass through immigration on foot, your vehicle will be waiting for you on the other side. Remember Tibet is two hours and fifteen minutes ahead of Nepal, so you have to set off early if you want to catch the bank in Khasa before it closes, though most people – on both sides of the border – use moneychangers instead. Rates on either side of the border are similar, though not great, and – as always with moneychangers – make sure you get the right amount, and are not palmed off with dirty or torn notes.

If you're **entering Nepal** from Tibet, it's best to set off early from Khasa if you plan to make Kathmandu. Visas are easily available at Nepali immigration, but watch out for overcharging.

To Jiri

The 110km road **to Jiri** gives a marvellous foretaste of the immense country that's in store if you're on your way to Everest. It's very narrow and winding, with some unbelievable ups and downs, making it a gruelling **bus** journey of anywhere from ten to thirteen hours from Kathmandu. On a mountain **bike** it

---

Tamangs

Tamangs, Nepal's largest ethnic group, making up around twenty percent of the population, dominate the central hills between elevations of around 1500m and 2500m. With their origins in Tibet (Tamang means "horse trader" in Tibetan), the group follow a form of Buddhism virtually indistinguishable from Lamaism, though most also worship clan deities, employ shamans and observe major Hindu festivals. Despite their numbers, they remain one of Nepal's most **exploited** groups, a situation dating back to the Gorkhali conquest in the late eighteenth century. Much of their land was appropriated, leaving the Tamangs as tenant farmers, bonded labourers, freelance woodcutters or stuck in menial jobs serving the new aristocracy – the latter they performed so efficiently the government came to view them as a strategic asset, prohibiting them from serving in the Gurkha regiments. The Tamangs today remain an underclass, locked into low-wage or exploitative jobs (rikshaw wallahs, carpet makers and porters, for example), or simply locked up (surveys suggest a disproportionate number are in prison).

Entering Tibet

You can't officially enter Tibet (China) from Nepal without a Tibetan visa, and must also be part of an official organized tour. Rules are strictly enforced: you have no chance of getting in without the correct paperwork. See p.145 for details.

would be a marathon. On a **motorcycle**, though, it's an absolute magic-carpet ride – this has to be one of the world's great motorcycle journeys.

This route has a reputation for **theft** from the roofs of buses, so keep an eye on your stuff. **Charikot** is a good place to break up the journey; the *Charikot Panorama Resort* (℡04/942 1245, ✉binda_c@hotmail.com; ❻ full board), just above town, has sweeping views and tasteful en-suites.

Jiri

Most people come to **JIRI** for the Everest trek, and few spend more than a night here. The bazaar is a busy place, with trucks dropping off supply shipments and porters assembling to carry impossibly heavy loads out into the hinterland of Solu and Khumbu. Saturday is particularly colourful, as Jirels (the local indigenous group), Sherpas, Tamangs and Newars descend from the hills for the weekly market in the old bazaar, about 3km back up the road.

In 1958 the Swiss established the **Jiri Multi-Purpose Development Project**, a ground-breaking scheme based on the view that development needs are interrelated and can't be tackled separately. The programme established a hospital, a technical school, an experimental farm, managed forests and other facilities. But it was the Swiss-built road that brought the greatest material boost to Jiri, and it has now been extended south via the major Khimti Khola hydroelectric project to the district capital of **Manthali**. It is also being bulldozed on from there towards Okhaldhunga, an important bazaar town in the eastern hills.

At least a dozen no-nonsense trekking **lodges** are grouped around the western end of the bazaar. There's little to distinguish between them; *Cherdung Lodge* (❶) has relatively clean but spartan rooms with shared baths. Don't expect hot water. **Shops** sell Nepali porter gear (small backpacks, jackets, socks etc) and lodge owners can arrange porters and guides. Book return bus tickets as soon as possible for the next day's departures, as seats go quickly.

The Tribhuwan Rajpath and Daman

Nepal's most magnificent and hair-raising highway, the **Tribhuwan Rajpath** (usually just called the Rajpath, which means "King's Way") heads west out of the Kathmandu Valley and then hurls itself, through an astounding series of switchbacks, straight over the Mahabharat Lek to the Terai. En route it passes through lush stands of rhododendrons and takes in superb views of the Himalayas. Mountain bikers regard the road, and the culminating viewpoint of **Daman**, as something of a holy pilgrimage.

Built by Indian engineers in the mid-1950s, the Rajpath was the first highway to link Kathmandu to the outside world – before that, the prime ministers' automobiles had to be portered from India, fully assembled, by two-hundred-strong teams of coolies. At the time, India was on the brink of war with China and preferred to make any route through Nepal as inconvenient as possible to reduce the risk of invasion. King Tribhuwan, who owed his crown to India, agreed to allow the road to be built right over the highest ridge in the entire area, rationalizing it by saying it would help the development of remote villages. Since the faster Mugling/Narayangadh route was completed, however, the road has become something of a backwater – though its importance as the sole alternative route out of the valley was underlined during the monsoon in 2000, when the Prithvi Highway was closed by a landslide.

The Rajpath is poorly served by public transport, with only six **buses** (as well as more numerous shared Jeeps) making the through trip between Kathmandu and Hetauda (see p.319) every day. From Kalanki, on the outskirts of Kathmandu, there are also several daily buses that travel as far as Palung, from where it's an hour's walk up to Daman. Infrequent trucks take on passengers, but nearly all of them are heading south to Hetauda after delivering their cargo to Kathmandu – fully laden vehicles bound for Kathmandu take the safer, quicker and less diesel-drainingly steep Prithvi Highway.

The lack of traffic makes the Rajpath a perfect route for a **mountain bike** (see p.415) or motorcycle: challenging, varied and scenic. A good time to do this route is in April, when the **rhododendrons** are in bloom. The Rajpath is also famed for its many varieties of **orchids**, most of which bloom in March–June or in September–October.

Along the Rajpath

For its first 26km, the Rajpath follows the heavily used Prithvi Highway towards Pokhara. Leaving the Kathmandu Valley through its ugliest and most industrial corridor, it slips over a low point in the rim (good views here of Manaslu, Boudha, Ganesh and Langtang) and descends to **Naubise** (945m), near the bottom of the deep, wrinkled Mahesh Khola Valley. This first stretch is a real drag: traffic is heavy, and the descent to Naubise is a slow crawl behind smoke-belching trucks. Nepali restaurants are plentiful in Naubise and a few places have inexpensive rooms.

At Naubise the Rajpath leaves the Prithvi Highway and forks off to the left, climbing relentlessly for 30km to Tistung (2030m) before descending into the **Palung Valley** and its tidy terraces (spinach – *paalung* – and potatoes are local specialities). The turning for Markhu and the Kulekhani Reservoir appears on the left 4km past Tistung, and the Newari village of **Palung**, at 1745m, is 5km beyond that. Very basic food and lodging can be had in **Shikharkot**, 2km further on, but unless you're desperate it's worth toiling up the final, tough 10km to spend the night in Daman (see opposite).

Three kilometres beyond Daman, the Rajpath crosses the pass of **Sim Bhanjyang** (2488m) – often icy in winter – where it enters a landscape of plunging hill country and begins a relentless 2000m descent to the valley below. These south-facing upper slopes of the Mahabharat Lek are dramatically greener and wilder than those on the other side – they wring much of the moisture out of the prevailing winds, and are frequently wreathed in fog by afternoon.

The road passes through successive zones of mossy jungle, pine forest and finally terraced farmland before reaching the **Bhimphedi** turning, 40km from Sim Bhanjyang. The electric transformers seen near here relay power from the Kulekhani hydroelectric dam north of Bhimphedi, an important source of power for Nepal. The devices that look like ski lifts are ropeways, one bringing quarried limestone down to the big cement plant in **Hetauda** and the other, now disused, for ferrying raw materials up to Kathmandu. Hetauda (see p.319) is 10km further on.

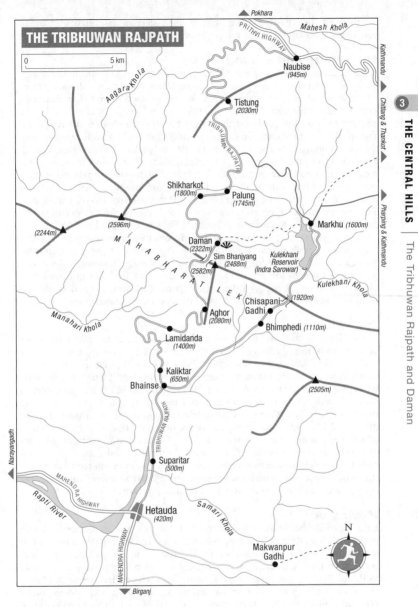

THE TRIBHUWAN RAJPATH

0 — 5 km

▲ Pokhara

Mahesh Khola

PRITHVI HIGHWAY

Naubise
(945m)

Aagara Khola

Tistung
(2030m)

TRIBHUWAN RAJPATH

Shikharkot
(1800m)

Palung
(1745m)

(2596m)

(2244m)

Markhu *(1600m)*

M A H A B H A R A T   L E K

Daman
(2322m)

Sim Bhanjyang
(2488m)

Kulekhani
Reservoir
(Indra Sarowar)

(2582m)

Kulekhani Khola

Manahari Khola

Aghor
(2080m)

Chisapani
Gadhi

(1920m)

Bhimphedi *(1110m)*

Lamidanda
(1400m)

Kaliktar
(650m)

Bhainse

(2505m)

TRIBHUWAN RAJPATH

▲ Narayangadh

Suparitar
(500m)

MAHENDRA HIGHWAY

Rapti River

Samari Khola

MAHENDRA HIGHWAY

Hetauda
(420m)

Makwanpur
Gadhi

N

▼ Birganj

Daman

Higher and farther back from the mountains than its rivals, **DAMAN** (2322m) is the most comprehensive of the Himalayan viewpoints surrounding Kathmandu. Sitting below the Rajpath's highest point, the hamlet overlooks the peaceful Palung Valley towards a magnificent spread of peaks. However, the mountains will probably be in clouds when you arrive: an overnight stay is obligatory to see them in their best morning light. Bring a sleeping bag in winter, unless you've got reservations at the deluxe *Everest Panorama Resort*.

The village and around

A signboard announces you're in Daman, but blink and you'll miss it. The village is a loose gathering of houses, a couple of agricultural research facilities, a seismic station and – its one unmissable landmark – an enclosed **view tower** that looks as if it might have been built for air traffic control purposes. Operated by the adjacent *Daman Mountain Resort*, the tower offers the best views in the village (for a small fee). On good days you can see seven 8000m peaks from here, along with the closer, and hence more prominent, 7000m peaks of Himalchuli, Ganesh Himal and Langtang. Uniquely among the Himalayan viewpoints, the view of the entire range is unbroken by foothills. A couple of high-powered **telescopes** give awesome close-ups of the peaks from this angle: the magnified view of Everest is almost identical to the one you get from Kala Pattar, ten days into the Everest trek. The view from the tower also gives you a good feel for the topography of the central hills and the Kathmandu Valley, from Phulchoki to the Trisuli Valley.

An even more sweeping vista can be had from the *Everest Panorama Resort*, a thirty-minute walk up the Rajpath, which also happens to be a fine spot for breakfast or lunch. One hairpin turn below the *Everest Panorama*, a signposted path winds through oak and rhododendron forest to a Buddhist **gompa** (allow twenty minutes). Run by a Bhutanese lama, the monastery is small and unembellished, but the view from its meditation perch is awesome.

Practicalities

Daman lacks the facilities for travellers that Nagarkot and Dhulikhel have. For **accommodation**, there's not much choice, and all of it is expensive for what you get. *Hotel Daman & Lodge* (☎05/754 0387; ❶–❷), one of a handful of family-run, shoestring places, provides no-frills digs and plenty of *daal bhaat*, while the *Daman Mountain Resort* (☎01/443 8023; ❸–❹) is an aged hotel in need of a little loving care, with safari-style tents (very cold in the winter) and simple rooms. If you want to stay in style, book into the *Everest Panorama Resort* (☎05/762 1480, ⓦwww.everestpanoramaresort.com; ❽), 2.5km above Daman, which has comfortable en suites and cute "honeymoon" cottages; all with private balconies and heaters. There's a good restaurant and a spa with a steam bath, Jacuzzi and massage treatments. Both resorts may offer substantial discounts if you turn up at the door. In all likelihood, you'll **eat** wherever you're staying, as there are only a few basic Nepali snack places in Daman.

Moving on

Heading **to Kathmandu** by public transport can be a pain, as the buses heading over from Hetauda are often standing-room only, and standing on a bus on this road is no fun. Shared Jeeps also ply the route, though you face the same problem of finding a seat. Alternatively, if you're travelling light, you can walk to Palung, less than an hour below Daman, from where there are several buses, spread out through the day until late afternoon, to Kathmandu. Moving on to **Hetauda** you should be able to squeeze onto any of the morning buses coming up from Kathmandu, Palung and Markhu. For more details on **travel from Kathmandu**, see pp.142–146.

These transport peculiarities make a good case for **walking** or **biking** down instead. Departing from the Rajpath about 500m down from the view tower, a walking trail descends to the western shore of the Kulekhani Reservoir in three to four hours, and continues from there to the Kathmandu Valley.

4

The Western hills

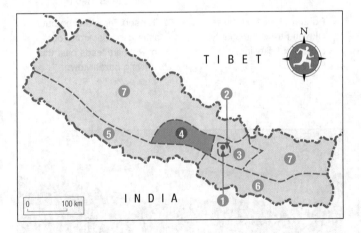

CHAPTER 4 # Highlights

✳ **Manakamana** Swoop up to this lofty, wish-fulfilling temple in Asia's longest cable-car ride. See p.226

✳ **Gorkha** Gorgeously carved historic temple-palace, perched high on a ridge. See p.228

✳ **Bandipur** A charming Newari hamlet, with breathtaking views of the Himalayas. See p.231

✳ **Pokhara** Relax by the serene lake and trawl the shanty bazaar of Lakeside. See p.234

✳ **Paragliding** Fly like a bird from Sarangkot, a world-famous spot for paragliding. See p.248

✳ **Sarangkot to Naudaada** Get a taste for trekking, and a classic panorama of the Annapurna range, on this easy ridgetop amble. See p.253

✳ **Begnas and Rupa Tal** Walk the wooded trail rising up between Pokhara's lesser-known lakes. See p.257

✳ **Tansen** The stunning but little-used backroad out of Pokhara leads past this thriving bazaar town. See p.259

▲ Phewa Tal, Pokhara's myth-shrouded, backpacker-friendly lake

The Western hills

The **Western hills** are Nepal at its most outstandingly typical, with roaring gorges, precariously perched villages and terraced fields reaching to improbable heights, and some of the most graceful and accessible peaks of the Himalayas for a backdrop.

Yet in this, Nepal's most populous hill region, people are the dominant feature of the landscape. Magars and Gurungs, the most visible **ethnic groups** (see *The people of Nepal* colour section), live in their own villages or side by side with Tamangs, Hindu castes and the usual smattering of Newari merchants. Life is traditional and close to the earth, but relatively prosperous: houses are tidy and spacious, and hill women festooned with the family gold. The prosperity comes, indirectly, from an unlikely quarter, as the western hills were historically the most important recruiting area for **Gurkha soldiers** (see p.225).

The chief destination is the laid-back lakeside resort of **Pokhara**, Nepal's major trekking hub. Most visitors are understandably intent on heading straight for the mountains (trekking, rafting and mountain biking are described in Chapters Seven to Nine), but it's well worth sidestepping to the historic hilltop fortress of **Gorkha**, the pilgrimage site of **Manakamana** and the increasingly popular hamlet of **Bandipur**. Beyond Pokhara, on the road to the Indian border, the charming bazaar town of **Tansen** lies at the southern edge of the hills. All of these make excellent bases for **day hikes**.

Two main roads cut a swath through the hills: the **Prithvi Highway** (Prithvi Rajmarg), running west from Kathmandu to Pokhara, and the **Siddhartha Highway** (Siddhartha Rajmarg), which carries on from Pokhara to the Indian border.

Heading west: the Prithvi Highway

Weaving through the heart of the hills, the **Prithvi Highway** is the best-maintained and fastest road between Pokhara, Kathmandu and the Terai – a status that makes it all the more dangerous, as bus drivers compete to slice minutes off journey times. Nepal's second trunk road when it was built with

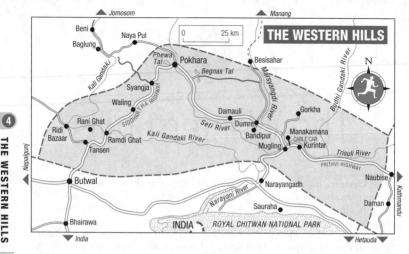

Chinese assistance in 1973, the Prithvi Highway has played a crucial role in modernizing the country, opening up the western hills and enabling Pokhara to develop into Nepal's second tourist city.

The road stays near the bottom of deep valleys for most of its 200km. There are few towns of consequence, but many **rafting** parties come this way to paddle Nepal's most popular river, the Trisuli, which the highway parallels for about 50km, or to put in on the Seti, which it crosses at Damauli. **Trekkers** going around Annapurna turn off for Lamjung at Dumre.

In addition, three **cultural destinations** just off the highway – **Manakamana**, **Gorkha** and **Bandipur** – offer further reasons to break the journey. Not many people visit them, because it means giving up their seat on the tourist bus, but continuing on by public bus is an experience in itself, and easily bearable given the short distances involved. The danger from traffic puts off most potential **cyclists**, though it's easy enough to put your bike on the roof for the most trying leg, from Kathmandu to Naubise.

Manakamana to Bandipur

After parting with the Tribhuwan Rajpath at Naubise (see p.218), the highway soon joins the **Trisuli River** at Bhaireni, one of several rafting put-in points. Keep an eye out for magnificent, spidery suspension bridges and precarious ropeways spanning the river; you might also spot funeral pyres on the sandy banks. Lorries parked in the riverbed are collecting stones; these are then broken up by hand by families of workers, attracted by the chance of earning $2 a day. The solid, three-storey farmhouses seen here generally belong to Baahuns and Chhetris, while the humbler mud-and-thatch huts are typical Tamang or Magar dwellings.

You'll see small sugar cane plantations and the tall, angular *simal* (the silk cotton or kapok tree), which produces red flowers in early March and pods of cotton-like seeds in May. Most tourist buses make a breakfast and a mid-morning pit stop for *daal bhaat* at isolated fancy restaurants where the prices will be inflated by commission. Public buses break for lunch at **Mugling**, a ghastly crossroads at the junction of the Trisuli and Marsyangdi rivers that exists mainly to provide *daal bhaat* and prostitutes to long-distance drivers. Traffic bound for the Tarai also turns south here for the gradual 34km descent to Narayangadh.

Just past Mugling, the Prithvi Highway crosses the Trisuli and heads upstream along the Marsyangdi, passing the massive **Marsyangdi Hydroelectric Project** powerhouse. The spur road to **Gorkha** (see p.228) leaves the highway at **Abu Khaireni**, 7km west of Mugling, while **Dumre**, 11km beyond, is the turning for two side roads: one north to **Lamjung's Besisahar**, the starting point of the Annapurna Circuit, and one south to **Bandipur** (see p.231).

Damauli, 8km west of Dumre, is marked out by its position overlooking the confluence of the Madi and Seti rivers. In reverence of this union, there is a complex of shrines set back from the road, and to the left of them is **Byas Gupha**,

The Gurkhas

An elite Nepali corps within the British and Indian armies for almost two centuries, the **Gurkha regiments** have long been rated among the finest fighting units in the world. Ironically, the regiments were born out of the 1814–16 war between Nepal and Britain's East India Company: so impressed were the British by the men of "Goorkha" (Gorkha, the ancestral home of Nepal's rulers) that they began recruiting Nepalis into the Indian Army before the peace was even signed.

In the century that followed, Gurkhas fought in every major British military operation, including the 1857 **Indian Mutiny**. More than 200,000 Gurkhas served in the two world wars, (often earmarked for "high-wastage" roles – sixteen thousand have died in British service) earning respect for their bravery: ten of the one hundred **Victoria Crosses** awarded in World War II went to Gurkhas. Following India's independence, Britain kept four of the ten regiments and India retained the rest. More recently, Gurkhas have distinguished themselves in Cyprus, the Falklands and as UN peacekeepers.

Recruits hail mainly from the Magar, Gurung, Rai and Limbu ethnic groups, from Nepal's middle hills. Most boys from these groups have traditionally dreamt of making it into the Gurkhas, not only for the money, but also for a rare chance to see the world and return with prestige and a comfortable pension. Those who fail can always try in the lower-paid Indian regiments; the Nepali army is considered the last resort.

Gurkhas used to be Nepal's major source of remittances, sending home $40 million annually, but changes in **pension equality** and the right to reside in the UK have changed lifestyle patterns, with many Gurkha families moving to Britain, especially to educate their children. In addition, the Gurkhas' long and faithful service to Britain is winding down. The only remaining **training centre** is in Pokhara, where thousands of would-be recruits still try out for places.

It remains to be seen how the removal of the Gurkhas' cash injection will affect the economy of cities like Pokhara and Dharan; already the need for cash to set up in the UK has seen many families sell up their houses for peanuts, sending market prices plummeting. The increase in other work migration (mostly to the Middle East) has made up for the remittance shortfall at a national level, at least – supplying $2 billion in remittances in 2007/8 and spreading profits through a much wider cross-section of the population.

The **Gurkha Memorial Museum** can be found in Pokhara, next to the Gurkha camp. Photographs of medal-winners line the walls, attached to short paragraphs of no-nonsense prose that describe act after extraordinary act of old-fashioned courage performed by Gurkha soldiers in British service.

a cave where Byas (or Vyasa), the sage of the Mahabharat, is supposed to have been born and lived.

After crossing the Madi, the Prithvi Highway rises and then descends gradually to rejoin the broad Seti Valley, finally reaching Pokhara. Begnas and Rupa lakes, off to the right of the highway on the approach to Pokhara, are described on p.257.

Practicalities

All of the roadside towns – Kurintar, Mugling, Dumre and Damauli – have plentiful **accommodation**, most of it noisy and insalubrious.

There are, however, a few **resort hotels**, which make the best places to stay if you can't get to Gorkha, Manakamana or Bandipur. Some make the most of the warm riverside location, such as the *River Side Springs Resort* ❼ (☎056/540 129). which provides the most luxurious **accommodation** anywhere between Kathmandu and Pokhara. What really makes the place is its palatial pool and long, sandy Trisuli River frontage. The nearby *Manakamana Village Resort* (☎056/540 150, ✉om@hons.com.np; ❺) is a more affordable alternative, although it is rather close to the highway. Perched on a hilltop in Dhading near Malekhu, with amazing views of the Ganesh Himal, the *Shreeban Nature Camp* (☎01/622 0359 or 01/425 8427, ☽www.shreeban.com.np; ❻) offers climbing, handgliding, trekking and mountain biking.

For **food** along the route, bog standard *daal bhaat* reigns king, but lots of places do chow mein, fried rice and all kinds of weird and wonderful snack foods, at anything from dirt-cheap to highly inflated prices.

Manakamana

Just about every Nepali has either been to **MANAKAMANA** (Ma–na–kaa-ma-na) or hopes one day to go. Located on a prominent ridge high above the confluence of the Trisuli and Marsyangdi rivers, the village is home to Nepal's famous wish-fulfilling temple. Each year over half a million people make the journey, the wealthier of them speeding up the hillside with a bird's-eye view

Farming in the hills

The **farming** methods practised along the Prithvi Highway are fairly representative of those employed throughout the hills. The land is used intensively but sustainably: trees and bamboo are pruned for fodder; livestock, fed on fodder, pull ploughs and provide milk and manure; and manure is dolloped onto the fields as fertilizer. Goats, chickens and pigs recycle scraps into meat and eggs.

The average hill family's half-hectare holding is fragmented into several plots located at different elevations, often far apart. The typical household owns only simple hand tools – its only beast of burden a buffalo or ox – and grows just seventy percent of the food it needs each year. Tractors will probably never be appropriate for the vast majority of farms in Nepal's hills. Most farmers barter surplus grain for odd essentials such as salt, sugar, pots and pans, and have little to do with the cash economy. Some supplement their incomes with portering work or **seasonal labour** in the Terai or India, and increasingly further abroad in the Middle East; often incurring huge debt to secure a job with manpower agencies. Some return with watches and modern appliances but the unlucky or the unenterprising fall into further debt and may lose their land as a result.

in the swish **cable car** service. Completed in 1998, at a cost of $7.5 million, the line is one of the few developments targeted at Nepali tourists.

One of its less appealing results has been the transformation of an attractive village into a cluster of concrete hotels, but the car (daily 9am–noon & 1.30–5pm; $12, children $8 and 130 rupees for bringing a goat to his first, and last, pilgrimage) does allow visitors to travel in comfort. The gondolas are international-ski-resort standard with 360-degree views and the ride takes just ten minutes to ascend the 2.8km-long line. Any bus will drop you off at the turning for the base station, which is marked by a big brick archway just off the highway, halfway between Kurintar and Mugling. Be prepared for long queues on Saturdays. Sadhus and poorer pilgrims still toil up the walking route on the other side of the hill, starting from Abu Khaireni. **Walking up** this way takes about five hours – you can stay overnight in a simple lodge along the way.

The village and around

From the cable-car station, a path leads between stalls of Hindu souvenirs, toys and snacks up to the famous **Manakamana Devi** temple, set in a square and overlooked by a huge sacred magnolia. Tradition has it that the goddess Bhagwati rewards those who make the pilgrimage to her shrine by granting their wishes; she's especially popular with Newari newlyweds, who pray for sons. The place goes into overdrive on Saturday mornings, when the vast majority of pilgrims come to perform animal sacrifices; locals raise goats, chickens and pigeons specifically for this. The festivals of Dasain (in Sept–Oct) and Nag Panchami (in July–Aug) bring even greater numbers of celebrants.

Manakamana is also famous for its **mountain views**: from high points around the village you can see a limited panorama from Annapurna II and Lamjung Himal across to Peak 29 and Baudha of the Manaslu Himal. If you're game for more, you can continue 45 minutes further up the ridge to another temple, the **Bakeshwar Mahadev Mandir**, and then another fifteen minutes to **Lakhan Thapa Gupha**, a holy cave near the highest point of the ridge, from where the views are tremendous on clear mornings. The cave is named after the founder of the Manakamana temple, a seventeenth-century royal priest whose descendant is still the chief temple *pujari* today, making offerings including the famous local oranges, which come into season in November and December.

Practicalities

You can **stay** at several resorts nearby on the main road (see p.226) or in Manakamana itself, where dozens of lodges vie for pilgrims' business. You're unlikely to have any trouble finding a room, except on Friday or Saturday nights when you must stake your claim early. Decent budget options include the standard but friendly *Black & White Hotel* (☎064/460 028; ❷) and the ambitiously-named *Malla Fulbari Resort & Fulpati Restaurant* (☎064/460 056; ❷), which is simple but reasonably far away from the noise of the temple bells. **Food** is mostly a matter of low-grade *daal bhaat* or Indian-style variations, though in season the *Thakali Café* just above the temple has some other Nepali and the usual Continental offerings, as does the cleanest-looking option, *Manakamana Café*, at the foot of the cable car.

Moving on from Manakamana, board any local bus plying the Prithvi Highway – it's only three bearable hours to either Kathmandu or Pokhara. The old walking route, done in reverse, is a good way to approach Gorkha. The path leaves from the entrance gate to the ridge-set *Manakamana Village*

Resort, descending steeply over 1000m to reach the busy junction town of **Abu Khaireni**, in the Marsyangdi valley. The descent should take less than three hours, and from Abu Khaireni there are frequent local buses to Gorkha, less than an hour away. A more ambitious hike would be to take the old porters' path that bends north along the ridge from the Bakeshwar Mahadev Mandir, reaching Gorkha in around four hours' walking time from Manakamana.

Gorkha

Despite its status as the cradle of the nation, **GORKHA** remains strangely untouristed, even though the 24-kilometre paved road up from Abu Khaireni makes it a relatively painless half-day's ride from Pokhara, Kathmandu or Chitwan. Conscious of its tourist potential, the government has spruced up Gorkha's main monuments, but the lower town remains a fairly ordinary roadhead bazaar with a handful of rundown hotels.

As the ancestral home of the Nepali royal family, Gorkha occupies a central place in Nepali history. Hunched on the hilltop above the bazaar is its link with that splendid past, the **Gorkha Durbar**, an architectural tour de force worthy of the flamboyant Gorkha kings and the dynasty they founded. Unless you're setting straight off on a trek or just finishing one, you'll have to spend the night here. The Durbar and its agreeable surroundings can easily soak up a day, and hikes around the area could keep you busy for another couple.

Direct **bus** services connect Gorkha with Kathmandu, Pokhara, Narayangadh, Sonauli and Birganj, but it's easy enough to take a tourist bus from Pokhara or Kathmandu to Abu Khaireni and ride a local bus from there. All buses terminate at Gorkha's modest bus park just west of the bazaaar. If you're

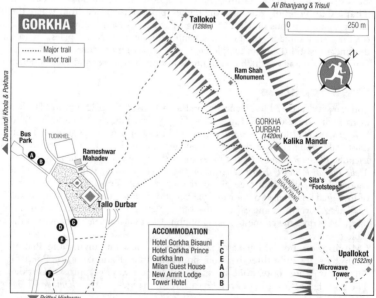

pedalling, bear in mind it's a 900m ascent from Abu Khaireni to Gorkha, and it gets steeper as you go.

Some history

In a sense, Gorkha's history is not its own. A petty hill state in medieval times, it was occupied and transformed into a Himalayan Sparta by outsiders who used it as a base for a dogged campaign against Kathmandu and then, having won their prize, restored Gorkha to obscurity. Yet during those two centuries of occupation, it raised the nation's most famous son, **Prithvi Narayan Shah**, and somehow bred in him the audacity to conquer all of Nepal.

Prithvi Narayan's ancestors came to Gorkha in the mid-sixteenth century, having been driven into the hills from their native Rajasthan by Muslim invaders, and soon gained a reputation as a single-mindedly martial lot. His father launched the first unsuccessful raid on the Kathmandu Valley in the early eighteenth century, and when Prithvi Narayan himself ascended to the throne in 1743, at the age of twenty, he already had his father's obsession fixed in his mind. Within a year, he was leading Gorkha in a war of expansion that was eventually to unify all of present-day Nepal, plus parts of India and Tibet. Looking at the meagre terraces of Gorkha today, you can imagine what a drain it must have been to keep a standing army fed and supplied for 27 years of continuous campaigning. The hardy peasants of Gorkha got little more than a handshake for their efforts. After conquering the valley in 1769, Prithvi Narayan moved his capital to the bright lights of Kathmandu, relegating Gorkha to a mere garrison from which the later western campaign was directed. By the early nineteenth century, Gorkha had been all but forgotten, even as an alternative spelling of the name – Gurkha – was becoming a household name around the world.

The town and around

Nestled on a shelf beneath a steep ridge, most of the bazaar stretches along two parallel lanes, separated by the old **Tallo Durbar** (Lower Palace). Built in around 1750, this imposing Newari-style edifice served as the kingdom's administrative headquarters, while the upper Durbar housed king and court. It is now a museum (Mon & Wed–Sun: summer 10am–5pm; winter 10am–4pm; Rs50; Rs20 for SAARC country members) of the Shah dynasty leading up to Prithvi Narayan and beyond, with limited exhibits of old royal decrees, coins, pots and weapons, surrounded by contrasting landscaped gardens.

The road joining the two main lanes runs past Gorkha's modest Tudikhel (parade ground) and a small temple precinct. The gilded figure kneeling atop a pillar facing the onion-domed **Rameshwar Mahadev Mandir** is Prithvi Pati Shah; grandfather of Prithvi Narayan Shah, he established most of the temples and shrines still in use around the town, including the Kalika temple in the upper Durbar.

Most shops sell the usual imported bric-à-brac, though the jewellers are worth a look for their heavy gold earrings and *tilari* (decorated gold tubes strung on a necklace).

The Gorkha Durbar

It's a brisk, 250m ascent up a steep stone stairway to the **Gorkha Durbar** from Pokharithok, the junction just east of Tallo Durbar. At the top of this route – once the royal approach to the palace – you can marvel at the grand staircase that's one of the Durbar's most distinctive features. It must have cowed visiting vassals into submission – a neat trick for a tinpot realm that could barely muster

150 soldiers at the time of Prithvi Narayan's first campaign. Entrance to the Durbar is through a doorway on its western side, reached by a path to the left of the retaining wall. No leather is allowed in the compound.

Conceived as a dwelling for kings and gods, the fortress remains a religious place, and first stop in any visit is the revered **Kalika Mandir**, occupying the left (western) half of the Durbar building. Its interior is closed to all but priests – others would die upon beholding Kali's terrible image, say the priests. Sacrifices are made in the alcove in front of the entrance daily except on *Ekadasi* (every fifteen days). After the twice-monthly observance of *Astami*, which is celebrated with special gusto in Gorkha, the paving stones are sticky with blood. Most worshippers arrive cradling a trembling goat or chicken and leave swinging a headless carcass. Chait Dasain, Gorkha's biggest annual **festival**, brings processions and more bloodletting in late March or early April, as does the tenth day of Dasain in October.

The east wing of the Durbar is the historic **palace**, site of Prithvi Narayan's birthplace and, by extension, the ancestral shrine of the Shah kings. Though predating the Gorkhali conquest of Kathmandu, the exceptional eighteenth-century brick- and woodwork palace bears the unmistakable stamp of Newari craftsmanship. Two rooms are now open to the public and you can see what is claimed to be Prithvi Narayan's **throne**.

The remaining space within the fortress walls is fairly littered with other Hindu shrines. By the exit is a small temple built around the holy **cave of Gorakhnath**, the centre for worship of the shadowy Indian guru who gave Gorkha its name and is regarded as a kind of guardian angel by the Shah kings. As a young man, Prithvi Narayan Shah is said to have prayed to the guru for success, and was answered in a dream (some say he came in person, and at this spot) by an old man who offered the young prince a bowl of curd. Haughtily, Prithvi Narayan let it fall to his feet (though some say he spilled it by accident), whereupon Gorakhnath revealed himself, saying that the future king would conquer everywhere he set his foot. If he had accepted and eaten the curd, the guru admonished, he would have conquered the world. Sadhus of the Gorakhnath cult are known as *kaanphata* ("split-ears"), after an initiation ceremony in which they insert sticks in their earlobes – a walk in the park compared to some of the other things they get up to in the name of their guru. *Kaanphata* priests sometimes administer ashen *tika* from the shelter above the cave.

Viewpoints and forts

The views are good from the Durbar, but carry on for much better ones. Exit the compound through a door to the east and descend to **Hanuman Bhanjyang** (Hanuman Pass), a small notch in the ridge named after the valiant monkey king whose image guards the popular shady rest stop. Cross the main trail (a branch of the Pokhara–Trisuli porter route) and follow a steep, stone-paved path up for just a couple of minutes to an awesome vantage point where you can stand in a pair of stone "footsteps" (ascribed to Ram, his wife Sita, Gorakhnath himself and even – by Buddhists – to Padma Sambhava) and, weather allowing, snap a postcard picture of the Durbar and the mountains to the north. From this angle, the Durbar looks like Nepal's answer to Mad Ludwig's castle. The Himalayas seen from here stretch from the Annapurnas (and even Dhaulagiri, which from this angle is to the right of Annapurna I and Machhapuchhre) to Ganesh Himal, with the pyramids of Baudha and Himal-chuli occupying centre stage. Come early to catch the sunrise.

From Hanuman Bhanjyang it's another half-hour hike to **Upallokot** (Upper Fort – though it's now more like a hut), a 1520m eyrie at the highest, easternmost point of the ridge. To get to it you have to walk through a fenced microwave relay facility, and views are unfortunately restricted by vegetation. At the other end of the ridge stands **Tallokot**, another watch post with limited views. You can easily stroll there from the Durbar, passing a small Ganesh shrine and a new monument to **Ram Shah**, the seventh-generation ancestor of Prithvi Narayan Shah who is reckoned by some to have been the progenitor of the Shah title. The views from this monument are also excellent.

Longer walks

There are three main options for longer hikes. One with a unique cultural dimension is the route to **Manakamana** (see p.226), which starts on an unpaved side road off the main Gorkha road about 4km down from the town, and takes four hours. It's easily possible to return via the cable car and bus the same day.

The high road through **Hanuman Bhanjyang** gives access to the country east of the Durbar, descending gently for about an hour and a half to Ali Bhanjyang (where you can find tea and snack food), then ascending along a ridge with fabulous views to Khanchok Bhanjyang after about two and a half hours. This would be about the limit for a day hike, but given an early start you could continue down to the subtropical banks of the Budhi Gandaki at Arughat, a long day's 20km from Gorkha, and find basic lodging there – at this point you'd be a third of the way to Trisuli.

Alternatively, follow the main trail west out of Gorkha village, which reaches the untrammelled **Daraundi Khola valley** after about an hour and a half. Continuing on for another three hours brings you to Khoplang, a beautiful hill village with lodgings. For trekking from here, see Chapter Seven.

Practicalities

There's little choice of **accommodation** in Gorkha. Two overpriced hotels that have seen better days offer gardens and views across the valley. The better option is *Gurkha Inn* (☎064/420 206 or 01/444 0091; ❹), which has some character, and the nicer garden. *Hotel Gorkha Bisauni* (☎064/420 107, 01/428 7382, ✉gh_bisauni@yahoo.com; ❹, dorm beds ❷) is in greater need of renovation. The usual local lodges are found near the bus park: *Milan Guest House* and *Tower Hotel* (both ❶) are reasonably clean.

For **food**, the choice is fairly limited. The restaurants at *Gurkha Inn* and *Gorkha Bisauni* do reasonable Western fare, while plenty of places near the bus park serve up the usual *momo*, chow mein or all-you-can-eat *daal bhaat*. There's a **bank** on the main road, but it will usually exchange only US dollars cash.

Bandipur

Its grand houses perched improbably on a ridge above the Pokhara highway, with breathtaking views of the Himalayas, the hilltop bazaar of **BANDIPUR** has become an increasingly popular tourist stopover between Kathmandu and Pokhara. At the time of writing several renovations for boutique hotel accommodation were underway: it's still fairly undeveloped, but Bandipur could have a chic future.

From Pokhara, Kathmandu or Narayangadh, take any bus heading along the Prithvi Highway and get off at Dumre, from where you can pick up a ride in a crowded jeep. Book ahead and the more expensive hotels will pick you up from the roadhead. You could also take the historic **trail** to Bandipur, immortalized in

▲ The atmospheric former trading centre of Bandipur

a poem by the late King Mahendra. The walk takes two to three hours, beginning 500m east of the main Dumre intersection and climbing through shady forest punctuated by very civilized rest shelters and waterspouts.

Accommodation

Bandipur's numerous **guesthouses** are situated right in the main bazaar and include both simple lodgings and boutique hotels.

Bandipur Guest House ☎065/690 634.
Occupying a seventy-year-old Neoclassical mansion, this is the most atmospheric of the budget options, but only has bucket-wash facilites. ❶
Bandipur Mountain Resort ☎065/690 024 or 01/422 0162, ✉island@mos.com.np. Located at the beautiful northern end of the *tudikhel*, offers pricey and comfortable accommodation and has a rocky terrace for taking in the views; they are building a new stone-clad hotel nearby and also arrange nature treks down to Chitwan National Park. ❼
Hills Heaven Restaurant & Lodge ☎974/600 2641. Basic guesthouse, but provides a warm welcome and a hot shower. ❶

Old Inn ☎065/520 110 or 01/470 0426, ✉raftnepl@himenco.wlink.com.np. Run by Himalayan Encounters, this upmarket place has beautifully restored rooms, all beams and slate floors. The facilities need a bit of tweaking considering the price, but it offers a unique experience, with traditional food and guide costs included in full board. ❺–❼
Pradhan's Family Guests' Accommodation ☎065/520 106, krishnaprd@hotmail.com. Simple place; the proprietor speaks excellent English. ❶

The town and around

Bandipur was once a prosperous **trading centre**, and its substantial buildings, with their Neoclassical facades and shuttered windows, speak of past glories.

Originally a simple Magar village, it was colonized in the 1800s by Newars from Bhaktapur, who took advantage of its malaria-free location to develop it into an important stop along the India–Tibet trade route. Bandipur hit its heyday in Rana times and in 1945, as a measure of its prestige, it was granted special permission to have its own library (the converted eighteenth-century building still stands). In the 1950s, the eradication of malaria made Terai travel easier, reducing the town's importance, and the 1973 completion of the Prithvi Highway shifted commerce to Dumre, leaving Bandipur a semi-ghost town.

Sitting in a saddle at 1000m beneath dramatic limestone hills, Bandipur's quiet main **bazaar** is oriented from southwest to northeast. Hiking up, you approach the bazaar from the northwest, first passing the **tudikhel** (parade ground), perched exhilaratingly on a rock outcrop with a sheer drop to the east. The view to the north is stunning: you're looking at a map of the first half of the Annapurna Circuit, with the Marsyangdi valley straight ahead and the Annapurna and Manaslu ranges behind.

Bandipur has several temples. The main **Khadga Devi Mandir**, reached by bearing left up the steps at the north end of the bazaar, houses a holy sword supposedly given to a local king by Lord Shiva himself. The sword is displayed on the seventh day of Dasain but bound in cloth because locals believe that anyone looking at the blade hidden beneath will die instantly. The shrine of **Thani Mai**, Khadga Devi's "sister", is of more interest for its awesome views – it's at the top of Gurungche Daada, the limestone hill southwest of the bazaar.

Day hikes around Bandipur could fill up several days. The obligatory destination is **Siddha Gupha**, Nepal's biggest cave, which incredibly was discovered only in 1987. It's 10m wide, 400m long and full of stalactites, not to mention a sizeable bat population. You'll need to bring your own torch/flashlight. It takes about an hour and a half to walk to the cave from Bandipur – the route is not well signposted, but you can hire a guide for around Rs150. A trail also leads up to it from the Prithvi Highway at Bimalnagar, 1km east of Dumre. A hike to Siddha Gupha can be combined with a visit to another nearby cave, **Patale Dwar** ("Portal to the Underworld") – supposedly a geologic wonder. You can also visit the **silk farm**, an easy half-hour walk from the town.

Other, longer hikes go through pretty, cultivated hills and traditional Magar villages, and are worth considering as alternatives to leaving Bandipur by bus. The village of **Rankot**, two hours' hike from Bandipur, is one of the most scenic. You can walk **to Damauli** via the Chabda Barahi Mandir in about five hours, the last part of it on a motorable road. If you follow the crest, you'll be rewarded by panoramic views of the Annapurnas.

Practicalities

All the guesthouses have basic menus, but **eating** options are currently fairly limited in Bandipur. The *Old Inn* has opened a little café opposite its lodge, with slightly higher prices and standards than the competition.

Moving on from Bandipur, it shouldn't be too hard to get down to Dumre, either on foot or by shared jeep – the upmarket hotels provide a transfer. Frequent buses pass through Dumre on their way between Kathmandu and Pokhara, and Manakamana or Gorkha are only about an hour away.

Pokhara

The Himalayas form the highest, sheerest rise from subtropical base to icy peaks of any mountain range on earth, and nowhere is the contrast more marked than at **POKHARA** (Pok-hur-ra). Spreading down a lush valley to the lakeshore, on clear days it boasts a nearly unobstructed view of the 8000m-plus Annapurna and Manaslu ranges, just 25km to the north. Dominating the skyline, in beauty if not in height, is the double-finned 6997m summit of Machhapuchhre ("Fish-Tailed") – so named for its twin-peaked summit, though only one is visible from Pokhara.

Nepal's main resort area lolls beside **Phewa Tal** (Phewa Lake), well outside the actual town of Pokhara. This is Nepal's little budget paradise: carefree and culturally undemanding, though extremely touristy, with a steaks-and-cakes scene rivalling Kathmandu's. New businesses pop up like mushrooms after each monsoon, and disappear just as quickly; cheap places go upmarket, great views get blocked, and what's hot today may be dead tomorrow. No guidebook can keep up with all the changes, so take all recommendations with a pinch of salt.

As the main destination served by tourist buses and internal flights, Pokhara is usually the first place travellers venture to outside the Kathmandu Valley. For **trekkers**, it's the gateway to Nepal's most popular trails; for **rafters** and **kayakers**, it's Nepal's river-running headquarters; for paragliders and mountain bikers it's one of the best spots on earth; and for everyone else, it's the most relaxing place in Nepal that you don't have to trek to get to. **Day-trips** around the Pokhara Valley beckon, and if Pokhara town is short on temples and twisting alleys, you might find that a relief after Kathmandu's profusion. At 800m above sea level it's both cooler than the plains in summer and warmer than Kathmandu in winter; it's also less protected from the prevailing rains and receives about twice as much as the capital.

Orientation, arrival and information

To get your bearings, start with the tourist areas of **Lakeside** and **Damside**, set along the eastern and southeastern edges of **Phewa Tal**, where you'll find the vast majority of budget lodgings and restaurants. The **tourist bus park** lies at the northern edge of Damside, and the **airport** begins just to the northeast.

Northeast of the lake, **Pokhara Bazaar** is maddeningly diffuse, sprawling a good 6km along two main north–south roads and a ladder of cross streets from **Mustang Chowk** in the south, past **Prithvi Chowk**, home of the **public bus park**, to **Purano (Old) Bazaar** on the high ground to the north.

Arrival

Tourist **buses** arrive at their own bus park near Damside; Greenline buses continue on to a depot at the southern end of Lakeside. It's a pretty easy walk from the bus park to most lodgings, but the touts, who go into a feeding frenzy at the arrival of Westerners, make this all but impossible. Don't be surprised if they insist that your guesthouse burned down last week or if your driver tries to earn commission by taking you to a different one. If you do allow a tout to entice you with an offer of a free taxi ride, expect to pay more for the room – if you don't the fare will be inflated to at least Rs150, depending on your destination and bargaining skills.

You'll be spared most or all of this hassle if you arrive by **public bus** as they all terminate at the main bus park, east of Prithvi Chowk. A taxi ride to

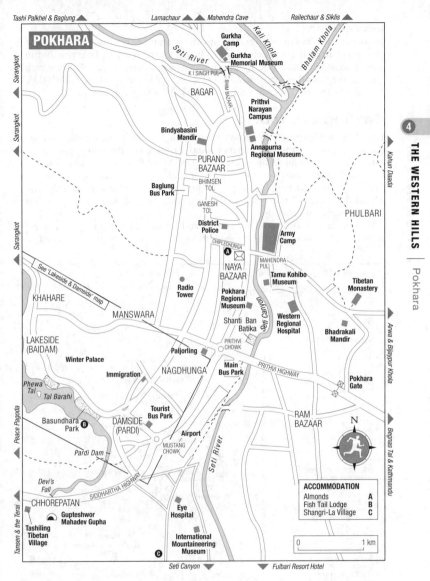

Lakeside/Damside from here should cost around Rs100. **Flying** to Pokhara from Kathmandu cuts out the hardships of the journey (see p.143 for airline info). Take the earliest flight available before clouds obscure the peaks – the mountain views are stupendous if you bag a seat on the right-hand side of the plane. At the time of writing, taxi fares from the airport were fixed at Rs150 for Damside and Rs200 for central Lakeside. In the airport food and drink are extortionate, while a registered moneychanger usually offers fairly decent rates.

Information

Innkeepers are the best sources of up-to-the-minute information. Anything else you might need is contained in the standard tourist **map** of Pokhara, sold in most bookstores. Better are Mappa/Karto Atelier's *Pokhara Town & Valley* map and the very detailed series of 1:25,000 sheets published by HMG/FINNIDA, though the latter is easier to find in Kathmandu before you go.

Getting around

Poor local transport makes getting around Pokhara time-consuming. A cross-town journey on one of Pokhara's **local buses** takes the better part of an hour. There are four main routes: all start or end at the Prithvi Narayan Campus near the north end of the bazaar, and go to Lakeside (via Mahendra Pul), Damside (via Chipledhunga), Chhorepatan (via Mustang Chowk) and Mahendra Cave. Catch buses in Damside near the *German Bakery* and at various points in Lakeside.

Taxis wait at several spots in Lakeside and Damside. They're more expensive than in Kathmandu and are metered, though drivers can be very reluctant to

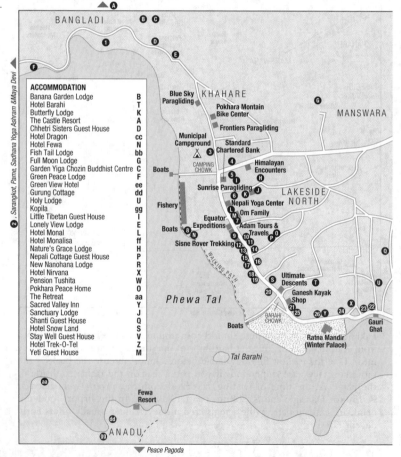

ACCOMMODATION

Banana Garden Lodge	B
Hotel Barahi	T
Butterfly Lodge	K
The Castle Resort	A
Chhetri Sisters Guest House	D
Hotel Dragon	cc
Hotel Fewa	N
Fish Tail Lodge	bb
Full Moon Lodge	G
Garden Yiga Chozin Buddhist Centre	C
Green Peace Lodge	F
Green View Hotel	ee
Gurung Cottage	dd
Holy Lodge	U
Kopila	gg
Little Tibetan Guest House	I
Lonely View Lodge	E
Hotel Monal	L
Hotel Monalisa	ff
Nature's Grace Lodge	H
Nepali Cottage Guest House	P
New Nanohana Lodge	R
Hotel Nirvana	X
Pension Tushita	W
Pokhara Peace Home	O
The Retreat	aa
Sacred Valley Inn	Y
Sanctuary Lodge	J
Shanti Guest House	Q
Hotel Snow Land	S
Stay Well Guest House	V
Hotel Trek-O-Tel	Z
Yeti Guest House	M

use them. For day-trips around the valley it might make sense to hire a taxi for the day, which should cost about $30 including petrol – let someone at your guesthouse do the negotiations.

A **bicycle**, rentable all over Lakeside and Damside, increases mobility tremendously. Cheap bikes go for about Rs150 a day. A **mountain bike** with gears is more practical for exploring the valley, although the ones for rent on the street aren't very good – for better quality, try the outfits mentioned on p.248. For zipping around the valley consider renting a **motorcycle**; in Lakeside prices range from Rs250 a day (not including fuel) up to Rs500 a day for the newest bikes in Gurung Motorbike Hire, next to *Mamma Mia* restaurant. Next to the *Punjabi* restaurant in Lakeside, Adam Tours and Travels (℡061/461 806, ⓦwww.adamnepal .com) is an efficient agency for booking bus or flight tickets or arranging a taxi.

Accommodation

Pokhara is glutted with cheap and moderately priced options, the majority with clean rooms, friendly staff and good breakfasts. Some of Nepal's classiest **luxury hotels** are also found in Pokhara: these are grouped together on p.240.

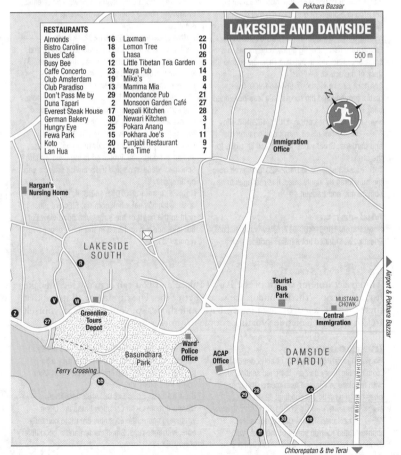

▲ Pokhara Bazaar

LAKESIDE AND DAMSIDE

RESTAURANTS			
Almonds	16	Laxman	22
Bistro Caroline	18	Lemon Tree	10
Blues Café	6	Lhasa	26
Busy Bee	12	Little Tibetan Tea Garden	5
Caffe Concerto	23	Maya Pub	14
Club Amsterdam	19	Mike's	8
Club Paradiso	13	Mamma Mia	4
Don't Pass Me by	29	Moondance Pub	21
Duna Tapari	2	Monsoon Garden Café	27
Everest Steak House	17	Nepali Kitchen	28
German Bakery	30	Newari Kitchen	3
Hungry Eye	25	Pokara Anang	1
Fewa Park	15	Pokhara Joe's	11
Koto	20	Punjabi Restaurant	9
Lan Hua	24	Tea Time	7

0 _____ 500 m

N

Immigration Office

Hargan's Nursing Home

LAKESIDE SOUTH

Tourist Bus Park

MUSTANG CHOWK

Greenline Tours Depot

Central Immigration

Airport & Pokhara Bazar

Ward Police Office

ACAP Office

DAMSIDE (PARDI)

Basundhara Park

SIDDHARTHA HIGHWAY

Ferry Crossing

Chhorepatan & the Terai ▼

Just about all independent travellers stay in hip **Lakeside** or quieter **Damside**. If you're looking for the chilled-out lakeside vibe that made Pokhara's name, consider staying further afield in semi-rural **Bangladi**, or across the lake in **Anadu**. In general, the views are better the further south you go. Pokhara's **municipal campground** is right by the lake and popular with overland groups, but you'd be better off working out a deal with one of the guesthouses along the back lanes of Lakeside.

The listings start with the most popular accommodation area, which we've divided into Lakeside North and Lakeside South. These are not actual place names, but correspond to areas with distinctive personalities.

Lakeside North

With its strip of high-rise guesthouses, shack restaurants and curio shops, the **northern** portion of Lakeside is like a relaxed, spread-out version of Kathmandu's Thamel. Avoid rooms overlooking the main drag, as you'll be tormented by early-morning buses.

Inexpensive

Hotel Monal ☎061/461 459. Cool, clean rooms set around a pleasant garden, with friendly staff. Good value. ❸

Nepali Cottage Guest House ☎061/461 637. Family-run place offering a few large rooms in a small but rather grand building shoehorned into the thick of the action. ❷

Pokhara Peace Home ☎061/464 960. Quiet, restful grounds and big rooms on a less-developed back lane. ❸

🏃 **Sanctuary Lodge** ☎061/462 407. Tiny family-run place with traditional rooms and gardens. Great value for a place so close to the strip. ❷

Yeti Guest House ☎061/462 423. Sheltered from the main drag by jungly trees, this manages to be both central and tranquil. ❸

Mid-range

Hotel Barahi ☎061/460 617, ⓦwww.barahi.com. Friendly, well-priced hotel (rates include a/c);

rooms in the new stone wing have more character and upper ones have mountain views. The sizeable swimming pool is open to non-residents for a small fee. ❻

Butterfly Lodge ☎061/461 892, ⓦwww .butterfly-lodge.com. Lovely, spacious garden, and clean, homely rooms, the more expensive ones (❸) kitted out in traditional style. ❶

Little Tibetan Guest House ☎061/461 898, ⓦwww.littletibguesthouse.com. Set back behind a quiet garden, with sparkling new rooms furnished in characterful Tibetan style. ❸

Nature's Grace Lodge ☎061/207 177. Small, tucked-away place with simply furnished rooms and an in-house pub. Profits go to the Child Welfare Scheme; village-stays and treks to visit projects can be arranged. ❸

Hotel Snow Land ☎061/462 384, ⓔsnowland@cnet.wlink.com.np. Efficient place right in the heart of the strip, with good views of the lake and a/c and tubs in the more expensive rooms (❺). ❹

Lakeside South

Things get quieter **south** of the Royal Palace and you can actually see the lake from the strip – the mountain views are better too. The flipside of all this is that there's less choice of restaurants, bars and shops, so you may find yourself trekking up to Lakeside North a couple of times a day.

Inexpensive

Holy Lodge ☎061/463 422, ⓔholylodge@bb .com.np. Big, leafy garden, thatched seating area with fireplace in winter. Clean rooms; the cheap ones are in a rustic old building. ❷–❸

🏃 **Pension Tushita** ☎061/621 222, ⓦwww .tushitanepal.com. Clean rooms and uninterrupted rooftop views of the lake, with Japanese hot bath and cuisine. Their shop sells

reliable organic products, including wild honey, coffee and rhododendron juice, and they also have an interesting eco-farm you can visit 6km south from Lakeside. ❷–❹

Shanti Guest House ☎061/463 645. The standard rooms with common baths are clean, white and spare; the en suites are more comfortable, with nice rugs. Small garden and a good little library. ❷

Mid-range

New Nanohana Lodge ☎061/464 478, ⓔmsnr @mos.com.np. Spotless rooms, pleasant big balconies, lovely terrace garden. Popular with Japanese, partly for the deep Japanese-style bathtubs in the top rooms. ❷–❹

Hotel Nirvana ☎061/463 332, ⓔnirvanapkr @wlink.com.np. Huge, thoughtfully decorated and spotlessly clean rooms overlooking spacious balconies and a garden. The friendly and know ledgeable owners also run treks. ❸–❺

🏃 **Sacred Valley Inn** ☎061/461 792, ⓔsvalley@cnet.wlink.com.np. Large, very

clean, balconied rooms with views in a homely building in a good location – close enough to the action, but on the quiet side of town. Good value, and the owners (same as *Nirvana*) are friendly and knowledgeable. ❷–❹

Stay Well Guest House ☎061/463 624. Friendly and quiet, in a cute little castle of a building. The deluxe rooms are lovely, with huge windows looking out on mountain views. ❷

Hotel Trek-O-Tel ☎061/464 996. Well furnished, odd-shaped a/c rooms with terracotta floors in a tight little complex right on the lakefront. Classy act, with uniformed, much-namasteing staff. ❼

Khahare, Bangladi and beyond

The area north of Holland Chowk (the main crossroads near the municipal campground) is well-known to long-termers and hippies. **Khahare**, the more southerly part of this area, is almost a suburb of Lakeside – if a bit quieter and slightly less commercialized. **Bangladi**, further north, preserves some of the undeveloped ambience of old, with simpler facilities, and the lake is more visible. Taxis can get to any of the guesthouses listed below, but they'll charge more than the standard fare to Lakeside.

Inexpensive

Banana Garden Lodge ☎061/464 901. Bungalow rooms ranging from the monastic to the spartan, set among pleasant gardens. Friendly and inexpensive, hence often full. ❶

Garden Yiga Chozin Buddhist Centre ☎061/462 923. Suitably basic accommodation is provided in this meditation retreat centre – house rules to be respected. ❶

🏃 **Green Peace Lodge** ☎061/462 780, ⓔgreenpeacelodge@hotmail.com. Basic but friendly, in a unique location right by the lake, with its own boats and a semi-resident traveller population. An annexe with plusher rooms is oddly isolated in a rice-paddy field round the next bend in the road. ❶

Lonely View Lodge ☎984/602 3090. A nice combination of rural location and proximity to town. Beautiful garden/orchard, excellent views, friendly family, and a cool atmosphere. ❷

Mid-range

🏃 **The Castle Resort** ☎061/461 926, ⓦwww.pokharacastle.com. The hot 15min walk up from Khahare is worth it for this fantastical castle with a small swimming pool. It offers a beautiful viewpoint of the Lake and rural surroundings, nice cottages for peaceful retreat and a fair-priced menu. ❻

Chhetri Sisters Guest House ☎061/462 066, ⓦwww.3sistersadventure.com. Success has brought a smart guesthouse to these infamous sisters, pioneers of trekking for women, whose training courses have raised the standard of all guiding in the region. Light airy rooms in wood and brick, with paintings of local scenes. ❺

Full Moon Lodge ☎061/461 511. A unique place in an above-it-all location (access by a steep set of steps). The garden area is brimming with kitsch Hindu statues and unusual touches, and the rooms are a good size. ❷

Damside

Damside is isolated both from the town and the tourist razzmatazz of Lakeside. The mountain views are better, but it's questionable whether they compensate for the limited choice of bars and restaurants. Damside is very popular with Japanese tourists, which is an interesting cultural feature in itself. A popularity pitch is being made by a street festival on Friday evenings.

Inexpensive

Green View Hotel ☎061/464 844. Looks like the worst kind of concrete mansion, but the flashy

frontage conceals a friendly, family-run guesthouse. Secluded, very flowery garden and a roof view. ❶

Mid-range

Hotel Dragon ☏061/462 630, ⓦwww
.himalayadragonhotel.com. Slightly overbearing
complex, but there's a pretty garden and the rooms
have cosy Tibetan furnishings. Also has more
expensive rooms (❺) with a/c. ❸

Hotel Monalisa ☏061/463 863. A bit more
upmarket than its rivals, in a good location
overlooking the neck of the lake, with the
mountains behind. Popular with Japanese
visitors. ❸–❹

Across the lake: Anadu

Anadu, directly across the lake from Lakeside, is not one of Nepal's friendliest
villages, but it's certainly peaceful and there's a certain bohemian attraction to
staying in a place that can only be reached by boat. (Actually, you can walk to
Anadu from the highway on the other side of the ridge behind, but let's not
spoil the illusion.) Furthermore, the views from here are better than they are
from anywhere in Lakeside, the water is clean, and there's a great hike (to the
Peace Pagoda) right out your back door. Most of the places can be reached in
about twenty minutes' rowing from the palace area of Lakeside. A big new resort
project that languished during the conflict had resumed construction at the
time of writing.

Gurung Cottage (no ☏). Awfully primitive (cold
water and *daal bhaat* only), but certainly
secluded. ❶

Kopila ☏061/621 369. The clear budget
winner in Anadu: awesome views, shady

(though unkempt) grounds, good (though slow)
restaurant, and hot water. ❷–❸

The Retreat ☏01/421 2860, peter@ad-asia.com.
Good, homely getaway for long-stay and self-
catering meditators. Email for more details.

Pokhara Bazaar and resort hotels

Most of Pokhara's poshest places are uninspiring and located in the vicinity of
the **airport**. Though these hotels do provide a bit of welcome luxury and a
lovely environment to relax in, don't expect perfection.

Fish Tail Lodge Opposite Lakeside South
☏061/465 071, ⓦwww.fishtail-lodge.com.
Lakeside's original deluxe hotel: dated, but has
fabulous grounds and an unrivalled view of the
lake, with a classic profile of the mountains behind.
Access by rope ferry. ❽

Fulbari Resort and Spa 4km south of the
airport ☏061/432 451, ⓦwww.fulbari.com.
Humungous wannabe top-of-the-range complex

overlooking the stupendous Seti gorge, with a
golf course, a swimming pool, six restaurants,
tennis courts, etc. ❾

Shangri-La Village 1.5km south of the airport;
see map, p.235 ☏061/462 222, ⓦwww
.hotelshangrila.com. Beautifully designed complex
of deluxe Nepali houses scattered through expen-
sively landscaped grounds. A serene pool for
supreme lazing is open to all; service is slow. ❾

Phewa Tal (Phewa Lake)

Much of Pokhara's tourist scene is bunched around tranquil **Phewa Tal**.
According to a local legend, the lake covers the area of a once-prosperous valley,
whose inhabitants one day scorned a wandering beggar. Finding only one
sympathetic woman, the beggar warned her of an impending flood: as the
woman and her family fled to higher ground, a torrent roared down from the
mountains and submerged the town – the "beggar" having been none other
than the goddess Barahi Bhagwati. The woman's descendants settled beside the
new lake and erected the island shrine of **Tal Barahi**.

The other, geological explanation is that the entire Pokhara Valley, like the
Kathmandu Valley, was submerged about 200,000 years ago when the fast-rising
Mahabharat ridge dammed up the Seti River. Over time, the Seti eroded an
ever-deeper outlet, lowering the water level and leaving Phewa Tal and several

The people of Nepal

The number of travellers who return from Nepal and say that, for all the breathtaking scenery, it was the people they liked best, is astonishing. The friendliness of Nepalis is proverbial, as is their toughness and proud independence. Yet as well as these national character traits, Nepal also has a continent's worth of ethnic groups. Much of this diversity is owed to the country's unique situation, poised between the Buddhist, Mongoloid peoples of Tibet, north of the Himalayan wall, and the Hindu Indo-Aryans of the Subcontinent.

Baahuns and worshippers at Dakshin Kal ▲

Wearing the *topi* and doing *namaste* ▼

Caste Hindus

The majority of Nepalis descend from Hindus who fled the Muslim conquest of northern India – or their converts among existing hill peoples. They're called **Parbatiyas** ("Hill-dwellers") or **caste Hindus**, since nearly all were high-caste **Baahuns** and **Chhetris** (see p.433) who had the most to lose from the advance of Islam. Well-educated and ambitous, they largely subjugated the hill tribes they encountered, imposing Hinduism's strictures on the role of women and the consumption of meat and alcohol, and bequeathing the country's *lingua franca*, Nepali. In the countryside, Baahuns in particular tend to live in well-spaced, two-storey farmhouses. The minority *dalit* (oppressed or "untouchable") castes, by contrast, occupy meaner dwellings, often on the edge of villages.

The hilly heartlands

Each area of the Central Hills is the cultural homeland of a distinctive ethnic group: **Gurungs** and **Magars** in the west (see p.257), and **Rais** and **Limbus** in the east (see p.388). Roughly a third of Nepalis belong to these *janajaati* or "national" groups, sometimes called the "hill tribes". Mongoloid features and Tibeto-Burman languages are signs of their distant ancestral origins.

The *janajaati* worship nature gods and local spirits, and some employ shamans, but most have been influenced by Hinduism or Tibetan Buddhism. **Social mores** are more relaxed than for orthodox Hindus: women have more independence, for instance, and meat and home-distilled raksi are consumed enthusiastically. Print skirts, heavy gold jewellery and *pote malla* (strands of glass beads) are traditional dress for women; men have mostly abandoned the elfish *daura suruwal* (shirt and jodhpur pants) of old, but *topis* (colourful fez-like hats) are still worn proudly.

Mountain peoples

Nepal's most famous ethnic group, the **Sherpas** (see p.380), make up less than one percent of the population. Alongside other "Bhotiya" peoples of more recent Tibetan origin, such as the **Humlis** of Humla, the **Lo-pa** of Mustang and the **Tamangs** of the central hills, they live at the harshest, highest altitudes, herding yaks and growing barley, buckwheat and potatoes – or guiding mountaineers. All follow the Tibetan school of **Buddhism** (see p.435), and their villages of stone houses, chortens, prayer walls and prayer flags are all distinctively Tibetan. Tibetan looks aside, Bhotiya people are recognizable by their clothing, especially the rainbow aprons (*pangden*) and wraparound dresses (*chuba*) worn by married women – who have a relatively strong voice in the community.

Terai peoples

Until recently, the flat Terai, in the south of the country, was sparsely populated by forest-dwelling groups like the **Tharus** (see p.270), **Danuwars** and **Majhis**. The Tharus are something of an ethnological mystery, divided by puzzlingly different local cultures but united by Mongoloid features, a genetic resistance to malaria and a name. After the malaria-control programmes of the 1950s, the Terai was opened up for several million gung-ho immigrants from the hills and India alike. The incomers from the south retain close cultural links with India, and refer to themselves as **Madheshis**.

▲ *Janajaati* girl

▼ Tharu people harvesting, Terai

▼ Chhetri houses, Solu Khumbu

Bhotiya woman ▲

Baahun man making rice doughnuts, Tansen ▼

The Newars of the Valley

The Kathmandu Valley has its own indigenous group: the **Newars** (see p.180), whose tight-knit communities are recognizable by their distinctive architecture of russet-pink brick, tiled roofs and dark, richly carved wood. Newars are now found across Nepal, as their enterprising **merchant class** founded the bazaars around which so many hill towns grew. The Newars could be said to represent a mixture of all Nepal's cultures: they are Hindus and Buddhists at the same time; they look by turns "Indian" and "Tibetan". But it would be more true to say that they created the culture which is Nepal – including the culture of extraordinary religious and ethnic tolerance, which persists today, in the teeth of a surge in ethnic assertiveness.

Rana Tharu women, Terai region ▼

Ethnic identity

The monarchy was long the source and symbol of Nepal's nationhood. When it fell, in 2006, it was like the removal of the keystone of an arch: there seemed little reason for Nepal's scores of ethnicities and cultures to hang together any more. In fact, trouble had been brewing for years. The hill peoples had long resented the loss of ancestral lands and the erosion of their culture, while the Madheshis of the Terai seethed at being politically sidelined. In their campaign for power, the Maoists had encouraged regional separatist and ethnic identity movements. When they entered government in 2008, they reaped what they had sown as seemingly every ethnic group clamoured and, sometimes, fought for its separatist slice of the power cake. Nepal's famed traditions of peaceful co-existence suddenly looked vulnerable.

Nautical pursuits

Boating (or just floating) on Phewa Tal is the easiest way to get away from the business of getting away from it all. **Rowing boats**, which hold six easily, can be rented all along the eastern shore. Prices are supposed to be fixed at Rs200 per hour or Rs500 per day, but "discounts" are possible. Fibreglass **sailboats**, available from *Hotel Fewa*, south of the fishery, cost Rs250 per hour or Rs950 per day; wooden ones are somewhat less. At least one operator rents **pedalos** (Rs250 per hour, Rs950 per day), and some rafting companies (see p.247) rent out **kayaks** for about Rs750 a day or less for a few hours. Motorized boats aren't allowed on the lake.

Swimming is best done from a boat, as much of the shore is muddy and bacteria counts are sometimes unhealthy due to sewage seeping from a couple of prominent Lakeside hotels. That said, Phewa Tal's water is fairly clean for a subtropical lake, largely because the monsoon rains flush it out each year. The stuff floating on the surface at certain times of year is pollen, not sewage. Stay away from the dam area, as the **current** is deceptively strong.

An obvious first destination is **Tal Barahi**, the island shrine located a few hundred metres offshore from the palace. While the temple itself is modern and not much to look at, it's a popular spot with Nepalis, visitors and locals alike.

From the island it's a little bit further again to the far shore which, with dense jungle, manic monkeys and few places to put ashore, is best observed from the water. If you want to walk around on the other side, make for **Anadu**, the diffuse Gurung village that covers the hillside directly opposite Lakeside, twenty- to thirty-minutes' row from the palace. You'll often meet Nepali picnic parties and the area is popular with local lads enjoying beers and snacks before returning by boat, singing merrily.

smaller lakes as remnants. Phewa was further enlarged by the installation of **Pardi Dam** in 1967, which brought electricity and irrigation to the valley, and gave Damside its name.

Like most Himalayan features, Phewa Tal is geologically very young and fast-changing. Its watershed is steep and highly prone to erosion, so the streams that feed it carry massive quantities of suspended **sediments**. When the sediments reach the lake, they settle out: the Harpan Khola, the lake's main tributary, has already deposited a "delta" that covers the western third of the lake's former surface. Water hyacinths started to appear on the shore a decade ago, and have now expanded so much that they cover a huge part of the lake if nothing is done; locals organize regular clearing sessions.

Lakeside (Baidam)

Next to eating, promenading along **Lakeside**'s pipal-shaded main drag is the favourite pastime in Pokhara. For years many hotels and restaurants have flourished next to the Phewa Tal, taking advantage of a government that profited from turning a blind eye on building in restricted areas. With the new political situation the idea of destroying offending constructions – basically everything on the west side of the main street next to the lake – has increasing support. In summer 2008 a paved walkway around the shore was opened up, running from Camping Chowk nearly up to the boat hub at Barahi ghat, opening up views of the lake as it runs past the fish farm and seasonally blooming lotuses. The scheme's instigators, the Young Communist League (YCL) would like to expand the trail to some 14km, reaching round to Phewa Tal's opposite edge – thus changing the whole experience of the lake's shore.

Basundhara Park, Lakeside's biggest patch of open space, is the venue for the annual **Annapurna Festival** (usually held in April), a cultural event featuring music, dance and food.

Midway along the strip sits Ratna Mandir, previously the winter **Royal Palace**. At the palace's northern edge, a road leads down to the lake and **Barahi ghat**, the main launching site for boats to Tal Barahi. North of Lakeside, in the area known as **Khahare**, the lake again becomes visible from the main road, which you can follow along the attractive and less developed northern shore. Side trails lead up to Sarangkot (p.252) from there.

Pokhara Bazaar

Until it was linked to the outside world by the Prithvi Highway in 1973, **Pokhara Bazaar** was a small Newari market town along the trade route from Butwal to Mustang. The once-tight bazaar has now spread into a city of over 100,000, with traffic and all the rest, but thanks to its gardens and the surrounding natural wonders, it doesn't feel congested.

The northern bazaar

Most of Pokhara was destroyed in a fire in 1949, but original remnants, with simple variants on the typical stacked-together Newari style, can still be seen in the pleasant **Purano Bazaar**, which runs from Bhimsen Tol up to Bag Bazaar. Perched on a hillock in the middle of this area is the **Bindyabasini Mandir**, a quiet temple complex more noteworthy for its sweeping mountain views than its collection of shrines. The featured deity, Bindyabasini, is an incarnation of Kali, the mother goddess in her bloodthirsty aspect. Animal sacrifices are common, particularly on Saturdays and the ninth day of Dasain in October. Bindyabasini has a reputation as a bit of a prima donna: in one celebrated incident, her stone image began to sweat mysteriously, causing such a panic that the late King Tribhuwan had to order special rites to pacify the goddess. The 1949 fire allegedly started here, when an offering burned out of control.

Tucked away in one corner of the Prithvi Narayan Campus at the northeastern part of town, the **Annapurna Regional Museum** (Sun–Fri 9am–12.30pm & 1.30–5pm, closes 4pm in winter; free) offers a feeble treatment of Nepal's natural history that's really meant for local schoolkids, though the display of Himalayan butterflies is interesting. An adjacent **information centre**, maintained by the Annapurna Conservation Area Project, contains some enlightening dusty exhibits about wildlife, geology, ethnic groups and culture in the ACAP area. If you're interested in the Gurkhas' history and legacy (see p.225), you can pay a visit to the **Gurkha Memorial Museum** (daily except Wed 8am–4.30pm; Rs150), next to the Gurkha camp.

Along the Seti River

Immediately east of town lies the dramatic **Seti River gorge**. One of the best places to see it, amazingly, is just north of the ugly main bus park. Walk north past Shanti Ban Batika, a park/picnic spot and turn right down a path; the river emerges from its narrow confines here to produce a sizeable canyon. If you plan to visit Mahendra cave and the bat cave to the north of Pokhara, stop off at K.I. Singh Pul for the most impressive view of the gorge.

Two nearby museums are worth visiting if you're in the area. The **Pokhara Regional Museum** (daily except Tues 10am–5pm, Friday closes at 3pm; Rs10), located south of Mahendra Pul, is small but quite well done, with informative displays and commentary on Nepali ethnic groups. The tiny **Tamu Kohibo Museum** (daily 10am–4pm; Rs20) sits on the opposite side of the canyon, and is reached by a lane heading down from Mahendra Pul. Dedicated to the shamanic traditions of Gurung culture, it gives an intriguing introduction to an important ethnic group. For more on Gurungs and Nepali shamanism, see p.257 and p.441.

Other sights

At the extreme southern end of the bazaar, the worthwhile **International Mountaineering Museum** (Mon & Wed–Sun 10am–5pm; Rs300) houses models of famous peaks, mannequins of renowned climbers, an exhibit of historical mountaineering equipment and information on the geology, flora and fauna of the Himalayas and other ranges.

If you're in this neighbourhood, especially on a mountain bike, set aside at least a little time to check out the dramatic **Seti canyon**. There's an access point near the mountaineering museum, and the road following the river southeast from there makes an excellent jaunt.

Chhorepatan

About 2km west of Damside, a trio of sights in the roadside suburb of Chhorepatan might just tempt you away from the lake. **Devi's Fall** (Rs10) marks the spot where the Pardi Khola – the stream that drains Phewa Tal – enters a grottoed channel and sinks underground in a sudden rush of foam and fury. In the autumn following a good monsoon it can be very impressive. The spot is perhaps more interesting as a source of pop mythology: known to locals as **Patale Chhango** (roughly, "Waterfall to the Underworld"), the sinkhole's name is supposed to be a Nepalification of Devin, the name of a Swiss woman said to have drowned while

▲ Pokhara hugs the shore of Phewa Tal

skinny-dipping with her boyfriend in 1961. The name "Devi" may be a casualty of the transliteration system, or possibly part of the Nepali propensity to deify everything that moves – *devi* means "goddess". The whole story sounds like a fabrication to warn local youth to shun promiscuous Western ways.

On the opposite side of the highway, a signposted path leads for a few metres between houses and curio stalls to **Gupteshwor Mahadev Gupha** (Rs20), a cave-shrine dedicated to Shankhar, who incorporates both Shiva and his consort Parbati as male and female halves of one figure. Guided by a dream vision, a priest discovered the idol in 1992, since when the cave has attracted increasing numbers of devotees. Enshrined in a large womblike chamber, the black Shankhar figure is a natural rock form dolled up with a carved Naga (snake) crown. Local religious authorities have prohibited photography inside the cave, whatever guides may say.

The adjacent Tibetan settlement of **Tashiling** has some 750 residents. Walk to the far end of the compound, past the school, *gompa* and curio stalls, to reach the community's small carpet-weaving hall; a short walk beyond brings you to an abrupt drop and a glorious panorama of the valley of the Phusre Khola.

Eating

Restaurants are everywhere in Pokhara and, while there's not much nightlife after around 10.30pm, the congenial restaurants and cafés around the lake are easy places to make friends and find trekking partners. Candle-light (often imposed by load-shedding) adds to the romance. Most tourist restaurants boast a more or less standard menu, featuring an implausible selection of improvised **non-Nepali** dishes and local fish prepared umpteen different ways.

For something much cheaper, try one of the myriad **momo** shacks and, for a real change of scene, Pokhara Bazaar has a number of Indian restaurants – *Almonds* is the most popular. The usual greasy spoons serving Nepali or **Tibetan** food are scattered throughout the city. Watch out for the **juice** sellers: they'll dilute the juice with (unsafe) water and sugar behind the scenes.

Chautaara

A uniquely Nepali institution found in every hill vilage, the **chautaara** is a resting place that serves important social and religious functions. The standard design consists of a rectangular flagstoned platform, built at just the right height for porters easily to set down their *doko*, while two trees provide shade.

Chautaara are erected and maintained by individuals as an act of public service, often to earn religious merit or in memory of a deceased parent. Commonly they'll be found on sites associated with pre-Hindu nature deities, often indicated by stones smeared with red *abhir* and yellow *keshori* powder. The trees, too, are considered sacred. Invariably, one will be a **pipal**, whose Latin name (*Ficus religiosa*) recalls its role as the *bodhi* tree under which the Buddha attained enlightenment. Nepalis regard the pipal, with its heart-shaped leaves, as a female symbol and incarnation of Laxmi, and women will sometimes fast and pray before one for children. It's said no one can tell a lie under the shade of a pipal, which makes the trees doubly useful for village assemblies. Its "husband", representing Shiva Mahadev, is the **banyan** (*Ficus bengalensis*), another member of the fig genus, which sends down Tarzan-vine-like aerial roots which, if not pruned, will eventually take root and establish satellite trunks. A *chautaara* is incomplete without the pair; occasionally you'll see one with a single tree, but sooner or later someone will get around to planting the other.

Longer day-trips and overnights from Pokhara are covered in "The Pokhara Valley", p.250.

Places described here as inexpensive will charge Rs200 or less per person for a full dinner, not including alcohol. Moderate restaurants will run to Rs200 –400, expensive ones to over Rs400. For a real post-trek splurge, the *Shangri-La Village Hotel*, outside town (see p.240), does an eat-as-much-as-you-like buffet for around Rs800 at weekends, and you can use the swimming pool.

Lakeside North

Almonds Among the best restaurants for Indian food on Lakeside, and popular with locals. The branch in the main bazaar is even better. Inexpensive.

Bistro Caroline The food isn't quite French, but it's about as good as it gets in Pokhara, and there's a wine list – at a price. Expensive.

Everest Steak House Lively rooftop place serving beef in every conceivable form; the huge garden is pleasant for daytime seating. Moderate.

Hungry Eye A pricier, tour-group version of the other standard-menu restaurants on the strip, with reliable food. The nightly culture show is hardly discreet, but does at least feature genuine, and well-performed Nepali songs and dances. Expensive.

Koto Serves reasonably authentic Japanese food, including sushi and sticky rice. Excellent set menus. Moderate to expensive.

Lemon Tree Sophisticated atmosphere and good service, with one or two better-than-average dishes (try the cannellini), safe shakes and excellent fish. Moderate.

Little Tibetan Tea Garden A good range of Tibetan food, along with the usual Western stuff, in a lovely little bamboo grove. Inexpensive.

Mamma Mia Relaxed wicker interior open to the street. Serves surprisingly good home-made pasta with fresh sauces. Inexpensive.

Mike's It was the ultimate tranquil spot, until the YCL (Young Communist League) paved a road through it, but it still has the closest seating to the lake. Best for breakfast or lunch, with large portions of authentic American-style *huevos*, waffles, eggs Benedict, etc. Good margaritas, too. Moderate.

Moondance The epicentre of Lakeside eating, with dishes you won't find elsewhere (Thai food, wonderful almond fish), and a lively atmosphere. Good for chilled after-dinner drinking and a game of pool too. Moderate.

Newari Kitchen Specialises in Newari dishes, but has a good range of Continental food; try the Newari set, the *momo* or the walnut

pate. The atmosphere is boosted by the company of swallows – there's a nest inside the premises. Moderate.

Punjabi restaurant Pure vegetarian, offering delicious Indian curries in a cozy atmosphere. Inexpensive.

Pokhara Joe's Nice coffee, cheesecake and brownies with ice cream – a good place to while away time with a book.

Tea Time One of Lakeside's original hangouts, good for daytime people-watching, drinks and board games. Moderate.

Lakeside South

Cafe Concerto Authentic pizza, lasagne, gnocchi and other Italian dishes (their tiramisu is the real McCoy), plus tolerable wine. and a mellow atmosphere. Moderate.

Lan Hua Chinese food popular with locals – the set menu is super value if you're very hungry. Moderate.

Laxman Large indoor/outdoor hangout, one of the pioneers of the cosy-wicker decor now so prevalent around Lakeside. Steaks, pastas, serious cakes. Pool and snooker tables. Moderate.

Lhasa Good range of Tibetan specialities, including the strange, hot alcohol *tongba* and Tibetan nail soup. Moderate.

Monsoon Garden Cafe Lovely garden for relaxing and enjoying classy breakfasts and lunches, and afternoon cream teas. Open till 6pm. Moderate.

Khahare and Bangladi

Lakeside Garden Worth it just for the beautiful setting in a tranquil corner of the lake. Decent standard dishes, and great *momos*, but the real draw is the superb (and pricey) Korean menu. Moderate to expensive.

Duna Tapari Khapaundi, near Pame bazaar. An atmospheric Nepali restaurant (the name means "leaf plate", and it's often referred to as such) serving fish snacks with spicy sauce. Sit on the red mud floor and enjoy a beautiful view of the lake. Closes around 8.30pm.

Damside

Don't Pass Me By Lovely patio seating right beside the lake. Competent all-round food, excellent for breakfast. Inexpensive.

German Bakery Tolerable croissants and Damside's premier cake display. Inexpensive.

Nepali Kitchen Caters to the local Japanese traveller contingent with tasty soups, snacks and fish and noodle dishes. Dingy inside. Inexpensive.

Fewa Park Unbeatable location, with thatched pavilions scattered around a lawn that slopes down to the lake. Better for breakfast or lunch, as insects can be troublesome at night. Moderate.

Nightlife

While nightlife around Pokhara usually just means a second helping of pie and another pirate DVD, a good way to break the routine is to catch a **culture show**. The *Hungry Eye* and a few other tourist restaurants put on free dinner music performances by local folk troupes. *Hotel Dragon* and *Fish Tail Lodge* host more-elaborate music and dance programmes nightly in the high season. Tickets cost Rs100–200 and are available through agents.

Blues Café Lakeside North. Popular with local (male, inevitably) youth and young traveller crowd. Sometimes Nepali bands, pool and other games.

Busy Bee Lakeside North. Nice open-air bar that's as busy as the name says, and with a group rocking every night.

Club Amsterdam Lakeside North. Well-stocked bar, pool table, satellite TV above the bar – all the trappings of a studenty pub back home.

Club Paradiso Lakeside North. The place for the happening young crowd in Pokhara, getting down on the dancefloor – funky car deco.

Maya Pub Lakeside North. Current after-hours favourite for cocktails and music. Serves good, moderately-priced pastas, sizzlers and vegetarian dishes, too.

Shopping

Shopping is still a mainly outdoor activity in Lakeside and Damside. Local specialities include **batiks** (dyed wall hangings) wooden **flasks**, **dolls** in ethnic dress and fossil-bearing **shaligram** stones from the Kali Gandaki. Hand-stitched **wall hangings** in simple Tibetan designs are attractive. Persuasive Tibetans peddle their wares in Lakeside's cafés, but these aren't produced locally, and **carpets** are best purchased at the Tibetan villages.

Kashmiris have colonized Lakeside, with **boutiques** touting "Asian" art: mainly high-priced carpets and cheap papier-mâché and soapstone widgets. Other than that, you'll find the usual range of tourist bait, most of it imported from Kathmandu. The **bookshops** and stalls can muster a good selection of secondhand stuff – the best is Mandala bookshop near the palace.

Activities

Pokhara has emerged as the outdoor-recreation capital of Nepal. It's the gateway to some of the best **treks** in the world, and an increasing number of travellers are coming here for **rafting**, **kayaking**, **paragliding** and **mountain biking** as well. Pokhara is also a pleasant setting for meditation or yoga studies.

Trekking

There are any number of ways to get to the start of a **trek** out of Pokhara. Most people take a taxi to **Suikhet (Phedi)**, **Naya Pul** or **Beni**. The fare to Naya Pul – the most popular gateway – should be about Rs1000. Cheaper but much slower local buses depart hourly from the Baglung bus park. You can also enter the region by hiking straight in from Lakeside, via **Sarangkot** (see p.252), or by hiring someone to row you across the lake and upriver to a point below Naudaada.

Those trekking the Annapurna Circuit typically start at Besisahar, reached by taking a bus to **Dumre** (on the way to Kathmandu – see p.225), from where buses and jeeps shuttle the rest of the way. An alternative trailhead is **Begnas Tal** (see p.257), reached by taxi or local bus from Chipledhunga in the bazaar.

Recommending **trekking agencies** in Pokhara is even riskier than in Kathmandu. Anyhow, you don't need an agency to trek the Annapurna region unless you're doing something unorthodox. **Guides** and **porters** can be hired through almost any trekking agency or equipment shop.

Three Sisters Adventure Trekking (☎061/461 749, ⓦwww.3sistersadventure .com) nabbed National Geographic's ecotourism award for their efforts at empowering women and helping local people develop tourism in remote areas. In addition to the classic trails, they offer treks off the beaten track, like starting from the Annapurnas and hiking through the less visited western districts to Mount Kailash in Tibet. They can arrange female guides and porters; it's best to book in advance.

If you're going trekking you'll almost certainly be heading into the Annapurna Conservation Area (**ACAP**), and will want to pay the Rs2000 **entry fee** in advance, as it costs double when bought at an entry post. ACAP's office is situated in Damside, in the same room as Nepal Tourism (Sun–Fri 9am–5pm, closes 4pm in winter); you'll need a passport photograph. See Chapter Seven for full details on trekking preparations and routes; you'll need a passport photograph. See Chapter Seven for full details on trekking preparations and routes.

The ACAP office is a good place to find potential **trekking partners**. You'll sometimes see messages at Lakeside restaurant notice boards as well, but don't worry too much if you don't hook up with anyone before you leave – you'll meet tons of people as soon as you start walking. Pokhara's selection of rental **trekking equipment** is as good as Kathmandu's, and you'll pay for fewer days by renting locally. Ex-expedition gear tends to be top quality but it's more lived-in than worn-in, while new kit, usually imported from farther east, looks better than it wears.

Rafting and kayaking

Pokhara is within striking distance of no fewer than four **rafting** rivers – the Kali Gandaki, Trisuli, Seti and Marsyangdi. The Kali is probably the most popular trip out of Pokhara; the Trisuli is better done out of Kathmandu, since the starting point is closer to there and the river flows towards Pokhara. The Seti is best known as the venue for **kayak** clinics, which are organized by several companies; kayaks can be rented from most of the places listed below (from $10 without gear). See Chapter Eight for more detail about rivers, rafting and kayaking. The box on p.241 has information on **boating** on Phewa Tal.

Many **river operators** have offices in Lakeside but most don't have enough of a track record to be worthy of recommendation. The following are the more reputable companies.

Equator Expeditions ☎061/462 999, ⓦwww .equatorexpeditionsnepal.com. Rafting trips with kayak support, also four-day (registered) kayak courses on the Seti. Experienced Western and Nepali guides, good equipment.
Ganesh Kayak Shop ☎061/462 657, ⓦwww .ganeshkayak.com. If you're in Nepal to kayak independently, this should be your first stop. The shop has a wide variety of kayaks and associated gear for rent, as well as hydrospeeds. It recently opened an exciting trip on the Upper Seti, which

only takes half a day, and also runs Seti kayak clinics.
Himalayan Encounters ☎061/461 873, ⓔrafting &trekking@himenco.wlink.com.np. Classy, professional and expensive, this is Nepal's longest-serving rafting operator, with experienced Nepali guides.
Ultimate Descents ☎061/463 240, ⓦwww .udnepal.com. Nepal's biggest river operator – operating as part of Adventure Centre Asia – has had its ups and downs, but is still good on the river. Also offers Seti kayak clinics.

Other outdoor activities

Local **mountain-biking** possibilities are described in Chapter Nine, and possible routes are also indicated briefly throughout the "Pokhara Valley" section of this chapter (see p.250). It's surprisingly hard to hire good mountain bikes in Pokhara, but you can try your chance in the numerous places around the lake where they hire bikes. Pokhara Mountain Bike Center (T 980/413 4788, W www.nepalmountainbike.com) offers more than twenty rides in the Pokhara valley, and other trips in the Annapurnas, Tansen or Manakamana, and gives free professional mountain-bike training to Nepali children.

Paragliding is an increasingly popular activity – see box below. If you want a sensational closer look at the Annapurnas, fly with the Avia Club Nepal (T 061/462 192, W www.aviaclubnepal.com). Their ultralight **aircraft** can carry one passenger at a time. The price is 57 euros (they also accept dollars) for a fifteen-minute flight, 167 euros for an hour: an unforgettable experience.

Kids and their parents will get the most out of **pony trekking**. Many outfits run short rides beside the lake at around $15 for a half-day, $25 for a full day; book through any agent. You can also play **tennis** at the *Hotel Barahi* in Lakeside, **swim** in their pool or the ones at *Shangri-La Village* or *Fulbari Resort and Spa*, where **golf** at a nine-hole course is an option. The eighteen-hole Himalayan Golf Course (T 061/695408) was set up by an ex-Gurkha major; sheep keep the fairways trim.

You can also have a rooftop **Japanese hot bath** (*ofuro*), while admiring the sunset over the Annapurnas at *Pension Tushita* (T 061/621 222). Order three hours in advance. The Japanese tend to have it at forty-five degrees, but if you don't want the lobster experience, try five less.

Meditation and yoga

Many spiritual centres last only a season or two in Pokhara. **Sadhana Yoga Ashram** (E yogisanga@yahoo.com), is the most popular, and now runs a basic centre on a hillock north of Lakeside offering one-day yogic cleansing and longer residential courses. **Garden Yiga Chozin Buddhist Centre** (T 061/462 923) is a very peaceful facility a short walk north of Lakeside, where teachers come up in season from Kopan monastery, outside Kathmandu. They run regular residential courses and teachings (retreats, daily yoga, t'ai chi and reiki

---

Paragliding

Paragliding companies based in Pokhara adopted standard prices in 2008, which set the price of a 20–30 minute flight at 65 euros and 1hr flight at 95 euros (dollars are, of couse, accepted). All launch jumps from Sarangkot, and conduct 9/10-day courses for beginners, with prices ranging from 1000 to 1200 euros. The Nepal Open Paragliding championship takes place every year between Dec and Jan, attracting pilots from all over the world. Recommended operators, all with their own speciality, are listed below.

Blue Sky Paragliding T 061/464 737, W www.paragliding-nepal.com. Offers acrobatic tandem rides and an exciting range of cross-country adventures.

Frontiers Paragliding T 061/522 127, W www.parahawking.com. Flight options include parahawking with a trained bird of prey to guide you up the thermals. You can also drop by the *Maya Devi* village restaurant and even learn to handle the birds.

Sunrise Paragliding T 061/463 174, W www.sunrise-paragliding.com. Qualified jumpers can try out para-treks, which involve hiking up to various local summits and floating back down.

sessions) designed for mainly Western participants. The **Nepali Yoga Centre** in Lakeside is run by women and has had very good reports.

Introductory classes are sometimes free, while short sessions usually **cost** a few hundred rupees. Expect to pay $15–30 per day for residential courses. Other courses can easily be found by checking notice boards around Lakeside and Damside.

Listings

Banks and money Standard Chartered in Lakeside handles foreign exchange (Sun–Thurs 9.45am–4.15pm, Fri 9.45am–1.15pm) and has an ATM, while several in the main bazaar have ATMs.

Haircutting Pokhara has a preponderance of barbers, who do not only haircuts but also shaves and massages (see below). A basic trim should cost from around Rs30, but establish the price and exact extent of services beforehand.

Hospitals, clinics and pharmacies Several pharmacies in Lakeside and Damside do stool tests, though incorrect diagnoses are common. One or two also offer ayurvedic medicine. In an emergency head for the new Manipal Teaching Hospital (☎061/526 416), with a staff of Indian-trained doctors. Closer to hand, but more chaotic, is the Western Regional Hospital (☎061/520 066), also known as the Gandaki Hospital – its ER looks terrible, but quite a few Western-trained doctors work there. Have your hotel phone ahead to make sure a doctor is on duty. Padma Nursing Home, on New Rd, is good for non-emergency treatment.

Laundry Most lodges take laundry for a few rupees per item and machines are springing up all over Lakeside.

Massage Seeing hands (☎061/522 478) is reputed, and ethical as it employs blind therapists. Sanjay Lama, who can be found at Rainbow Thanka Art Gallery (☎061/462 132, 984/602 0163), is recommended for many types of massage and physical therapy. Barbers, who mostly come

from India, are well-versed in traditional head massage, and usually offer neck, back and full-body too. The specialists charge around Rs1000 per hour and the barbers less.

Media International newspapers and magazines are available in bookshops. The English-language Nepali papers mostly arrive around noon, on the morning flights from Kathmandu.

Post Tourist book- and postcard shops sell stamps – Europe Rs25, US Rs30. Many shops and hotels will take mail to the post office; they're mostly trustworthy. In any case, the trip to the main post office in Mahendra Pul (Sun–Thurs 10am–5pm or 4pm in winter, Fri 10am–3pm) is an eye-opener. They've got a tiny poste restante department, but it may not be as reliable as the one in Kathmandu.

Provisions Mini-supermarkets along the Lakeside strip anticipate your every need: chocolate, tinned food, bread, cheese, wine, spirits, toiletries, batteries, etc. Mahendra Pul ones are much cheaper if you plan to go to town.

Visa extensions For visa extensions, go to the Immigration office, between Ratna and Shahid Chowk. Application hours are Sun–Thurs & 10.30am–1pm (12.30pm in winter), Fri 10am–noon; visas are ready later the same day. Trekking or travel agents can handle the paperwork for a commission of about Rs300, but it's hardly worth it. Passport photos are available in minutes from photo shops around Lakeside and near the Immigration office (about Rs200 for four).

Moving on

Buses link Pokhara with Kathmandu via the Prithvi Highway, and with the Terai and India via the Siddhartha Highway. All the major domestic airlines connect Pokhara with Kathmandu.

Buses

Several companies operate tourist buses and minibuses from Pokhara to **Kathmandu**, which usually leave around 7am. The fare is around Rs400, which is about twice the price of public buses, but the tourist services are more comfortable and somewhat faster and safer, and they pick up passengers in Lakeside and Damside. More expensive ($18 or so) luxury coaches offer air conditioning and an alternative 8.30am departure; operators change from year to year, but Greenline is the most established. A handful of companies also run tourist buses to Sauraha (for **Chitwan National Park**); the fare is Rs300, or $12 for Greenline's luxury bus. Microbuses can't really be recommended as they have a high number of crashes, due to their macho, minute-slicing driving techniques.

Buses and night buses to the Indian border at **Sonauli** aren't technically tourist services, but they do pick up passengers in Lakeside/Damside. There are no other tourist buses.

All tourist and night buses can be booked through **ticket agents**, found throughout the tourist areas; costs and commission are fairly standard. Buses serving the Prithvi and Siddhartha highways depart from the **main bus park**, and tickets are sold from the booking hall at the top of the steps on the west side. For services along the Baglung Highway, you need to buy tickets from the separate **Baglung bus park**, located on the western side of the bazaar. However, Baglung buses have a reputation for reckless driving, so it's preferable to take a taxi to the start of a trek.

If you're heading **to India**, read the section on ticket agents in Basics (p.27) first.

Private vehicles

Long-distance travel by **private vehicle** is more expensive than the usual daily rental rate, since you have to pay for the car and driver to return to Pokhara even if you're travelling only one way. For most journeys the most economical option will be a taxi; jeeps and vans can also be arranged. Rates for a taxi or similar are around $100 to Kathmandu, $90 to Chitwan, and $120 to Lumbini/Sonauli. Travel agencies can arrange rentals, but it may be easier to have your hotel or guesthouse do it.

Flights

There are **internal flights** from Pokhara to Kathmandu ($96) and Jomosom ($82), and in the past there have been flights to Manang in the trekking season as well. It's easier to use an agent than book direct. Mountain-view excursions and flights to Dolpo are usually available only on a charter basis.

The Pokhara Valley

Day-trips around the **Pokhara Valley** make excellent training for a trek. Start early to make the most of the views before the clouds move in and the heat builds, and bring lunch and water. If you're feeling adventurous, you can **stay overnight** at Sarangkot, Tashi Palkhel or Begnas Tal.

The World Peace Pagoda and beyond

The **World Peace Pagoda**, a local landmark which crowns the ridge across the lake at an elevation of 1113m, provides one of the most satisfying short hikes in the area. The views from the top are phenomenal, and since there are several routes up and back, you can work this into a loop that includes boating on the lake and/or visiting Chhorepatan. A basic up-and-back trip can be done in two to three hours, so you can leave after breakfast and be back in time for lunch.

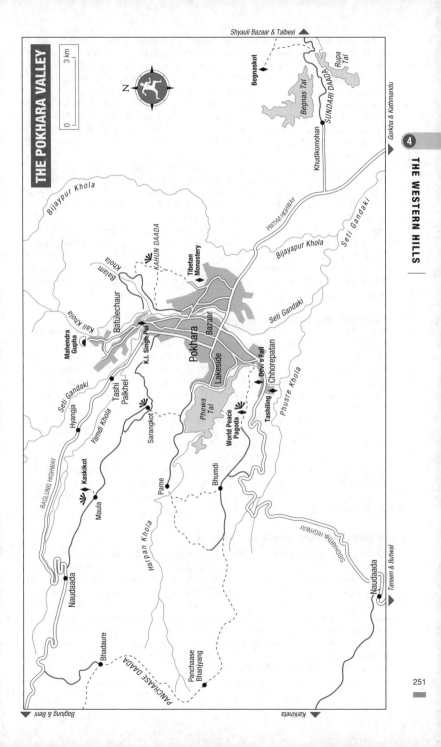

The easiest approach is by trail **from Damside**. Cross the river on a footbridge just downstream of the dam, then follow the path as it bears left and passes a small shrine before beginning a gradual ascent up the back (south) side of the ridge. Don't take all your valuables or walk alone, and check with locals before leaving as there are some reports of robberies in the forest here. The way is somewhat obscure at first, but soon becomes a fine wide path through chestnut forest until the final ascent. The climb is steeper **from Anadu**, the village across the lake (reached by boat from Lakeside). If descending this way, you should have no trouble getting a canoe back to Lakeside.

Standing more than 40m tall, the so-called **pagoda** looks like a cross between a stupa and a lighthouse. It seems rather grandiose for a religious shrine, but if it helps achieve its stated aim (world peace) then more power to it. The Japanese Buddhist organization that funded the monument maintains an adjacent monastery. The **view** from here is just about the best wide-angle panorama you can get of this part of the Himalayas, and certainly the only one with Phewa Tal and Pokhara in the foreground. Over on the far left you'll see the towering hump of Dhaulagiri and its more westerly sisters, in the middle rises the Annapurna Himal and the graceful pyramid of Machhapuchhre, and off to the right are Manaslu, Himalchuli and Baudha. Small cafés provide refreshment.

Routes beyond the pagoda

To make an easy day-trip of the walk you can **loop around Phewa Tal**. From the pagoda, keep walking along the ridgeline past Rani Ban Retreat and along a rough road to the village of Bhumdi, where another road descends to the highway and a trail leads down to the sluggish Harpan Khola at Pame, 3km upstream of Phewa Tal. For a longer hike, continue further west beyond Bhumdi to the end of the road before descending to the Harpan Khola.

A superb two-day trek offering supreme views climbs on from Bhumdi up to **Panchaase Daada**, the prominent forested ridge west of Phewa Tal. From the top of the path, a trail follows the ridge northwest to Panchaase Bhanjyang, where you can stay at one of a handful of basic **lodges**. The next morning, continue up to the high point of the ridge (2509m) and on north to Bhadaure and the Baglung Highway, where you can pick up a bus past Naudaada back to Pokhara. Very few foreigners venture into this area, so a good map or knowledgeable guide is recommended.

Sarangkot and beyond

Sarangkot, a high point (1590m) on the ridge north of Phewa Tal, is the most popular of the mountain viewpoints around Pokhara. The peaks appear even closer from here than from the Peace Pagoda, though not quite as many of them are visible. Sarangkot has a substantial little village near the top that can provide lodging – many people hike up in the afternoon, spend the night and then catch the views first thing in the morning, when it's most likely to be clear. As with the hike to the Peace Pagoda, there are various routes to the top and at least one route further along the ridge once you're up there, so a number of different itineraries are possible. You will have to pay Rs25 to access Sarangkot, and the local children will pester you for money.

Getting there

There are two principal **hiking routes** up Sarangkot. The tougher one heads straight up **from Lakeside**, a long, steep climb with no mountain views until the very top – if you're running late you might miss them altogether. Follow the road north from Lakeside as it bends around the lake, goes up and down a small hill and traverses a large cultivated area. Two kilometres beyond Halland Chowk the trail, marked by a painted stone, forks off to the right; when in doubt, stay on the flagstoned path and keep heading generally towards the summit. You'll be doing well to make it from the trailhead to the top in less than two and a half hours.

The easier route starts near the **Bindyabasini temple** in the bazaar, a Rs200 taxi ride from Lakeside. A paved road goes from there to within a half-hour's hike of the top, so if you want to take the easier route, you can have the **taxi** take you as far as the end of the road (Rs800 one-way). Compared to the Lakeside approach this is a gentler ascent, and the scenery – both mountains and lake – gets better and better as you go. That said, it's also far more commercialized, with offers of cold drinks, curios and guide services all along the upper stretch.

The village and summit

The **village** of **Sarangkot**, nestled just below the summit, has teashops, handicrafts sellers and something like a dozen **lodges** with views of the lake. All have electricity and most can provide hot washing water by the bucket. *Lake View Lodge* (T 980/413 1949; ❷) and *Hotel Annapurna & Sherpa* (❷) are simple but fairly well established. Several simple restaurants line the path up to the top, some with excellent views. Several paragliding companies (see p.248) launch jumps from here.

For the **summit**, continue another ten minutes up to the remains of a fort. *Kot* means "fort" in Nepali, and you'll find that as the area was once divided among warring principalities, many hills are called Something-kot. If you've hiked up from Lakeside, the sudden view here will come as a staggering revelation. The peaks seem to levitate above their blue flanks, the gathering clouds add a quality of raw grandeur, while to the south, Phewa Tal shimmers in the hazy arc of the valley.

Routes beyond Sarangkot

A road connects Sarangkot with Naudaada, about 10km further west on the Baglung Highway, making all sorts of longer trips beyond Sarangkot possible. A few villages are located along the way, notably Maula, the starting point of a flagstoned path up to **Kaskikot**, seat of the kingdom that once ruled the Pokhara Valley, perched on a craggy brow of the ridge with views as big as Sarangkot's. A stone enclosure and a house-like Kali temple are all that remain of the citadel of the Kaski kings, which fell to the Gorkhalis without a fight in 1781. **Naudaada** is another 4.5km west of Maula, and the first place from which Machhapuchhre's true fishtail profile can be seen. Two or three nice little lodges offer trekking-style accommodation along the road between Maula and Naudaada. You'll probably catch a bus from Naudaada back to Pokhara, but other interesting variations are possible, including walking down from Maula to Pame or west along the main road from Naudaada and then south to Panchaase Daada (see p.252).

The Baglung Highway and Tashi Palkhel

Heading northwest from the bazaar, the **Baglung Highway** provides the chief access for treks in the Annapurna region and rafting trips on the Kali Gandaki.

Most people are only whizzing through on their way to their respective adventures, however, and other than a few mountain bikers returning from Sarangkot, towns along the road see few foreign faces. The highway follows the **Yamdi Khola** valley, which has been transformed by a hydroelectric project and a roadside smattering of modern concrete dwellings, which emanate like a comet's tail from Pokhara Bazaar.

Tashi Palkhel (Hyangja)

With twelve hundred residents – eighty of them monks – **Tashi Palkhel** (commonly known as **Hyangja**) is the largest and the least commercial of Pokhara's Tibetan settlements. The entrance is clearly marked, about 4km northwest of the north end of Pokhara Bazaar on the Baglung Highway. Get there by bike, taxi (Rs500) or a bus from the Baglung bus park.

A path past curio sellers draws you naturally to the community's large **gompa** (monastery), where resident monks usually gather for chanting at 6am and 4pm, and all day during festivals. The *gompa* is of the Kagyu-pa sect, and portraits either side of the Buddha statue inside the hall depict the Dalai Lama and the late Kagyu leader, the sixteenth Karma Lama; smaller figures behind represent the one thousand Buddhas believed to exist during the present age. Opposite the monastery, a broad quadrangle is the focal point of Tashi Palkhel's **carpet industry**, which is successful enough to employ local women from outside the Tibetan community as weavers. No one minds if you wander around. You can even specify your own designs, which can be turned into a workable pattern and woven within a fortnight – ready for when you come back from that trek. The community also has a school to which Tibetan children from all over Nepal come as boarders, an old people's home, a clinic and community hall.

Tashi Palkhel's cooperative **guesthouse**, the *Tibetan Yak* (❷), can supply very basic rooms; hot showers are sometimes available, and camping is possible. Get **food** at the guesthouse or at one of the smoky, buttery holes-in-the-wall nearby. **Handicrafts** can be purchased at the cooperative shop in the guest-house compound, whose profits support community projects, as well as from private shops and freelance vendors. Even if you're perfectly healthy, the **Tibetan medicine centre** is worth a visit, as long as you can find someone to help you over the language barrier.

To Beni

The Baglung Highway is smoothly asphalted as far as **Baglung**, 72km from Pokhara, and rough but passable into **Beni**, 10km further on. Most rafting trips on the Kali start at Baglung, but at certain times of year some companies put in farther up near Beni.

A seasonal dirt road, regularly destroyed by the monsoon's landslides, forces its way up the Thak River to Jomosom, and right into Mustang. Jeeps, tractors and motorbikes now ride on what was one of the best walking trails. As the road is improved, buses will join the traffic and the Annapurna landscape will be changed forever. See p.392 for the route into trekking country.

Combined with a visit to Sarangkot, the Baglung highway makes for an enjoyable two-day-plus bike ride or motorcycle cruise. You can stay overnight in **Nayapul** or in one of the nice lodges at **Birethanti** (off the highway, at the boundary of the Annapurna Conservation Area).

Mahendra Gupha and the Kali Khola

While it just about scrapes its description as a geological wonder, **Mahendra Gupha** (Mahendra Cave; Rs15) is probably best thought of as a base from

Tibetans in exile

Thirty years ago, Dervla Murphy worked as a volunteer among **Tibetan refugees in Pokhara**, and called the account she wrote about her experiences *The Waiting Land*. Pokhara's Tibetans are still waiting: three former **refugee camps**, now largely self-sufficient, have settled into a pattern of permanent transience. Because Pokhara has no Buddhist holy places, most Tibetans have remained in the camps, regarding them as havens where they can keep their culture and language alive. Many plainly don't see the point of moving out and setting up permanent homes in Nepal when all they really want is to return to their former homes in Tibet.

The settlements – Tashi Palkhel, Tashiling and Paljorling – are open to the public, and a wander around one is an experience of workaday reality that contrasts with the otherworldliness of, say, Boudha or Swayambhu. You'll get a lot more out of a visit if you can get someone to show you around.

At the time of the **Chinese invasion** of Tibet in 1950, the Tibetans now living in Pokhara were mainly peasants and nomads inhabiting the border areas of western Tibet. The political changes in faraway Lhasa left them initially unaffected, but after the Dalai Lama fled Tibet in 1959 and the Chinese occupation turned violent, thousands streamed south through the Himalayas to safety. They gathered first at Jomosom, where the terrain and climate were at least reminiscent of Tibet, but the area soon became overcrowded and conditions desperate. Under the direction of the Swiss Red Cross, three **transit camps** were established around low-lying Pokhara and about two thousand refugees were moved down.

The first five years in the camps were marked by rationing, sickness and unemployment. Relief came in the late 1960s, when the construction of Pardi Dam and the Prithvi and Siddhartha highways provided work. A second wave of refugees began around the same time, after the United States' detente with China ended a CIA operation supporting Tibetan freedom-fighters based in Mustang. Since then, the fortunes of Pokhara's Tibetans have risen with the local **tourism** industry, and carpet-weaving and handicraft sales have become the main source of income, especially for women. Many men work seasonally as porters or guides, where they can make better money than in the camps. A small but visible minority have become smooth-talking curio salespeople, plying the cafés of Lakeside and Damside, but whereas Tibetans have by now set up substantial businesses in Kathmandu, opportunities are fewer in Pokhara, and prosperity has come more slowly.

which to explore the valleys north of Pokhara. To get there, pass K.I. Singh Pul (Bridge) at the top end of Pokhara, head north past the Gurkha camp, turn right up a paved road 600m beyond the bridge, and follow it for about 3km to the end. The climb is relentless and if you're on a one-speed bike you'll have to push some of the way (the reward comes on the way back). A taxi will charge about Rs400 return.

Water percolating through the valley's limestone sediments has created a honeycomb of caves extending up to 2km from the main entrance, though a guided tour of the illuminated part only takes ten to fifteen minutes. The cave used to be well known for its stalactites, but these have unfortunately been ransacked by vandals; a few surviving **stalagmites** are daubed with red *abhir* and revered as *shivalinga* because of their resemblance to phalluses. A café near the entrance serves food in a pleasant garden setting.

A more adventurous and impressive trip is to **Chamere Gupha** (Bat Cave; Rs15 plus something for the guide), about ten minutes' walk along a side road. It's a bit of a tight scramble up out of the main chamber, where thousands of bats hang from the ceiling. Bring your own torch/flashlight, or rent one from the ticket seller.

About 1km south of Mahendra Cave, the road from Pokhara passes through **Batulechaur**, a village locally famous for its **gaaine**. Wandering minstrels of the old school, *gaaine* are still found throughout the hills, earning their crust by singing ballads to the accompaniment of the *sarangi*, a four-stringed, hand-hewn fiddle: "I have no rice to eat/let the strings of the *sarangi* set to," runs the *gaaine's* traditional opening couplet.

Kahun Daada and the Bhalam Khola

If the view from **Kahun Daada**, the hill east of Pokhara, is a shade less magnificent than Sarangkot's, a lookout tower near the top gives you a better crack at it, and trails up to it are totally uncommercialized. The easiest and most interesting starting point is the **Tibetan monastery**, which stands on a hill 2km east down the main road from Mahendra Pul (in Pokhara Bazaar). At the top of a breathless couple of hundred steps at the base of Kahun Daada, the Karma Dhubgyu Chhokhorling Nyeshang Korti occupies a breezy spot with valley views east and west. Around thirty monks inhabit the modern monastery, which contains all the usual Vajrayana paraphernalia. Next to the *gompa*, on the top of a hill, is the Newari temple of Bhadrakali, an angry aspect of the goddess Parvati; the temple is rustically surrounded by bougainvilleas. From the *gompa*, follow the east track and take the second main turn on the right.

The trail to the lookout tower starts at the bottom of the steps, initially following a road that hugs the western base of the ridge for about 1km, and then climbs through several lazy settlements collectively known as **Phulbari**. Keep heading towards the tower (1444m), which is visible most of the way – it takes about an hour and a half from the monastery. From the half-finished concrete platform, you can contemplate the tremendous force of the Seti River and its tributaries, which tumble out of the Annapurna Himal clouded with dissolved limestone (*seti* means white) and, merging at the foot of the Kahun Daada, split the valley floor in a bleached chasm.

The tidily terraced side valley of the **Bhalam Khola**, immediately north of Kahun Daada, is also well worth exploring. To get there directly from the tower, it's better to backtrack towards the monastery until you pick up the first main northbound trail. It's also accessible by a rough (bikeable) track heading northwards on the east side of the Seti River. The power of erosion can readily be seen from this route as it passes the confluence of the Bhalam, Seti and Kali rivers, where they undercut old gravel beds, leaving sheer, mossy cliffs.

Begnas and Rupa Tal

With Lakeside and Damside so overdeveloped, it's strange that **Begnas Tal** and **Rupa Tal**, twin lakes 15km east of Pokhara, haven't taken off as tourist destinations. Begnas Tal, the bigger of the two, is framed by meticulously engineered paddy terraces, while Rupa, behind the ridge, remains pristinely hidden in a bushy, steep-sided valley. Come prepared to spend the night: several lodges can put you up, and trails open up a wealth of outstanding walking opportunities.

A **taxi** to Begnas Tal costs about Rs600 one way. **Local buses**, departing every fifteen minutes from the main bus park in Pokhara, take up to an hour and tend to be crowded. By **bicycle**, the first stretch along the Prithvi Highway is horribly polluted and fairly terrifying. After 10km, turn left at the signpost, and it's a pleasant three-kilometre ride down a straight road to the end of the line, a dumpy hamlet called **KHUDIKOMOHAN** (often referred to as Begnas).

Gurungs and Magars

Once active trans-Himalayan traders – the Chinese occupation of Tibet put paid to that – **Gurungs** are a common sight around Gorkha and Pokhara, where many have invested their Gurkha pensions in guesthouses and retirement homes. The majority of Gurungs who don't serve in the military keep sheep for their wool, driving them to pastures high on the flanks of the Himalayas, and raise wheat, maize, millet and potatoes.

Traditional pursuits such as hunting and honey-gathering are being encroached upon by overpopulation, while the Gurung form of shamanism is coming under pressure from the advance of Hinduism and Buddhism. Gurungs employ shamans to appease ghosts, reclaim possessed souls from the underworld, and guide dead souls to the land of their ancestors – rituals that contain clear echoes of "classic" Siberian shamanism and are believed to resemble those of pre-Buddhist Tibet.

A somewhat less cohesive group, **Magars** are scattered throughout the lower elevations of the western hills and in some parts of the east. A network of Magar kingdoms once controlled the entire region, but the arrival of Hindus in the fifteenth century brought swift political decline and steady cultural assimilation. After centuries of coexistence with Hindu castes, most Magars employ Baahun priests and worship Hindu gods just like their Chhetri neighbours, differing only in that they're not allowed to wear the sacred thread of the "twice-born" castes. Despite the lack of unifying traits, group identity is still strong, and will probably remain so as long as Magars keep marrying only within the clan.

Begnas Tal

Begnas Tal is just around the corner from the bazaar, up the road to the left immediately before the cul-de-sac where the buses stop. Just after the gate and ticket booth (Rs10 entrance fee), a plain block of basic lodge-restaurants looks across to the southern shore of the lake. The dam stretches away to the left, below which there is a governmental **fish farm** and research centre - concrete holding tanks fed by water from the lake. Fish farming has become big business here; Chinese carp, native *sahar* and *mahseer are* packed off to city restaurants – those that the white egrets don't get, at any rate. Phewa-style **boats** are rented out beside the lake just beyond the dam (Rs250 per hour); with tent-shaped Annapurna II for a backdrop, the paddling here scenic, and you'll practically have the lake to yourself. A good destination is the wooded peninsula at the north side of the lake, which is a **bird sanctuary**.

Rupa Tal and Paachbaiya Daada

Getting to **Rupa Tal** involves a little more effort than Begnas Tal, and the lake is far more secluded as a result. Every hour or two, **buses** from Begnas's bazaar negotiate the switchback road that leads along **Sundari Daada**, the ridge that separates the two lakes, but most people will prefer to **hike**. A handful of quirky, trekking-style **lodges** are scattered along the ridge.

The rough road leads north from the far end of the bus park at Begnas bazaar and ascends the side of the ridge steeply. Hikers can turn left up to the ridge-top after about twenty minutes; cyclists and buses (just) stick to the road. Begnas Tal is visible first, on the left, and then Rupa Tal comes into view after the highest point is passed, about 45 minutes from the bus park. Local belief has it that the lakes are husband and wife, and that an object thrown into one lake will eventually appear in the other. The things that look like fences peeping above the water of both lakes are more fish farms – Rupa Tal is said to be particularly rich in nutrients. It's not such a good choice for swimming, however, as the lake margins are being progressively choked with mud and water hyacinths. In another ten minutes or so the trail rejoins the road as it descends to the half-dozen shops of the village called **Sundari Daada**, after the ridge it sits on. This is the jumping-off point for just about all explorations in this area.

Just short of Sundari Daada, a trail to the left leads steeply down to Begnas Tal and *Begnas Lake Resort*, where you can get a boat back to the dam area. A bit further along the road, a trail leading off to the right, signposted "Karputar", descends to the north end of Rupa Tal and the village of Talbesi – this route makes an attractive alternative way into the Annapurna Circuit, and offers the possibility of a steep side trip to the hilltop viewpoint of **Rupakot**. Another 1km down the road, a trail to the left leads up to another village called Begnas and then to **Begnaskot** (about three hours from Sundari Daada), an even better viewpoint of the Annapurnas and lake from the grassy crest of the ridge; this trail is part of the Royal Trek.

Practicalities

A couple of **guesthouses** and snack joints are clumped near the dam, but *Hotel Daybreak* (❶), perched on a bluff above the other buildings, has better views and cleaner, brighter rooms.

Far more idyllic are the indescribably peaceful **lodges** strung along the Panchbhaiya Daada trail. The simple chalets of *Rupa Viewpoint* (❶), accessed by a path leading off to the right, just after the highest point of the road, are tacked onto a farmhouse home. Slightly more upmarket, *Dinesh's House* (❷), near the top of the ridge, is a sort of bed-and-breakfast, set among beautifully kept gardens; while *Robin's Nest*, immediately above, is an ordinary guesthouse with a tourist menu and a fabulous view from its rooftop terrace.

Another steep path leads down from the ridge to the seriously posh *Begnas Lake Resort and Villas* (☎061/560 030, ⓦ www.intertours_nepal.com/begnas; ❽), which spreads down through the forested southeastern shore of Begnas Tal; most guests come by boat. An even fancier outfit run by the Tiger Tops luxury lodge group, *Tiger Mountain Pokhara Lodge* (☎01/436 1500, ⓦ www.tigermountain .com; $150 per night; ❾), is located along the ridge to the northwest of Begnas Tal, and offers naturalist-led treks ($150 per night). All meals, activities and transportation to and from Pokhara are included in the price.

The **food** served by the guesthouses is pretty unexciting compared to what's on offer in Pokhara, although you can usually get a few tourist items as well as the Nepali standards.

South of Pokhara

The only through-road beyond Pokhara, the **Siddhartha Highway** (Siddhartha Rajmarg), points south: a slow, uncomfortable, but occasionally rewarding journey to the Terai. In 160km it negotiates countless twists and turns and landslide paths, and often claims a tyre or an axle. Six hours would be a fast run. Although it's the most direct route between Pokhara and the Indian border, most buses travel via Narayangadh, to the east. Cyclists, however, will enjoy the light traffic.

Entering the Amdhi Khola watershed, the Siddhartha Highway wriggles tortuously across the side of the valley. After the bazaar of **Syangja**, the valley draws in and the hills rear up spectacularly in places. Signs of erosion are evident everywhere: these hills are geologically very unstable.

Near Syangja, you can hike up four hours of steep trail from Arjunchaupari to the cultural Gurung village of Sirubari, where you can stay in villagers' homes. A viewpoint next to Sirubari displays a huge rank of the Himalayas. It is also possible to reach the place by jeep from Pokhara, but it takes half a day on a dirty road. The best option is to arrange a visit with an agency, as you will be received with much fanfare.

Beyond **Waling**, the highway climbs gradually and then begins its descent to the Kali Gandaki, first passing the access road to the huge new **Kali Gandaki "A" Project**, which provided Nepal with surplus power for the first time – and like it or not, is now the finishing point for rafting trips on the river. The Siddhartha Highway crosses the river at **Ramdi Ghat**, the site of many caves, before climbing almost 1000m to its highest point. A few kilometres beyond is the turning for **Tansen** (see below). From there it's an hour's descent to Butwal and the Terai (covered in Chapter Five). This last forty-kilometre stretch is particularly prone to landslides and so is often in dreadful shape.

Tansen and around

Once the seat of a powerful kingdom, the hill town of **TANSEN** (Palpa) now seems little more than a bazaar town stranded in the hills. Tourism comes a low second to trading, yet slowly, almost reluctantly, Tansen yields its secrets: clacking *dhaka* looms glimpsed though doorways; the potters of Ghorabanda; the view from Srinagar Hill; the superb day hikes and bike rides in the surrounding countryside. If you're coming from India, Tansen makes a far more authentic introduction to Nepal than Pokhara, and at an altitude of 1370m, it's usually pleasantly cool after the heat of the plains.

Tansen's **history** goes back to the early sixteenth century, when it was known as Palpa, and the Sen clan of princes, already established at Butwal, chose it as a safer base from which to expand. Makunda Sen, Palpa's legendary second king, allegedly raided Kathmandu and carried off two sacred Bhairab masks, only to be cut down by a plague sent by the Pashupatinath *linga*. Chastened by the king's death, his successors formed an alliance with Gorkha, which bought them breathing space when the latter began conquering territory in the mid-eighteenth century. Aided by a friendly Indian rajah, Palpa staved off the inevitable until 1806, when it became the last territory to be annexed to modern Nepal. Tansen remains the headquarters of Palpa District, and many still refer to the town as Palpa.

The **bazaar** was set up by Newari merchants from the Kathmandu Valley to take advantage of the trade route between India and Tibet. That business was killed off by the road, which passes a few hundred metres below town, but the Newars have smoothly switched to retailing Indian-manufactured goods to the local Magar people.

Arrival and information

Public **buses** serve the Siddhartha Highway between Pokhara and Butwal. Coming from Pokhara or Sonauli/Bhairawa you've also got the option of taking a faster and more comfortable quasi-tourist bus. However, these buses

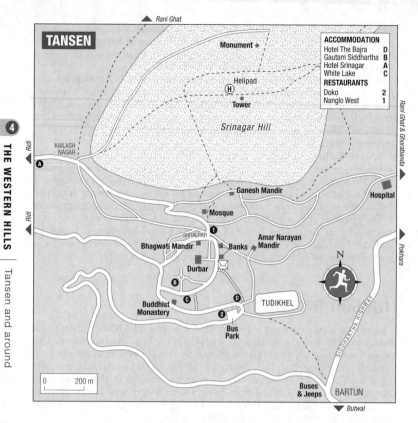

don't leave the Siddhartha Highway, so you have to get off at Bartun, the village at the start of the three-kilometre Tansen spur road. Jeeps and buses shuttle almost nonstop from the roadside to Tansen, leaving as soon as they're full.

There are no taxis or rickshaws in Tansen, although the better hotels can arrange **motorcycle** or **vehicle hire**. It should be possible to rent an ordinary bicycle through guesthouses. One of the two **banks** on Bank Street, Rastriya Banijya or Nepal Bank (Mon–Thurs & Sun 10am–2pm, Fri 10am–noon), should be able to change US dollar and sterling traveller's cheques.

Accommodation

You pay roughly double in Tansen what you'd pay for the same class of **accommodation** in Pokhara. Hot water and electricity are always intermittent, the town is under a permanent water shortage, and there's nothing very fancy, though two places try. Don't settle for the lodges near the bus park, which are noisy and a steep slog from the centre.

Hotel the Bajra ☎075/521 522. A big place with decent, if slightly shabby, rooms and a friendly owner. Just far enough from the bus park to avoid the worst of the noise, but hardly secluded. ❶

Gautam Siddhartha Guest House ☎075/520 280. A fairly primitive Nepali lodge in a relatively quiet but uninteresting neighbourhood. ❶

Hotel Srinagar ☎075/520 045. Great location on Srinagar Hill, with views nearby, but facilities and service aren't great for the price. It's a good 20min above town, so call ahead to arrange transport. ❺

White Lake ☎075/520 291. Pretty ordinary, but nevertheless the top hotel in Tansen itself, and used to dealing with foreigners. Decent *daal bhaat* too. ❸–❺

The Town

Tansen spills down the flank of Srinagar Hill, the southernmost flank of the Mahabharat range. The **bus park** occupies the lowest, newest level, from which a path leads steeply up through a modest bazaar. Things improve once you've found your way to the **upper town**, although the palace, slapped together by British architects from Kolkata at the end of the nineteenth century, was ruined during a 2006 skirmish (see box, p.262), and is now being rebuilt. **Shitalpati**, the hub of the busy upper town, is overlooked by a reminder of Tansen's grand past, the **Mul Dhoka** (main gate) – tall enough for elephants and their riders to pass through, and reputedly the biggest of its kind in Nepal. West of here lie Tansen's oldest neighbourhoods, with lovely, quirky old houses. An undistinguished modern **Bhagwati Mandir** enshrines the hostess of Tansen's biggest festival, the Bhagwati Jaatra (late Aug to early Sept), which, in addition to its religious function, commemorates an 1814 battle in which Nepal routed British troops near here. The cobbled lane going east from Shitalpati leads down to the nineteenth-century **Amar Narayan Mandir**, a pagoda-style temple that's the stopping place for sadhus on their way to Janai Purnima festivities at Muktinath in late July or early August.

Keep an eye out for **dhaka weavers**, who work at wooden treadle looms shaped like upright pianos. Many shops in the bazaar sell nothing but *dhaka*, which is woven in many hill areas by shuttling coloured threads back and forth across a constant vertical background to form repeating, geometric patterns that allow for almost infinite improvisation. A good-quality Palpali weave will set you back Rs400 a metre. The fabric's most famous use is in the archetypal *dhaka* or *Palpali topi*, the colourful hat worn by millions of

▲ Tansen bazaar

Nepali men, and the garish crowning glory of Nepal's national dress. You can pick up a ready-made "Nepali cap" for as little as Rs50 – or up to Rs400 for a model that's made to measure. Tansen is also known for **thailo**, a woman's purse made from *dhaka* with two coloured pairs of drawstrings – and **karuwa** – heavy, bulbous brass water vessels, which cost Rs200–2000 depending on size.

Tansen's solitary **mosque** isn't much to look at, but does recall the somewhat surprising presence of a settled Muslim population, descendants of bangle-sellers.

Eating

🦐 *Nanglo West* provides a culinary oasis in Tansen. Overlooking Shitalpati, it has comfy indoor and outdoor tables, and serves excellent Newari food. Only the *White Lake* hotel and *Hotel Srinagar* are alternatives in the tourist food department. *Doko Restaurant* serves a good range of *momo* and other Newari dishes, and there's the usual swarms of *daal bhaat* and snack stalls all around the town.

Around Tansen: Srinagar Hill and beyond

The best thing about Tansen is getting out of it to **explore** the outlying hill country and Magar villages. People on the trail will likely greet you with delighted smiles and the full palms-together *namaste*.

The first stop on most excursions is **Srinagar Hill**, north of town. The most direct route, which takes about half an hour on foot, starts from a small Ganesh temple above Shitalpati, but you have to zigzag a bit to get to the temple. From *Hotel Srinagar* it's an easy twenty-minute walk east along the ridge. The top (1525m) is planted with thick pine forest – catch the view from the helipad or the open area west of *Hotel Srinagar*. The peaks appear smaller and hazier from here than they do from Pokhara, but the Dhaulagiri and Annapurna ranges are still impressive, and Machhapuchhre's true "fishtail"

Tansen attack

Walking around the streets concealing the palace, you may notice a fair number of holes and even metal rounds in the walls of neighbouring houses. These are the result of the most dramatic offensive conducted by the Maoists during the conflict. On the evening of January 31, 2006, thousands of fighters of the People's Liberation Army (PLA) launched parallel attacks on Srinagar Hill and the barracks and town below, paralyzing the Royal Nepalese Army and setting free the jailbirds. On the top of the hill, a patrol took shelter in the *Srinagar Hotel* and the now-renovated building was severely damaged by a storm of bullets.

Back in the middle of the town, the PLA fired from the houses surrounding the palace; the rooftop of the *Nanglo* restaurant opposite the main entrance, for example, was used by the fighters. The palace was targeted because it housed the office of the district government administration, and the district police station. By the middle of the night, the pride of the Palpali was reduced to ashes; the Mul Dhoka, the iconic towering main gate, was also damaged. The PLA took full control of the town's heart but, in classic guerrilla style, returned to the hills at dawn, taking many (subsequently released) hostages from the police and army. During the fight, several PLA and Nepalese Army soldiers and policemen were shot down, but miraculously for such an urban attack, only one civilian was killed. However, the palace's destruction has left deep scars in the inhabitants' psyche. The building is under reconstruction, and is supposed to stand again by 2011.

profile is visible from this angle. On the southern side, beyond Tansen, lies the luxuriant Madi Valley, layered with paddy fields owned by Tansen's Newari landlords. The area north of the helipad, just below the summit, has been turned into a large municipal park.

All three routes described below pass through farmland and are heavily used by villagers, so it's fairly easy to find your way with just enough Nepali to ask directions. You may prefer to take a guide – ask your innkeeper – or consult the HMG/FINNIDA maps for the area. *Hotel Srinagar* has some excellent route plans, which include detailed maps. Numerous other hikes are possible from Tansen, including taking the old trading route to Butwal, which passes the ruins of the old Sen palace at Nuwakot.

Rani Ghat

It's a 14km round-trip to **RANI GHAT**, the site of a fantastically derelict palace along the Kali Gandaki. The trail begins 200m east of *Hotel Srinagar* and descends through an immensely satisfying landscape of farmland, trailside hamlets and, finally, a jungly gorge with impressive waterfalls. The circuit itself takes at least four or five hours, but you'll want to set aside the whole day (it's quite an uphill climb on the way back).

Set in a tranquil spot beside turquoise Kali Gandaki, Rani Ghat is the site of occasional cremations. But the main attraction here is the spooky old **palace**, built in the late nineteenth century by a former government minister who, according to the custom of the day, was exiled to Palpa after a failed coup. Perched atop an outcrop overlooking the river, it was abandoned to the elements for many years. You get a great view of it from the distressingly long suspension bridge that crosses the river here.

Rani Ghat itself isn't really a village, just a couple of *chiya pasal* that offer only very limited food and emergency shelter. Bring a lunch and picnic on the tranquil, sandy beach.

To Ridi Bazaar

RIDI BAZAAR makes an equally eventful all-day outing, either on foot (13km one-way, with the option of bussing back) or by bike (60km round-trip). From *Hotel Srinagar*, walk west to a fork at a police checkpost, bear right and in half an hour you'll reach Chandi Bhanjyang; turn left here and descend through a handsome canyon before rejoining the unpaved road for the last 7km. On a bike, stay on the main road all the way.

Set on the banks of the Kali Gandaki, Ridi is considered sacred because of the wealth of **shaligrams** – fossil-bearing stones associated with Vishnu – found in the river here. It is said that if a person were cremated at Ridi and his ashes sprinkled into the river, they would congeal to form a *shaligram*, and if the stone were then made into a likeness of Vishnu, the devotee would be one with his god. The spiral-shaped ammonite fossils typically found in *shaligram* are 150–200 million years old, dating from a time when the entire Himalayan region lay under a shallow sea.

During the **festival** of Magh Sankranti (Jan 14 or 15), Ridi is a pilgrimage site for ritual bathing. Celebrations of the *ekadashi* of Kaattik (the eleventh day of the "bright fortnight" around the full moon of Oct–Nov) include processions and dancing. The colourful commercial end of town lies across a stream that joins the Kali Gandaki here, while the magical eighteenth-century **Rishikesh Mandir** is south of the stream, just above the bus stop. According to legend, the idol inside the squat temple, a form of Vishnu, was fished out of the river and originally bore the likeness of a young boy, but over the course of years has matured into adult form.

Several **buses** a day head back to Tansen, taking two and a half hours, but you may have to wait some time, as most ply the route in the morning only. You can stay overnight if you get stuck. The return journey can be combined with a visit to **Palpa Bhairab**, up a short path from the pretty Newari village of Bhairabsthan, 8km before Tansen. So many animal sacrifices are performed at this temple, especially on Saturdays and Tuesdays, that it's often compared with that of Dakshin Kali in the Kathmandu Valley. Its much-feared Bhairab image is kept in a small chamber at the far corner of the compound; the gilded *trisul* (trident) here is claimed to be the biggest in Asia, and pilgrims have left a large number of smaller replicas at its base.

Ghorabanda

The most interesting of the villages east of Tansen, **GHORABANDA** is locally famous for its **potters**. It's just off the Siddhartha Highway, 3km north of the Tansen turning, but without your own wheels you'll have to walk. Take the dirt road from the Amar Narayan temple towards the United Mission Hospital, bear right onto a trail after about 500m, descend and then contour through extensive paddy – you'll drop down to the highway after about 2km, with Ghorabanda another 1km further along the road. Ghorabanda's notoriously drunken potters, members of the Kumal ethnic group, throw their almost spherical water jugs on heavy clay flywheels. The farmhouses and potteries of Ghorabanda spread down the hill from the highway.

Travel details

Day buses

Gorkha to: Abu Khaireni (every 30min; 1hr); Birgunj (2 daily; 7hr); Kathmandu (10 daily; 5hr); Narayangadh (14 daily; 2hr 30min); Pokhara (3 daily; 3hr); Sonauli (1 daily; 7hr).

Pokhara to: Baglung (31 daily; 3hr); Bartun for Tansen (14 daily; 5hr); Begnas Tal (every 20min; 45min); Beni (8 daily; 4hr); Besisanar (2–3 daily; 4hr 30min); Birgunj (10 daily; 8hr); Butwal for Sonauli* (20 daily; 7hr); Gorkha (3 daily; 3hr); Jagatpur (2 daily; 11hr); Janakpur (2 daily; 11hr); Kakarbhitta (1 daily; 14hr); Kathmandu* (75 daily plus 12 tourist buses; 5–7hr); Narayangadh (every 30min; 4hr).

Tansen to: Butwal (every 30min; 2hr); Kathmandu (1 daily; 11–12hr); Pokhara (3 daily; 6hr).

* Tourist bus service also available.

Night buses

Pokhara to: Birgunj (2 daily; 10hr); Butwal for Sonauli (2 daily; 10hr); Dhangadhi for Bardia (2 daily; 15hr); Janakpur (1 daily; 12hr); Kakarbhitta (3 daily; 16hr); Kathmandu (5 daily; 6–7hr); Mahendra Nagar (1 daily; 16hr); Nepalgunj (1 daily; 14hr).

Tansen to: Kathmandu (1 daily; 11–12hr).

Flights

Pokhara to: Bhairawa (1 daily); Jomosom (3–9 daily); Kathmandu (16–17 daily); Manang (0–3 weekly).

Charter flights from Pokhara to Bharatpur, Chitwan, 246 Dolpo, Jumla, and mountain flights are also available.

The Western Terai

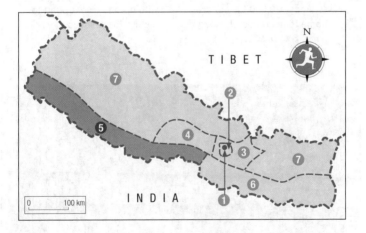

CHAPTER 5 # Highlights

✳ **Chitwan National Park**
Spot the endangered Asian
one-horned rhino from the
back of an elephant.
See p.269

✳ **Sauraha, Chitwan** Watch
the sun go down over the
teeming jungle from a "beach"
bar. See p.270

✳ **Bis Hajaar Tal, Chitwan**
Away from the tiger- and
rhino-hunting crowds, the
swampy "20,000 Lakes" are
home to hundreds of exotic
birds. See p.287

✳ **Devghat** Devout Hindus
come to die at this holy
confluence, spanned by
a dramatic suspension
footbridge. See p.288

✳ **Lumbini and Tilaurakot** Visit
the birthplace of the Buddha,
before meditating among the
ruins of his childhood home.
See p.293 & p.299

✳ **Bardia National Park** Take a
guided walk into the jungle,
with no one else around to
disturb the animals.
See p.302

▲ Chitwan National Park

5

The Western Terai

I n a country best known for the Himalayas and Sherpas, the lowland, Indian-influenced **Terai** gets short shrift from most guidebooks. A narrow strip of flatland extending along the length of Nepal's southern border – including several *dun* (inner Terai) valleys north of the first range of hills – the Terai was originally covered in thick, malarial jungle. In the 1950s, however, the government identified the southern plains as a major growth area to relieve population pressure in the hills, and, with the help of liberal quantities of DDT, brought malaria under control. Since then, the jungle has been methodically cleared and the Terai has emerged as Nepal's most productive agricultural and industrial region, accounting for around half its GDP and supporting about half its population. The jungle barrier that once insulated Nepal from Indian influences as effectively as the Himalayas had guarded the north, making possible the development of a uniquely Nepali culture, has disappeared. An unmistakable Indian quality now pervades the Terai, as evidenced by the avid mercantilism of the border bazaars, the chewing of *betel*, the mosques and orthodox Brahmanism, the jute mills and sugar refineries, and the many roads and irrigation projects built with Indian aid.

Fortunately, the government has set aside sizeable chunks of the **western Terai** in the form of national parks and reserves, which remain some of the finest **wildlife and bird havens** on the subcontinent. Dense riverine forest provides cover for predators like tigers and leopards; swampy grasslands make the perfect habitat for rhinoceros; and vast, tall stands of *sal*, the Terai's most common tree, shelter huge herds of deer. Of the region's wildlife parks, the deservedly popular **Chitwan** is the richest in game and the most accessible, but if you're willing to invest some extra effort, **Bardia** and **Sukla Phanta** further to the west make quieter, more jungly alternatives.

The region's other claim to fame is historical: the Buddha was born 2500 years ago at **Lumbini**, and his birthplace is appropriately serene. Elsewhere in Lumbini, important archeological discoveries have been made at **Tilaurakot** and several other outlying sites.

Four **border crossings** in the western Terai are open to foreigners. As it's on the most direct route between Kathmandu and Varanasi, and fits in well with visits to Lumbini and Chitwan, **Sonauli** is still the most heavily used. Less popular are the crossing points south of **Nepalgunj** or Dhangadhi. Alternatively, on the far western frontier, **Mahendra Nagar** is only around twelve hours from Delhi, but it's an arduous journey to Kathmandu (though you can visit Bardia and Sukla Phanta on the way).

Bus connections to the Terai from Kathmandu and Pokhara are well developed via **Narayangadh**. The Terai itself is traversed by the **Mahendra**

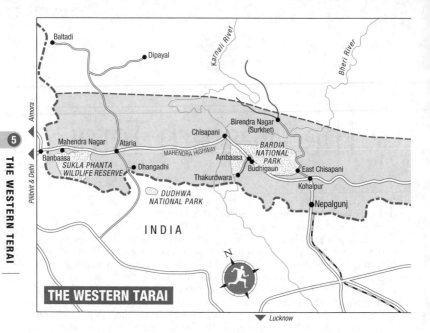

THE WESTERN TARAI

Lucknow

Highway (the Mahendra Rajmarg in Nepali), a thin line of tarmac stretching from the far west to the far east, with offshoot roads connecting to the district capitals in between. Traffic drops off west of Butwal, which makes for peaceful **cycling**, but potentially long waits for bus connections. Internal **flights** aren't expensive; Nepalgunj is the air hub for western Nepal, and there are numerous less useful airstrips in the areas as well.

The **weather** in the Terai is at its best from October to January – the days are more pleasantly mild during the latter half of this period, though the nights and mornings can be surprisingly chilly and damp. However, the wildlife viewing gets much better after the thatch has been cut, from late January, by which time the temperatures are starting to warm up again. It gets really hot (especially in the far west) in April, May and June. The monsoon brings not only rain but mosquitoes, malaria and leeches, and many roads become impassable at this time. From July to September the monsoon makes a lot of the more minor, unpaved roads very muddy and difficult to pass, and some rivers burst their banks.

There are a number of armed **Madhesi** groups in the Terai, who continue to carry out attacks. Tourists are not targets, however, and aside from the odd *bandh* or traffic blockade, you are unlikely to be affected by their activities.

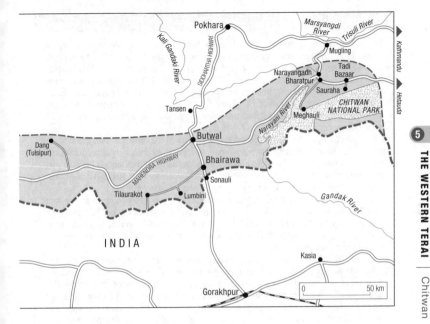

Chitwan

CHITWAN is the name not only of Nepal's most visited national park but also of the surrounding *dun* valley and administrative district. The name means "Heart of the Jungle" – a description that, sadly, now holds true only for the lands protected within the park and community forests. Yet, the rest of the **valley** – though it's been reduced to a flat, furrowed plain – still provides fascinating vignettes of a rural lifestyle. Really ugly development is confined to the wayside conurbation of **Narayangadh/Bharatpur**, and even this has left the nearby holy site of **Devghat** so far unscathed.

The best – and worst – aspects of **Chitwan National Park** are that it can be visited on the cheap, and that it's easy to get to. It is high on the list of "things to do in Nepal", so unless you go during the steamy season you'll be sharing your experience with a lot of other people.

If you want to steer clear of the crowds, and don't mind making a little extra effort, try avoiding the much-touted tourist village of **Sauraha** and heading instead for **Ghatgain** or **Meghauli**, a little further west. Or, if you've got the money (around $200 a night per person, all-in) go for pampered seclusion at any one of the luxury lodges and tented camps inside the park itself.

Tharus

Two great mysteries surround the Terai-dwelling **Tharus**, Nepal's second largest ethnic group: where they came from and how they became resistant to malaria. Some anthropologists speculate that they originally migrated from India's eastern hills, which would account for their Hindu-animist beliefs, but doesn't fully explain the radically different dialects, dress and customs of different Tharu groups. Isolated by malarial jungle for thousands of years, bands of migrants certainly could have developed their own cultures, but then why would the name "Tharu" survive with such consistency?

Further confusing the issue are the **Rana Tharus** of the far west, who claim to be descended from high-caste Rajput women sent north by their husbands during the Muslim invasions – the husbands never came for them, so they ended up marrying their servants. (There is some circumstantial evidence for this: Rana Tharu women are given extraordinary autonomy in marriage and household affairs.)

In terms of the malarial resistance, red blood cells seem to play a part – the fact that Tharus are prone to sickle-cell anaemia may be significant – but little research has been done. At least as significant, Tharus boost their immunity by common sense precautions, such as building houses with tiny windows to keep smoke in and mosquitoes (and ghosts) out.

Skilled hunter-gatherers, Tharus have in modern times become farmers, and livestock raisers, fishing rivers, clearing patches in the forest and warding off wild animals. Their famed whirling stick **dance** evokes their uneasy, but respectful, relationship with the forest spirits. Their homes are made of mud and dung plastered over wood-and-reed frames, giving them a distinctive ribbed effect. In the west, half a dozen families or more often still live in the traditional communal longhouses.

The Tharus have fared poorly in recent years, largely reduced to sharecropping. Their distinct culture remains strong in the far west, but in other areas is being drowned out by dominating influences from elsewhere in Nepal and India. Like indigenous people throughout the world, the Tharus' traditional skills and knowledge of the environment seem to count for little these days.

Sauraha

Spectacularly situated on the banks of the Rapti River, opposite a prime area of jungle, **SAURAHA** (pronounced *So*-ruh-hah) is one of those unstoppably successful destinations at which Nepal seems to excel. In some lights it looks like the archetypal budget safari village, with its folksy guesthouses spread out along a few dusty roads at the edge of the forest; at other times, you could half-close your eyes and imagine yourself in a miniature, jungly Thamel. There's still a lot to recommend it though, not least the ease of access into the park, but each year, Sauraha loses a little more of what once made it so enjoyable: electricity has replaced lanterns and fire light, resort hotels are displacing local lodges (and village homes) and restaurants with tourist menus are springing up in place of local *daal bhaat* joints.

Getting there

Several daily **tourist buses** run to Sauraha's bus park from Kathmandu, Pokhara and Sonauli (via Bhairahawa). The fare is around Rs300 and the journey takes about six hours; minibuses and the comfortable Greenline Tours (☎056/560 267; $18, including lunch) cost more. When you arrive, touts will have prepared the usual ambush and will take you by battered **Jeep** to their own guesthouse, making every effort to win your business on the way. You don't have to stay at their place, of course, but – as they will argue – you may as well have a look. Otherwise a lift into town by Jeep should cost around Rs50.

There are more frequent connections with **Tadi Bazaar**, on the Mahendra Highway, 6km north of Sauraha. Hotel touts offering rides often meet buses during the day, but you can alternatively get a rikshaw (roughly Rs50), horse and cart (roughly Rs150) or Jeep (roughly Rs350 per vehicle) into Sauraha.

It's also possible to **fly** to Bharatpur (see p.287), about 15km west of Tadi Bazaar, though the journey to Chitwan isn't so taxing that this is really necessary. A flight from Kathmandu costs around $86.

Accommodation

Sauraha has a great tradition of "camp"-style **accommodation**: the best guest-houses here are like rustic little country clubs, with simple mud-and-thatch bungalows, airy dining pavilions and shady gardens or open lawns. Unfortunately, many have forsaken traditional designs and natural materials for concrete, and some of the newer places, with their regimental rows of bunkers and little or no shade, look more like prison camps than jungle camps.

The deciding factor when choosing a place to stay in Sauraha is usually **location**. The largest share of lodgings line up shoulder to shoulder along the village's main north–south strip which is handy for restaurants and the park entrance, though relatively noisy and crowded. The ones overlooking the river avoid those drawbacks, and are especially peaceful around sunset, although they are further away from the park and restaurants. Other places scattered in the area east of the park entrance provide a good combination of seclusion and convenience. A number of places have materialized along the peaceful road leading westwards to the Elephant Breeding Project, though many have had trouble winning business due to the relative inconvenience of staying here.

Booking ahead may weaken your bargaining position, and if you call a lodge's Kathmandu office you'll almost certainly be quoted a package rate. If you just turn up, you won't be short of offers of a room; there are many more guest-houses in Sauraha than the selection listed below.

A reminder: Sauraha is not the only place to stay – see the later "Alternative bases" section (p.276).

About budget packages

The best advice is: avoid them! A two-night, three-day Chitwan safari **package**, booked via any Kathmandu or Pokhara travel agency, gives you only a day and a half in the park, and you'll have little control over the programme of activities. You'll be locked into staying at a lodge that has little incentive to work for your business (and every incentive to cut corners, since it has to give the booking agent between forty and sixty percent), you'll be served inferior set meals, and you probably won't get to choose your guide. Additionally, a $70-odd package is likely to be slightly more expensive than doing the same thing on your own, and saves you hardly any trouble since Chitwan is incredibly easy to visit independently. If you must be bound by an itinerary, at least book directly with the lodge itself.

A package tour of Chitwan can also be combined with a **raft trip** on the Trisuli River, bookable through rafting operators in Kathmandu and Pokhara, but, for the reasons set out above, it's still a bad idea to book the Chitwan stay as part of the raft trip. And a raft won't take you all the way to the park no matter what the salesman says: Narayangadh is normally the end of the line.

Budget lodges

Many of Sauraha's **budget lodges** are pretty similar to each other, not least in name: most offer rooms in concrete bungalows with thatched roofs arranged around attractively subtropical gardens. Most have private bathrooms (generally with solar-powered hot water systems) and mosquito nets (use them, and have any holes sewn up), though you may have to pay more for a ceiling fan (and certainly will for air conditioning).

Competition is extremely keen in this category, so **prices** will often drop dramatically when occupancy is low, and discounts can generally be negotiated. The best strategy is to decide on a guesthouse in advance and try to get a ride with a Jeep that's going directly there; if you don't like it you can always move in the cool of the following morning.

Chitwan Resort Camp ☏056/580 082, ✉crc @mail.com. Bungalows house clean, straightforward rooms, and there are nice communal areas in the garden where you can sit under thatched roof "umbrellas". ❸

Chitwan Safari Camp and Lodge ☏056/580 078. Excellent, welcoming, locally owned budget option, surrounded by fields. Basic but cheerful rooms, with private baths, are set amongst a shaded garden which features a *bodhi* tree. ❷

Jungle Wildlife Camp ☏056/580 093, ✉junglewcamp@yahoo.com. Under renovation at the time of research, this Dutch-Nepali venture has tasteful rooms in a peppermint-coloured building, a good restaurant and a peaceful riverside location. Keep an eye out for the crocodile on the opposite bank. ❷–❹

Hotel Rainforest ☏056/580 007, ⊛www .hotel-rainforest.com. Amiable owner and a range of rooms: the smartest have beige décor and two private verandas/balconies with mountain views; those in the next class down are similar, but lack views; and the cheapest are plain but clean. ❷–❺

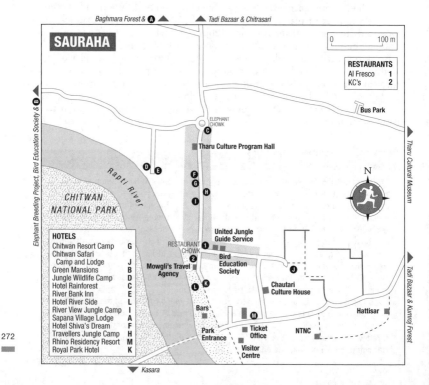

River Bank Inn ☏056/580 450, @riverbankinn @gmail.com. In a pretty spot overlooking the river, this new, well-run lodge has large, modern rooms and two elephants. The friendly owner is a font of local knowledge – particularly regarding birds – and can organise volunteer placements. ❷–❹

Hotel River Side ☏056/580 009, @hriverside @hotmail.com. The interior of this professional hotel is much more attractive than the exterior: there is a selection of rooms from standard options with tubs to "cottage-style" rooms with lovely river views. ❸–❺

River View Jungle Camp ☏056/580 096, @rvjcsauraha@hotmail.com. The name is a little misleading as you have to walk right to the end of the garden to see the river, but there is a lookout tower for guests to use. The red-brick rooms have corrugated iron roofs and are shaded by rows of tropical trees. ❹

Sapana Village Lodge ☏056/580 308, ⓦwww.sapanalodge.com. Backed by a Dutch development project, *Sapana* aims to support the local Tharu community, both through employment opportunities and by giving visitors an insight into Tharu life via cooking classes, fishing trips and homestays. The hacienda-style lodge, in a sedate riverside location, has delightful rooms with plenty of local touches. ❺

Hotel Shiva's Dream ☏056/580 369, ⓦwww .foresthideaway.com. *Shiva's Dream* is a professional lodge with informative management and staff, and a choice of clean, comfortable a/c and non a/c rooms, all with private facilities. It has a similarly good sister lodge in Bardia (see p.306). ❸–❹

Travellers Jungle Camp ☏056/580 013, ⓦwww.travellersjunglecamp.com.np. A popular, good-value place with brown and beige buildings and its own elephant stand: the most expensive rooms have a/c and tubs, and even the standard ones have TVs (should you need one). ❹

Moderate and expensive lodges

Price is not necessarily an indicator of quality in Sauraha. Some lodges charge deluxe prices for budget facilities, on the theory that package tourists will never know the difference. However, the ones listed here are a cut above the budget pack: you should be able to count on superior grounds, good food, reliable hot water, a Jeep in good working order, experienced guides, and small touches like a library and slide shows.

These lodges get by mainly on expensive package business, but they'll usually take you on an accommodation-only basis if you just show up, with substantial discounts out of season, potentially up to fifty percent.

Green Mansions ☏056/580 088. Named after a WH Hudson novel, and close to the Elephant Breeding Centre, *Green Mansions* has peaceful, manicured gardens, an atmospheric dining hall and spacious en suites with stylish bathrooms. ❼

Royal Park Hotel ☏056/580 061, ⓦwww .royalparkhotel.com.np. Cute buildings with terraces and lattice dividers sit in ample grounds, which also feature a tiny plunge pool. Opt for the (no more expensive) second-floor rooms with high ceilings and extra space. ❻

Rhino Residency Resort ☏056/580 095, ⓦrhino@residency.wilkn.com.np. The green and white en suites, decorated with bird pictures, are probably the smartest outside the park, and there's a pool and plenty of lime trees. However, the preserved creatures in jars in the lobby are a little off-putting. ❼

The village

The fast-changing cluster of shops and hotels that make up Sauraha "**village**" constitute most of the action here, though there's little to do except shop, eat and plan excursions. The national park **visitor centre** (daily 6am–6pm) has a modest but informative display on the ecology of the park and the local Tharu culture. The **Tharu Cultural Museum** (daily 6am–6pm; Rs25), a 15–20-minute walk east of the bus stand, is also worth a visit. It has an interesting collection of exhibits and paintings, including agricultural, fishing and clothing items, and displays on dance, religion and festivals. If this whets your appetite and you want to get more of a flavour of Terai village life, find yourself a bicycle (see box below) and put as much distance between you and Sauraha as the heat allows.

Small **shops**, stalls and a "German" bakery stock food and other items (beer, batteries, toilet paper, postcards, crafts and so on), and there are a handful of fairly good bookshops. The **Community Souvenir Shop**, opposite the park visitor centre, sells some useful books and maps, as well as mementos; the town's curio shops sell mainly geographically inappropriate

Tharu village tours and bike rides

Guided **Tharu village walks** out of Sauraha can be rather voyeuristic, especially when you consider how many tourists have trooped through the homes before you. For cultural tours with more sensitivity, try Mowgli's Eco Adventure Tours (☎056/580 201, ⑩www.mowglieco adventure.com), just south of Restaurant Chowk, which uses 25 percent of its profits to fund conservation education programmes for local people. The company runs jungle walks through the park to **Maadi**, an authentic Tharu village towards the Indian border, where you can participate in a homestay. It's possible, but trickier, to do this independently: four or five daily buses run between Gita Nagar (see below) and Maadi, taking around 3 hour 30 minute, and asking around in Sauhara may yield a homestay – this is pretty difficult to organise however, and almost certainly not worth the effort. Mowgli also organises interesting treks and homestays in the Chepang Hills.

You can also learn about real Terai village life by hopping on a **bike** and just getting lost on the backroads to the east and west of Sauraha. Stopping at any village and asking *chiya paunchha?* (where can I get a cup of tea?) will usually attract enough attention to get you introduced to someone.

In November, when the rice is harvested, you'll be able to watch villagers cutting the stems, tying them into sheaves and threshing them; or, since it's such a busy time of year, piling them in big stacks to await threshing. January is thatch-gathering time, when huge bundles are put by until a slack time before the monsoon when there s time to repair roofs. In early March, the mustard, lentils and wheat that were planted after the rice crop are ready; maize is then planted, to be harvested in July for animal fodder, flour and meal. Rice is seeded in dense starter-plots in March, to be transplanted into separate paddy fields in April.

From Sauraha, the most fertile country for exploration lies to the east: heading towards Tadi along the eastern side of the village, turn right (east) at the intersection marked by a health post and you can follow that road all the way to **Parsa**, 8km away on the Mahendra Highway, with many side roads to villages en route. Given a full day and a good bike or motorcycle, you could continue eastwards from Parsa along the highway for another 10km, and just before Bhandaara turn left onto a track leading to **Baireni**, a particularly well-preserved Tharu village. Another 10km east of Bhandaara lies **Lothar**, from where you can follow a trail upstream to reach the waterfalls on the Lothar Khola, a contemplative spot with a healthy measure of birdlife.

For a short ride west of Sauraha, first head north for 3km and take the first left after the river crossing, which brings you to the authentic Tharu villages of **Baghmara** and **Hardi**. If you're game for a longer journey, pedal to Tadi and west along the Mahendra Highway to Tikauli. From there, the canal road through Bis Hajaar Tal leads about 10km through beautiful forest to **Gita Nagar**, where you join the Bharatpur Jagatpur road, with almost unlimited possibilities from there. A good route is to continue due west from Jagatpur on dirt roads all the way to Meghauli, though you may have to ford a river on the way, impossible on a motorbike from June/July until at least late November. Don't overlook the possibility of an outing to Devghat (see p.288). For more on Tharu culture, see box, p.270.

items, but if you search around you can find some locally produced Tharu handicrafts.

A couple of **moneychangers** have offices on the strip, though their rates are a couple of percent lower than what you can get in a **bank**. The nearest ATM is in Tadi Bazaar. International **telephone** and **internet** services are available, but again, charges here are significantly higher than in Kathmandu or Pokhara. The **post office** is at the intersection east of the bus stand, but bookshops will take letters there for franking. There's a **pharmacy** on Restaurant Chowk and a private clinic in Tadi Bazaar, but if you're really ill, make for the hospital in Bharatpur (see p.287)

Bikes can be rented on the main strip for about Rs200 a day. **Motorcycles** cost from around Rs500 to rent for the day, excluding fuel, and make a great way to get to park entry points further afield, such as Ghatgain or Meghauli (see p.276 & p.277), or to make a day-trip to Devghat (see p.288).

Chitwan **maps** are helpful if you're planning to do any unguided excursions outside the park: Mappa/Karto Atelier's map is the best.

Eating

Guesthouse dining rooms are generally not particularly exciting, while the handful of **restaurants** in and around Sauraha's so-called Restaurant Chowk serve a mix of fresh fish, Indian and Nepali dishes, and variable attempts at Western fare. *Al Fresco* is worth a look, but *KC's*, which is owned by the same family, is probably the best, and certainly the most popular. It has an Indian chef, a proper *tandoor* and quality North Indian food, in a pleasant setting. You could also visit one of the classier guesthouses or go for inexpensive local fare at one of the *bhatti* on the main drags.

Nightlife

Some of Sauraha's rooftop restaurants advertise "happy hours" and are good for **evening drinks**, but nothing stays open very late. At **sunset**, head to the "beach" on the riverbank by the park entrance, where a few shifting bars spring up every season serving beers, cocktails and snacks on the sandy shore. Watching the sun go down over the jungle is one of Chitwan's more relaxing activities, but you'll have to get away from the bars to enjoy it in peace.

Sauraha's trademark entertainment is the **Tharu stick dance**, a mock battle in which participants parry each other's sticks with graceful, split-second timing. The original purpose of the dance, it's said, was simply to make a lot of racket to keep the wild animals away at night. It still forms a traditional part of Tharu celebrations of Phaagun Purnima (the full moon of Feb–March), but the version you're likely to see is a more contrived tourist show put on for package groups at Sauraha lodges.

The Tharu Culture Program Hall (see map, p.272) puts on nightly **culture shows** at 7.30pm featuring regional music and dance for tourist consumption (Rs80). Some of the smarter lodges host similar performances, often included in the package price.

Moving on

Leaving Sauraha is easy by **tourist bus**. For a small commission, your guesthouse or a travel agent on the main strip can arrange tickets. Agents in Sauraha can also arrange **air tickets** from Bharatpur to Kathmandu.

If your next destination isn't Kathmandu, Pokhara or Sonauli/Bhairahawa you'll have to get yourself to Tadi, and from there catch a **public bus** heading

▲ Sauraha "beach" bar

in your direction, which may well mean standing – all public buses start their journeys elsewhere, so you can't usually book seats at Tadi. Long-distance buses pass roughly every half-hour in both directions; your guesthouse should be able to advise on the timings of relevant services. Public buses leave Tadi for Naray-angadh/Bharatpur (where you'll have a much greater selection of onward services) every fifteen minutes or so; there are also regular services to Kathmandu.

Alternative bases

It's increasingly easy (though still not very popular) to avoid Sauraha altogether and base yourself in one of two villages along the park's northern boundary, just to the west. **Ghatgain** and **Meghauli** are much quieter and less developed than Sauraha, but also have guesthouses, guides, elephants and entry checkposts (though Jeeps are more difficult to come by). You can also do a jungle trek (see p.283) from Sauraha to either village. Those with deeper wallets can seek seclusion in one of the **luxury lodges and camps** inside the park itself (see opposite).

Ghatgain

There are four simple lodges, one upmarket resort and little else in the sleepy village of **GHATGAIN**, on the north bank of the Rapti River, 16km west of Sauraha. Close by is a good patch of jungle, two interesting lakes (Lami Tal and Tamar Tal) and the Kasara park headquarters, 4km downriver. The **park** starts on the other side of Rapti River from the village: guides (who guesthouses can provide) will take you across by dugout canoe and you pay your entry fee, if you haven't already got a ticket (see p.281). Numerous elephants are based in this area.

To get here, take any **bus** for Jagatpur and ask to be let off at Patihani (if that doesn't ring a bell, ask for *Safari Narayani*). It's then a fifteen-minute walk south to Ghatgain. Express buses run to Jagatpur from Pokhara (2 daily), and local buses trundle from Narayangadh roughly hourly (1hr) until mid afternoon.

Once at Ghatgain, most locals will be able to point you towards any of the four budget **lodges** (❶–❷), which are close together in the heart of the village, making the most of the stunning river view. *Riverview Lodge* (☎984/506 9589) is the pick of the bunch, with neat, clean rooms, well-tended garden, welcoming owner and good *daal bhaat*; at the time of research, a set of more modern rooms was being built. *Ghumtee Riviera Lodge* (☎984/508 2847) is another friendly place, with a tiny garden and bucolic location, while *Sunset View Lodge* (☎056/620 948) is a fair alternative, with a choice of shared or private squat toilets. *Wild Discover Hotel* (☎974/501 6627) is newer but not as well kept. By contrast, the package-only *Safari Narayani Lodge* (☎056/693 486, Ⓔsafarinarayani@wlink.com.np; ❼–❽) has a giant pool, en suites and a palm-filled garden.

Meghauli

Some 19km west of Ghatgain, **MEGHAULI** sits opposite Bhimle, an area of the park just across the Rapti River, which boasts superb rhino and tiger habitat and birdwatching. In early December Meghauli's airstrip, 1.5km south of the village centre, hosts the **Elephant Polo Championship**, which is well worth adjusting your schedule to see.

It's a two-day trek from Sauraha, or about two hours by local **bus** from Narayangadh (roughly every half-hour). Buses stop at the easternmost end of the village. The Bhimle guard post, where you can pay the park entrance fee, is 3km into the park and you will need to hire a guide (available from your guesthouse) to ferry you across the river.

Beyond the airstrip (just follow the signs) is *Chital Lodge* (☎984/515 5667; ❷), which has a lovely location, knowledgeable owner and star fruit trees in the garden; the little wooden huts, however, are poorly maintained. *Rhino Resort* (☎056/620 134, Ⓦwww.rhinoresort.com.np) is a good-value package place with twee rooms and riverside viewpoint.

Luxury lodges and tented camps

The **luxury lodges** and **tented camps** inside Chitwan National Park are among Nepal's most expensive lodgings. The owners pay the government massive fees to stake out exclusive concession areas and as a result you really feel like you've got the park all to yourself. Some are lavish lodges with permanent facilities, others are more remote tented camps offering camping in the softest sense, with fluffy mattresses, solar-heated showers and fully stocked bars, and some are both. The prices quoted below, which are per person based on double occupancy, include all activities, meals and tax, but most resorts offer various other packages, perhaps with transport included, or as part of a wider tour. **Book ahead**, either online, through an agent or by calling directly. Your accommodation will arrange your travel there and back by private vehicle, plane or raft, which costs extra unless otherwise stated below.

At the time of research, there were suggestions that some of the current concessions might not be renewed in the coming years. Perhaps in anticipation of this, many upmarket hotel groups are buying land outside the park boundaries, particularly in the countryside beyond Jagatpur, an area that seems likely to take off in the not too distant future.

Chitwan Jungle Lodge ☎01/444 2240, ⓦwww .chitwanjunglelodge.com. Accommodation is in individual, thatched huts raised on stilts at *Chitwan Jungle Lodge*, which is situated near the Rapti River. $220 per person for a two-night, three-day package.
Gaida Wildlife Camp ☎01/421 5431, ⓦwww .gaidawildlife.com. Located uncomfortably close to Sauraha, on the north side of the Rapti River, *Gaida* has a series of uniform thatched-roof bungalows. You can sometimes see crocodiles and rhinos from the comfort of the lodge. $135 per person per night.
Island Jungle Resort ☎01/422 0162, ⓦwww .islandjungleresort.com.np. Simple but comfy rooms, with bird murals on the walls, at a wonderful site on an island in the middle of Narayani River – something which makes it excellent for wildlife spotting. $200 for two-night, three-day package.
Machan Wildlife Resort ☎01/422 5001, ⓦwww .nepalinformation.com/machan. Wooden bungalows kitted out with furnishings made by local Methyl women, and a sublime swimming pool formed by a natural stream. The sister lodge, *Machan Paradise View*, outside the park, however, is disappointing. $285 for a two-night, three-day package.
Temple Tiger ☎01/422 1637, ⓦwww.catmando .com/temple-tiger. Camp at the west end of the

park, particularly good for wildlife sightings, offering stilted huts with nice Tharu touches and viewing terraces. Around $250 per person per night.
Tiger Tops Jungle Lodge ☎01/436 1500, ⓦwww.tigermountain.com. Founded in the 1960s, *Tiger Tops* was the first – and is still the most fashionable – lodge at Chitwan. The lodge, with rooms in treehouses or bungalows, is pure jungle Gothic, and the location and service are both excellent. Around $340 per person per night.
Tiger Tops Tharu Lodge ☎01/436 1500, ⓦwww.tigermountain.com. An off-shoot of the original *Tiger Tops*, with architecture inspired by the traditional Tharu longhouse and an emphasis on cultural activities outside the park, as well as wildlife viewing and safaris. Around $170 per person per night.
Tiger Tops Tented Camp ☎01/436 1500, ⓦwww.tigermountain.com. Another *Tiger Tops* camp, close to the Reu River, providing the veneer of roughing it, without any compromise in comfort: the luxury safari tents have attached bamboo bathrooms, and there's a library and viewing platform. Around $220 per person per night.

Chitwan National Park

Whether the **CHITWAN NATIONAL PARK** has been blessed or cursed by its own riches is an open question, and the coexistence of the valley's people and wildlife has rarely been easy or harmonious, even before the creation of the national park. In the era of the trigger-happy maharajas, the relationship was at least simple: when Jang Bahadur Rana overthrew the Shah dynasty in 1846, one of his first actions was to make Chitwan a private hunting reserve. The following century saw some truly hideous **hunts** – a visiting King George V, during an eleven-day shoot in 1911, killed 39 tigers and 18 rhinos.

Still, the Ranas' patronage afforded Chitwan a degree of protection, as did malaria. But in the early 1950s, the Ranas were thrown out, the monarchy was restored, and the new government launched its **malaria-control programme**. Settlers poured in and **poaching** went unpoliced – rhinos, whose horns were (and still are) valued for Chinese medicine and Yemeni knife handles, were especially hard-hit. By 1960, the human population of the valley had trebled to one hundred thousand, and the number of rhinos had plummeted from one thousand to two hundred. With the Asian one-horned rhino on the verge of extinction, Nepal emerged as an unlikely hero in one of conservation's finest hours. In 1962, Chitwan was set aside as a **rhino sanctuary** (becoming Nepal's first national park in 1973) and, despite the endless hype about tigers, rhinos are Chitwan's biggest attraction and its greatest triumph.

Chitwan now boasts around 408 **rhinos** and the park authorities have felt confident enough to relocate some to Bardia National Park. A number were killed by poachers during the civil war, but now the soldiers are back at their posts in the park the problem has declined (though it has not been eradicated).

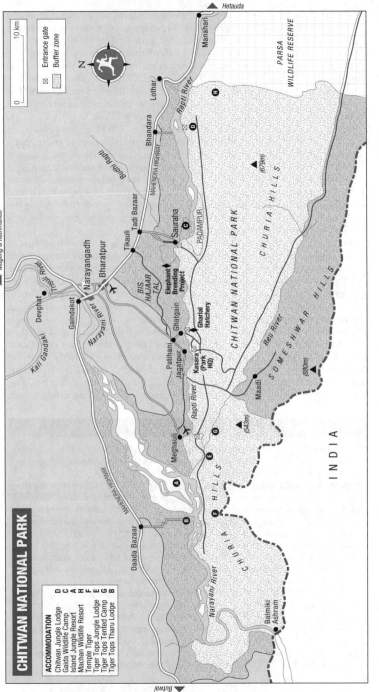

CHITWAN NATIONAL PARK

ACCOMMODATION

Chitwan Jungle Lodge	**D**
Gaida Wildlife Camp	**C**
Island Jungle Resort	**A**
Machan Wildlife Resort	**H**
Temple Tiger	**F**
Tiger Tops Jungle Lodge	**E**
Tiger Tops Tented Camp	**G**
Tiger Tops Tharu Lodge	**B**

There are thought to be around one hundred **tigers** in the park, though a census was being carried out at the time of research to get a more precise figure.

Chitwan also supports at least four hundred **gaur** (Indian bison) and provides a part-time home to as many as 45 wild **elephants**, who roam between here and India. Altogether, 56 mammalian species are found in the park, including sloth bear, leopard, langur and four kinds of deer. Chitwan is also Nepal's most important sanctuary for **birds**, with more than five hundred species recorded, and there are also two types of **crocodile** and over one hundred and fifty types of **butterfly**. (For more detail on Terai wildlife, see p.455.)

But Chitwan's seesaw battle for survival continues. While its forest ecosystem is healthy at the moment, **pollution** from upstream industries is endangering the rivers flowing into it: gangetic dolphins have disappeared from the Narayani, and gharial crocodiles hang on only thanks to human intervention (see p.285). With well over three hundred thousand people now inhabiting the Chitwan Valley, human **population** growth represents an even graver danger in the long term. **Tourism** has picked up again, after dropping off considerably during the civil war – the key issue will be to ensure the development this results in is handled in a sensitive, sustainable manner.

The key to safeguarding Chitwan, everyone agrees, is to win the support of local people, and there's some indication that this is beginning to happen. Some local groups run awareness-raising programmes, particularly targeting children, but there has been little government action in this regard. Another pressing problem for the local area – and the country as a whole – is a lack of investment in infrastructure, notably roads.

Communities living in the 750 square kilometres around the park receive some state financial support, and compensation is paid for damage caused by wild animals (safety has improved but one or two people are still killed each year). The **National Trust for Nature Conservation** (formerly the King Mahendra Trust; Ⓦ www.ntnc.org.np), funded by several international agencies, is active in general community development efforts such as building schools, health posts, water taps and appropriate technology facilities, as well

Park people

A procession of bicycle-toting locals crossing the Rapti at dusk, wading or being ferried across the river before disappearing into the trees of the national park on the far side, was once a familiar Sauraha scene.

In the late 1990s, over twenty thousand people lived within the park boundaries, mainly in **Padampur**, the area immediately opposite Sauraha. Inevitably, villagers were forced to compete with the park's animal population for forest resources and the ever-increasing number of wild animals would regularly raid farmers' crops, causing widespread damage and even deaths. The situation became increasingly unsustainable, and the government finally decided to **relocate** Padampur's villagers from the park itself to Saguntole, around 10km north of the national park, which extends from Bis Hajaar Tal towards the hills of the Mahabharat Lekh. This programme – completed by the mid-2000s – has left Chitwan itself free of human settlement.

This has inevitably raised troubling issues. Foremost is that people have been forced to leave their homes to make way for animals and the tourists that come to see them. A great deal of knowledge, and the cultural beliefs that go with it, has been, if not lost, then undoubtedly threatened. There are concerns about water supply in Saguntole and allegations of corruption surround the villagers' compensation payments. The move could also accelerate the destruction of a vital wildlife corridor, one of the few that still connects the plains and the hills.

as in conservation education and training for guides and lodge-owners. They have also been instrumental in helping set up **community forests** (see p.286) around Chitwan and the prospect of collecting hefty entrance fees from these is turning local people into zealous guardians of the environment.

When to visit

Chitwan is by far the most popular of Nepal's national parks, although how busy it actually gets is heavily influenced by the **season**. October and November are relatively cool (though still pleasantly warm) but the most popular activities can get booked up, the tall grass makes sightings much rarer, and there's something depressing about your main confrontation with wildlife being another trained elephant topped by tourists. Tourist numbers tail off in December and January, but after the grass is cut (usually in late Jan), visitors flock in to take advantage of the easy sightings, particularly in March. From April onwards, the park gets almost unbearably hot – particularly in the steamy monsoon months of July, August and September – but at least you'll have the place to yourself.

Park practicalities

There are no formal **park entrances** to Chitwan, as the boundary is formed by the river. In **Sauraha**, daily park **entry permits** (Rs500) are purchased at the ranger's office (daily 6am–6pm) to the left of the visitor centre. You will need a separate permit for each day you wish to enter the park and there are no discounts for longer visits. Once you've got your permit, your guide will then take you across the river and into the national park by canoe or, in low water, by wading. From **Ghatgain**, you can get permits from the Kasara headquarters (daily 6am–6pm). There's no ranger's office at **Meghauli**; once across the river your guide will help you buy one from the guard post on the other side.

Permits are valid for one day only, but allow you free access to the **community forest** areas the following day as well. These lie outside the national park proper, but as they form part of the raft of activities offered in Sauraha, they're described below.

Guides

Guided activities such as jungle walks, elephant rides, canoe trips and Jeep safaris vie for your attention once you arrive in the vicinity of the park. In fact, for safety reasons (see box, p.282), visitors are not allowed to enter the park on foot without a certified **guide**. For the most part, Sauraha's guides are keen and personable, and some of them are among Nepal's finest. Most are well versed in what tourists want to know, while the best are more than capable of explaining the park's animals, birds, butterflies, trees, plants and indeed its entire ecosystem in competent English. Their knowledge of species (especially birds) can be encyclopedic.

Guides are **certified** by the National Trust for Nature Conservation as "senior", "junior" or "assistant", and should be able to show their credentials. However, this isn't a very good indicator of **experience**, because it only takes a year or so to reach senior status – the question you need to ask prospective guides is how many years they've been guiding in Chitwan. Unfortunately, leading tourists through a jungle full of two-ton horned animals is a hazardous occupation, and anyone with any sense gets out of it as soon as they can, so it may be hard to find someone with more than three or four years' experience.

Staying alive in the jungle

Lodge owners and guides often play down the risks associated with tracking wildlife, but **safety** is a serious issue in Chitwan, and rarely a year goes by without one or two fatalities in the park. There are no emergency medical facilities in or near the park – the closest hospital is in Bharatpur, a minimum two-hour evacuation when you add up all the stages, which means if there's major bleeding the patient is essentially out of luck.

The greatest danger comes from **rhinos**, who have a tendency to charge at anything they perceive to be a threat. If a rhino is about to charge it lowers its head and takes a step back; if it does, try to run in a zigzag path and throw off a piece of clothing (the rhino will stop to smell it), or hide behind – better yet, climb – the nearest big tree. **Sloth bears** can also be dangerous if surprised. Fortunately, there is little danger to visitors from **tigers**. If a bear or tiger charges, climb a small tree – so they can't climb it after you. Don't get anywhere near a mother with young ones of any of these species.

The best safety tip is to get an experienced **guide**, but even they can't guarantee invulnerability. Most guides are young and gung-ho, and in their eagerness to please will sometimes encourage tourists to venture too close to animals. No matter how competent, a guide can't know where all the animals are, nor, in an emergency, assist more than one person at a time. For this reason most reputable guides will limit **group size** to four clients.

Note that less experienced guides are also apt to speak less English. (If your guide yells *look*, that means "hide" in Nepali!)

To **find a guide**, ask other travellers if they've found someone they can recommend. Every lodge has its own in-house guides, or you could hire one through United Jungle Guide Service (☏056/580 034), a syndicate of freelancers; other services are just one-man outfits. The Bird Education Society (☏056/580 113, ✉besnepal@wlink.com.np), with its main office near the Elephant Breeding Centre and a smaller branch near Sauraha's Restaurant Chowk, can put you in touch with excellent, committed guides but, obviously enough, they tend to specialize in birds. Every Saturday they run free birdwatching tours (donation appreciated); contact them in advance to book a place. Freelance guides tend to have more experience, but there are some excellent in-house guides. Another reason to go with one of your lodge's guides is that it will probably be easier to put together a group, which lowers the per-person cost. Guide **fees** depend on the activity and, to some extent, on the experience of the guide, and are detailed in the relevant sections below.

Activities inside the park

Promises of "safari adventure" in Chitwan can be misleading. While the park's **wildlife** is astoundingly concentrated, the dense vegetation doesn't allow the easy sightings you get in the savannas of Africa (especially in autumn, when the grass is high). Many guides assume everyone wants to see only tigers and rhinos, but there are any number of birds and other animals to spot which the typical safari package may not cover, not to mention the many different ways to simply experience the luxuriant, teeming jungle: **elephant rides**, **Jeep tours**, **canoe trips** and **jungle walks** each give a different slant.

The following **activities** are most commonly done inside Chitwan National Park so you'll need to add the cost of an entry permit to the prices quoted. All activities can, and in most cases should, be arranged through your lodge, or via a guide service in Sauraha. Book the night before, or even earlier during the cut-throat months of October, November and March.

Jungle and bird walks

Walking is the best way to observe the park's prolific **birdlife**. The Chitwan region is an important stopover spot for migratory species in December and March, as well as being home to many year-round residents – look for parakeets, Indian rollers, paradise flycatchers, kingfishers, hornbills, cranes and literally hundreds of others. The Bird Education Society is an excellent source of local information.

Walking allows you to appreciate the smaller attractions of the jungle at your own pace: orchids, strangler figs, towering termite mounds or tiger scratchings. You are virtually guaranteed to see a **rhino**, and deer and monkeys are easy to spot, but tiger sightings are rare: maybe one or two a week.

The best **season** for walking is spring, when the grass is shorter, though at other times of year you can compensate by spending more time in the *sal* forest and riverine habitats. No matter when you go, carry lots of water. The **cost** for a morning's walk is Rs350–500 per person (depending on the guide's level of experience and the number of clients), and Rs700–1000 for a full day. An all-day walk doesn't necessarily increase your chances of seeing game – most of the rhinos hang out close to Sauraha – but it gets you further into the park where you aren't running into other parties every two minutes. In cool weather some guides lead all-day walks in the Churia Hills, where you may see gaur (Indian bison) as well as deer, monkeys and a huge number of bird species.

Jungle treks

To get well clear of the Sauraha crowds you need to walk for two or more days, overnighting en route outside the park – think of it as a **jungle trek**. Staying with the trekking analogy, there's a "teahouse" route in the park, plus any number of other possibilities if you stay in private homes. The Churia Hills are best for birds, while the teahouse route is excellent for animals. There's a fair chance of seeing bears in the Maadi Valley.

The teahouse route follows the forest road from **Sauraha to Kasara** and on **to Meghauli**, or vice versa. It takes two days of roughly equal length, or you could just do one half or the other. The Sauraha–Kasara leg is more commonly trekked, and is also the route taken by Jeep tours out of Sauraha. There are of course no teahouses inside the park, but you can spend nights at Meghauli and Ghatgain (see p.276 & p.277). It's also possible to carry on trekking for a further two days (you could also start from Meghauli), overnighting at **Maadi**, in a beautiful valley just inside the park's southern boundary and then returning to Sauraha. This allows you to get to less-visited parts of the park's interior, such as Tamar Tal, which is excellent for birdwatching. You can return to Sauraha by local bus or arrange to have a Jeep take you back. Go with a guide who's done this trek before – most haven't. The **cost** of a jungle trek is simply the guide's daily rate (Rs500–1000), plus his food and lodging.

Jungle trek itineraries are limited by the fact that **camping** is not allowed inside the park (except at the luxury lodges). The next-best thing to camping in the park is to spend a night in an observation tower in one of the community forests (see p.286).

Elephant rides

In terms of cost per hour, a Jeep's a better deal, but how often do you get to **ride an elephant**? The pachyderm's stately gait takes you back to a time, as recently as the early 1950s, when this was the way foreign delegations entered Nepal. The *phanit* (driver) sits astride the animal's neck, giving it commands with his toes, periodically walloping its huge skull, and attentively fending branches out of passengers' way. An elephant is the safest way to get around in the grasslands – especially in summer and autumn, when the grass towers eight metres high – and it's the best way to observe **rhinos** and possibly wild boar or sloth bear without scaring them off, since the elephant's scent masks your own.

Only elephants owned by the National Park (and those belonging to the luxury lodges and tented camps inside Chitwan) are allowed in the park itself. Just a handful of rideable animals are kept at Sauraha, with many others on patrol duty. National Park-owned elephants are also kept near Ghatgain and Meghauli and, as fewer people stay at these locations, it is easier to organise elephant rides in the park from here.

Fortunately there are many more elephants owned privately or by lodges, and they can be used for rides in the **community forests** (see p.286); bear in mind though that there's a fair bit of road plodding before you get into the trees. The chance of seeing rhino and deer is at least as good as in the areas of the park that government elephants reach, but other wildlife is usually more scarce. Rides in the community forests cost the same as those in the park (Rs1000 per person) but last up to twice as long (around two hours). Safaris run in the early morning, or late afternoon.

One activity not to be missed is **elephant bathtime**: everyday between around 11am and noon, many of Sauraha's elephants are taken down to the Rapti River for a good scrub down – and the best part is that tourists can join in this magical experience. There is currently no charge for this, though there is some talk of levying a small fee in the future. Elephant bathtime is great fun, and very popular, but do take care as these huge animals can inadvertently hurt you.

Over the Christmas and new year period, Sauraha stages an **Elephant Festival**, with elephant races and football matches which are free to watch. Note that elephants don't work on major holidays, such as the eighth and ninth days of Dasain, and Lakshmi Puja.

Canoe trips

Floating down either of the Sauraha area's two rivers in a dugout **canoe** gives you your best shot at seeing **mugger crocodiles** (which, unlike the pointier-snouted gharials, prefer such marshy areas), and is also a relaxing way to watch birds and look for occasional wildlife on the shore. It's best done in winter, when the water is cool and the muggers sun themselves on the gravel banks; ruddy shelducks may be seen in profusion at this time, too. In hot weather, the outing is less rewarding, though you'll be assured of plenty of birds.

The standard itinerary is to depart from near the Baghmara Community Forest and float down the **Budhi Rapti** (Old Rapti) River to the Elephant Breeding Project (see p.287), then walk or catch a Jeep back to your lodging. The trip isn't actually within the park itself, but a park permit is required. The time spent on the water is relatively brief, and if you're not in the first couple of canoes that morning or afternoon you may not see much. Somewhat longer trips on the main **Rapti River** are more worthwhile, though there's a tendency to pack too many people into one boat.

Canoe trips **cost** from Rs500 per person per hour. You can often return either through the park or outside the park via the Elephant Breeding Centre.

Jeep rides

Hiring a **Jeep** (or more often a battered army surplus vehicle) for a half-day gives you the chance to get deep into the jungle, but it is relatively disruptive, and will set you back around Rs4000 for a four-seater. If you can't get a group together, sign up for a half-day **Jeep tour** (Rs1000, including a guide), which can be pretty cramped as eight or nine people can be packed in. The **best months** are from February to April, after the grass has been cut and the new shoots attract the deer.

For big game, you're limited to what you can see through the dusty wake of the Jeeps in the midmorning or afternoon, which pretty much means **deer**, though **rhinos** can often be seen too. The standard Jeep tour includes a stop at **Lami Tal** (Long Lake), which should be a prime spot for watching **birds** and **mugger crocodiles**, but things get pretty sleepy in the heat of the day. The tour continues to the gharial crocodile breeding project and Kasara Durbar.

Kasara and the gharial crocodile breeding project

Chitwan National Park's headquarters lie at **Kasara**, about 15km west of Sauraha. Jeep tours generally pass through, taking in the crocodile breeding project, but it's not somewhere you'd go out of your way to visit.

Overlooking a small army base, **Kasara Durbar** was constructed in 1939 as a royal hunting lodge, and now serves as the park's administrative headquarters. There is a meagre **museum** (daily 9am–6pm; free), with a collection of skulls and school project-like displays. Baby rhinos, orphaned by the work of poachers, can sometimes be seen roaming freely and begging for food near here pending relocation.

A well-used signposted track leads about 300m west from Kasara Durbar through light forest to the **gharial crocodile breeding project** (9am–6pm; Rs100), which is Kasara's only real attraction, (see box below). Nearby, an aggressive, orphaned (now adult), tiger is kept in a painfully cramped wooden cage.

Activities outside the park

Large patches of jungle still exist outside the park in Chitwan's heavily populated buffer zone, albeit in a less pristine state. The areas designated as **community forests** were originally conceived to reduce the need for residents of this critical strip to go into the park to gather wood, thatch and other resources, but they're now nearly as rich in flora and fauna as Chitwan itself.

Gharials

The longest of the world's crocodiles – adults can grow to more than seven metres from nose to tail – the **gharial** is an awesome fishing machine. Its slender, broom-like snout, which bristles with a fine mesh of teeth, snaps shut on its prey like a spring-loaded trap. Unfortunately, its eggs are regarded as a delicacy, and males are hunted for their bulb-like snouts which are believed to have medicinal powers.

In the mid-1970s, there were only 1300 gharials left. Chitwan's project was set up in 1977 to incubate eggs under controlled conditions, thus upping the survival rate – previously only one percent in the wild – to as high as 75 percent. The majority of hatchlings are released into the wild after three years, when they reach 1.2m in length; more than five hundred have been released so far into the Narayani, Koshi, Karnali and Babai rivers. Having been given this head start, however, the hatchlings must then survive a growing list of dangers, which now include not only hunters but also untreated effluents from upstream industries and a scarcity of food caused by the lack of fish ladders on a dam downstream in India. Counts indicate that captive-raised gharials now outnumber wild ones on the Narayani, which suggests that without constant artificial augmentation of their numbers they would soon become extinct. A few turtles can also be seen at the breeding centre.

Two forests, Baghmara and Kumroj on the outskirts of Sauraha, offer alternatives to entering the park itself, and the **elephant rides**, particularly, are often no less rewarding.

Another community forest, the **Bis Hajaar Tal** wetland area, is one of the best areas – inside or outside the park – for **birdwatching**, though the growth of water hyacinth in the area has reduced numbers. There are plenty of animals, but it's one of the few areas of jungle that can be visited independently with relative safety – though, as always, you'll probably get more out of it in the company of a good guide.

The community forests

Closest to Sauraha, **Baghmara Community Forest** is a good place to see rhinos and birds; you can also combine your visit with a trip to Bis Hajaar Tal, which it borders, or the Elephant Breeding Project, just to the south. Its main entrance is 1km west of Sauraha. **Kumroj Community Forest** (also written as Kumrose), 2km east of Sauraha, is further away from most lodges and you'd probably only visit it on an elephant ride, though the route from Sauraha is partially forested.

Both Baghmara and Kumroj have concrete *machaan* (observation towers) where you can **spend the night** – good for nocturnal viewing if the moon is out. Guides will charge around Rs1000–1500 for an overnight trip. As in the park, a guide is required to enter either of the community forests on foot.

Asian elephants

In Nepal and throughout southern Asia, **elephants** have been used as ceremonial transportation and beasts of burden for thousands of years, earning them a cherished place in the culture – witness the popularity of elephant-headed Ganesh, the darling of the Hindu pantheon. Thanks to this symbiosis with man, Asian elephants (unlike their African cousins) survive mainly as a domesticated species, even as their wild habitat has all but vanished.

With brains four times the size of humans', elephants are reckoned to be as **intelligent** as dolphins. What we see as a herd is in fact a complex social structure, consisting of bonded pairs and a fluid hierarchy. In the wild, **herds** typically consist of fifteen to thirty females and one old bull, and are usually led by a senior female; other bulls live singly or in bachelor herds. Though they appear docile, elephants have strongly individual personalities and moods. They can learn dozens of commands, but they won't obey just anyone; as any handler will tell you, you can't make an elephant do what it doesn't want to do. That they submit to such apparently cruel head-thumping by drivers seems to have more to do with thick skulls than obedience.

Asian elephants are smaller than those of the African species, but still formidable. A bull can grow up to three metres high and weigh four tons, although larger individuals are known to exist. An average day's intake is 200 litres of water and 225kg of fodder – and if you think that's impressive, wait till you see it come back out again. All that eating wears down teeth fast: an average elephant goes through six sets in its lifetime, each more durable than the last. The trunk is controlled by an estimated forty thousand muscles, enabling its owner to eat, drink, cuddle and even manipulate simple tools (such as a stick for scratching). Though up to 2.5cm thick, an elephant's skin is still very sensitive, and it will often take mud or dust baths to protect against insects. Life expectancy is about 75 years and, much the same as with humans, an elephant's working life can be expected to run from its mid-teens to its mid-fifties; training begins at about age five.

The **Bis Hajaar Tal** (Twenty Thousand Lakes) area is Nepal's second-biggest natural wetland, and provides an important corridor for animals migrating between the Terai and the hills. The name refers to a maze of marshy oxbow lakes, many of them already filled in, well-hidden among mature *sal* trees. The area teems with birds, including storks, kingfishers, eagles and the huge Lesser Adjutant. The forest starts just west of Baghmara and the Elephant Breeding Project and reaches its marshy climax about 5km northwest of there. To explore this area, have a guide lead you in on foot from the breeding project, and allow a full day.

National Park (single day) **entry tickets** are valid for two days in the community forests.

The hattisar (elephant stables) and Elephant Breeding Project

The majority of Chitwan's elephant workforce is housed at the government **hattisar** (elephant stables), on the northwestern edge of Sauraha. The best time to visit is mid-afternoon, when the elephants are sure to be around for feeding time.

Sauraha lodges offer Jeep tours out to the **Elephant Breeding Project** (Rs50), 4km west of the village, where baby elephants are the main attraction. Just inside the project is a small room with photos and nuggets of information about elephants, including verbal commands: for example *mail* means "stand-up", while *baith* means "sit down".

Until the mid-1970s, Nepal's Parks Department commonly bought its elephants from India, where they were captured in the wild and trained in captivity. As the wild population shrank, this procedure became increasingly unaffordable, so the government began breeding and training its own elephants, first at the old *hattisar* and then, in 1988, establishing this separate facility, where elephants can mate in peace and mothers and babies can receive special attention. At any given time the **project** is home to a couple of breeding bulls, ten to fifteen cows, and usually a number of calves. The young elephants need to spend as much time as possible with their mothers to become socialized into elephant society, so it's best to arrive here in early morning or late afternoon – in the middle of the day they're usually off on educational trips to the river and the jungle.

You can visit the project independently either on foot or bicycle, though you have to cross the Budhi Rapti just before you get there; it's fordable for most of the year, and a **boatman** will ferry you across in high water. You're better off coming with a guide, though, who'll be able to explain the goings-on and then take you on to Bis Hajaar Tal.

Narayangadh and around

It's hard to travel far in Nepal without passing through **NARAYANGADH**: the Mugling–Narayangadh highway has made it the gateway to the Terai and the country's busiest crossroads. What was once a far-flung intersection is now a kilometre-long strip of diesel and *daal bhaat* (and a hotbed of prostitution). Its sister city, **BHARATPUR**, continues to the east without a visible break, though as the headquarters of Chitwan District, Bharatpur is tangibly more upmarket, and fast becoming an educational and medical hub: it boasts a university and two medical colleges, as well as an airstrip. Unflattering as all that may sound, you may have occasion to pause in the area, and the side trip to the sacred confluence of **Devghat**, 5km upstream of Narayangadh, makes for a refreshingly cultural outing from Chitwan.

Buses serving the northward Mugling Highway (to and from Pokhara, Gorkha and Devghat) have their own bus park at the north end of Narayangadh. All other express buses serving the Mahendra Highway stop at the fast-food parade just east of Pulchowk (the intersection of the Mugling and Mahendra highways). There are two additional bus parks for local services: buses and minibuses to Tadi Bazaar (for Sauraha) and eastern Chitwan District start from Sahid Chowk, about 500m east of Pulchowk; minibuses to Meghauli and Jagatpur start from just north of Sahid Chowk – walk north for 50m, take the first right down a small lane, and it's on the left after 200m. Flights for Kathmandu (4 daily; $86) leave from Bharatpur's **airstrip**, just south of the Mahendra Highway.

Rikshaws should take you anywhere within Narayangadh and Bharatpur for Rs50 or less.

Devghat

DEVGHAT (or Deoghat), 5km northwest of Narayangadh, is many people's idea of a great place to die. An astonishingly tranquil spot, it stands where the wooded hills meet the shimmering plains, and the Trisuli and the Kali Gandaki **rivers** merge to form the Narayani, one of the major tributaries of the Ganga (Ganges). Some say Sita, heroine of the Ramayana, died here. The ashes of King Mahendra were sprinkled at this sacred *tribeni* (a confluence of three rivers: wherever two rivers meet, a third, spiritual one is believed to join them), and scores of *sunyasan*, those who have renounced the world, patiently live out their last days here hoping to achieve an equally auspicious death and rebirth. Many retire to Devghat to avoid being a burden to their children, to escape ungrateful offspring, or because they have no children to look after them in their old age and perform the necessary rites when they die. *Pujari* (priests) also practise here and often take in young candidates for the priesthood as resident students. There were suggestions that a hydroelectric project could be built just downstream of the confluence, but fortunately these plans appear to have fallen by the wayside.

Buses shuttle every couple of hours (30min) between Narayangadh and Devghat, but it's quite pleasant to **walk**. Head north from the Pokhara bus park along the main highway to Mugling and after 1km turn left on a paved road under an arch – Devghat is at the end of the road, about 5km through forest. Either way, you come to the Trisuli and cross it by a dramatic suspension footbridge, which was immortalized in the classic Nepali film *Kanchhi*, when the heartbroken lover attempted suicide from it. From the far side of the bridge, bear left up and into the village. You can also cross the river further downstream by **dugout canoe** – for the return trip, the ferryman, if he thinks he can be spared from his duties, might even consent to take you all the way back to Narayangadh for a suitable fee.

Dozens of small shrines lie dotted around the village, but you come here more for the **atmosphere** than the sights. Vaishnavas (followers of Vishnu) congregate at Devghat's largest and newest temple, the central *shikra*-style **Harihar Mandir**, founded in 1998 by the famed guru Shaktya Prakash Ananda of Haridwar. Shaivas (followers of Shiva) dominate the area overlooking the confluence at the western edge of the village.

To get to the confluence, turn left at a prominent *chautaara* at the top of the path leading through the village: **Galeshwar Ashram**, on your right as you walk down the steps, and **Aghori Ashram**, further downhill on the right, are named after two recently deceased holy men. One of them, the one-armed Aghori Baba, was a follower of the outrageous Aghori tradition (see p.155) and was often referred to as the "Crazy Baba", claiming to have cut off his own arm after being instructed to do so in a dream. Various paths lead upstream of the confluence, eventually arriving at **Sita Gupha**, a sacred cave that is closed except on Makar Sankranti, and **Chakrabarti Mandir**, a shady temple area housing a famous *shaligram* that locals say is growing.

A huge **pilgrimage** is held at Devghat on Makar Sankranti (Jan 14 or 15), while Shiva Raatri, falling on the new moon of February–March, brings many Indian devotees. At other times, sadhus and pilgrims do *puja* at the point where the rivers meet – cremations are also held here – and old-timers meditate outside their huts in the sun. Be sensitive to the residents, and don't disturb them or touch anything that might be holy: many are orthodox Baahuns and your touch is considered polluting.

Practicalities

The last bus back to Narayangadh leaves Devghat around 6pm. If you get stuck, a couple of teahouses near the Trisuli bridge on the Devghat side can provide really bare-bones lodging, but frankly, Devghat is the sort of place that visitors should leave in peace after the sun goes down and most of its **accommodation** is fairly crummy and often seedy.

For something more salubrious, head for one of the resort-style hotels in Bharatpur, across the bridge to one of a couple of riverside guesthouses on the more peaceful west bank of the Narayani, or to one of the more upscale places on the outskirts of town. **Food**, plentiful but not wildly exciting, can be found all around Pulchowk. Standing out slightly from the greasy spoons and whisky shacks are *Royal Rest House's* restaurant and *Kitchen Café*, towards the bridge in Pulchowk. A considerable step up in class is the *Central Palms Hotel* restaurant, which has a range of international dishes, including particularly good Indian meals.

▲ Holy confluence at Devghat

Central Palms Hotel New Rd, Pulchowk, Narayangadh ☏ 056/526 070. An eye-catching white circular construction, with surprisingly swish, contemporary en suites, pool, well-equipped gym and one of the best restaurants in town. ❼

Hotel Global Bharatpur ☏ 056/525 514. *Hotel Global* has large, cared-for grounds and comfortable, but a little worn, en suites, the best of which are in bungalows and boast terraces and tubs. ❻–❽

Island Jungle Resort Bharatpur ☏ 056/520 730. The huge *sal* trees and lush gardens do give a jungle-like feel, if you block out the road noise. The decent – though a bit gloomy – rooms are arranged in bungalows and there's a pool. ❺

Royal Rest House Pulchowk, Narayangadh ☏ 056/521 442. A reasonable choice above a restaurant: rooms with private facilities – including tubs – are clean enough, though some lack natural light, so ask to see a few. ❸–❹

Hotel Satanchuli Behind the Pokhara bus park, Narayangadh ☏ 056/521 151. The best-situated budget option, especially for those visiting Devghat, with clean and simple rooms with private baths. ❷

Uncle's Lodge West of Narayani bridge, Narayangadh ☏ 056/501 121. Head to this riverside lodge for the warmest welcome in town. The economical rooms have hot showers, there's a family atmosphere, and "Uncle" himself (Narenda Regmi) offers plenty of help and advice. ❷

Lumbini Terai

Hordes of travellers hurry through this ancient part of the Terai, west of Chitwan, but few take the time to look around. It's best known, unfairly, for **Sonauli**, the main tourist border crossing between Nepal and India. Yet only 20km away is one of Nepal's premier destinations, **Lumbini**: birthplace of the Buddha and the site of ruins going back almost three thousand years.

Two highways – the Siddhartha and the Mahendra – connect the region with Pokhara and the rest of the Terai, and buses between Sonauli and Kathmandu are frequent. The journey to Lumbini takes a little extra effort, as you will need to take a connecting bus from Bhairahawa/Sonauli, but is well worth it.

Butwal to Sonauli

Westwards from Narayangadh, the Mahendra Highway runs across a washboard of cultivated fields, briefly climbs over a jungle-cloaked spur of the Churia Hills, and passes long stretches of heavily used but seemingly healthy forest. It's a relatively painless 110km to Butwal.

Butwal

Crouching uninvitingly at the point where the Tinau river spills out onto the plains, **BUTWAL** is an ugly modern town of convenience. It's the hub of the Lumbini administrative zone: north lies Pokhara; south is Sonauli and the Indian border; and to the west, the Mahendra Highway barrels along towards Nepalgunj and Nepal's western border.

Placed at the start of an important trade route to Tibet as well as the pilgrim trail to Muktinath, the **tax post** at Butwal was for centuries a tidy little earner for Palpa (Tansen) and then Kathmandu. Much later, it came to be a staging post for Gurkha soldiers. In the early nineteenth century, Nepal and the East India Company fell into a dispute over the territory around Butwal. In the subsequent two-year **war with Britain** (see p.422), Nepal scored several improbable early victories but was eventually forced to surrender. Under the resulting treaty, the Terai territories from Butwal west were ceded to the British (Nepal struck a deal to get the disputed land around Butwal back the same year).

Many **buses** originate or terminate at this busy crossroads – see p.313 for routes and frequencies. Express services are based at the bus park, to the south of town on the main Sonauli road (the Siddhartha Highway), but some buses stop off at "Traphik Chowk", a busy crossroads 500m north on the same highway. The bus park has a reputation for petty theft so keep an eye on your belongings. Local buses use the old bus park, four blocks to the west of Traphik Chowk.

Practicalities

Butwal has some ghastly highway-side dives, but there are a few fairly professional **hotels**. Bhairahawa (see below), however, is a much better place to stay. If rupees are really tight, *Hotel Gandaki* (℡071/540 928; ❶), one block west of Traphik Chowk, is bleak, but just about habitable for a night. A further block west is *Hotel Green Land* (℡071/543 411; ❹–❺), which offers solid mid-range rooms with attached baths and a certain style. Just south of the local bus park, *Hotel Sindoor* (℡071/540 381, ✉hsindoor@nec.com.np; ❸–❺) is friendly, efficient and one of the most peaceful options in town, though the more expensive air-conditioned rooms are overpriced.

Hotel Green Land has a decent **restaurant**, and there are a few *bhojanalaya* around Traphik Chowk. *Nanglo West*, inconveniently located around 2km north of *Hotel Sindoor*, is worth a visit for its unusual Nepali/Newari food.

Bhairahawa (Siddhartha Nagar)

Half an hour south by bus, **BHAIRAHAWA** (or **SIDDHARTHA NAGAR**) is less frenetic than Butwal, and a better place to stay than Sonauli. Its bazaar **supports** a sizeable minority of Muslim traders and, like so many border towns, exists primarily to peddle imported goods to acquisitive Indians.

Bhairahawa's three main streets form an upright triangle: the eastern side is the Siddhartha Highway (which continues north to Butwal and south to the Indian border), Bank Road runs along the south, and Narayanpath along the west. *Hotel Yeti* stands on a roundabout at the southeastern apex of the triangle and is a handy landmark; rikshaws and shared Jeeps bound for Sonauli wait here. The road to Lumbini breaks west from the highway about 1km north of the *Hotel Yeti*, just north of the triangle's northern apex.

Practicalities

Bhairahawa has some decent **accommodation** options. *Hotel Yeti* (℡071/520 551, ✉hotelyeti@ntc.net.np; ❻–❼), on the corner of the border highway and Bank Road, is a bit of a monolith, but staff are professional and the en suites (a/c or non a/c) in muted colours are much the best in town. A portrait of Queen Elizabeth II greets you in the lobby of *Hotel Glasgow* (℡071/523 737; ❹–❺), on Bank Road, a well-run mid-range hotel, offering homely en-suites with TVs and writing desks. *Hotel Mt Everest* (℡071/520 410; ❷–❹), also on Bank Road, is overpriced, but still the pick of the budget lodges with clean but cramped standard rooms and larger ones with a/c and TV: both are noisy, however, and have squat toilets.

Pawan Misthan Bhandar, on Main Road, just south of Bank Road, is a bustling local joint serving inexpensive South Indian **food** like *dosas* and all manner of fried, sticky and sugary delights – there's no real menu and you may have to share a table, but that's all part of the fun. Nearby *New Kasturi* is a virtual re-run. The restaurants at hotels *Yeti* and *Glasgow* offer more variety.

Moving on

The **bus park**, for all express services, lies 500m south of *Hotel Yeti* on the main Siddhartha Highway, but some local buses still drop off and pick up in town, at the main crossroads by *Hotel Yeti*. Buses (and minibuses and Jeeps) to Kathmandu leave every ten to thirty minutes until about 8pm; departures to Pokhara are almost as frequent.

Cars and **Jeeps** can be rented by the day (Rs3000–5000) or for the journey to Lumbini (Rs600–700 one way) or Tilaurakot (about Rs2500 return) – arrange through the better hotels or any travel agent in the town centre.

Travel agents can also book internal **flights** from Bhairahawa airport (also known as Gautam Buddha airport), 10km north of town, to Kathmandu (5 daily; $120).

Sonauli (Belahiya) and the border

The little border scrum of **SONAULI** (Soo-*no*-li; technically the Nepali side is known as **BELAHIYA**) is the most popular border crossing between Nepal and India, and while it's not quite as awful as Raxaul/Birgunj (see p.320), there's no need to linger: all the main tourist facilities and transport connections are in Bhairahawa, 5km north. There is a small **tourist office** right on the Nepali side of the border (daily except Sat, 10am–5pm).

Indian currency is readily accepted in Sonauli, and sometimes in Bhairahawa, but not beyond. There are several government-approved **moneychangers**, all keeping long hours, at the border, and numerous banks in Bhairahawa. If changing Nepali into Indian rupees, make sure the moneychanger hasn't offloaded torn notes on you, which are hard to pass in India.

The border

The **border** is officially open round the clock, but you may have trouble tracking down the immigration officers early in the morning or at night. Nepali visas are available on the border but Indian visas have to be obtained in advance (see p.145). Figure on a total of half an hour to get through Nepali and Indian border formalities unless you're crossing with a vehicle; appalling traffic jams on the Nepali side mean this can take hours. Nepal is fifteen minutes ahead of India.

Leaving Nepal is a simple enough matter of getting off whatever transport brought you here from Bhairahawa and walking across the border. South of Indian immigration, an easy 200m walk from the Nepali side, public and private buses depart almost hourly to Gorakhpur (3hr) between about 5am and 11am. There's generally a daily tourist bus to Varanasi (10–12hr), as well as fairly regular public buses. There are also buses to Lucknow (12hr). From Gorakhpur you can make broad-gauge **train** connections throughout India. It also has an airport.

If you're **entering Nepal**, make straight for Bhairahawa (see p.291), the starting point for all buses to elsewhere in the country. Local buses, microbuses and Jeeps make the ten-minute journey almost continuously (around Rs10 in either currency); a rikshaw costs about Rs40. Many buses continue to Butwal (around Rs40). See the Bhairahawa section for more advice on onward travel – and note that there are no air-conditioned tourist buses through to Kathmandu, whatever agents in Gorakhpur may say. A smart alternative is to continue on past Bhairahawa to nearby Lumbini (see below): Sonauli's one-man-and-a-desk "travel agencies" can arrange Jeeps to Lumbini (Rs600–700 one-way) and other destinations. If you're coming from Varanasi, set off as early as possible if you want to carry on into Nepal the same day.

Lumbini

After I am no more, Ananda! Men of belief will visit with faithful curiosity and devotion to the four places – where I was born … attained enlightenment…gave the first sermons … and passed into Nirvana.

The Buddha (c.543–463 BC)

For the world's one billion Buddhists, **LUMBINI**, 22km west of Bhairahawa, is where it all began. The **Buddha's birthplace** is arguably the single most important historical site in the country – not only the source of one of the world's great religions but also the centre of Nepal's most significant **archeological finds**, dating from the third century BC. With only modest ruins but powerful associations, it's the kind of place you could whizz round in two hours or rest in for days, soaking up the peaceful atmosphere of the wooded park and its scattering of monasteries, founded by countries from all over the Buddhist world.

The Buddha has long been a prophet without much honour in his own country, however, and the area around Lumbini is now predominantly Muslim. The main local **festival** is a Hindu one, commemorating the Buddha as the ninth incarnation of Vishnu – it's held on the full moon of the Nepali month of Baisaakh (April–May). Celebrations of **Buddha Jayanti** (the Buddha's birthday) are comparatively meagre because, as the local monks will tell you with visible disgust, Buddhists from the high country think Lumbini is too hot in May.

Pilgrims used to stick to the more developed Indian sites of Bodh Gaya, Sarnath and Kushinagar, but in the 1970s the government, with the backing of the United Nations, authorized a hugely ambitious **master plan** for a **religious park** consisting of monasteries, cultural facilities, gardens, fountains and a tourist village. After a glacially slow start, the plan is finally starting to take shape under the direction of (or perhaps in spite of) the Lumbini Development Trust (w www.lumbinitrust.org). Roads enter the master-plan area from several directions, with the **main entrance gate** at the southeastern edge. A road leads from there to the **Sacred Garden**, which contains all the archeological treasures associated with the Buddha's birth. To the north of the Sacred Garden, two "**monastic zones**" are filled by an international array of temples, overlooked by the grand Shanti Stupa, or Peace Pagoda. Alongside, a miniature wetland reserve has been established for the endangered sarus crane, and 600,000 trees have been planted throughout the site, attracting many birds and animals.

Of course there is ample cause for scepticism, not least when it comes to the nakedly commercial aspirations of the Nepali government – transforming the **airport** at Bhairahawa into an international terminal has even been mooted – yet if the remaining plans come off, Lumbini could grow to be quite a cosmopolitan religious site. Japanese tour groups have already added Lumbini to their whirlwind tours of the Buddhist holy places.

Lumbini is much more enjoyable in early morning and late afternoon, when it's cool and peaceful. If you only see it in the heat of the day, with tour groups and school parties trooping around and the sounds of construction activity

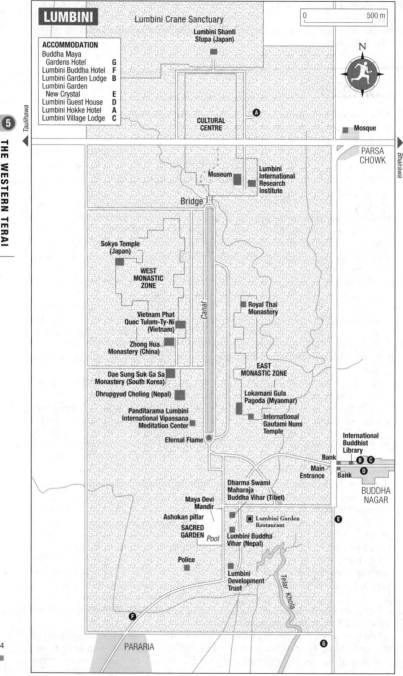

LUMBINI

Lumbini Crane Sanctuary

Lumbini Shanti
Stupa (Japan)

0   500 m

N

ACCOMMODATION
Buddha Maya
  Gardens Hotel   G
Lumbini Buddha Hotel   F
Lumbini Garden Lodge   B
Lumbini Garden
  New Crystal   E
Lumbini Guest House   D
Lumbini Hokke Hotel   A
Lumbini Village Lodge   C

CULTURAL
CENTRE

Mosque

PARSA
CHOWK

Museum

Lumbini
International
Research
Institute

Bridge

Sokyo Temple
(Japan)

WEST
MONASTIC
ZONE

Canal

Royal Thai
Monastery

Vietnam Phat
Quoc Tulam-Ty-Ni
(Vietnam)

Zhong Hua
Monastery (China)

EAST
MONASTIC
ZONE

Dae Sung Suk Ga Sa
Monastery (South Korea)

Dhrupgyud Choling (Nepal)

Lokamani Gula
Pagoda (Myanmar)

Panditarama Lumbini
International Vipassana
Meditation Center

International
Gautami Nuns
Temple

Eternal Flame

International
Buddhist
Library

Bank

Main
Entrance

Bank

BUDDHA
NAGAR

Dharma Swami
Maharaja
Buddha Vihar (Tibet)

Maya Devi
Mandir

Ashokan pillar

SACRED
GARDEN   Pool

Lumbini Garden
Restaurant

Lumbini Buddha
Vihar (Nepal)

Police

Lumbini
Development
Trust

Telar Khola

PARARIA

Indian Border

Taulihawa

Bhairawa

emanating from the temples, you'll probably be disappointed. For this reason it's highly recommended to stay overnight.

Getting there

If you're travelling between Kathmandu and India, it's easy to stop in Lumbini along the way: there are a handful of day buses (9–11hr) to and from Kathmandu and a single night bus. A tourist bus to the capital departs in the high season at 7am. Coming from anywhere other than Kathmandu, first go to Bhairahawa or Sonauli, where you can pick up a **Jeep**. The fare should be Rs600–700 one-way, or Rs1000 for a return trip with an hour or two's waiting time. Consider having it take you first to Tilaurakot (see p.299), dropping you in Lumbini on the way back (about Rs1500).

Local buses (every 30min; 1hr) trundle between Bhairahawa's bus station (you can also pick it up from the start of the westbound road to Lumbini), and Pararia, the village immediately south of the master plan area, stopping at the main east gate and Buddha Nagar on its way round the park. The last bus from Bhairahawa leaves around 6pm; from Lumbini the final one departs about 5.30pm.

The Sacred Garden

The **Sacred Garden**, where the Buddha was reputedly born, was by all accounts a well-tended grove in his day. Consecrated soon after his death, at least one monastery was attached to it by the third century BC when Ashoka, the great North Indian emperor and Buddhist evangelist, made a well-documented pilgrimage to the spot. Ashoka's patronage established a thriving

---

The Buddha: a life

The year of the Buddha's **birth** is disputed – it was probably 543 BC – but it's generally accepted that it happened at **Lumbini** while his mother, Maya Devi, was on her way to her maternal home for the delivery. He was born Siddhartha Gautama ("he who has accomplished his aim"), the son of a king and a member of the Shakya clan, who ruled the central Terai from their capital at Tilaurakot (see p.299). Brought up in his father's palace, Prince Siddhartha was sheltered by his father from the evils of the world, until, at the age of 29, he encountered an old man, a sick man, a corpse and a hermit: old age, sickness and death were the end of life, he realized, and contemplation seemed the only way to understand the nature of suffering.

Siddhartha revolted against his former life of pleasure and fled the palace, leaving behind his wife, child and faithful servant – not to mention his horse, which another legend says promptly died of a broken heart. Passing through the east gate of the palace, he shaved his head and donned the yellow robe of an ascetic. He spent five years in this role before concluding that self-denial brought him no closer to the truth than self-indulgence. Under the famous *bodhi* tree of Bodh Gaya in India, he vowed to keep meditating until he attained **enlightenment**. This he did after 49 days, at which time Siddhartha became the Buddha, released from the cycle of birth and death. He made his way to Sarnath (near Varanasi in India) and preached his **first sermon**, setting in motion, Buddhists believe, *dharma*, the wheel of the truth. Although he is said to have returned to Kapilvastu to convert his family (and according to some stories he even put in an appearance in the Kathmandu Valley), the Buddha spent most of the rest of his life preaching in northern India. He **died** at the age of eighty in Kushinagar, about 100km southeast of Lumbini, saying "all things are subject to decay. Strive earnestly". For a fuller account of Buddhism, see Religion, p.435.

religious community, but by the time the intrepid Chinese traveller Hiuen Tsang visited in the seventh century it was limping, and must have died out after the tenth century.

The garden was lost for at least six hundred years, and its **rediscovery**, in 1896, solved one of the last great mysteries of the Orient. Europeans had been searching in earnest for the site since 1830, but it wasn't until 1893, when a Nepali officer on a hunting expedition claimed to have found a related Ashokan relic some miles to the west, that the first solid clue came to light. The race was on. Two main rivals, A. A. Führer of the Archeological Survey of India, and Austin Waddell, a British military doctor serving in Calcutta, each pursued various trails based on their interpretations of the writings of Hiuen Tsang and other early pilgrims to Lumbini. In the end, the site was found more by chance than by science. In 1896, Führer's Nepali escort, General Khadga Shamsher Jung Bahadur Rana, suggested they rendezvous in Pararia before proceeding to the intended dig site. While awaiting Führer's arrival, the general was led by locals to an ancient pillar near the village and had his peons begin excavating it. The pillar was already known to at least one British official in the area, who had investigated its visible inscriptions and dismissed them as "medieval scribblings", but no one had ever bothered to dig below the surface. When Führer saw the much older inscription revealed by General Rana's excavations, he immediately recognized the pillar as the one described by the early travellers, and claimed credit for the find in his reports. Although he was later stripped of his credentials for his falsifications, he continues to be known as the discoverer of Lumbini.

The Maya Devi Mandir and sculpture

Centrepiece of the Sacred Garden, the **Maya Devi Mandir** (roughly 10am–5pm, though times may vary; Rs50, camera Rs75) contains brickwork dating back to 300 BC, making it the oldest known structure in Nepal. A restoration project was completed in 2003, surrounding the original bricks by a simple building, which you can walk around if you remove your shoes.

Excavations done in the course of the restoration confirmed earlier speculation that the known Gupta period (fourth to sixth centuries AD) temple sat atop foundations from the earlier Kushana and Maurya periods. In fact, the lowest foundation seems to indicate a **pre-stupa structure** of a kind that existed at the time of the Buddha, suggesting that the site was venerated well before Ashoka's visit and adding further weight to Lumbini's claim as the Buddha's birthplace. Near the lowest level, archeologists also found a reddish-brown, 70cm-long stone that some believe is the "**marker stone**" Ashoka is reputed to have placed at the precise location of the Buddha's birth. In a sign of the times, it is now covered by a bullet-proof glass case.

The excavation and restoration of the Maya Devi Mandir has been something of a botched chapter in the annals of archeology. The project, launched in 1990, was originally conceived as a simple "renovation", which was supposed to mean trimming back a large **pipal tree** whose roots had been interfering with the temple for many years. But with little public consultation, the Japan Buddhist Federation, the organization leading the effort, unilaterally launched a full-scale excavation and cut down the tree, which had been regarded by many as a living link with the Buddha's day.

The temple derives its name from Maya Devi, the Buddha's mother. It houses a famous bas-relief **sculpture** (the so-called nativity scene) depicting her and the newborn Buddha in the Mathura style (from the fourth or fifth century AD). The sculpture's features are so worn, due to the flaky quality of the sedimentary stone used to make it, that archeologists at first dismissed it as

Hindu because locals were worshipping the image as the wish-fulfilling goddess Rumindei (believed to be a corruption of "Lumbini Devi").

The Ashokan pillar and other remains

West of the temple, the **Ashokan pillar** is the oldest monument in Nepal. It's not much to look at – it resembles a smokestack – but the inscription, recording Ashoka's visit in 249 BC, is the best available evidence the Buddha was born here. Split by lightning sometime before the seventh century, its two halves are held together by metal bands. Pillars were a sort of trademark of Ashoka, serving the dual purpose of spreading the faith and marking the boundaries of his empire: this one announces that the king granted Lumbini tax-free status in honour of the Buddha's birth. The carved capital to this pillar, which early pilgrims describe as being in the shape of a horse, has never been found; the weathered stone lying on the ground beside the pillar is the lotus- or bell-shaped "bracket" upon which it would have rested.

The square, cement-lined **pool** just south of the Ashokan pillar is supposed to be where Maya Devi bathed before giving birth to the Buddha. Heavily restored **brick foundations** of buildings and stupas around the site, dating from the second century BC to the tenth century AD, chart the rise and fall of Lumbini's early monastic community. The two mounds north and south of the garden aren't ancient, they are archeological debris removed during amateur excavations in the 1930s led by Field Marshal Kesar Shamsher Rana.

Around the master plan area

A walk northwards from the Sacred Garden soon hits the highlights of the slowly unfurling master plan. An elevated path passes through what's supposed to be a reflecting pool encircling the Sacred Garden, and beyond burns an **eternal flame**, a symbolic remembrance of the "Light of Asia".

From here you can follow the kilometre-long central canal past the East (Theravada) and West (Mahayana) **Monastic Zones**, where 41 plots have been set aside for temples and monasteries representing each of Buddhism's major sects and national styles of worship. Many have already been built, and some are quite impressive – the Burmese (Myanmar) **Lokamani Gula Pagoda**, done in the style of Rangoon's famous Shwedagon temple, the Chinese **Zhong Hua Monastery**, a sort of mini Forbidden City featuring a big Buddha statue, and the eye-catching white **Royal Thai Monastery** are highlights. There seems to be more than a bit of religious one-upmanship going on here, and the area may someday turn into a Buddhist Disneyland, but it's still interesting to see so many different manifestations of Buddhism assembled in one place. Several of the monasteries offer meditation sessions, courses and retreats, including – for serious students – the **Panditarama Lumbini International Vipassana Meditation Centre** (☎071/621 084, ⓦwww.panditarama-lumbini.info).

The canal ends at what is being billed as Lumbini's **Cultural Centre**, which at the time of writing was decidedly lacking in culture, or for that matter, any sign of life at all. The tubular buildings of the Japanese-built **Lumbini International Research Institute** and **museum** (daily except Tues 10am–5pm; Rs50, camera Rs75) with terracotta, religious manuscripts, coins and sculptures are in place, while the planned restaurants and shops remain stubbornly on paper. If you can find one – try asking at the research institute – it's well worth hooking up with one of the Lumbini Development Trust's archeologists, who sometimes freelance as guides.

North of the Cultural Centre, the white-and-gold **Lumbini Shanti Stupa** (Peace Pagoda) soars 41m over the parkland. The impressive monument was finally completed in November 2001 by Nippozan Myohoji, an endearing Japanese Buddhist organization that is also responsible for the Peace Pagoda in London's Battersea Park, as well as seventy other stupas around the world. Beyond, the **Lumbini Crane Sanctuary** (open 24hr, free) is one of the last refuges of the beautiful sarus crane, the world's tallest flying bird, and one of its most endangered. As many as ninety of Nepal's 200–300 sarus cranes reside here from time to time, along with storks, egrets and other arboreal birds. The Lumbini master plan area is itself something of a bird sanctuary, thanks to its wetlands and forests, with 165 species recorded.

Practicalities

Lumbini's **accommodation** is spread thinly over a wide area. The pleasant village of Buddha Nagar (or Mahilwar), strung along a side road near the main eastern gate, offers a cluster of simple guesthouses, while a number of luxury hotels have opened around the park. To really get close to the spirit of the area, stay in one of the **monasteries**: the Nepali (Theravada), Korean and Tibetan monasteries, among others, shelter pilgrims informally for a modest donation but are sorely lacking in things like bedding. You may be invited to join the monks (or nuns) for meals.

At the time of research, there were no **restaurants** around the Sacred Garden area – though the *Lumbini Garden Restaurant* may reopen in the future – but there are plenty of cheap eateries dotted around the entrances to the religious park. The guesthouses and hotels all have restaurants – easily the best (though suitably expensive) is the *Hokke's*, which serves outstanding Japanese food.

Nepal Credit and Commerce Bank and Siddhartha Development Bank stand opposite each other in Buddha Nagar, on the corner of the main road, and both have **foreign exchange** facilities.

Most hotels and lodges can organise **guided trips** to nearby villages where you can see local life first-hand. Good places to visit include Tenuhawa, which has a mosque, Ekala's Shiva temple, and Madhuvani, for a glimpse of Biraha culture.

Buddha Maya Gardens Hotel Just beyond the southeast corner of the park ☎071/580 220, ⊛www.ktmgh.com. Part of the *Kathmandu Guest House* stable, *Maya Gardens* has the appearance of a modern palatial villa, offering smart en suites with a few Buddhist touches, ample grounds and a meditation "grotto". ❼

Lumbini Buddha Hotel South of the Sacred Garden ☎071/580 114, ⊜lbuddha@mos.com.np. Lovely location in a shady grove near the Sacred Garden, this upper budget/lower mid-range hotel has decent rooms in salmon-coloured buildings with corrugated iron roofs. It's popular with visiting Buddhist monks, so book ahead. ❹

Lumbini Garden Lodge Buddha Nagar ☎071/580 146. The exposed concrete in the hall and stairway is a bit off-putting, but the rooms are fine, although a little barren. They have green and white tiled floors and some overlook the fields. The friendly owner speaks English. ❷

Lumbini Garden New Crystal Near Buddha Nagar ☎071/580 145, ⊜lumcrystal@ntc.net.np. Follow an avenue of palms up to this large red brick establishment, which apes the very best in airport hotels. Staff are amiable and the en suites are comfortable but bland. ❼

Lumbini Guest House Buddha Nagar ☎071/580 142. This popular and good-value place is one of a cluster of budget lodges in Buddha Nagar. Neat and tidy rooms come with TVs and attached baths. ❷

Lumbini Hokke Hotel Near the Shanti Stupa ☎071/580 136, ⊛www.theroyal residency.net. Aimed at wealthy Japanese pilgrims, the *Hokke* has a serene air, with lotus ponds in the gardens, special "*ofuro*" Japanese bath, excellent restaurant and a choice of Western and Japanese-style en suites. For the less sedate, there's also a karaoke lounge. ❽

Lumbini Village Lodge Buddha Nagar ☎071/580 432, ⊜lumbinivillagelodge@yahoo.com. Clean, straightforward rooms with pink interiors and private baths – though those on the top floor are overpriced. There's also a dorm (Rs150), internet café, rental bikes (Rs100 per day) and an owner well attuned to travellers' needs. ❷–❹

Tilaurakot and around

The ruins of **TILAURAKOT**, 24km west of Lumbini, are believed to be the remains of ancient **Kapilvastu**, seat of the ancient Shakya kingdom and the childhood home of Prince Siddhartha Gautama. Tilaurakot gets far fewer visitors than Lumbini, yet its ruins are at least as interesting, and its history arguably even more so. Shaded by mango, *kusum* and *karma* trees, they have a serenity that Lumbini has begun to lose.

Admission to the **excavation** site is free, and the lonely guards will probably be happy to give you a tour around the grounds (donation expected, up to Rs100 is reasonable) Among the remains are a couple of stupa bases, thick fortress walls and four gates. Looking out across the ruins from the **eastern gate** could hardly be a better place for a moment's meditation, as it's said to be from here that the Buddha walked out on nearly thirty years of princely life to begin his search for enlightenment. It's doubtful this is literally the ruins of the palace of King Suddhodana, the Buddha's father, for the style of bricks used aren't thought to have been developed until the third century BC, but it may well have been built on top of it; assuming the earlier structure was made of wood, no trace of it would remain. Indian archeologists argue that Piprahwa, just south of the border, is the true site, but excavations at Tilaurakot in 2000 uncovered potsherds and terracotta beads contemporaneous with Buddha's lifetime, helping to corroborate the Nepali claim.

A small **museum** (daily except Tues 10am–5pm; Rs15), opposite the start of the side road to the Tilaurakot site, displays some of the three thousand coins found in the area (including one bearing the Shakya name), together with pottery spanning three distinct periods and a thousand years. Even older pottery discovered in caves near Jomosom, high in the Himalayas, is for some reason also displayed here.

Other archeological sites

Tilaurakot is only one of several archeological sites dating to the time of the Buddha which are scattered in the countryside surrounding Taulihawa. **Niglihawa**, 10km northeast of Taulihawa, is the location of a broken Ashokan pillar associated with one of the mythical Buddhas of a previous age. **Sagarhawa**, 5km further to the northwest, contains an ancient water tank identified as the site of a notorious Shakya massacre. The Ashokan pillar and brick stupa at **Gotihawa**, 6km south of Taulihawa, commemorate another previous Buddha, while the *pokhari* at **Kudan**, 2km southwest of Taulihawa, is said to be where the Buddha returned after his enlightenment to preach the *dharma* to his father and young son.

Practicalities

The easiest way to get to Tilaurakot is by **Jeep** from Sonauli or Bhairahawa (Rs2500 or so return, depending on waiting time), which enables you to hit Lumbini en route. Don't get locked into a rushed half-day tour of Lumbini and Tilaurakot, though – negotiate plenty of waiting time, and consider staying over at Lumbini on the way back. Getting there by public transport, you're stuck with the irregular **buses** (roughly hourly; 1hr) which make their way from Bhairahawa to **Taulihawa**, 22km beyond Lumbini on the same road; you can flag these down at Lumbini's Parsa Chowk, but don't expect to get a seat. From the centre of Taulihawa, rikshaws are usually available to take you the last 3km along the main northbound road to an obvious intersection where the museum is on the left and a paved road on the right leads 400m to the site. On a bike it takes less than two hours to get from Lumbini to Tilaurakot.

Some Buddhists make a pilgrimage circuit of all these sites, but this is only practical in a vehicle rented in Bhairahawa (and driven by someone who knows the way to all the sites). This will cost you around Rs2500, depending on your negotiating skills and is pretty easy to do; just ask at one of the hotels.

Basic **food** is available at Taulihawa. If you get stuck, you can **stay** at the basic *New Siddhartha Guest House* (❶–❷) just north of the town centre along the road to Tilaurakot, which has pretty basic, boxy rooms with shared facilities.

The Far West

Nepal's remote **far west**, linked to the rest of the country by the Mahendra Highway, is slowly opening its doors to travellers. It's still a hell of a haul to get here from Kathmandu, but Delhi is just twelve hours by bus from the far western border crossing, and the smooth, fast road between the two passes two of the richest wildlife parks in Nepal, **Bardia National Park** and **Sukla Phanta Wildlife Reserve**. The partly Muslim city of **Nepalgunj** is the largest city in the west, and the hub for all flights to more remote airstrips. The Mahendra Highway makes good time to Nepalgunj, 250km west of Butwal, crossing the Duduwa Hills (350m ascent) and following the green and pleasant valley of the Rapti River (no relation to the river of the same name in Chitwan). North of here lies Dang, home of the white-clad Dangaura Tharus and fine cycling country. The last 40km to Kohalpur, the turning for Nepalgunj and Birendra Nagar, passes through the Kusum–Ilaka forest, which is being eyed as a potential extension area of Bardia National Park.

Nepalgunj

Industrial and transport hub of the far west, **NEPALGUNJ** is Nepal's most Muslim city. The presence of Muslims in the Terai is hardly surprising, since the border with India, where Muslims comprise a significant minority, was only determined in the nineteenth century. Until just prior to the 1814–16 war with the British, this area belonged to the Nawab of Oudh, one of India's biggest landowners; after Nepal's defeat it was ceded to the East India Company and only returned to Nepal as a goodwill gesture for services rendered during the Indian Mutiny of 1857. A fair few Muslims fled to Nepalgunj during the revolt – Lucknow, where the most violent incidents occurred, is due south of here – and others filtered in during the Rana years, seeing chances for cross-border trade. The resulting permanent Muslim community is self-contained, but maintains business and family links with India. Indeed, the entire city feels Indian.

In the heart of the sprawl is **Tribhuwan Chowk**, the lively but dilapidated intersection of the city's two main shopping thoroughfares, south of which the Indian-style Janaki Mandir sits in the middle of the road like a toll booth. The

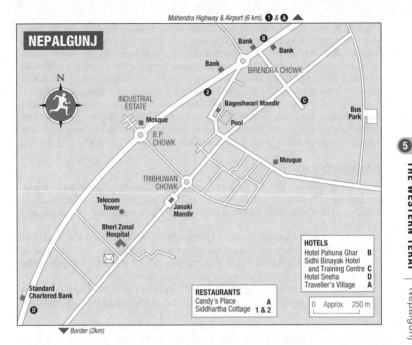

NEPALGUNJ

N

Bank Ⓑ
Bank
Bank
BIRENDRA CHOWK

INDUSTRIAL ESTATE
❷ Bageshwari Mandir Ⓒ
Mosque
Pool
B.P. CHOWK
Bus Park

Mosque

TRIBHUWAN CHOWK

Telecom Tower
Janaki Mandir

Bheri Zonal Hospital

Standard Chartered Bank
Ⓓ

HOTELS
Hotel Pahuna Ghar **B**
Sidhi Binayak Hotel
  and Training Centre **C**
Hotel Sneha **D**
Traveller's Village **A**

RESTAURANTS
Candy's Place **A**
Siddhartha Cottage **1 & 2**

0   Approx.   250 m

Border (2km)

Muslim quarter lies northeast of Tribhuwan Chowk and is worth a wander. The mosques in this area are disappointingly modern, though, and out-of-bounds to non-believers. Hindu worship and trade is centred around the nondescript **Bageshwari Mandir**; behind the temple is a large pool with a jaunty, kitsch statue of Mahadev (Shiva) in the middle.

The **bus park** has been inconveniently banished to the extreme northeast end of the city, a twenty-minute walk away. There are **banks** with ATMs on the main road either side of Birendra Chowk.

Accommodation

Hotel Pahuna Ghar Near Birendra Chowk ☏081/522 358. Clean and compact marble-floored rooms, with TVs, fans, attached showers and squat toilets. Those at the back are partially shielded from the road noise, but you'll find it hard to block out the early morning call to prayer from the nearby mosque. ❸

Sidhi Binayak Hotel and Training Centre Southeast of Birendra Chowk ☏081/527 551. Staffed by hospitality students, service here is inevitably inconsistent, but the mint-green en suite rooms with TV and comfy chairs are good value (though the mattresses are firm to say the least). ❸

Hotel Sneha South of the centre ☏081/520 119, ✉hotel@sneha.wlink.com.np. Nepalgunj's smartest hotel, popular with NGO staff, is set back from the road, behind well-tended gardens. The en suites, housed in a whitewashed building, have a touch of class, but are a bit overpriced. ❻–❼

Traveller's Village Northeast of town towards the airport ☏081/520 858. Near the UN compound, *Traveller's Village* has a vaguely Mediterranean feel, with shady gardens, climbing plants, decorative photos of Nepal's varied ethnic groups and decent en suites. There's also an excellent restaurant. ❹–❺

Eating

Nepalgunj's busiest **eating** areas are around Birendra Chowk and Tribhuwan Chowk, where there are scores of *dhabas* and a few sweet shops. In the evenings, vendors in the bazaar dish up curd and *raabri*, a local speciality made from sweetened cream flavoured with cardamom and saffron. If you're feeling homesick, head to ✳ *Candy's Place*, at *Traveller's Village*, for delicious pancakes with maple syrup, hygienic salads, steaks, burgers and lemon meringue pie. There is a collection of restaurants with almost identical menus – a mix of Chinese, Indian and Italian dishes – between B.P. Chowk and Birendra Chowk. A step above is *Siddhartha Cottage*, known to local expats as "Sid's Place", with stand-out, reasonably-priced North Indian food, which you can enjoy in the pleasant garden out back. The owners are planning to move the restaurant from its town centre location to a new setting outside of town, about a kilometre beyond *Traveller's Village*.

Moving on

Westbound **bus** services are frequent, and depart from the main road north of the bus park. Fewer, but still regular, buses head east, mostly travelling at night because of the distances involved. See p.313 for a rundown of routes, and consider flying.

Two local buses leave at around 11.45am and 3.30/4pm (4hr) for Thakurdwara and Bardia National Park. Hiring a car to Bardia can cost as little as Rs2500, though you'll probably end up paying around Rs3500. Try one of the travel agents strung along the main road, and negotiate hard.

Nepalgunj is the hub for **flights** in Nepal's western region, including those to trekking regions such as Jumla and Dolpo (see p.314 for flight info). At the time of writing, there was some talk that Nepalgunj could lose some or all of its flights to mountain airstrips, which would be a significant blow for the city.

Almost every private airline flies the Kathmandu–Nepalgunj route at least daily, and NAC (☎081/520 767) serves the mountain airstrips. All the airlines have offices around Birendra Chowk or B.P. Chowk, or have your hotel make the booking. The **airport** is 6km north of town, reachable by shared tempo or rikshaw.

The **border crossing** of Jamunaha, 5km south of Birendra Chowk, is open to tourists and you can get there by rikshaw. There's little at the border besides immigration and customs offices. Buses connect Rupaidia, the town on the Indian side of the border, with Lucknow (7hr).

Bardia National Park and Thakurdwara

With Chitwan becoming increasingly mass-market, **BARDIA NATIONAL PARK**, northwest of Nepalgunj and the largest area of undisturbed wilderness left in the Terai, beckons as an unspoilt alternative. Budget lodging is available, but there's nothing like Chitwan's commercialism, and the park's distance from Kathmandu is likely to shield it from the masses for many years to come. The area was particularly badly affected during the civil war, and Bardia district had the highest rate of "**disappearances**" in the whole country.

In 2001, the government announced plans for a huge eastward **extension** of Bardia that would increase the park's area by half as much again to nearly 1500 square kilometres (it's currently 968 sq km), but this is yet to happen.

Most of Bardia's lodgings are within walking distance of the park headquarters at **Thakurdwara**, 12km off the highway in a game-rich corner of the park near the Geruwa River.

Ecologically, Bardia spans a greater range of habitats than Chitwan, from thick riverine forest and *sal* stands to *phanta* (isolated pockets of savanna) and dry

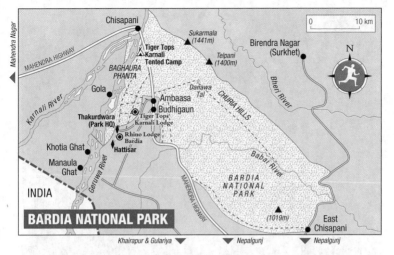

BARDIA NATIONAL PARK

upland slopes. The **Geruwa**, a branch of the awesome **Karnali River**, forms the park's western boundary and major watering hole, and the density of wildlife and birds along this western edge is as great as anywhere in Asia. The **Babai River** drains the core area to the east of Thakurdwara, forming a sanctuary-like *dun* valley teeming with game, but it is out of bounds to visitors.

Bardia was once hailed as a conservation success story: **rhinos**, hunted to extinction here in the early twentieth century, were reintroduced in the mid-1980s and numbered about fifty at the turn of the century. However, with a reduced army presence in the park during the civil war, poaching became a serious problem again. (A number of ex-army personnel were also implicated in poaching activity.) Security is now much tighter, and there are around 22 rhinos in the park. The **tiger** population was also badly affected by the poaching; there are now believed to be 25–30. You'll be lucky to get a sighting – it's said a tiger is a hundred times more likely to see you than you are to see it. Because of the park's remoteness, and minimal human disturbance, tiger experts regard it as the most promising place in Nepal in which to maintain a viable breeding population. For the same reasons, the park has also become an important sanctuary for between 27 and 45 migratory **wild elephants**.

The Geruwa is one of the few places anywhere where you may be able to get a peep at rare **gangetic dolphins**; three to six still survive in the river's deep channels. You can also fish for huge **mahseer**. By 1989, the mugger and gharial **crocodile** populations in the river were reduced to less than a dozen of each species, but a successful project to release juveniles raised from hatchlings means they can now be easily spotted in winter. Five species of **deer** – spotted, sambar, hog, barking and swamp – are abundant, along with **langurs** and **wild pig**. **Nilgai** ("blue bull"), bovine-looking members of the antelope family, roam the drier upland areas, while more than two hundred graceful, corkscrew-horned **blackbuck** (featured on the back of Nepal's ten-rupee note) survive in an unprotected grassland area south of the park. More elusive are sloth bear, leopard and other nocturnal creatures, as well as the endangered hispid hare. The park is also home to nearly four hundred bird species, three of which – the Bengal florican, the lesser florican and the sarus crane – are endangered. The commonest sight of all around Bardia are

▲ Bardia National Park

sandy-coloured **termite mounds**, which reach their greatest height – up to 2.5m – in the *sal* forest here.

Thakurdwara

A sleepy collection of Tharu farming settlements, **THAKURDWARA** is archetypal Terai. The main centre is a kind of village green where local buses stop, encircled by a small bazaar known locally as the "mandir" because of its temple. Most visitors never stray this far from the park headquarters, however, which lie about 1km north of the bazaar. There are few facilities for either locals or tourists, and while most guesthouses have electricity, few village homes are similarly equipped.

The small mandir near the bus stop is the focus of a modest *mela* (religious fair) held on the first day of the month of Magh (mid-Jan). A few other park-related points of interest are scattered in and around the leafy headquarters compound, but most of the action is inside the park. In short, it's a lot like Sauraha was in the good old days: quiet, remote and adventurous.

Tourism will inevitably change Thakurdwara, but conservationists are already taking steps to ensure it doesn't repeat Sauraha's mistakes, and the National Trust for Nature Conservation is working on ways to help ensure local people benefit from the park (see box, p.307).

Getting there

From Kathmandu, the quickest and easiest way to get to Thakurdwara and Bardia is to **fly** to Nepalgunj and travel the rest of the way by car or Jeep (2hr 30min). Even if you don't want to spend the money on the flight, consider renting a **vehicle** in Nepalgunj or Mahendra Nagar.

The next quickest, but by no means easiest, way to get to Bardia **from Kathmandu or Pokhara** is to take a night bus bound for Dhangadhi or Mahendra Nagar, getting off at Ambaasa, the tea-shack turning for Thakurdwara. This is a hell of a way to come – aside from the usual miseries of night travel, it's hard not to fret about missing the stop in the dark, despite the reliability of the ticket-boys, since night buses pass Ambaasa between around 3am and 6am. One night bus also runs direct from Kathmandu to Thakurdwara.

If you have the time, it's far more relaxing to take a **day bus**, and overnight in Lumbini (see p.293) on the way. Day buses from Butwal, Nepalgunj, Dhangadhi and Mahendra Nagar pass Ambaasa on their way to other destinations, and direct local services to Thakurdwara originate in Nepalgunj. Night buses heading eastwards from Mahendra Nagar or Dhangadhi should also get you to Ambaasa before dark.

Some guesthouse Jeeps wait at Ambaasa specifically for the arrival of prospective pre-dawn guests, ready to ferry them the final 12km to Thakurdwara. You'll get a free ride if you stay in their guesthouse for a night; otherwise it's a steep Rs500–1000 flat fee. If you book your guesthouse ahead, you should get a free pick-up from Ambaasa.

Finally, without a doubt the most enjoyable way to get to Bardia is by **raft** down the Karnali River (see p.402). Most commercial trips on the Karnali include the option of finishing up with two or more nights at a Bardia lodge.

Accommodation

If you're picking up a Jeep in Ambaasa, you may not have too much choice about where you spend your first night. Don't worry: most **lodges** are very similar, and all are acceptable. Pioneered in (and steadily disappearing from) Sauraha, the formula is simple: mud-and-thatch huts arranged around a garden, with a simple dining pavilion serving *daal bhaat* and approximations

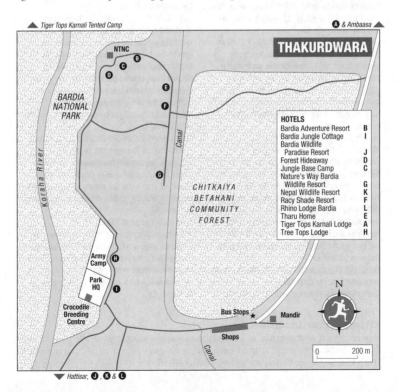

of Western dishes. A few places have more hotel-like concrete bungalows, and most have solar-heated water. All except the most basic can arrange access to Jeeps, fishing rods, guides, elephants and the like. Many lodges offer **packages**, but as in Chitwan, these provide little benefit for their added cost (see p.271). *Tiger Tops*, the only place to stay in the park itself, is well worth it if you've got the money.

Just over half the lodges in Thakurdwara at the time of writing are listed, but bear in mind that as visitor numbers are so small, places here are particularly prone to sudden closure.

Bardia Adventure Resort ☎084/429 721, ⓦwww.bardia-adventure.com. Attractive individual cottages set in a garden abundant with palm trees. There's also a creeping plant-covered lookout tower for guests to use. ❷–❸

Bardia Jungle Cottage ☎084/429 714. Thakurdwara's original budget lodge, run by a knowledgeable former assistant park warden. Cross a humped-back bridge to find rustic cottages and a nice dining area with exposed tree trunks propping it up. ❷

Bardia Wildlife Paradise Resort ☎084/692 083, ⒺBardia_tiger47@yahoo.com.au. Thatched huts with private or shared facilities, enlivened by rugs and easy chairs: opt for the one with the eye-catching "temple-style" roof. The riverside location, 1km south of Park HQ, is appealing and there's an airy dining area. ❷–❸

🏃 **Forest Hideaway** ☎084/620 237, ⓦwww.foresthideaway.com. This deservedly popular lodge has knowledgeable, professional staff, a back-up generator to cope with power cuts, internet access, superb banana pancakes and a range of comfortable rooms in mud-walled huts, all with reliable hot water supply in the evenings. ❷–❹

Jungle Base Camp ☎084/690 487, Ⓔjunglehukum@gmail.com. Standard mud huts with thatched roofs and private baths, surrounded by bamboo trees. The cosy open-sided dining area is accessed via two mini bridges. ❷–❸

Nature's Way Bardia Wildlife Resort ☎084/690 682. Under renovation at the time of research, the peaceful *Nature's Way* is surrounded by fields and has clean and simple rooms with private baths. It's run by a helpful Nepali naturalist and his English business partner. ❷

Nepal Wildlife Resort ☎084/690 490, Ⓔraaika@mos.com.np. The carpeted rooms are a bit more comfortable, if less atmospheric, than the norm at

this riverside lodge, 500m south of Park HQ. Off its tree-studded path there is also a viewing tower and an echoing dining hall. ❸

Racy Shade Resort ☎084/690 486, ⓦwww.racyshade.com. The more expensive rooms (named after Hindu gods) have rugs and fairly modern attached baths, while the cheaper options (named after animals) are also decent. The atmosphere is normally lively around the bar. ❸

Rhino Lodge Bardia ☎084/690 489, ⓦwww.rhinolodgebardia.com. In a secluded location close to the *hattisar*, 3km south of Park HQ, *Rhino Lodge* has a tree-filled garden and a proper bar in its dining rooms. Its concrete cottages with modern baths and interiors display a little more flair than the budget lodges. ❹

Tiger Tops Karnali Lodge and Tented Camp ☎01/436 1500, ⓦwww.tigermountain.com. The lodge sits outside the park in a serene location, with stylish but not luxurious rooms, while the tented camp, inside the park, overlooking the Geruwa River, offers a good, old-fashioned safari experience. You can split your stay between the lodge and the camp, and service at both is excellent. $315–325 per person per night, including all activities. ❾

Tharu Home ☎084/429 722, Ⓔtharuhome@ntc.net.np. Run by four energetic twenty-somethings, this lodge has some of the cheapest, no-frills rooms in Bardia, with shared or attached baths (these are cold water, but there's a single hot water shower across the garden). Internet access is also available. ❷

Tree Tops Lodge ☎974/800 4076, Ⓔtreetops1@rediffmail.com. Close to the army barracks, amid scrubby grounds, *Tree Tops* has mud-walled cottages with thatched roofs. A few only have a sheet separating the bathroom from the bedroom, which may offer too little privacy for some. ❸

Other practicalities

There are no **restaurants** in Thakurdwara, only a couple of snack stalls in the bazaar. Most people eat at their own lodge, or drop in at a neighbouring place if it's looking lively (however lodges advise guests not to walk around after dark without a guide because elephants and rhinos sometimes escape from the park). Guesthouses can **change money** informally. **International calls** can be made from any guesthouse with a phone and from shops in the bazaar. Charges are relatively expensive. There's a local **health post** and pharmacy near the bus stop; the nearest hospital is in Nepalgunj.

Moving on

The simplest and quickest way to move on from Thakurdwara is to have your guesthouse make your travel arrangements for you. Lodges can book seats on **night buses** to Kathmandu and Pokhara, which pass through Ambaasa in the afternoon and early evening. They charge Rs100 or so commission on top of the cost of the bus ticket, but it's well worth paying for a guaranteed seat, and almost impossible to do it yourself.

Making your own way is slower: two **local buses** run to Nepalgunj from Thakurdwara bazaar (7am & 9am; 4hr) and there is – less reliably – one direct to Kathmandu (ask at your guesthouse for details). From Nepalgunj, there are frequent services to Kathmandu and Pokhara.

Otherwise, get off at Kohalpur, the turnoff 13km north of Nepalgunj, where you can book seats on the day express buses bound for Butwal and destinations east. You should also be able to book a night bus at Kohalpur, but there's less to

---

Bardia in the balance

Nepal's wildlife parks never sit easily with the inhabitants of nearby villages, who not only are barred from their former woodcutting areas but also must cope with marauding animals. In the case of **Bardia National Park**, the potential for resentment is especially high, because the government actually reintroduced rhinos to the area, giving local farmers a headache they thought they'd gotten rid of. It's estimated that half the crops in fields adjoining Bardia are damaged by wildlife (primarily by rhinos and elephants). While local people are still occasionally injured and even killed by wild animals, safety has improved since an electric fence was installed around part of the park.

As in Chitwan (see p.278), Bardia's long-term viability depends as much on human factors as ecological ones, and recent initiatives have reflected this. The UN-sponsored **Parks and People Project**, which worked on community development in the buffer zones adjoining the park, came to an end in 2001, but the **National Trust for Nature Conservation** is continuing many of its initiatives, and between thirty and fifty percent of the National Park's income is spent in the buffer zones. The number of local Tharu people involved in Bardia's tourism trade has also increased in recent years.

People-centred activities have to be balanced with the needs of the wildlife. **Chitkya Community Forest**, along the eastern border of the park, is being managed to allow it to regenerate naturally, providing a source of firewood and increased habitat for animals in the park. Elsewhere, the problem is rather that bushes and trees encroach on the vital grassland needed by deer and tigers, and locals are given controlled access to collect wood.

Other projects prioritize the needs of animals over humans. A notable one aims to create wildlife corridors linking eleven national parks including Sukla Phanta, Bardia and Chitwan in Nepal, and Dudhwa and Corbett National Parks in India. Such corridors reflect natural migration patterns, and are seen as vital for maintaining viable breeding populations. They are threatened, however, by deforestation and population growth, which runs the risk of leaving animals marooned in separate national parks. Wildlife corridors are seen as the only way for animal populations to be able to exchange genes without the aid of trucks and tranquillizer guns.

do while you wait. Heading west, get off at Ambaasa and flag down any bus that's going. You should be able to get to Mahendra Nagar before dark, though you may end up having to change buses at Chisapani or Atariya (the turning for Dhangadhi). Your lodge may also be able to arrange cars to Nepalgunj (Rs2500–3500) or book **plane** tickets.

Activities in and around the park

Bardia's menu of activities is similar to Chitwan's, and you'll find lengthier descriptions in that section (see pp.282–285). All **access to the park** is via the main headquarters entrance, crossing the Koraha River from there. Park **entry permits** cost Rs500 per day; you can buy them from the **ticket office** inside the headquarters compound, or have your guesthouse do it for you. The same goes for elephant ride tickets and vehicle and fishing permits.

While you're at the HQ, stop by the park's **Crocodile Breeding Centre** (Rs30), where gharials, mugger crocodiles and black turtles are raised from eggs before being released into local waters, the **Tharu Museum** (daily except Sat 10am–4pm; Rs50), which provides a basic introduction to local culture, and the **Visitors' Information Centre** (daily 7am–sunset), with interesting displays on the park's flora and fauna.

Also keep an eye out for **Shiva Ram**, a 10–11-year-old tame rhino, orphaned as a calf, who wanders round the HQ and army base, occasionally resting his head on the rangers' parked motorbikes. He's pretty docile and can be petted, though you should be careful.

Walks

Although rhino danger is somewhat lower here than in Chitwan, it would still be extremely foolish to enter the park on foot without a **guide**. Hire one through your lodge, or ask who's available at the park office. **Prices** depend on experience, but expect to pay around Rs650 for a full day. Although Bardia guides generally speak less English and are less well trained than those at Chitwan, they know the territory and can keep you out of harm's way. See p.282 for jungle safety tips.

Most walks inside the park take a northerly bearing from Thakurdwara, roughly paralleling the Geruwa River through mixed grassland and jungle. Some of the best rhino habitat, as well as areas favoured by wild elephants, is found in the riverine corridor between Thakurdwara and **Gola**. Tigers, bears, boars, nilgai and dolphins may be sighted, and you're assured of seeing deer, monkeys and all manner of birds. The track to **Baghaura Phanta**, about 7km northeast of Thakurdwara, is a prime birdwatching route.

To watch Bardia's hardest-working employees enjoying some down-time, visit the government **hattisar** (elephant stable; Rs50), outside the park about forty minutes' walk south of the HQ. At the time of writing there were six baby elephants, and ten adults: the best time to visit is before 9am or after around 4pm; at other times most of the elephants are at work or being trained. Remaining outside the park, the road continues southwards along the river past **Manaula Ghat** and **Khotia Ghat**, the latter being one of the best places to look for dolphins.

Camping isn't allowed inside the park (except at *Tiger Tops*), which limits the scope for longer hikes. However, guides have developed a two-day trek from Ambaasa to **Danawa Tal** and then up to **Telpani** (1400m), a high point along the crest of the ridge that forms the park's northern boundary, where you can camp out and then return via Chisapani the next day. Another possibility for a nocturnal experience is to arrange with a guide to sleep out in a **machan** (tower) in Chitka Community Forest; bring a mosquito net.

Elephant rides

You can arrange **elephant rides** yourself at the HQ ticket office, or have your guesthouse do it for you. The **charge** is Rs1000 per person per hour, for up to three hours. Rides must be **reserved** the day before, but it may be advisable to book a day or two in advance if there are many other tourists in the village, as only ten rideable elephants are kept here, and not all of them may be on duty on any given day. Of the lodges, only *Tiger Tops* owns its own elephants. Departures are in the early morning and late afternoon from a platform at the far end of the HQ compound.

Jeep rides

A **Jeep** might or might not increase your chances of surprising game, but it will certainly enable you to penetrate the more remote parts of the park where the animals aren't as wary of humans. Inevitably, however, vehicles disturb much of the wildlife you've come to see. Most lodges have their own Jeeps, with prices beginning at around Rs2000 per person, or Rs7000–8000 for the whole vehicle, for four hours. Jeep safaris run 7–11am and 2–6pm.

Most trips are confined to the network of tracks in the park's western sector, which take you through *sal* forest and the grasslands of **Baghaura Phanta** and give access to pristine stretches of river and rich wildlife habitat. Given more time you could continue north to Chisapani to look for gharials and dolphins. From Ambaasa, you can follow a track eastwards to **Danawa Tal**, a wetland at the base of the foothills where rhinos and elephants are sometimes spotted.

Nepal's only herd of blackbuck antelope congregates around a big *phanta* well south of the park at **Khairapur**, 32km from Thakurdwara by road and most easily reached by vehicle. From Thakurdwara, drive north to Ambaasa, then 3km south along the Mahendra Highway to Budhigaun, and then take the road south from there – look for the herd on your left as you approach Gulariya. Blackbucks were thought to be extinct until three were sighted here in 1973; by 2008 the herd was estimated at more than two hundred. Most lodges can organise trips here.

River trips

Once on the River Geruwa, you've got just as good a chance of seeing dolphins, muggers, monkeys and birds as you would on foot, and you may even be lucky enough to glimpse an elephant or tiger. A couple of lodges have **rafts**, and others will book you on one of them if places (around Rs2000 per person) are available. Another option is a half-day **dugout canoe** ride, costing Rs400–600 per person.

Fishing

The Karnali/Geruwa is renowned for its **mahseer**, a sporting fish related to carp and weighing up to 40kg. If you catch one, release it: the *mahseer* population is declining due to pollution, dams, barriers and a general lack of headwaters protection. The Babai is superb for *mahseer* and *goonch*, another huge fish. Be alert for crocodiles.

Fishing is allowed everywhere on the Karnali and Geruwa rivers (you can fish as part of a raft trip), but on the Babai, it's restricted to the waters below the dam (the Mahendra Highway crossing). You'll need a **fishing permit**, which costs Rs500 per day and can be obtained from the ticket office at Park HQ. The more switched-on lodges can provide fishing gear, but if you're at all interested in angling you'll want to bring your own – and strong tackle.

Bike rides and Tharu villages

Some guesthouses in Thakurdwara rent **bicycles** (for around Rs180 per day), which open up a host of possibilities for exploring the surrounding countryside. Two dirt roads head south from Thakurdwara and take you through numerous traditional Tharu villages. The one past the *hattisar* and on along the riverbank to Khotia Ghat (see p.308) gets far more tourist traffic. Cycling north along the road to Ambaasa is also a possibility, but not advisable alone, due to the presence of wild animals. Given more time and a packed lunch, you could conceivably cycle to Chisapani or some of the other spots normally only reached by Jeep. It might be worth joining a guided **village tour** (Rs300 for 2–3hr) to learn more about local Tharu culture, if you can get past the human-zoo aspect of it. Lodges can also organise **Tharu cultural perform-ances** (including the special Bardia *chokara* dance) which are sometimes included in the package price.

West of the Karnali River

The "far west" of Nepal, beyond the **Karnali River**, is a foreign land for most Nepalis – a remote, underdeveloped region which has long been neglected by the Kathmandu government. In fact, Delhi is closer than the Nepali capital by bus and, until the completion of the Karnali bridge in the mid-1990s, the region was literally cut off altogether in the monsoon, the Karnali effectively forming Nepal's western border. The region makes for some great off-the-beaten track travelling, though there's a distinct lack of facilities and communicating with local people can be difficult.

The westernmost section of the Mahendra Highway was finally completed in 2000, after a twitchy Indian government insisted on replacing the Chinese who were originally contracted to do the job. Twenty-two major bridges (many of which were subjected to Maoist attacks during the civil war) carry just 215km of asphalt, but the road now at least lives up to its alternative name of the East–West Highway, bringing new trade and industry to the region. The little-visited **Sukla Phanta Wildlife Reserve**, which lies just outside the relatively laid-back

---

The Karnali

The Mahendra Highway emerges from Bardia National Park to vault the mighty **Karnali River**, surging out of a gap in the rugged foothills, on what is reputed to be the longest single-tower **suspension bridge** in the world. The exotic design of this World Bank-funded structure appears to have been dictated mainly by the foreign contractors need for a showcase project, but it's an impressive sight as you rush along the tarmac. Look out for gharial crocodiles basking on the rocks as you pass over.

An even bigger showcase project may be in the pipeline for the Karnali: the construction of a mammoth **dam** upstream of the bridge has been mooted, as has a – far simpler – tunnel across the neck of a major bend on the Upper Karnali. As with many large infrastructure projects in Nepal, however, moving from the planning stage to the building stage can be an interminably long process. See p.446 for more on hydroelectric projects in Nepal.

border town of **Mahendra Nagar**, is an excellent place to visit for the adventurous (and resourceful) traveller.

Mahendra Nagar

The Mahendra Highway ends at **MAHENDRA NAGAR**, a border town with a good deal of spark thanks to day-tripping shoppers from India. Its bustle is only a border aberration, however, for the outlying region is one of the more traditional parts of the Terai. Rana Tharu (see box, p.270) sharecroppers work the fields, maintaining an apparently happy symbiosis with their old-money landlords, and their villages, scattered along dirt tracks north of the Mahendra Highway, still consist of traditional communal longhouses.

Mahendra Nagar is laid out in an unusually logical grid south of the highway, with the **bus park** at the northwestern end. Walk south from the bus park for 500m and you come to a roundabout: to the left (east) is Main Road, the street with the bazaar, and to the right (west) is the road to the **airstrip** (3.5km) and Sukla Phanta Wildlife Reserve (see p.312).

Mahendra Nagar has several decent **accommodation** options, the pick of which is *Hotel Opera* (☎099/522 101, ⓦwww.hoteloperanepal.com; ❸–❺), near the main *chowk*. There's a range of bright en suites, with modern bathrooms, TVs and phones; the best ones have nice touches like tea- and coffee-making facilities. Alternatively, try *Hotel Gangotri Plaza* (☎099/524 444, ⓦwww.hotelgangotri .com.np; ❹–❺), close to the bus park, which has carpeted rooms with private baths, a restaurant and money exchange facilities. Both hotels can help organise visits to Sukla Phanta. Basic but acceptable rooms can be found at *Royal Guest House* (☎099/523 799; ❷), opposite the bus park.

Several *dhaba*, concentrated mainly along the first lane leading off the bazaar, do a fair range of Nepali and Indian **food**. Rastriya Banijya Bank, 250m south of the bazaar on the third lane, can **change** Indian rupees and US dollars, but other currencies may be beyond its abilities. Indian currency is readily accepted – and unofficially exchanged – everywhere in Mahendra Nagar.

The border

The **border** begins 6km west of Mahendra Nagar, reached by shared tempo, rikshaw, or bus. A rough road traverses the one-kilometre no man's land between the Nepali and Indian immigration posts. From Indian immigration you can catch a rikshaw across the wide Mahakali River along the top of a huge flood-control/irrigation barrage and then a further 4km to Banbaasa, the first Indian town. The border is officially open 24 hours, but you may have trouble finding the immigration officials at night or early in the morning.

Banbaasa is relatively friendly for a border town, but accommodation is poor, and since crossing the border can be fairly time-consuming, you'll want to make an early start from Mahendra Nagar to avoid being stuck there. Buses connect Banbaasa to Bareli (the nearest broad-gauge rail station; 2hr 30min), Almora (6hr), Naini Tal (7hr), Haridwar (9hr) and Delhi (10hr). Narrow-gauge trains from Banbaasa are slow and infrequent, so you're better off taking a bus.

If you're **entering Nepal**, visas are available at the border. Refer to p.313 for onward bus information. The travel agent's booth next to immigration can book through-tickets, including Jeep transport, to Bardia National Park. There are direct night buses and a single marathon day bus from Mahendra Nagar through to Kathmandu, but unless you're on urgent business you'd do better to make the journey in stages.

Sukla Phanta Wildlife Reserve

The great tracts of natural grassland (*phanta*) in Nepal's extreme southwest could almost be mistaken, albeit on a smaller scale, for the savannas of East Africa. **SUKLA PHANTA WILDLIFE RESERVE**, southeast of Mahendra Nagar, is dotted with them, and touring the reserve is, for once, really like being on safari. Always a difficult place to reach, Sukla Phanta was even more cut off during the civil war, and as a result attracts barely a trickle of visitors. The park is home to one of the world's largest populations of **swamp deer** – sightings of a thousand at a time are common – as well a number of **wild elephants** and several rhinos. The **tiger** population has declined dramatically from 20–50 in 2005 to an estimated 6–14 in 2008 as a result of poaching; a sad turn of events for a park that once boasted one of the highest densities of the species in Asia. Sukla Phanta remains astonishingly rich in **birds**, with 470 species having been counted here, one of the highest concentrations in Nepal. Rare species include the Bengal florican and the giant hornbill.

Several four-wheel-drive tracks crisscross the reserve, making itineraries flexible, but the first stop is bound to be the **Sukla Phanta** at the southwestern end, a rippling sea of grass that turns silvery-white in October (*sukila* means white in the local Tharu dialect). You're virtually guaranteed **swamp deer** here, and in quantity – make for the view tower in the middle and scan for them with binoculars. As *barasingha* ("twelve-pointer"), the swamp deer was

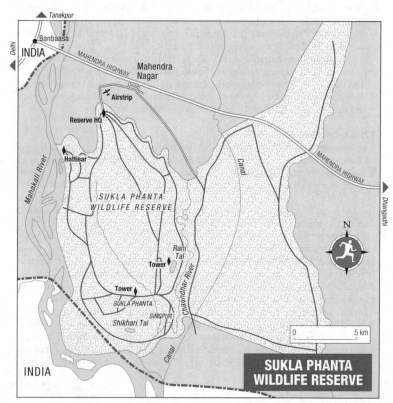

one of Kipling's beloved *Jungle Book* animals – "that big deer which is like our red deer, but stronger" – and common throughout the plains and hills. Today it's an endangered species, finding safety in numbers in the *phanta* and particularly the boggy parts where seasonal fires don't burn off the grasses.

Having seen your obligatory *phanta*, make a beeline for **Rani Tal** (Queen's Lake), near the centre of the reserve. Surrounded by riotous, screeching forest, the lake – a lagoon, really – is like a prehistoric time capsule, with trees leaning out over the shore, deer wading shoulder-deep around the edges and crocodiles occasionally peering out of the water-hyacinth-choked depths. In the early morning, the **birdlife** is amazing: a dazzling display of cranes, cormorants, eagles and scores of others. You can watch all the comings and goings from a tower by the western shore. Nearby is an overgrown **brick circle**, 1500m in circumference, which locals say was the fort of Singpal, an ancient Tharu king (Rani Tal is said to have been his queen's favourite spot).

Park practicalities

The Sukla Phanta Reserve **entrance** is 5km southeast of Mahendra Nagar, not far from the airstrip. The **entry fee** is Rs500 per day, with opening hours from around 8am to sunset. The best **time to visit** is after the *phanta* is burned back in mid-November; after April it's too tall to see anything.

At the time of research, there was nowhere to stay at the park, although at least one **hotel** was in the process of being built. It is possible to camp at selected areas in the park (Rs500 per person); ask at a few travel agencies to see what they can arrange. Alternatively you can stay in Mahendra Nagar, **rent a vehicle** (about Rs4000 per day, plus entry fees and permits) from one of the better hotels and visit for the day.

Travel details

Day buses

Bhairahawa to: Birgunj (4 daily; 8hr); Butwal (every 10min; 1hr); Janakpur (1 daily; 10hr); Kathmandu (every 10min; 8–9hr); Lumbini (every 30min; 1hr); Taulihawa (for Tilaurakot; hourly; 1hr).
Butwal to: Bartun (for Tansen; every 15min; 2hr); Bhairahawa (every 10min; 1hr); Birgunj (4–6 daily; 7hr); Dhangadhi (1–3 daily; 9hr); Janakpur (2 daily; 9hr); Kathmandu (every 10min; 6–7hr); Mahendra Nagar (2–4 daily; 11hr); Nepalgunj (7–8 daily; 6hr); Pokhara (18–20 daily; 7hr).
Lumbini to: Bhairahawa (every 30min; 1hr); Kathmandu* (4 daily; 9–11hr).
Mahendra Nagar to: Butwal (2–4 daily; 11hr); Dhangadhi (every 30min; 1hr); Kathmandu (1 daily; 16–17hr); Nepalgunj (6–7 daily; 5–7hr).
Narayangadh to: Bandipur (2–3 daily; 5hr); Devghat (every 2hr; 30min); Gorkha (hourly; 2hr 30min); Jagatpur (hourly; 1hr); Kathmandu (every

20min; 4–5hr); Meghauli (1–2 hourly; 1hr); Pokhara (every 30min; 4hr).
Nepalgunj to: Dhangadhi (8 daily; 6hr); Kathmandu (4 daily; 13hr); Mahendra Nagar (6–7 daily; 5–7hr).
* Tourist bus service also available

Night buses

Bhairahawa to: Biratnagar (1 daily; 13hr); Birgunj (1 daily; 10hr); Janakpur (1 daily; 11–13hr); Kathmandu (every 30min; 10–11hr).
Butwal to: Birgunj (3 daily; 10hr); Janakpur (3 daily; 12hr); Kathmandu (every 30min; 9–10hr); Mahendra Nagar (3–4 daily; 12hr); Nepalgunj (5–6 daily; 8hr); Pokhara (5–6 daily; 10hr).
Lumbini to: Kathmandu (1 daily; 10–11hr).
Mahendra Nagar to: Biratnagar (1 daily; 22hr); Birgunj (1 daily; 16hr); Butwal (3–4 daily; 11hr); Kathmandu (5 daily; 16–17hr); Pokhara (2 daily; 16hr).
Narayangadh to: Kakharbitta (2 daily; 12–14hr).

Nepalgunj to: Kathmandu (16 daily; 13hr); Pokhara (4 daily; 13–14hr).

Flights

Note that services are subject to cancellation and change.

Bhairahawa to: Kathmandu (5 daily).

Kathmandu to: Bhairahawa (5 daily); Bharatpur (4 daily); Dhangadhi (2 daily); Meghauli (1 daily); Nepalgunj (5–6 daily).

Nepalgunj to: Bajhang/Chainpur (1 weekly); Birendra Nagar/Surkhet (1 weekly); Chaurjhari/Jajarkot (3 weekly); Dhangadhi (1 weekly); Dolpo/Dunai (3 weekly); Jumla (1–2 daily); Kathmandu (5–6 daily); Rukum (4 weekly); Simikot (1 daily).

The Eastern Terai and hills

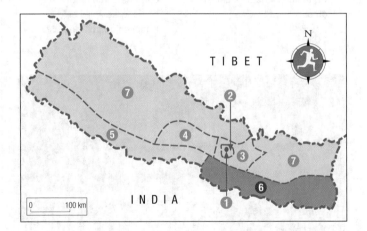

CHAPTER 6

Highlights

✳ **Janakpur** Join the pilgrims in this fascinating holy Hindu city. See p.323

✳ **Janakpur Women's Development Centre** The place to learn about and buy Maithili folk art. See p.328

✳ **Koshi Tappu Wildlife Reserve** Ride in a dugout through the sandy, estuary-like river channels, alive with waterbirds. See p.329

✳ **Bhutanese Refugee Camps** Untainted Bhutan? Hear the other side of the story. See p.331

✳ **Dhankuta** The tidiest and prettiest of the eastern hill towns. See p.336

✳ **Hile** Come to the end of the tarmac at this airy, frontier-like bazaar, swarming with different ethnic groups. See p.336

✳ **Walking near Basantapur** Tremendous views and an exceptional diversity of rhododendron species. See p.337

✳ **Ilam** Nepal's finest tea gardens perch among the steep, green hills below Kanchenjunga. See p.338

▲ Janaki Mandir temple in Janakpur

The Eastern Terai
and hills

The **Eastern Terai** – the southern flatlands east of Chitwan – is lusher and more tropical than the west, but also more populous, more industrial and more Indian. Although the foothills are usually within sight, the main east–west highway sticks to the plains, where the way of life is essentially identical to that of Bihar and West Bengal just across the border; in many parts of this region, Nepali is the second or even third language, after Maithili, Bhojpuri or other North Indian dialects.

Most travellers only flit through here on their way to the border crossings of **Birgunj** (for Patna) and **Kakarbhitta** (for Darjeeling), and outside these places you won't find a speck of tourist hype. The cities are admittedly awful, with one outstanding exception: **Janakpur**, a famous Hindu pilgrimage centre which provides the exoticism of India without the attendant hassles. Although large tracts of jungle are less common east of Chitwan, birdwatchers can check out **Koshi Tappu Wildlife Reserve**, straddling the alluvial plain of the mighty Sapt Koshi river.

The few visitors that get to the **eastern hills** tend to be trekkers bound for the Everest or Kanchenjunga massifs, or rafters running the Sun Koshi. Most other potential visitors are put off by the prospect of a twenty-odd-hour bus trip from Kathmandu, but the journey is far more enticing if you're entering Nepal from the east anyway. By turns riotously forested and fastidiously terraced, the hills are great for day-hiking. Just two all-weather roads serve the area, one climbing to the lovely Newari town of **Dhankuta** and rowdier **Hile**, and the other crawling up the steep green slopes to **Ilam**, Nepal's tea-growing capital.

Buses make good time through the eastern Terai on the Mahendra Highway, and the Dhulikhel–Sindhuli Highway, if it's ever completed, will make getting to the east even easier. However, most of the places described in this chapter are located on side roads, thus requiring various degrees of extra toil to get to. Also, **tourist facilities** in this region are minimal, and you won't find much Western cuisine making this a particularly rewarding stretch of Nepal. The **haat bazaar**, or weekly market, is specific to eastern Nepal, and it's worth trying to coincide with one or two of these pan-cultural extravaganzas.

The Eastern Terai

For travellers coming by road from other parts of Nepal, **Hetauda** is the gateway to the Eastern Terai. The **Tribhuwan Rajpath** highway enters the town from the north and continues south to the Indian border at Birgunj. East of Hetauda, the highway barrels along the plains all the way to Nepal's easternmost border, at Kakarbhitta, and is well-served by buses serving the three big cities of the eastern Terai: **Birgunj**, Nepal's unappealing trade capital, **Biratnagar**, an industrial centre that holds little interest for the visitor, and **Janakpur**, the holiest of Terai towns.

The Rajpath: Hetauda to Birgunj

For centuries the only developed corridor through the Terai, the gentler southern section of the **Tribhuwan Rajpath** was, before air travel, every foreigner's introduction to Nepal. A narrow-gauge railway used to run from Raxaul, the last Indian station, as far as Amlekhganj; dignitaries were transported from there by elephant over the first band of hills to Hetauda before being carried the rest of the way to Kathmandu by donkey or sedan chair. Those few who made the journey during Nepal's isolation years before 1951 did so only by invitation of the prime minister or king. The construction of the Rajpath in the 1950s eliminated the need for elephants and sedan chairs, but the railway wasn't decommissioned until the 1970s.

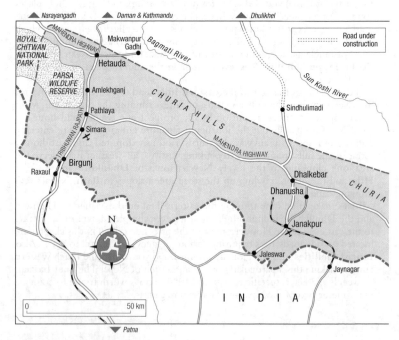

If you're arriving from **India**, the Rajpath makes an exhilarating introduction to Nepal, particularly if coupled with an overnight stay in Daman, from where there's a superb Himalayan panorama. The dramatic northern section of the Tribhuwan Rajpath, including Daman, is covered in Chapter Three.

Hetauda

Clumped around the junction of the Mahendra Highway and the Rajpath, **HETAUDA** is still a staging–post on the India–Kathmandu route. It's a restless place, where Indian trucks rumble through with fuel and bulk goods bound for Kathmandu, and buses stop at all hours. Prostitution is common, helping make the city a link in the transmission of AIDS from India to Nepal. Among Nepalis, Hetauda is probably most famous for its cement plant and its industrial estate, responsible for much of Nepal's prodigious beer production. In fairness, though, Hetauda's roads are brightened up by lines of deep–green *ashok* trees and much of the surrounding area is dominated by *sal* forest.

The centre of Hetauda is **Mahendra Chowk**, a four-way intersection with the Mahendra Highway coming in from the west and the Rajpath from the north. There is nothing much to do in Hetauda, but it's possible to visit the orchid and avocado garden of *Motel Avocado & Orchid Resort* (see below).

Practicalities

Hetauda's busy **bus park** is 150m southwest of Mahendra Chowk. If you're trying to get to Daman or Kathmandu, only six buses serve this route. Fortunately, ✈ *Motel Avocado & Orchid Resort* (☎057/520 235, ✉avocado@wlink.com .np; ❷) compensates for Hetauda's shortcomings, with a range of rooms from budget cells to smart suites with attached bath (❻). Located in a quiet compound

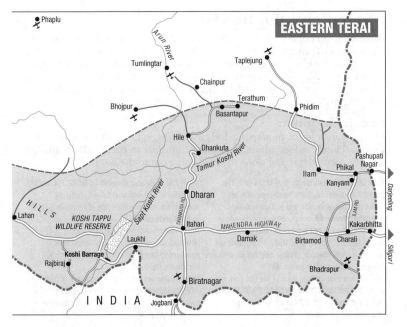

500m north of Mahendra Chowk, the grounds include an orchid garden and a small grove of avocado trees planted by displaced Californians when this was the USAID guesthouse. Running a distant second, *Lidolun* (☎057/520 937; ❸–❻), south of Mahendra Chowk opposite Standard Chartered bank, has a good range of well-kept rooms, some with a/c. There are several cheaper choices north of Mahendra Chowk (such as *Neelam Lodge*; ❶) or west of it (*Hetauda Rest House*; ❶). **Food** outside the guesthouses is unexceptional, but you'll find a number of tea stalls and *sekuwa* (kebab) vendors near *Neelam Lodge*.

South to Birgunj

Heading south over the low **Churia Hills**, the Rajpath enters a strange landscape of stunted trees and steeply eroded pinnacles. These hills are the newest wrinkle in the Himalayas, heaved up as the thirty-million-year-long collision between the Indian and Asian continental plates ripples southwards – less than half a million years old, they're so young that the surface sediments haven't yet been eroded to expose bedrock.

Leaving the hills, the road passes **Amlekhganj**, the former rail terminus (now Nepal's main fuel depot), and 4km further on, the entrance to **Parsa Wildlife Reserve**, an annexe of Chitwan National Park, providing secondary habitat for many of its sub-adult tigers. The forest is also a shelter for elephants, sloth bears, blue bulls, leopards and three hundred species of birds – including the giant hornbill. It is possible to visit the park (entrance Rs650), but facilities are limited – there's a small guesthouse at the headquarters and it is possible to camp (Rs300 per person per night).

The Mahendra Highway branches off east at **Pathlaya**, while **Simara** heralds a dreary succession of factories and fields that continues all the way to Birgunj. Simara has an **airstrip**, with six daily flights to Kathmandu ($80); a taxi to or from Birgunj will cost Rs700.

Birgunj and the border

BIRGUNJ isn't one of the best places in Asia to spend time, but it sure beats Raxaul, its evil twin across the border. The town has exploded in the last ten years on the back of cross-border trade with India, its population having almost tripled since 2001. The construction of a $29m Inland Container Depot, connected by broad-gauge railway line to Raxaul and ultimately Kolkata, should keep Birgunj's accelerator pedal pressed firmly to the floor.

Accommodation

There's quite a lot of comfortable **lodging** in Birgunj, but it's pricey for what you get. Hotels and guesthouses are grouped mainly in the humdrum market area of Adarsh Nagar, and along the road going out to the bus park.

Hotel Classic Adarsh Nagar ☎051/524 070. The budget feel doesn't suit the most-expensive a/c rooms (❹), but otherwise this is a reasonable mid-range choice. ❷

Hotel Diamond 200m west of the bus park on the road to the clock tower ☎051/527 465. Stands out from most of its cheaper, grottier neighbours, with well-kept if unattractive rooms. ❶

Hotel Heera Plaza 500m west of the bus park on the road to the clock tower ☎051/523 988. Swanky expense-account kind of place not far from the bus park, offering a/c isolation. ❸

Hotel Kailas Adarsh Nagar ☎051/522 384. Large, professional and well maintained, if slightly anonymous, with a wide range of rooms in addition to the standards. ❷

Hotel Makalu Adarsh Nagar ☎051/523 054, ✉hmakalu@mos.com.np. This central hotel manages to be both professional and friendly. Rooms are top-notch. ❹

Hotel Vishwuva Next to the bus park ☎051/527 777. A relatively new hotel with all facilities and a swimming pool. The best – and most expensive – option in town. ❻

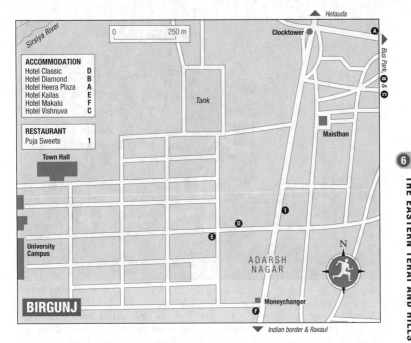

The Town

Unless you have business interests, there's no reason to come here except to cross the border to or from Varanasi or Kolkata. Even then, you're more likely to use Sonauli (see p.292) because of its better connections within Nepal. You could probably kill a few hours in the old-ish market area around **Maisthan**, a mother-goddess temple just off the main drag.

Buses connect Birgunj with Kathmandu, Pokhara and a few major Terai cities (see p.340). The new bus park is located almost 1km east of the clocktower. Rikshaws and shared *tongas* (horse carts) provide transport from there (Rs 40).

All the better hotels – notably the *Kailas* and the *Makalu* – have fine tandoori **restaurants**, while the nearby *Puja Sweets* serves up tempting assortments of Indian goodies. You'll also find *sekuwa*, *momo*, fried fish and other street food in stalls around the town centre. Branches of Standard Chartered and other **banks** are found in Adarsh Nagar, and most of them have ATMs; nearly all businesses in Birgunj accept Indian rupees at the official rate. There are a few phone-cum-internet shops in Adarsh Nagar.

The border

The **border** is 2km south of Birgunj, and **Raxaul**, the first Indian town, sprawls for another 2km south of it. Horrendous traffic jams are a regular occurrence here – if you're driving it can take hours to physically get through, leaving aside the paperwork. Rikshaws charge about Rs40 (Rs25 Indian) to ferry passengers from Birgunj through to Raxaul's train station. The border is open 24 hours, but if you arrive between 7pm and 5am you'll probably have to search around for someone. If you're entering Nepal and you don't already have a visa, make sure you have the correct change in cash (US dollars). Indian visas are not available at the border.

▲ Border gate, Birgunj

Raxaul is the terminus of a rail line and has daily direct train service to Kolkata (around 20hrs), departing in mid-morning; for other destinations, change at Patna (5hr). Buses also depart for Patna several times a day.

East to Kakarbhitta

Resuming its eastward journey at Pathlaya, the Mahendra Highway cuts through extensive forest alternating with farmland. Timber and sugar are the area's key exports. After 55km the highway crosses the Bagmati River, its volume here about ten times bigger (and cleaner, thanks to dilution) than in the Kathmandu Valley. East of the turn-off for Janakpur, things become increasingly Indian and, for a long stretch after the nondescript market town of Lahan, there's very little to remind you that you're in Nepal.

The landscape changes markedly at the **Sapt Koshi**, Nepal's biggest river. The road crosses the **Koshi Barrage**, a network of dykes and flood-control gates. In 2008, a flood submerged the region (see opposite) and the water nearly vanished from the barrage's area and took another path. The flood caused significant damage to local communities and wildlife, and the surrounding fertile fields were turned into a desert of sand. The barrage, however, still looks much as it did before the flood. The gangetic dolphins (see box, p.329) - who sometimes could be seen fishing and playing in the outflow – disappeared, and a few of them reappeared unexpectedly in faraway rivers. The **Koshi Tappu Wildlife Reserve** was badly affected, but with a few seasons and a good monsoon it may return to being a popular area for bird enthusiasts.

The landscape is particularly flat east of the Sapt Koshi to Itahari, a major junction town between the hills and the Terai and the turning for **Biratnagar**, Nepal's second-biggest city. There's little reason to come here, unless you're changing planes for one of the flights on into the eastern hills. Even if you're changing buses, it's better to do so at Itahari, as it's a main junction for buses, and for Dharan as well (see p.334). There's a surprisingly well furnished supermarket next to the main *chowk* in Itahari.

For its final leg, to the border at **Kakarbhitta**, the Mahendra Highway traverses the more picturesque districts of **Morang** and Jhapa. Once renowned for its virulent malaria, Morang's forest has now been almost entirely cleared and the land homesteaded by immigrants from the hills; the half-timbered houses are the work of transplanted Limbus. **Jhapa**, further east, is known for tea cultivation: its shaded plantations are a reminder that Darjeeling is barely 50km away as the crow flies, and Ilam (see p.338), Nepal's prize tea-growing region, sits in the hills just north of here. Though the roadside bazaars are monotonously similar in this area, the countryside is idyllic: banana trees and thatched-roof houses on stilts give it a classically Asian look.

Janakpur and around

JANAKPUR, 165km east of Birgunj, is the Terai's most fascinating city. Also known as **Janakpurdham** (*dham* denoting a sacred place), it's a holy site of the first order, and its central temple, the ornate Janaki Mandir, is an obligatory stop on the Hindu pilgrimage circuit. Although Indian in almost every respect, the city is, by Indian standards, small and manageable: motorized traffic is all but

The Koshi flood

On August 18, 2008, due to poor maintenance of the Koshi barrage, the Sapt Koshi river broke its embankment, submerging crops, sweeping away over three thousand houses and displacing more than fifty thousand people. The terrible flood cut the eastern Terai in two, sweeping away chunks of the Mahendra Highway and forcing people to cross on dangerously overloaded boats near Laukhi – some died in the attempt. The consequences were even more disastrous in India where thousands died. Ironically the barrage, constructed in 1964 by the Indian government, was supposed to protect the state of Bihar from possible floods; though neither India nor Nepal took the necessary measure to keep the sand from piling up at the flood control gate – just a few kilometres north of the barrage.

The Koshi wildlife reserve (see p.329), while not directly in the flood's path, was significantly affected. Blue bulls, who generally live on higher ground and are skilled swimmers, managed to save their own skin, but the grassland habitat of a variety of mammals and reptiles, as well as the breeding colonies of herons, egrets and storks, was partially submerged. Except the Koshi camp in the quieter Northern area, all the other park camps were still closed at the time of writing. In the South, the wildlife was significantly disturbed by the work to repair the road and the embankments. Thousands of temporary shelters have sprung up in the area and there are several camps of **displaced people** around the park that are intensively using its resources. The atmosphere as it is now may not be very conducive to serene birdwatching. Foreign visitors may not be perceived so much as tourists in love with nature, but as international donors who've come to help the flood victims. However, many displaced families have already gone back to their homes, the camps have considerably reduced in size, and the Koshi reserve may be fully operational in a near future.

In February 2009, the river was finally brought back to its original course; three stranded **dolphins** (see p.329) were rescued by the Nepalese Army and released back into the Koshi. The road was temporarily repaired and vehicles started to flow again. This being said, the next monsoon may easily wash away the temporary road – which is nothing but sand for the moment – if preventive measures are once again not taken.

banned from the centre, tourist hustle is largely absent and the poverty isn't oppressive. The surrounding countryside is delightful, and Janakpur's short, rickety **railway** – the only passenger railway still operating in Nepal – makes for an unusual way to experience it.

Hindu mythology identifies Janakpur as the capital of the ancient kingdom of **Mithila**, which controlled a large part of northern India between the tenth and third centuries BC. The city features prominently in the Ramayana, for it was here that **Ram** – the god Vishnu in mortal form – wed **Sita**, daughter of the Mithila King Janak. In Janakpur, where the two command almost cult status, the chant of "Sita Ram, Sita Ram" is repeated like a Hindu Hail Mary, and sadhus commonly wear the tuning-fork-shaped *tika* of Vishnu. Mithila came under the control of the Mauryan empire around the third century BC, then languished for two millennia until Guru Ramananda, the seventeenth-century founder of the sect of Sita that dominates Janakpur, revived the city as a major religious centre.

Despite the absence of ancient monuments to confirm its mythic past – no building is much more than a century old – Janakpur remains an attractive city. Religious fervour seems to lend an aura to everything; the skyline leaves a lasting impression of palm trees and the onion domes and pyramid roofs of local shrines. Most of these distinctively shaped buildings are associated with **kuti** – self-contained pilgrimage centres and hostels for sadhus – some five hundred of

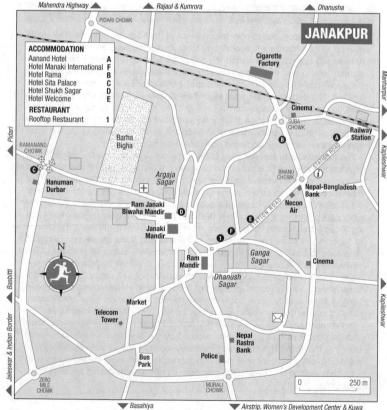

which are scattered throughout the Janakpur area. The city's other distinguishing feature is its dozens of **sacred ponds**, which here take the place of river ghats for ritual bathing and *dhobi*-ing. Locals claim the roughly rectangular tanks go back to Ram's day, although it's more likely they've been dredged over the centuries by wealthy merit-seekers.

Janakpur is a long haul from Kathmandu – ten or more hours by **bus** – and only six services (three of them night buses) ply the route. If and when it is completed, the new Dhulikhel–Sindhuli Highway is expected to bring the travel time down to eight or nine hours, making Janakpur more accessible. In the meantime, your only other options are to break the journey in Hetauda or Birgunj (the latter is better for getting a seat on to Janakpur) or fly. Buddha Air and Agni Air **fly** daily from Kathmandu ($110).

Arrival and information

Janakpur lies 25km south of the Mahendra Highway. It's a small city with a few main roads extending outwards from a compact core. **Station Road**, which runs from near the **Ram Mandir** northeast to the train station, is the nearest thing to a commercial thoroughfare, and contains virtually all of Janakpur's lodgings and restaurants. Another important road heads northwest past the main **Janaki Mandir** to **Ramanand Chowk**, which is turning into something of a main entrance to the city. The main **bus park** is an easy rikshaw ride southwest of the centre. The **airstrip**, 2km further to the south, is a longer, more tedious ride (around Rs100).

The **tourist office** (Sun–Thurs 10am–4pm, Fri 10am–3pm) may be useful for learning about upcoming festivals. It's on Station Road, 50m east of Bhanu Chowk, on the first floor.

Nepal Rastra **bank**, at the southern end of town, exchanges some foreign currencies. Nepal Bangladesh Bank, at Bhanu Chowk, can change cash but not traveller's cheques. Everest Bank, near Janaki Mandir, and Invest Bank, behind Hotel Rama, have ATMs. Many shops along Station Road offer **phone** services, and a couple of them have **email**.

Accommodation

Janakpur's few **lodgings** are aimed more at Indian pilgrims than Western visitors, and are all of the crummy, concrete variety. Keep a distance from the *kuti* around the Janaki Mandir, as their loudspeakers create a hell of a racket. While the scarcity of accommodation normally doesn't present a problem, you need to **book** well ahead during the big festival times.

Aanand Hotel Station Rd ☎041/523 395. A perpetually half-completed building with the rudiments of a garden seating area, quite far away from the temple. The smarter rooms with hot water are more expensive. ❷

Hotel Manaki International ☎041/521 540, ⓔ hotelmanaki2009@hotmail.com. A smart white building, with rooms with attached bathrooms, a/c and TV. The UN Office of the High Commissioner for Human Rights has his office in it. ❸–❼

Hotel Rama Near Suba Chowk ☎041/520 059. A quiet, formal and clean option in town, though it's rather far from the sights. The more expensive upstairs rooms (❺) are quite spacious and have hot water and a/c. ❸

Hotel Sita Palace By Ramanand Chowk ☎041/527 626. A relatively new hotel with "deluxe" (by Terai standards; ❺) and standard rooms. Unfortunately, it's a bit far away from the temple and situated next to the noisy main road. ❹–❺

Hotel Shukh Sagar ☎041/520 488. Great central (but noisy) location overlooking the Janaki Mandir. Reasonably clean, with a good sweet shop/ vegetarian restaurant downstairs. ❶

Hotel Welcome Station Rd ☎041/520 646. The staff here have lots of experience in dealing with foreigners. Wide range of rooms, from poky boxes to spartan a/c suites (❺). ❶

The City

Central Janakpur is remarkably car-free. Though the city is easy enough to navigate on foot, **rikshaws** wait in efficient ranks all over town; you'll rarely pay more than Rs10–20 for short distance. You may be able to rent a **bicycle** informally through your hotel.

The Janaki Mandir

A palatial confection of a building in the Mughal style, the **Janaki** (pronounced Jaa-nuh-kee) **Mandir** is supposed to mark the spot where a golden image of Sita was discovered in 1657 and, presumably, where the virtuous princess actually lived. The present plaster and marble structure, erected in 1911 by an Indian queen, is already looking a little mouldy. Its outer building encloses a courtyard and inner sanctum, where at least twice a day (generally 8am and 4pm) priests draw back a curtain to reveal an intricate silver shrine and perform various rituals for attending worshippers; non-Hindus are allowed to watch. It's an enchanting place at night and early in the morning, when the devout gather in lamplit huddles and murmur haunting hymns. The temple is also a traditional place for boys to undergo the ritual of *chhewar* (the first shaving of the head), and male dancers in drag, who are often hired to perform at the ceremony, may sometimes be seen here.

Climb the stairs to the roof of the outer building for a view of the central courtyard and the dense, brick-laned Muslim village butting right up against the temple's rear wall. North of the temple, the modern, Nepali pagoda-style **Ram Janaki Biwaha Mandap** (Ram Sita Wedding Pavilion) houses a turgid tableau of the celebrated event.

Other sights

The city's oldest, closest quarter lies to the south and east of the Janaki Mandir – making your way through this area, with its sweet shops, *puja* stalls and quick-photo studios, you begin to appreciate that Janakpur is as geared up for Indian tourists as Kathmandu is for Western ones. The main landmark here, the pagoda-style **Ram Mandir**, isn't wildly exciting except during festivals (see below). Immediately to the east, **Dhanush Sagar** and **Ganga Sagar** are

---

Janakpur's festivals

Janakpur's atmosphere is charged with an intense devotional zeal. New shrines are forever being inaugurated and idols installed, while *kuti* loudspeakers broadcast religious discourses and the mesmerizing drone of *bhajan*. Pilgrimage is a year-round industry, marked by several highlights in the festival calendar:

Parikrama As many as 100,000 people join the annual one-day circumambulation of the city on the day of the February/March full moon, many performing prostrations along the entire eight-kilometre route. The pilgrimage coincides with the festival of Holi, when coloured water is thrown everywhere and on everyone.

Ram Navami Ram's birthday, celebrated on the ninth day after the March/April full moon, attracts thousands of sadhus, who receive free room and board at temples.

Chhath Women bathe in Janakpur's ponds and line them with elaborate offerings to the sun god Surya at dawn on the third day of Tihaar (Diwali) in October–November. Women in the villages surrounding Janakpur paint murals on the walls of their houses.

Biwaha Panchami The culmination of this five-day event – Janakpur's most important festival – is a re-enactment of Ram and Sita's wedding at the Janaki Mandir, which draws hundreds of thousands of pilgrims on the fifth day after the new moon of November/December.

Maithili painting

For three thousand years, Hindu women of the region once known as Mithila have maintained a tradition of **painting**, using techniques and motifs passed from mother to daughter. The colourful images can be viewed as fertility charms, meditation aids or a form of storytelling, embodying millennia of traditional knowledge.

From an early age **Brahman girls** practise drawing complex symbols derived from Hindu myths and folk tales, which over the course of generations have been reduced to *mandala*-like abstractions. By the time she is in her teens, a girl will be presenting simple paintings to her arranged fiancé; the courtship culminates with the painting of a **kohbar**, an elaborate fresco on the wall of the bride's bedroom, where the newlyweds will spend their first nights. Depicting a stalk of bamboo surrounded by lotus leaves (symbols of male and female sexuality), the *kohbar* is a powerful celebration of life and creation. Other motifs include footprints and fishes (representing Vishnu), parrots (symbolic of a happy union), Krishna cavorting with his milkmaids, and Surabhi, the Cow of Plenty, who inflames the desire of those who milk her. Perhaps the most striking aspect of the *kohbar* is that, almost by definition, it is ephemeral: even the most amazing mural will be washed off within a week or two. Painting is seen as a form of prayer or meditation; once completed, the work has achieved its end.

Women of all castes create simpler **wall decorations** during the autumn festival of Tihaar (Diwali). In the weeks leading up to the festival they apply a new coat of mud mixed with dung and rice chaff to their houses and add relief designs. Just before Lakshmi Puja, the climactic third day of Tihaar, many paint images of peacocks, pregnant elephants and other symbols of prosperity to attract a visit from the goddess of wealth. Until Nepali New Year celebrations in April, the decorations are easily viewable in villages around Janakpur.

Paintings on paper, which traditionally play only a minor part in the culture, have become the most celebrated form of Maithili art – or Madhubani art, as it's known in India, where a community-development project began turning it into a marketable commodity in the 1960s. More recently, the **Janakpur Women's Development Center** (see p.328) has helped do the same in Nepal, making Maithili paintings a staple of Kathmandu tourist gift shops. Many artists concentrate on traditional religious motifs, but a growing number depict people – mainly women and children in domestic scenes, always shown in characteristic doe-eyed profile.

considered the holiest of Janakpur's ponds. The sight of Hindus performing ritual ablutions in the fog at sunrise here is profoundly moving.

Walk westwards from the Janaki Mandir to the highway and you reach **Ramanand Chowk**, the nucleus of many of Janakpur's *kuti* and a major sadhu gathering place during festivals. A four-way arch bearing a statue of Guru Ramananda, the saint responsible for Janakpur's modern fame, marks the intersection that bears his name. Two well-known establishments, Ramanand Ashram and Ratnasagar Kuti, are located west of here but, like most *kuti*, they are closed to non-Hindus.

Hanuman Durbar, a small *kuti* 150m south of Ramanand Chowk on the west side, was home until 1998 to the world's biggest (well, fattest) rhesus monkey, worshipped as Hanuman the monkey god. Priests still proudly display photos of the late great monkey, and they are optimistically fattening up another one as his replacement.

Around Janakpur

The surrounding countryside is inhabited by Hindu castes and members of the Tharu and Danuwar ethnic groups, and features some of the most meticulously kept farmland you'll see anywhere. You can ride the narrow-gauge **railway** east or west and, during the cooler winter months, great bike rides can be made along several roads radiating out from the city.

The Janakpur Women's Development Center

Hindu women of the deeply conservative villages around Janakpur are rarely spared from their household duties, and, once married, are expected to remain veiled and silent before all males but their husbands. Fortunately, their rich tradition of folk art (see box, p.327) offers them an escape. The nonprofit **Janakpur Women's Development Center** (Sun–Thurs: mid-Feb to mid-Nov 10am–5pm; mid-Nov to mid-Feb 10am–4pm; free), 3km south of town, provides a space for women from nearby villages to develop. Founded in 1989, with assistance from several international aid organizations, the artists' cooperative helps its fifty-odd members turn their skills into income – and the fact that some have gone on to start their own companies is a sure sign of the project's success. But more importantly, the centre empowers women through training in literacy and business skills, and support sessions in which they can share their feelings and discuss their roles in family and society.

Initially specializing in Maithili paper art, the centre now has separate buildings for sewing, screen-printing, ceramics and painting. Visitors are welcome to meet the artists and learn about their work and traditions. A **gift shop** sells crafts made on the premises, as well as the JWDC's own booklet, *Master Artists of Janakpur*.

The centre is a fifteen-minute rikshaw (Rs50) or bike ride from Janakpur. Head south towards the airport and make a left turn about 1km after Murali Chowk. Bear right after about 200m, passing through the well-kept village of **Kuwa**. Set in a walled compound, the centre is on the right after about 500m. If in doubt, ask for Nari Bikas Kendra (Women Development Center), or just have a rikshaw-wallah take you – they all know the way.

The Janakpur Railway

Janakpur's **narrow-gauge railway** is an excellent way to get out into the country. On a misty winter's morning, the ride past sleepy villages and minor temples is nothing short of magical. Built in the 1940s to transport timber to India from the now-depleted forest west of Janakpur, the railway these days operates primarily as a passenger service.

Janakpur station, at the top of Station Road, is the terminus for two separate lines, each about 30km long: one eastbound to **Jaynagar**, just over the border in India, and the other westbound to **Bijalpura**. In general the Jaynagar service runs three times a day (departing at around 7am, noon and 3pm and returning to Janakpur at around noon, 2pm and 6pm) and takes two to three hours one way. The Bijalpura service runs only once a day, departing Janakpur in the late afternoon and returning the next morning. That makes the Jaynagar line the more feasible for a day-trip: you could ride all the way to Khajuri (last stop before the border) and then catch the train as it passes through on the way back. The **fare** to Jaynagar is Rs29 in second class or Rs50 in first. Arrive early for a seat; on the way back you'll probably end up riding on the roof.

Other villages

Dozens of villages dot the land around Janakpur at regular intervals, each with its own mango grove and a pond or two. Subsistence farming – livestock, grains, vegetables and fish – is virtually the only occupation here. You can explore south towards **Nagarain** or west to substantial **Khurta**, but the most rewarding day trip heads north from Suba Chowk to Dhanusha (Dhanushadham), an important pilgrimage site 18km from Janakpur. According to the Ramayana, it was here that King Janak staged an Arthurian contest for the hand of his daughter, Sita, decreeing that the suitors prove themselves by lifting an impossibly heavy bow. After all others had given up, Ram picked up the bow with ease, and broke it in two for good measure. Villagers can point you to a walled compound encircling a volcanic rock that's said to be a piece of the bow.

There are also several picturesque villages on either side of the main road that connects Janakpur to the Mahendra Highway. The loveliest is **Kumrora**, on the right about 4km north of Pidari Chowk, a tidy Brahman settlement with particularly expressive wall murals.

Eating and drinking

If you enjoy Indian **food**, *Hotel Welcome* and *Hotel Rama*'s restaurants do beautiful meals, while various places around the Janaki Mandir offer pure vegetarian food. For Nepali fare, the line of places around the corner from *Hotel Welcome*, on Station Road, is just the ticket. For Indian sweets, take your pick from a host of *mithai pasal* near the Janaki temple. Western dishes can be had at the *Rooftop Restaurant*, on Station Road.

Moving on

For **bus** frequencies and travel times from Janakpur, see p.340. Note that Sajha tickets are purchased at Ramanand Chowk, not at the bus park – the Sajha bus to Kathmandu sets off from here too. Tickets for night buses to Kathmandu are also sold from desks along Station Road near the *Aanand Hotel*, but go to the bus park for a better seat assignment. Buddha Air, just off Bhanu Chowk (☎041/525 021), flies daily from Janakpur to Kathmandu ($110). Rikshaws charge about Rs100 from the market to the airport.

Koshi Tappu Wildlife Reserve

Straddling a floodplain of shifting grassland and sandbanks north of the Koshi Barrage, **Koshi Tappu Wildlife Reserve** is the smallest of the Terai's parks. There are no tigers or rhinos, nor even any jungle – but **birdwatchers** can have a field-day here. Koshi Tappu is one of the subcontinent's most important wetlands, and thanks to its location just downstream from one of the few breaches in the Himalayan barrier, it's an internationally important area for waterfowl and waders.

Some 465 **bird** species, many of them endangered, have been counted here. Flocks of up to fifty thousand ducks used to be seen in winter and spring, though numbers have been lower in recent years. Most of Nepal's egrets, storks, ibises, terns and gulls are represented, as are at least five globally threatened species, including the black-necked stork, red-necked falcon, swamp frankolin and the impressive lesser adjutant, one of the world's largest storks. November

Nepal's river dolphins

Nepal's susu, or **gangetic dolphins**, belong to one of only three species of freshwater dolphins in the world and, like their cousins in the Amazon and Indus, are highly endangered. A small, isolated population survives in the far west of Nepal, downstream of the **Chisapani gorge** in the Karnali River. Before the 2008 flood, dolphins used to cavort openly in the outflow of the **Koshi Barrage**, less than a dozen kilometres from Koshi Tappu Wildlife Reserve. Whether these practically blind animals (they use echo-location), revered in myth as "messenger kings", return in numbers, or go the way of the now-extinct Yangtze Dolphin, remains to be seen.

and December are the optimum months to see winter migrants, and mid-February to early April are best for the late migratory species.

The reserve was established to protect one of the subcontinent's last surviving herds of **wild buffalo**, believed to number 150–170 animals. However, wildlife experts are concerned about the number of domestic buffalo getting into the reserve and mating with the wild ones. There are **mugger** crocodiles and many species of **turtle** and **fish**, as well as blue bull, wild boar, langur and spotted deer and, before the flood, **Gangetic dolphins** could sometimes be seen playing in the water above or below the barrage. Dolphins have since been seen in the Koshi again, and it's thought that at least three of them are definitely there.

With no rhinos or large carnivores, Koshi Tappu is comparatively safe to enter **on foot**, but take a guide and local advice: wild elephants have been known to maraud in this area. Rides on **elephants** (Rs1000 per hour) and trips in **canoes** (from Rs2500) can also be arranged at the reserve headquarters. Between the channels of water lie a number of semi-permanent islands of scrub and grassland that are the main stomping ground for blue bull. (*Tappu* means "island" in Nepali, which is an accurate description of this floodplain in the wet summer months.) Blue bulls are big animals with very sizeable horns – those of a mature bull can measure over two metres from tip to tip – and while they normally run away at the first scent of humans, you have to make sure not to threaten them or block their escape route.

Park practicalities

The reserve is marked by a sign beside the Mahendra Highway, about 12km east of the Koshi Barrage – or, if you're coming from the other direction, 3km west of Laukhi. From here an access road leads 3km north to the **reserve headquarters** where you will find a museum. An **entry permit** costs Rs500 per day.

Most of the few foreigners who visit Koshi Tappu come on fairly expensive **package tours**, flying in and out of Biratnagar and staying in one of the small

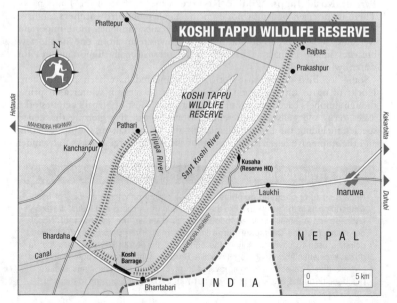

KOSHI TAPPU WILDLIFE RESERVE

Lhotshampas: Nepal's other refugees

Every visitor to Nepal knows about Tibet. But few have heard of its Bhutanese **refugees**, who far outnumber Tibetans in Nepal. Some 107,000 ethnic Nepalis, forcibly expelled from Bhutan in 1991-92, are effectively interned in eastern Nepal, pawns in an obscure political stalemate.

Members of Nepali hill groups, notably Rais and Limbus, began migrating into Bhutan in significant numbers in the mid-nineteenth century, eventually accounting for at least a third of Bhutan's population and earning the designation **Lhotshampas** (southerners). However, during the mid-1980s, the continued influx of ethnic Nepalis and a rise in Nepali militancy in neighbouring Darjeeling and Sikkim gave rise to a wave of Drukpa nationalism. The Drukpas were quick to make scapegoats of the Lhotshampas who, not coincidentally, controlled lands that were emerging as the economic powerhouse of Bhutan.

In 1988, after a national census was taken, the government began a process of **systematic discrimination** against anyone who couldn't provide written proof of residency in Bhutan in 1958. A campaign of **ethnic cleansing** gathered momentum, culminating in 1991 when "illegal" families were evicted from their lands. Opponents of the regime had their citizenship revoked, and they and their families were harassed, imprisoned, tortured and raped.

The refugees fled initially to India, but receiving little encouragement there, most continued on to Nepal. As their numbers swelled, the Nepalese government, wanting to keep the problem out of sight, established **refugee camps** at Timai (just east of Kakarbhitta), Goldhap (south of Birtamod), Pathari (southeast of Itahari) and, biggest by far, Beldangi I, II and II (north of Damak). Since then, a number of international and Nepali NGOs have built housing, schools, health posts and other essential facilities in the camps under the direction of the UN. Conditions are fairly liveable, but residents are desperately poor, dependent on aid or scarce labouring work.

The crisis shows no signs of being resolved anytime soon. India has closed its borders to refugees attempting to return of their own accord. In 2008, a new resettlement campaign permitted eight thousand refugees to emigrate – mainly to the US. One third of them have agreed to emigrate, while the others are still desperate to return to their homes in Bhutan. Preparing for a long haul, aid agencies have shifted their focus from relief work to income-generation projects that will give the refugees some independence.

tented camps. *Koshi Camp* (☎01/4429 609, ⓦwww.kosicamp.com), is located just outside the northeastern corner of the reserve, near the village of Prakashpur, and is reached via a separate road. Due to its location, the Koshi Camp was less affected by the flood's consequences than the other camps, which were disturbed by the presence of displaced people and by the reparation of the road and embankments. *Aqua Birds Unlimited Camp* (☎01/443 4705, ⓦwww.aquabirds.com.np), is just a few minutes' walk from the reserve headquarters. *Koshi Tappu Wildlife Camp* (☎01/422 6130, ⓦwww.koshitappu.com) is situated in a private jungle not far from the Sapt Koshi river. All camps provide accommodation in deluxe twin-bedded tents with solar hot-water showers, serve decent food and have experienced guides. All meals, activities and transportation to and from Biratnagar are included in the price (around $100–150 per night). The reserve is not really developed for independent travellers, however.

Biratnagar

Biratnagar, the second largest city in Nepal, is an industrial town close to the border and pretty much deprived of any charm. Industry here was deeply shaken by the Madhesi movement – which paralyzed the whole Terai for a month in 2008. In 2009, protests and *bandhs* (strikes) by various minorities and political groups (most recently the Tharus) reached such an extreme that industrialists reacted by conducting their own *bandhs* against the *bandhs*, and Biratnagar was eventually declared a "*bandh*-free" area. *Bandhs* in the area can seriously disrupt travel and block the highway.

The main reason visitors pass through is in order to catch a flight to Kathmandu or anywhere in the Eastern hills. The **airport** is situated 3kms north and the bus station 500m south of Mahendra Chowk. East of Mahendra Chowk is Traffic Chowk, a central point on Main Road, where you will find a few **internet cafés**. A short distance north, on the same road, after the small but lively Hanuman temple, there are a few **banks** with ATMS.

Accommodation

As well as the more formal accommodation listed below, you'll find several cheap and basic lodges near the bus station, like *Geetanjali* (**②**).

Hotel Namaskar On Main Rd, 100m south of Traffic Chowk ☎021/521 199. Quietly set back from the noise of the street, this hotel's better appointed rooms come with TV and a/c. (**⑤**). The restaurant is worth trying. **③**

Hotel Swagatam Half a kilometre south of the bus station on Malaya Rd ☎021/524 450. This pink hotel offers comfortable rooms with TV, bathroom

and a/c, and its Art Deco restaurant serves tasty curries. **③**–**⑤**

Hotel Xenial Just behind the bus station ☎021/530 250. The poshest option in town, with all facilities and a small – but dubious – swimming pool. The restaurant is rather dark and offers a good range of Continental food and heavy Indian curries. **⑤**–**⑧**

Moving on

By **bus**, Biratnagar is one hour from Dharan and three hours from Kakarbhitta. Regular buses also leave for Kathmandu, Dhankutta, Hile and Janakpur. Kathmandu is also well served by different **airline companies** ($125) and there are also few flights a week to Taplejung and to all the Eastern hill districts. **Taxis** may cost up to Rs300 to drop you at the airport. You can book a bus or plane ticket from any agency near Mahendra Chowk.

Kakarbhitta

Once-sleepy **KAKARBHITTA** is the municipal capital of Nepal's easternmost district. It's mainly a gateway for people, and most of those using it are Indians, hopping over from Darjeeling for some shopping, or heading to Biratnagar for business; the presence of over 107,000 Bhutanese refugees in camps west of here (see box, p.331) contributes to the flow. In addition, the villages situated on both sides of the border receive some perfectly legal migrants just passing by: **wild**

The people of the Terai

Alongside the mysterious Tharu (see box, p.270), the Eastern Terai is home to the **Danuwars**, who are widely distributed across the region, and the **Majhis**, who live in riverside settlements between the Bagmati and the Sun Koshi. Both groups traditionally rely more on fishing than hunting or farming. Most of the Terai's **Hindu** caste families are first- or second-generation immigrants from India, and maintain close cultural, linguistic and economic ties with their homeland. In addition, a significant number of **Muslims** inhabit the western Terai, especially around Nepalgunj, where they're in the majority. Most are farmers, tailors or shopkeepers.

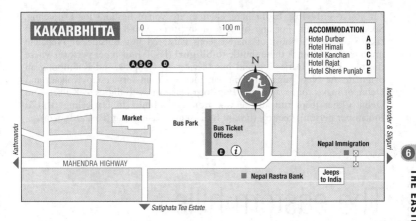

KAKARBHITTA

0   100 m

N

ACCOMMODATION
Hotel Durbar   **A**
Hotel Himali   **B**
Hotel Kanchan   **C**
Hotel Rajat   **D**
Hotel Shere Punjab **E**

Kathmandu

Indian border & Siliguri

Market

Bus Park

Bus Ticket Offices

Nepal Immigration

MAHENDRA HIGHWAY

Nepal Rastra Bank

Jeeps to India

Satighata Tea Estate

elephants. Every year a few people are trampled to death and houses get destroyed by the furious pachyderms, who liberally help themselves to the grain stock.

If you have some time on your hands, the pleasantly green Satighata tea estate is just ten minutes' walk south of Kakarbhitta, and a Buddhist monastery run by Tamangs can be visited on the way. Don't be afraid to go there: the chances you'll meet any marauding elephants are very slim.

Practicalities

All of Kakarbhitta's **accommodation** is within spitting distance of the bus park. *Hotel Durbar* (☏023/562 384; ❺) is the best option in town but unfortunately only has four rooms, and the cheapest are non air-conditioned. The friendly *Hotel Kanchan* (☏023/562 384; ❶–❻) has a good range of rooms, from shared-bath, air-conditioned options to mid-range, fan-cooled rooms. *Hotel Rajat* (☏023/562 033; ❶–❻) has good facilities, including an internet connect, decent restaurant and a small garden/parking area, and offers a similar range of rooms to the *Kanchan*.

Most guesthouses have their own **restaurants**, among which *Hotel Rajat*'s is probably the best. Moneychangers and lodges will swap Nepalese and Indian rupees at the market rate, but to change hard currency you'll have to use the **bank** (Nepal Rastra, on the south side of the highway).

Bus tickets for travel within Nepal can easily be purchased from the desks lining the east side of the bus park. Night buses to Kathmandu and Pokhara leave Kakarbhitta in staggered intervals between 3pm and 5.30pm, but book at least a couple of hours ahead to be sure of a good seat. Dharan and Janakpur make good intermediate destinations from here on the safer daytime buses. Travel agents around the bus park can book **flights** to Kathmandu from Bhadrapur ($156). Bhadrapur's airstrip can accommodate only very small planes, and you'll need to rent a taxi for around Rs700 to get there (1hr). Biratnagar has more frequent and reliable flights, but is more than three hours away by bus.

Just up from *Hotel Shere Punjab*, the **tourist office** (Sun–Thurs 10am–5pm, Fri 10am–2pm) may be able to advise on onward travel.

The border

The wide Mechi River forms **the border**, about 500m east of town. Formalities are pleasantly relaxed, and Nepalese immigration is open 24 hours a day, though it may be hard to find anyone after dark. Make sure you have the correct cash in US dollars (see p.63) – if you have anything else they'll make you go to the bank.

If you're **entering India** here, chances are you're heading for Darjeeling, Sikkim or Kolkata. For any of these destinations, you'll probably be best off taking one of the host of shared jeeps clustered just outside of Nepalese immigration. Most of these shuttle to **Siliguri** (Rs30 Indian per person), where the toy train to Darjeeling and bus services to Gangtok and Kalimpong all originate. At New Jalpaiguri you can pick up train services to Kolkata and Delhi, or make your way to the **Bagdogra** airport, with flights to Kolkata and Delhi. Other jeeps run all the way from Kakarbhitta to Darjeeling (Rs170 Indian per person), Gantok (Rs200 Indian) and Kalimpong (Rs150 Indian).

The eastern hills

Two main roads link the Terai with the hills east of the Sapt Koshi – the **Dhankuta road**, leaving the Mahendra Highway at Itahari, and the **Ilam road**, beginning at Charali. **Bus** services are more fickle than along the Mahendra Highway, but this is made up for by the availability of **shared jeeps**, which are faster than buses and don't cost much more.

The Dhankuta road

Call it development, or colonialism by another name, but the big donor nations have staked out distinct spheres of influence in Nepal. Despite the closure of the Gurkha Camp at **Dharan**, the bustling gateway to the eastern hills, almost half the British Army's Gurkha recruits still come from the area, and the old ties are strongly felt. Britain's aid programme, based in the airy ridge-top bazaar of **Dhankuta**, has been handed over to the Government, but agriculture, forestry, health and cottage industries are still in operation. The biggest and most obvious British undertaking is the **road** to Dharan, Dhankuta, Hile and beyond, which was constructed with £50 million of British taxpayers' money. While there are few grand monuments or temples, this region is a bastion of traditional Nepali hill culture. The bazaar towns of **Hile** and **Basantapur**, in particular, give a powerful taste of what lies beyond the point where the tarmac runs out.

Dharan and around

From the Mahendra Highway, the Dhankuta road winds languidly through forest as it ascends the Bhabar, the sloping alluvial zone between the Terai and the foothills. **DHARAN**, 16km north of the highway, sits a slightly cooler 300m above the plain.

Dharan hit world headlines in 1988 when an **earthquake** killed seven hundred people and flattened most of the town. In late 1989 another crisis occurred when the **British Army**, foreseeing forces reductions, pulled out of the town and handed its Gurkha Camp back to the government. Would-be recruits must now travel to Pokhara to compete for even fewer places in the regiments (see p.225). Fortunately, Dharan has bounced back smartly. Earthquake-damaged areas have

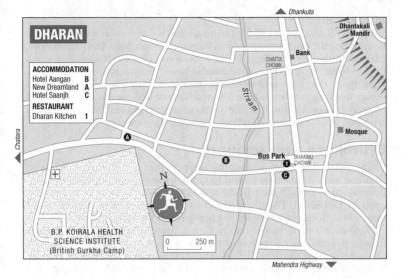

DHARAN

ACCOMMODATION
Hotel Aangan   **B**
New Dreamland   **A**
Hotel Saanjh   **C**
RESTAURANT
Dharan Kitchen   **1**

Dhantakali
Mandir

Bank

CHATTA
CHOWK

Stream

Mosque

Bus Park   BHANNU
      CHOWK

Chatara

N

0   250 m

B.P. KOIRALA HEALTH
SCIENCE INSTITUTE
(British Gurkha Camp)

Mahendra Highway

been rebuilt, the city's western half has grown into a neat little enclave of retired Gurkhas' bungalows, and the Gurkha Camp is now a fancy medical institute.

Yet Dharan's **bazaar**, which runs the length of the main street between Chatta and Bhanu chowks, remains as earthily Nepali as ever. For many people throughout the eastern hills this is still the proverbial Bright Lights, where they come to sell oranges by the sackload. In the area northeast of central Bhanu Chowk, you'll see hill women investing the family fortune in gold ornaments and shops selling silver coins to be strung into necklaces.

An easy path leads up to the modest **Dantakali Mandir**, on a low ridge just east of the bazaar, and continues on to two other temples, Buddhasubbha and Bindyabasini. **Chatara**, 15km west of Dharan, is the finishing point for rafting trips on the Sun Koshi. Walk an hour north of here and you'll reach the sacred confluence of **Barahakshetra**, site of a temple to Vishnu incarnated as a boar (Barahi) and an annual pilgrimage on the day of the full moon of October–November.

Practicalities

Accommodation in Dharan is fairly poor and made worse by bus-park noise. The *Hotel Aangan* (☎025/520 640; ❸) is a reasonably quiet place, with good facilities, clean, decently furnished rooms, hot water and TVs in the more expensive rooms (❹). *Hotel Saanjh* (☎025/522 010; ❶) is similar but smaller, noisier and darker. Far from the bus station and next to the golf course, ⚘ *New Dreamland* (☎025/525 024; ❷–❹) is situated in a quiet suburb where brick abodes and little gardens show the influence of Britain on ex-Gurkha soldiers. It's the best hotel in town, with air-conditioned, TV and attached or non-attached bathrooms.

Several **restaurants** do quite tasty Nepali, Indian and even Continental dishes. The restaurants at the *Aangan* and *Saanjh* hotels are worth trying. Some of the best places for eating, though, are the *Dharan Kitchen*, with a good range of Nepalese, Indian and Continental food, and the ⚘ *Jojola Khaja Ghar* – an atmospheric Newari restaurant with a large variety of moderately priced dishes.

You'll find an **ATM** in the Tamu complex, next to the bus park, and in Nabil bank further north.

Moving on

Buses run from the bus park to Biratnagar and Kakarbhitta at least every half-hour during the day, less frequently to Birgunj. To reach other Terai destinations, change at Itahari or Biratnagar. If you want to go straight to Kathmandu, you'll have to book ahead on one of the few day buses, which leave very early, or the night buses that leave mid-afternoon. Buses to Dhankuta and points north depart from the eastern side of Bhannu Chowk and are basically local and chronically overcrowded; it can be a real ordeal getting a seat, but shared **jeeps** are faster, more comfortable and only slightly more expensive.

Dhankuta and around

From Dharan the road switchbacks abruptly over a 1420-metre saddle at Bhedetar, with dramatic views and some competent roadside restaurants, then descends to cross the Tamur Koshi at Mulghat (280m) before climbing once again to **DHANKUTA**, stretched out on a ridge at 1150m. Though you'd never guess, this is the administrative headquarters for eastern Nepal.

Dhankuta is a small, predominantly Newari town, with shady *chautaara* and a friendly, well-to-do feel. Steps lead up from the bus park to the main **bazaar**, which climbs north along the ridge. The lower half of the bazaar, up to the police station, is paved and reasonably active; the upper half is quieter and more picturesque, lined with whitewashed, tiled and carved Newari townhouses. The outlying area is populated by Rais, Magars and Hindu castes, who make Dhankuta's **haat bazaar**, on Thursdays, a tremendously vivid affair. The **Dhankuta Museum** (Mon, Wed–Fri & Sun 10am–5pm; closes at 4pm mid-Nov to mid-Feb; Rs10), near the top of the bazaar, displays ethnic and archeological artefacts of eastern Nepal. To get to it, walk up the flagstoned bazaar to the four-way intersection of Bhim Narayan Chowk, marked by a statue, then follow the road to the right around and down for 250m – the museum is above the road on the left, signposted in Nepali.

Although you can't see the Himalayas from here, the area makes fine **walking** country. In **Santang**, a Rai village about 45 minutes southeast of town, women can be seen embroidering beautiful shawls and weaving *dhaka*, which is as much a speciality of the eastern hills as it is in the west (see p.261). You can walk to Hile in about two hours by taking short cuts off the main road: stick to the ridge and within sight of the electric power line.

Practicalities

The cheapies in the bazaar are cold-water outfits with minimal command of English, but pleasantly traditional wooden interiors. *Hotel Suravi* (☎025/520 204; ❷) and *Hotel Anjuli* (☎025/520 366; ❷), both situated in the main street, are the cleanest and best options. Plenty of places in the bazaar do *daal bhaat*, *pakauda* and the like, and one or two can rustle up *momo*, *thukpa* and curries.

Hile and beyond

Most buses to Dhankuta continue as far as **HILE** (*Hee*-lay), 15km beyond Dhankuta and 750m higher up along the same ridge. This spirited little settlement is one of the most important staging areas in eastern Nepal.

Poised over the vast, hazy Arun Valley, Hile's bazaar strip straggles up the often fog-bound ridge, drawing a swirl of ethnic peoples who walk in from miles around to trade: Tamangs and Sherpas from the west, Newari and Indian traders from the south, and Rais from their heartland of the roadless hillsides all around. The most visible minority, however, are Bhotiyas (see p.361) from the northern highlands, who run a number of simple wooden lodges. One of the most exotic things you can do in Nepal is sit in a flickering Bhotiya kitchen sipping hot millet beer from an authentic **tongba**: unique to the eastern hills, these miniature wooden steins with brass hoops and fitted tops look like they were designed for Genghis Khan.

Other than drink a *tongba*, or maybe visit a couple of *gompas*, the only thing to do in town is browse the bazaar. Hile's **haat bazaar**, on Thursday, is lively, but not as big as Dhankuta's. Most visitors are here to trek, and magnificent **views** can be had just a half-hour's hike from Hile – as long as you're up early enough to beat the clouds. Walk to the north end of the bazaar and bear right at the fork up a dirt lane; after 100m a set of steps leads up to join the Hattikharka trail, which contours around the hill. The panorama spreads out before you like a map: to the northwest, the Makalu Himal floats above the awesome canyon of the Arun; the ridges of the Milke Daada zigzag to the north; and part of the Kanchenjunga massif pokes up in the northeast.

Encouraged by a liberalized market, some landowners in this area have begun to cultivate tea. You can visit the **Guranse tea estate**, whose main entrance is just down the road from the bazaar.

Practicalities

Hile's **lodges** are pretty savvy about catering to foreigners. Of the half-dozen Bhotiya places in the bazaar (all ❶), *Hotel Gajur* is perhaps the most atmospheric, and its kitchen is legendary for *momo*, *sokuti* and *tongba*. Many stalls at either end of the bazaar also do Nepali/Tibetan **food** such as *momo*, *sokuti* and chow mein. The Rastriya Banjiya **bank**, opposite the small *gompa* at the southern end of the bazaar, can change cash and traveller's cheques.

Moving on

When it's time to **move on**, you can get a night bus direct to Kathmandu, but it's a brutal eighteen-hour ride. If possible, break the journey into two or more days, with stops in Janakpur and/or Chitwan. Buses leave Hile every half-hour for Dharan (last bus down is at 5.30pm), from where you can pick up onward connections. From Hile, you can also reach Basantapur and go up to Chainpur by bus.

Turning round isn't obligatory, however, as dirt roads penetrate further and further into the hills each year. From the northern end of the bazaar, **jeeps** and the occasional battered bus bump and rev their way down a road which reaches the **Arun river**, passing the agricultural research station at Pakhribas en route.

Most buses from Dhankuta rumble north and east on another dirt road as far as **Basantapur**, a dank, almost Elizabethan bazaar that lies a dusty 21km – nearly three hours by bus – from Hile. You get tremendous views of the Makalu massif for much of the way, and Kanchenjunga pops into view near the end. The hills above Basantapur are a delight for walking, with mixed pasture and dense mossy forest, rhododendrons, orchids and jasmine, and plenty of friendly villages. A local factory produces a rather nice rhododendron juice that you can find easily in Basantapur, alongside Nepal's only wine (berry not grape), called Hinwa. As long as the road isn't blocked by snow or landslides, you can pick up a shared jeep from Basantapur to **Tehratum**, a four-hour ride to the east, from where the road will eventually be extended through to Phidim, Taplejung and Ilam. Another road, rougher at the time of writing but due for improvements as we went to press, continues north from Basantapur towards the beautiful Newari towns of **Chainpur** and **Tumlingtar**, halfway to the Tibetan border. The first bus reached Chainpur in October 2008 and was welcomed by an overjoyed crowd, blessing it with flowers.

The Ilam road

Like the Dhankuta road, the **Ilam road** keeps getting longer: originally engineered by the Koreans to connect the tea estates of Kanyam and Ilam with the Terai, it now goes all the way to Taplejung, the most common starting point for Kanchenjunga treks. The road is pitched and in excellent shape as far as Ilam, but it's extremely steep and entails a couple of monster ascents.

A few express **buses** to Ilam come through from Dharan, but a more frequent, crowded service begins from Birtamod, located on the Mahendra Highway 8km west of the actual start of the road at Charali. The 78km journey takes about four hours by bus; shared **jeeps**, also departing from Birtamod, are somewhat faster and more comfortable. Be sure to catch the bus or jeep in Birtamod, as you won't get a seat if you try to board in Charali.

After traversing lush lowlands, the road begins a laborious 1600m ascent to Kanyam. At Phikal, a few kilometres further on, a pitched side road leads steeply up for 10km to **Pashupati Nagar**, a small bazaar at 2200m just below the ridge that separates Nepal and India here. Shared jeeps wait at the turnoff at Phikal, from where the road descends 1200m in a series of tight switchbacks to cross the Mai Khola before climbing another 700m to Ilam (1200m).

Ilam and around

To Nepalis, **ILAM** (Ee-lam) means tea: cool and moist for much of the year, the hills of Ilam district (like those of Darjeeling, just across the border) are perfect for it. The bazaar is fairly shoddy, though it does contain some nice old wooden buildings, and there are no mountain views from anywhere very close by. There are, however, plenty of **hikes** and some good **birdwatching**. Settled by Newars, Rais and Marwaris (a business-minded Indian group with interests in tea), Ilam was eastern Nepal's main centre of commerce at one time and the Thursday *haat bazaar* here still draws shoppers from a wide radius.

A single tourist **hotel**, *Green View Guest House* (☎027/520 103; ❶) has clean, large and well-furnished rooms with windows looking out over the tea gardens, and geyser hot water. *Danfe Guest House* (☎027/520 048; ❶), just down the road, is a classic bare-bones trekking inn, but with a superb location in among the tea bushes. Simple **meals** are available at loads of places along the main drag. Two places that can be recommended for *daal bhaat*, *momo* and *tongba* are *Changwa Hotel*, about midway along the bazaar, and *Kanchanjhangha Restaurant*, a tiny, welcoming wooden shack near the top end.

Ilam's **tea gardens** carpet the ridge above town and tumble down its steep far side and between April and November you can watch the pluckers at work. Nepal's first tea estate, it was established in 1864 by a relative of the prime minister after a visit to Darjeeling, where tea cultivation was just becoming big business. Marwaris soon assumed control of the plantation, an arrangement that lasted until the 1960s when the government nationalized this and six other hill estates. In 1999, however, the government sold the estates to an Indian company. As a result, the 140-year-old tea factory in Ilam town has been closed and workers have lost their pensions, but production is increasing

To actually try tea and see how it's made, you'll need to return back down the main road as far as Paltangemor (1hr 30min by jeep). The Kanyam **tea factory** here, built using British aid money in 1985, is the largest in the district. Staff are not quite used to visitors yet, so you may need to ask around for the manager, but once inside you're likely to be welcomed with a short (free) **tour** and a cup of tea.

The plucked leaves are loaded into "withering chutes" upstairs, where fans remove about half their moisture content. They're then transferred to big rolling

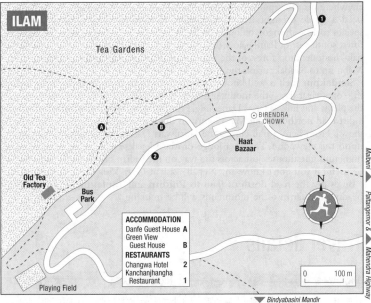

machines to break the cell walls and release their juices, and placed on fermentation beds to bring out their flavour and colour. Finally, most of the remaining moisture is removed in a wood-fired drying machine, and the leaves are sorted into grades. Ilam's premium tea compares favourably with Darjeeling's, and indeed most of it is exported to Germany to be blended into "Darjeeling" teas. Transport up to Ilam and down to Birtamod passes frequently, but you may have to stand on a local **bus**, or wedge yourself into a shared jeep.

Beyond Ilam

The Ilam area is noted for its greenness – higher up, the jungle is exuberant, and the slopes fertile. Keep an eye out for **cardamom**, which grows in moist ravines and has become an important cash crop here. Another common cash crop cultivated in this area is **broom grass**, which is used to make traditional Nepali brooms. Locals produce a surplus of milk here, which you'll see being transported in canisters on horseback to local cheese factories. Rais make up the majority of villagers, followed by Baahuns, Chhetris and Limbus.

Rewarding **walks** set off in several directions. From the tea gardens, you can contour westwards and cross the Puwamai Khola, ascending the other side to Sanrumba, site of a Tuesday market, with views of Kanchenjunga from further along the ridge. A trail heading east from Ilam descends to cross the Mai Khola, where the annual Beni Mela attracts thousands of Hindus on the first day of Magh (mid-Jan), and continues on to Naya Bazaar. Atop a wooded ridge north of Ilam, the sacred pond of Mai Pokhri can be reached by walking or hitching along the road towards Phidim and turning right at Biblete, 2km from the bazaar, from where it's another two hours' ascent, passing through rhododendron and magnolia forest; a shorter trip could be made by riding a shared jeep one-way.

The **Mai Valley**, which Ilam overlooks, is renowned for its **birds**: the dense, wet habitat and abundant undergrowth provide cover for some 450 species. To see anywhere near that number of species you have to move around a lot, and you'll need a guide brought from Kathmandu, Chitwan or Koshi Tappu. Lowland species such as drongos, bulbuls and flycatchers are best observed in the Sukarni forest southwest of Ilam, below the Soktim tea estate. Temperate birds inhabit the oak-rhododendron forest of the upper Mai Valley to the northeast of Ilam, from Mabu up to Sandakpur on the Indian border, at elevations of 2000m to 3000m.

Sandakpur itself is well known in India for its sunset and sunrise views, taking in – on a clear day – the mountains from Kanchenjunga to Everest, and views of the plains and hills as far as Darjeeling. From Biblete, jeeps can be hired to follow a dirt road north (passing Mai Pokhri on the way) until it peters out at Maima-jhuwa. From here, a trail climbs the Goruwala Daada, taking around four hours up to the viewpoint. There's a lodge on the Nepalese side of the border – and numerous guesthouses just across the way, on the Indian side. A local guide would be useful if you don't know any Nepali – ask at *Green View Guest House* in Ilam.

Buses ply the road north of Ilam to **Phidim** and **Taplejung** – most people heading this far into the mountains will be trekking.

Travel details

Day buses

Biratnagar to: Birgunj (8 daily; 6hr); Dhankuta (4 daily; 4hr); Dharan (every 10min; 1hr 30min); Janakpur (7 daily; 6hr); Kakarbhitta (every 10min; 3hr); Kathmandu (10 daily; 10hr).
Birgunj to: Bhairahawa (8 daily; 8hr); Biratnagar (8 daily; 6hr); Butwal for Sonauli (4 daily; 6hr); Dharan (8 daily; 8hr); Gorkha (5 daily; 7hr); Janakpur (every 20min; 4hr); Kakarbhitta (12 daily; 8hr); Kathmandu (8 daily; 8hr); Pokhara (5 daily; 8hr).
Dhankuta to: Basantapur (every 30min; 3hr); Biratnagar (4 daily; 3hr); Dharan (every 30min; 3hr); Hile (every 30min; 30min).
Dharan to: Basantapur (every 30min; 6hr); Biratnagar (every 15min; 1hr 30min); Birgunj (3 daily; 8hr); Dhankuta (every 30min; 3hr); Hile (every 30min; 3hr 30min); Ilam (3 daily; 6hr); Janakpur (5 daily; 6hr); Kakarbhitta (every 15min; 3hr); Kathmandu (10 daily, 14hr).
Hile to: Basantapur (every 30min; 2hr 30min); Dhankuta (every 30min; 30min); Dharan (every 30min; 3hr 30min); Kakarbhitta (7 daily; 5hr).
Ilam to: Birtamod (every 1hr; 3hr); Dharan (4 daily; 6hr); Phidim (every 3hr; 4hr).
Janakpur to: Bhairahawa (5 daily; 9hr); Biratnagar (7 daily; 6hr); Birgunj (every 20min; 4hr); Butwal (2 daily; 9hr); Dharan (1 daily; 6hr); Kakarbhitta (7 daily; 7hr); Kathmandu (4 daily; 11hr).
Kakarbhitta to: Biratnagar (every 20min; 3hr); Birgunj (2 daily; 8hr); Birtamod (every 10min; 30min); Dharan (every 15min; 3hr); Hile (3 daily; 5hr); Janakpur (7 daily; 7hr); Kathmandu (9 daily; 14hr); Pokhara (5 daily; 15hr).

Night buses

Biratnagar to: Bhairahawa (1 daily; 14hr); Birgunj (2 daily; 10hr); Kathmandu (8 daily; 14hr).
Birgunj to: Bhairahawa (2 daily; 10hr); Biratnagar (2 daily; 9hr); Butwal for Sonauli (3 daily; 10hr); Kakarbhitta (2 daily; 13hr); Kathmandu (12 daily; 12hr); Mahendra Nagar (1 daily; 16hr); Pokhara (3 daily; 10hr).
Dhankuta to: Kathmandu (2 daily; 17hr).
Dharan to: Kathmandu (6 daily; 15hr).
Hile to: Kathmandu (1 daily; 18hr).
Ilam to: Kathmandu (2 daily; 20hr).
Janakpur to: Bhairahawa (2 daily; 12hr); Butwal (2 daily; 12hr); Kakarbhitta (2 daily; 11hr); Kathmandu (8 daily; 11hr); Nepalgunj (2 daily; 14hr); Pokhara (2 daily; 16hr).
Kakarbhitta to: Bhairahawa (4 daily; 14hr); Birgunj (2 daily; 13hr); Janakpur (2 daily; 11hr); Kathmandu (6 daily; 15hr); Narayangadh (2 daily; 12hr); Nepalgunj (2 daily; 19hr).

Flights

Biratnagar to: Bhojpur (1–3 weekly); Kathmandu (10–15 daily); Lamidanda (2–4 weekly); Phaplu (2 weekly); Taplejung (2–5 weekly); Tumlingtar (2 weekly).
Kathmandu to: Bhadrapur (5 daily); Janakpur (4 daily); Lamidanda (4 weekly); Lukla (up to 19 daily); Phaplu (6 weekly); Simara (6 daily); Tumlingtar (1-2 daily).

Trekking

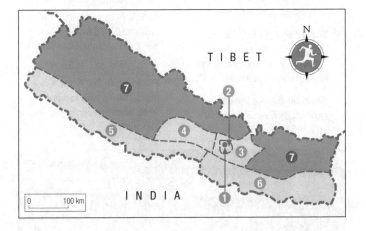

CHAPTER 7

Highlights

* **The Annapurna Sanctuary**
One of the most popular
treks, and for good reason:
the trail slowly penetrates a
steep gorge, emerging into a
secret mountain cirque.
See p.364

* **Foothill approaches** Many
trekkers come for the
mountains, but they go away
with powerful memories of
the terraced hills, the cultural
heartland of Nepal.
See p.368 & p.385

* **The Thorung La** Crossing
this 5415-metre pass is the
exhilarating high point of the
Annapurna Circuit. See p.372

* **Khumbu** Even if it wasn't
capped by Everest, the lofty
and colourfully Buddhist

Sherpa country of Khumbu
would be one of the highlights
of Nepal. See p.378

* **Going off-piste** Whether
you do it with the help of a
guide, an agency or simply a
willingness to embrace truly
local accommodation, simply
stepping off the main trail is
one of the most rewarding
things you can do. See p.386

* **Pangpema** Base camp
for the north face of
Kanchenjunga, deep in a
protected wilderness – you
can't get more remote than
this. See p.389

* **Phoksundo Tal** A jewel-like
alpine lake made famous by
Peter Matthiessen's *The Snow
Leopard*. See p.391

▲ Trekking in the Everest foothills

Trekking

T he soaring Himalayas are, to many travellers' minds, the whole reason for visiting Nepal. With eight of the world's ten highest peaks – including, of course, Everest – Nepal's 800-kilometre link in the Himalayan chain literally overshadows all other attractions. More than just majestic scenery, though, the mountains have always exerted a powerful spiritual pull. In Hindu mythology, the mountains are where gods go to meditate, while the Sherpas and other mountain peoples hold certain peaks to be the very embodiment of deities, and mountaineers are often hardly less mystical.

You can **walk** just about anywhere in Nepal – the country's trail network is far more extensive than its roads – but most visitors to the mountain areas stick to just a few well-established **trekking routes**. They have good reasons for doing so: the classic trails are popular because they offer close-up views of the very tallest peaks, dramatic scenery and fascinating local cultures, while lodges and other amenities make it possible to go without carrying a lot of gear or learning Nepali. However, with popularity comes commercialization and a loss of much of what once made these treks special. Genuine "teahouse" shacks, or *bhattis*, for instance, where you sit round the fire with a local family sipping a mug of *chhang*, are now rare on the most popular trails, and some newer lodges are as sophisticated as ski chalets. For those who put a high priority on getting away from it all, however, there are plenty of less-developed routes, and going out of season can make a huge difference.

On popular trails you can eat and sleep for less money than you'd spend in Kathmandu. Trails are often steep, to be sure, but you walk at your own pace, and no standard trek goes higher than about 5500m (the *starting* elevation for most climbing expeditions). That said, trekking is not for everybody – it's demanding, sometimes uncomfortable, and it does involve an element of risk.

When to trek

Where you go trekking will depend to a great extent on the time of year. The following seasonal descriptions are generalizations, of course: Annapurna is notoriously wetter than regions further east, and **climate change** – which is already hitting the Himalayas hard – is having unpredictable effects. In 2006, for instance, the winter in Khumbu was completely, abnormally dry, and serious snowstorms arrived in April, after the spring.

The peak seasons
Autumn (early Oct to early Dec), is normally dry, stable and very clear, although there can be the odd shower or freak autumn storm. It gets progressively colder

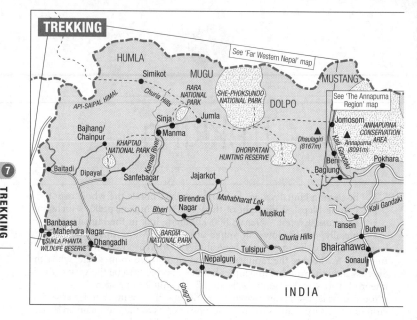

Map labels: TREKKING, HUMLA, Simikot, MUGU, See 'Far Western Nepal' map, MUSTANG, RARA NATIONAL PARK, SHE-PHOKSUNDO NATIONAL PARK, DOLPO, See 'The Annapurna Region' map, API-SAIPAL HIMAL, Churia Hills, Sinja, Jumla, Jomosom, ANNAPURNA CONSERVATION AREA, Bajhang/Chainpur, Manma, Dhaulagiri (8167m), Annapurna (8091m), Kali Gandaki, KHAPTAD NATIONAL PARK, DHORPATAN HUNTING RESERVE, Beni, Pokhara, Baitadi, Dipayal, Sanfebagar, Jajarkot, Baglung, Kamali River, Birendra Nagar, Mahabharat Lek, Kali Gandaki, Bheri, Musikot, Tansen, Butwal, Banbaasa, Mahendra Nagar, BARDIA NATIONAL PARK, Churia Hills, SUKLA PHANTA WILDLIFE RESERVE, Dhangadhi, Tulsipur, Bhairahawa, Nepalgunj, Sonauli, Ghagra, INDIA

at night higher up, but the chill is rarely severe until December and daytime temperatures are pleasantly cool for walking; at low elevations it can be distinctly hot. The fine conditions mean that the main Annapurna and Everest trails will be busy: porters will charge top dollar and flights will be tight. In 2008, admittedly a bumper year, guides were even being sent ahead to book up lodges in the Everest region, and some independent trekkers were forced to carry on up the trail to the next village to find a bed. The other drawback is the general lack of greenery on the freshly ploughed terraces in the Middle Hills. In general, this is a good time to think about getting off the beaten track.

After winter, temperatures and the snow line rise steadily during **spring** (Feb–April). The warmer weather also brings more trekkers, though not nearly as many as in autumn. The main factor that keeps the numbers down is a disappointing haze that creeps up in elevation during this period, plus the occasional sudden downpour (or freak snowstorm) and sometimes unpleasant afternoon winds. By April, you probably won't get good views until you reach 4000m or so, though this is also the time when the most colourful rhododendrons bloom, generally between 2000m and 3000m.

The off seasons

Winter (Dec–Jan) is for the most part dry and settled, albeit colder. When precipitation does fall, the snow line drops to 2500m and sometimes lower. Passes over 4000m (including the highest on the Annapurna Sanctuary and Circuit treks) may be uncrossable due to snow and ice, and some settlements described in trekking guidebooks may be uninhabited. High-altitude treks, such as Everest, require good gear and experience in cold-weather conditions, as temperatures at 5000m can drop below minus 20°C and heavy snow can fall; if you're up to it, however, this can be a magical time to trek. Some treks see

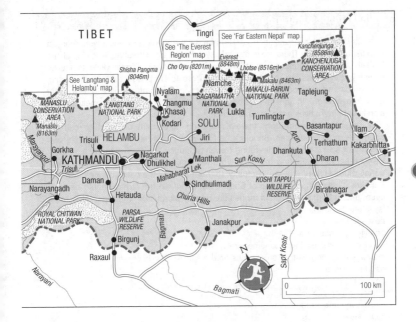

something like twenty or thirty times the numbers of trekkers in autumn as in midwinter, and below 2000m, temperatures can be quite spring-like, though valleys are often filled with fog or haze.

During May and June it gets hotter, hazier and increasingly unsettled. The warming Asian landmass has begun drawing air up from the south, ushering in the **pre-monsoon** – a season of erratic weather and increasingly frequent afternoon storms. The trails and lodges again begin to empty out. This is a time for going high, but be prepared for rain, especially in traditionally wet areas such as Annapurna and far eastern Nepal.

Few foreigners trek during the **monsoon** (mid-June to early Sept), because of the rain, mud, leeches, travel difficulties and general lack of mountain views. (The leeches along the middle-elevation trails are not for the squeamish!) However, treks in the Himalayan rain shadow and in Nepal's far west are sheltered from the brunt of the monsoon. Even in wet areas, mornings are often clear, wildflowers and butterflies can be seen in abundance, the terraces and forests are a luscious green and the soundscape – dripping leaves, roaring rivers – magical. Authentic Nepali culture is more in evidence, too, as the summer off-season is when locals return to their farming and other traditional activities. Note also that the monsoon isn't consistently rainy: it builds up to a peak in July and August, then tapers off again.

Conditions in the post-monsoon **harvest** season (roughly mid-Sept to early Oct) are hard to predict: it all depends on the timing of the rains. If you're lucky, you can enjoy clear, warm weather and gloriously empty trails. At lower altitudes it can be hot and sticky, however, and you may face an extended monsoon tail, with clouds obscuring the peaks and heavy afternoon showers or snow flurries higher up.

The spelling and pronunciation of **Himalayan place names** has given many a traveller a headache. There are competing systems for transliterating from Nepali into English, and many names in mountain regions are taken from Tibetan dialects or even unwritten languages, so the possibilities can proliferate chaotically. When reading from maps and guidebooks, or asking for directions, keep an open mind as to what might mean where. In general, this book follows the most widely used spellings, but significant alternatives are given in brackets.

As regards **pronunciation**, there's not even agreement on what to call the country – or its mountains. Should it be Nuh-*pawl*, as it has been in English for a century or so, or Nay-paal, imitating Nepali pronunciation? Is the range a singular Hi-*maal*-ee-yuh (reflecting the local word for mountain, *himal*) or the more traditional, plural Him-*uh-lay*-ers? Actually, that one's easy: the name derives from the Sanskrit *hima laya*, or "Abode of Snow", not *himal*, so the stress should be fairly even; and in English mountain ranges are usually plural, like "the Alps". Hee-maa-lay-ahs it is, then.

besi – lower
bhanjyang – pass, col
chorten – stone religious monument/reliquary
deurali – meeting point, often of paths on the saddle or side of a hill
danda – hillside
gao – village
gompa – monastery
himal – mountain range
kosi – river
khola – stream
la – mountain pass
lekh – watershed range of hills, ridge
mani wall – wall of stones inscribed with prayers
phedi – settlement at the foot of a hill
pokhari – lake
ri – peak
tal – lake

Trekking Basics

This section explains the **practicalities** of independent and organized treks: the costs you can expect, the specialist books and maps you may need, the preparations you'll have to make before setting off and health matters to be mindful of. It's designed with particular emphasis on the nuts and bolts of **independent trekking**. Route descriptions follow on p.362.

Trekking independently

Trekking independently – making all your own arrangements, carrying your own pack and staying in lodges – saves money and may give you more freedom or flexibility on the trail. In terms of route choice, however, it's more limiting than an organized trek.

Doing it yourself gives you more **control** over many aspects of the trek: you can go at your own pace, stop when and where you like, choose your travelling companions and take rest days or side-trips as you please. The downside is that you have to spend a day or three lining up bus or plane tickets, renting equipment, buying supplies and perhaps tracking down a porter or guide. A more serious drawback is that you're effectively confined to the more popular trails; trekking to remote areas is difficult unless you speak Nepali or you're prepared to deal with considerable porter logistics.

Life on the trail is described later, but an independent trek is likely to be less comfortable than one arranged through an agency. Lodges can be noisy and lacking in privacy, and there may be long waits for food of dubious quality. The active **social scene** in lodges goes a long way to compensating for this, however – even if you start out alone, you'll quickly meet up with potential companions.

By not being part of a group, you're better placed to learn from Nepali ways rather than forcing local people to adapt to yours. Equally important, a high proportion of the money you spend goes directly to the local economy (whereas most of the money paid to trekking agencies goes no further than Kathmandu, and often finds its way overseas). However, as an independent trekker you must guard against contributing to **deforestation**. If you or your porters or guides order meals cooked over wood fires, you encourage innkeepers to cut down more trees. Fortunately, kerosene is replacing wood in the most popular areas. See the box on p.360 for tips on minimizing your environmental impact.

Costs

The biggest single cost is likely to be **transport**. Public buses to the major trailheads usually cost anything up to about Rs500, but if you choose to hire a taxi or, where it's possible, buy a seat in a shared jeep to get further up the trail, the costs can mount up. Single plane fares to mountain aistrips are almost all in the $90–150 range, though tickets to some of the very remotest airstrips can be a little more expensive, and if you need to touch down anywhere on the way, you have to buy a separate ticket. Kathmandu to Pokhara tickets are cheaper (see p.143).

Unless you seek out luxurious lodges, the cost of **lodging** is negligible (see p.360), and there's very little else to spend your money on besides a porter or guide (if you choose to hire one) and **food**. Provisions (for those camping) and basic, local meals are both inexpensive; well off the beaten track, you could struggle to spend Rs500 ($6) a day. On the major Everest and Annapurna trails, however, food costs can add up surprisingly and the daily budget could easily rise to Rs1600 ($20) if you order pizzas, chips and the like – not counting things like beer, soft drinks and chocolate, which go up in price as you ascend away from the nearest road. A single beer can sell for more than $5 in some remote locations. Hiring a porter will add considerably to your daily cost (see p.348).

Guides

Guides are only strictly necessary on esoteric routes, but any trek will be enlivened by the company and local knowledge of a good guide, who may well take you on unusual side trips to visit the homes of family and friends. The best have detailed knowledge of wildlife and local culture: check it out before you sign them up. Guides can also cramp your style, however, by steering you to certain lodges, and they may restrict your contact with local people by conducting all negotiations on your behalf. Many guides are willing to carry gear as well, but this isn't always the case: ask.

The **hiring** process is informal, so shop around: ask for recommendations from fellow travellers or people who have just returned from Nepal, visit the Kathmandu Environmental Education Project, KEEP (see p.80) or go through an agency. Guesthouses almost always have guide contacts, too. Try to interview more than one candidate, and take the time to talk a while, maybe over tea or a meal, to get a feel for whether you'll get along. You're going to be spending a lot of time together. A guide who's actually from the area you plan to trek in is preferable to one who's not, because he or she will have family and friends along the way and will be respected by the local people.

Trekking agencies pay their guides a pittance of $10–15 a day (which doesn't leave them much after costs) and are likely to charge you at least $20. If you're employing a guide directly, $15–20 would be a fair wage, with guides funding their own expenses. Guides on longer treks and those with good language skills or perhaps wildlife expertise may command slightly higher wages. Be clear whether or not any agreed amount includes food and drink: it may avoid problems if guides pay for themselves. And don't pay too much up front: fifty percent is pretty standard. Expect to give your guide a **tip** equivalent to about one day's extra pay for each week worked, assuming the work was well done.

If you've never hiked before, don't try to organize a trek off the well-trodden routes.

Finding a guide familiar with a particular area will be hard, and transporting him with a crew of porters and supplies to the trailhead a major (and expensive) logistical exercise. Getting a trekking agency to do it might not cost much more.

Porters

Porters are an important part of the Himalayan economy, and there's no shame in hiring one. With a porter taking most of your gear, you only have to carry a small pack containing the things you need during the day; this can be a great relief at high elevations, and it may be essential in remote mountain areas, where tents, cooking equipment and serious amounts of food may have to be brought in.

Hiring a porter is simple enough: just ask at your guesthouse, a reputable trekking agency or an equipment-rental shop. Hiring someone off the street is riskier, but it will save you money and the porter will end up better-off too. Another strategy is simply to wait till you get to the trailhead or airstrip: there are usually porters (and guides) waiting for work at the starting points of the popular treks, and they usually know the area better than someone hired in Kathmandu. If you start out without help and change your mind later, you may be able to hire a porter at one of the major trailside towns, such as Namche and Manang.

A typical daily **wage** for a porter is about Rs500 ($6) a day, though those hired on the Annapurna or Everest treks or through agencies or middlemen may cost around fifty percent more. Porters who speak English – few do – may command higher fees,

especially if you're expecting them to do informal guiding. Porters generally pay for their own food and lodging; be aware that this can cost them anything from Rs300 to Rs500, so **tips** are crucial. You should tip anything from ten to twenty percent, and many trekkers also give spare gear or clothing at the end of the trek, or make donations to organizations like KEEP.

Organized trekking

Organized treks are for people who haven't got the time or inclination to make their own arrangements, or who want to tackle ambitious routes that can't be done independently. They **cost** from $35 to $150 a day, depending on the standard of service, size of the group, remoteness of the route, whether you're in tents or lodges, and whether you book the trip in your home country or in Kathmandu. The price should always include a guide, porters, food and shelter, although cheap outfits often charge extra for things like national park fees and transport, and may cut other corners as well. The lower the price, the more wary you need to be.

A trek is hard work however you do it, but a good company will help you along with a few **creature comforts**: you can expect appetizing food, "bed tea" and hot "washing water" on cold mornings, camp chairs and a latrine tent with toilet paper. Depending on the size of your party, a guide, *sirdar* (guide foreman) or Western trek leader will be able to answer questions and cope with problems. Trekking groups usually sleep in **tents**, which, while quieter than lodges, may be colder and are certainly more cramped.

A few bad apples

There are very occasional reports that guides have **sexually harassed** female clients. It's partly the result of fairly widespread Nepali perceptions of Western sexual mores, and partly an unfortunate consequence of the fact that a number of women do hook up with Nepali boyfriends, leading to overeager expectations. While the vast majority of Nepali guides are meticulously respectful, there are always a few bad apples – and there have been instances of outright assault. The best way to avoid problems is to follow the recommendations of people you trust, insist on meeting the guide before hiring, bring along a trekking partner, and nip any unwanted advances in the bud with a frank "I don't want to sleep with you". You might also consider hiring a female guide – see p.247.

The **responsibilities** of employing a porter or guide cannot be overstated. Porters, especially, are some of the poorest people in Nepal. Most do a backbreaking job only because they have no alternative, and the vast majority are illiterate and landless. They are typically able to get work for less than eighty days a year, and are at significant risk of injury or ill-health. When hiring, don't over-negotiate: Rs100 a day is trivial to you, but can make a huge difference to your porter. You should also ensure your porter has health and life **insurance**: agencies should do this as standard; if you're hiring independently this can be easily and inexpensively arranged through an agency. For more information, speak to the International Porter Protection Group (IPPG) – contactable via the Himalayan Rescue Association in Kathmandu (see p.81).

Several porters die needlessly each year, typically because their *sahib* (pronounced "sahb") thought they wouldn't mind sleeping outside in a blizzard. You must make sure your employees are adequately **clothed** for the journey – on high-altitude treks, this will mean buying or renting them good shoes and socks, a parka, sunglasses, mittens and a sleeping bag. Establish beforehand if something is a loan. You must check they have proper **shelter**. If they get **sick**, it's up to you to look after them – including making sure they are not paid off and sent down without anyone checking on their fitness first. Since many porters hired in Kathmandu and Pokhara are clueless about altitude-related problems, it's your responsibility to educate them. It's also important not to **overload** porters. Some are capable of bearing wondrous loads, but thirty kilograms is an accepted maximum; it may need to be reduced according to your porters' age and condition.

The daily routine of eating as a group can get monotonous, and gives you **less contact** with local people. There's something to be said for safety in numbers, but trekking with a group imposes a somewhat **inflexible itinerary** on you, and if you don't like the people in your group, you're stuck.

In theory, organized treks are more **environmentally sound**, at least in the national parks and conservation areas, where trekkers' meals are supposed to be cooked with kerosene. Sometimes, however, cooks use wood so they can sell the kerosene at the end of the trek – and, worse still, for each trekker eating a kerosene-cooked meal, there may be two or three porters and other staff cooking their *bhaat* over a wood fire.

But the main advantage of organized trekking is it enables you to get **off the beaten track**: there's little point in using an agency to do a very popular trek. A number of companies now offer "wilderness" or "nature" treks, which forsake the traditional village-to-village valley routes for obscure trails along uninhabited ridgelines or through forested areas, often with experienced wildlife enthusiasts as guides. Shop around and you'll also find special-interest treks based around Tibetan Buddhism, birdwatching, rhododendron-viewing, and trail construction or cleanup. Many companies also run trips that combine trekking with rafting, cycling and wildlife-viewing.

Agents and operators

Small **budget operators** in Kathmandu and Pokhara, charging from around $35 a day for non-camping treks (which means, three meals a day, food, lodging, guides and porters), are notoriously hard to recommend: many are fly-by-night setups who represent themselves as trekking specialists when in fact they're merely agents, taking a commission and providing very little service for it. A few of the more established budget companies run scheduled treks, but again, usually only to the most popular areas. In this category, names change often and standards can quickly rise and fall. A good place to start your search would be KEEP's list of member trekking agencies and its trekker logbooks (see p.80).

Trekking companies in Nepal speak the green lingo as fluently as anyone, but in many cases their walk doesn't match their talk. Here are some specific **questions** to put to them to find out what they're actually doing to minimize their impact on the environment. You may not find a company able to answer every question, but the exercise should help establish which outfits are genuinely concerned.

• Do they carry enough kerosene to cook all meals for all members of the party, including porters?

• What equipment do they provide to porters? Tents, proper clothing, shoes, UV sunglasses?

• Do they separate trash and carry out all non-burnable/non-biodegradable waste?

• How many of their staff have certificates from the Kathmandu Environmental Education Project's eco-trekking workshop? Failing that, have they attended courses with the Trekking Agencies' Assocation of Nepal (TAAN) or Nepal Mountaineering Association?

• Do staff have wilderness first-aid training?

Kathmandu's **big operators** mainly package treks on behalf of overseas agencies, but they may allow "walk-ins" to join at a reduced price. They offer treks specifically for the local market, typically priced at around $50–70 a day for camping treks, or $10–25 more for Everest Base Camp. (For agencies in Kathmandu, see p.136.) Request brochures to make sure your schedule coincides with theirs; for customized treks to exotic areas, make contact several months in advance.

Booking through an **overseas agency** lets you arrange everything before you leave home, and may not cost all that much more: expect to pay upwards of £60/US$90 per day. Some agencies have their own Nepali subsidiaries in Kathmandu, others effectively subcontract. Overseas agencies will look after all your arrangements up till the time you leave your home country, and will also play a part in maintaining quality-control in Nepal. Some may allow you to join up in Kathmandu at a reduced price. See pp.20–24 for names and addresses.

Information, books and maps

The **main trails** are generally so clear that you could easily embark on a trek with nothing more than this book – certainly if you were planning on hiring a guide. But this chapter is not intended to take the place of a detailed guidebook to an individual trek, still less a full-size, fold-out map with contour lines, minor trails and all the rest – and if you're venturing into **mountain areas**, buying both would be a very good idea, for safety's sake alone. The best specialist books and maps are therefore reviewed below.

Information and websites

The best sources of current trekking **information** are the Kathmandu Environmental Education Project and the Himalayan Rescue Association. Both have offices in Kathmandu (see p.80): KEEP is off Tridevi Marg, at Jyatha Thamel; HRA is at Dhobichaur, Lazimpath, north of the Royal Palace. HRA also maintains two rescue and information posts at Pheriche (Everest region) and Manang (Annapurna), with a seasonal post at Thorung Phedi.

These are nonprofit organizations that rely on membership dues and donations to do their work. Both have libraries of trekking-related books, logbooks full of comments from returning trekkers (invaluable for tips on routes and trekking agencies), staff who can advise on trail conditions and equipment, and notice boards for finding trekking partners and used equipment. KEEP also sells books and maps, iodine water-purification tablets and biodegradable and other trekking-related items; exhibits in the office give a primer on trekkers' impact on the environment and culture.

ⓦwww.everestnews.com Expedition reports, climber profiles and extensive info on Everest and other major peaks.

@ **www.high-altitude-medicine.com** Good info on high-altitude health, with links.

@ **www.himalayanrescue.org** The Himalayan Rescue Association's site: the best information on health, altitude and helicopter rescue.

@ **www.ippg.net** The International Porter Protection Group builds shelters, provides warm clothing and medicine and offers excellent online guidelines on the ethical employment of porters.

@ **www.keepnepal.org** Tips on environmentally sensitive trekking from the Kathmandu Environmental Education Project.

@ **www.lonelyplanet.com/thorntree** Their books may be a bit sketchy, but LP's online forum is a very useful resource for travellers exchanging information or seeking trekking partners.

@ **www.mountainexplorers.org** The International Mountain Explorers Connection's website features trip reports, a newsletter, information on volunteer opportunities and on the Porter Assistance Project, which provides warm clothing to porters.

@ **www.nepalmountaineering.org** Information on trekking and expedition peaks from the Nepal Mountaineering Association, which runs the permit scheme as well as mountaineering courses.

@ **www.taan.org.np** Site of the Trekking Agents' Association of Nepal, with useful (if not always up-to-date) information on permits, fees and other bureaucracy.

Specialist guidebooks

All trekking **guidebooks** and general books on the Himalayas can easily be bought in Kathmandu or Pokhara. Given how infrequently most trekking guides can realistically be updated, it's worth going on the date of the last revision as much as your individual preference for the style. For general books on Nepal, its history, wildlife, people and ecology, see p.462.

Stan Armington *Trekking in the Nepal Himalaya* (Lonely Planet). The Microsoft of trekking guides, with treks divided into fixed days – which can be limiting. The style is clear, if uninspiring, and the maps are good. Unless you're doing lots of treks, it might make more sense to buy a dedicated, single-region guidebook.

Stephen Bezruchka *Trekking in Nepal: A Traveler's Guide* (Cordee/The Mountaineers). Dated (from 1997) but still the most culturally sensitive book on trekking, containing background pieces on Nepali language, culture and natural history.

Bob Gibbons and Sian Pritchard-Jones *Mustang: A Trekking Guide* (Pilgrims, Nepal).

Still the best guide to Mustang, despite its 1993 publishing date. The authors also wrote the definitive guide to the Mount Kailash trek, heading out from Simikot into Tibet.

Margaret Jefferies *Highest Heritage: The Mount Everest Region and Sagarmatha National Park* (Pilgrims, Nepal). Superbly detailed guide to the Everest region, covering Sherpa culture, landscape, history and wildlife, as well as giving shortish trekking itineraries.

Jamie McGuinness *Trekking in the Everest Region* and *Trekking in Langtang, Helambu and Gosainkund* (Trailblazer, UK). Guides to all the routes by a hugely experienced leader of treks and climbs. The Trailblazer series has a friendly, usable feel, with hand-drawn maps and a chatty tone.

Bill O'Connor *The Trekking Peaks of Nepal* (o/p). Describes climbing routes and trek approaches for eighteen trekking peaks.

Kev Reynolds *Annapurna, Everest, Manaslu, Kangchenjunga, Langtang, Gosainkund & Helambu and Manaslu* (Cicerone). Cicerone publishes well-written guides to all these areas, all by the indefatigable Reynolds, with plentiful colour photos, simple but easily readable maps, detailed route guides and lots of cultural background.

Bryn Thomas *Trekking in the Annapurna Region* (Trailblazer, UK). A good, workmanlike guide to this popular region from Traiblazer (see the comments on Jamie Guinness's title, above), though the 100 pages of trek descriptions are rather overshadowed by general information on Nepal, Kathmandu, Pokhara and so on. Reviews of trekking lodges are unusually detailed.

Maps

Nepal's trekking regions are fairly well **mapped**, although you get what you pay for – and none currently shows an up-to-date road network. The best product for a particular trek will vary from year to year, as companies leapfrog past each other with new editions. Currently, the locally produced (and widely available) NepaMaps series is the clearest and is fairly up-to-date, although there are some howling errors and the maps can't be relied upon for off-trail route-finding. National Geographic do a similar job with their "Nepal Adventure Map" series, though they only cover the Annapurna, Everest and Langtang regions. The pricier Geo-Buch ("Schneider") maps of the Everest and Langtang/Helambu areas have much more reliable contours and topographical details, though they're way out of date for villages and roads.

For more obscure treks, try the HMG/ FINNIDA maps, produced by His Majesty's Government (as labelled) in co-operation with a Finnish aid agency – they're superb and not too expensive, though they're not designed specifically for trekking and are only patchily available in tourist bookshops.

Permits, fees and red tape

Trekking permits are no longer required for most areas, including all the standard routes in the Annapurna, Everest and Langtang/ Helambu/Gosainkund areas. You will, however, need to register for a TIMS card – a kind of trekkers' register – and pay a national park or conservation area entry fee. Organized treks will do this for you. Before setting off on any trek, **register with your embassy** in Kathmandu, as this will speed things up should you need rescuing. You can have KEEP or the Himalayan Rescue Association forward the details to your embassy.

National Park and Conservation Area fees

If your trek goes through any of the **national parks** or conservation areas, and almost all treks do, you'll have to buy an **entry ticket.** The proceeds go towards important conservation work, from tree nurseries and path maintenance to local education on sustainable lodge-management. Fees for all national parks are Rs1000; Langtang and Everest's Sagarmatha National Park fees are payable at the entry check posts at Dhunche and Monjo, respectively. The Annapurna Conservation Area Project charges Rs2000 entry, which you should pay in advance at the ACAP offices in Kathmandu (in the Tourist Service Center, Exhibition Rd, Bhikruti Mandap; see p.80), or Pokhara (in the Tourist Service Centre, Damside, near the airport; see p.247); bring your passport and a passport photograph. If you don't buy an ACAP permit in advance, you'll be charged double at the park gate. Children under ten receive free admission to all parks.

The TIMS card

Since 2008, trekkers have been obliged to provide themselves with a TIMS card. The **Trekkers' Information Management System**

is designed to make sure the government knows if a trekker goes missing or needs rescuing, and to keep an eye on rogue companies. On organized tours this will be done for you by the agency. Independent trekkers can get their card from the Nepal Tourism Board offices in Kathmandu (see p.80) and Pokhara (conveniently placed in the same building as the ACAP office, where you need to pay your park entry fee; see p.247) or through TAAN, the Trekking Agencies' Association of Nepal, which has offices in Maligaon, Kathmandu, and Lakeside, Pokhara. It may be more convenient to go through a registered trekking agency, which should pass on no (or little) more than the Rs200 the government charges. Whether you're on an organized trek or not, you'll need your passport and two passport photos – the latter easily and inexpensively obtained in Thamel and Lakeside. Some independent trekkers have managed fine without a TIMS card in the past, but you may save yourself problems by obtaining one.

Fees for remote areas

Permits are still required for treks that pass through certain **remote areas**, and these can only be arranged through registered agencies – and, in practice, on fully equipped camping treks. The fee-paying areas are: Lower Dolpo, in the northwest, Kanchenjunga, in the far northeast and Gauri Shankar, just west of the Everest region ($10 per person per week); Chekampar and Chunchet, below Ganesh Himal, north of Gorkha (Sept–Nov $35 per person for 8 days; Dec–Aug $25); Manaslu, just east of Annapurna (Sept–Nov $70 per person for a week, then $10 per day; Dec–Aug $50/$7), Simikot, in far western Humla district, on the way to Mount Kailas and Tibet ($50 per week, then $7 per day). At the top end of the scale are Mustang, north of Annapurna, and Upper Dolpo ($500 per person for the first ten days, thereafter $50 per day).

Equipment

Having the right **equipment** on a trek is obviously important, though when you see how little porters get by with, you'll realize

Trekking peaks and mountaineering

Thirty-three lesser summits, ranging in elevation from 5550m to 6654m, are designated as **trekking peaks**. They fill the gap between standard hikes and full-on mountaineering expeditions: some are little more than snowy, breathless plods, others technical, multi-day rock and ice climbs. You need to be especially fit and able to cope with very cold and potentially stormy conditions; previous climbing experience is preferable for the easier peaks, and essential for the harder ones. Above all, acclimatization is crucial: many agency expeditions don't allow enough time, and many clients fail to summit – or worse – as a result.

The most popular trekking peaks are in the **Everest** region. Imja Tse, aka Island Peak (6160m), is busy and relatively straightforward; Lobuje East (6119m) is a demanding ridge climb; Mera Peak (6654m) is the highest of all trekking peaks, and thus among the most dangerous – even if technically it's a walk. In the **Annapurna** region, popular peaks include Pisang (6091m), a moderately difficult peak with rocky sections near Manang; and Tharphu Chuli, aka Tent Peak (5663m), dramatically situated in the Annapurna Sanctuary. There are two categories of peak: "Group B" peaks are the original eighteen trekking peaks; "Group A" mountains were only opened to climbing parties in 2002, and may offer more of a sense of breaking new ground. They're distinguished only by bureaucracy, with harder and easier climbs in both groups.

Climbing a trekking peak takes more time than most standard routes – three to four weeks is typical – and inevitably **costs** more, especially if you go with an agency. Contributing to the expense is the peak **permit**. Group B peaks cost $350 for a group of 1–4 people, with an extra $350 for 5–8 people, plus $40 per person, and an extra $510 for 9–12 people, plus $25 per person; Group A peaks costs $500 for up to seven members, plus $100 per additional person, up to a maximum of 12 in the party. Fees are payable to the official Nepal Mountaineering Association (NMA) through a certified guide or authorized trekking or travel agency. You'll also have to pay the salaries of a NMA-certified **sirdar** and at least a few porters, and transportation and equipment for both trekkers and staff. Some peaks are located in restricted areas, for which an additional permit fee is payable. The **sirdar** can help with logistics and advise on what extra equipment to bring or obtain in Kathmandu. It will take several days to a week to organize a trekking peak expedition from scratch in Kathmandu.

Another hundred-odd higher peaks are open only to **expeditions**, which must comply with additional regulations and pay higher fees (up to $25,000 for one climber, in the case of Everest Southeast Ridge in peak season). Fees are much lower than they were before 2002, however, averaging $1000–2000, and there are deep discounts for small groups climbing out of season. Some peaks in the mid- and far-west are now royalty-free.

Further information on trekking and expedition peaks is available from the Nepal Mountaineering Association, Nagpokhari, Naxal (☎01/443 4525, ⓦwww.nepal mountaineering.org). Scores of agencies offer guided or organized trips, some arranged around a mountaineering courses. Among the bigger players in Kathmandu are: Asian Trekking, Thamel Northeast (☎01/442 4249, ⓦwww .asian-trekking.com); Equator Expeditions, Thamel Northwest (☎01/435 6644, ⓦwww.equatorexpeditionsnepal.com); Highlander Trekking and Expeditions, Thamel (☎01/470 0563, ⓦwww.highlandernepal.com); and Thamserku Trekking, in Basundhara, on the Ring Road (☎01/435 4491, ⓦwww.thamserkutrekking.com).

high-tech gear isn't essential. Bring what you need to be comfortable, but keep weight to a minimum. The list below is intended mainly for independent trekkers staying in lodges. If you're planning to camp, you'll need more,

and if you're trekking with an agency you won't need so much.

By **renting** bulky or specialized items in Nepal, you'll avoid having to lug them around during the rest of your travels. Kathmandu has dozens of rental places, while Pokhara's fewer shops inevitably offer a more limited selection; if you're trekking in the Everest region, you can rent high-altitude gear in Namche. Even in Kathmandu, you might have trouble finding good gear of exactly the right size during the busy autumn trekking season. You'll be expected to leave a deposit. Inspect sleeping bags and parkas carefully for fleas (or worse) and make sure zippers are in working order. You can also **buy** equipment quite cheaply (see p.135).

Clothes should be lightweight, versatile and breathable (cotton gets very sweaty), especially on long treks where conditions vary from subtropical to arctic. Many first-time trekkers underestimate the potential for extremes in temperature. What you bring will depend on the trek and time of year, but in most cases you should be prepared for sun, rain, snow and very chilly mornings; dress in layers for maximum flexibility. Note too that high-altitude trekking days are short, so you may spend many hours lounging around in the cold. As explained on p.53, Nepalis have innately conservative attitudes about dress. For minimum impact, women should consider wearing calf-length dresses or skirts rather than trousers and a top that covers the shoulders; men should wear a shirt and long pants (shorts tradition-ally indicate low status, though this is less of an issue nowadays along the popular trekking routes). Both sexes should wear at least a swimsuit when bathing, preferably a T-shirt too.

For **footwear**, hiking boots are pretty essential, providing better traction, ankle support and protection than anything else. A pair of trainers, sports sandals or flip flops are useful for rest days and airing your feet. Bring plenty of socks, because you'll be changing them often.

A **sleeping bag** is strongly recommended. Most lodges will supply quilts or blankets on demand, but you don't know who used the bedding last or what surprises might lurk therein. A three-season bag is adequate for mid-elevation treks; above 4000m, or in winter, you'll need a four-season bag and possibly a liner.

Camera equipment involves a trade-off between weight and performance – and cold weather and stunning views can really eat up batteries, with no possibility of recharging. If you're taking an SLR body, be sure to bring a polarizing filter to cope with the Himalayan skies and snowfields.

Health, emergencies and safety

Guidebooks tend to go overboard about the **health** hazards of trekking, particularly altitude sickness. Don't be put off – the vast majority of trekkers never experience anything worse than a sore throat (common in high, dry air) and a mild headache. That said, trekking can be physically demanding, and may take you a week or more from the nearest medical facilities.

Children, seniors and people with disabili-ties have all trekked successfully, but a certain **fitness** level (or, failing that, bloody mindedness) is required. Don't allow yourself to be talked into biting off more than you can chew or you'll have little fun and could get into trouble. If you're in any doubt about your ability to cope with strenuous walking, see your doctor. It's certainly worth checking that your **insurance** policy doesn't exclude trekking, which may be listed as a hazardous sport. Check the policy on helicopter rescue as well.

Stomach troubles

The risk of **stomach troubles** is particularly high while trekking, and water is the usual culprit: you need to drink lots of fluids on the trail. Innkeepers normally boil water and tea, but not always for long enough, and at high altitudes the boiling point of water is so low that a longer boiling time is necessary. All running water should be assumed to be contaminated – wherever you go, there will be people, or at least animals, upstream.

Treating water (see p.49) is not only the best line of defence against illness, it also reduces your reliance on boiled or bottled water, both of which cause significant environmental problems in mountain areas. For tips on diagnosing and treating stomach upsets, see p.49.

Minor injuries

Most minor injuries occur while walking downhill; **knee strains** are common,

What to bring

All the items listed below can be purchased in Kathmandu, though branded, top-quality clothing and gear is rarely much less expensive than at home. Kit marked (*) can be rented.

Essentials

Backpack* – one with a frame and hip belt is best

Sleeping bag*

Medical kit – see p.356

Toiletries – including biodegradable soap/shampoo

Water bottle, plus **iodine** tablets or solution and/or a **water-purification system** – see p.49

Torch/flashlight – the ones mounted on a headstrap are very useful; spare batteries are available on main trails

Sunglasses – a good UV-protective pair, ideally with side shields if you expect to be in snow

Sunscreen, **lip balm** – at altitude you'll need SPF30+, or zinc oxide

Map and **guidebook**

Footwear and specialist clothing

Hiking boots* – leather or Gore-Tex boots are best

Thermals – warm, breathable (not cotton) long johns and vests are essential for high-altitude or winter treks

Sun hat and **warm hat** – helpful at both low and high elevations

Wool sweaters or **fleeces** – fleece dries quickly and stays warm when wet; close-fitting layers are much warmer than loose ones

Bandana – to use as a handkerchief, sweatband or scarf

Mittens/gloves – the warmest have thermal liners and a waterproof outer shell

Outer jacket – breathable waterproofs are best, and provide good wind protection; you're unlikely to need waterproof trousers outside the wet season

Down or fibre-filled jacket* – natural down provides unbeatable warmth; down overtrousers and booties take it to the next level

Gaiters* – if snow is likely on passes

Other useful items

Day pack – if a porter is carrying your main pack

Sleeping mat* – if you're likely to sleep in basic lodges or local homes

Toilet paper – see "Conservation Tips", p.360

Whistle – for emergencies

Sewing kit

Stuff sacks – handy for separating things in your pack and for creating a pillow when filled with clothes

Plastic bags – a big one to cover your pack in the rain, small sealable ones for many uses; you can buy more durable "canoe bags"

Candles

A book, journal or game/pack of cards – trekking days can be short, leaving long afternoons

Snack food – biscuits and chocolate can be bought along the way on the major treks

Telescoping hiking poles* – may be useful for keeping your balance and protecting the knees on descents

Ice axe/crampons* – may be needed for icy passes in winter, but you'll need to know how to use them

especially among trekkers carrying their own packs. If you know your knees are weak, bind them up with crepe (ace) bandages as a preventive measure, or hire a porter. Good, supportive boots reduce the risk of **ankle sprains** or twists, but the best prevention is just to pay careful attention to where you put your feet. A walking stick or hiking pole(s) can help, as can using Nepali technique: smaller, pitter-patter steps on steeper slopes.

It's hard to avoid getting **blisters**, but make sure your boots are well broken-in. Some people swear by two pairs of socks. Airing your feet and changing socks regularly also helps: you can have one pair on while the other dries on the back of your pack. Apply protective padding (eg moleskin) to hotspots as soon as they develop, making sure to clean and cover blisters so they can heal as quickly as possible.

Altitude

At high elevations, the combination of reduced oxygen and lower atmospheric pressure can produce a variety of unpredictable effects on the body – known collectively as **acute mountain sickness (AMS)** or, colloquially, **"altitude sickness"**. Barraged

by medical advice and horror stories, trekkers all too often develop altitude paranoia. The fact is that just about everyone who treks over 4000m experiences some mild symptoms of AMS, but serious cases are very rare, and the simple cure – descent – almost always brings immediate recovery. The syndrome varies from one person to the next, and strikes without regard for fitness – in fact, young people seem to be more susceptible. For further advice on AMS, visit the Himalayan Rescue Association's aid posts at Manang (on the Annapurna Circuit) and Pheriche (on the Everest trek).

Prevention

The body can acclimatize to some very high elevations but it takes time and must be done in stages. The golden rule is don't go **too high too fast**. Above 3000m, the daily net elevation gain should be no more than 300–400m. Take mandatory acclimatization days at around 3500m and 4500m – more if you're feeling unwell – and try to spend them day-hiking higher. These are only guidelines, and you'll have to regulate your ascent according to how you feel. Trekkers who fly directly to high airstrips have to be especially careful to acclimatize.

First-aid checklist

This is a minimum first-aid kit, and won't cope with serious injuries or emergencies. Most of the items can be purchased inexpensively in Nepal. For self-diagnosis of diarrhoea or dysentery, and antibiotics and drugs to treat it, see p.50.

For injuries

Plasters/Band-Aids – in large and small sizes

Gauze pads, sterile dressing, surgical tape – for wounds and large blisters

Moleskin or **"Second Skin"** – synthetic adhesive padding for blisters

Elastic support bandages – for knee strains, ankle sprains

Antiseptic cream – for scrapes, blisters, insect bites

Tweezers, scissors

For illnesses

Ibuprofen – pain relief for swollen joints and strained muscles

Throat lozenges – sore throats are common at high elevations

Diarrhoea tablets – blockers, such as Imodium; consider also bringing antibiotics for bacterial diarrhoea (see p.50)

Oral rehydration formula – to replace fluids lost due to diarrhoea

Allergy tablets – if you need them (especially in spring)

Diamox – consider carrying this drug, for treatment of AMS (see opposite)

- Know the early symptoms of acute mountain sickness (AMS) and be willing to recognize when you have them
- Never ascend to sleep at a higher altitude if you have any AMS symptoms
- If symptoms are worsening while at rest, descend immediately, no matter how late in the day

Drink plenty of **liquids** at altitude, since the air is incredibly dry – unless you pee clear, you're probably not drinking enough. Keeping warm, eating well, getting plenty of sleep and avoiding alcohol will also help reduce the chances of developing AMS.

Symptoms

AMS usually gives plenty of warning before it becomes life-threatening. **Mild** symptoms include headaches, dizziness, racing pulse, nausea, loss of appetite, shortness of breath, disturbed sleep and swelling of the hands and feet. One or two of these symptoms is a sign that your body hasn't yet adjusted and you shouldn't ascend further until you start feeling better; if you do keep going, be prepared to beat a hasty retreat if the condition gets worse.

AMS is defined as **moderate** if the headache becomes severe and medication doesn't help, the nausea verges on vomiting, and coordination starts to suffer. At this point you want to start descending, as **severe AMS symptoms** can develop from moderate ones within hours; these can include all of the above, plus shortness of breath even while at rest, difficulty walking, mental confusion or lethargy, bubbly breathing or coughing, and bloody sputum. The worst case scenario is High Altitude Pulmonary or Cerebral Odema (HAPO/ HACO), or potentially fatal build-up of fluids in the lungs or brain.

Descent and Diamox

The only cure for AMS is **immediate descent**. Anyone showing moderate or severe symptoms should be taken downhill immediately, regardless of the time of day or night – hire a porter or pack animal to carry the sufferer if necessary. Recovery is usually dramatic, often after a descent of only a few hundred vertical metres.

Acetazolamide (better known under the brand name **Diamox**) improves respiration at altitude, and can therefore accelerate acclimatization. (It also stimulates breathing, evening out the disturbing peaks and troughs of "periodic breathing" during sleep at altitude.) Some doctors recommend a **preventive dose** (125mg twice a day) for people trekking at high elevations, though note that unpleasant side effects such as numbness, tingling sensations (Nepali guides call it *jhum jhum*) and light-headedness are not uncommon. To **treat AMS**, the dosage is 250mg twice a day. Note that diamox is a diuretic, so it's all the more important to keep hydrated while taking it. And note too that while it can accelerate acclimatization, it won't stop AMS symptoms worsening if you keep on ascending.

Other dangers

Other altitude-related dangers such as hypothermia and frostbite are encountered less often by trekkers, but can pose real threats on high, exposed passes or in bad weather. Common-sense **precautions** bear repeating: wear or carry adequate clothing; keep dry; cover exposed extremities in severe weather; eat lots and carry emergency snacks; and make for shelter if conditions get bad.

The symptoms of **hypothermia** are similar to those of AMS: slurred speech, fatigue, irrational behaviour and loss of co-ordination. Low body temperature is the surest sign. The treatment, in a word, is heat. Get the victim out of the cold, put him or her in a good sleeping bag (with another person, if necessary) and ply with warm food and drink.

Frostbite appears initially as small white patches on exposed skin, caused by local freezing. The skin will feel cold and numb. To treat, apply warmth (*not* snow!). Avoid getting frostbite a second time, as this can lead to permanent damage. **Snowblindness** shouldn't be a worry as long as you're equipped with a good pair of sunglasses. On snowy surfaces you'll need proper glacier glasses with side shields.

Avalanches can be a serious hazard in certain areas, such as the Annapurna Sanctuary and the Thorung La. If you don't know how to recognize avalanche zones or gauge avalanche danger, ask for a crash course at one of the HRA posts.

Emergencies

Ninety-nine percent of the time, trekking in Nepal is a piece of cake and it's hard to imagine something going wrong. But while few trekkers ever have to deal with **emergencies** – illness, AMS, storms, missteps, landslides and avalanches are the main causes – they can happen to anyone. In non-urgent cases, your best bet is to be carried by porter or pack animal to the nearest **airstrip** or **health post**, although bear in mind that medical facilities outside Kathmandu and a few other major cities are very rudimentary. Locals are the best source of information as to the nearest and quickest way to access health care.

Where the situation is more serious, send word to the nearest village with a phone, satellite phone or police radio transmitter to request a **helicopter rescue**. Satellite phones are increasingly common on the trails, so the message could be relayed inside a couple of hours. Write and repeat your message as clearly as possible, indicating the severity of the problem as well as your location. Note that it could be 24 hours between an accident and a helicopter reaching you, partly because many helicopters can only fly in the early morning. A typical rescue costs in the region of $3000, and they won't come until they're satisfied you'll be able to pay; being registered with your embassy (or, failing that, a good trekking agency) will speed the process of contacting relatives who can vouch for you.

Crime and personal safety

In terms of crime and personal safety, Nepal's hills are probably among the safer parts of the world. Travellers occasionally report luggage stolen or rifled on a bus to the roadhead, a tent or bedroom looted, or boots vanishing from outside a bedroom. Violent crime is more unusual, though inevitably every year there are a few muggings-with-menaces and attacks (including sexual assaults). Due to its accessibility and the volume of tourism, the Annapurna region has a slightly worse reputation than other areas.

During the **Maoist** conflict, many trekkers encountered groups of gun-toting *Maobaadis* (Maoists) and were "asked" to contribute to the cause. Emboldened by the general decline in law and order in the hills, some **groups** took to posing as Maoists and effectively mugging trekkers. Nepal is still politically volatile – other, more localized armed groups seem to spring up all the time – and banditry has not entirely vanished from the hills, so seek up-to-date advice before travelling: both official travel warnings (see p.64) and online message boards. Upon arrival in Kathmandu, consult with the Kathmandu Environmental Education Project (see p.80) on the current safety of areas where you plan to trek. Trekking alone is ill-advised at the best of times.

Trekking life

A trek, it's often said, is not a wilderness experience. Unlike most other mountain ranges, the Himalayas are comparatively well settled, farmed and grazed – much of their beauty, in fact, is man-made – and the trails support a steady stream of local traffic. If you're trekking independently, you'll probably be sleeping and eating in lodges and making equal contact with locals and other foreigners. You'll need a good deal of **adaptability** to different living situations, but the payback comes in cultural insights, unforgettable **encounters**, and, of course, **breathtaking scenery**. Nepal does have a lot of unsettled backcountry, of course, and it's possible to experience it if you're willing to camp and carry your own supplies; this is easier to do with the aid of a trekking agency.

Getting there

The trailhead is typically reached at the end of a long, bumpy bus ride (or a short, bumpy flight), and **getting there** is an

Trekking with children

The potential problems when considering whether to go **trekking with children** are obvious: will they walk? Will he/she let a porter carry them? What if they get sick? What if the weather is bad? Yet trekking with kids may be one of the best things you or they ever do – especially if there are lots of children together. Delights lie round every corner: chickens, goats, jingling donkey trains, frogs, bugs, waterfalls, caves, temples, prayer wheels – all that plus being the centre of attention everywhere they go.

Routes Stick to easy ones and don't take a young child above 3500m due to the risks of AMS. The standard treks generally offer more comforts and easier access to emergency services, although a good agency can help you take children off the beaten track.

Pace depends on the age and sportiness of your youngest. Plan on modest days, stopping by mid-afternoon. That said, many children are up for much longer walks than they might be willing to try at home.

Health and safety Trekking has most of the same hazards as a weekend camping trip. The extra concern is tummy bugs: teach kids to drink only boiled or purified water, keep hands and foreign objects out of mouths, and wash hands frequently (sanitary wipes come in handy). Establish clear ground rules about not wandering off, not running, not venturing close to dropoffs, and staying clear of animals. Bathroom arrangements in the more primitive trekking inns may put children off.

Food and drink Some kids love **daal bhaat** – they can eat it with their fingers – but many turn up their noses. Familiar Western dishes are found on the main trails. A water-purifying travel cup is a handy device, or consider bringing neutralizing powder to remove the taste of iodine from purified water.

Transportation Hours on winding mountain roads is a recipe for car-sickness and misery. If possible, rent a more comfortable vehicle, or fly.

Porters Consider a porter for each child. Almost all porters are great playmates/babysitters, despite the language barrier, and they can carry the child for all or part of the trek in a customized **doko**. Make sure any porter you hire is agile, conscientious and sober, and treat him or her well.

What to bring Bring the same range of clothes for your child as for yourself, only more and warmer – and don't rely on renting locally. Bring a few lightweight games or toys; crayons are ideal. You probably won't need as many books as you might think, as bedtime comes early.

integral part of the experience. This is also a big factor in deciding where to trek, as the going and returning can eat up two days or more. Even if you fly, bad weather can halt flights for days. Helicopters carry only charter groups.

General information on bus and air travel is given in Basics (see pp.26–33). Specific advice on travel to each trek is given in the trek descriptions later in this chapter.

Trails

Most walkers take the Himalayas in easy stages, from one glass of *chiya* to the next. It's best to set off early each morning to make the most of the clear weather, as clouds usually roll in around midday. Pad your schedule for rest days, weather and contingencies, and try to make time for at least one side trip. Walking even a few steps away from the main trail can take you back virtual decades, in terms of development and commercialization, and some of the most fascinating or beautiful sights – monasteries, villages, waterfalls, glaciers – are tucked away up side valleys.

Trails can be steep and rough, and footbridges sometimes alarming. You may occasionally **get lost**, but not for long: all but the highest and most remote trekking routes pass through populated areas, and stopping to chat and ask directions is part of the fun. If you must **trek alone**, stay within sight of other people and spend nights in the company of others, as they can help you if you get hurt and can detect signs of AMS or hypothermia. Nepalis think all lone travellers are a bit odd, so you might find it worthwhile teaming up with others just to avoid the constant question, *Eklai?* ("Alone?"). Be sure to read "Cultural hints" on pp.52–55; again, *don't* give pens or rupees to children, whether they ask or not – if you do, every trekker will be hounded for handouts.

Lodges

Trekking lodges, sometimes called "teahouses", are efficient operations, with English signs, menus and usually an English-speaking proprietor. Many are family homes, typically run by the matriarch, with a stone-and-wood annexe for lodging and a dining room off the family kitchen. In the Annapurna and Everest regions, some have become distinctly fancy: you may find glazed sun-terraces, electric lighting, kerosene heaters, telephones (satellite or otherwise), solar-powered hot showers, a Western toilet and even wi-fi.

Most lodges follow the Nepali tradition of providing inexpensive accommodation (anything from Rs50 and up for a bunk bed) so long as you eat your meals in-house – though note that lodge (and food) prices in the **Annapurna region** are officially agreed (see p.364), prices rise steeply as you gain altitude, and the Everest Base Camp route is relatively expensive. "Luxury" lodges, mostly found on the most popular Annapurna and Everest regions, tend to cater to organized group treks, but may accept walk-ins in quiet periods; expect to pay anything from $5 to $20. An appealing alternative is the **community lodge**, set up on sustainable principles with the aim of spreading the benefits of tourism more widely.

You'll find fewer comforts on **less-trekked trails**, where lodgings are likely to be basic dormitories, or a bench by the kitchen fire, and meals are eaten amid

---

Conservation tips

The main environmental problem in the Himalayas is **deforestation**, and trekking puts an additional strain on local wood supplies: it is estimated that one trekker consumes, directly and indirectly, between five and ten times more wood per day than a Nepali. In addition, walkers leave **litter**, strain local **sanitation systems** and contribute to water **pollution**. The following are suggestions on how to minimize your impact on the fragile Himalayan environment.

Where the choice exists, eat at places that cook with kerosene, electricity or propane instead of wood.

Bring plenty of warm clothes so you (and your porter) are less reliant on wood fires to keep warm.

Try to time your meals and co-ordinate your orders with other trekkers; cooking food in big batches is a more efficient use of fuel.

If trekking with an agency, see that all meals are cooked with kerosene or propane, and complain if they aren't.

Avoid hot showers except in inns where the water is heated by electricity, solar panels or fuel-efficient "back boilers".

Treat your own drinking water rather than relying on bottled or boiled water. Plastic water bottles can't be recycled in Nepal and pose a serious litter problem in trekking areas. Water sterilized by boiling uses precious wood or other fuel.

Use latrines wherever possible. Where there's no facility, go well away from water sources, bury your faeces and burn your toilet paper. Better yet, use water, as Nepalis do.

Use phosphate-free soap and shampoo, and don't rinse directly in streams.

Deposit litter in designated rubbish bins, where they exist. Elsewhere, carry back all non-burnable litter: tins, plastic bottles and especially batteries.

The inhabitants of Nepal's northernmost, highest-altitude regions are culturally very close to their Tibetan cousins, on the other side of the range. While many have developed their own local identities, most famously the Lo-pa of Lo (better known as Mustang) and the Sherpas of Khumbu, the Everest region (see p.378), Nepalis collectively call these peoples **Bhotiya**. This usually, broadly, "Tibetan", but usually conveys an unfortunate derogatory sense of "unwashed hicks from the sticks who can't speak Nepali properly".

Farmers, herders and trans-Himalayan traders, the highland peoples eke out a living in the harsh climate by growing barley, buckwheat and potatoes, and herding yaks and yak hybrids. Their villages vary in appearance: those in the west are strongly Tibetan, with houses stacked up slopes so that the flat roof of one serves as the grain-drying terrace of the next, while in the east houses are more likely to be detached and have sloping, shingle roofs. Like Tibetans, they traditionally take their tea flavoured with salt and yak butter, and married women wear trademark rainbow aprons (**pangden**) and wraparound dresses (**chuba**). That said, jogging pants with a fleece or down jacket is practically a uniform in tourist areas.

Almost all highland ethnic peoples are **Tibetan Buddhists** (see p.437). Their **chortens** (stupa-like cremation monuments), **mani** walls (consisting of slates inscribed with the mantra **Om mani padme hum** – see p.438), gompa (monasteries) and prayer flags (**lung ta**: literally, "wind horse") are the most memorable man-made features of the Himalayas. Unencumbered by caste, highlanders are noticeably less tradition-bound than Hindus, and women are better off for it: they play a nearly equal role in household affairs, speak their minds openly, are able to tease and mingle with men publicly, and can divorce without stigma. Trekkers are likely to encounter many highland women capably running their own tourist lodges and businesses while their husbands are off farming, yak herding or guiding.

eye-watering smoke. Known as *bhattis*, or teahouses, such places rarely advertise themselves, but once you've spent a little time off the beaten track you'll start realizing that almost every trailside house with an open front is potential shelter. In fact, in many parts of Nepal it's possible to ask for food or lodging in private homes – though people in very remote areas, and high-caste Hindus, may not be comfortable with the notion.

Private rooms are usually available along the popular routes, but elsewhere – and at altitude – **dormitory** accommodation is the norm: unroll your sleeping bag early to reserve your place. Beds normally have some sort of padding, but a foam mat may come in handy, especially if you get caught out in high season and end up on the dining room floor.

Recommending specific trekking lodgings is beyond the scope of this chapter. Your best advice will be from trekkers coming the other way.

Food and drink

Trekking cuisine is a world unto itself. Although lodges' plastic-coated menus promise tempting international delicacies, items often turn out to be permanently *paindaina* (unavailable), and you'll notice that the spring rolls, enchiladas, pizzas and pancakes all bear more than a passing resemblance to chapatis. But at any rate, eggs, porridge, muesli and even apple pie are reassuringly familiar, and goodies like chocolate and biscuits are always available. In highland areas you'll be able to eat such Tibetan dishes as *momo*, *thukpa* and *riki kur*, and instead of porridge you might be served *tsampa* (see p.40). At lower elevations, *daal bhaat*, chow mein, packet noodles and seasonal vegetables are the standard offerings.

Food **costs** depend on what you eat and where you go. A full dinner of *daal bhat* at a local *bhatti* costs around Rs300 in Annapurna and Langtang, but you can pay that much for a single plate of chips or small pizza, and on the main Everest trails prices are easily half as much again – and more like double when you get higher up. Budget for a minimum of $15 a day on trekking routes, or up to $30 if you want to order Western dishes, beers and so on.

When **ordering**, bear in mind that the cook can only make one or two things at a time, and there may be many others ahead of you: simplify the process and save fuel by co-ordinating your order with other trekkers. *Daal bhaat* may be the quickest choice, but only if it's already cooked; if it's not, you may find yourself waiting till all the Western orders are done. Most innkeepers expect orders to be placed several hours in advance, and there's usually a notepad floating around for keeping a tally of everything you've eaten. Eating dinner at a lodge other than the one where you're staying is very much frowned upon. Pay when you leave, and be sure to bring plenty of small money on the trek, since innkeepers often have trouble making change.

Tea and hot lemon are traditionally the main **drinks** on the trail. Bottled soft drinks, water and even beer are common along the popular routes, but the price of each bottle rises by Rs15–25 for each extra day it has to be portered from the nearest road. Don't miss trying *chhang*, *raksi* and *tongba* (see Basics, p.41), and the delicious apple cider and apple *raksi*, occasionally available in the Everest region and elsewhere.

Sanitation

Off the established routes or at higher elevations, you'll have to **bathe** and do **laundry** under makeshift outdoor taps or in a tin bucket, using freezing cold water (which explains why hot springs are such major attractions). Most lodges in the Annapurna and Everest regions have solar or electric-heated showers. Others will offer washing water that has been heated on a wood fire. Most lodges provide outdoor **latrines** (*chaarpi*), and a few even have indoor flush **toilets**, but don't be surprised if you're pointed to a half-covered privy hanging over a stream, or simply to a paddock.

The treks

Almost two-thirds of trekkers make for the **Annapurna region**, north of Pokhara, with its spectacular scenery, ease of access and wealth of treks of different lengths and difficulties. The **Everest region**, in the near east of the country, is one of Nepal's most exciting areas, but altitude and distance from the trailheads make shorter treks less viable; roughly a quarter of trekkers walk here. The **Helambu** and **Langtang** regions are less dramatic but conveniently close to Kathmandu, attracting a little under ten percent of trekkers. This leaves vast areas of **eastern and far western Nepal** relatively untrodden by visitors. To walk in these areas you'll need either to be prepared to rough it, and live like a local, or pay to join an organized trek with tents and accept the compromises that go along with that. With a good agency, you can go just about anywhere – and increasing numbers of trekkers are getting off the beaten track. There's even a proposal to create a Great Himalayan Trail along the entire length of Nepal – though it will be many years before such a route could be serviced by lodges.

The following sections give overviews of the areas and describe the major trekking routes within them, but for step-by-step, turning-by-turning descriptions you'll need a route-specific guidebook (see p.351).

The Annapurna region

The **Annapurna region**'s popularity is well deserved: nowhere else do you get such a varied feast of scenery and hill culture and the **logistics** are relatively simple. Treks all start or finish close to Pokhara, which is a relaxing place to end a trek and a handy place to start one, with its clued-up guesthouses, equipment-rental shops and easy transportation to trailheads. With great views just two days up the trail, short treks in the Annapurnas are particularly feasible, and good communications mean the region is also relatively **safe**, from the point of view of medical emergencies – although sporadic muggings in the Birethanti–Ghandruk–Ghorepani triangle mean that **trekking alone is inadvisable**. Tourism is relatively sustainable, too, thanks to ACAP, the Annapurna Conservation Area Project. The inevitable consequence is commercialization. The popular treks in this region are a well-beaten track, and unless you step aside from them you're more likely to be ordering bottled beer from a laminated menu than drinking homebrew with locals.

The **Annapurna Himal** faces Pokhara like an icy, crenellated wall, 40km across, with nine peaks over 7000m spurring from its ramparts and Annapurna I above all at 8091m. It's a region of stunning diversity, ranging from the sodden bamboo forests of the southern slopes (Lumle, northwest of Pokhara, is the wettest village in Nepal) to windswept desert (Jomosom, in the northern rain shadow, is the driest).

The *himal* and adjacent hill areas are protected within the Annapurna Conservation Area Project (ACAP), for which you have to pay a Rs2000 **entry fee** (see p.352). A quasi-park administered by a non-governmental trust, ACAP aims are to protect the area's natural and cultural heritage and ensure sustainable benefit for local people. To take the pressure off local forests, the project has set up kerosene depots and installed microhydroelectric generators, and supports reforestation efforts. Lodge owners benefit from training and low-interest loans, enabling them to invest in things like solar water heaters and efficient stoves. Safe drinking-water stations, rubbish pits, latrines, health posts

▲ The Annapurna region

and a telephone service have all been established on the proceeds of park entry fees. ACAP also sets **fixed lodge prices** (Rs200, or Rs500 with attached bathroom), and agreed menu prices (which vary by area), to prevent undercutting and price wars; these prices should be respected rather than negotiated.

The Annapurna Sanctuary

The aptly named **ANNAPURNA SANCTUARY** is the most intensely scenic short trek in Nepal, and one of the most well-trodden – there are lodges and tea stops at hourly intervals or more frequently, until the highest sections at least. The trail takes you into the very heart of the Annapurna range, passing through huge hills in Gurung country with ever-improving views of the mountains ahead, then following the short, steep Modi Khola, making for a narrow notch between the sheer lower flanks of Machhapuchhare and Hiunchuli. Then, you pass into the most magnificent mountain cirque: the Sanctuary. Wherever you stand, the 360-degree views are unspeakably beautiful, and although clouds roll in early, the curtain often parts at sunset to reveal radiant, molten peaks.

The Sanctuary is an eight- to twelve-day round trip from Pokhara. The actual distance covered isn't great, but **altitude**, **weather** and **trail conditions** all tend to slow you down. The trail gains more than 2000m from Ghandruk to the top, at 4100m, so you'd be wise to spread the climb over four days – and dress for snow. Frequent precipitation makes the higher trail slippery at the best of times, and in winter it can be impassable due to snow or avalanche danger.

There are two main approaches, both converging on the major village of Chhomrong after two or three days' walk (though hardy types have made it in one exhausting day).

Treks at a glance

This list omits treks that require agency or extensive porter support.

Trek	Days*	Best Months	Elevation (m)
Jomosom/Kali Gandaki	5–7	Oct–April	1100–3800
Helambu	3–8	Oct–April	800–3600
Poon Hill	4–6	Oct–April	1100–3200
Machhapuchhare	5–7	Oct–April	1100–3700
Siklis	4–7	Oct–April	1100–2200
Rara	6–8	Oct–Nov, April–June	2400–3500
Langtang	7–12	Oct–May	1700–3750
Annapurna Sanctuary	8–12	Oct–Dec, Feb–April	1100–4130
Annapurna Circuit	12–21	Oct–Nov, March–April	450–5380
Everest (Lukla fly-in)	14–18	Oct–Nov, March–May	2800–5550
Manaslu Circuit	14–20	Oct–Nov, March–May	550–5200
Gosainkund	4–7	Oct–Dec, Feb–May	1950–4380
Everest (Jiri walk-in)	21–28	Oct–Nov, March–April	1500–5550
Everest (Eastern route)	28+	Nov, March	300–5550

* Not including transport to and from the trailhead.

The Phedi approach

Arguably the most satisfying approach route begins at **Phedi** (1160m), a mere twenty-minute taxi drive west of Pokhara. From here the trail ascends the wooded Dhampus ridge, climbing steeply up the last hour to Pothana (1900m), where you're rewarded with fine views of the mountains, including Machapuchhare, the "Fish Tail" mountain. From the col at **Bhichok Deurali** (2080m), a well-paved trail descends again through thicker rhododendron forest, then contours and gently switchbacks through cultivated hillsides around the village of **Tolka** (1700m) before reaching **Landruk**, a substantial Gurung village with wonderful views of Annapurna South. From here the trail follows the Modi Khola upwards, crossing the river at **New Bridge** (1340m) and climbing steeply above Jhinu Danda and Chhomrong.

The Nayapul alternative

A slightly more direct approach leaves the Jomosom road at the **Nayapul** bridge, sloping down to the well-to-do town of **Birethanti** (1050m), where you enter the Annapurna Conservation Area – sign in at the gate. From here, the trail pushes up the steep, terraced west bank of the **Modi Khola**. You can either climb to the major settlement of **Ghandruk** (1940m) – given those 900m of ascent, this is likely to be enough for one day – or stay low in the Modi Khola valley, leaving the main trail at Syauli Bazaar and bypassing Ghandruk on the way up to **New Bridge**. From Ghandruk, the usual trail detours west to the crest of the fine **Komrong Danda** (2654m), joining the Ghorepani trail (see p.368) at **Tadapani** (2630m) before descending to **Kimrong** (1890m), then contouring up to **Chhomrong**, with its distinctly upmarket lodges.

Difficulty	Comments
Easy to moderate	Spectacular, varied but very commercial and somewhat spiritually undermined by the new road.
Moderate	Easy access, uncrowded, varied; only modest views.
Moderate	Easy access, excellent views; very commercial.
Moderate	Easy access; a little-trekked route through fields and forest.
Moderate	Easy access; uncrowded village trek.
Moderate	Fly in; must be prepared to camp; pristine lake and forest.
Moderate	Beautiful alpine valley close to Kathmandu.
Moderate to strenuous	Spectacular scenery, easy access; acclimatization necessary.
Strenuous	Incredible diversity and scenery; high pass requires care and acclimatization; jeep descent from Muktinath makes "half-circuit" possible.
Strenuous	Superb scenery; flights can be a problem; acclimatization necessary.
Strenuous	Little-trekked, remote alternative to the Annapurna Circuit.
Strenuous	Sacred lakes; usually combined with Langtang or Helambu.
Very strenuous	Wonderful mix of hill and high-elevation walking, but with a lot of up-and-down; can save time by flying one way.
Very strenuous	Similar, but with an even greater net vertical gain.

From Chhomrong to the Sanctuary

At **Chhomrong** (2170m), you should visit the ACAP post to bone up on Acute Mountain Sickness and find out about weather and conditions higher up the trail. The path can get dangerously slippery, and the **avalanche risk** is very real, especially in spring and in the areas immediately above Hinku and Deurali. **Altitude**, of course, can kill (see p.356) – or at least stop you reaching

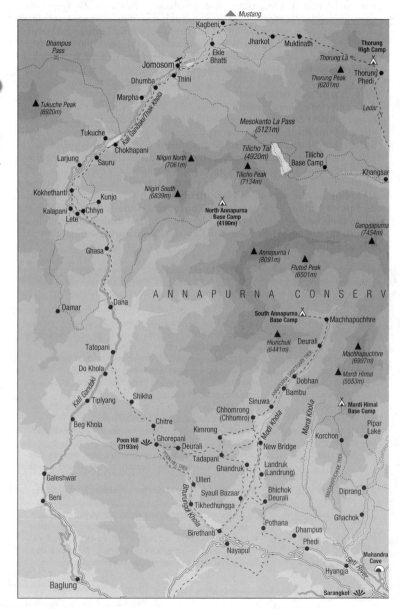

the Sanctuary. There are clusters of small **lodges** at Sinuwa, Bamboo, Doban, Himalaya, Deurali, Macchapuchhare Base Camp and Annapurna Base Camp, and you'll have to pace yourself not by fitness but acclimatization. Actual walking time from Chomrong is in the region of twelve hours, but you should plan to spread the trip over three or four days. Be aware that in the autumn peak season, lodges can fill up early, especially higher up, and some

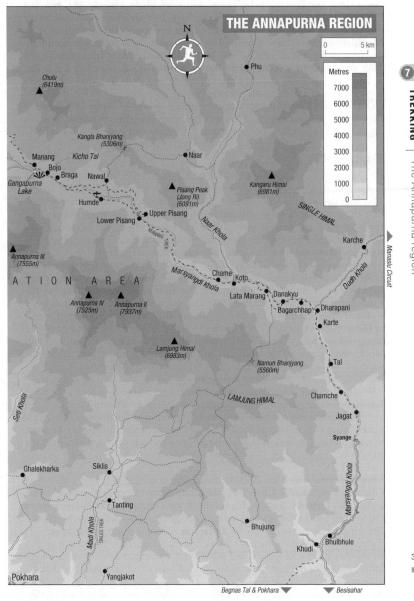

THE ANNAPURNA REGION

N

0   5 km

Metres
7000
6000
5000
4000
3000
2000
1000
0

TREKKING | The Annapurna region

Manaslu Circuit

Chulu
(6419m)

Phu

Kangla Bhanjyang
(5306m)

Kicho Tal

Naar

Manang
Bojo
Braga   Nawal
Gangapurna
Lake
Humde

Pisang Peak
(Jong Ri)
(6091m)

Kangaru Himal
(6981m)

SINGLE HIMAL

Upper Pisang

Lower Pisang

Naar Khola

MANANG TREK

Karche

Annapurna III
(7555m)

ATION   AREA

Marsyangdi Khola

Chame
Koto

Lata Marang   Danakyu

Dudh Khola

Annapurna IV
(7525m)

Annapurna II
(7937m)

Bagarchhap   Dharapani

Karte

Lamjung Himal
(6983m)

Namun Bhanjyang
(5560m)

Tal

LAMJUNG HIMAL

Chamche

Jagat

Syange

Seti Khola

Ghalekharka   Siklis

Tanting

Madi Khola

SIKLES TREK

Bhujung

Marsyangdi Khola

Khudi   Bhulbhule

367

Pokhara   Yangjakot

Begnas Tal & Pokhara ▼   ▼ Besisahar

trekkers often end up sleeping on the dining room floor; make sure you have a warm sleeping bag.

The route above Chhomrong is simple and spectacular: you are ascending the deep and forested Modi Khola valley, with the mountains, notably the splendid swoop of Machhapuchhare, looming white at the head of the gorge. As you ascend, past lodge clusters at Sinuwa (2360m), **Bambu** (2310m), Dobhan (2600m) and Himalaya (2920m), the oak and rhododendron forests slowly give way to bamboo. The avalanches are at their worst above **Deurali** (3239m), and the trail may be diverted to the opposite bank or shut altogether – ask before proceeding up. Once past this sanctuary "gate", you stumble across moraines to **Machhapuchhare Base Camp** (3700m). A good tip is to sleep here and do the final ascent and descent in one long day, thus avoiding an uncomfortable high-altitude night at **Annapurna Base Camp** (4100m). Note too that lodges at both get impossibly crowded in peak season, and shut altogether after heavy snowfall, especially from early December.

Descending is astonishingly fast, compared to going up – two fairly leisurely days down to Chhomrong. It makes sense to return along the alternative approach route, or you can make a longer loop via Ghorepani and Poon Hill (see below).

Poon Hill

The Himalayan viewpoint of **POON HILL** (3193m) provides a tempting destination amid the steep, lush hill country between Pokhara and the Kali Gandaki. This trek doesn't take you right in among the mountains but, weather permitting, there are outstanding vistas and handsome Gurung and Magar villages. The **trails** are wide and well maintained (though steep in places), the lodges are large and comfortable, and the altitude shouldn't present any problems – though you will need **warm clothes** at night. Rain gear is also advisable.

Most people do Poon Hill as a loop from Pokhara, starting at **Birethanti** (1050m), just below the roadside settlement of **Nayapul**. From here it's two shortish but relentlessly uphill days up the Bhurungdi Khola valley via the handsome Magar village of **Ulleri** (1960m) and some fine rhododendron forest to **Ghorepani** (2860m) or, a little higher up, the thrumming cluster of lodges at **Ghorepani Deurali**. There's no need to set your alarm at either, as you'll be awakened at 4am by the daily stampede of Poon Hill sunrise-seekers. If clouds block your view, as they often do, it's worth hanging on for an extra day for the sight of Annapurna South apparently looming over Annapurna I, and the hump-shouldered pyramid of Dhaulagiri.

Beyond Deurali, the trail descends the thriving, terraced valley of the Ghar Khola, before crossing the Kali Gandaki on a splendid suspension bridge and arriving at the busy town of **Tatopani** (1190m) after a day's walk. There are banks (no ATMs as yet), restaurants, a health post and all the other facilities you might need, as well as the hot springs from which the town gets its name (it means "hot water" in Nepali), and frequent buses and jeeps down to Beni and Pokhara.

For a slower return to Pokhara, head east from the old, lower village of Ghorepani, making for Ghandruk – one long or two short days' walk. The first section to **Deurali** (not to be confused with the Deurali above/north of Ghorepani) is a fine ridge walk, with great views of Dhaulagiri and Machhapuchhare; the descent to **Tadapani** (2630m) is steep and slippery. At Tadapani you join the Ghandruk route described under the Nayapul approach to the Annapurna Sanctuary (see p.364), but you could easily make a longer loop, crossing to the east bank of the Modi Khola to rejoin the road at Phedi.

For information on getting to Pokhara from Kathmandu, see p.142. Heading **west of Pokhara**, buses to Phedi (45min), Nayapul (2hr), Baglung (3hr 30min) and Beni (4hr 30min) all leave from the Baglung bus park, 4km from Lakeside. Departures are at least every half-hour as far as Baglung; buses through to Beni leave more like hourly, with the majority heading off in the morning. Buses to Phedi can also be picked up in Harichowk, Bagar, 5km from Lakeside. A taxi to the Baglung Bus Park from Lakeside costs roughly Rs150, or Rs200 to Bagar, but many trekkers commission taxis all the way to the roadhead, thus saving around a third of the travel time – depending on road conditions, and the driver. Taxi costs are variable, but in the region of Rs800 to Phedi, Rs1500 to Nayapul and Rs3500 through to Beni. Heading up the rough road above Beni towards Jomosom, jeep prices will change dramatically depending on the road conditions; ask around in Pokhara before setting off.

Heading towards **Manang and the Marsyangdi valley**, the main bus terminus is Besisahar, a bustling district centre with at least a dozen lodges, a bank, a hospital and so on. It's probably best reached by tourist bus to Dumre on the Prithvi Highway, on the way between Pokhara and Kathmandu; you can then pick up a bus (or hire a jeep) for the 43km (3hr by bus) north to Besisahar. There are also direct public buses from Kathmandu (7 daily; 7–8hr) and Pokhara (2–3 daily; 4hr 30min) – slower, but you don't have the hassle of changing at Dumre. The quickest option, of course, is a direct taxi from Pokhara (3hr); expect to pay around Rs4000. From Besisahar, frequent jeeps (and some public buses) can now take you north; at the time of writing rough road had replaced the trail as far as Syange, some two hours up the road – though transport was mostly stopping some way short of the village.

The fast – and decidedly thrilling – alternative is to **fly**. From Pokhara there are flights to Jomosom (3–9 daily), on the northwestern side of the Annapurna range, and Manang (0–3 weekly), or rather, to the Humde airstrip, at least three hours below Manang. The Manang/Humde option is much less reliable: flights from Pokhara run only two or three times a week, even in high season, and they're usually on the same plane as made the trip to Jomosom; strong winds at either airstrip can mean the flight is cancelled. Plus if you start your trek this high you're asking for altitude problems.

The Jomosom trek: the Kali Gandaki and Muktinath

The trek down (or, for a few, up) the **Kali Gandaki** gorge from the pilgrim site of **Muktinath** and the busy regional capital of **Jomosom** was for many years the classic Himalayan sampler, and the most developed stretch of trail in Nepal, with food and lodging closer to what you'd find in Thamel than the usual hill fare. Since the construction of a road from Beni to Jomosom, on the west bank of the Kali Gandaki (see p.399), many would-be trekkers have gone elsewhere. Yet it's still perfectly possible to do the trek – sticking mostly to the opposite, eastern side of the valley – and guides can show you some fantastic **day-hikes** and overnight trips up from the valley floor: little-trekked trails lead to North Annapurna Base Camp, the Dhaulagiri Icefall (way out west of Larjung) and the high-level Dhampus Pass (5182m), the key to Dolpo.

Many trekkers choose to fly to Jomosom and walk down, but you'll have more sense of arrival (and acclimatize better) if you do the trek the hard way. The best approach route is now from Nayapul to Tatopani via **Poon Hill** (for a full description, see p.368).

Tatopani to Ghasa

From Tatopani to Muktinath is at least four days' walk (or a day in a succession of jeeps). A definitive new route is yet to be firmly established – so seek local

The Annapurna Circuit and the new road

As of 2009, the legendary **Annapurna Circuit** no longer exists. Or not as it once did: a challenging three-week, off-road trek encircling the Annapurna massif. A road now extends from Baglung all the way up the Kali Gandaki gorge, on the western half of the Annapurnas, to Jomosom and Muktinath. A second road, meanwhile, is creeping steadily up the Marsyangdi valley, on the eastern side of the circuit. It will be many years before the full circle is joined (and the potentially deadly altitude of the Thorung La pass, at the top of the circuit, makes the idea of future vehicle tours unlikely), yet the roads have nevertheless changed everything.

It's not all bad news. The Jomosom side was already over-developed for some tastes, and many trekkers are doing a **two-week half-circuit**, walking up the Marsyangdi, crossing the pass, then treating themselves to a jeep ride down from Muktinath or Jomosom to Pokhara, via Beni. At the time of writing, the 83km road was unpaved and very rough, and there were some impassable sections, so travellers were walking between one jeep drop-off point and the next pick-up along. Landslides (and a lack of money for stabilisation measures and tarmac) mean this is likely to be the situation for some years to come, but seek local advice.

Guides have established an **alternative route** on the eastern bank of the Kali Gandaki, mostly out of sight and earshot of the road. **New treks** are also being developed in less-visited areas, such as Dolpo, Jumla, Manaslu, Dhaulagiri and the Dhorepetan Hunting Reserve (see Remote and restricted areas, p.386), potentially spreading the economic benefits of tourism more widely. And of course the road is bringing a new generation of tourists. Indian pilgrims are already heading up to Muktinath in unprecedented numbers, further increasing the colour and fervour already associated with this pilgrimage site.

advice or take a guide – but it's possible to leave the road thirty minutes' walk out of Tatopani and stay on the **eastern bank** of the Kali Gandaki from there. The main settlements (and most of the trekking lodges) are on the western side, but temporary wooden bridges make criss-crossing relatively simple – in the dry season, at least. To access the east-bank towns when the river is high, you may have to make strategic crossings at the permanent suspension bridges and resign yourself to walking on the road for some stretches. The alternative is to stay east at all times, taking camping equipment or seeking accommodation in local homes; that said, lodges are already springing up to serve the eastern route and it's likely to be feasible all the way through by the winter season of 2010, though landslides are a perennial problem.

Above **Tatopani** (1190m), where the trail from Poon Hill joins the road up from Beni, the route passes into the world's deepest gorge, the **Kali Gandaki**, with the 8000-metre hulks of Dhaulagiri and Annapurna towering on either side. It's an awesome sight, even from a vehicle. Some agencies are taking a tough, high-level route out west (you'll need camping equipment), climbing west from Tatopani onto a high ridge at **Damar**, and switchbacking before descending to **Kalapani** (2530m). Most trekkers simply follow the valley up, however. Opposite the old Magar village of **Dana**, you enter the steepest, sheerest part of the gorge, the gateway to Mustang.

Ghasa to Muktinath

At **Ghasa** (2010m), you enter **Lower Mustang** district and the homeland of the Thakali people (see opposite) – from here on up, the river is known locally as the **Thak Khola**. At the village of **Chhyo**, opposite Lete (2480m), alternative trails divert inland slightly, climbing steeply either up to Titi Tal and then down to the well-established trekking village of **Kokhetanti** (2545m), or continuing up to **Kunjo** and crossing a high ridge at some 3800m, then descending to the trail north of Kokhetanti. Both trails then join and follow the river up, passing the settlements of Sauru, Chokhopani, Dhumba, Thini and Ekle Bhatti to Kagbeni (2800m). It would be a pity not to cross over short of Dhumba to handsome, stony **Marpha** (2670m), which sits amid apricot and apple orchards – the cider and brandy are famous – but you'd do as well to bypass the increasingly hectic town of **Jomosom** (2720m), unless you need to buy supplies, visit the doctor, bank or police, or seek some respite – it's a major administrative centre with scores of fancy hotels.

Above Thini, the trail is mostly shared with a rough road, though a guide can show you alternative routes. At the romantic fortress town of **Kagbeni**, with its medieval buildings and terracotta Buddhist figures, you're on the edge of the Tibetan plateau. The main Himalayas chain looms magnificently to the south. Upper Mustang, to the north, requires an expensive permit to visit (see p.352), but it's an open-access, 1000-metre climb (or jeep ride) up a side valley to poplar-lined **Muktinath** (3760m), one of the most important religious sites in the Himalayas – and a pilgrim boomtown. The Mahabharata mentions it as the source of mystic *shaligrams*; a priest will show you around the Vishnu temple, with its 108 water spouts and pilgrims bathing in the freezing water. Further down the trail, a Buddhist shrine shelters two perpetual flames. Yartung, a madly exotic **festival** of horseriding, is held at Muktinath around the full moon of August–September.

Manang and the Marsyangdi Valley

The **Marsyangdi Valley**, which curls around the east side of the Annapurna range, has long been the less commercialized half of the Annapurna Circuit, trekked only by the hardcore few intending to cross the 5415m pass of the Thorung La and descend towards Jomosom. With the opening of the road on the western side of the range, it is set to eclipse its wealthier cousin. Starting in subtropical paddy at about 500m, the trail ascends steadily. If you're crossing the Thorung La, you'll need proper boots, gloves and very warm clothes, and a four-season sleeping bag for a night spent above 4400m.

Thakalis and Manangis

A small but economically powerful clan, **Thakalis** are the ingenious traders, innkeepers and pony-handlers of the Thak Khola in the Annapurna region. Their entrepreneurial flair goes back at least to the mid-nineteenth century, when the government awarded them a regional monopoly in the salt trade. When Nepal opened to the outside world, many branched out into more exotic forms of commerce, such as importing electronics from Singapore and Hong Kong, while others set up efficient inns in the western hills. Similarly, the **Manangis** (or Manang-ba) of the upper Marsyangdi, the next valley to the east of the Thak Khola, built early trading privileges into a reputation for international smuggling and other shady activities. Women have traditionally run most of the trekking lodges in both of these valleys, while their well-travelled husbands spent most of their time away on business. In recent years, the relaxation of import restrictions and currency controls has deprived these groups of their special status, and many traders have returned to their home villages. Both groups could arguably be classified as Bhotiyas (see p.361), but their languages are more akin to Gurung than to Tibetan; Manangis are Buddhists, while Thakalis' religion blends Buddhism with Hinduism and shamanism.

The main **trailhead** is at Besisahar, but in good conditions jeeps penetrate the valley as far as Syange (see below). With a guide, you could also walk in two to three days from Begnas Tal, via Nalma Phedi and Baglungpani, to Khudi, just north of Besisahar.

The Upper Marsyangdi to Manang and the Thorung La

Above the riverside settlement of **Syange**, the road is (or was at the time of writing) left behind, and the trail passes from terraced farmland into the gorge of the **Upper Marsyangdi**; and it's three or four marvellous days' walk up to Manang, mostly through Buddhist country. The trail crosses astonishing suspension footbridges and passes along dramatic walkways blasted into the rock, all the time climbing through successive climatic zones: temperate forest, coniferous forest, alpine meadows and finally the arid steppes of the rain shadow. The walk from Chame to **Manang** – the high route via Upper Pisang avoids the bizarre stretch of unconnected road below – is spectacular and shouldn't be rushed. The sight of the huge, glacier-dolloped Annapurnas towering almost 5000m above the valley will stay with you forever. Manang's architecture, like that of all the older villages here, is strongly Tibetan.

The **Thorung La** (5416m) is iffy to impossible from late December till early March, while the lower parts of the trek are uncomfortably warm from April onwards. Snow can block the pass at any time of year, so be prepared to wait it out or go back down the way you came. If you're going for it, make sure you visit Manang's Himalayan Rescue Association post for information on weather conditions, AMS and suggested pacing of the route. It's only six or seven hours to **Thorung Phedi** (4450m), the last cluster of lodges before the pass, but you should spread the ascent over a least two days – perhaps making day-trips from Manang (see p.371). Thorung Phedi and the worryingly high **Thorung High Camp** (4925m) are grotty places where you'll be woken up at 3am by trekkers who've been told (wrongly) that they have to clear the pass by 8am. The climb up the pass, and the knee-killing 1600-metre descent down the other side to **Muktinath** (see p.369) is a tough but exhilarating day.

Side trips from Manang

Manang makes a fine base for exploratory day-hikes around the Upper Marsyangdi valley – ideal for acclimatizing if you're crossing the Thorung La, and worthy as destinations in their own right. The **gompa** at Manang, Bojo and Braga, all within half an hour of each other, are well worth visiting, and you could add on a short stroll from Manang to **Gangapurna Lake** and the fine viewpoint two hours above. **Kicho Tal** (4950m), an icy lake where *bharal* (blue sheep) have been sighted, makes a fine day hike.

Two tricky hours from Manang, **Khangsar** (3734m) is the highest permanent village in the Marsyangdi valley; it has a couple of lodges. Four or so demanding hours above there's a single, icy lodge at **Tilicho Base Camp** (4150m), where an overnight would make possible a steep continuation towards the astounding, often iced-over **Tilicho Tal** (4920m), a further three hours up. It's not a trip for the inexperienced; still less is the high, snowy, dangerous, two-day route (camping required) through to Jomosom (or Marpha), via crossings of the frozen lake and the **Mesokanto La** (5121m).

Other Annapurna region treks

The following three treks have little in common with the well-serviced routes described above. You'll typically find only Nepali food and lodging, or will need to camp – and possibly stay in people's homes for at least some nights. If you're not trekking with an agency, you'll probably want to go with a guide.

Of course, there are scores of possibilities beyond the three treks described here. The **Khopra Lake** trek, on the shoulder of Annapurna South above Ghorepani and Tadapani, could soon rival Poon Hill in popularity, with its views from Khyar Lake (4880m). Increasing numbers of trekkers are exploring west of the Kali Gandaki towards the **Dhaulagiri** massif and the little-visited **Dhorpatan Hunting Reserve**; beyond that, of course, there's Dolpo (covered in Far Western Nepal; see p.390).

The Machhapuchhare trek

Guides in Pokhara have recently started advertising a new loop route directly north of Pokhara, towards the south faces of Mardi Himal and **MACCHAPUCH-HARE**, with fine views of the Annapurna wall. The usual approach route heads up the upper valleys of the Seti Khola, leaving a spur road just above **Hyangja** (20min by taxi from Pokhara), and passing through lush, terraced farmland around the Gurung villages of **Ghachok** and **Diprang** (1440m), where there's a community lodge. A choice of steep paths lead up through forest (one passes **Pipar Lake**, prime pheasant habitat with a stunning view of Machhapuchhare, looming just to the north) to a high ridge dripping with rhododendrons and alive with birds, which you can follow up to the minor peak at **Korchon** (3682m), and potentially on up in the direction of **Mardi Himal Base Camp** (4120m). Most treks descend the ridge before dropping to the Mardi Khola at the village of Ribang. The trek takes five to seven days, and requires camping and supplies.

The Siklis trek

The **SIKLIS TREK** probes an uncrowded corner of the Annapurna Conservation Area under the shadows of Lamjung Himal and Annapurna II and IV. The main itinerary takes about a week, starting at Begnas Tal (see map, p.366) and heading north to the Madi Khola, then following the river's west bank up to well-preserved **Siklis** (1980m), Nepal's biggest Gurung village. After backtracking a bit you strike westwards over the thickly forested ridge that separates the Madi and Seti drainages and then descend via **Ghalekharka** and the Sardikhola to the Seti Khola, returning towards Hyangja via Ghachok (see above). Many other variations are possible. As part of an effort to develop this into a model eco-trekking route, ACAP has funded the construction of a small museum and cultural centre in Siklis, as well as a community lodge for non-camping trekkers. Other lodges may soon make this trek possible without the necessity of camping or staying in local homes – ask or, preferably, hire a guide.

Manaslu Circuit

It takes up to three weeks to trek the **MANASLU CIRCUIT**, a challenging route east of the Annapurna area that ventures into the extremely remote Manaslu Conservation Area and over a 5200-metre pass. This trek is well worth considering if you were thinking of doing the Annapurna circuit and were put off by the new road or the increased commercialization. It is officially restricted to organized groups with camping equipment and supplies, however – though there are simple *bhattis* or teahouses most of the way round. However you go, an authorized agency will need to arrange your trekking permit (Sept–Nov $70 per person for a week, then $10 per day; Dec–Aug $50/$7).

The trek traditionally starts in Gorkha, though a road now bypasses the first two days east to **Arughat** – which can also be reached by roads coming up from Benighat, on the main Kathmandu–Pokhara highway, and Dhading. From

Arughat (530m), the first eight days climb steadily up the **Burhi Gandaki** valley, passing through deep Gurung country. (A fascinating side-trip would be east of Philim up to the stunning, forested and intensely Buddhist Tsum valley, which penetrates behind the 7000-metre peaks of **Ganesh Himal**.) Beyond **Deng** (1800m) the valley starts to turn east and you enter the high, Tibetan country of Nupri; it's roughly four more days up through increasingly lofty, Buddhist country to the splendid **Larkya La** (5213m), on the very shoulder of Manaslu – the pass can be snowy and dangerous. The descent is very fast: two steep days down the Dudh Khola to the Marsyangdi valley just above **Dharapani** (1860m), from where the road coming up from Besisahar (see p.369) is less than a day away.

Helambu, Langtang and Gosainkund

Trekking **north of Kathmandu** is curiously underrated and relatively uncrowded. The most accessible of all the trekking regions, it's well suited to one- or two-week itineraries. What it lacks in superlatives – there are no 8000-metre peaks in the vicinity (unless you count Shisha Pangma, across the border in Tibet) – it makes up for in base-to-peak rises that are as dramatic as anywhere. Langtang, in particular, delivers more amazing views in a short time than any other walk-in trek in Nepal, with the possible exception of the Annapurna Sanctuary.

Two distinct basins and an intervening *lek* (ridge) lend their names to the major treks here; each stands on its own, but, given enough time and good weather you can mix-and-match them. **Helambu** is closest to Kathmandu, comprising the rugged north–south valleys and ridges that lie just beyond the northeast rim of the Kathmandu Valley. North of Helambu, running east–west and tantalizingly close to the Tibet border, lies the high, alpine **Langtang Valley**, which in its upper reaches burrows spectacularly between the Langtang and Jugal Himals. **Gosainkund** comprises a chain of sacred lakes nestled in a rugged intermediate range northwest of Helambu. One practical inconvenience is that the connections between these three treks aren't reliable – winter snow may block the passes between Helambu and the other two – and done on their own, the Langtang and Gosainkund treks require you to retrace your steps for much of the return journey.

Food and lodging here are less luxurious than in the Annapurna and Everest regions, but never a problem on the main trails. All these routes take you into **Langtang National Park**, for which there's an Rs1000 entry fee.

Langtang

The **LANGTANG TREK** can be done in as little as a week, but day-hikes in the upper valley should detain you for at least another two or three days, and given more time you'll want to add Gosainkund to the itinerary. Most people start at **Syaphru Besi** (1400m), a very "local" and very bumpy nine-hour bus ride from Macha Pokhari, near Kathmandu's Gongabu Bus Park (2 buses daily; leaving early in the morning; Rs475). The first two days of the trek are spent climbing briskly up the gorge-like lower Langtang valley, probably overnighting at **Lama Hotel** (2470m) or **Ghoratabela** (2970m). Oaks and rhododendron give way to peaceful hemlock and larch forest; after ascending an old moraine, snowy peaks suddenly loom ahead and the gorge opens into a U-shaped glacial valley – prime yak pasture. Spring-time is excellent for flowers here, and in autumn the berberis bushes turn a deep rust colour. Two Bhotiya villages occupy the upper valley: **Langtang**

Tamang Heritage Trail

Perhaps trying to compensate for the lack of celebrity peaks, many agencies arrange **cultural treks** in the Langtang area, with nights spent in village homes, visits to religious sites and monasteries, and evening "cultural shows" – which are generally much better than they sound. There's often a strong emphasis on wildlife viewing and sustainable tourism. In all, these treks offer a refreshing change from the relentless altitude- and view-bagging mentality behind the big-name Annapurna and Everest trails. The area northwest of Syaphru Besi, in particular, has been developed as a **Tamang Heritage Trail**. The usual route is a four- to six-day circuit, via Gatlang, Tatopani, with its hot springs, Timure and Briddim. The route may change, however, as at the time of writing the Chinese were completing a sixteen-kilometre road between Syaphru Besi and Rasuwagadhi, on the Tibet border.

(3300m), the bigger of the two, makes a good place to spend an extra night and acclimatize, while **Kyanjin Gompa** (3750m) boasts a small monastery, a cheese "factory" (fabulous yogurt) and a cluster of chalet-lodges which fill up early in high season.

The **Langtang Glacier** is further up the valley – a long day's round-trip, as there are no lodges. From a rocky viewpoint at 4100m, a little beyond the yak pasture at Numthang, you can see ice and moraine spreading up the high valleys, hemmed in by snowy peaks. Equally tempting are the ascents of either **Tsergo Ri** (4984m), a challenging, six- or seven-hour round trip which offers an awesome white wilderness of peaks or **Kyanjin Ri** (4773m), which stands a mere two hours or so above Kyanjin Gompa.

You can **return** by crossing into Helambu over the Kangja La (see p.378), but most people go back down the valley, perhaps varying the last leg by turning off to Thulo Syaphru (where the trail to Gosainkund branches off) and down to Dhunche.

Gosainkund

GOSAINKUND can be trekked on its own in as little as four days, but because of the rapid ascent to high elevation – 4380m – it's best done after acclimatizing in Langtang or Helambu. Combined with either of these, it adds three or four days; a grand tour of all three areas takes sixteen or more days.

From either Dhunche (served by three buses daily from Kathmandu's Gongabu Bus Park, leaving in the early morning) or Thulo Syaphru (on the Langtang trek), trails ascend steeply through mossy rhododendron forest to the monastery and cheese factory of **Sing Gompa** at 3250m. The climb from Dhunche is particularly brutal. Above Sing Gompa, the trail ascends through tall fir stands before emerging above the tree line for increasingly panoramic views of the high peaks (Laurebinayak is a beautiful place to stop) and finally entering the barren upper reaches of the Trisuli River, where glacial moraines and rockslides have left a string of some half-dozen **lakes** (*kund*). Several lodges sit by the shore of **Gosainkund**, the most sacred of the lakes and renowned among Nepali Hindus. A famous legend recounts how Shiva, having saved the world by drinking a dangerous poison, struck this mountain-side with his *trisul* to create the lake and cool his burning throat. During the full moon of July–August, Janai Purnima, a massive Hindu **pilgrimage** is held at Gosainkund. In good weather you can climb **Surya Peak** (5144m), on the northeast side of the Laurabinayak La – the pass two hours southeast of Gosainkund; the views are superb.

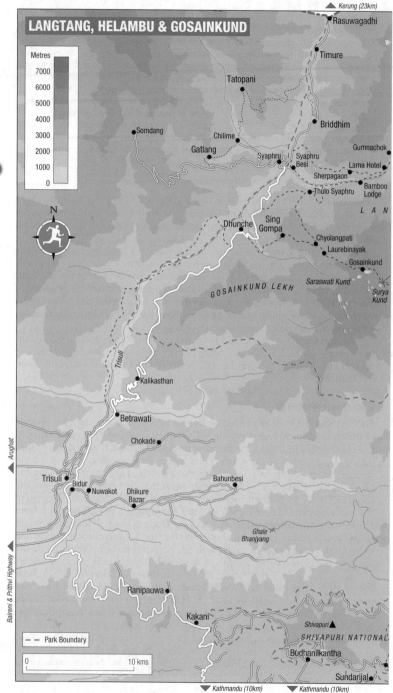

LANGTANG, HELAMBU & GOSAINKUND

Metres
7000
6000
5000
4000
3000
2000
1000
0

N

Kerung (23km)

Rasuwagadhi

Timure

Tatopani

Briddhim

Somdang

Chilime

Gatlang

Syaphru

Gumnachok

Syaphru
Besi

Lama Hotel

Sherpagaon

Bamboo
Lodge

Thulo Syaphru

L A N

Dhunche

Sing
Gompa

Chyolangpati

Laurebinayak

Gosainkund

GOSAINKUND LEKH

Saraswati Kund

Surya
Kund

Trisuli

Kalikasthan

Betrawati

Chokade

Bahunbesi

Arughat

Trisuli

Bidur

Nuwakot

Dhikure
Bazar

Ghale
Bhanjyang

Baireni & Prithvi Highway

Ranipauwa

Kakani

Shivapuri

SHIVAPURI NATIONAL

– – Park Boundary

0   10 kms

Budhanilkantha

Sundarijal

Kathmandu (10km)   Kathmandu (10km)

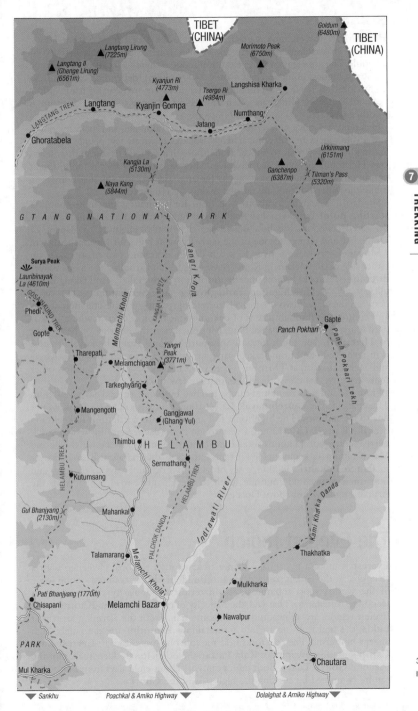

TIBET
(CHINA)

Goldum
(6480m)

TIBET
(CHINA)

Langtang Lirung
(7225m)

Morimoto Peak
(6750m)

Langtang II
(Ghenge Lirung)
(6561m)

Kyanjun Ri
(4773m)

Tsergo Ri
(4984m)

Langshisa Kharka

LANGTANG TREK

Langtang

Kyanjin Gompa

Numthang

Jatang

Ghoratabela

Urkinmang
(6151m)

Kangja La
(5130m)

Ganchenpo
(6387m)

Tilman's Pass
(5320m)

Naya Kang
(5844m)

GTANG   NATIONAL   PARK

Yangri Khola

Surya Peak

Lauribinayak
La (4610m)

Melamchi Khola

KANGJA LA ROUTE

GOSAINKUND TREK

Phedi

Gapte

Gopte

Panch Pokhari

Yangri
Peak
(3771m)

Tharepati

Melamchigaon

Tarkeghyang

Mangengoth

Gangjawal
(Ghang Yul)

Panch Pokhari Lekh

Thimbu   H E L A M B U

Sermathang

HELAMBU TREK

Indrawati River

HELAMBU TREK

Kutumsang

PALCHOK DANDA

Kami Kharka Danda

Gul Bhanjyang
(2130m)

Mahankal

Talamarang

Melamchi Khola

Thakhatka

Mulkharka

Pati Bhanjyang (1770m)

Chisapani

PARK

Melamchi Bazar

Nawalpur

Mul Kharka

Chautara

▼ Sankhu   Poachkal & Amiko Highway ▼   Dolalghat & Arniko Highway ▼

7

TREKKING

377

Helambu

HELAMBU (or Helmu) is great for short treks: access from Kathmandu is easy, and an extensive trail network enables you to tailor a circuit to your schedule. The area spans a wide elevation range – there's a lot of up-and-down – but the highest point reached is only 2700–3200m (depending on route), so acclimatization is rarely a problem. Winter treks are particularly feasible. The peaks of Langtang Himal are often visible, but the views aren't as close-up as in other areas.

Helambu was once considered a hidden, sacred domain, and its misty ridges and fertile valleys are still comparatively isolated; relatively few people trek here, and with so many trails to choose from, those that do tend to spread themselves out. Helambu's people call themselves **Sherpa**, although they're only distant cousins of the Solu-Khumbu stock. Tamangs (see p.216) are also numerous, while the valley bottoms are farmed mainly by Hindu castes.

Sundarijal, a taxi or local bus ride from Kathmandu, is the most common **starting point**, but alternative trailheads include Sankhu, Kakani and Nagarkot. To get deeper into the hills faster, take the Arniko Highway to Banepa or Dhulikhel, and change to one of the fairly frequent buses for Melamchi Bazaar.

Most trekkers make a five- to seven-day loop around two main ridges on either side of the Melamchi Khola, staying high – and avoiding the mega water-diversion Melamchi Project under construction in the valley – and taking in the villages of **Melamchigaon**, **Tarkeghyang** and **Sermathang**. The walk between the second two is especially rewarding, passing picturesque monasteries and contouring through forests of oak, rhododendron and *lokta*, whose bark is used to make traditional paper. From Melamchigaon, the return loop heads west to **Tharepati**, then south towards Shivapuri National Park. The fast alternative is to take a side trail from Tarkeghyang, heading down to the Melamchi Khola and Melamchi road at **Thimbu**, where you can pick up a jeep. Countless other trails strike west and east to villages that see few trekkers.

From Helambu, Gosainkund can be reached by a long, rugged day's walk from Tharepati, via the **Laurebinayak La (**4610m); this pass can be tricky in winter due to ice and snow. The high route to Langtang heads north from Tarkeghyang over the **Kangja La** (5130m), a very tough three-day traverse for which you'll need a tent, food, crampons and ice axe (it may be impassable between Dec and March). From Tarkeghyang, lesser trails cut across the Indrawati basin and over to **Panch Pokahri** (3800m), a set of lakes two or three days to the east, and from there you could continue south to the Chautara road, which joins the Arniko Highway just above Dolalghat.

The Everest region

Everest is more a pilgrimage than a trek: a tough personal challenge with a clear goal at the end, it passes deep into Buddhist Sherpa country, among some of the world's most sublime peaks. In terms of popularity, the region runs second to Annapurna. That said, the majority of trekkers in **Solu-Khumbu**, the Everest region, are all heading up the same trail. From the alarming airstrip at **Lukla**, the trail leads north into mountainous **Khumbu**, the dizzyingly high Sherpa homeland. The trail forks near the top: one route leads to **Everest Base Camp** and the viewpoint of **Kala Pattar**; the other, less trodden, makes for the beautiful **Gokyo Lakes**. Both high points are about eight days from Lukla, and can be combined by crossing the high pass of the **Cho La**.

Getting to Everest

Most trekkers fly to **Lukla** from Kathmandu. There are up to twenty flights a day, even though the airstrip is one of the world's most alarming – or thrilling, depending on your point of view – a distressingly short uphill runway apparently heading into the mountain halfway up the Dudh Koshi gorge. At least it's got tarmac these days and they've cleared away the plane wreckage that used to festoon it. The old problems of flights cancelled because of bad weather and trekkers queuing to get out, however, remain.

The dedicated few walk from the nearest roadhead, at **Jiri** (see p.217). All transport departs from the City Bus Park in Kathmandu (see p.143), leaving very early in the morning. Tata Sumo jeeps are quickest (8–9hr), and some will take you on the rough road that now stretches beyond Jiri as far as **Bhandar** – potentially cutting the first two days off the trek, though at the cost of six or so very uncomfortable hours. Otherwise, the once-daily "Super Express" bus (10hr) is preferable to the ordinary public buses (12hr). At the time of writing, jeeps cost Rs810 to Jiri, the express bus Rs475.

It's also possible to **fly** to **Phaplu**, four days east of Jiri, and a couple of hours below Junbesi. It's not much cheaper than flying all the way to Lukla, three days further on, but it would allow for a fascinating detour to Solu-Khumbu's rarely visited capital, Salleri, a long strip of two-storey houses strung out on a green hillside, with a thriving Saturday bazaar at its bottom end. The longer, eastern approaches to Everest are described on p.386.

Relatively few trekkers now take the switchback hike from the roadhead at **Jiri** through **Solu**, the lower, greener, more populous and more ethnically diverse country to the south. It's a stunning route, and offers a great way to acclimatize, but the extra five to seven days' walking is too much for many people. You should leave slack in your schedule even if you're flying, though, as getting a place on a plane out of Lukla can be problematic if bad weather causes cancellations to stack up.

To get a good look at Everest, you'll have to spend at least four nights above 4000m and at least one at around 5000m. At these altitudes, there is a serious risk of developing **acute mountain sickness** (AMS) and you must know the signs (see p.356). Everest is also the **coldest** of the major treks, so you'll need a good sleeping bag, several layers of warm clothes, and sturdy boots that will keep out snow. The rental shops of **Namche Bazaar** (or Namche for short), in Khumbu, allow you to stock up on high-altitude gear and return it on the way back down. Because of weather, the **trekking "window"** is especially short in Khumbu – early October to mid-November, and late March to late April – and this, in turn, creates a seasonal stampede on the trails and at the Lukla airstrip. Winter isn't out of the question, but it's just that much colder.

While Everest isn't as heavily trekked as Annapurna, its high-altitude **environment** is even more fragile. Khumbu, with less than four thousand inhabitants, receives anything from ten to twenty thousand trekkers a year, and probably twice as many porters. Lodge-building almost destroyed the Blue Pine and Silver Fir forests around Lukla, and the demand for firewood is many times the regeneration capacity of the area. Near trekking villages, up to half the juniper shrubs have vanished in smoke. The **Sagarmatha National Park**, which covers most of Khumbu, has done some fine work in reforestation (funded by the Rs1000 entry fee), but it can't be said often enough: have as little to do with wood-burning as possible.

The popular trails through Solu-Khumbu are well-equipped with **lodges**, some basic, some fancy and surprisingly expensive – until you consider the costs of portering in all supplies this far. Prices rise as you ascend; near the top, most lodges offer basic bunk beds only. The main Jiri–Lukla–Namche–Base Camp route is very straightforward, as is the alternative high-level spur, to the Gokyo lakes, but a **guide** is advisable for pretty much anything else. Solu-Khumbu is the easiest area in Nepal to hire a **woman porter** – a Sherpani – although few speak enough English to serve as guides.

Everest Base Camp

From **Lukla** (2840m), the trail powers north up the Dudh Koshi ("Milk River") before passing into Khumbu and the Sagarmatha National Park (Rs1000 entry fee) at **Jorsale** (2740m), and bounding up to lofty **NAMCHE** (3450m), where Khumbu and the serious scenery start. Nestled handsomely in a horseshoe bowl, the Sherpa "capital" has done very well out of mountaineering and trekking over the years, and shops sell (or rent) absolutely anything a trekker could desire. There's also a bank (with, astonishingly, an ATM), a post office, a bakery, a place calling itself "the world's highest bar", and even internet access. Try to make your trip coincide with the **Saturday market**, which draws Tibetans from the north and **Rais** from the south, or visit the national park **visitors' centre**, perched on the ridge east of town, which contains an informative museum. **Thami**, a beautiful few hours' walk west of Namche, makes an excellent side trip.

There are numerous possibilities above Namche, including passing through the relatively untouristy and unusually flat settlements of **Khumjung** (3780m) and Khunde. The main route contours to Sanasa (where the trail to Gokyo

---

Sherpas

Nepal's most famous ethnic group, the **Sherpas** probably migrated to Solu-Khumbu four or five centuries ago from eastern Tibet; their name, locally pronounced *sharwa*, means "People from the East". Until the arrival of the potato in the 1830s, whose calories enabled a settled lifestyle, they were nomads, driving their yaks to pasture in Tibet and wintering in Nepal. (Sherpa potatoes today are famously delicious, eaten boiled in their skins, with a little salt and chilli.) Cross-border trade is now very much one-way, with everything from butter, noodles and meat to electronics, carpets and cement making its way south from Tibet.

Sherpas maintain the highest permanent settlements in the world – up to 4700m – which accounts for their legendary hardiness at **altitude**. From the 1900s, Sherpas worked as high-altitude expedition porters, gaining a reputation as "tigers of the snows" and learning climbing techniques. In 1953, Tenzing Norgay became one of the first two men to reach the top of Everest, achieving worldwide fame for his people. The break couldn't have come at a better time, for trans-Himalayan trade was soon cut short by the Chinese occupation of Tibet. Since then, Sherpas have deftly diversified into tourism, starting their own trekking and mountaineering agencies, opening lodges and selling souvenirs and equipment. Forty years ago, Namche Bazaar was a cluster of stone, wood and slate huts; now every single roof is metal, all windows are glazed and some lodges are palatial.

Canny commercialism doesn't mean Sherpas aren't devout **Buddhists**, and most villages of note support a *gompa* and a few monks (or nuns). But there are a few animist elements as well: they revere Khumbila, a sacred peak just north of Namche, as a sort of tribal totem, and regard fire as a deity (it's disrespectful to throw rubbish into a Sherpa hearth). Sherpas eat meat, of course, but in deference to the *dharma* they draw the line at slaughtering it – they hire people of other groups to do that.

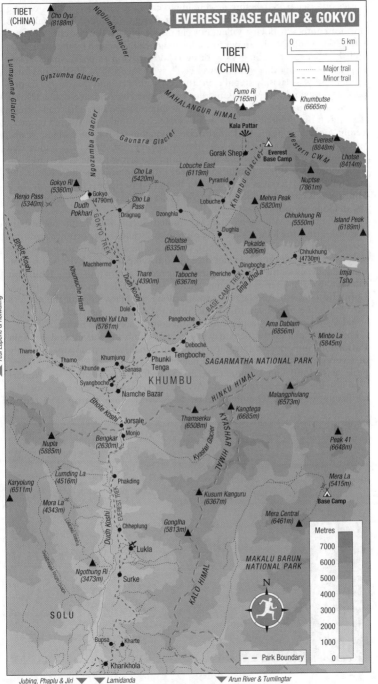

EVEREST BASE CAMP & GOKYO

TIBET
(CHINA)

| 0 | 5 km |

.... Major trail
- - - - - Minor trail

TIBET
(CHINA)

Cho Oyu
(8188m)

Ngojumba Glacier

Lumsumna Glacier

Gyazumba Glacier

Ngozumba Glacier

MAHALANGUR HIMAL

Pumo Ri
(7165m)

Khumbutse
(6665m)

Gaunara Glacier

Kala Pattar

Western CWM

Everest
(8843m)

Lhotse
(8414m)

Gorak Shep

Everest
Base Camp

Renjo Pass
(5340m)

Gokyo Ri
(5360m)

Gokyo
(4790m)

Cho La
(5420m)

Lobuche East
(6119m)

Pyramid

Nuptse
(7861m)

Dudh
Pokhari

Cho La
Pass

Lobuche

Mehra Peak
(5820m)

Chhukhung Ri
(5550m)

Island Peak
(6189m)

Dragnag

Dzonghla

Bhote Koshi

GOKYO TREK

Cholatse
(6335m)

Dughla

Pokalde
(5806m)

Chhukhung
(4730m)

Dudh Koshi

Machhermo

Thare
(4390m)

Taboche
(6367m)

Pheriche

Dingboche

Imja Khola

BASE CAMP TREK

Imja
Tsho

Khumjuche Himal

Dole

Pangboche

Ama Dablam
(6856m)

Minbo La
(5845m)

Khumbi Yul Lha
(5761m)

Deboche

Tengboche

SAGARMATHA NATIONAL PARK

Thame

Thamo

Khumjung

Khunde

Sanasa

Phunki
Tenga

HINKU HIMAL

Syangboche

KHUMBU

Namche Bazar

Malangphulang
(6573m)

Bhote Koshi

Jorsale

Monjo

Thamserku
(6508m)

KYASHAR HIMAL

Kangtega
(6685m)

Nupla
(5885m)

Bengkar
(2630m)

Kyashar Glacier

Peak 41
(6648m)

Karyolung
(6511m)

Lumding La
(4516m)

Phakding

Mera La
(5415m)

Mora La
(4343m)

EVEREST TREK

Kusum Kanguru
(6367m)

Base Camp

Chheplung

Gonglha
(5813m)

Mera Central
(6461m)

Lukla

Dudh Koshi

Ngothung Ri
(3473m)

Surke

MAKALU BARUN
NATIONAL PARK

Metres
7000
6000
5000
4000
3000
2000
1000
0

SOLU

KALO HIMAL

N

Bupsa

Kharte

- - - Park Boundary

Kharikhola

Jubing, Phaplu & Jiri ▼ ▼ Lamidanda

▼ Arun River & Tumlingtar

◄ Tesi Lapche & Rolwaling

breaks off – see p.384), before descending to cross the genuinely milky-looking Dudh Koshi ("Milk River"), at **Phunki Tenga** (3250m). The trail veers northeast into a tributary valley and climbs steeply to **Tengboche** (3860m), where the wildlife-rich juniper forest has long been protected by the local lamas and there's a show-stealing view of everybody's favourite peak, Ama Dablam (6828m) – the "mother with a jewel box", as Sherpas call it. Tengboche's large monastery was lavishly rebuilt in the early 1990s, and has a fascinating permanent exhibition. Mani Rimdu (see p.45), the Sherpa dance-drama festival, is held here on the full moon of November–December. The trail briefly descends through birch and fir forest to Deboche, a settlement with a nunnery, before ascending again to **Pangboche**, containing Khumbu's oldest *gompa*, where for a donation the lama will show you some yeti relics. (The higher trail leading west out of Pangboche allows you to cut across to the Gokyo trek, on the opposite side of the Dudh Koshi valley.) After crossing the Imja Khola, the trail follows the terraces of the valley floor to **Pheriche** (4250m), site of a Himalayan Rescue Association post (AMS talks are held every afternoon during the trekking season).

Above Pheriche, the stone and slate-roofed Sherpa settlements are strictly seasonal – trekking lodges aside. The route now ascends more gently, apart from a steep spurt up to **Dughla** (4620m), which is where acclimatization problems set in for many trekkers. Do not ascend with symptoms of AMS (see p.356). Immediately above the trail climbs the stony terminal moraine of the **Khumbu Glacier**, passing a series of monuments to Sherpas killed on Everest, to reach **Lobuche** (4930m). Another day's march along the grassy edge of the glacier's lateral moraine brings you to **Gorak Shep** (5180m), the last huddle of lodges – and a cold, probably sleepless night in uncomfortably bunk rooms.

The payoff comes the next day, when you climb up the mound of **Kala Pattar** (5545m): the extra height provides an unbelievable panorama, not only of **Everest** (8848m) but also of its neighbours Lhotse (Nepal's third-highest peak, at 8516m) and Nuptse (7861m), as well as the sugarloaf of Pumori (7165m), the "daughter mountain". A separate day-trip can be made across the thrillingly ice-spired Khumbu Glacier to **Everest Base Camp**. The trail is

▲ The view from Kala Pattar

In 1841, while taking routine measurements from the plains, members of the Survey of India logged a previously unnoted summit which they labelled simply Peak XV. Fifteen years later, computations revealed it to be the world's highest mountain, at 29,002ft, or 8840m. The estimate was later revised upwards to 8848m, though two surveys in the last ten years have tried to revise the figure again to either 8850m or 8844m. Take your pick; it's still the highest. The British named it after **Sir George Everest**, head of the Survey of India from 1823 to 1843, and it was decades before anyone troubled to find out the local, Sherpa name: **Chomolungma**. Usually translated as "Mother Goddess", this is actually a contraction of *jomo miyo langsangma*, one of five sister mountain gods, known to Sherpas for her agricultural bounty. There's also a Nepali name, Sagarmatha, from the Sanskrit for "Forehead of the Sky", but it was invented in the 1960s by a Hindu-nationalist Nepali government. The Chinese use the Sherpa name, rendered as "Zhumulangma". To avoid confusion, this book goes with the usual international term: Everest.

Politically off-limits until the early twentieth century, the climb to the summit was first attempted from the Tibetan side in 1922 by a British party that included **George Mallory**, who famously justified his attempt on the mountain "because it is there". Two years later, Mallory and Andrew Irvine reached at least 8500m before probably falling to their deaths from the Second Step – a barrier that would likely have thwarted any attempt with the equipment of the day; a 1999 search found Mallory's body. Several more attempts were made until World War II suspended activities, and the Chinese invasion of Tibet in 1950 closed the northern approach to mountaineers.

With the opening of Nepal in 1951, a race between Swiss and British teams was on. The mountain was finally scaled via the South Col by New Zealander **Edmund Hillary** and Sherpa **Tenzing Norgay** in a British-led expedition in 1953. Throughout the next two decades, increasingly big expeditions put ever greater numbers of men – and women, starting with **Junko Tabei** of Japan in 1975 – on the top. From the mid-1970s, smaller, quicker "alpine-style" ascents began to grab the headlines. **Reinhold Messner** was one of two climbers to reach the summit without oxygen in 1978, and in 1980 he made the first successful solo ascent of Everest.

After Messner's landmark achievements, climbing became a matter of finding new and ever-harder routes, or setting new records for youngest/oldest/fastest ascents, or descending on **skis** (Davo Karnicar in 2000), **snowboards** (Marco Siffredi and Stefan Gatt in 2001) or **paragliders** (Bertrand and Claire Bernier Roche; eight minutes from summit to base camp). Or indeed going up repeatedly: professional guide-climber **Appa Sherpa** had summited eighteen times at the time of writing. Between the first ascent in 1953 and 1990, some three hundred people had climbed Everest. At the time of writing, the tally of summiteers was nearing four thousand.

Everest has most often hit the headlines in recent years due to **pollution** – well-climbed areas of the mountain are littered with old ropes, tents, oxygen canisters and even bodies – and a few notorious **tragedies**. The most controversial was the storm of 1996, chronicled in Jon Krakauer's *Into Thin Air* (see p.466), in which eight climbers died in a single day – partly due to the fixed ropes up the southeast ridge being so congested with clients on commercial expeditions that climbers were too slow getting up, and too late making their descent. Stuck above the blizzard, respected guide Rob Hall was able to radio his wife to say goodbye: "Sleep well my sweetheart", he told her, "Please don't worry too much." In 2006, new controversy flared when it was revealed that a number of expeditions passed by the frostbitten and disoriented climber David Sharp without trying to rescue him.

well-trodden by climbing expeditions and their yaks and porters, so you don't need any technical equipment beyond stout boots. Some climbers are happy to have well-wishers, but many are wary of trekkers, preferring to stay focused on the climb ahead.

The Gokyo Lakes spur and Cho La

The scenery is every bit as good at **Gokyo Lakes**, in the next valley to the west, and noticeably quieter. The route breaks off the main Base Camp trail at **Sanasa**, on the edge of Khumjung village, following the Dudh Koshi due north to Gokyo, a cluster of lodges set beside the immense Ngozumba Glacier – the biggest in Nepal. It can be done in a long day if you're fit and acclimatized; two or three if you're not – there are lodges at frequent intervals all the way up. Several brilliant-blue lakes, dammed up by the glacier's lateral moraine, dot the west side of the valley above and below Gokyo. The high point is an overlook, **Gokyo Ri**, surveying a clutter of blue teeth – Cho Oyu, Everest and Lhotse are just the ones over 8000m – and the long grey glacier tongue.

It's possible to be in Gokyo in two days from Gorak Shep (or vice versa), if you can manage the strenuous **Cho La** (5420m). There are a couple of simple lodges at **Dragnag** (4700m), four hours from Gokyo, on the opposite side of the glacier, and a couple more at **Dzonghla**, two to three hours from Dughla or Lobuche (4910m). But the high, middle section, crossing the pass, has to be done in one long day (unless you have tents): that's six to eight hours, or more in bad conditions or if you suffer from altitude problems – which is all too likely this high. The pass is usually snowy on the eastern side, where you have to cross onto a glacier, with some tricky and slippery sections. Don't attempt it if you're in any doubt about the weather, or your own condition, and team up with a group. In good conditions crampons aren't usually necessary, but an ice axe may be very handy – and a guide or at least a thorough understanding of the route is essential.

Yaks and yetis

The **yeti** ("man of the rocky places") has been a staple of Sherpa and Tibetan folklore for centuries, with some authoritatively describing three different kinds: the grey or reddish haired, man-like *drema*, who portends disaster; the huge, bear-like *chuti*, which preys on livestock; and the red or golden-furred *mite*, which sometimes attacks humans. Stories of hairy, ape-like creatures roaming the snowy heights first came to the attention of the outside world when explorers reported seeing mysterious moving figures and large, unidentified footprints in the snow. Captivated by the reports, an imaginative Fleet Street hack coined the term "abominable snowman", but it wasn't until 1951, during the first British Everest expedition from the Nepal side, that climber Eric Shipton took clear **photographs** of yeti tracks. Since then, several highly publicized **yeti-hunts**, including one led by Sir Edmund Hillary in 1960, have brought back a wealth of circumstantial evidence but not one authenticated sighting, spoor or hair sample. Oversized footprints could be any animal's tracks, melted and enlarged by the sun. Meanwhile, "yeti" scalps kept at various *gompas* have been revealed to be stitched-together animal skins, while the skeletal hand at Pangboche is likely to be a human relic.

If there are large, hairy creatures in the Himalayas, they're probably bears or yaks. The true, wild yak (or nak, for a female) is a shaggy, long-horned relative of the cow with an incredible capacity for altitude. It's quite a rare beast, and you're much more likely to see zopkio (male) and dzum (female) crossbreeds, recognizable by their more even temper, forward-curving horns and lowing – yaks can only grunt.

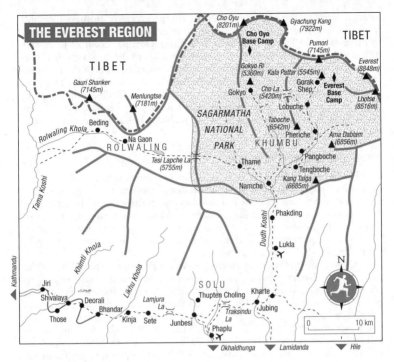

Solu: the Jiri walk-in

The **JIRI WALK-IN** follows the historical route that all Everest mountaineers had to take before it was possible to fly to Lukla. Cutting across the lay of the land, the trail bobs between tropical valleys as low as 1500m and alpine passes as high as 3500m, but the sense of excitement as you get closer to the mountains proper makes all the gruelling legwork worthwhile – not to mention the fitness and acclimitization you'll accrue. A few glimpses of peaks – notably Gauri Shanker (7145m) – urge you along during the first five or six days, although the lasting images of the Solu region are of tumbling gorges, rhododendron forests and terraced fields hewn out of steep hillsides. Expect to walk for seven days to reach Lukla, not counting side-trips, or eight to Namche Bazaar. The bulk of traffic through Solu consists of porters humping in gear for trekking groups and expeditions flying into Lukla, and this is reflected in the relatively no-frills **food and lodging** available.

There are a number of variations on the route – for which it's worth getting a dedicated guidebook – but essentially you're switchbacking over three passes, each bigger than the last. After the steamy, bustling riverside bazaar of **Shivalaya** (1770m) you climb over the pass at **Deurali** (2710m) – an alternative side-route takes you higher, via the cheese factory at **Thodung** (3091m) – and down via the handsome village of **Bhandar** (2190m) to another settlement on the warm valley floor: **Kinja** (1630m). Most people choose to break the monumental third climb that lies ahead into two parts by spending their third night out of Jiri at **Sete** (2575m), halfway up to the **Lamjura La** (3530m), a pass where you first taste the scale of the mountains ahead. From there, it's a long descent through forest to the idyllic quasi-alpine Sherpa village of **Junbesi** (2680m). Most trekkers are understandably impatient to get up to Everest, but a side trip to the powerfully Tibetan **Thubten Chholing Gompa**, north of Junbesi, is well worth it, and it's possible to spend many days in the area. Less than two hours above Junbesi, **Everest View** gives the first serious view of the Khumbu range, with Everest itself apparently subsidiary to the nearer peaks. The next pass, **Traksindho La** (3071m), finally takes you into the Dudh Koshi Valley and, at **Jubing**, an attractively bamboo-festooned Rai village below, the trail bends north towards Everest. Two days later, it sidesteps Lukla and joins the well-trodden route to Khumbu.

The eastern routes

The **EASTERN ROUTE** to or from Everest is sometimes treated as an exit by trekkers who want to avoid the long backtrack to Jiri, but there's no reason why the itinerary can't be done in reverse, except perhaps that it's better to gain some confidence before tackling this less-trekked region. Another factor to consider is the **season**: try to do the lower section of the trek when it's cooler. The route is equipped with **lodges** and a guide isn't needed, but don't expect many English signs or much fancy food.

From the Everest region, the **route** (shown on the map on p.385) leaves the Jiri walk-in at **Kharte**, about a day south of Lukla, and heads southeastwards to reach Tumlingtar five to seven days later, crossing three passes over 3000m. Part of this stretch traverses the Makalu-Barun Conservation Area (see p.388), and the Rs1000 entrance fee may be required at a checkpost. The first half of the trek passes through tangled hills inhabited mainly by Rais; after reaching the last and highest pass, the Salpa Bhanjyang (3350m), it descends steadily to the deep, hot valley of the Arun – the traditional Rai homeland, though with a strong Hindu-caste presence. After crossing the river at a mere 300m, it's a short day to **Tumlingtar**, a busy bazaar overlooking the Arun River; from here there are flights most days to Kathmandu ($65), or you can pick up a local bus for the tortuous journey back via Chainpur and Basantapur to Hile (see p.336) – perhaps detouring up the Milke Daada (see opposite).

The Okaldhunga and Lamidanda alternatives

As well as the route to the **Phaplu** airstrip (see p.379), there are two **alternative eastern routes** south of the Everest country. One breaks off the Jiri walk-in at the Tragsindho La and heads for three to five days through heavily populated country to **Okaldhunga**, a bustling bazaar town; there's an airstrip here, **Ramjatar**, and a new, rough road coming up from the south, joining the Mahendra Highway a little east of Janakpur. The other route aims roughly due south from Jubing, down the Dudh Koshi then across the big hills on the eastern side of the valley and over to **Lamidanda** airstrip. Flights are roughly daily; if you can't get on one, a combination of rough roads and trails continue south to the Terai or east to Bhojpur, Nepal's most famous *khukuri*-making centre – from where a rough road just about connects through to Hile.

Remote and restricted areas

Treks in **far eastern** and **far western** Nepal are mostly restricted to two kinds of traveller, both adventurous in their own way. The majority come on organized camping treks with agencies – in fact, this is obligatory for those areas that

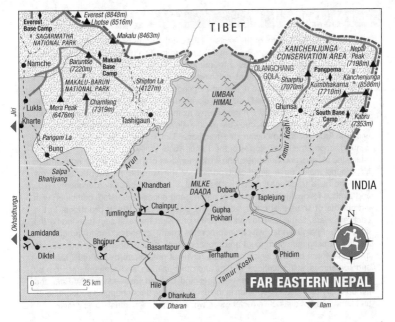

require a permit (see p.352). The minority are independent trekkers prepared either to carry tents and food and negotiate with porters, or to seek food and lodging in local homes and basic lodges. Independent travel is difficult in the west, where food shortages, relatively low population and cultural barriers can be problematic. **Access** is a problem on both sides of the country. In the east, Basantapur, the principal trailhead, is some 24 hours by **bus** from Kathmandu. Journey times to the far West by road – where there are roads – don't even bear calculating. **Flights**, therefore, are worth looking into. Few cost little more than $100 one-way, though some remote areas require two flights to reach.

Far eastern Nepal

Ethnically, eastern Nepal is even more diverse than the Annapurna region: Rais and Limbus (see p.388) are dominant in the hills, while Sherpas, Tamangs and other highlanders inhabit the high country, and Hindu castes the valleys. Makalu, Kanchenjunga and other big peaks provide stunning **views** from most high points. Flora and fauna are also of great interest to specialists especially the **butterflies** and other insects of the upper Arun Valley, and the **rhododendrons** of the Milke Daada. The east is relatively well-off, so in the settled areas, especially in the region around the Newari bazaar towns of Bhojpur, Chainpur and Khandbari, **food** and **lodging** is easy to come by – making fine country for adventurous trekkers who like exploring places that aren't written up in guidebooks. The serious mountain treks to Makalu and Kanchenjunga, however, require expedition-scale planning, official permits and agency support.

The Milke Daada

A long north–south ridge famed for its spectacular views and rhododendrons, the **MILKE DAADA** can be linked up with a visit to the fine bazaar town of Chainpur for a fine trek of seven or so days, going no higher than 3500m. From

Rais and Limbus

The traditional inhabitants of the eastern hills are the Kirati peoples, usually labelled either **Rai** or **Limbu**, though Rai is really an honorific title meaning "chief" and Rais and Limbus divide themselves into numerous *thars*, or clans. There are over two-dozen Rai languages – an astonishing number in a population of around half a million. The orally transmitted myths and legends of the Rais and Limbus differ from clan to clan, but largely agree that each clan is descended from one of ten (or more, or less) "brothers" who took different routes as they migrated to Kirat, probably from the east. Rais traditionally occupy the middle-elevation hills between the Dudh Koshi and the Arun River. Limbuwan, the traditional Limbu homeland, lies further east, centred around the lower slopes of the Tamur Koshi Valley.

Like the Magars and Gurungs of the west, members of these staunchly independent hill groups make up a significant portion of the **Gurkha regiments**, and army pensions have traditionally boosted the local, virtually subsistence economy. Rais and Limbus follow their own forms of nature- and ancestor-worship, combined with ingredients of shamanism, but increasingly also embrace **Hindu practices**. In the past few years, some have joined the ranks of a Kirat revivalist sect founded by the late Guru Phalgunanda, which incorporates many orthodox Hindu practices – including abstinence from meat and tobacco. Such behaviour is somewhat alien to traditional Kirati culture, which seems to have set great store by the ritual raising – and sometimes, still, sacrifice – of pigs and other animals, and even greater store by the liberal drinking of home-brewed beer and distilled raksi. Unusually, Rais and Limbus bury their dead (cremation is the usual practice throughout the subcontinent), and Limbus erect distinctive rectangular, whitewashed monuments over graves.

Basantapur (p.337) the route heads north, initially following a rough road then continuing north on paths through the lush cloudforest of the Milke Daada, past the lakes at **Gupha Pokhari** (2890m). Various trails to the bazaar town of **Chainpur** branch off to the west; from there you can hitch a jeep ride to the airstrip at Tumlingtar or return to Hile. Alternatively, you could head east from Gupha Pokhari to Taplejung airstrip. Both Tumlingtar and Taplejung airstrips have more frequent and reliable connections to Biratnagar, in the Eastern Terai, than to Kathmandu.

Basic **food and lodging** can be found along most of this route, but the absence of lodges north of Gupha Pokhari limits an independent trekker's ability to explore higher up the Milke Daada.

Makalu Base Camp

Much of the **MAKALU BASE CAMP** trek passes through the wild and remote **Makalu–Barun National Park** (Rs1000 entry fee) and the contiguous **Makalu–Barun Conservation Area**. Established in 1992, the park is intended to stem the growing human pressure around the base-camp area and preserve one of the most botanically diverse and wildlife-rich areas in the Himalayas. The usual starting point is the airstrip at **Tumlingtar**, though a marathon road trip could get you there (and even beyond, up to Khandbari) via Dharan, Hile and Basantapur. There are alternative routes on either side of the Arun for the first three or four days, but only one route above there for the next seven days or so (for which a tent and food are required) to the base camp, so you're obliged to retrace your steps most of the way back. The highest days take you over the Barun aka the **Shipton La** (4127m), and into the remote Upper Barun valley, whose lofty beauty is often compared to the Annapurna Sanctuary.

Kanchenjunga

The most incredible trek in this part of Nepal is to the foot of **KANCHEN-JUNGA**, the third-highest peak in the world at 8586m. Kanchenjunga is an expensive trek because it's officially restricted to agency-organized groups and, given its remote location in the extreme northeastern corner of the country, it involves up to three weeks' walking, or more if you plan to visit both south and north sides. Unofficially, it may be possible to do this trek independently, with an agency organizing your permit ($10 per week), and porters carrying your supplies for the upper elevations – there are basic *bhattis* to stay and eat in lower down. There's a Rs1000 fee to enter the **Kanchenjunga Conservation Area**.

The starting points are either the roadhead at **Basantapur** (see p.337), initially following the trail up the Milke Daada, or, saving three days, the airstrip at **Taplejung** – which has occasional direct flights from Kathmandu but is more efficiently served via Biratnagar (see p.331), in the Eastern Terai.

The trek passes deep into Limbu country (see p.388), forking a few days northeast of Taplejung, one trail going to the so-called North Base Camp at **Pangpema**, the other to the South Base Camp and the Yalung Glacier. (The high passes connecting the two are distinctly tricky propositions, and not to be considered by the inexperienced.) Both routes offer terraced hills, wildlife-rich forests and a serious taste of unspoiled Nepali hill culture, along with fabulous views. The northern trail takes you deeper into the high mountains for longer – up to a week longer, with all the problems and risks that entails.

Far western Nepal

West of Dhaulagiri, the Himalayas retreat north into Tibet, while the foothill zone broadens, the climate becomes drier and the people poorer. The northern third of the region, left in the rain shadow of the Himalayas, receives little monsoon moisture – in every way but politically, this highland strip is part of Tibet. Jagged Himalayan grandeur isn't so much in evidence, but there's a wildness and a vastness here, and the feeling of isolation is thrilling. Treks in the **far west** are well off the beaten track: they're a chore to get to, they require a

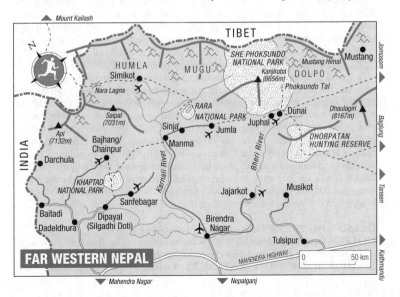

FAR WESTERN NEPAL

lot of preparation and, with the exception of Rara Lake, you'll find that very few Westerners have gone before you. All that might appeal if you're an experienced trekker looking for new challenges, but if you're a first-timer without agency support, forget it.

Logistics make or break a trek in the far west. Given the distances involved, you'll probably want to **fly** to the starting point, but the usual problems of confirming bookings are generally worse in this area. **Food and lodging** are in uncomfortably short supply, so you'll need to bring a tent, cooking utensils and at least some provisions. You should be prepared to carry it all yourself, because **porters** here are a fickle lot and often can't be spared from their farmwork. **Guides** familiar with the area are also scarce, so don't venture out without a reasonable command of Nepali. If you go on an **organized trek** you may not be entirely insulated from these inconveniences, and for this reason agencies may try to steer you towards more easterly destinations.

As roads gradually penetrate into the far west, trekking is becoming easier. The three treks described below are the most realistic possibilities.

Rara National Park

RARA NATIONAL PARK is the best known of the far western trekking areas. The usual itinerary is a loop that starts and ends at Jumla airstrip, three to four days' walk from the lake; most tours take about eight days for the trip. The country is a sea of choppy, mostly forested mountains, offering only glimpses of Himalayan peaks, but the highlight is Nepal's largest lake, a lofty blue jewel surrounded by a wilderness area of meadows and forests of blue pine and rhododendron.

To get to the trailhead you first have to **fly** to Nepalgunj and then from there to **Jumla**; flights are supposed to be daily in season, but are often cancelled. There is also an airstrip at **Talcha**, less than three hours from the lake beside Gumgarhi, the remote capital of Mugu district, but flights up from Nepalgunj are irregular and most people choose to walk from Jumla. The overland alternative is to head up from **Birendra Nagar** (Surkhet) towards Jumla, which is either a week to ten days' walk each way or a horrendously, unpredictably long bus journey – 48 hours isn't unrealistic – on the grandiously named Karnali Highway, via Dailekh, Kalikot and **Sinja**, where the ruins of the capital of the twelfth- to fourteenth-century Khasa dynasty can be viewed across the river. There are **lodges** in Jumla and a bunkhouse at the lake; in between, there are a few teahouses where you might be able to stay, but camping is more pleasant and certainly more reliable – especially as food can be in short supply. The **park fee** is Rs1000.

Technical difficulties aside, Rara makes a fair compromise between the popular treks and the really obscure ones, and in a way combines the best of both worlds: like the popular treks, Rara is given detailed route descriptions in the trekking books, so you can do it without an organized group or even a guide, yet it's remote enough to ensure that you'll see few – if any – other foreigners. Starting at Jumla (2400m), the route crosses two 3500-metre ridges before reaching pristine **Rara Lake** at 3000m. The park is one of the best places in Nepal to see **wildlife**, including Himalayan black bear, tahr, goral, musk deer and the rare red (lesser) panda; the lake itself is home to many species of waterfowl. Autumn and spring are the best seasons, and Rara is particularly worth considering in May and June, when the weather elsewhere is getting too hot or unpredictable.

Dolpo and She-Phoksundo National Park

DOLPO (sometimes written Dolpa) is an enormous, isolated district northwest of Dhaulagiri and bordering Tibet, the western half of which has been set aside as **SHE-PHOKSUNDO NATIONAL PARK**, Nepal's biggest. The park protects an awe-inspiring region of deep valleys, unclimbed peaks, remote monasteries and rare fauna. The best **time to go** is September, with May–June and October–November close behind.

Dolpo was the setting of Peter Matthiessen's *The Snow Leopard* (see p.462), and for many years the book was as close as most foreigners were allowed to get to it. It's now open to trekking, but only by organized groups. Unofficially, it might be possible to arrange a trekking permit for **Southern (Lower) Dolpo** through an agency and do everything else independently. The permit costs $10 per week, and a trek there will take a week to ten days. There are some lodges in Lower Dolpo, but it's a food-deficit area so you'll need to bring several days' worth of provisions. Guides and porters can be hired near the airstrip. The agency-trekking requirement for **Northern (Upper) Dolpo** is strictly enforced, and the permit is much more expensive: $500 for the first ten days, $50 per day thereafter.

Most people fly into Juphal, the airstrip for Dolpo District, from Nepalgunj. Flying into or out of Jumla, about five days' walk further west, is also possible. From Juphal the route heads east to Dunai and then

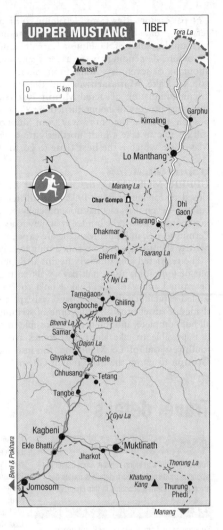

north, entering the park after about a day (Rs1000 **entry fee**) and reaching the village of Ringmo and the stunningly blue **Phoksundo Tal** after another two days. There are plenty of day-hiking opportunities around the lake. Beyond lies Northern Dolpo.

Humla and Mount Kailash

Tucked away in the extreme northwestern corner of Nepal, **HUMLA** is high, dry and strongly Tibetan. Snowcapped peaks hem the district in on three sides and shut out most outside influences, including the monsoon. It's open only to organized groups, and the permit costs $50 for the first week, $7 per day thereafter. This area often experiences serious spring and early-summer famines, so it's essential to bring all the food you'll need – and then some.

Nepal Airlines **flies** from Nepalgunj to **Simikot** (Humla's district headquarters) most days of the week in season. The most popular trek from here heads west up the valley of the Humla Karnali Nadi, struggling over the 4580m Nara La before descending to the river again and the **Tibet** border at Hilsa; it's about six or seven days' walk. From Sher, on the Tibetan side, a jeep will take you to **Lake Manasarowar** and the starting point for the three-day-plus circumambulation of sacred **Mount Kailash**. (The Humla Karnali trail is in the long process of being turned into a road, which will one day make it possible to drive the entire way from Simikot; those who prefer to walk will still be able to take a high, northerly route via Talung Lake to the border.) In May–June, which is the **best time** to go, the wildflowers are out of this world.

Upper Mustang

UPPER MUSTANG, the high-desert headwaters of the Thak Khola, was closed to foreigners until 1992, and still retains much of its medieval Tibetan culture – even if its raja has now officially been deposed and Chinese goods are now pouring across the border via a new road (the border is closed to foreigners). Permits to trek in Upper Mustang are expensive – $500 for the first ten days, $50 per day thereafter – and are issued only to agency-organized groups.

The restricted area officially begins at Kagbeni, and groups usually fly in and out of Jomosom, just a half-day's walk to the south. From there up the high, desertified valley of the Thak Khola to **Lo Manthang** (3840m), the lofty, walled capital, it's about five days' walk, past wind-eroded cliffs in astonishing shades of russet brown. At the time of writing, the road up from Jomosom was all but complete, and it'll soon be possible to make the trip both ways in a jeep. It is possible to take alternative routes avoiding the road, however – hiking southwest out of Lo Manthang, for instance, via the Chogo La and **Ghar Gompa** to rejoin the main trail at Ghemi.

Travel details

Buses

Buses in Nepal's trekking regions are a useful but laborious mode of transport; details & routes are given in the relevant accounts in this chapter.

Flights

Biratnagar to: Lamidanda (3 weekly); Taplejung (2–5 weekly); Tumlingtar (0–2 weekly)

Kathmandu to: Biratnagar (10–15 daily); Lamidanda (4 weekly); Lukla (up to 19 daily); Nepalgunj (5–6 daily); Phaplu (4–6 weekly); Pokhara (16–17 daily); Taplejung (0–1 weekly); Tumlingtar (5 weekly)

Nepalgunj to: Juphal/Dolpo (1 weekly); Jumla (0–1 daily); Simikot (1–2 weekly); Talcha for Rara Lake (0–1 daily)

Pokhara to: Jomosom (3–9 daily); Kathmandu (16–17 daily); Humde/Manang (0–2 weekly).

Rafting and kayaking

* **Kayak school** How cool is it to be able to say you learned to kayak in the Himalayas? See p.398

* **Kali Gandaki descent** Fly to Jomosom, in the bitingly cold Himalayas, trek or take a jeep down the magnificent gorge of the upper Kali Gandaki valley, then raft your way into the jungle national park at Chitwan. See p.399

* **The Seti** A tame, picturesque, easily accessible river, warmed by geothermal springs. See p.400

* **The Bhote Koshi** A short adrenaline rush on the steepest and hardest of Nepal's raftable rivers, which plunges down from the Tibetan border. See p.400

* **The Marsyangdi** A magnificent, continuously technical stretch of river – last chance before the dam breaks it into two.... See p.401

* **The Sun Koshi** The perfect introduction to rafting in Nepal: eight varied days through remote hill country. See p.401

* **The Tamur** Six days of challenging whitewater in the far east, with the option of trekking to the put-in point through the beautiful eastern hills. See p.403

▲ Raft and support kayak, the Bhote Koshi

Rafting and kayaking

Thanks to the Himalayas, Nepal has some of the best and most scenic whitewater on earth. A few of the longer trips are world classics, offering the experience of a lifetime. As well as the tranquillity of being deep in the countryside, away from towns and roads, rafting offers the thrills, laughter and companionship that comes from shooting rapids. Then there's the sheer escapism of life on the river: camping on white-sand beaches, campfires under the stars, warm water (most rivers in Nepal are at lower, semitropical elevations), jungle-clad slopes, wildlife and birds. Some of the remoter trips, meanwhile, entail mini-treks through little-visited areas just to get to the put-in point. It's also worth mentioning that almost all rivers in Nepal are clean, and there are almost no nasty biting insects on the beaches (mosquitoes are very rare).

When to go

Time of year makes an enormous difference: water volume during the height of the monsoon (July & Aug) is ten or more times greater than in February and March, making the major rivers off-limits to all but experts. The water is more manageably exciting in late October to November, which is the peak rafting season, and becomes mellower (but colder) from December through to April or May, when snowmelt begins to add to flows again.

Winter isn't as chilly as you might think, since most raftable river sections are below 500m elevation, but it's a slow time for tourism generally in Nepal, so many river operators don't run trips then. March and April are the best months for long, warm days and excellent birdwatching. However, different rivers are at their best at different times of the year – for example, the Sun Koshi is actually quite good starting in late September – so which river you go on will depend to a large extent on when you're in Nepal. Note that a given trip will take less time in high water than when the water is running more slowly.

Information, books and maps

You'll be able to get most or all of your questions answered by your rafting company, assuming you're going on an organized trip. Independent rafters and kayakers, however, should get hold of a copy of *White Water Nepal*, by Peter Knowles and David Allardice, which is dated but still provides comprehensive river descriptions and hydrographs, maps, and advice on logistics. For more information, updates and links to operators, visit Ⓦwww.raftnepal.org or the website of the Nepal River Conservation Trust, Ⓦwww.nepalrivers.org. Himalayan Map House publishes rafting maps for the more popular rivers (such as the Sun Koshi and Trisuli), showing rapids, put-in points and so on. For other areas, trekking maps (see p.351) can keep you oriented.

Rafting operators and agents

A fairly sophisticated river-running industry exists in Nepal, with dozens of Nepali and Western-associated **rafting operators** offering both scheduled and customized trips. Unless you're an experienced kayaker (see opposite) or are on some sort of a self-organized expedition, you'll go with one of these companies. The standards of most operators exceed international guidelines, but you get what you pay for, and Nepal has its share of rip-off artists.

A few of the more reputable Nepal-based operators are listed in the Kathmandu and Pokhara sections (p.136 & p.247). These deal with bookings from overseas, but they'll also take walk-in clients, and if you can muster up a few friends you can arrange your own customized departure. Booking with an agency in your own country (see pp.20–24) is more expensive, but it guarantees arrangements – and in high season the best trips are fully booked months in advance.

Some of the cut-price outfits in Kathmandu and Pokhara aren't bad, but making recommendations would be misleading – companies come and go, and standards rise and fall from one season to the next. Shop around, and press operators hard on the criteria given below. Only use a company belonging to the **Nepal Association of Rafting Agents**, a trade body that sets safety standards, requires its members to employ only trained and licensed guides, and handles complaints.

Many places advertising rafting trips are merely **agents**, who usually don't know what they're talking about and who will add their own commission (low or high) to the operator's price, so you're strongly advised to **book directly with the rafting operator**. Another reason for dealing directly with the operator is that you can find out who else is booked on the trip, which might well influence your enjoyment.

Costs

Trips booked in Nepal **cost** $25 to $80 a day, depending on the river, number of people in the party, and standard of service. For trips on the Trisuli and Kali Gandaki (the most popular rafting rivers), upmarket companies typically charge $30–40 a day to a walk-in customer, which should include transport to and from the river by private bus, good, hygienic meals and a mat in a tent. Budget outfits offer these trips for around $25 a day, but at that price you can expect to travel by local bus and be served pretty unappetizing food – or even pay for your own bus tickets and meals. Other more remote rivers cost $10–20 a day extra. These prices assume full rafts, which hold up to seven paying passengers each.

When reckoning cost per day, bear in mind that a "three-day" trip is rarely three days of solid rafting: you may be travelling to the river most of day one, with just an hour spent on the river that afternoon, rafting for maybe four hours on day two, and then travelling back on your last day.

Your travel **insurance** policy should cover the proposed activity: if you're away from main roads then helicopter rescue may be needed, and no helicopter will take off without cash in hand or the assurance of repayment by an insurance company. Leave a copy of your travel policy with the operator, highlighting the emergency contact number.

Note that at the time of writing, government **rafting permits** were no longer required. There was talk of reintroducing them, however, so check locally.

Equipment and safety

Most companies use **paddle rafts**, in which everyone paddles and the guide steers from the rear – lots of group participation and fun. On less exciting oar trips, the guide does all the work, giving the clients the chance to sit back and enjoy the scenery.

Your rafting company will advise on what to **bring**, but you'll definitely need a swimsuit, sunglasses, suntan lotion, rubber-soled shoes or sport sandals, a change of clothes and shoes for camp, a towel, a head torch/flashlight and spare batteries. T-shirts and shorts are standard river wear, but if the weather is likely to be cold and/or wet, bring thermal tops and trousers; the better companies furnish wetsuits, thermal tops and paddling jackets. Tents, foam mattresses and waterproof bags are normally supplied, but you need to bring your own sleeping bag (rentable in Kathmandu or Pokhara). Some companies provide special waterproof barrels for cameras, but you might prefer to buy a disposable waterproof camera in Kathmandu or Pokhara.

By and large, rafting is reasonably **safe** with a much better accident rate than, say, mountain-biking or skiing (or, for that matter, trekking). However, there are few government controls on Nepal's low-end operators and in the early 2000s there were a couple of fatalities – the first in two decades, mind you. Make sure the company supplies lifejackets, helmets and a full first-aid kit, and satisfy yourself that the rafts are in good running order and that there will be a safety demonstration. There must be a minimum of **two rafts**, in case one capsizes. In high-water conditions or on any river more difficult than class 2, the rafts should be self-bailing and there should be **safety kayakers** to rescue "swimmers". Most important of all, **guides** must be trained, certified, have experience guiding on the stretch of river in question, and speak adequate English – there should be an opportunity to meet guides before departure.

Rafters have the same responsibilities to **the environment** as trekkers, particularly regarding firewood, sanitation and litter – see the tips on p.360.

Kayaking and other river sports

Nepal has taken off as one of the world's leading destinations for recreational **kayaking**, and is now recognized as the best country for whitewater multi-day trips. There are rivers for all abilities, including beginners.

Most visiting kayakers start by booking on a rafting trip for a warm-up – often on the Sun Koshi or Kali Gandaki rivers. If you book on as a kayaker, the rafting company will normally provide you free use of a kayak as part of the deal, or give you a discount of around $10 a day if you have your own boat. If you're thinking of **bringing your own kayak**, talk to others who've visited Nepal recently, as some have ended up paying high excess-baggage charges on the way back. There's a wide selection of modern kayaks available for **rent** at around $15 a day in both Kathmandu and Pokhara – the latter has become quite a thriving centre for kayakers, with an excellent rental outlet (Ganesh Shop). It's worth bringing all your own kayaking gear with you, but this also is available for rent if necessary.

Kayak schools are a recent development in Nepal, mostly operating out of Pokhara and offering a half-day introduction on Phewa Tal and another four-days' practice and paddling on the nearby Seti River, with rafting support. The Seti is warmed by geothermal springs, making it a very pleasant place to practice rolling. Other kayak schools operate out of the riverside resorts on the Bhote Koshi and upper Sun Khoshi rivers, not far from Kathmandu. Typical price for a five-day course is around $300, which includes tuition, gear, food, transport, raft support and camping – that's great value.

While not so popular, another conveyance for enjoying Nepal's whitewater is the **hydrospeed**, a sort of boogie board for swimming down rivers. Pokhara's Ganesh Shop rents out hydrospeeds with wetsuits and helmets for $15 a day. It also rents out inflatable canoes (known as "**duckies**") and **catarafts** for those planning a do-it-yourself trip.

The rivers

Your choice of **where to raft** will be largely dictated by what the rafting companies are running when you're in Nepal. But within that context, consider what you're after in a river trip – thrills, scenery, culture, relaxation – as well as how much time and money you're willing to invest.

Note that a number of hydroelectric dams and diversions are either proposed or under construction; this may eventually shorten or eliminate some popular routes, and put more pressure on the remaining ones. Roads, on the other hand – which are often built to access new dams – can open up previously unrunnable river sections by creating new put-in and take-out points.

The descriptions that follow are given roughly in order of popularity/accessibility. Note that the stated grades are only a guideline, and river levels – and difficulties, therefore – can fluctuate dramatically at any time of year.

The Trisuli

Perhaps fifty percent of all raft trips are on the **Trisuli**, west of Kathmandu, and this is an obvious choice if your time or budget is limited. Most itineraries are two or three days. The Trisuli has some rapids of medium difficulty (Class 3+)

River classifications

Below is a summary of the international classification system of rafting river difficulty.

Class 1 Easy. Moving water with occasional small rapids. Few or no obstacles.

Class 2 Moderate. Small rapids with regular waves. Some manoeuvring required but easy to navigate.

Class 3 Difficult. Rapids with irregular waves and hazards that need avoiding. More difficult manoeuvring required but routes are normally obvious. Scouting from the shore is occasionally necessary.

Class 4 Very difficult. Large rapids that require careful manoeuvring. Dangerous hazards. Scouting from the shore is often necessary and rescue is usually difficult. Kayakers should be able to roll. Turbulent water and large irregular waves may flip rafts. In the event of a mishap, there is significant risk of loss, damage and/or injury.

Class 5 Extremely difficult. Long and very violent rapids with severe hazards. Continuous, powerful, confused water makes route-finding difficult, and scouting from the shore is essential. Precise manoeuvring is critical and for kayakers rolling ability needs to be 100 percent. Rescue is very difficult or impossible, and in the event of a mishap there is a significant hazard to life.

Class 6 Nearly impossible. Might possibly (but not probably) be run by a team of experts at the right water level, in the right conditions, with all possible safety precautions, but still with considerable hazard to life.

and good scenery, though it's hardly wilderness – the main road to Kathmandu follows it the entire way, and in October and November you'll have to share the river (and perhaps your beach campsite) with many other parties. Some operators have their own fixed campsites or lodges, ranging from private, green, semi-luxurious safari-style resorts to windblown village beaches complete with begging kids and scavenging dogs. Check out the camps and lodges carefully, especially with regard to how close a camp is to the noisy highway.

When booking, ask where the put-in point is: anything starting at Kuringhat or Mugling will mainly be a relaxing float. The best whitewater section is upstream of Mugling, from Charaundi to Kuringhat, and this can be done as a full-on half-day trip (perhaps as a break in the journey from Kathmandu to Pokhara).

The Trisuli lies between Pokhara, Kathmandu and Chitwan National Park, so it might make sense to incorporate your raft trip into your travel schedule. Your rafting company will normally be able to help you with logistics and look after your luggage. However, rafting all the way to Chitwan isn't allowed, so you'll have to travel from Narayanghat to the park by vehicle.

The upper Kali Gandaki

The **upper Kali Gandaki** is Nepal's second most popular rafting river and provides an exciting three- or four-day itinerary out of Pokhara. Serious whitewater (Class 4) starts soon after the put-in point near Baglung and continues for the whole trip to the take-out at the dam at the confluence with the Andi Khola. This section of water is away from roads and civilization, and offers excellent upriver views of the Annapurnas and Dhaulagiri. However, it's a popular stretch of river, and camping beaches are limited in number, well used, and may be squalid. There have been quite a few accidents on this river, so choose your operator carefully.

The Kali Gandaki is probably at its best for rafting at low and medium flows: mid-October to mid-December and March to April. It's a good idea to think

Nepal's rivers at a glance

River	Class	Volume	Total days
Trisuli	2/3+	Big	1–4
Upper Kali Gandaki	4-	Med	4
Marsyangdi	4+	Med	6
Sun Koshi	4-	Huge	10
Upper Sun Koshi	3	Med	2
Bhote Koshi	4+	Med	2
Seti	3-	Small	3
Lower Kali Gandaki	2	Med	5
Karnali	4	Huge	10
Tamur	4	Med	11
Bheri	3+	Med	8–10
Arun	4-	Big	4

Relative volumes are given because the actual flows vary so enormously according to season.
Total days = days from Kathmandu or Pokhara and back.

about adding this raft trip onto the end of a trek in the Annapurna region. Consider flying to Jomosom, trekking or taking a jeep (see p.369) down the Kali Gandaki to Baglung, and then continuing down the river on a rafting trip – a journey from the highest mountains on earth to the jungle lowlands.

The Seti

Another river easily reached from Pokhara, the **Seti** offers a gentler alternative to the upper Kali Gandaki. It's a fairly tame (Class 3-) but very picturesque river, taking two or three days to float from Damauli to near Narayanghat. This is a better choice than a similar trip starting on the Trisuli, as it takes you away from the road and has a fine green jungle corridor and beautiful white-sand beaches for camping. It's a popular choice for birdwatching groups, who often schedule it into their itinerary from Pokhara to Chitwan. The water temperature is incredibly warm, making it a popular choice for winter trips and for kayak clinics.

The Bhote Koshi

The **Bhote Koshi**, which runs alongside the Arniko Highway to the Tibetan border northeast of Kathmandu, is probably the steepest and hardest commercial rafting river in Nepal. In low water it's like a pinball machine (and you're the ball); in medium flows it's more like being flushed down the U-bend of a toilet. A few companies specialize in this deviant experience, offering it as a one- or two-day trip out of Kathmandu (it's only a three-hour drive) using road support and empty rafts. If you have previous rafting experience or are just looking for an adrenaline rush, then this is the one for you. It's a cooler river, so if you are running it in the winter months between December and late February then look for a company that provides wetsuits and paddle jackets. The Bhote Koshi is best booked as a two-day trip, staying the night at one of the comfortable riverside resort camps (see box, p.402).

River days	Scenery/wildlife rating	Overall rating	Elevation (start/finish)
1–4	*	**	330m/170m
3	**	**	750m/500m
4	***	**	850m/370m
8	**	***	625m/105m
1	*	**	730m/650m
1–2	**	***	1020m/760m
2	**	**	345m/190m
4	**	**	370m/170m
8	***	***	560m/195m
6	**	***	635m/105m
6–8	***	**	770m/195m
3	**	**	290m/115m

The overall rating is a somewhat subjective score of the river as a rafting trip, taking into account whitewater, scenery, logistics and cost:

*** = highly recommended
** = recommended
* = specialist interest

The Marsyangdi

The **Marsyangdi** has only been commercially rafted in recent years, but it is a magnificent, blue whitewater river with a spectacular mountain backdrop. Kayakers rave about it. It's a full-on, continuously technical river, like a large nonstop slalom, needing experienced river staff and shore support. Companies normally run it as a four-day trip from near Khudi (along the Annapurna Circuit trek) down to the Kathmandu–Pokhara highway, and many combine this with a scenic three-day trek from Begnas Tal (near Pokhara) to Khudi. The river is particularly beautiful in November, when levels are reasonably low and the mountain views are usually clear. Work is almost completed on a dam at Phaliya Sanghu, some 14km by road south of Beisisahar; this will break the Marsyangdi into two sections of whitewater, separated by a short drive around the dam.

The Sun Koshi

Widely acknowledged as one of the ten best rafting trips in the world, the **Sun Koshi** is the most popular of several longer floats in Nepal, and logistics are fairly easy, making it one of the cheapest in terms of cost per day. It's an eight-day run beginning at Dolalghat, three hours east of Kathmandu, and ending at Chatara, near Dharan in the eastern Terai. If you're planning to go on from Nepal to Darjeeling, this raft trip cuts out most of the twenty-hour bus ride to the eastern border.

Relatively few companies do scheduled trips on the Sun Koshi, so you're less likely to see other parties, and the camping on beautiful white-sand beaches is great. The river traverses a remote part of the country, flowing through a varied landscape of jungle-clad canyons, arid, open valleys and sparse settlements. Unlike most rivers, which start out rough and get tamer as they descend, this one starts gently, affording a chance to build up experience and confidence prior to a steady diet of increasingly exciting whitewater (Class 3–4). This makes

The Bhote Koshi resorts

In the last few years, several companies have bought land on the banks of the Bhote Koshi and upper Sun Koshi and built fixed safari-style **riverside camps**, with luxuriant gardens, flush toilets, showers, hammocks, restaurants and bar areas. Only two- to three-hours' drive from Kathmandu, each of these mini-resorts offers its own mix of activities: all do rafting, but there is also canyoning, kayaking, trekking, rock-climbing, bungy-jumping, and mountain-biking available. They also regularly host adventure events such as mountain-bike races and the Nepal International Kayak Rodeo (held annually in Nov). If you just want to stay and hang out at the camp, then typical daily rates are around $30 for food, accommodation and transport to and from Kathmandu. Many overseas rafting and kayak groups now go straight from the Kathmandu airport to one of these riverside resorts. Full reviews of all the resorts can be found in Chapter Three, p.214.

it an especially good choice for those doing their first river trip. It's at its best for rafting at medium to high flows – from mid-September to late October and in May and early June. Note that a new main highway is being built alongside the top 40km of the Sun Koshi; once complete (and no one knows when this will be), it'll allow shorter six-day trips on the river and will also probably halve the return time from the take-out.

Upper Sun Koshi (Lower Bhote Koshi)

Only two hours' drive from Kathmandu, the **upper Sun Koshi** (the section above Dolalghat, often mistakenly called the lower Bhote Koshi) makes an easier alternative to the Bhote Koshi, especially at higher water levels. There are two different sections: the top one is a fun Class 3 whitewater run, the lower a mellow, scenic, flat-water float. The river is clean and blue with green valley sides, and the nearby highway is relatively quiet, so this stretch of river is an ideal choice for a half-day rafting trip close to Kathmandu, and makes a welcome escape from the city if you stay overnight at one of the resort camps on the riverside. This is a another popular river for kayak schools.

The Karnali

Nepal's biggest and longest river, the **Karnali** provides perhaps the finest trip of its kind in the world. Way out in the remote far west, it requires a long bus ride to Birendra Nagar (many groups fly to Nepalgunj) and then about three- hours' rough bus ride to the small village of Sauli. From here it is either a two-hour trek to the river or, if the road is in good shape, you can drive onto Dungeshwar right on the Karnali. Most rafting trips last eight days, with challenging, big-water rapids, superb canyons, pristine wilderness and plentiful wildlife. The biggest rapids (Class 4) come in the first three days, with the river gradually mellowing after that. You can raft the Karnali right into Bardia National Park, where wild elephants, tigers, crocodiles and rhinos may sometimes be seen from the river. Pulling into a luxury safari camp and being met with a tray of cold beers makes a magnificent climax to this long river trip; many parties take the opportunity to spend a few extra days watching wildlife in Bardia.

The Karnali is best run at low to medium levels – it's a particularly good choice in March and April, though the nature of the channel makes it lively at all times outside of high water. There are plentiful driftwood supplies for campfires, so this makes it a popular choice for overseas kayak groups around

Christmas. It's also renowned as Nepal's premier fishing river, with giant *mahseer* (a freshwater perch) and catfish.

The Tamur

Only recently opened to rafting, the **Tamur** offers six days of fabulous and challenging whitewater in a remote and scenic valley in eastern Nepal, coupled with a highly scenic trek. The river is at its best in medium flows – it would be a nightmare at high levels – with the optimum time (after a normal monsoon) being the middle of October to the middle of November. Note that the final day of the trip from Mulghat (where a highway crosses the river) can be added as an exciting extra day to a Sun Koshi trip.

▲ Rafting in Nepal is as much about stunning mountain backdrops as whitewater

The trip starts with a twenty-hour bus ride to Basantapur, followed by a four-day walk in along a high ridge with wide panoramas of Kanchenjunga and the Everest peaks – often described as one of the most beautiful treks in Nepal. It is possible to fly from Kathmandu to Taplejung, only a couple of hours' hike from the put-in point at Dobhan, but flights may be delayed by weather, so it's more reliable to fly to Biratnagar and then take a taxi or bus from there to the Basantapur trailhead. You can even drive via Ilam and Taplejung to a village just 45min from the put-in, but it's a wearyingly long journey on an unreliable road.

The Bheri

The **Bheri** offers a shorter and easier alternative to the Karnali, of which it's a tributary. It's one of the most scenic rivers in Nepal, with golden cliffs, green jungle, crystal-clear green water, white-sand beaches, excellent fishing and good birdwatching, all coupled with a powerful current and sparkling rapids of moderate difficulty. Access is from the Nepalgunj–Birendra Nagar road, a total of about fifteen hours of bus travel from Kathmandu (via Nepalgunj). Few companies raft the Bheri at the moment, but if roads improve it is likely to become more popular.

The lower Kali Gandaki

The **lower** section of the **Kali Gandaki**, starting from Ramdi Ghat on the Siddhartha Highway, offers a longer alternative to the Seti. It's a medium-volume and relatively easy river, with the same beautiful scenery as the Seti, and it flows through a completely unspoilt and untouristy valley of pretty villages, small gorges and jungle-backed beaches. Although the river is easily accessible, it takes longer to get to than the Seti (five hours from Pokhara to the put-in at Ramdhi Ghat), making it less crowded – ideal as the perfect river for a relaxed, romantic, away-from-it-all break. Like the Seti, this is probably a good choice for a do-it-yourself trip in a "duckie" (inflatable canoe), rentable in Pokhara.

The Arun

A powerful and famous river that dominates eastern Nepal, the **Arun** offers a shorter and easier alternative to the Sun Koshi, with big rapids of moderate difficulty and a fine jungle corridor. A few companies offer trips on this little-travelled river, but the necessity of flying in to Tumlingtar, near the put-in point, makes it relatively expensive for such a short trip.

This chapter was updated by David Allardice.

Mountain biking

CHAPTER 9

Highlights

* **The Jomosom Highway**
Nepal's newest road offers
the possibility of a descent
through the world's deepest
gorge. **See p.411**

* **Shivapuri National Park**
Seldom-travelled unpaved
roads thread through a forest
preserve in the Kathmandu
Valley's northern reaches.
See p.412

* **The Arniko Highway** The
road to the Tibet border, with

cool stopovers and side trips
and the option of rafting.
See p.414

* **The Tribhuwan Rajpath** A
classic monster climb and
descent, with the possiblity
of some delightful return
routes. **See p.415**

* **Begnas Tal** This fine lake
is the gateway to miles of
pastoral backroads east of
Pokhara. **See p.416**

▲ The Pokhara Valley with Machhapuchhare behind

Mountain biking

The best way to see Nepal, it has long been said, is to walk. Nowadays, due to the availability of rental mountain bikes, route information and organized tours, **mountain biking** is a serious alternative. Bikes provide a more intimate experience than a speeding jeep or bus and they get you places at a more exciting pace than trekking.

Despite Nepal's Himalayan mystique, it's not all steep: the Kathmandu Valley's slopes are generally easy, and the Terai is just plain flat. The longer and more scenic routes do tend to require a high level of fitness, and there are monster ascents (and descents) for those who relish that sort of thing, but there are also plenty of relaxed village-to-village rambles and downhill rides. Mountain bikes are pretty much the only option: even major roads, where you could otherwise get away with a hybrid or robust tourer, have frequent potholes and damaged sections.

Tour operators and bike-shop gurus are continually pioneering new off-road rides. Meanwhile, **road construction** is creating routes and giving access to many others, producing an exponential increase in the possibilities. On the downside, traffic is becoming a serious problem near cities. In the Kathmandu Valley, especially, what was once a pleasant ride may now be choked and frightening. The rapid pace of change also makes it hard for any guidebook to keep up, so seek the latest information locally from someone in-the-know.

No special **paperwork** is required, though biking is not permitted in most national parks and some conservation areas. For details of access to restricted remote areas, and potential dangers and annoyances on seriously off-road trails, see Trekking (p.343).

When to go

If you have a choice, go for **October to December**, when there's little chance of rain and visibility is good. It gets gradually cooler but never gets very cold at biking elevations – in fact, even in December and January the days can be sunny and even warm anywhere up to about 3000m, though snow may occasionally be encountered as low as 2000m. December and January also happen to be the most comfortable months for cycling in Pokhara and the Terai. The shortening days are a factor, though: by December you'll need to be off the roads or trails by 4.30pm or so.

From **January to March** the days lengthen and grow warmer. This too is a good time for biking. In April, May and the first part of June, the weather keeps getting hotter, the road conditions dustier, the air hazier – and afternoon showers become more common. On the plus side, you can take advantage of long daylight hours. The monsoon (**mid-June to late Sept**) is hot and damp; the mountains are usually hidden by clouds, and the trails are wet or muddy. This is prime riding time in Tibet and Mustang (see p.392), however, both of which are shielded from the rains by the Himalayas.

Another seasonal consideration is the **Himalayan Mountain Bike (HMB Adventures) Race Series,** usually held in November, organized by one of the better-known tour operators; see Ⓦ www.hmbadventures.com.

Information and maps

Bike shops in Kathmandu and Pokhara have up-to-date **information** on trails and roads, though of course they're in business mainly to sell tours, and won't divulge all their secret routes.

There is no dedicated mountain-biking guidebook, but James Giambrione's *Kathmandu Valley Bikes & Hikes* gives reasonable if dated coverage of this area. A map is crucial, but shouldn't be relied upon absolutely – and maps go out of date fast in Nepal. Nepamaps does a 1:50,000 scale *Biking Around Kathmandu Valley* map, and a 1:75,000 *Biking Around Annapurna* map, both available in Kathmandu. Coverage of the former extends beyond the valley into the Central Hills, and bike trails are marked, if not always entirely accurately; the latter has been made hopelessly out of date by the new road to Jomosom (see p.411). Otherwise, you'll have to rely on trekking maps (see p.351).

Tours and cycling independently

Like trekking, mountain biking can be done **independently** or as part of a **tour.** With mountain biking, the specialized equipment involved and the difficulty of route-finding makes the latter an attractive option.

Organized tours

An **organized bike tour** will save lots of pre-departure time and headaches, and maximize the chances that all will go more or less according to plan. The itinerary will be well planned, avoiding the dead ends and wrong turns that inevitably come with a self-organized trip. Decent bikes and all the necessary gear will be provided, and guides will take care of maintenance and on-the-spot repairs. Guides can also show you trails you'd never find on your own and help interpret Nepali culture and ask or answer questions. On longer tours, a "sag wagon" will tote heavy gear, provide emergency backup, and whisk you past the busier or less interesting stretches of road.

A one-day trip will typically cost $20–25, while longer excursions work out to $45–90 per day, including vehicle support and accommodation. Generally, you get what you pay for – and it's worth checking exactly what you're getting. Many overseas companies offer mountain-bike tours, but almost all are actually organized by a few **operators** in Kathmandu (see p.137), and you can save money by booking directly with them. They usually require a minimum of four people for vehicle-supported tours, but shorter customized trips can be organized for just one or two people.

Cycling independently

Cycling independently takes a certain pioneering spirit and a greater tolerance for discomfort. It's up to you to rent or bring your own equipment and to arrange food and accommodation; if starting from Kathmandu, you'll need to organize transport out of the city or else put up with some ugly traffic. You'll definitely make mistakes finding your own way, which might mean spending more time than you'd intended, getting lost or having to backtrack. However, you'll have more direct contact with local people than you would with a group.

Day-trips in the Kathmandu and Pokhara valleys are the easiest to do on your own, since you can rent bikes in both cities. Though you probably won't find the more obscure trails, you'll no doubt stumble upon others. If you're riding **long-distance** without vehicle support, you'll have to tote your own gear and may find yourself spending nights in primitive lodges where little English is spoken and foreigners are considered the evening's entertainment. This will be par for the course if you're on a long tour of the Subcontinent, though, and the going is certainly easier in Nepal than in India: the roads, for the most part, are less busy, and there's less staring, hassling and risk of theft.

Equipment

Since good (and not-so-good) bikes can be rented in Nepal, you'll probably be better off not bringing a bike from home unless you plan to do a lot of riding. However, certain clothing and accessories are worth taking with you, especially if you can also use them when trekking or rafting.

Renting or buying a bike in Nepal

Chinese- and Indian-made bikes are available from streetside vendors for Rs150–200 per day. Superficially, they look the part – some even have suspension – but they're heavy and often uncomfortable, components are flimsy, maintenance may be poor, and they rarely come with a helmet. If you find such a bike in a fairly new condition, you could get away with a day-trip or overnight loop but they're not really fit for rough roads. Don't ride this kind of bike further than you're prepared to walk back with it.

For hard or long-distance riding you'll need a **real mountain bike**, which can be rented from specialist bike shops/tour operators in Kathmandu and Pokhara (but nowhere else). These bikes are not top of the line but they're reasonably well maintained, and feature decent components. A helmet and basic tool kit should come with the bike. The daily rate will be Rs500–1000, depending on quality and features; you'll be expected to leave a passport or something of value as security. You'll generally have to pay for damage or above-normal wear-and-tear. Be sure to reserve these bikes as far ahead as possible, especially during busy times; choice is definitely limited in the peak season.

Whichever kind of bike you rent, it's your responsibility to check it over before setting off. **Check** brakes and pads, test spoke tension (they should all be taut), ensure that tyres have sufficient tread and are properly inflated (check inflation while sitting on the bike), test the chain for tautness, and work the bike through its gears to see that the derailleurs function smoothly. Check that there's a bell – you'll be using it a lot.

You may be able to **buy** a decent used bike from a departing traveller, especially towards the end of the autumn or spring seasons – check noticeboards in Kathmandu or Pokhara or websites such as ⓦ www.hmbadventures.com. Alternatively, you could buy new and sell on yourself: good-quality bikes from manufacturers such as Giant and Trek can be bought in Kathmandu for $300 and up.

Bringing a bike from home

For any long-distance tour, you'll obviously want to bring your own bike. However, don't bring a bike unless you have the time, energy and commitment to use it a lot. **Airlines** (both international and domestic) now generally impose a 25kg weight limit, with extortionate rates for extra kilos, so check the costs and allowances when you book your ticket – and pack light. Returning home, make sure to clean off mud or soil to avoid problems at customs; a good local operator can wash, service and pack your bike post-tour. Soft bike bags are worth considering; you'll be expected to deflate the tyres and swivel the handlebars parallel with the frame. Nepali (and Chinese/Tibetan, if you're cycling that way) customs may want verbal assurance that the bike will be returning with you when you leave the country, but this shouldn't be a problem and should not cost money. Domestic airlines' willingness to accept bikes as baggage is always dependent upon available luggage space, so check in early.

Clothes and other equipment

Other than a helmet and water bottle, no special gear is necessary for day-trips, though enthusiasts may want to pack their own saddle, pedals and shoes. Long-distance riders should give careful thought to equipment, however. Cycling **clothing**, shoes and gloves aren't easily obtainable in Nepal, nor is good water-proof/windproof outerwear. Note that tight Lycra clothing is embarrassing or offensive to many Nepalis, especially when worn by women, so wear a pair of comfortable shorts and a T-shirt over body-hugging rental gear.

A **helmet** and water bottle will come with a better rental bike. If renting a cheaper one, you could buy a helmet in a Kathmandu department store and make do with a mineral-water bottle. Be sure to have iodine for water purification (see p.49). **Panniers** and racks can be rented from the better bike shops, and camping equipment from trekking shops. Daypacks and waist-packs are sold all over tourist areas, and you can pick up bungy cords in motorcycle accessory shops. If you do much riding in Kathmandu, wear a face mask to protect against dust and pollution – good (expensive) ones are sold in department stores.

A good **lock** and cable are essential, especially if bringing a fancy bike from home. Local bike shops sell cheap, less effective locks. Bring bikes inside at night. Puncture-repair places are everywhere on the roads, but travel with your own **patch kit**, inner tube(s), pump and basic tool kit, especially if riding off-road.

Repairs and service

At least two of the Kathmandu tour operators (Himalayan Mountain Bike Adventures and Dawn Till Dusk) have **workshops** with trained bike mechanics, a full range of tools and even a stock of spare parts. These are good places to go for servicing. Local bike **repair shops**, found in every town and crossroads, are equipped mainly to fix basic local bikes, but they can patch any sort of flat (puncture) and are often remarkably adept at performing improvised repairs and mini-tune-ups. Just be sure to ask the price first: a puncture repair should cost Rs20–30.

Riding conditions

Given the incredible variety of the country, it's hard to generalize, but this section describes the major riding conditions you're likely to encounter. Be aware that conditions on Kathmandu's city streets are downright awful.

Highways

The scarcity of **highways** in Nepal means that all heavy-vehicle traffic converges on those few roads. Add the lack of consideration or attention afforded to cyclists by drivers and you'd be best advised to avoid busy roads altogether. Fortunately, the unpleasant stretches are limited mainly to the central Kathmandu–Pokhara and Mugling–Birgunj routes, and alternative routes are increasingly possible. Although highway cycling always entails dust and exhaust fumes, the traffic diminishes noticeably as you get further from Kathmandu; the eastern and particularly the far-western portions of the Mahendra Highway are delightfully rural.

If you want to skip a busy section or avoid backtracking, take a **bus** or a **taxi**. The latter come in especially handy in the Kathmandu Valley, where comparatively short lifts can get you past the urban blight. It's usually no problem to load your bike on the roof of a public bus, though you may need to tip Rs50–100 or so, depending on the distance and your negotiating skills. Tourist buses will charge slightly more. Lay the bike down flat and tie and lock it down securely (bungy cords are useful for this). Improvise padding (use your pack) to save your frame and derailleurs, and supervise the loading so that other luggage isn't laid on top.

Lesser roads and trails

Nepal's surprising number of paved and unpaved secondary **roads** mostly see very little traffic. There's also a burgeoning number of half-completed or half-washed-out jeep tracks, especially in the hills south of Kathmandu. With a good map to locate them, the possibilities are almost unlimited.

Although there are zillions of off-road **trails**, most aren't suitable for mountain-biking because they're too steep, stepped and heavily used by humans and animals. One notable exception is the Annapurna Circuit, a fair proportion of which is ridable – and there's now a road round its Western half, opening the amazing possibility of a flight to Jomosom and a descent through the Kali Gandaki gorge to Pokhara. A few bikers have "ridden" trekking trails to Everest Base Camp and elsewhere, but the mountainous national parks (with the exception of the Annapurna Conservation Area) are now officially out of bounds for bikes.

There are some excellent single-track rides, but finding them is tricky without a tour guide. If you go off-road, give people and livestock **priority**, slow down around all signs of habitation and signal your approach by ringing your bell or yelling *"Saikal aiyo!"* ("Cycle coming!"). It will often be necessary to dismount. Maintain a watchful eye for children, who like to grab hold of the back of bikes and run alongside, or throw stuff at your spokes. Be careful around buffalo and other livestock because it's easy to send them stampeding down a narrow trail – or be knocked off. If you manage to kill an animal you'll be liable for its replacement value.

Pedestrians and other hazards

Traffic culture in Nepal is communitarian and fatalistic: it's everyone's job to work their way around everyone else, hoping for the best. Horns and bells are integral parts of the system: sounding them sends the message, "I'm here". On a bicycle, you're near the bottom of the pecking order. Cars and buses will squeeze you off the road, motorbikes will approach head-on, and taxis will suddenly veer around obstacles with no apparent regard for your presence. It won't take you long to discover that there are few road rules, that the police have little control, and if you hit someone you'll probably be asked to pay compensation, whether it was your fault or not. The single saving grace is the **slow speed** at which most vehicles travel. However, smooth new highway surfaces are tempting many to go faster, especially young motorbike riders.

Route-finding and timing

Little **English** is spoken in the rural areas that are best for riding, so learn to ask the way to the next destination or village on your route in Nepali (see p.467). Don't point when asking directions, as many people will say yes out of courtesy, even if they don't know – it's better to put your hands in your pockets and ask "Which way to?" Do this several times to be sure you've got the right answer.

Don't ask how far it is to a given destination – rather, ask how long it takes to get there. The answer will be a rough walking time in hours; you'll somehow have to convert that to riding time. With so many **gradients** and variable **road conditions**, distances on the map bear little relation to actual time.

Routes

The following **itineraries** are grouped as being out of either Kathmandu or Pokhara, since those are the only places where you can rent a decent mountain bike. If riding further afield, seek expert advice in Kathmandu (ask in a bike shop) and find the most up-to-date map possible. If you're planning a long-distance bike tour then you'll probably combine Nepal with India or Tibet – those routes are summarized on p.414.

Rides in the Kathmandu Valley

Kathmandu is not the best place to be based if you're planning to do much biking around the valley. For rides toward the south, you'll make a cleaner escape from the traffic by staying in Patan. The highly ridable eastern valley and rim routes are best explored from Bhaktapur, Nagarkot, Dhulikhel or Panauti. Refer to the map on p.150 unless otherwise indicated.

Shivapuri National Park

Shivapuri National Park (Rs250 entry fee), which afforests Kathmandu Valley's northern rim, offers some superb possibilities. The scarcely used network of dirt roads begins right at the Budhanilkantha entrance. The road to the left snakes generally westwards for at least 15km, at which point the hill resort of Kakani is only about 2km further east along the ridge by a trail with some challengingly technical sections (some carrying required). This ride is more enjoyable done from Kakani to Budhanilkantha. For a shorter loop starting and ending in Budhanilkantha, ride to the Tokha Hospital and then descend along a steep, sandy road.

The road to the right (east) of the Budhanilkantha gate contours and climbs out of the valley, passing the monastery of Nagi Gompa and reaching the watershed's easternmost point at Jhule after about 20km. From Jhule you can bike southwards to Nagarkot, or make a jarring, stone-paved descent to the valley floor at Sankhu, a ride of 45 to 60 minutes. Alternatively, you can stay on the park road for another 8km beyond Jhule, rounding the Shivapuri ridge and reaching Chisopani, a village on the main Helambu trekking trail, from where you can cycle the long way to Nagarkot. Along this route, accommodation is available in Mulkharka, Chisopani, Chuaki Danda and of course Nagarkot.

Nagarjun Ban variations

Nagarjun Ban, an annexe of Shivapuri National Park, offers wilderness-style riding under a beautiful canopy of trees. At the time of writing, ex-king Gyanendra had taken up residence within the park, so access is occasionally restricted – and solo riders are usually prohibited for safety reasons. Seek local advice before committing to the following rides through the park.

Entering via the southern gate, you embark on a challenging 18km ascent on a jeep trail; the last 2km increases in gradient to reach a final elevation of 2096m. The return trip to the north gate is an additional 12km via a less established trail.

A marvellous section of trail leads to Nagarjun's western entrance from Sitapaila, a village west of Swayambhunath. Contouring high above the Mahesh Khola, this sometimes narrow single-track provides excellent riding for intermediate and above riders. The road beyond Ichangu Narayan, a temple northwest of Swayambhunath, links with this trail beyond the village of Baralgaun. Once in the forest park, keep to your left and you'll come out at the northern gate, on the main road to Kakani.

Another way to get to or from Nagarjun is via Tokha, a well-preserved village reached by trail from the Ring Road at Gongabu. From Tokha you can proceed in a north-northwest arc along excellent undulating dirt trails and through traditional villages all the way to the southern gate. Even if you skip Nagarjun, this is a great day on the bike, and can be extended all the way east through to Budhanilkantha (roughly 1hr 30min from the southern gate).

The Lele Valley

The Bungamati, Chapagaun and Godavari roads provide the backbones for some easy loops through the southern valley; see p.176 for ideas. For something a bit harder and longer, head east from Chapagaun past the Bajra Barahi temple (this track eventually meets the paved Godavari road), then strike south on a smaller road that crosses a steep, forested ridge and enters the **Lele Valley**. From there, you can choose from a number of trails heading south into little-visited hill country. Just south of Tika Bhairab (see p.178), a rough road passes the *Malla Alpine Resort* and ascends to more than 2000m at Tinpani Bhanjyang before descending via Bhattedanda and Makwanpurgadhi to Hetauda and the Terai. Conditions are highly variable, however, and there's no bridge over the Bagmati, so you won't be able to get right through during the monsoon.

The Lakuri Bhanjyang

The 30km road connecting Patan with Panauti is a superb intermediate-level ride that can be done in either direction. From Patan, ride out of town on the road past Sundhara and the Eastern Stupa. The first section to Lubhu, a brickmaking and handloom centre 6km beyond the Ring Road, is busy and uninteresting, but the pavement soon peters out and the road climbs as a jeep track before commencing a serious 500-metre switchback ascent to the **Lakuri Bhanjyang**. On a clear day, the view of the valley and mountains is splendid. The second half of the ride is a sweet descent through the rural valley of the Bebar Khola and its scattered Tamang, Chhetri and finally Newar settlements to Panauti, where you can spend the night. From there you can link up with Dhulikhel and Namobuddha area rides (see below), on paved or dirt roads.

Around Nagarkot

From **Nagarkot**, the options before you are almost unlimited. Rough roads and trails radiate in all directions: northwest to Sankhu; southwest to Changu Narayan; south to Nala and Banepa; east to Hiuwapati, Sipaghat and Panchkhal; and north to Chisopani and the Helambu trails. All these routes are described in the Nagarkot section (see p.203). However, there are endless forks, many of which lead to dead-ends or treacherous descents, so don't bike alone.

Unless you're a very strong rider, the ascent to Nagarkot will probably be all you care to do in a day, and in any case you'll want to spend the night for the views the next morning. Most bike tour operators run popular two-day trips, including transportation up, an overnight stay, and the amazing descent back to the Kathmandu Valley, taking more pleasant back roads.

Dhulikel, Namobuddha and Panauti

Dhulikel is the traditional starting point of a very popular circuit to the Buddhist stupa of **Namobuddha** and (optionally) on to the Newar town of **Panauti**. Panauti is perhaps the better starting point nowadays, given the increasing urbanization around Dhulikhel. The so-called Namobuddha circuit, which offers several hours of biking, is described on p.210.

The Arniko Highway and the Tibet border

The **Arniko Highway** from Kathmandu to the **Tibet border** at Kodari is an adventurous three- to five-day round-trip. The road gets much quieter and better for cycling after heavy traffic turns off at Dhulikhel for the southward road to Sindhuli, Bardibas and the Tera – so consider approaching via Nagarkot, Nala or across the Lakuri Bhanjyang. From Dhulikhel, the Arniko Highway descends 600m and then ascends more than 800m to the border. You can make a fascinating side-trip by making uphill off the main highway to Palanchowk, the gateway to further rides down to the Sun Koshi River.

If you want to cross the border on a bike, you'll have to join a tour (see p.145). Some companies offer adventurous excursions into and back out of Tibet, notably Himalayan Mountain Bikes' "World's Longest Downhill", a twelve-day round-trip from Kathmandu which descends from the Yarle Shungla (Tibet) to Dolaghat (Nepal) – or 4380m over 157km.

The Trisuli Road

The **Trisuli Road** heads northwestwards out of the valley, skirting the hill station of Kakani before plunging nearly 1500m to Trisuli Bazaar and the subtropical valley of the Trisuli River.

Kakani is usually considered an overnight ride, since it has (limited) accommodation and mountain views that are best seen in the morning. From there you can connect to Shivapuri National Park: head east past the agricultural station, carry on for a short distance to the park entrance (Rs250 fee) and then you'll be on a nice dirt track with some short rutted climbs; at a fork, the high trail leads to Nagi Gompa and Chisopani, while the lower one descends to Budhanilkantha and the road to Kathmandu. From Trisuli, rural roads and tracks extend for miles in several directions: east to the historic forts of Nuwakot and beyond, south and then east up the Tadi Khola, west up the lovely Samari Khola towards Gorkha, and north up to the Langtang trailheads (see p.374).

The Tribhuwan Rajpath

The spectacular and little-used **Tribhuwan Rajpath** racks up a total elevation gain of more than 1700m from Kathmandu to a cloudforested pass through the Mahabharat Lek, before descending an even more dizzying 2300m to the Terai. For a map and detailed route account, see pp.217–219.

For a classic two-days-plus loop out of Kathmandu, make for **Daman**, a mountain viewpoint just below the pass. It's a very long day's ride up the Rajpath, taking between six and nine hours in the saddle, almost all of it climbing. Even if you're an expert you'll want to skip the first traffic-choked, oil-slicked 26km – put your bike on a bus as far as Naubise, where the Rajpath branches off from the main Kathmandu–Pokhara highway. After overnighting in Daman, you can return via Markhu, the Kulekhani Reservoir and Pharping (see p.174) in the southern Kathmandu Valley.

Dakshinkali, Pharping and the Kulekhani Reservoir

The sealed **Dakshinkali** road strings together some fascinating cultural sights (see p.175) and while the ride out is largely uphill, it's gradual. The return, of course, is a fine descent. You can explore further – potentially as far as the Terai – on one of two roads (see box below). The major route, now used by jeeps almost year-round, heads south from the Dakshinkali gate, making for Hetauda – 60km in all from Kathmandu.

The slightly longer and rougher road is better for bikers. It heads broadly west and uphill from Pharping (see p.174), making for Markhu (1600m), a small, newly built village (with lodges) on the northeastern shore of the Kulekhani Reservoir (see map, p.219). From Markhu, you can return to Kathmandu via a rough road heading northeast for Thankot, on the Prithvi Highway; a longer but better-graded route heads 13km northwest on a good, pine-shaded road to join the Tribhuwan Rajpath 15km north of Daman (see p.219). From Markhu, you can also head south along the shore of the reservoir, crossing the dam then climbing a 1920m pass on the Mahabharat Lek range and heading down a steep valley to the historic but now pleasantly sidelined town of Bhimphedi (where there's more accommodation); from Bhimphedi, a paved road descends to join the Tribhuwan Rajpath at Bhainse, some 8km north of Hetauda, in the Terai.

Cycling in the Terai

From Hetauda, Kathmandu's gateway to the Terai, it's a half-day's ride west along the busy Mahendra Highway to **Chitwan National Park**, where there are many flat village trails to explore by bike (see p.278). Moving on to Pokhara requires travelling via Narayanghat and the Prithvi (Kathmandu–Pokhara) Highway – worryingly busy in the mornings, but nonetheless beautiful, especially between Mugling and Pokhara. Another option is just to put your bike on a bus. Heading east out of Hetauda, the Mahendra Highway is sometimes interestingly rural, sometimes rather urbanized, and always flat. There's a good network of lovely rural tracks around **Janakpur**.

Rides based in Pokhara

The "Pokhara Valley" account (see p.250) gives more detail on roads and bikeable destinations in that area. Here are a few recommended itineraries.

Sarangkot and beyond

The hilltop viewpoint of **Sarangkot** makes a great focus for an intermediate-level day-trip or overnight. From the Bindyabasini temple in the bazaar, follow the paved road 8km westwards to Sarangkot town and lodges, where there's a junction: the hilltop viewpoint is another 3km along to the right, while the left-hand fork leads to Naudaada.

The preferred way down is via Naudaada. The first 10km is an enjoyable track that contours along the south side of the ridge through forest, terraced farmland and villages. The track finally reaches Naudaada on the Baglung Highway; at which point you can either return to Pokhara, or continue deeper into the hills, potentially all the way up the Kali Gandaki to Jomosom (see p.369), though you may have to carry your bike some of the way.

Begnas and Rupa Tal

An unpaved road follows a ridge between two beautiful lakes, **Rupa Tal** and **Begnas Tal**, and then westwards to Besisahar. A network of trails is developing in this region that can offer one or several days' riding – inquire at Pokhara bike shops, and get hold of the most up-to-date map you can find. Good prospects include the trail north of Begnas Tal through Begnaskot and Kalikasthan (this is the Royal Trek), where a road leads back to Pokhara. Heading east of Begnas Tal, it's a 40km rough-road trip through Bhorletar and Sundaar Bazaar on the way to the paved road at Besisahar; from there you could head on up the new road up the Marsyangdi valley (the eastern side of the Annapurna Circuit) or return to Pokhara (with a side-trip to Bandipur).

The Seti River

Unpaved roads head downstream along the **Seti River**, with dramatic overlooks of the canyon and views of the mountains. The road on the south side of the canyon goes on for many easy, downhill miles, and leads to some more-remote trails further to the southeast.

To the Terai: Chitwan, Lumbini, Bardia and Sukla Phanta

The easiest route to **the Terai** is along the Prithvi Highway to Mugling and then south from there to Narayangadh, which is only a short hop from **Chitwan National Park**. It does get heavy traffic, but is mostly downhill and you can pedal it in a day.

A more adventurous and strenuous route follows the winding, scenic Siddhartha Highway southwards to Butwal. This ride requires some long stints in the saddle and several overnight stops. It's a fast downhill ride from Tansen to Butwal, and from there it's a flat and easy couple of hours to the Buddha's birthplace, **Lumbini**. West of Butwal, the Mahendra Highway leads through a beautiful *dun* valley towards the relatively undeveloped far west, the traffic lightening as you go.

This chapter was revised with help from Peter Stewart.

Contexts

Contexts

History

For a tiny Himalayan backwater, Nepal has played a surprisingly pivotal role in Asian history. In its early days, the country reared the Buddha; much later, its remarkable conquests led it into wars with Tibet and Britain. Its name and recorded history go back nearly three thousand years, although it has existed as a nation for barely two hundred: before 1769, "Nepal" referred only to a kingdom based in the Kathmandu Valley. Some rural people still talk about it as such.

The rise of the Himalayas

Nepal's history – its ethnic migrations, its crops, its development and politics today – is founded on its extraordinary **landscape**. The **Himalayas**, which march across the country's northern border, are a kind of cataclysmic, geo-scale crumple zone. Despite being astonishingly young – a mere half a million years old – they're already so high that they have created the desertified **Tibetan plateau**, parts of which lie within the northwestern borders of Nepal.

The body and cultural heart of Nepal – and its capital, Kathmandu – lies in the **Middle Hills**, or Pahar, a muscular belt of green created as much by water as plate tectonics. Beginning deep within Tibet, the Karnali, Kali Gandaki and Arun rivers have carved some of the world's deepest and grandest **gorges** through the country. Towards Nepal's southern edge, the geologically more recent uprising of the **Mahabharat Lek** and **Churia Hills** has formed a last barrier, forcing the great southbound rivers to make lengthy east–west detours before they flood out across the flat **Terai** region, and on into India.

Earthquake danger in Nepal

The **earthquakes** which periodically trouble Nepal are all-too-tangible proof that the Himalayas are still rising, forced ever upward by the movement of the Indian Subcontinent plate as it drives into the greater Asian plate at a rate of 2cm per year. Tremors of magnitude 4 and 5 occur a dozen or so times a year, while the most recent major earthquake, in 1988, registered a terrifying 8.3 on the Richter scale and killed seven hundred people in the eastern part of the country. When a similar quake hit Kathmandu in 1934, it destroyed a quarter of the capital's buildings and killed some seventeen thousand people inside a single minute, its power amplified by the Valley's soupy soil.

If a major earthquake struck the Kathmandu Valley today, the damage would be far greater. The population has soared, and nearly six thousand concrete houses are built every year – sixty percent of them officially thought to be "highly unsafe". Unnervingly, tourist guesthouses, built ever upwards in unceasing competition for roof-top airspace, may be among the main contenders for collapse. Recent seismic studies, moreover, predict that a **major earthquake**, one that hits eight or more on the Richter scale, is due to hit Nepal "soon" – which is to say at any time within the next fifty years. Local experts contend that the less populated (and much less visited) western region is a more likely target than Kathmandu, thanks partly to the tension release of 1934, but it's enough to make you think twice about spending a great deal of time in the Valley.

Ancient migrations

According to the Newars, who have lived here longest of all, the Kathmandu Valley was once filled with a primordial lake. Geologists agree that a lake dried up some 100,000 years ago. Whether the valley itself was inhabited is uncertain, but hilltop shrines such as Swayambunath may once have existed to rise above the waterline. Archeologists have found simple stone tools in the Churia hills, to the south, which date back at least 100,000 years.

Folk myths suggest that most of Nepal's current ethnic groups arrived as migrant hunter-gatherers. (Many preserved those ways of life until around the seventeenth century.) Semi-mythological genealogies talk about the warlike **Kiranti** (or Kirati) people who, by the sixth or seventh century BC were controlling the eastern hills – where they remain today – and the Kathmandu Valley. By this time, Hindus from the south were clearing the malarial jungle of the Terai, founding the city-states of **Mithila** (modern Janakpur), the scene of many of the events in the Ramayana epic, and **Kapilvastu** (now Tilaurakot), where the Buddha spent his pre-enlightenment years during the sixth century BC.

During the first millennium, the hills were populated from all sides. The **Khasas** steadily pushed eastward into what would become western Nepal, bringing their Indo-Aryan Nepali language and Hindu religion with them. From Tibet and the north came waves of migrants: first the **Tamangs**, then the **Gurungs**, in about 500 AD. At first these northerners were animists, practising nature worship and Shamanism; after Buddhism took root in Tibet, they reimported their version of the religion into its original homeland. The last Tibetans to cross the passes into Nepal were the **Sherpas**, from the 1530s onwards.

The ethnic groups of the hills largely kept themselves to themselves. The Kathmandu Valley, by contrast, acted as a giant ethnic mixing bowl. Even the Valley's "indigenous" **Newars** speak a language, Newari, whose Tibeto-Burman roots have come under strong Sanskrit (Indian) influences, and the Newars' genes seem to be as mixed as their language.

The Licchavis and Thakuris

In the second century AD, the **Licchavi** clan, of north Indian origin, overthrew the Kirants and established their capital and their dynasty at Deopatan (modern Pashupatinath), exploiting the Valley's position as a trading entrepôt between India and Tibet. Although Hindus, the Licchavis endowed both Hindu and Buddhist temples and established Nepal's longstanding policy of religious tolerance. No Licchavi buildings survive, but Chinese travellers described "multi-storeyed temples so tall one would take them for a crown of clouds" – perhaps a reference to the pagodas that would become a Nepali trademark. Sculptors, meanwhile, ushered in a classical age of stonework, and Licchavi statues still litter the Kathmandu Valley.

The earliest stone inscription, dated 464 AD and still on view at Changu Narayan, extols the Licchavi king **Mandev** (often spelled Manadeva), the legendary builder of the Boudha stupa. The greatest of the Licchavi line, **Amsuvarman** (605–621) was said to have built a splendid palace, probably at present-day Naksal in Kathmandu. But by this time Nepal had become a vassal of Tibet, and Amsuvarman's daughter, Bhrikuti, was carried off by the Tibetan king. She is popularly credited with introducing Buddhism to Tibet, as a result.

The Licchavi era came to a close in 879. The three centuries that followed are sometimes referred to as Nepal's **Dark Ages**, though Nepalese chronicles record a long list of **Thakuri kings**, who may have been puppets installed by the various powers controlling the Terai. Nonetheless, learning and the arts continued to thrive, and from the eleventh century onwards the Kathmandu Valley became an important centre of tantric studies (see "Religion", p.429).

The Khasas and Mallas

From the twelfth century, the great regional power was based in Sinja, in the Karnali basin near modern-day Jumla. The **Khasa empire**, at its height, controlled the Himalayas from Kashmir to present-day Pokhara. The resurgence of the Kathmandu Valley – then known as "Nepal" – began when the Thakuri king of Bhaktapur, Arideva, took the title **Malla**, probably in the year 1200. The name came to be associated with three major dynasties across more than five centuries, presiding over a golden age of Nepali culture.

The early Mallas had to defend their nascent kingdoms against destructive raids by Khasas and, in 1349, Muslims from Bengal. Yet trade and the arts flourished. Arniko, the great Nepali architect, was even dispatched to teach the Ming Chinese to build pagodas. **Jayasthiti Malla** (1354–95) inaugurated a period of strong central rule from Bhaktapur, and legendarily imposed the caste system. Malla power reached its zenith under **Yaksha Malla** (1428–82), who extended his domain westwards to Gorkha and eastwards as far as present-day Biratnagar. Upon his death, the kingdom was divided among three sons, and for nearly three centuries the independent city states of Kathmandu, Patan and Bhaktapur (and occasionally others) feuded and competed, building ever more opulent palaces and temples in a battle of regal theatricality.

While the Valley flourished, new powers were arising in the West. A steady stream of Rajasthani princes fled the Muslim conquest of North India, seeking conquest or refuge in the hills, and by the early fifteenth century the Khasa empire had fragmented into a collection of petty provinces. Those in the Karnali basin came to be known as the **Baaisi Rajya** (Twenty-two Kingdoms), while those that ruled over subjugated Magar and Gurung states further east, in the Gandaki basin, became the **Chaubisi** (Twenty-four). Khasa peoples, meanwhile, began migrating eastward towards and into the Kathmandu Valley, laying down the ethnic foundations of Nepal's long-dominant **Parbatiya**, or caste-Hindu population.

Gorkha conquest

The Chaubisi and Baaisi confederacies were small, weak and culturally backward, but politically stable. Then **Gorkha**, the most easterly territory, began to have ambitions. Under the inspired, obsessive leadership of **Prithvi Narayan Shah** (1722–75), the Gorkhalis launched a campaign that was to take 27 years to conquer the Valley kingdoms of "Nepal", and as long again to unite all of modern Nepal.

Prithvi Narayan hoped to create a single pan-Himalayan kingdom, a bastion of Hindu culture in contrast to north India, which had fallen first to the Mughals and then the British. He first captured Nuwakot, a day's march northwest of Kathmandu. From there he directed a ruthless twenty-year **war**

of attrition against the Valley. Kirtipur surrendered first, following a six-month siege. Its inhabitants had their lips and noses cut off as punishment for resistance. Desperate, the Kathmandu king, Jaya Prakash Malla, sought help from the British East India Company. It was to no avail: of the 2400 soldiers loaned by the Company, only eight hundred returned to India. On the eve of Indra Jaatra in 1768, Jaya Prakash, by now rumoured to be insane, let down the city's defences and **Kathmandu fell** to the Gorkhalis without a fight. Patan followed, two days later, and Bhaktapur the following year; by 1774 the Gorkhalis had marched eastwards all the way to Sikkim.

Suspicious of Britain's ambitions in India and China's in Tibet – he called his kingdom "a yam between two stones" – Prithvi Narayan closed Nepal to foreigners. The gates would remain almost entirely shut until the 1950s. Instead, Nepal turned in on itself, embroiling in a series of bloody **battles for succession** which set the pattern for the next two hundred years. Yet when they weren't stabbing each other in the back, the Shahs managed to continue the wars of conquest. Lured on by promises of land grants – every hillman's dream – the Nepali army became an unstoppable fighting machine, and by 1790 Nepal stretched far beyond its present eastern and western borders.

Expansion was finally halted first by a brief but chastening **war with Tibet** and then, in 1814, by a clash with **Britain**'s East India Company after Nepal annexed the Butwal sector of the Terai. It took Britain two years and heavy losses before finally bringing Nepal to heel. The 1816 **Treaty of Segauli** forced Nepal to accept its present eastern and western boundaries and surrender much of the Terai. Worst of all, it had to accept an official British "resident" in Kathmandu. Yet so impressed were the British by "our valiant opponent" that they began recruiting Nepalis into the Indian Army, an arrangement which continues today in the famed **Gurkha regiments** (see p.225). Britain restored Nepal's Terai lands in return for its help in quelling the Indian Mutiny of 1857.

Rana misrule

The intrigues and assassinations which bedevilled the Kathmandu court during the first half of the nineteenth century culminated in the ghastly **Kot massacre** of 1846, in which more than fifty courtiers were butchered in a courtyard off Kathmandu's Durbar Square. Behind the plot was a shrewd young general, **Jang Bahadur Rana**, who seized power and proclaimed himself prime minister for life. He later made the office hereditary, in a move that speaks volumes about the court: his title was attached to a grade of kingship, Shri Tin Maharaja (short for Shri Shri Shri Maharaja), or His Three-Times-Great Highness the King.

The Shah king may have had five Shris before his title but the Ranas held all the power. For a century, they remained authoritarian and isolationist, building almost no roads or schools, only overweening Neoclassical palaces. They kept on careful good terms with the British, but only allowed a handful of foreigners to actually enter Nepal – and usually only as far as Chitwan. Even the British resident was corralled within the Kathmandu Valley. The eastern and western tracts of the country were treated as colonies, the religious and land-tenure customs of the hill tribes subject to ever-greater "sanskritization" – meaning colonization by Parbatiya, or caste-Hindu, culture. Peasants migrated ever-further eastward across the hills, and south into the Terai's jungle in search of ever-scarcer land. Slash-and-burn agriculture gave way to subsistence farming, while the Tibetan salt and trade networks were increasingly bypassed by the new British route via Darjeeling. Newar merchants fanned out across Nepal, meanwhile, establishing bazaars where they could sell imported goods. And from the early twentieth century, the population began to grow.

Chandra Shamsher Rana, who came to power in 1901 by deposing his brother, is best known for building the thousand-roomed Singha Durbar and (belatedly) abolishing slavery and the practice of *sati*, or widow-burning. He also built Nepal's first college and hydroelectric plant, along with suspension bridges on the hill trails and the celebrated **ropeway** connecting Kathmandu with the Terai. India's railway network was joined to Nepal in the inter-war years, but never penetrated more than a few miles into the Terai. Factories were established around Biratnagar in the 1930s, and Nepal's first airstrip arrived in 1942.

The monarchy restored

The absurdly anachronistic regime could not hope to survive the geopolitical seismic shifts of the postwar era. In 1947 the British quit India. In 1949, the Communists took power in China – and within two years had taken over in **Tibet**. Seeking stability, Nepal signed a far-reaching "**peace and friendship**" **treaty** with India in 1950. Despite the upheavals that were to follow, it remains the contentious basis for all relations between the two countries.

In 1950, the **Nepali Congress Party**, which had recently been formed in Kolkata, called for an armed struggle against the Ranas. Within a month, King Tribhuwan had requested asylum at the Indian embassy and was smuggled away to Delhi. Sporadic fighting and political dealing continued for two months until the Ranas, internationally discredited, reluctantly agreed to enter into negotiations. Brokered by India, the so-called **Delhi Compromise** arranged for Ranas and the Congress Party to share power under the king's rule. Power-sharing squabbles between Ranas and Congress factions, however, ensured that the compromise was ineffective and short-lived. Tribhuwan himself died in 1955, and the promised Constituent Assembly, which was supposed to write a new democratic constitution, never came to fruition.

Crowned in 1955, **King Mahendra** pushed through a constitution which guaranteed him emergency powers, and ultimate control of the army. Long-delayed elections were eventually held in 1959, but this "**experiment with democracy**" was too successful. Under Prime Minister **B.P. Koirala** the Nepali Congress Party began bypassing palace control; in response, Mahendra banned political parties, jailed the Congress leaders and created the "partyless" **panchaayat** system. His national assembly, elected ultimately from local village councils (*panchaayat*), served in practice as a rubber stamp for royal policies and a conduit for corruption and cronyism. The regime only survived on **foreign aid** and by playing off India and China against each other.

King Birendra assumed his father's throne in 1972, immediately declaring Nepal to be a **Zone of Peace**, a Swiss-style neutrality pledge which won international plaudits – but antagonized India. Birendra made minor concessions towards political reform throughout his reign, and was widely admired, but it became clear in the 1980s that he could neither curtail ever-growing corruption – which involved his own family – nor keep the lid on simmering discontent.

Development under the Shahs

Under the three Shah kings, Nepal's **population** exploded: from 8.4 million in 1954 to 18.5 million in 1991. Much of that growth was absorbed in the flat Terai region, bordering India, where the jungle was cleared for farmland and malaria sprayed out of existence. But slowly, the land began to run out. So too did forest – a crucial fuel and fodder resource for farmers in the hills. Up to a third of Nepalis lacked sufficient food, and the majority of men would migrate in winter in search of paid employment. The Kathmandu Valley's population trebled to well over a million by 1991, and over a million more crossed the border into India. Piecemeal **development projects** failed to stimulate growth, instead bloating the bureaucracy and distorting the budget so that during the peak dependency era, in the late 1980s, forty percent of all government spending derived from foreign aid.

Royal rule was not entirely disastrous for Nepal. Literacy rates stood at a dismal forty percent by 1991 – but it was an improvement on the five percent rate of fifty years earlier. In the same period, infant mortality fell from an appalling twenty percent to a merely shocking ten percent. Notwithstanding huge problems over tariff and trade agreements with India, industrial estates were established at Balaju, Birgunj and Hetauda, and **carpet-weaving**, a trade largely controlled by Tibetan refugees, employed up to 250,000 people by the mid-1980s. But **tourism** was perhaps the most conspicuously successful of Nepal's endeavours. The kingdom which had once accepted a single British resident was welcoming four thousand visitors in 1960, 100,000 in 1976, at the close of the hippy era, and – due to a new kind of tourism cleverly marketed as **trekking** – 250,000 by the early 1990s.

Democracy and discontent

The **panchaayat** government might have tottered on for many more years if it hadn't been for a trade and migration dispute with India, whose government punished Nepal with a virtual **blockade** through most of 1989. The government might still have ridden out the crisis had it not been for the inspiration provided by China's failed pro-democracy movement at Tiananmen Square, and the successful revolutions in Eastern Europe.

The banned opposition parties united in the **Movement to Restore Democracy**, calling for a national day of protest on February 18, 1990 – the anniversary of the first post-Rana government, a date already known as Democracy Day. Street clashes with police and the arrest of leading opposition figures did little to contain the desire for change, and the **Jana Andolan** ("People's Movement") gathered pace. On March 31, the Newari inhabitants of Patan took control of their city. On April 6, the king promised constitutional reform – but his move failed to placate the 200,000 people marching up Kathmandu's Durbar Marg towards the Royal Palace. After the army fired into the crowd, **killing** dozens, the king's hand was forced. He dissolved his cabinet, lifted the ban on political parties and invited the opposition to form an interim government.

Once again, calls for a constitution to be written by a Constituent Assembly were bypassed; and once again the king clung onto key powers as constitutional monarch – and Nepal remained officially a Hindu state, not a secular one. However, the old Rastriya Panchaayat was replaced by a true bicameral Parliament, and free **elections** were held in May 1991. Again, the Nepali Congress Party, under **Girija Prasad Koirala**, younger brother of B.P. Koirala, came out on top. The challenge from Nepal's several Communist parties, however, was strong: they maintained their traditional strongholds in the east and, incredibly, captured the Kathmandu Valley. For the next five years, power swung between Congress and the **Communist Party of Nepal–United Marxist-Leninist (CPN-UML)**. No matter who was in power, political infighting and horse-trading for the powers of patronage and the proceeds of corruption took precedence over the real business of government. The impoverished millions living outside the Kathmandu Valley seemed all but forgotten.

Maoists and massacres

Between 1990 and 2000, Nepal certainly developed. The road network doubled in size, phones proliferated, literacy rose by twenty percent (to 58 percent) and infant mortality improved substantially. But **growth** was quickly swallowed up by **demographics**, and hope was increasingly replaced by cynicism. By the end of the decade half a million young Nepalis were leaving school and seeking work each year, but few had any hope of finding employment. In the roadless hills, meanwhile, where three-quarters of the population lived, development still seemed a world away.

In February 1996, members of the **Nepal Communist Party (Maoist)** broke with what they considered to be Nepal's failed democratic system, launching a "**People's War**" from their base in the midwestern hill districts of Rolpa and Rukum. The Congress government paid little heed – a miscalculation that it would regret. The Maoists picked off police stations and district offices one at a time, financing their operations by robbing banks and demanding protection money. Political enemies were intimidated or killed. Political friends were won by aggressive development programmes: schools, courts and health posts were run with renewed efficiency, land redistributed and programmes empowering women, lower castes and minorities launched. Five years later the rebels effectively controlled nearly a quarter of the country's 75 districts, and had infiltrated another half.

In 2001, Maoist leader Pushpa Kamal Dahal – better known by his nom de guerre **Prachanda** ("the Fierce") – issued his preconditions for peace: a Constitutional Assembly with seats for Maoists, and the abolition of the monarchy. Girija Prasad Koirala's government responded by creating a paramilitary **Armed Police Force** with broad powers to combat the rebels. As yet, parliament was unwilling to cross the political Rubicon by letting the Army out of its barracks. It owed its loyalty to the king, after all.

The monarchy was soon to enter politics for a very different reason. On the evening of June 1, 2001, King Birendra, Queen Aishwarya and seven other members of the royal family were **massacred** in the Narayanhiti Royal Palace by the heir to the throne, Prince **Dipendra**, who then turned the gun on himself. Dipendra survived on a life-support machine for almost two days, during which time the country boiled with anxiety, speculation and conspiracy theories. When Dipendra's death and his uncle **Gyanendra's ascension** were finally announced, **riots** broke out.

Nepal in crisis: the royal regime

The royal massacre gave the Maoists a golden opportunity to tap into anti-monarchist feelings. Gyanendra was known to be sharper-nosed and harder-line than his brother, and his son Paras, now crown prince, was widely loathed. The Maoists stepped up their offensive, even bombing the hitherto safe Kathmandu Valley and flexing their muscles in the capital by successfully enforcing a general strike. **Peace talks** in the summer of 2001 proved merely to be an interlude, a classic Maoist tactical manoeuvre allowing them to regroup prior to launching a new wave of coordinated attacks.

The Congress party, as ever, seemed more concerned with infighting than government. When **Sher Bahadur Deuba** took over from Girija Prasad Koirala in July 2001, his was the eleventh government in as many years. In November 2001, the new king proved his critics right by declaring a **state of emergency** in which he suspended civil liberties, began imprisoning thousands of dissidents, and mobilized Nepal's **army**. Aggressive "search and destroy" operations took Nepali troops deep into the hills. In response, the Maoist People's Liberation Army began to target dams, telecommunications facilities

The royal massacre

The **royal massacre** of June 1, 2001 – in which **Crown Prince Dipendra** killed most of his family, including his father, the king – traumatized and ultimately transformed the nation. The Shah dynasty had created Nepal back in the eighteenth century, and the monarchy was seen as the very bedrock of national identity, holding dozens of ethnic groups and castes together in peaceful coexistence. The king was regarded as an incarnation of the god Vishnu, a supreme patriarch whose very existence proclaimed Nepal's uniqueness – as the last Hindu kingdom, when all of India had fallen to either the Mughals or the British.

Most monstrous of all, the alleged killer was the king's own son. In a culture where parents still command the highest respect from their children, and where murder is rare, such a crime was almost unimaginable. Nepalis felt grief, anger and deep shame at the egregious breaking of taboos. But above all they felt **disbelief**. Could the crown prince really have done it? Based on the testimony of survivors and palace employees, it's known that before an untypical family gathering, Dipendra was drinking whisky and smoking hashish laced with an unnamed "black substance" – presumably opium. Shortly after, he had to be helped to his room. A few minutes later, he entered the billiard room where the royal family was assembled, dressed in camouflage fatigues with an automatic weapon in each hand. He opened fire, coolly targeting the king first and then other members of his family. He then retreated to the garden where he apparently shot his mother, who had fled, and finally himself.

His motivations seemed oddly run-of-the-mill. Dipendra was apparently furious with the queen for opposing his marriage plans with his girlfriend, **Devyani Rana**. He was also known to have a lethal temper, a fetish for weapons, a predilection for alcohol and drugs, and – observers concluded – a propensity for violent psychotic outbursts. It seemed clear-cut. But the hastily produced **High Level Committee Report**, delivered just two weeks after the tragedy, was riddled with unanswered – indeed unasked – questions. Why was the first response of the royal aides de camp on duty that night to call a doctor, rather than to overpower the attacker, and why did it take them ten minutes to do that? Why were no post-mortems performed on the victims? Why did Dipendra, who was right-handed, shoot himself behind the left ear? Why did a soldier throw the weapon lying next to Dipendra's body into a pond?

Conspiracy theorists thought it no accident that Gyanendra, alone among the immediate family, was absent from the palace that evening, and that his unpopular son Paras, who was present, escaped unhurt. Others connected the killings with the Maoists – who in turn claimed it was a plot co-ordinated by the CIA and its Indian counterpart, RAW. Whoever did it, some said, killed Dipendra and replaced him with a stand-in wearing a lifelike mask (which would account why Dipendra reportedly neither spoke nor showed any expression during the rampage). Others held Dipendra was a patsy, drugged and given weapons by the real perpetrators and then bumped off afterwards. Whatever the truth, the damage done to the institution of the monarchy was severe – if not fatal.

and other infrastructure. A regional insurgency by a fringe political party was escalating into **civil war**. By 2004, the Maoists were strong enough to be able to blockade Kathmandu for an entire week.

Before the war was over, it would kill some fourteen thousand Nepalis, leaving the economy in tatters, the tourist industry in ruins and the Kathmandu Valley straining at the seams with villagers fleeing the fighting in the hills. Nepalis had given up hope. The Maoists, it seemed, could not hope to take control of the capital and win outright. The army could not militarily defeat a movement whose roots ran deep into the roadless hills. The government, meanwhile, was collapsing in a series of failed administrations, postponed elections and compromises with an ever-more interventionist Royal Palace.

The People's Movement (part II)

In February 2005, Gyanendra snapped, **seizing power** and imposing martial law; as a result, the previously fractious political parties united against him. As the **Seven Party Alliance (SPA)**, the politicians signed an understanding with the Maoists: they would back Maoist demands for a Constituent Assembly and drop support for the monarchy; the Maoists, in return, would announce a ceasefire. Everyone would mobilize against Gyanendra's regime.

During the winter of 2005–06, the scale and belligerence of the protests, rallies and strikes grew – as did the aggression of the government response. Hundreds of political leaders were arrested and once again, Nepalis died under government bullets. **Bandhs**, or complete shut-downs of the Valley, became commonplace. By early April it was like 1990 all over again – indeed, the movement became known as **Jana Andolan II** (Second People's Movement) though others preferred to call it the **Loktantra Andolan** (Democracy Movement). During April, hundreds of thousands of Nepalis came out onto the streets of Kathmandu day after day, in the face of aggressively enforced curfews. On April 21, Gyanendra played his last card, asking the leaders of the SPA to name a new prime minister. With Maoist guns behind them, the SPA could afford to call the king's bluff, and three days later parliament was duly reinstated under Girija Prasad Koirala.

After ten years of war and stagnation, the pace of political change was now astonishing. Parliament quickly moved to scrap the 1990 constitution and hold elections for a **Constituent Assembly**. The king's powers were dramatically curtailed, and Nepal was declared to be no longer a kingdom. The Maoists had what they wanted, and in November 2006 they formally ended their insurgency, agreeing to put their weapons under UN supervision and send their combatants into UN-monitored cantonments. The Maoists' leaders, meanwhile, took their places in an interim government.

Towards a red dawn?

All of Nepal was determined that, this time, democracy would be made to work. But without Gyanendra's regime to unite them in opposition, the political parties were free to squabble. And without the monarchy to bind the country, the tensions that had been building between ethnic groups for years could break out. From late 2006, activists in the Terai launched the **Madheshi Andolan**, or "Movement for Madhesh", to fight for the rights of ethnically and culturally

Indian people, or Madheshis, against the historic dominance (or indifference) of hill peoples and the Kathmandu elite. A host of political parties and pressure groups sprang up, some aspiring to regional autonomy, others demanding a separate state – *ek pradesh, ek madhesh* ("one state, one Madhesh"), as the slogan went. In 2007 and 2008, the major Terai towns were the site of bomb blasts and violent clashes between activists and both Maoist cadre and police, and mass strikes and *bandhs* (shutdowns) paralyzed the entire region in early 2009.

In April 2008, the Maoists won an astounding victory in the **Constituent Assembly elections**, taking 220 seats, over a third of the total. It was not an outright majority but the Maoist bloc was still double the size of that of either Congress or the CPN-UML. Many Nepalis had voted cannily – or desperately – in order to keep the peace process alive, but it was clear that Prachanda's radical programme had genuine support. Nepal was duly transformed into a **republic** in May 2008, and Gyanendra was given three days to quit the Narayanhiti palace, which was designated a national museum. In August, Comrade Prachanda – who increasingly used his proper name, Pushpa Kamal Dahal – became the first Prime Minister of the secular **Federal Democratic Republic of Nepal**.

Hope and realities

High hopes for the new government quickly came up against intractable **realities**. Attempting to merge those former adversaries, the Royal National Army and the People's Army, proved predictably difficult. So too did persuading self-serving politicians to stop fighting long enough to even *discuss* writing the new **constitution**. Girija Prasad Koirala's Nepali Congress Party quickly established itself as an official, obstructive opposition while the Maoists began to split over issues such as the extent of federalism, and whether the new Nepal would officially be a *People's* Republic. And across the country, highly politicized youth and ethnic identity groups proliferated, posing a serious threat to stability. Some were armed. A few actually called themselves armies, and began employing Maoist-style tactics.

But what really got the people down was power: not political power, but **electricity**. By spring 2009, Nepal's puny power industry was on its knees. Poor maintenance, lack of new projects coming on stream, "pilferage" of power, the disastrous flooding which broke the **Koshi Barrage** in August 2008 (killing thousands in India) and an unprecedented winter drought resulted in scheduled "load shedding" – ie power cuts – which blacked out the capital for up to twenty hours a day. The effect on industry – already feeling the first chill wind of global **recession** – was catastrophic; the effect on Kathmandu's morale was, if anything, even more severe.

As ever, **tourism** held out the greatest economic hope. Thousands, it seemed, had just been waiting for the conflict to end. In 2008, 800,000 foreigners visited Nepal (roughly one for every Nepali working in the tourism sector), and the trails were once again buzzing with trekkers. Longer-term, however, Nepal's problems seem to be intensifying. Population growth continues apace – power cuts have apparently fuelled a new baby boom – and **climate change** is starting to hit. The larger glaciers have lost up to half their volume in the last fifty years, and the rate of attrition is increasing. The risk of catastrophic outburst flooding from glacial lakes (**GLOF** events) is ever more serious, and landslips, flooding and erosion are gathering pace.

Religion

Nepal stands at an extraordinary crossing point of religions. For long the Subcontinent's last great **Hindu kingdom**, it was also the **birthplace of Buddhism** and its Buddhist communities – Sherpas, Tibetan refugee monks – are internationally celebrated. In theory, you can judge a Nepali's religion by altitude. The Madheshi peoples of the plains, and the Parbatiyas of the Middle Hills are fairly orthodox Hindu. In the hilly heartland of the country, Nepal's ethnic groups intertwine Hinduism with ancient animist traditions and shamanistic practices, often worshipping local gods under nominally Hindu names. Tibetan-style Buddhism prevails on the ridge-tops and in the high Himalayas – and of course in the large and vibrant Tibetan refugee communities of Kathmandu and Pokhara. In the Kathmandu Valley, the Newars practise their own extraordinary, tolerant mix of the two main religions, bound together by Nepal's vibrant Tantric legacy.

Long supported by the monarchy and Brahmin-dominated government, many Hindu institutions are now facing a more uncertain future. Elements within the Maoist movement are aggressively **secular**, and in 2008 the government attempted to throw traditional priests out of the Pashupatinath temple and withdrew funding for key Kathmandu festivals. By contrast, **minority Buddhist** and **indigenous religious groups** are enjoying something of a renaissance. **Tibetan Buddhism** attracts generous foreign funding, while reform movements within the ethnic groups of the hills are asserting political and religious independence, rejecting the creeping Hinduization of past decades and turning back to local traditions.

Hinduism

Hinduism isn't so much a religion as **dharma**, meaning duty, faith – an entire way of life. Hindus seek the divine not in books or prayer meetings but in the ritual rhythms of the day and the seasons – festivals are hugely

---

Aum

"AUM" is a word that represents to our ears that sound of the energy of the universe of which all things are manifestations. You start in the back of the mouth, "ahh," then "oo," you fill the mouth, and "mm" closes the mouth. When you pronounce this properly, all vowel sounds are included in the pronunciation. AUM. Consonants are here regarded simply as interruptions of the essential vowel sound. All words are thus fragments of AUM, just as all images are fragments of the Form of forms. AUM is a symbolic sound that puts you in touch with that resounding being that is the universe. If you heard some of the recordings of Tibetan monks chanting AUM, you would know what the word means, all right. That's the AUM of being in the world. To be in touch with that and to get the sense of that is the peak experience of all. A-U-M. The birth, the coming into being, and the dissolution that cycles back. AUM is called the "four-element syllable". A-U-M – and what is the fourth element? The silence out of which AUM arises, and back into which it goes, and which underlies it.

From *The Power of Myth*, by Joseph Campbell, reproduced with permission of Doubleday.

important – and in the very fabric of family and social relationships. Having no common church or institution, Hinduism's many sects and cults preach different dogmas and emphasize different scriptures, and worshippers can follow many paths to enlightenment. By absorbing other faiths and doctrines, rather than seeking to suppress them, Hinduism has flourished longer than any other major religion.

According to the philosophical **Upanishads,** the soul (*atman*) of each living thing is like a lost fragment of the universal soul – **brahman**, the ultimate reality – while everything in the physical universe is mere illusion (*maya*). To reunite with *brahman*, the individual soul must go through a **cycle of rebirths** (*samsara*), ideally moving up the scale with each reincarnation. Determining the soul's progress is its **karma** – its accumulated "just desserts" – which is reckoned by the degree to which the soul conformed to **dharma** in previous lives. Thus a low-caste Hindu must accept his or her lot to atone for past sins, and follow *dharma* in the hope of achieving a higher rebirth. The theoretical goal of every Hindu is to cast off all illusion, achieve release (*moksha*) from the cycle of rebirths, and dissolve into *brahman*.

The Hindu pantheon

Hinduism's earliest known origins lie in the **Vedas**, sacred texts composed in India in the first and second millennia BC. They tell stories of a pantheon of nature gods and goddesses, some of whom are still in circulation: Indra (sky and rain) is popular in Kathmandu, while Surya (sun), Agni (fire), Vayu (wind) and Yama (death) retain bit parts in contemporary mythology. As the messenger between the gods and humanity, Agni was particularly important, and sacrifice was thus a major part of Vedic religion. Gradually, the Vedic gods were displaced by the **Brahminical "trinity"**: Brahma the creator, Vishnu the preserver and Shiva the destroyer. Every locality has its own forms, often derived from ancient nature worship. Even today, many ancestral spirits of the Nepali hill peoples are being given Hindu names, their worship adapted to fit more conventional rituals – a process known as Hinduization. When pressed, Nepalis often refer to their local deities as aspects of Mahadev (Shiva), Vishnu or one of the other mainstream gods, either out of respect for foreigners' potential bewilderment or out of a widespread notion that they all boil down to one god in the end. Shaivism, or the worship of Shiva, is the most widespread devotional cult in Nepal, as part of the Tantric legacy (see box, p.435).

In art and statuary, the most important gods can easily be identified by certain trademark implements, postures and "vehicles" (animal carriers). Multiple arms and heads aren't meant to be taken literally: they symbolize the deity's "universal" (omnipotent) form. Severed heads and trampled corpses, meanwhile, signify ignorance and evil.

Vishnu

Vishnu (often known as **Narayan** in Nepal) is the face of dignity and equanimity, typically shown standing erect holding a wheel (*chakra*), mace (*gada*), lotus (*padma*) and conch (*sankha*) in his four hands, or, as at Budhanilkantha, reclining on a serpent's coil. A statue of **Garuda** (**Garud** in Nepal), Vishnu's bird-man vehicle, is always close by. Vishnu is also sometimes depicted in one or more of his ten incarnations, which follow an evolutionary progression from fish, turtle and boar to the man-lion **Narasimha**, a dwarf, an axe-wielding Brahman and the legendary heroes **Ram** and **Krishna**, as portrayed in the much-loved epics, the Mahabharata and Ramayana.

Ram is associated with **Hanuman**, his loyal monkey-king ally, while blue-skinned Krishna is commonly seen on posters and calendars as a chubby baby, flute-playing lover or charioteer. Interestingly, Vishnu's ninth *avatar* is the Buddha – this was a sixth-century attempt by Vaishnavas to bring Buddhists into their fold – and the tenth is Kalki, a messiah figure invented in the twelfth century as Muslims took the upper hand in India. Vishnu's consort is **Lakshmi**, the goddess of wealth, to whom lamps are lit during the festival of Tihaar. Like Vishnu, she assumed mortal form in two great Hindu myths, playing opposite Ram as the chaste princess Sita, and opposite Krishna as the passionate Radha.

Shiva

Shiva's incarnations are countless but to many devotees he is simply **Mahadev**, the Great God, and he is the pre-eminent divinity in Nepal. The earliest and most widespread icon of Shiva is the **linga**, a phallic stone fertility symbol often housed in a boxy stone *shivalaya* ("Shiva home"), often garlanded in marigolds and dusted with red *abhir* powder, and sometimes encircled in a *yoni*, or vulva symbol. Shiva temples can be identified by the presence of a *trisul* (trident) and the bull **Nandi**, Shiva's mount.

Many sadhus worship Shiva the *yogin* (one who practises yoga), the Hindu ascetic supreme, who is often depicted sitting in meditative repose on a Himalayan mountaintop. In his benign form as **Pashupati** ("Lord of the Animals"), he occupies Pashupatinath as his winter home. As **Nataraja**, lord of the "dance" of life, he maintains and destroys the cosmos. As the loving husband of Parvati and father of Ganesh, he represents family life – the divine couple can be seen leaning from an upper window of a temple in Kathmandu's Durbar Square. Nearby stand two famous statues of the grotesque **Bhairab**, the Tantric (see p.435) interpretation of Shiva in his role as destroyer: according to Hindu philosophy, everything – not only evil – must be destroyed in its turn to make way for new things. Bhairab alone is said to take 64 different forms.

Mahadevi – the mother goddess

The mother goddess is similarly worshipped in many forms, both peaceful and wrathful. Typically, she is the consort of Shiva, and represented as the vulva-like **yoni** symbol. In Nepal she is widely worshipped as **Bhagwati**, the embodiment of female creative power, and in the Kathmandu Valley she takes physical form as the **Kumari**, a young girl chosen to be her virginal incarnation. She is appeased by sacrifices of uncastrated male animals, a practice far more common in Tantric Nepal than in more orthodox India. In art, she is most often seen as **Durga**, the many-armed demon-slayer honoured in the great Dasain festival; as angry **Kali** ("Black", but often painted as dark blue), the female counterpart of Bhairab, wearing a necklace of skulls and sticking out her tongue with bloodthirsty intent; as the **Saptamatrika** she takes the form of seven (or sometimes eight) ferocious "mothers". On a more peaceful level, she is also **Parbati** ("Hill", daughter of Himalaya), Gauri ("Golden") or just **Mahadevi** ("Great Goddess").

Ganesh and others

Several legends tell how **Ganesh**, Shiva and Parbati's son, came to have an elephant's head: one states that Shiva accidentally chopped the boy's head off, and was then forced to replace it with that of the first creature he saw. The god of wisdom and remover of obstacles, Ganesh must be worshipped first to ensure offerings to other gods will be effective, which is why a Ganesh shrine or stone will invariably be found near other temples. Underscoring Hinduism's great sense of the mystical absurd, Ganesh's vehicle is a rat.

Of the other classical Hindu deities, only **Annapurna**, the goddess of grain and abundance (her name means "Full of Grain"), and **Saraswati**, the goddess of learning and culture, receive much attention in Nepal. Saraswati is normally depicted holding a *vina*, a musical instrument something like a sitar.

Prayer and ritual

In practice, Hinduism is chiefly concerned with the performance of day-to-day rituals. **Puja**, a gift to the divine which acts as worship, is particularly important. It can be done before a shrine in the home – and should in fact be performed first and last thing – at a public temple, or simply on an ad hoc basis: when encountering a sacred cow in the street, for instance, or while whizzing past a particular shrine on a motorbike. In a more formal *puja*, offerings (*prasad*) are made to the chosen god: flowers (usually marigolds), incense sticks, light (in the form of butter lamps), *abhir* (coloured powder) and "pure" foods such as rice, milk or sweets. In return for the *puja*, the worshipper often receives a mark (*tilak*, or *tika* in Nepali) on the forehead, usually made of sandalwood paste, ash or coloured powders.

If the day is regulated by *puja*, the year is measured out in seasonal festivals. The most important Nepali festivals, **Dasain** and **Tihar** (see p.44), both take place in the autumn. Life, meanwhile, is marked by key **rites of passage** (*samskaras*). Among the most important in Nepal are the ceremony for a baby's first rice and the *upanayana* or "**rebirth**" rite for higher-caste (Baahun and Chhetri) pubescent boys. The boy's head is shaved (except for a small tuft at the back) and he is given the sacred thread (*janai*) to wear sash-like over one shoulder, next to the skin, signifying his twice-born status. In some communities, especially Newari ones, girls may undergo *barha*, a purification rite around the time of first menstruation. **Weddings** are hugely important and correspondingly lengthy, involving endless processions, gifts and offerings. In Nepal, they're often loudly signalled by a live band – either the traditional Nepali ensemble of *sahanai* (shawm), *damaha* (large kettledrum), *narsinga* (C-shaped horn), *jhyaali* (cymbals) and *dholaki* (two-sided drum) or, for more urban types,

Hindu bhajan and Tantric hymns

The most visible form of Hindu sacred music is **bhajan** – devotional hymn-singing, usually performed in front of temples and in the half-covered loggias, or *sattals*, of rest houses. *Bhajan* groups gather on auspicious evenings to chant praises to Ram, Krishna or other Hindu deities and to recite classical devotional poetry. Like a musical *puja*, the haunting verses are repeated over and over to the mesmeric beat of the tabla and the drone of the harmonium. The group of (male) singers usually follows one lead voice, gradually coming together as the hymn accelerates to a triumphant, energising conclusion. During festivals, round-the-clock vigils are sometimes sponsored by wealthy patrons.

Bhajan is mostly a Hindu import, but Newars have their own style, often sung in the Newari language and sometimes even invoking Newari Buddhist deities. Some Newari Buddhist priests still also sing esoteric **Tantric hymns** which, when accompanied by **mystical dances** and hand postures, are believed to have immense occult power. The secrets of these are closely guarded by initiates, but a rare public performance is held on Buddha Jayanti, when five *vajracharya* costumed as the Pancha Buddha dance at Swayambhu.

The pace of change

Nepal's unique allure has long been defined by its inaccessibility and by its trekking trails. Until the 1950s, the only way even to get to the capital was to walk. There were a few, rare exceptions. VIPs were carried in on palanquins and, for a few heady decades in the 1930s and 40s, the royal elite could cruise on Kathmandu's few roads in cars dismantled and imported piecemeal from India – either on the backs of porters or on an astonishing 42km ropeway. Everyone else came on foot, and only a handful of Westerners were ever allowed in at all.

The gates open

The earthquake of Indian independence, in 1948, inevitably sent aftershocks up into Nepal. Kathmandu could no longer remain a medieval kingdom, walled off from the world by its fortress mountains. The first **plane** landed in the Kathmandu Valley in 1953, and in the same year, the successful British Everest expedition made the long trek to Solu Khumbu, fording rivers as they went. Three years later, the tortuous, hairpinning **Tribhuwan Rajpath** was completed, connecting Kathmandu to its southern neighbour.

Nepal was at last opening itself to the world. Roads through the mighty central hills are nightmarishly difficult to build and maintain but, in the 1960s, the **Chinese** managed to bulldoze and dynamite the jolting Arniko Highway from the Tibetan border, right through the dramatic Bhote Koshi gorge. The bridges, it was said, were exactly strong enough to carry a Chinese tank. The Chinese also funded the Prithvi Highway, which joined Kathmandu with Pokhara – and **India** helpfully chipped in with a link from Pokhara to its own border, at Sonauli.

Bridges, airstrips and tarmac

Nepal was now joined to both its neighbours, but had to pray for **regional peace**. Sandwiched between two mighty and mutually suspicious giants, it could ill afford to become a battleground. New roads were built during the 1960s, but the more significant change was taking place in the hills, where scores of rivers and gorges were spanned by

Porter with a heavy doko ▲

Lukla airstrip ▼

Mule caravan, Annapurna region ▼

spidery suspension footbridges. They might tremble alarmingly but could save villagers hours or even days of walking. Airstrips were being hammered out in remote areas, too, bringing government, medicines and post to mountain regions. In the south, the plains and forests were pierced by the Mahendra Highway which, by the early 1980s, sped east–west though the Terai in one unbroken (if not smooth) ribbon.

Tractors, trucks, jeeps, buses

Then change seemed to slow. A few single tracks inched their way into the hills, then abruptly stopped. From the early 1990s, some communities decided they were unwilling to wait for the tarmac, and began blasting and digging on their own account. First a tractor would make its way through. Then came the trucks, pouring cheap utensils and Indian vegetables into the roadside markets – which soon shouldered aside the old hilltop bazaars. Overloaded jeeps followed, accompanied by overnight tea stalls. Finally, the first gaudy bus would roar and bounce its way through, generally to local rejoicing.

Thanks in part to the army, which sought to bring its military campaign into the Maoist heartlands, "feeder roads" gradually pushed their way up from the highways into the hills in the 2000s. "Green roads" crept towards the district capitals. But political and geographical instability meant that either protests or landslides could still blockade Kathmandu in a matter of moments. Building new routes from the capital remained the priority.

▲ Snowy mountain road near Muktinath

▼ Local bus negotiating an unpaved road

Jeep on a rough road ▲

Trekker and guide, Solu Khumbu ▼

Himalayan highways

As this guidebook was written, new roads were finally being completed in the famed Himalayan trekking areas. The extravagantly beautiful Kali Gandaki gorge has now been penetrated and, in a few years, it will be possible to drive to the Chinese border through once-forbidden Upper Mustang. The Trisuli road now creeps beyond the trailhead for the Langtang trek; before long it will reach Rasuwagadhi and the Tibetan border. New earthen roads bump their way south from the Kathmandu Valley, making for the Terai. And once the tarmac is dry, the Japanese-funded Sindhulimadi Highway will provide a fast route to India via the ancient town of Dhulikhel.

Nepal's future

Every part of Nepal that is touched by a road changes forever. Porters no longer people the trails. Nepalis can get to hospitals and universities. Cheap imports arrive in ever greater quantity. And what was once a country whose every step was measured at walking pace, whose people met and talked with each other (and with foreign visitors) on the hill trails, becomes a little more like the rest of the world.

Yak caravan near Everest ▼

The dawn of trekking

"Trekking" was the mid-1960s brainchild of former Gurkha officer, Colonel Jimmy Roberts. He thought tourists might enjoy the porter-supported walk-ins of mountaineering expeditions – without the climb at the end. Of course, Nepalis have been walking in the hills for centuries, and Nepal is crisscrossed by hundreds of everyday trails which aren't featured on any "trekking route". Few ever see a Western hiker.

a brass band in military-style uniforms. The other key rite is, of course, the **funeral**. Hindus cremate their dead, and the most sacred place to do so in Nepal is beside the river at Pashupatinath, just outside Kathmandu. Mourning sons are supposed to shave their heads and wear white.

Priests can be full-time professionals or simply the local Brahman. They officiate at the more important rites and festivals, and may also give private consultations for wealthier patrons at times of illness or important decisions. Temple priests preside over the act of **darshan** (audience with a deity), providing consecrated water for the devotee to wash him or herself and to bathe the deity, leading the *puja* and the symbolic offering of food to the deity, and bestowing the **tika** on the devotee's forehead.

The caste system

One of the Hinduism's unique features is the apartheid-like **caste system**, which theoretically divides humanity into four main *varnas*, or groups. The Rig Veda, Hinduism's oldest text, proclaimed that Brahmans had issued from the head and mouth of the supreme creator, Kshatriyas from his chest and arms, Vaishyas from his thighs and Sudras from his feet. In Nepal, the system is thought to have been instituted by the fourteenth-century king **Jayasthiti Malla**, who further subdivided his subjects into 64 hereditary occupations – a system which remained enshrined in Nepali law until 1964.

Discriminating according to **caste** is now illegal in Nepal, though most "higher" caste Hindus are still careful about ritual pollution, being careful not to accept food or water from lower castes, and avoiding physical contact with them. Marriage has been slowest to change: intercaste couplings are still shocking, often resulting in families breaking off contact – a serious punishment in a country where connections are everything. Escaping occupational caste has become much easier, but a low-caste person will still have difficulty running a shop, for example, since higher castes may well refuse to enter it.

The usual term for caste in Nepali is **jaat**, though it can signify ethnicity and traditional occupation, as well as caste in the proper sense. A further subdivision is **thar**, usually defined as a **clan**. Members of a *thar* have a common surname, which may or may not indicate common lineage, but may often indicate a hereditary occupation and position in the social hierarchy – and may enforce caste-like rules regarding marriage.

Baahuns

Although **Baahuns** (Brahmans) belong to the highest, priestly caste, they're not necessarily the wealthiest members of society, nor are they all priests. However, their historic ability to read and write has long given them a significant edge in Nepali society, and they have tended to occupy the best government and professional jobs – even half the Maoists' leaders belong to the caste. Rural Baahuns have a reputation for aggressive moneylending that is sometimes deserved.

Baahuns are supposed to maintain their caste purity by eschewing foods such as onions, hens' eggs and alcohol, and they are technically prohibited from eating with lower castes – including foreigners – or even permitting them to enter the house. In practice, the stricter rules are only followed by traditional families in the remote West of Nepal. Priest-work – which usually consists of reading Sanskrit prayers and officiating over rites for fixed fees – is usually a family business. Some Baahuns make a full-time living out of it, others officiate part-time alongside other work.

Chhetris

The majority of **Parbatiyas** – the descendants of Hindus from India who live in the hills – are **Chhetris**. They are ranked in the classical caste system as Kshatriyas, the caste of warriors and kings. Like Baahuns, they rank among the "twice-born" castes, because men are symbolically "reborn" at thirteen and thereafter wear a sacred thread (*janai*) over one shoulder. While Baahuns usually claim pure bloodlines and exhibit classic, aquiline "Indian" features, many Chhetris have more mixed parentage. Some descend from the Khasa people of the western hills, others are the offspring of Baahun and Khasa marriages and are known as the Khatri Chhetri, or "KC" for short. Those whose Khasa ancestors didn't convert or intermarry are called **Matwaali Chhetris** – "alcohol-drinking" Chhetris – but because they follow a form of shamanism and don't wear the sacred thread, they're sometimes thought to be a separate ethnic group. Chhetris who claim pure Kshatriya blood – notably the aristocratic **Thakuri** subcaste of the far west, who are related to the former royal family – can be as twitchy about caste regulations as Baahuns. Chhetris have long been favoured for commissions in the military and, to a lesser extent, jobs in other branches of government and industry. Significantly, the Shah dynasty was Chhetri, and their rule owed much to the old warrior-caste mentality.

Dalits – "untouchables"

A significant number of Sudras – members of the "untouchable" caste – immigrated to Nepal's hills over the centuries. The members of this caste are now known as **Dalits**, or "the oppressed", and they certainly suffer severe disadvantages in Nepali society, being typically landless and uneducated, and lacking access to education, health facilities or representation in government. Many villages have an attached Dalit hamlet, often a cluster of smaller, meaner dwellings lacking the terracotta-and-white two-tone decoration of their neighbours Although untouchability was officially abolished in 1963, Dalits threaten orthodox Hindus with ritual pollution, and in many parts of the country they're not allowed to enter temples, homes or even tea stalls. Another name for the dalits is the **occupational castes**, as they fall into several occupation-based *thars*, such as the Sarki (leatherworkers), Kami (blacksmiths), Damai (tailors/musicians) and Kumal (potters). While the importance of their labour traditionally helped offset their lowly status, nowadays they cannot compete with imported manufactured goods. Many are turning to tenant farming, portering and day-labouring to make ends meet.

The ethnic groups of the hills

The ethnic peoples of the hills, or **janajaatis**, don't quite fit into the caste system, as their roots typically lie outside the Hindu homeland, to the north and west. Internal migration has led to much intermixing, however, and most hill peoples now live alongside caste Hindus: Gurungs and Magars in the mid-West (see p.257), Tamangs in the central hills (see p.216), Rais and Limbus in the east (see p.388). As a result, the *janajaatis* have been given a place half inside Nepal's caste system: practices such as eating meat and drinking alcohol have placed them below Chhetris but above Dalits. This puts them roughly on a par with foreigners (*bideshis*), incidentally – though Westerners are technically untouchable.

Each ethnic group has its own indigenous myths, beliefs and ritual practices, often centring around nature worship, propitiation of spirits, shamanism and veneration of ancestors. Many Rais and Limbus, however, are partly or largely "Hinduized" in terms of religion, while Magars and Gurungs have been more strongly influenced by Tibetan Buddhism. (Tamangs, Sherpas and other mountain groups are usually fairly orthodox Buddhists.) In recent decades,

movements have sprung up to assert "authentic" religious identities for the
ethnic groups of the hills, but these often owe as much to Hindu reform
movements as to genuine tribal tradition.

Buddhism

The Buddha was born Siddhartha Gautama in what is now Nepal (see p.293)
in the fifth or sixth century BC. His teachings sprang out of Hinduism's ascetic
traditions, adapting its doctrines of reincarnation and *karma*, along with many

Tantrism

Nepal's highly coloured religious practices owe much to the feverish influence of
Tantrism, a ritualistic and esoteric strain of religion which courses through the religious
blood of Hindus and Buddhists alike. The Tantric cults originated in the Shiva worship
of Nepal and the surrounding Himalayan regions in around the eighth and ninth
centuries, but their influence soon spread across India, pervading both Hinduism and
Buddhism. When India succumbed to first Islamic and then British overlords, Nepal
became not just the last remaining Hindu kingdom, but the bastion of Tantric traditions.
Tibet, meanwhile, developed its own distinctively Tantric version of Buddhism.

So strong did Tantrism become in Nepal, that the entire Kathmandu Valley – then
known as **Nepal mandala** – could be conceived as a kind of interactive map of the
divine cosmos, studded with religiously supercharged sites and temples. Many sites
are dedicated to the chief objects of Tantric worship: the "Great God" Shiva, and his
female counterpart Shakti, the mother goddess. In Nepal, they are often depicted in
art as the fierce god Bhairab and his terrifying consort Kali, and sometimes seen
locked in a fierce sexual embrace which symbolizes the creative unity of the male and
female principles: masculinity is conceived as passive and intellectual, female as
active and embodied; together, they sustain the life force of the universe.

Buddhist tantra, known as **Vajrayana** ("Thunderbolt Way"), reverses the symbolism
of these two forces and makes the male principle of "skill in means" or compassion
the active force, and the female principle of "wisdom" passive. In tantric rituals, these
forces are symbolized by the hand-held "lightning-bolt sceptre" (*vajra*; *dorje* in
Tibetan), which represents the male principle, and the bell (*ghanti*), representing the
female. Expanding on Mahayana's all-male pantheon, Vajrayana introduces female
counterparts to the main Buddha figures and some of the *bodhisattva*, and
sometimes depicts them in sexual positions.

Tantra has nothing to do with the Western invention of "**tantric sex**". Or almost
nothing: some extreme Hindu followers turned orthodoxy on its head by embracing
the forbidden, seeking spiritual liberation by means of transgression. Ascetics from
the Kapalika Tantric sect took up residence in cemeteries, following "left-hand" ritual
practices such as the consumption of meat and alcohol, and the use of sexual fluids
in sacrifice. But these now-notorious rituals were always rare, and Tantrism today is
chiefly concerned with using rituals to speed up the search for enlightenment or
union with the divine. Quasi-magical techniques are passed from teachers to
initiates, who progress upwards through levels of understanding. Through meditation
and the practice of yoga, the body's energy can be made to ascend through the
seven (or sometimes six) *chakras* or psychic nodes, beginning at the perineum and
ending at the crown of the head, where blissful union with the god Shiva can be
achieved. **Mantras**, or sacred verbal formulas, are chanted; worship is intensified
with the use of **mudras** (hand gestures). Arcane geometrical diagrams known as
yantras or **mandalas** are drawn to symbolize and activate divine principles.

yogic practices, but rejecting the caste system and belief in a creator God. The essence of the Buddha's teaching is encapsulated in the **four noble truths**: existence is suffering; suffering is caused by desire; the taming of desire ends suffering; and desire can be tamed by following the **eightfold path**. Wisdom and compassion are key qualities, but the ultimate Buddhist goal is **nirvana**, a state of non-being reached by defeating the "three poisons" of greed, hatred and delusion.

Buddhism quickly became a full-time monastic pursuit but it also evolved a less ascetic, populist strand known as **Mahayana** ("Great Vehicle"), which took root in Nepal from around the fifth century. Reintroducing elements of worship and prayer, Mahayana Buddhism developed its own pantheon of *bodhisattva* – enlightened intermediaries, something akin to Catholic saints, who have forgone *nirvana* until all humanity has been saved. Some were a repackaging of older Hindu deities. Nepal – and especially the Newar people of the Kathmandu Valley (see p.180) – gradually developed its own unique blend of Hindu and Buddhist traditions, with a strong **Tantric** flavour (see p.435). Buddhism reached its apogee in the medieval Malla dynasty, but following the Mughal invasion of India, the arrival of orthodox Hindus from the south and west increasingly diluted the Buddhist part of the mix. When the Hindu Shah dynasty took control of Nepal, in the latter half of the eighteenth century, Buddhism went into a long decline. The fortunes of Buddhism in Nepal only recovered thanks to the arrival of another wave of refugees, this time **Tibetans** fleeing the Chinese takeover during the 1950s. They brought with them their own unique form of the religion, **Vajrayana**. As a relatively structured typeset of beliefs and practices, it is now far stronger and more visible than the indigenous Nepalese strains.

Tibetan Buddhist ritual music

More astounding, even, than the polychrome decor of a **Tibetan Buddhist** monastery is its crashing, thumping, rasping ritual music. At the core of the ritual is the recital or hymn-like **chanting of texts**, which usually begins with the master, or cantor, and spreads in rhythmic ripples down the rows of monks. Monks from the Gelug-pa order (see p.438), most dramatically, use the extraordinary overtone or "throat-singing" technique; this ultra-low, growling tone produces rich harmonics sometimes called the *gyü-ke*, or "Tantric voice". Alongside the virtue regarded as inherent in the recitation of holy texts, such demanding vocal techniques create their own meditational discipline.

In the Tibetan Tantric tradition chanting alternates antiphonically with **instrumental music**, whose crashes and blasts and bangs punctuate and disrupt the hypnotic vocal line, seeking to lift the mind out of its ordinary groove. Music can represent fierce protective Buddhas or calming, peaceful ones, and different instruments have different ritual significance or uses. The *dung-dkar* conch, for instance, embodies the clear voice of the Buddha. The *rkang-gling* trumpet, traditionally made from a human thighbone, is apparently like the whinnying of horses on their way to paradise. Cymbals can be soft and peaceful (*gsil-snyan*) or brassily fierce (*rol-mo*). The *rgna*, or double-drum with its distinctively crooked beater, typically leads the orchestra. Oboe-like *rgya-gling* shawms play intense, microtonally sliding melody lines, while the long (up to ten feet long), alpenhorn-like *dung* trumpets play sustained, almost subsonic rasping notes in discordant pairs. The *dril-bu* hand bell and *damaru* rattle drum usually mark off different sections of the ritual. (The *damaru* is a particularly powerful instrument: commonly used by shamans in Nepal, it may be made of two human half-skulls, and the pair of pellet beaters should ideally contain male and female pubic hairs.)

Increasing numbers of lavishly endowed **gompas**, or monasteries, have sprung up all over Nepal in the last twenty years, thanks to the growing wealth of the Tibetan community and the generous sponsorship of Western followers. Rather like medieval cathedrals, *gompas* are vehicles for esoteric religious symbolism as much as places of worship. Fierce guardian demons (*dharmapala*) flank the entrance, while the interior walls are riotously covered in paintings of deities, Buddhas and geometric *mandalas*, and hung all over with silken **thangka** icons. Gorgeous banners of brightly coloured silk brocade hang from the ceiling, often with elaborately carved and gilded cornices and panelling. On low trays, butter lamps burn pungently alongside heaps of rice piled onto three-tiered silver stands, rows of incense sticks and offerings of fruit, money, flowers and conical dough cakes called *torma* – sacrifices of a uniquely vegetarian kind. The eye is inevitably drawn, however, to the golden statues of **Buddhas** and **bodhisattvas** which line the altars. Often mistaken for deities, these provide a focus for meditation as well as an object of devotion. The most popular figures are **Shakya-muni**, the historical Buddha; **Avalokiteshwara** (**Chenrezig** in Tibetan), a white male figure with four arms (or, sometimes, a thousand), who represents compassion; **Tara**, a white or green female figure, also representing compassion; **Manjushri**, an orange-yellow male youth gracefully holding a sword above his head, who represents wisdom; and the founder of the monastery's sect, perhaps the Nyingma-pa's Padma Sambhava, better known as **Guru Rinpoche**. Though these figures are peaceful and benign, there are also wrathful bulging-eyed figures wearing human skins and bearing skulls filled with blood; they symbolize the energy and potency of the enlightened state, and the sublimation of our crudest energies.

Vajrayana – Tibetan Buddhism

Buddhism was originally exported from Nepal to Tibet, courtesy of the Licchavi princess **Bhrikuti**, who married Tibetan emperor Songstän Gampo in the seventh century. At the time, Tibet was under the sway of a native shamanic religion known as **Bön**, and Buddhism absorbed many of Bön's symbols and rituals. (Even today vestiges of the **Bön** tradition may be encountered while trekking in Nepal: for example, a follower of Bön will circle a religious monument anticlockwise, the opposite direction to a Buddhist.)

Buddhism only really took off in Nepal and Tibet in the eighth century, however, thanks to the founding father **Padmasambhava**. Better known as **Guru Rinpoche** or "Precious Teacher" – and recognizable in paintings by his wide-eyed stare, and the thunderbolt symbol and skull-cup he holds in each hand – he introduced magical and ritualistic practices from the Tantric cult (see p.435) that was then sweeping across South Asia. In doing so, he apparently meditated in just about every cave in the region, frequently leaving foot or handprints in the rock as signs of his passing.

Bön and Tantra proved an explosive mix, giving rise to the spectacular branch of Buddhism now known as **Vajrayana**, or "thunderbolt way" Buddhism. It takes its name from the *vajra* or thunderbolt (*dorje* in Tibetan), a diamond sceptre or dagger used in Tantric rituals to signify indestructability. True to its Tantric roots, Vajrayana placed great emphasis on close contact with a **lama**, or spiritual guide, who steers the initiate through the complex meditations and rituals, and progressively reveals teachings at ever higher and more esoteric levels. (It's sometimes called Lamaism for this reason.) The most important lamas are regarded as **tulkus**, reincarnations of previous teachers.

C

CONTEXTS | Religion

Four main sects developed in Tibet, all now represented in Nepal. The oldest, founded by Padmasambhava, is the Nyingma-pa sect – known as the "**Red Hats**" for obvious reasons. The Sakya-pa and Kagyu-pa orders emerged in the eleventh and twelfth centuries – the latter inspired by the Tibetan mystic Marpa and his enlightened disciple Milarepa, who also meditated his way around Nepal. The Gelug-pa sect, or "**Yellow Hats**", led by the Dalai Lama, is the only one that takes a significantly different theological line. Born out of a fifteenth-century reform movement to purge Lamaism of its questionable religious practices, it places greater emphasis on study and intellectual debate.

Vajrayana disciples make heavy use of quasi-magical rituals, such as the ringing of bells, the reading aloud of holy texts and the chanting of **mantras** or sacred syllables – most importantly, *Om mani padme hum* (pronounced "om mani peme hung" in Tibetan and meaning "Hail to the jewel in the lotus"). In part, these rituals are aids to **meditation**, the most important action of all, but they also serve to accelerate the passage of the disciple towards the ultimate goal: enlightenment.

The most visible sign of Vajrayana Buddhism is the **stupa** (*chorten* in Tibetan), a dome-like stone structure which serves to enshrine the relics of the saints and to act as a giant abstract representation of Buddhist beliefs. Around Kathmandu's Swayambhu stupa, for instance, stand five statues representing the transcendent or *dhyani* (meditating) Buddhas. Stupas are also surrounded by **prayer wheels and prayer flags**, Tibetan innovations which allow written mantras to be not spoken but spun or fluttered into the air.

Newari religion

Ask a Newar whether he's Hindu or Buddhist, the saying goes, and he'll answer "yes": after fifteen centuries of continuous exposure to both faiths, the Newars of the Kathmandu Valley have concocted a unique synthesis of the two. Until the eighteenth century, most Newars held fast to the original monastic form of Tantric Buddhism – as the *bahal* of Kathmandu and Patan still bear witness. Gradually, the Kathmandu Valley became "**Hinduized**" thanks largely to the Hindu kings who ruled it. The monasteries largely disappeared, and the title of Vajracharya (Buddhist priest) became a hereditary subcaste much like that of the Baahun (Brahman) priests. When Newars refer to themselves as **Buddha margi** (Buddhist) or **Shiva margi** (Hindu), they often do so only to indicate that they employ a Vajracharya or Baahun priest. Yet many *jyapu* (farmers) will attend Hindu festivals and use Vajracharyas as well.

Animal sacrifice is an important part of Hindu – but not Buddhist – Newari religious practice (see p.176). Newari priests don't perform sacrifices, but they do preside over the rituals that precede them. Similar ceremonies and feasts are held at private gatherings of patrilineal groups during the Newars' many **festivals** (see pp.42–45) and during **digu puja**, the annual reunion based around the worship of the clan deity (*digu dyo*).

Many other members of Newari society function in spiritual capacities, either as full-time parapriests or in bit parts during rites of passage and festivals. Members of the Vajracharya subcaste, **Gubhajus** are Tantric healers who employ *vajrayana* techniques and accoutrements to cure ailments caused by malevolent spirits. **Baidyas** play a similar role but draw from a more diverse range of Hindu, Buddhist and shamanic techniques including *jhar-phuk* ("sweeping" away bad influences and "blowing" on healing mantras), *puja*, amulets and ayurvedic medicines. **Jyotish** – astrologers – specialize in helping clients deal with planetary influences and their corresponding deities (see box opposite).

A visit to the astrologer

His name is Joshi – in Newari society, all members of the astrologer subcaste are called Joshi – and to get to his office I have to duck through a low doorway off a courtyard in the old part of Patan and feel my way up two flights of wooden steps in the dark, climbing towards a glimmer of light and the sounds of low murmuring. At the landing I take off my shoes and enter the sanctum. Joshi-ji doesn't even look up. He's sitting cross-legged on the floor behind a low desk, glasses perched on the end of his nose, scowling over a sheaf of papers and, except for his Nepali-style clothes, looking exactly the way I'd always pictured Professor Godbole in *A Passage to India*. Shelves of books and scrolls are heaped behind him, and over in one corner a small shrine is illuminated by a low-watt bulb and a smouldering stick of incense.

To Newars, the **astrologer** is a counsellor, confessor, general practitioner and guide through the maze of life. He acts as mediator between the self and the universe (which are one), and his prognostications are considered as important as a priest's blessings and as vital as a doctor's diagnosis. He knows most of his clients from birth. For new parents, the astrologer will prepare complex planetary charts based on the baby's precise time and place of **birth**, together with a lengthy interpretation detailing personality traits, health hazards, vocational aptitude, characteristics of the ideal marriage partner, and a general assessment of the newborn's prospects. When a **marriage** is contemplated, he will study the horoscopes of the prospective couple to make sure the match is suitable to determine the most auspicious wedding date. During an **illness**, he may prescribe a protective amulet, gemstone or herbal remedy corresponding to the planets influencing the patient. He may also be consulted on the advisability of a business decision or a major purchase.

Although it's misleading to speak in terms of planetary "influences", the *karma* revealed by an astrologer's **horoscope** strongly implies the future course of one's life. The astrologer's role is to suggest the best way to play the hand one was dealt. Hindu astrology recognizes the usual twelve **signs of the zodiac**, albeit under Sanskrit names, and assigns similar attributes to the planets and houses as in the West. The basic **birth chart** indicates the **sun sign** (the sign corresponding to the sun's position at the time of birth), the ascendant (the sign rising above the eastern horizon at the time of birth) and the positions of the moon and the five planets known to the ancients, plus a couple of other non-Western points of reference. The positions of all of these are also noted in relation to the twelve **houses**, each of which governs key aspects of the subject's life (health, relationships and so on). Where Western astrologers use the **tropical zodiac**, in which Aries is always assumed to start on the spring equinox (March 21, give or take a day), Hindu astrologers go by the **sidereal zodiac**, which takes all its measurements from the *actual* positions of the constellations.

In practice, if you have a horoscope done in Nepal, you'll probably be presented with a beautifully calligraphed scroll detailing all these measurements in chart and tabular form, using both tropical and sidereal measurements. **Interpretation** of the chart is an intuitive art requiring great eloquence and finesse. The astrologer can draw on numerous texts but at the end of the day, the usefulness of the reading comes down to his own skill and experience. As I found on my visit to Joshi-ji, the specifics aren't everything. The astrologer isn't peddling facts; he's offering insight, hope, reassurance and a dash of theatre.

David Reed

The Newari pantheon

All the Hindu and Buddhist deities already discussed are fair game for Newars, along with a few additional characters of local invention. Some deities specialize in curing diseases, others bring good harvests – as far as Newars are concerned, it doesn't matter whether they're Hindu or Buddhist so long as they do the job.

The widely worshipped **Ajima**, or **Mai**, the Newars' grandmother goddess, is both feared as a bringer of disease and misfortune and revered as a protectress against the same. There are innumerable Ajimas, each associated with a particular locality. Some are also worshipped as Durga, Bhagwati or Kali, including the **Ashta Matrika**, the eight mother goddesses, whose temples in and around Kathmandu are considered especially powerful. Similar are the Tantric **Bajra Yoginis** (or Vajra Joginis), who command their own cults at four temples around the Kathmandu Valley. Local manifestations of Ajima are represented by clusters of round stones (*pith*) located at intersections and other strategic places. Chwasa Ajima, the Ajima of the crossroads, has the power to absorb death pollution, which is why Newars traditionally deposited possessions of deceased persons at crossroads. **Nag** (snake deities), who control the rains and are responsible for earthquakes, may be similarly indicated by modest roadside markers.

Machhendranath, the rainmaker *par excellence*, is known by Buddhist Newars as **Karunamaya**, and associated with Avalokiteshwara, the *bodhisattva* of compassion. Depending on his incarnation (he is said to have 108), he may be depicted as having anything up to a thousand arms and eleven heads. **Kumari**, the "Living Goddess", is another example of Newari syncretism (religious fusing): although acknowledged to be an incarnation of the Hindu goddess Durga, she is picked from a Buddhist-caste family. **Bhimsen**, a mortal hero in the Hindu Mahabharat, who is rarely worshipped in India, has somehow been elevated to be the patron deity of Newari shopkeepers, both Hindu and Buddhist. **Manjushri**, the *bodhisattva* of wisdom, plays the lead part in the Kathmandu Valley's creation myth, and is often confused with Saraswati, the Hindu goddess of knowledge. He is always depicted with a sword, with which he cuts away ignorance and attachment, and sometimes also with book,

Supernatural forces

Nepal has a rich lore of **demons**, **ghosts** and **spirits** who meddle in human affairs and, like deities, must be propitiated to safeguard passage through their respective domains. Demons are sometimes thought to be the wrathful or perverted manifestations of deities, or more often as supernatural ogres, vampires and the like. Some demons, such as the *lakhe*, are regarded somewhat fondly, or, like the *betal*, can also serve as temple protectors. *Bhut pret* – restless ghosts – are thought to be the spirits of people who died an accidental or violent death and were not administered the proper funeral rites. Other evil spirits take the form of poltergeist-like dwarfs, furry balls, or temptresses with their feet pointing backwards; the design of traditional Newari windows is intended to prevent such spirits from entering the house. Since spirits are believed to attack mainly at night and are repelled by light, it is sometimes said that they are driven out when electricity arrives in a village.

Nepalis often blame their troubles on **witches** (*bokshi*), who are believed to be able to cast "black" tantric spells by giving the evil eye or reciting mantras over their victims' food. Evidence of bewitchment is often seen in bruises called "*bokshi* bites". "Witches" are usually neighbours, in-laws or other people known to their alleged victims. Although laws prohibit false accusations of witchcraft, this doesn't protect many people (particularly elderly women) from suffering unspoken fear and resentment for their alleged dark arts.

A final category of supernatural forces is negative **planetary influences** (*graha dosa*), caused by the displeasure of the deity associated with the offending planet.

bow, bell and *vajra*. **Tara**, the embodiment of the female principle in Vajrayana Buddhism, assumes special meaning for Newars, who consider her the deification of an eighth-century Nepali princess.

Shamanism

Shamans – sometimes called medicine men, witch doctors and oracles, or **jhankri** and **dhami** in Nepali – exist to mediate between the physical and spiritual realms. Shamanistic practices are often found alongside animism, or nature-worship, and the ethnic groups of Nepal's hills, including those who would unhestitatingly describe themselves as Hindu or Buddhist, will often turn to a *jhankri*. Urbane Nepalis may publicly ridicule the shaman in favour of more "modern" beliefs such as orthodox Hinduism, but many will privately call on a shaman to exorcise a new house or deal with a case of toothache. Even in Kathmandu, the shaman's double-headed drum can sometimes be heard beating behind closed doors.

Most ethnic groups clearly distinguish between the true shaman, whose duties, rituals and powers are concerned with the spiritual world, and other types of tribal priest, whose concerns may be with seasonal rituals, rites of passage or tribal myth, and whose roles have been more easily absorbed by mainstream religion. For all the many local variations, a *jhankri* – usually carrying a double-sided drum and often wearing a headdress of peacock feathers – is always unmistakable. And even across ethnic and religious divides, *jhankris* may come together on high hilltops or at lakes deep in the mountains for *melas*, or religious fairs.

The *jhankri* may be "called", or born, or both, and his (almost never her) main job is to maintain spiritual and physical balance, and to restore it when it has been upset. As a healer, he may examine the entrails of animals for signs, gather medicinal plants from the forest, perform sacrifices, exorcise demons, chant magical incantations to invoke helper deities, or conduct any number of other rituals. As an oracle, he may fall into a trance and act as a mouthpiece of the gods, advising, admonishing and consoling listeners. As the spiritual sentry of his community, he must ward off ghosts, evil spirits and angry ancestors – sometimes by superior strength, often by trickery. All this, plus his duties as funeral director, dispenser of amulets, teller of myths and consecrator of holy ground and so on, puts the *jhankri* at the very heart of religious and social life in the hills.

Few visitors to Nepal will encounter a *jhankri*, as their rituals are usually performed in homes, at night, and shamans have a tendency to guard their esoteric knowledge jealously, wrapping it up in archaic, poetic language that veers between the mystical and the mystifying. There are signs of new confidence, however, with a Gurung shamanic cultural centre and training school in Pokhara.

Islam and Christianity

A significant number of **Muslims** inhabit the western Terai, especially around Nepalgunj, where they're in the majority. **Musalmans**, as they're called in Nepal, form a distinctive cultural group. They have their own language (Urdu), clothing styles and customs – including the institution of **purdah** for women. In the hill areas, Nepali Musalmans are traditionally wandering traders. They specialize in selling bangles and in "teasing" cotton quilts, and they can often be heard in Kathmandu and other towns calling on housewives to come-buy-my-wares, or giving a prompting twang on the instrument of their cotton-teasing trade. Many are now farmers, tailors or run clothing shops.

Christianity barely registered in Nepal for centuries, due to a vigorously enforced ban on missionary conversions. The interdict was largely lifted in 1990, however, and since 2006 Nepal has been an officially secular state. The result has been a significant influx of evangelicals, mostly targeting lower castes and other disadvantaged groups – and a corresponding growth of churches, especially in the Kathmandu Valley. There may be as many as half a million Nepali Christians today.

Development dilemmas

Development – or *bikas*, in Nepali – has been the country's political mantra ever since the Ranas were booted out of office in 1950. And yet Nepal remains one of the world's poorest nations, with a per-capita income of just $470 (a figure largely created by migrant labourers in the Middle East), and a quarter of the population living on less than a dollar a day. On the UN's 2008 Human Development Index, Nepal ranked 145th out of 153 countries.

Everything seems stacked against Nepal. It is landlocked, and squeezed between two economic giants of neighbours. It has few natural resources. The steep terrain makes farming inefficient and communications difficult. Earthquakes and monsoons can undo dams, roads and other infrastructure as fast as they're built. A combination of Hindu fatalism, the caste system and a legacy of aristocratic paternalism has long kept the doors of opportunity tightly shut – the regime did essentially nothing for its people before 1951. Since then, governments have apparently prioritized corruption and clientism over development – despite the incredible efforts of aid workers and local activists.

The development industry

Everyone loves to give **aid** to Nepal. The country receives some $500–800 million annually in direct grants and concessionary loans, making it one of the world's leading aid recipients on a per-capita basis. Foreign aid accounts for a staggering 55–70 per cent of the money spent by Nepal's government on projects (capital expenditure), and around a quarter of total expenditure; the joke goes that the country can't *afford* to develop.

Aid comes in many forms. **Bilateral** (and multilateral) aid – money directly given or lent by foreign governments, invariably with political or commercial strings attached – has financed most of the roads, dams and airports in the country. Social programmes tend to be carried out by international **non-governmental organizations (NGOs)**, which can be anything from giants such as Oxfam, CARE and Save the Children to a couple of highly motivated people doing fieldwork and raising sponsorship money at home. Voluntary NGOs, such as Britain's Voluntary Service Overseas (VSO) and the US Peace Corps, generally slot volunteers into existing government programmes. Increasingly important are revenues from **international lending bodies** such as the World Bank and Asian Development Bank (ADB), which both provide direct grants and act as brokers to arrange loans for big projects with commercial potential – usually irrigation and hydroelectric schemes. The ADB, for instance, is now the source of over twenty percent of Nepal's foreign aid.

Many of these organizations do excellent work. But paying imported experts ten or twenty times more than Nepalis to do the same job causes resentment and distorts the local economy. And large organizations are effectively obliged to fund large-scale projects, which may not always be the most appropriate or efficient options. Foreign aid can also foster a crippling **aid dependency**. The latest fashionable philosophy, therefore, is to finance **local NGOs**, which supposedly have a better handle on local problems and solutions. The result has been an explosion in Nepali organizations, blurring the distinction between genuine, grass-roots organizations run by the heroically dedicated, and quasi-companies tailoring themselves to fit the latest development buzz-words: sustainable, small-scale, women-focused, environmental – whatever. Lack of co-ordination results in monumental inefficiency, and lack of scrutiny means that some aren't doing much besides writing grant proposals.

Population

Nepal's population, roughly 29 million at the time of writing, is growing at an annual rate of some 2.25 percent, which means that each year there are more than half a million more Nepalis to feed and employ – and indeed requiring health care, education, clean water, sewage disposal, electricity and roads. The growth rate will remain high as long as women remain comparatively ill-educated and low-status, and as long as children are needed to fetch water, gather fuel and tend animals – and to care for the aged parents in the absence of pensions or state support. Moreover, Nepalis tend to have large families because they can't be sure all their children will survive. Hindus, especially, keep trying until they've produced at least one son, who alone can perform the prescribed rites (*shradha*) for his parents after their death.

It's often said that "development is the best contraceptive", and indeed, there is a close correlation between rising standards of living and declining birth rates. Unfortunately, in most countries this so-called **demographic transition** involves a period of rapid population growth until the birth rate settles down to match the lower death rate. Nepal seems to be in the middle of just such a boom, and it is only managed by migration. The hill peoples, especially men, have long sought work in Kathmandu, the Terai and India. Nowadays, young Nepali men are as likely to emigrate to the Middle East, China and – for those who can afford to get there – the West. Even so, the country's urban population is exploding. The population of the Kathmandu Valley more than doubled between the early 1990s and late 2000s, reaching almost two million, by some estimates. It is set to continue rising at an unsustainable rate.

Health and sanitation

The average **life expectancy** is now 63, up from 43 in 1975 – though the poor can still expect to live some fifteen years less than the average. The figure is heavily influenced by the distressingly high rate of child mortality: almost one out of every twenty children in Nepal dies before he or she reaches the age of five. (Still, this is a vast improvement over 1960, when the figure was almost one in three. Cheap oral rehydration packets are largely responsible for saving these lives.) The chief cause of death is nothing more complicated than **diarrhoea**, itself the consequence of poor sanitation. The majority of rural Nepalis are obliged to defecate in the open; even in urban areas, toilets are often inadequately designed and sewage systems conspicuous by their absence or inefficiency. As a result around half of Nepalis have access to safe water from springs, wells or communal taps.

Surviving infancy is only the start. Around half of Nepali children are **malnourished** and suffer from unceasing hunger and a relentless series of infections – of which the permanently snotty nose of the rural child is just one outward sign. Parasitic infections are also rife. The incidence of **tuberculosis** has declined, though an astonishing 45 percent of the population is thought to carry the disease, with forty thousand people a year developing it actively leading to more than five thousand deaths. **Leprosy** is also becoming more rare, though Nepal still has one of the highest per-capita rates in the world. And mosquito spraying in the Terai has reduced **malaria** cases to about five thousand annually – compared with two million a year during the 1950s.

Nepal avoided the **HIV-AIDS** epidemic for many years, but sex workers, long-distance truck-drivers and seasonal migrants provided a channel for transmission of the disease from India – one recent study found that two thirds of women trafficked into India for sex work acquired HIV. The infection is common among the country's thirty thousand-odd injecting drug users and twenty to thirty thousand sex workers, and starting to spread into the general population as well: roughly seventy thousand Nepalis are currently living with HIV–AIDS.

There are no statistics on **alcoholism**, but it is certainly one of the major public health problems among men from the hill ethnic groups. Since the late 1990s, Maoist-affiliated women's community groups have aggressively tackled drinking, and in government the Maoists have introduced ever-more stringent regulation, but drinking culture is fairly embedded. Tobacco-use seems if anything even more entrenched: more than half of adult Nepalis smoke, and they're not enjoying low-tar brands.

In the face of all these problems, access to **health care** is extremely poor. Many parochial hospitals lack even a single resident doctor, since the vast majority of qualified physicians prefer to practise privately in the Kathmandu Valley. For most Nepalis, medical assistance means a local *jhankri* (see p.441) or health post that's a day or more's walk (or piggyback ride) down the trail and where the only person on staff may effectively be the janitor, or perhaps an assistant with some ayurvedic training.

Agriculture

About eighty percent of Nepalis still make their living from agriculture, on some of the most intensively cultivated land in the world. For some, this means farming must be the focus of development – especially given the population growth. Nepal has been a net importer of rice since the 1970s, and localized **food deficits** are a serious problem, especially in the remote northwestern districts of Humla and Mugu, where famines and emergency food airlifts are a regular spring occurrence.

Clearing new land for cultivation only adds to deforestation (see p.446), so **productivity** has been chased instead. **High-yielding seeds** and animal breeds such as the Jersey cross – fondly known as *bikasi gai*, or "development cow" – have had some success, while **pesticides** and chemical **fertilizers** are now widely used in the Kathmandu Valley and Terai. In the hills, however, it can be impossible or uneconomic to transport these inputs. Where fertilizers are used, they're often misapplied. **Irrigation** is a promising area, but the big canal systems underwritten by the government and foreign funders are often inefficient and poorly maintained, and tend to benefit only the bigger landholdings. Tractors and other **mechanized equipment**, similarly, are only really workable on bigger farms in the plains.

Thanks to subdivision across generations, many farms have simply become too small to feed a family – which is why so many Nepalis are now undernourished. Many small farmers are locked in a hopeless cycle of debt, or have been forced to sell or hand over their land to unscrupulous moneylenders. Supplying **credit** through the official Agriculture Development Bank has grown impossibly bureaucratic, but microcredit loan programmes look more promising. Allowing farmers to grow cash crops is another possible solution, but roads are needed if farmers are going to compete with Indian imports.

Areas under Maoist control during the ten-year war saw large areas of land seized and **redistributed**, sometimes turned over to farms working on a "cooperative" model. In government, the Maoists have come under pressure to return much of it, and whether or not their promises of country-wide, "scientific" **land reform** will bear fruit is uncertain. Even the lowering of existing ceilings on individual land ownership is in question.

Deforestation

An expanding population needs not only more land, but more **firewood** and more **fodder** for animals – which, in Nepal, is gathered by hand in the forest. The result is **deforestation**, which itself causes erosion and landslides, thus reducing productivity and contributing to flooding. In practice, there are counterbalancing forces: the further people have to walk to find firewood or fodder, the more likely they are to emigrate, taking pressure off the area's resources.

No one has a clear idea of the rate of forest loss in Nepal but certainly the government got it badly wrong when it **nationalized the forests** in the 1950s. Since the 1980s, however, the policy of sustainable, locally managed **community forestry** has slowed, halted or even reversed deforestation in some areas. The **Terai** is the notable exception: trees have been clear-felled across the south to make way for settlers and earn from timber, and the vast majority of the magnificent native forest has disappeared. Fortunately, large chunks are now protected by **national parks** and wildlife or forest reserves. Perhaps a quarter of Nepal's total land cover is woodland, although less than half of that is true, "primary" forest.

Efforts to reduce deforestation produced one apparently brilliant solution, the "**smokeless**" **chulo** (stove), which burns wood more efficiently. The brilliant side-effect, however – reducing levels of health-destroying kitchen smoke – turned out to be problematic: insects were no longer smoked out of traditional thatched roofs, leading to infestations and increased use of corrugated metal. The miracle stoves also emit less light, causing increased dependency on kerosene for lamps or electricity – both of which require hard cash to purchase.

Electricity

Nepal's steep, mountain-fed rivers have enormous hydroelectric potential – enough to power the British Isles, by some estimates. Unfortunately, getting materials and technical experts into the rugged backcountry, not to mention handling the Himalayan-scale seismic problems, has made this potential difficult to harness. Currently, forty percent of Nepalis have access to electricity, but 85 percent of it comes from imported coal and diesel, and power is rarely found in rural areas – at night the hills still remain largely swathed in darkness. And electricity is no miracle solution. As far as most rural Nepalis are concerned, wood is free, whereas electricity costs rupees – and electric appliances cost dollars. And electrification can actually add to the pressure on forests, because good lighting encourages people to stay up late, burning more wood to keep warm.

To satisfy demand growing at ten percent a year, and currently estimated at 800MW (megawatts), at peak, Nepal has to persuade international donors and lending bodies to finance **hydroelectric** projects. The idea of building huge-scale storage dams fell out of favour in 1995, after the World Bank finally withdrew from the monstrous (404MW) **Arun III** project, citing environmental and social concerns. The policy now is mostly to license private-sector companies to build mostly small- to medium-sized "**run-of-river**" diversions; in recent years, the 70MW Middle Marsyangdi project, on the east side of the Annapurna range and the 144MW Kali Gandaki A project, on the west, have both started production.

But much more is needed. Even leaving aside the goal of exporting power to India, Nepal cannot keep up with domestic demand. In fact, it actually imports power from its southern neighbour – a fact which became painfully clear after the Koshi flood of 2008, which washed out a crucial transmission line from India. Alongside a lack of proper maintenance, failure to build sufficient new capacity during the Maoist insurgency, and a strangely dry and warm winter, the Koshi flood helped precipitate an **energy crisis** in the winter of 2008/9. Electricity production fell to 286MW in late 2008, well under half the peak demand, and the country experienced unprecedented levels of **load-shedding** (scheduled power cuts), losing all power for anything up to eighteen hours a day. Industry was crippled, government and business slowed to crawling pace and even tourism began to feel the shock.

Numerous big dams and hydro-power projects are currently in talks, or under licence and seeking funding. The huge (and hugely controversial) 750MW West Seti dam – proposed by an Australian company and funded by the ADB alongside Indian and Chinese banks – may yet be built, in spite of (or, rather, ignoring) local and environmental concerns. And in 2009, the government announced tax incentive schemes for smaller-scale hydro projects and, rather desperately, approved the installation of diesel plants. Yet none of this helps hill areas too remote to be economically connected to the grid. Extending the country's relatively successful **microhydro** projects, which supply electricity for a few hundred households each, would make more sense. Locally manufactured **solar water-heaters** are also promising, as are **biogas** plants, tank-like super-composters of manure and agricultural waste which collect the gas given off for burning.

Roads and paths

Roads largely benefit the wealthy: bus owners, truckers, merchants, building contractors, big farmers with cash crops to sell, tourists hurrying to trekking regions… Porters and shopkeepers along the former walking route, meanwhile, lose out. Nevertheless, roads lie at the heart of Nepal's development strategy because it's hard to deliver services, administer projects, maintain order or even collect taxes in areas not served by them. The government has long had the goal of extending roads to each of its 75 district headquarters, and only a handful remain. (Even Solu Khumbu, the celebrated Everest district, has a road creeping towards it from Okaldhunga, in the south.) Each year many new roads are boldly etched into hillsides, only to be washed away in the next monsoon. Foreign donors subsidize road building but rarely fund maintenance, so as the road network grows it also detiorates.

Before road-building began, footpath improvement was the focus. Early trekkers in Nepal spent much of their time wading; today miniature suspension bridges span the rivers on all the major routes – even if their wooden planking

The end of the road

Gazing down from the hill, over terraces of paddy fields, we could see the first truck making its hesitant journey up the spiralling new dust road. Local people ran down the main street of the bazaar to meet the first iron monster to complete the ascent. Excitement about the road lasted quite a while. Then people became less frightened and awe-struck, and the verges were no longer dotted with rapt, admiring observers. Those who could afford the fare became seasoned travellers and were no longer to be seen vomiting out of the windows as the truck lurched along. In fact it became an accepted part of daily life – rather like the plane, it came and went, affecting few people.

But down by the airstrip, a shantytown of temporary shacks sprang up overnight with the coming of the road. Here was where all the goodies that came by truck from India were to be found: plastic snakes that wriggled, gilt hair-slides, iron buckets, saucepans and – best of all – fresh fruit and vegetables. For us foreigners, and the paid office workers, accustomed to going for weeks with nothing but potatoes and rice in the shops, it seemed like paradise. Every day more and more apples, oranges, onions, cabbages and tomatoes would make their way up the hill. There was even a rumour that ten bottles of Coca-Cola had been sighted in the bazaar.

One morning, as I was eyeing a big plastic bucket full of huge Indian tomatoes in a local shop, a woman pulled my arm. "Don't you want to buy mine?" she asked. And there, in her *doko*, were a few handfuls of the small green local tomatoes. Just a fortnight earlier I would have followed her eagerly, begging to be allowed to buy some. Now the shopkeeper laughed at her: who would want to buy little sour green tomatoes when there were big sweet red ones to be had? For women like her, trudging in for miles from one of the surrounding villages to sell her few vegetables, there was no longer a market. The influential bazaar shopkeepers negotiated deals with the Indian traders with their truckloads of vegetables. The new road meant new money for the shopkeepers – but less for the poor, whose livelihood was undermined and who had no way of buying the wonderful new merchandise.

There were other casualties, too. Gaggles of poor women, who had made a living out of carrying people's baggage from the airstrip to the bazaar, were once a common sight, haggling in angry, spirited voices over the price of their services. Ragged and downtrodden at the best of times, these women were reduced to silently and gratefully accepting any rate people were prepared to pay for their help.

I began to wonder about the road. But I needn't have worried. Soon the monsoon rains arrived and the swelling river took charge of things. Within days the bridge was completely washed away, leaving several trucks stranded on the wrong side of the river, never to return to India. The original truck continued to creak up and down the winding road between the airstrip and the bazaar, its fuel being hoisted across the river by rope-pulley, but became so overcrowded that one day it broke down halfway up the hill. As the road had been almost completely washed away by the rain, it was simply left there in the middle of the road.

When the monsoon ended, the truck was overgrown with creepers and made a very pleasant home for a local family. By then the grand new road was little more than a memory. The women porters went back to climbing regularly up and down the hill; the shantytown vanished as quickly as it had appeared; and everyone went back to eating rice and potatoes as before. Last I heard, a foreign-aid agency had decided to rebuild the road, with a proper bridge this time: in the interests of development.

Anna Robinson-Pant

Anna Robinson-Pant worked for three years as a VSO volunteer in Doti District, in the far western hills. Reproduced by permission of New Internationalist Publications ®www.newint.org.

has been borrowed for a spot of home improvement. Paths remain vital in most parts of Nepal, and footbridges put villagers within easier reach of jobs, health facilities and markets. Where funds don't allow for a bridge, there's always **the** *tar pul* or "wire bridge", a human-powered gondola that travels along a set of suspended wires.

Education

Education is one of Nepal's relative success stories: the result, perhaps, of how well respected it is in Nepali culture: "book is god", as the saying goes. The system has certainly come a long way in a short time: before 1951 schools only existed for the children of the ruling elite, and two percent of the population was literate. There are now government primary schools within walking distance of most villages, and secondary schools in most areas of denser population, and **literacy** has soared to 58 percent.

Of course, that's still an appalling figure by international standards. **Government schools** are chronically underfunded, especially in rural areas. Teachers may be unqualified, poorly trained, underpaid or simply absentee. Classes regularly number eighty or more, and are held in rooms with mud floors and no glazing. Toilet facilities, if they exist at all, are execrable – a major factor in putting children off school. Blackboards are sometimes made by scraping the insides of used batteries on old bits of wood. There are rarely enough benches, let alone desks – even though many children will be off school on any given day due to illness, the need for their labour in the fields, or lack of funds to buy a book or pen, or to find the modest subscription fee.

In these conditions it's no surprise that while three-quarters of young Nepalis now attend primary school, around half fail to finish. Girls and disadvantaged castes make up the bulk of the drop-outs. Secondary attendance is under a third, and many rural secondaries fail to get even one of their final-year students through their School Leaving Certificate (SLC). As a result, any family that can afford it sends its children away to one of the legion of private "**English medium**" boarding schools which have sprung up in the cities and towns, teaching in the English language. Those who make it to one of Nepal's **colleges** or **universities** often find that there's no work for them when they graduate. Frustrated by a lack of opportunities or just plain bored, the educated youth of the cities make up a growing class of angry young men.

Women, children and Dalits

Three groups in Nepal – women, children and Dalits ("untouchables") – have particularly low status, making them exceptionally vulnerable to exploitation. Rural women may still be considered their husband's or father's chattel. They work far harder than men, by and large: rising before dawn to clean the house, doing the hardest fieldwork and all of the cooking. Women wait for men to finish eating before they begin. Typically married off in their teens, women are often subject to institutionalized **domestic violence**. In orthodox Baahun families, low status is underpinned by religious sanction: the touch of a menstruating woman, for example, is considered as polluting as that of an untouchable. The status of women is generally slightly higher among the ethnic groups of the hills, and considerably so among Buddhists and in wealthy urban families, but even these women rarely enjoy true power-sharing.

It's estimated that each year, between five thousand and ten thousand Nepali girls and women – twenty percent of them under the age of sixteen – are **trafficked** into sexual slavery in India, where patrons prize them for their beauty and supposed lack of inhibition. To poor Hindu families in Nepal, a daughter is a serious financial burden; when a broker comes offering thousands of rupees for a pubescent girl, many agree. This trade is most pronounced in the central hills, where it has historical roots: Tamang girls were forced to serve as court concubines for generations. A sex worker may eventually buy her freedom, but few escape without acquiring HIV or are able to return to their home communities.

One solution to women's low status is to boost education and earning power. Two very successful efforts, the Bangladesh-based Grameen Bank and the Nepalese government's Production Credit for Rural Women programme, make **microcredit loans** to small, self-organizing groups of women, and support the borrowers with literacy, family-planning and other training. Another route is political. Legally, the position of women has vastly improved in recent years, with the **Maoists** being particularly vociferous about improving the status of women; female involvement in the insurgency has presented Nepal with a new and perhaps salutary image of women's empowerment.

However much their parents love them, children in poor families are counted as an economic resource from an early age. **Child labour** has always been essential in agriculture, and despite laws barring employment of anyone of fourteen or under, over half of all Nepali children between six and fourteen work. They are often porters, domestic servants and labourers in the carpet, brick and construction industries – menial or hazardous jobs, by and large – and some are forced into the sex trade. Children working in domestic service are also at risk of **sexual abuse**, and there are cases of foreign paedophiles preying on Kathmandu's numerous – and exceptionally vulnerable – **street children**.

Dalits – Nepal's "untouchables" (see p.434) – are still held back by poverty, lack of education and flagrant discrimination. Thanks in part to Maoist pressure, the Constitutional Assembly has taken significant steps to improve political representation, but it is unlikely that this kind of imposed political solution can quickly change attitudes at village level. The pre-Maoist democratic government did act dramatically in 2000 to free the **kamaiyas** (bonded labourers), victims of a system of indentured servitude prevalent in the mid- and far west. Unfortunately, it failed to accompany the liberation with any policy on land redistribution or job training, with the result that most *kamaiyas* found themselves suddenly homeless and jobless.

Industry and trade

Agriculture simply cannot absorb the country's growing workforce, and unemployment and underemployment are rife. Nepal also desperately needs to earn foreign exchange to pay for the imported technology and materials it needs for development. All of this means boosting **industry**, which in Nepal's case accounts for an unusually low proportion of gross domestic product.

Nepal has three religions, goes the saying: Hinduism, Buddhism and **tourism**. The latter is Nepal's top foreign-exchange earner (not counting massive remittances from **migrant workers**), the half-million-odd tourists bringing in some $250 million a year, and giving work to hundreds of thousands (the exact figures are unknown). The government hopes to attract a million tourists in **Visit Nepal Year**, proposed for 2011. But these numbers are not sustainable, and all tourism jobs tend to be both seasonal and intensely vulnerable to economic and political downturns. The fruits of tourism, so arbitrarily awarded, have turned legions of Nepalis into panhandlers, in much the same way that aid has done to politicians and institutions. And while tourism can claim some credit for shaping Nepal's environmental record, it has imposed its own ecological and cultural costs. Independent trekking may encourage tourists to spend money at the local level in rural areas, but it has placed an environmental strain on the fragile "honeypot" areas in the mountains.

Other countries in the region have used their low wages and high unemployment to attract the sweatshops of Western brand-name companies. Without a seaport, Nepal can't even do that. It achieved surprising success in the 1990s, however, with **carpet manufacture**, though volumes have since fallen due to quality-control problems, bad PR over child labour, saturation of the market and political instability. **Pashmina** (cashmere) items have seen similar rises and falls. Readymade **clothes** and **shoes**, by contrast, seem to be on the up. Beer and cigarettes, curiously enough, are two other success stories, alongside the more prosaic bricks and cement, and agricultural products like sugar and Himalayan **medicinal herbs** and essential oils – in which there is a thriving illegal market.

In many other industries, Nepal finds itself in a classic Third World bind. Even if it could fairly access external markets, it can't compete with high-volume market leaders in manufacture. But importing even modest amounts of high-value items quickly runs up a nasty trade deficit. The government therefore subsidizes the production of run-of-the-mill goods for domestic consumption, according to the economic theory of **import substitution**: for a country short on foreign exchange, a penny saved is a penny earned.

Nepal's main trading partner, India, is part of the problem as much as the solution. It levies high import duties to protect its own industries, thus benefiting Nepali border traders (who can sell imported goods for less than their Indian competitors), but crippling Nepali exporters (whose goods become uncompetitive with duty added on). The balance of power is so disproportionate that India can always present Nepal with take-it-or-leave-it **terms of trade**. Thus, when India imposed a "luxury tax" on Nepali tea leaves, it instantly pulled the rug from under the Nepali growers' market.

Kathmandu Valley problems

Solutions often create their own problems. For five decades, people have been trying to get Nepal to develop – now that it has, in the **Kathmandu Valley**, many are nervously fumbling for the "off" switch.

Kathmandu appears to be following in the footsteps of other Asian capitals, albeit on a smaller scale. Overpopulation and conflict has driven a growing **rural exodus**; new roads and bus services pull the landless poor away from their villages, while jobs in the tourism and manufacturing industries push them towards the Kathmandu Valley. Many immigrants land jobs in the big city, but there's no safety net for those who don't. They may end up squatting in the most primitive conditions imaginable – in unhealthy shacks on waste ground, in empty buildings, in the streets – and scrounging a living from the rubbish heaps or prostitution.

While poverty is a perennial problem in the valley, it's prosperity that's creating the brand-new headaches, starting with **traffic** and **pollution**. Industrial workers get to their factories by tempo or bus, while the more affluent drive their own motorbikes or cars. Goods must be moved by truck, and tourists take taxis. The result is ever-growing gridlock and an increasing smog problem from a fleet of vehicles that is doubling every six to eight years. Those who can afford to are moving out to the suburbs, and their commuting only worsens the problem. Vehicle emissions are blamed for an alarming increase in respiratory problems, which occur at twelve times the national average in Kathmandu. Health experts warn that children are particularly vulnerable to asthma, allergies and lead-related developmental problems caused by the appalling air quality. As discussed in the box on p.80, the causes of this environmental catastrophe are largely political, and require political will to solve. On the positive side, the dramatic success of electric-powered Safaa ("clean") tempos is providing a highly visible reminder that there are cleaner alternatives. Assuming there is power, that is: centralized "load shedding" ensured that half the fleet was off the road in the winter of 2008/9, as there simply wasn't time to recharge the tempos' batteries.

In Kathmandu, demand for **drinking water** vastly exceeds the supply, with the result that residents pump what water they can get up to rooftop storage tanks, and supplement it with deliveries by tanker. Leaks in underground pipes account for most of the shortfall, but development money, chasing the mega-project as ever, is all going to the controversial **Melamchi project**. The aim is to pipe water from the Helambu area northeast of the valley rim through a 27-kilometre tunnel, but the scheme is already thirteen years late, and demand is likely to have overtaken the new supply by the time it comes on tap. The project is also projected to cost more than $300 million – much of the money having leaked into politicians' pockets – and will desiccate irrigated farmland downstream of the tunnel mouth in the dry season. Citing these concerns, big donors withdrew one by one in the early 2000s; the Asian Development Bank was one of the few to stay the course, but insisted on the part-privatization of Kathmandu's water supply as a condition for its loan.

Water is not only scarce in the valley, it's also contaminated by **sewage** permeating the soil and infiltrating old, leaky pipes. Only thirty percent of the valley's sewage is properly treated, as municipal treatment plants don't operate properly. In many areas raw waste – or toxic effluents from carpet factories and the like – drains directly into rivers. **Rubbish** is another problem, and the Valley's municipalities still haven't agreed on a permanent dump: the Gokarna landfill in the Valley is full, and the "temporary" site established at Sisdol, 25km north of Kathmandu, is frequently closed off by protesting locals. Rubbish is often dumped in horrific landfills right beside the Bagmati River, or burnt, adding to air pollution.

The damage that has been done to the valley's **culture** in the name of progress is less easy to quantify, but is arguably more profound. Traditional architecture is only valued by a few. Members of the younger generation are drifting away from the religion of their parents. *Guthi* (charitable organizations) are in decline and have been forced to leave the upkeep of many temples to foreign preservationists. Tourism has robbed crafts of their ritual purpose and performance arts of their meaning. Work and schooling outside the home has loosened once-tight family ties, and the influx of strangers – especially refugees from the

Many aid workers blame Nepal's slow development on euphemistic "institutional problems". They speak of **bureaucrats** hoarding power so that project managers have to spend most of their time in Kathmandu queuing for signatures. They complain that Nepali managers settle into desk jobs in the capital, regarding field work as punishment and openly disdaining rural people. Important work is often left to untrained underlings, while managers pass their time in seminars and planning meetings. These traits aren't unique to Nepal, of course – and indeed many have been learned from aid organizations.

Nepal's gravest institutional problem is surely **corruption**. A government job with decision-making authority has long been regarded as a licence to collect "commissions". Byzantine bureaucratic procedures are devised precisely to elicit "speed money" from supplicants, opportunism being perpetuated by low salaries and, no doubt, the sight of piles of development loot. In the 1990s, the intense competition for power also **politicized** every branch of the bureaucracy: jobs were awarded on the basis of party loyalty, not merit, the appointees ordered to skim off as much as they could for the party (plus a bit for themselves) and given political cover to do so. Few scandals ever touched the elite. Since 2006, there has been little sign that the accession to power of former Maoists will change the prevailing political culture.

These institutional problems are common to most poor countries, but some may be unique to Nepal. One of Nepal's foremost anthropologists, Dor Bahadur Bista, controversially argued that along with Nepalis' beguilingly relaxed *ke garne* ("what to do?") attitude comes a crippling **fatalism**. Responsibility is supposedly passed on to higher-ups (whether a boss, an astrologer or a deity), and the relationship between present work and future goals glossed over, resulting in haphazard planning. Nepali society also values **connections** very highly. The cult of the *aafno maanche* (one's "own man'") makes it hard for minorities to advance, while the tradition of patronage ensures that loyalty is rewarded rather than skill or innovation.

Maoist conflict, including thousands of families whose homes were destroyed or requisitioned – has introduced social tensions and crime.

To an encouraging extent, valley residents are prepared to accept these problems as the price of progress: a little pollution or crime may seem a fair trade for improvements that keep children from dying and give people greater control over their lives. But, increasingly, Kathmanduites are worrying that they might have a "Silent Spring" in the making. What will be the effects on their children of growing up breathing air, drinking water and eating food that is not only contaminated with germs but also laced with chemicals and heavy metals?

The future

Many development workers succumb to periodic despair. Every solution seems to create more problems. Better health and sanitation increases population growth, for example – and will do until poverty and the status of women is addressed. In the meantime, agriculture has to be improved to feed all those new mouths, deforestation must be reversed to solve the fuel wood and fodder crisis, and industry developed. So **irrigation projects**, **roads** and **hydro-electric schemes** are needed – all requiring **foreign support**. If development is left entirely to Nepalis, **better education** is required, which means addressing the poverty that prevents children attending classes and teachers from working in rural areas.

Encouragingly, newcomers to the field tend to be the gloomiest. Older hands can see the slow successes behind the seemingly intractable problems. Literacy, life expectancy and access to healthcare are all up. **Community forests** are regreening the hills. Micro-hydro and micro-loan schemes are bringing power – real and metaphorical – into remote areas. And, most excitingly, Nepalis themselves are demanding change. **Women's groups** are combating domestic violence, alcoholism and gambling. **Environmentalists** are pioneering a renewed concern for woodland and wildlife. Activists are doing anything from building community trekking lodges and leading birdwatching walks for children to picking up litter in Kathmandu's Ratna Park – small steps, maybe, but signifying a refreshing culture of home-grown activism. For all the many problems besieging this terrifyingly young, post-monarchical republic, a smell of spring is undoubtedly in the air.

Wildlife

Nowhere in the world is there a transition of flora and fauna so abrupt as the one between the Terai and the Himalayan crest. In a distance of as little as 60km, the terrain passes from steaming jungle through monsoon rainforest and rhododendron highlands to glacial valleys and the high-altitude desert of the Himalayan rainshadow. As a result, Nepal can boast an astounding diversity of life, from rhinos to snow leopards.

Flora

Nepal's **vegetation** is largely determined by altitude and can be grouped into three main divisions. The **lowlands** include the Terai, Churia Hills and valleys up to about 1000m; the **midlands** extend roughly from 1000m to 3000m; and the **Himalayas** from 3000m to the upper limit of vegetation (typically about 5000m). Conditions vary tremendously within these zones, however: south-facing slopes usually receive more moisture, but also more sun in their lower reaches, while certain areas that are less protected from the summer monsoon – notably around Pokhara – are especially wet. In general, rainfall is higher in the east, and a greater diversity of plants can be found there.

The Terai

Most of the Terai's remaining **lowland forest** consists of **sal**, a tall, straight tree much valued for its wood – a factor which is hastening its steady removal. *Sal* prefers well-drained soils and is most often found in pure stands along the Bhabar, the sloping alluvial plain at the base of the foothills; in the lower foothills, stunted specimens are frequently lopped for fodder. In spring, its cream-coloured flowers give off a heady jasmine scent. Other species sometimes associated with *sal* include **saj**, a large tree with crocodile-skin bark; **haldu**, used for making dugout canoes; and **bauhinia**, a strangling vine that corkscrews around its victims.

The wetter **riverine forest** supports a larger number of species, but life here is more precarious, as rivers regularly flood and change course during the monsoon. **Sisu**, related to rosewood, and **khair**, an acacia, are the first trees to colonize newly formed sandbanks. **Simal**, towering on mangrove-like buttresses, follows close behind; also known as the silk-cotton tree, it produces bulbous red flowers in February, and in May its seed pods explode with a cottony material that is used for stuffing mattresses. **Palash** – the "flame of the forest" tree – puts on an even more brilliant show of red flowers in February. All of these trees are deciduous, shedding their leaves during the dry spring. Many other species are evergreen, including **bilar**, **jamun** and **curry**, an under-storey tree with thin, pointed leaves that smell just like their name.

Grasses dominate less stable wetlands. Of the fifty-plus species native to the Terai, several routinely grow to a height of eight metres. Even experts tend to pass off any tall, dense stand as "elephant grass", because the only way to get through it is on an elephant; the most common genera are *Phragmites*, *Saccharum*, *Arundo* and *Themeda*. Most grasses reach their greatest height just after the monsoon and flower during the dry autumn months. Locals cut **khar**, a medium-sized variety, for thatch in winter and early spring; the official thatch-gathering season in the Terai parks (two weeks in Jan) is a colourful occasion, although the activity tends to drive wildlife into hiding. Fires are set in March and April to burn off the old growth and encourage tender new shoots, which provide food for game as well as livestock.

The Middle Hills

The decline in precipitation from east to west is more marked in the **Middle Hills** – so much so that the dry west shares few species in common with the moist eastern hills. Central Nepal is an overlap zone where western species tend to be found on south-facing slopes and eastern ones on the cooler northern aspects.

A common tree in dry western and central areas is **chir pine** (needles in bunches of three), which typically grows in park-like stands up to about 2000m. Various **oak** species often take over above 1500m, especially on dry ridges, and here you'll also find **ainsilo**, a cousin of the raspberry, which produces a sweet, if rather dry, golden fruit in May.

Although much of the wet midland forest has been lost to cultivation, you can see fine remnants of it above Godavari in the Kathmandu Valley and around the lakes in the Pokhara Valley. Lower elevations are dominated by a zone of **katus** (*Castanopsis indica* or Nepal chestnut) and **chilaune** (*Schima wallichii*), the latter being a member of the tea family with oblong concave leaves and, in May, small white flowers. In eastern parts, several species of **laurel** form a third major component to this forest, while alder, cardamom and tree ferns grow in shady gullies.

The magical, mossy oak-rhododendron forest is still mostly intact above about 2000m, thanks to the prevalent fog that makes farming unviable at this level. **Khasru**, the predominant oak found here, has prickly leaves and is often laden with lichen, **orchids** and other epiphytes, which grow on other plants and get their nutrients directly from the air. It's estimated that more than three hundred orchid varieties grow in Nepal, and although not all are showy or scented, the odds are you'll be able to find one flowering at almost any time of year. **Tree rhododendron** (*Lali guraas*), Nepal's national flower, grows over 20m high and blooms with gorgeous red or pink flowers in March–April. Nearly thirty other species occur in Nepal, mainly in the east – the Milke Danda, a long ridge east of the Arun River, is the best place to view rhododendron, although impressive stands can also be seen between Ghodapani and Ghandrung in the Annapurna region. Most of Nepal's three hundred species of **fern** are found in this forest type, as are many medicinal plants whose curative properties are known to ayurvedic practitioners but have yet to be studied in the West. Also occurring here are **lokta**, a small bush with fragrant white flowers in spring, whose bark is pulped to make paper, and **nettles**, whose stems are used by eastern hill-dwellers to make a hard-wearing fabric.

Holly, **magnolia** and **maple** may replace oak and rhododendron in some sites. **Dwarf bamboo**, the red panda's favourite food, grows in particularly damp places, such as northern Helambu and along the trail to the Annapurna Sanctuary. **Cannabis** thrives in disturbed sites throughout the midlands.

The Himalayas

Conifers form the dominant tree cover in the **Himalayas**. Particularly striking are the forests around Rara Lake in western Nepal, where **Himalayan spruce** and **blue pine** (needles grouped in fives) are interspersed with meadows. Elsewhere in the dry west you'll find magnificent **Himalayan cedar** (*deodar*) trees, which are protected by villagers, and a species of **cypress**. Two types of **juniper** are present in Nepal: the more common tree-sized variety grows south of the main Himalayan crest (notably around Tengboche in the Everest region), while a dwarf scrub juniper is confined to northern rain-shadow areas. Both provide incense for Buddhist rites. In wetter areas, **hemlock**, **fir** (distinguished from spruce by its upward-pointing cones) and even the deciduous **larch** may be encountered.

One of the most common (and graceful) broadleafed species is **white birch**, usually found in thickets near the tree line, especially on shaded slopes where the snow lies late. Shivery **poplars** stick close to watercourses high up into the inner valleys – Muktinath is full of them – while **berberis**, a shrub whose leaves turn scarlet in autumn, grows widely on exposed sites. Trekking up the Langtang or Marsyangdi valleys you pass through many of these forest types in rapid succession, but the most dramatic transition of all is found in the valley of the Thak Khola (upper Kali Gandaki): the monsoon jungle below Ghasa gives way to blue pine, hemlock, rhododendron and horse chestnut; then to birch, fir and cypress around Tukche; then the **apricot** orchards of Marpha; and finally the blasted steppes of Jomosom.

Alpine vegetation predominates on the forest floor and in moist meadows above the tree line, and – apart from the dwarf rhododendron (some species of which give off a strong cinnamon scent and are locally used as incense) – many **flowers** found here will be familiar to European and North American walkers. There are too many to do justice to them here, but primula, buttercup, poppy, iris, larkspur, gentian, edelweiss, buddleia, columbine and sage are all common. Most bloom during the monsoon, but rhododendrons and primulas can be seen flowering in the spring and gentians and larkspurs in the autumn.

Mammals

Most of Nepal's rich **animal life** inhabits the Terai and, despite dense vegetation, is most easily observed there. Along the trekking trails of the hills, wildlife is much harder to spot due to population pressure, while very few mammals live above the tree line. The following overview progresses generally from Terai to Himalayan species, and focuses on some of the more charismatic or visible animals – anyone interested in identifying some of Nepal's 55 species of bats or eight kinds of flying squirrel will need a specialist guide.

The **Asian one-horned rhino** (*gaida*) is one of five species found in Asia and Africa, all endangered. In Nepal, about four hundred rhinos, or a quarter of the species total, live in Chitwan – down from over six hundred in 2000. Forty-eight were introduced to Bardia, but only half survived the period of instability. Rhinos graze singly or in small groups in the marshy elephant grass, where they can remain surprisingly well hidden.

Although trained **elephants** (*hatti*) are a lingering part of Nepali culture (see p.286), their wild relatives are seen only rarely in Nepal. Since they require vast territory for their seasonal migrations, the settling of the Terai is putting them in increasing conflict with man, and the few that survive tend to spend much of their time in India. About half of Nepal's elephants, some fifty animals or so, are found in Bardia.

Koshi Tappu is the only remaining habitat in Nepal for another species better known as a domestic breed, **wild buffalo** (*arnaa*), which graze the wet grasslands in small herds. Majestic and powerful, the **gaur** (*gauri gaai*), or Indian bison, spends most of its time in the dry lower foothills, but descends to the Terai in spring for water.

Perhaps the Terai's most unlikely mammals, **gangetic dolphins** – one of four freshwater species in the world – are present in small numbers in the Karnali and Sapt Koshi rivers (see box, p.329). Curious and gregarious, they tend to congregate in deep channels where they feed on fish and crustaceans, and betray their presence with a blow-hole puff when surfacing.

The most abundant mammals of the Terai, *chital*, or **spotted deer**, are often seen in herds around the boundary between riverine forest and grassland. **Hog deer** – so called because of their porky little bodies and head-down trot – take shelter in wet grassland, while the aptly named **barking deer**, measuring less than two feet high at the shoulder, are found throughout lowland and midland forests. **Swamp deer** gather in vast herds in Sukla Phanta, and males of the species carry impressive sets of antlers (their Nepali name, *barhasingha*, means "twelve points"). **Sambar**, heavy-set animals standing five feet at the shoulder, are more widely distributed, but elusive. Two species of antelope, the graceful, corkscrew-horned **blackbuck** and the ungainly **nilgai** (blue bull), may be seen at Bardia and Koshi Tappu respectively; the latter was once assumed to be a form of cattle, and thus spared by Hindu hunters, but no longer.

Areas of greatest deer and antelope concentrations are usually prime territory for the endangered Bengal **tiger** (*bagh*). However, your chances of spotting one of Nepal's hundred-odd tigers are slim: they're mainly nocturnal, never very numerous, and incredibly stealthy. In the deep shade and mottled sunlight of dense riverine forest, a tiger's orange- and black-striped coat provides almost total camouflage. A male may weigh 250kg and measure 3m from nose to tail. Tigers are solitary hunters; some have been known to consume up to twenty percent of their body weight after a kill, but they may go several days between feeds. Males and females maintain separate but overlapping territories, regularly patrolling them, marking the boundaries with scent and driving off interlopers. Some Nepalis believe tigers to be the unquiet souls of the deceased.

Leopards (*chituwa*) are equally elusive, but much more widely distributed: they may be found in any deep forest from the Terai to the timber line. As a consequence, they account for many more maulings than tigers in Nepal, and are more feared. A smaller animal (males weigh about 45kg), they prey on monkeys, dogs and livestock. **Other cats** – such as the fishing cat, leopard cat and the splendid clouded leopard – are known to exist in the more remote lowlands and midlands, but are very rarely sighted. **Hyenas** and **wild dogs** are scavengers of the Terai, and **jackals**, though seldom seen (they're nocturnal), produce an eerie howling that is one of the most common night sounds in the Terai and hills.

While it isn't carnivorous, the dangerously unpredictable **sloth bear**, a Terai species, is liable to turn on you and should be approached with extreme caution. Its powerful front claws are designed for unearthing termite nests, and its long snout for extracting the insects. The **Himalayan black bear** roams midland forests up to the tree line and is, if anything, more dangerous. **Wild boars** can be seen rooting and scurrying through forest anywhere in Nepal.

Monkeys, a common sight in the Terai and hills, come in two main varieties in Nepal. Comical **langurs** have silver fur, black faces and long, ropelike tails; you'll sometimes see them sitting on stumps like Rodin's *Thinker*. Brown **rhesus macaques** are more shy in the wild, but around temples are tame to the point of being nuisances. Many other **small mammals** may be spotted in the hills, among them porcupines, flying squirrels, foxes, civets, otters, mongooses and martens. The **red panda**, with its rust coat and bushy, ringed tail, almost resembles a tree-dwelling fox; like its Chinese relative, it's partial to bamboo, and is very occasionally glimpsed in the cloudforest of northern Helambu.

Elusive animals of the rhododendron and birch forests, **musk deer** are readily identified by their tusk-like canine teeth; males are hunted for their musk pod, which can fetch $200 an ounce on the international market. Though by no means common, **Himalayan tahr** is the most frequently observed large mammal of the high country; a goat-like animal with long, wiry fur and short horns, it browses along steep cliffs below the tree line. **Serow**, another goat relative, inhabits remote canyons and forested areas, while **goral**, sometimes likened to chamois, occurs from middle elevations up to the tree line.

The Himalaya's highest residents are **blue sheep**, who graze the barren grass-lands above the tree line year-round. Normally tan, males go a slatey colour in winter, accounting for their name. Herds have been sighted around the Thorung La in the Annapurna region, but they occur in greater numbers north of Dhorpatan and in She-Phoksundo National Park. Their chief predator is the **snow leopard**, a secretive cat whose habits are still little understood.

Amphibians and reptiles

Native to the Terai's wetlands, crocodiles are most easily seen in winter, when they sun themselves on muddy banks to warm up their cold-blooded bodies. The endangered **mugger crocodile** favours marshes and oxbow lakes, where it may lie motionless for hours on end until its prey comes within snapping distance. Muggers mainly pursue fish, but will eat just about anything they can get their jaws around – including human corpses thrown into the river by relatives unable to afford wood for a cremation. The even more endangered **gharial crocodile** lives exclusively in rivers and feeds on fish; for more on its precarious state, see p.285.

Nepal has many kinds of **snakes**, but they are rarely encountered: most hibernate in winter, even in the Terai, and shy away from humans at other times of year. Common cobras – snake charmers' favourites – inhabit low elevations near villages; they aren't found in the Kathmandu Valley, despite their abundance in religious imagery there. Kraits and pit vipers, both highly poisonous, have been reported, as have pythons up to twenty feet long. However, the commonest species aren't poisonous and are typically less than two feet long.

Chances are you'll run into a **gecko** or two, probably clinging to a guest-house wall. Helpful insect-eaters, these lizard-like creatures are able to climb almost any surface with the aid of suction pads on their feet. About fifty species of **fish** have been recorded in Nepal, but only *mahseer*, a sporty relative of carp that attains its greatest size in the lower Karnali River, is of much interest; most ponds are stocked with carp and catfish.

Birds

Over eight hundred **bird species** – one-tenth of the earth's total – have been sighted in Nepal. The country receives a high number of birds migrating between India and central Asia in spring and autumn and, because it spans so many ecosystems, provides habitats for a wide range of year-round residents. The greatest diversity of species is found in the Terai wildlife parks, but even the Kathmandu Valley is remarkably rich in birdlife. The following is only a listing of the major categories – for the complete picture, get hold of *Birds of Nepal* (see p.465).

In the **Terai** and lower hills, raptors (birds of prey) such as ospreys, cormorants, darters, gulls and kingfishers patrol streams and rivers for food; herons and storks can also be seen fishing, while cranes, ducks and moorhens wade in or float on the water. Many of these migratory species are particularly well represented at Koshi Tappu, which is located along the important Arun Valley corridor to Tibet. Peafowl make their meowing mating call – and peacocks occasionally deign to unfurl their plumage – while many species of woodpeckers can be heard, if not seen, high up in the *sal* canopy. Cuckoos and "brain fever" birds repeat their idiotic two- or four-note songs in an almost demented fashion. Parakeets swoop in formation; bee-eaters, swifts, drongos, swallows and rollers flit and dive for insects, while jungle fowl look like chickens as Monet might have painted them. Other oddities of the Terai include the paradise flycatcher, with its lavish white tailfeathers and dragonfly-like flight; the lanky great adjutant stork, resembling a prehistoric reptile in flight; and the giant hornbill, whose beak supports an appendage that looks like an upturned welder's mask.

Many of the above birds are found in **the midlands** as well as the Terai – as are mynas, egrets, crows and magpies, which tend to scavenge near areas of human habitation. Birds of prey – falcons, kestrels, harriers, eagles, kites, hawks and vultures – may also be seen at almost any elevation. Owls are common, but not much liked by Nepalis. Babblers and laughing thrushes populate the oak-rhododendron forest and are as noisy as their names suggest. Over twenty species of flycatchers are present in the Kathmandu Valley alone.

Nepal's national bird, the iridescent, multicoloured *danphe* (impeyan pheasant), can often be spotted scuttling through the undergrowth in the Everest region. *Kalij* and *monal*, two other native pheasants, also inhabit the higher hills and lower **Himalayas**. Migrating waterfowl often stop over at high-altitude lakes – ruddy shelducks are a trekking-season attraction at Gokyo – and snow pigeons, grebes, finches and choughs may all be seen at or above the tree line. Mountaineers have reported seeing choughs at up to 8200m on Everest, and migrating bar-headed geese are known to fly *over* Everest.

Invertebrates and insects

Perhaps no other creature in Nepal arouses such squeamishness as the **leech** (*jukha*). Fortunately, these segmented, caterpillar-sized annelids remain dormant underground during the trekking seasons; during the monsoon, however, they come out in force everywhere in the Terai and hills, making any hike a bloody business. Leeches are attracted to body heat, and will inch up legs or drop from branches to reach their victims. The bite is completely painless – the blood-sucker injects a local anaesthetic and anticoagulant – and often goes unnoticed until the leech drops off of its own accord. To dislodge one, apply salt or burn it with a cigarette; don't pull it off or the wound could get infected.

Over six hundred species of **butterflies** have been recorded in Nepal, with more being discovered all the time. Although the monsoon is the best time to view butterflies, many varieties can be seen before and especially just after the rains – look beside moist, sandy banks or atop ridges; Phulchoki is an excellent place to start in the Kathmandu Valley. Notable hill varieties include the intriguing orange oakleaf, whose markings enable it to vanish into forest litter, and the golden birdwing, a large, angular species with a loping wingbeat. **Moths** are even more numerous – around five thousand species are believed to exist in Nepal, including the world's largest, the giant atlas, which has a wingspan of almost a foot.

Termites are Nepal's most conspicuous social insects, constructing towering, fluted mounds up to eight feet tall in the western Terai. Organized in colonies much the same as ants and bees, legions of termite workers and "reproductives" serve a single king and queen. The mounds function as cooling towers for the busy nest below; monuments to insect industry, they're made from tailings excavated from the colony's galleries and bonded with saliva for a wood-hard finish. **Honey bees** create huge, drooping nests in the Terai and especially in the lush cliff country north of Pokhara. **Spiders** aren't very numerous in Nepal, although one notable species grows to be six inches across and nets birds (it's not poisonous to humans). **Fireflies**, with orange and black bodies, give off a greenish glow at dusk in the Terai. For many travellers, however, the extent of their involvement with the insect kingdom will be in swatting **mosquitoes**: two genera are prevalent in the lowlands, one of them *Anopheles*, the infamous vector of malaria.

Books

Most of these books are a lot easier to come by in Nepal, and some will only be available there. Where the UK and US publishers are different, the UK publisher is given first; books published in other countries are indicated accordingly. Out of print (o/p) titles may still be found in Nepal, or in libraries back home. Books marked with the ⭐ symbol are particularly recommended.

C

CONTEXTS | Books

Travelogue

Barbara Crossette *So Close to Heaven* (Vintage). A survey of the "vanishing Buddhist kingdoms of the Himalayas", including a chapter focusing on Nepal's Tibetans, Bhotiyas and Newars.

⭐ **Harka Gurung** *Vignettes of Nepal* (Sajha Prakashan, Nepal). This vivid travelogue, illuminated by a native's insights, is one of the best books written by a Nepali in English about his country.

⭐ **Toni Hagen and Deepak Thapa** *Nepal: The Kingdom of the Himalaya* (Himal Books, Nepal). No person alive has seen as much of Nepal as Hagen, who literally surveyed the entire country in the 1950s. His ground-breaking book was first published in 1961, and revised in 1999.

⭐ **Peter Matthiessen** *The Snow Leopard* (Vintage/Penguin). Matthiessen joins biologist George Schaller in a pilgrimage to Dolpo to track one of the world's most elusive cats, and comes up with

characteristically Zen insights and magnificent writing on landscape.

Dervla Murphy *The Waiting Land* (o/p). A personal account of working with Pokhara's Tibetan refugees in 1965, written in the author's usual entertaining and politically on-the-ball style.

⭐ **Charlie Pye-Smith** *Travels in Nepal* (Penguin, o/p). A curious and surprisingly successful cross between a travelogue and a progress report on aid projects. Mixes impressionistic writing with hard facts.

Barbara J. Scot *The Violet Shyness of Their Eyes: Notes from Nepal* (Calyx, US). An American woman crash-lands in the Nepali hills; the writing strikes a nice balance between observation and introspection.

Eric Valli and Diane Summers *Caravans of the Himalaya* (o/p). A journey along the old Nepal–Tibet trade route, packaged for maximum armchair impact. The authors' *Hunting for Honey* (o/p) also made a splash.

History and politics

Dor Bahadur Bista *Fatalism and Development* (Orient Longman, India). Controversial analysis of the cultural factors that stand in the way of Nepal's development, by the country's best-known anthropologist.

Jonathan Gregson *Blood Against the Snows* (Fourth Estate, UK).

Occasionally lurid account of the royal massacre, prefaced by rather dustier diggings into the history of Nepal's monarchy.

Michael Hutt *Himalayan People's War: Nepal's Maoist Rebellion* (Indiana University Press). Has dated fast since publication in 2004, but remains one of the most detailed academic analyses of the insurrection's origins and early years.

Percival Landon *Nepal* (Ratna Pustak Bhandar, Nepal). In two volumes, this was the most comprehensive study of the country at the time (1928) and is regarded as a classic – but having been commissioned by the Maharaja, it has a distinct political bias.

John Parker *The Gurkhas* (Headline, UK). One of many books lionizing Nepal's famous Gurkha soldiers.

Michel Peissel *Tiger for Breakfast* (Time Books International, India). This biography of Boris Lissanevitch, the Russian émigré who ran Kathmandu's first tourist hotel, opens a fascinating window on 1950s Nepal.

Anirban Roy *Prachanda, The Unknown Revolutionary* (Pilgrims, Nepal). Journalistic and anecdotal account of the Maoist leader, with lots of personal as well as political background.

David L. Snellgrove *Himalayan Pilgrimage* (o/p). A classic travelogue/ anthropological account of a trip through northwestern Nepal in the 1950s.

Ludmilla Tüting and Kunda Dixit *Bikas-Binas, Development-Destruction* (Ratna Pustak Bhandar, Nepal). Dated but classic collection of articles covering the whole gamut of dilemmas arising out of development, environmental degradation and tourism.

🏃 **John Whelpton** *A History of Nepal* (Cambridge University Press). The best and most up-to-date general history of Nepal, published in 2005.

Culture and anthropology

John Burbank *Culture Shock! Nepal* (o/p). Sensitivity training for tourists, with valuable insights into social mores, religion, caste and cross-cultural relations.

Broughton Coburn *Nepali Aama: Life Lessons of a Himalayan Woman* (Adarsh Books, India). Delightful study of an earthy old Gurung woman in a village south of Pokhara. Told in her own words, and includes photos.

Monica Connell *Against a Peacock Sky* (o/p). Beautiful, impressionistic rendering of life among the *matawaali* (alcohol-drinking) Chhetris of Jumla District, capturing the subtleties of village life in Nepal.

🏃 **Hugh R. Downs** *Rhythms of a Himalayan Village* (Book Faith India). An extraordinarily sensitive synthesis of black-and-white photos, text and quotes, describing rituals and religion in a Solu village.

William P. Forbes *The Glory of Nepal: A Mythological Guidebook to the Kathmandu Valley* (Pilgrims, Nepal). A lively retelling of myths from the Nepal Mahatmya and other medieval texts, linking them to modern-day locations.

Jim Goodman *Guide to Enjoying Nepalese Festivals* (Pilgrims, Nepal). All the arcane whys and wherefores of the Kathmandu Valley's festivals: authoritative, though not very user-friendly.

Eva Kipp *Bending Bamboo, Changing Winds: Nepali Women Tell Their Life Stories* (Book Faith India). Powerful oral histories and photographs of women from all over Nepal, revealing not only the country's amazing cultural diversity but also the universal trials of being a Nepali woman.

Robert I. Levy and Kedar Raj Rajopadhyaya *Mesocosm: Hinduism* and the *Organization of a Traditional Newar City in Nepal* (University of California, US). A heavy anthropological study of Bhaktapur, but its thesis – that the city's inhabitants collectively operate a sort of well-oiled cultural and spiritual machine – is fascinating.

Kathryn S. March *If Each Comes Halfway: Meeting Tamang Women in Nepal* (Cornell, US). Fascinating oral history collected from highland, rural Tamang women, with accompanying photographs.

Rashmila Shakya and Scott Berry *From Goddess to Mortal* (Vajra, Nepal). Fascinating window into the life of a *kumari*, as told by the ex-goddess herself.

🏃 **Mary Slusser** *Nepal Mandala: A Cultural Study of the Kathmandu Valley* (o/p). A gorgeous but exorbitant two-volume set, this is the definitive study of Newar culture and religion.

Religion

🏃 **Kevin Bubriski and Keith Dowman** *Power Places of Kathmandu* (Inner Traditions, US). A collaboration by two eminent authorities on Hindu and Buddhist holy sites. Rich colour photographs are accompanied by well-researched text.

🏃 **Claudia Müller-Ebeling, Christian Rätsch and Surendra Shahi** *Shamanism and Tantra in the Himalayas* (Inner Traditions, US). Impressive on-the-ground research and superb photographs make this a magnificent production – even if it is marred by a credulous stance.

🏃 **Georg Feuerstein** *Tantra: The Art of Ecstasy* (Shambhala). Clear-sighted and readable introduction to Tantra, dispelling the usual "tantric sex" myths and offering a vision of an alternative thread in Subcontinental spirituality.

James McConnachie *The Book of Love: In Search of the Kamasutra* (Atlantic/Metropolitan). Investigates the role of sex in Hinduism, touching on Tantra, and traces how those ideas became known in the West. By one of the authors of this guide.

Axel Michaels *Hinduism Past and Present* (Princeton, US). Heavyweight, but still one of the most insightful books on Hinduism. Written by a Nepal specialist, it focuses on living practices rather than texts and mythology.

Barbara Stoler Miller (trans) *The Bhagavad-Gita* (Bantam, US). A poetic English rendering of Krishna's teaching.

Stan Royal Mumford *Himalayan Dialogue: Tibetan Lamas and Gurung Shamans in Nepal* (University of Wisconsin, US). An account of myths and rituals practised in a village along the Annapurna Circuit – fascinating, once you get past the anthropological jargon.

R.K. Narayan (trans) *The Ramayana of Valmiki* (Penguin). One of the most engaging retellings of this magnificent tale. The Clay Sanskrit Library's seven-volume version offers an elegant, high-minded (and full-length) alternative.

John Powers *Introduction to Tibetan Buddhism* (Snow Lion, US). A thorough introduction for beginners.

Robert A.F. Thurman *Essential Tibetan Buddhism* (HarperOne, US). Weaves together classic texts with modern commentary; not for beginners.

Art and architecture

Lydia Aran *The Art of Nepal* (Sahayogi, Nepal). Good overview of Nepalese religion as well as stone, metal and wood sculpture and *thangka* paintings.

Hannelore Gabriel *Jewelry of Nepal* (o/p). A thorough cataloguing of traditional highland jewellery (less coverage is given to hill and Terai styles), with lavish illustrations.

Michael Hutt *Nepal: A Guide to the Art and Architecture of the Kathmandu Valley* (o/p). An in-depth discussion of iconography, design and construction, from one of the leading scholars of Nepal.

Eva Rudy Jansen *The Book of Buddhas: Ritual Symbolism Used in Buddhist Statuary and Ritual Objects* (Binkey Kok, Neths; Motilal Banarsidass, India) and *The Book of Hindu Imagery: The Gods and Their Symbols* (Weiser, UK; New Age, India). Good introductory guides to the iconography of religious statuary.

Jnan Bahadur Sakya *A Short Description of Gods, Goddesses and Ritual Objects of Buddhism and Hinduism in Nepal* (Handicraft Association of Nepal). This extremely handy pamphlet is fairly widely available in Nepal.

Fiction and poetry

Laxmi Prasad Devkota *Muna Madan* (Nirala, Nepal). The most famous work by one of Nepal's best-loved poets recounts the tragic, almost Shakespearean tale of a young Newari trader who leaves his young wife to travel to Lhasa.

Michael Hutt (ed) *Himalayan Voices: An Introduction to Modern Nepali Literature* (University of California Press; Indian Book Company, India). An excellent survey of Nepali poetry and fiction, with some commentary.

Manjushree Thapa *The Tutor of History* (Penguin, India). Tensions build before an election in a small roadside town between Kathmandu and Pokhara. Hugely vivid evocation of politics, social mores, alcoholism and a quintessentially Nepali struggle against what appears to be fate.

Samrat Upadhyay *Arresting God in Kathmandu* (Mariner, US). This acclaimed collection of stories, written by a Nepali living in the US, takes on typically introspective Nepali themes – jealousy, self-doubt, desire, family tension. Upadhyay's debut novel, *The Guru of Love*, tells a story of disturbed domesticity against the charged atmosphere of late-1990s Kathmandu.

Natural history

Richard Grimmett, Carol Inskipp and Tim Inskipp *Birds of Nepal* (Princeton University Press). The authoritative guide. The authors have published numerous shorter guides as well.

K.K. Gurung *Heart of the Jungle* (o/p). The essential guide to Chitwan's flora and fauna, written by the former manager of *Tiger Tops Jungle Lodge*.

George Schaller *Stones of Silence: Journeys in the Himalaya* (o/p). Written by the wildlife biologist who accompanied Peter Matthiessen on his quest for the snow leopard, this book provides a detailed view of ecosystems of the high Himalayas.

Rishikesh Shaha and Richard M. Mitchell *Wildlife in Nepal* (Nirala, India). Brief but handily illustrated guide, with a fascinating section on the history of hunting in Nepal.

Colin Smith *Illustrated Checklist of Nepal's Butterflies* (Rohit Kumar, Nepal). Beautiful colour plates show nearly six hundred species.

Adrian and Jimmie Storrs *Enjoy Trees* (Book Faith, India). Great beginner's guide to the more common flora of Nepal, covering flowers as well as trees, and with sections on medicinal and religious plants.

Mountains and mountaineering

For reviews of dedicated trekking guides, see p.351.

Chris Bonington and Charles Clarke *Everest: The Unclimbed Ridge* (Thunder's Mouth). The classic story of the bold but ill-fated first attempt of Everest's fearsome Northeast Ridge in 1982.

Maurice Herzog *Annapurna* (Pimlico/Lyons). One of the greatest true adventure stories ever written, describing the search for, and first successful ascent of, an 8000-metre peak. Herzog's dreamlike description of his summit stupor and the tale of the desperate descent are riveting.

Maurice Isserman and Stewart Weaver *Fallen Giants: A History of Himalayan Mountaineering* (Yale). This authoritative overview has great insights into the culture of mountaineering in different ages, but it has to cover too many climbs to be a truly gripping read.

Jon Krakauer *Into Thin Air* (Pan/Topeka). The best-selling first-person account of the 1996 Everest tragedy reads like a whodunnit and has all the elements of high tragedy: hubris, heroism, angry mountain gods, rivalry, vanity, triumph and agony.

Sherry Ortner *Life and Death on Mt Everest: Sherpas and Himalayan Mountaineering* (Princeton, US). The great anthropologist of the Sherpas brings all her knowledge to bear on this controversial topic, weaving some amazing stories as she does so.

H. W. Tilman *Nepal Himalaya* (Pilgrims, Nepal). A chatty account of the first mountaineering reconnaissance of Nepal in 1949–51. Tilman was one of the century's great adventurers, and his writing remains fresh and witty.

Miscellaneous

Jim Duff and Peter Gormly *The Himalayan First Aid Manual* (World Expeditions, Nepal). Handy pocket-sized booklet.

Jyothi Pathak *Taste of Nepal* (Hippocrene). Authoritative, comprehensive and mouth-watering cookbook.

Andrew J. Pollard and David R. Murdoch *The High Altitude Medicine Handbook* (Book Faith India). Everything you need to know for a trek.

Language

Language

Nepali

Basic Nepali is surprisingly easy to learn, and surprisingly useful: nearly all Nepalis who deal with tourists speak English, but almost all enjoy attempts to reciprocate. Off the beaten track, a few phrases are essential, as good English is rare.

Nepali is closely related to Hindi, so Nepalis and north Indians can usually get by – and many Nepalis in the Terai speak languages that are even closer to Hindi, such as Bhojpuri and Maithili. The ethnic groups of the hills and mountains speak utterly unrelated Tibeto-Burman languages – some Rai languages are only spoken by a few thousand people within a single valley – but almost all have adopted Nepali as a lingua franca. Fortunately for foreigners, many hill people use a relatively simple form of Nepali that's easy to learn and understand. Nepali is written in the **Devanaagari** script but signs, bus destinations and so on are usually written in English (see box, p.27).

There are lots of useful **phrasebooks** available in Kathmandu; internationally the choice is limited to Lonely Planet's useful *Nepal Phrasebook*. For a full-blown **teach-yourself book**, by far the best is *Teach Yourself Nepali*, by Michael Hutt and Abhi Subedi (Teach Yourself, UK), which comes with a CD; David Matthews' *A Course in Nepali* (SOAS, UK) offers a more literary perspective.

Pronunciation

Nepali has to be transliterated from the Devanaagari script into the Roman alphabet; the resulting spellings may vary, and aren't always exactly phonetic.

a as in "alone"
aa as in "father"
b sounds like a cross between "b" and "v"
e as in "bet"
i as in "police"
j as in "just"
o as in "note"

r lightly rolled; can sound like a cross between "r" and "d"
s can sound almost like "sh"
u as in boot
w sounds like a cross between "w" and "v"
z sounds like "dj" or "dz"

Nepali has lighter accents than English, but the accent almost always goes on any syllable with "aa" in it. If there's no "aa", it usually falls on the first syllable.

Vowels

The distinction between "a" and "aa" is important. *Maa* (in) is pronounced as it looks, with the vowel stretched out and open. *Ma* (I), by contrast, sounds shorter and more closed: something like "muh" or perhaps the "mo" in "mob"; *mandir* (temple) comes out like "mundeer".

Some Nepali vowels are nasalized – to get the right effect, you have to honk nasally, rather like a French "en". Nasalized vowels aren't indicated in this book, but they're something to be aware of: listen to a Nepali say *tapaai* (you) or *yahaa* (here) – it's like saying "tapaaing" or "yahaang", but stopping just before the end.

Aspirated consonants

The combinations "ch" and "sh" are pronounced as in English, but in all other cases where an "h" follows a consonant the sound is meant to be aspirated – in other words, give it an extra puff of air. Thus *bholi* (tomorrow) sounds like b'*holi* and Thamel sounds like *T'hamel*.

chh sounds like a very breathy "ch", as in "pitch here"; almost like "tsha"

ph sometimes sounds like an "f" (as in phone) but may also be pronounced like a breathy "p" (as in haphazard)

th is pronounced as in "put here" (as in Kathmandu, not as in think)

Retroflex consonants

The sounds "d", "r" and "t" occur in two bewildering forms, dental and retroflex; to Nepali ears, English "t" falls somewhere between the two. The retroflex sound is made by rolling the tip of the tongue back towards the roof of the mouth – a classic "Indian" sound. The dental form is like saying a "d" with the tip of the tongue right up against the teeth. An obvious example of a retroflex (and aspirated) "t" is Kathmandu, which sounds a little like a breathy "Kartmandu". Rarely, retroflexion changes meaning: *saathi* means friend, but with a retroflex "th" it means sixty.

A brief guide to speaking Nepali

Greetings and basic phrases

For advice on the nuances of some of these basic phrases, see "Cultural Hints" in Basics, pp.52–55. Separate words for "please" and "thank you" are rarely used, though **dhanyebaad** is increasingly common in tourist areas. Politeness is indicated by manner and the grammatical form of the verb.

Hello, Goodbye (formal)	Namaste
Hello (very formal)	Namaskar
Thank you (very formal)	Dhanyebaad
Yes/No (It is/isn't)	Ho/Hoina
Yes/No (There is/isn't)	Chha/Chhaina
How are things?	Kasto chha? or Sanchai chha?
It's/I'm OK, fine	Thik chha or Sanchai chha
OK!/Sure thing! (informal)	La!
OK!/Sure thing! (formal)	Hos!
What's your name? (to an adult)	Tapaaiko naam ke ho?
(to a child)	Timro naam ke ho?
My name is…	Mero naam…ho
My country is…	Mero desh…ho
I don't know	Malaai thaahaa chhaina
I didn't understand that	Maile tyo bujina
Please speak more slowly	Bistaarai bolnus
Please say that again	Pheri bolnus
I speak a little Nepali	Ali ali Nepali aunchha
Pardon?	Hajur?

No thanks	Pardaina (I don't want it)
I'm sorry, excuse me	Maph garnus
Let's go	Jaun (often sounds like djam)
It was an honour to meet you	Hajur lai bhetera dherai khushi laagyo
Thank you [very much] for everything	Sabai kurako laagi [dherai] dhanyabaad
See you again	Pheri betaaula

Forms of address

Excuse me… (more polite)	O… Hajur…
Elder brother	Daai; Daajyu (said to men your age or older; more respectfully)
Elder sister	Didi (women your age or older)
Younger sister	Bahini (women or girls younger than you)
Younger brother	Bhaai (men or boys younger than you)
Father	Buwa (a man old enough to be your father)
Mother	Aama (woman old enough to be your mother)
Grandfather	Baje (old men)
Grandmother	Bajei (old women)
Shopkeeper, Innkeeper	Saahuji (male)
Shopkeeper, Innkeeper	Saahuni (female)

Basic questions and requests

Whether you're making a statement or asking a question, the word order is the same in Nepali. To indicate that you're asking, not telling, raise your voice at the end.

Do you speak English?	Tapaailaai Angreji aunchha?
Does anyone speak English?	Kasailaai Angreji aunchha?
I don't speak Nepali	Ma Nepali boldina

Is/Isn't there [a room]?	[Kothaa] chha/chhaina?
Is [a meal/tea] available?	[Khaanaa/chiya] painchha?
Is [smoking] okay?	[Curot khaane] hunchha?
Please help me	Malaai madhat garnus
Please give me…	…dinus
I'm [hungry]	Malaai [bhok] laagyo
I'm not [hungry]	Malaai [bhok] laageko chhaina
I like…[very much]	Malaai…[dherai] manparchha
I want/don't want	Malaai…chaahi nchha/chaaidaina
What's [this] for?	[Yo] ke ko laagi?
What's the matter?	Ke bhayo?
What's [this] called in Nepali?	[yas] laai Nepali maa ke bhanchha?
What does [chiya] mean?	[chiya] ke bhanchha?
Really?	Hora?
How?	Kasari?
What?	Ke?
When?	Kahile?
Where?	Kahaa?
Who?	Ko?
Why?	Kina?
Which?	Kun?

Negotiations

How much does this cost?	Esko kati parchha?
How much for a [room]?	[Rum] ko kati parchha?
Is there somewhere I can stay here?	Mero laagi basne thau chha holaa?
How many people?	Kati jana?
For [two] people	[Dui] jana ko laagi
Only one person	Ek jana maatrai
Can I see it?	Herna sakchhu?
Go away! (to a child)	Jaau!
It's very/too expensive	Dherai mahango bhayo
Is there a cheaper one?	Kunai sasto chha?
I don't need/want it	Malaai chaaidaina

I don't have any change	Masanga khudra chhaina
Please use the meter	Meter-maa jaanus
Just a moment	Ek chin (literally, "one blink")
I'll come back	Ma pharkinchhu
Good job, Well done	Kyaraamro
Don't worry	Chinta nagarnus

Directions

Where is the…?	…kahaa chha?
Where is this [bus] going?	Yo [bas] kahaa jaanchha?
Which is the way/ trail/road to…?	…jaane baato kun ho?
Which is the best way?	Kun baato raamro chha?
How far is it?	Kati taadhaa chha?
Where are you going?	Tapaai kahaa jaanuhunchha?
I'm going to…	Ma…jaanchhu
Where have you come from?	Tapaai kahaabaata aaunubhaeko? – (also means "where are you from?")
Here	Yahaa
There/Yonder	Tyahaa/Utyahaa (the "u" is drawn out on a high note to indicate a long distance)
[To the] right	Daayaa [tira]
[To the] left	Baayaa [tira]
Straight	Sidhaa
Near/Far	Najik/Taadhaa

Time

What time is it?	Kati bajyo?
What time does the bus leave?	Yo bas kati baje jaanchha?
When does this bus arrive [in Kathmandu]?	Yo bas kati baje [Kathmandu-maa] pugchha?
How many hours does it take?	Kati ghanta laagchha?
[Two] o'clock	[Dui] bajyo
[Nine]-thirty	Saadhe [nau] bajyo
[Five] past [six]	[Chha] bajera [paanch] minet gayo (formal); chha paanch (informal)
[Ten] to [eight]	[Aath] bajna [das] minet bakichha
Minute	Minet
Hour	Ghanta
Day	Din
Week	Haptaa
Month	Mahina
Year	Barsaa
Today	Aaja
Tomorrow	Bholi
Yesterday	Hijo
Now	Ahile
Later	Pachhi
Ago, Before	Pahile
Next week	Aarko haptaa
Last month	Gayeko maina
[Two] years ago	[Dui] barsa aghi
Morning	Bihaana
Afternoon	Diuso
Evening	Belukaa
Night	Raati

Nouns

Bag, Baggage	Jholaa
Bed	Khat
Blanket, Quilt	Sirak
Bus	Bas
Candle	Mainbatti
Clothes	Lugaa
Ear	Kan
Eye	Akha
Food	Khaanaa
Foot	Khutta
Friend	Saathi
Hand	Haat
Head	Taauko
Hotel/Lodge	Hotel/Laj
House	Ghar
Job, Work	Kaam
Lamp	Batti
Mattress	Dasna, ochhan
Medicine	Ausadhi
Mistake	Galti
Money	Paisaa
Mouth	Mukh
Nose	Naak
Pain	Dukhyo

Problem	Samasya
Restaurant	Resurent, bhojanalaya
Road	Baato, rod
Room	Rum, kothaa
Shoe	Jutta
Shop	Pasal
Son	Chori
Stomach	Pet
Teahouse	Chiya pasal, chiya dokan
Ticket	Tikot
Toilet	Chaarpi (rural), toilet
Town, Village	Gaaun
Trail/Main trail	Baato/mul baato

Adjectives and adverbs

One tricky thing about Nepali adjectives: the ones that describe feelings behave like nouns. Thus to express the notion "I'm thirsty", you have to say *Malaai thirkaa laagyo* (literally, "To me thirst has been felt").

A little	Alikati, thorai
A lot	Dherai
After	Pachhi
Again	Pheri
All	Sabai
Alone	Eklai
Always	Sadai
Another	Aarko
Bad	Kharaab, naraamro
Beautiful	Sundari
Best	Sabbhandaa raamro
Better	Ajai raamro
Big	Thulo
Cheap	Sasto
Clean	Safaa
Closed	Banda
Cold (person or weather)	Jaado
Cold (liquid, food)	Chiso
Difficult	Gaaro
Dirty	Phohor
Downhill	Oraallo
Early	Chaadai
Empty	Khali
Enough	Prasasta
Expensive	Mahango

Far	Taadhaa
Few	Thorai
Full (thing)	Bhari
Good	Raamro
Heavy	Garungo
Hot (person or weather)	Garam
Hot (liquid, food)	Taato
Hungry	Bhok (laagyo)
Hurt	Dhukyo
Late	Dhilo
Less	Kam
Lost	Haraayo
Loud	Charko
Many	Dherai
More (quantity)	Aru
More (degree)	Ekdum, ajai
Near(er)	Najik(ai)
Never	Kahile paani
New	Nayaa
Noisy	Halla
Often, usually	Dheraijaso
Old (thing)	Purano
Old (person)	Budho (male), Budhi (female)
Only	Maatrai
Open	Khulaa
Quick	Chitto
Pretty, good	Ramaailo
Right (correct)	Thik
Similar	Jastai
Slowly	Bistaarai
Small	Saano
Soon	Chaadai, chittai
Stolen	Choreko
Strong	Baliyo
Tasty	Mitho
Terrible	Jhur
Thirsty	Tirkha
Tired	Thakai
Too much	Atti
Uphill	Ukaalo

Verbs

The following verbs are in the infinitive form. To turn a verb into a polite command (eg, "Please sit"), just add -s

(*Basnus*); for a request, replace the *-nu* ending with just *-u*, said through the nose, almost like "*Basun?*". For an all-purpose tense, drop the *-u* ending and replace it with *-e* (eg *jaane* can mean go, going or will go, depending on the context). The easiest way to negate any verb is to put *na-* in front of it (*nabasnus, najaane*).

Arrive	Aaipugnu
Ask	Sodhnu
Buy	Kinnu
Carry	Boknu
Close	Banda garnu
Come	Aunu
Cook	Pakaaunu
Do	Garnu
Eat	Khaanu
Feel	Laagnu
Forget	Birsinu
Get	Paunu, linu
Give	Dinu
Go	Jaanu
Hear, Listen	Sunnu
Help	Madhat garnu
Hurry	Hatar garnu
Leave	Chodnu
Lie (speak untruthfully)	Jhutho bolnu
Look, See	Hernu
Need	Chaahinu
Open	Kholnu
Receive	Paunu
Rent	Bhadama linu
Rest	Aaram garnu
Run	Daudinu
Say, Tell	Bhannu
Sleep	Sutnu
Speak	Bolnu
Steal	Chornu
Stop	Roknu
Think	Bichaar garnu, sochnu
Try	Kosis garnu
Understand	Bujnu
Wait	Parkhanu
Walk	Hidnu
Want	Chahanu
Wash (face, clothes)	Dhunu
Wash (body)	Nuhaaunu

Other handy words

Most of the following words are what we would call prepositions. However, those marked with an asterisk (★) are actually postpositions in Nepali, meaning they come *after* the thing they're describing (eg, "with me" comes out *masanga*).

Above, Over, Up	Maathi*
Behind	Pachhadi*
Below, Under, Down	Talla*
Each	Pratyek
From	Baata*
In, Inside	Bhitra*
In front of	Agaadi*
Near	Najik*
Out, Outside	Bahira*
That	Tyo
This	Yo
To, Towards	Tira*
With	Sanga*
Without	Chhaina*

Numbers

Unlike the English counting system, which uses compound numbers above twenty (twenty-one, twenty-two, etc), Nepali numbers are irregular all the way up to one hundred – the following are the ones you're most likely to use. A further complication is the use of quantifying words: you have to add *wotaa* when you're counting things, *jana* when counting people. Thus "five books" is *paanch wotaa kitaab*, "three girls" is *tin jana keti*. But note these irregular quantifiers: *ek wotaa* (once) = *euta; dui wotaa* (twice) = *duita; tin wotaa* (three times) = *tintaa*.

half	aada
1	ek
2	dui
3	tin
4	chaar
5	paanch
6	chha

Nepali numbers

?	?	?	?	?	?	?	?	?	??
1	2	3	4	5	6	7	8	9	10

7	saat	25	pachhis
8	aath	30	tis
9	nau	40	chaalis
10	das	50	pachaas
11	eghaara	60	saathi
12	baara	70	sattari
13	tera	80	asi
14	chaudha	90	nabbe
15	pandra	100	ek say
16	sora	1000	ek hajaar
17	satra	first [time]	pahilo [palta]
18	athaara	second	dosro
19	unnais	third	tesro
20	bis		

Days

Sunday	Aitabar	Thursday	Bihibar
Monday	Sombar	Friday	Sukrabar
Tuesday	Mangalbar	Saturday	Sanibar
Wednesday	Budhabar		

A glossary of food terms

Basics		Dudh	Milk
		Tel	Oil
Umaaleko [paani]	Boiled [water]	Marich	Pepper (ground)
Roti	Bread	Plet	Plate
Makhan	Butter	Sahuji	Proprietor (male)
Achhaar	Chutney, Pickle	Sahuni	(female)
Chiso	Cold	Bhaat	Rice (cooked)
Paakeko	Cooked	Chaamal	Rice (uncooked)
Taareko	Deep-fried	Chiura	Rice (beaten)
Phul	Egg	Nun	Salt
Khaanaa	Food	Piro	Spicy
Kaata	Fork	Chamchaa	Spoon
Gilaas	Glass	Chini	Sugar
Taato	Hot	Bhuteko	Stir-fried
Chakku	Knife	Guliyo	Sweet

Mithaai	Sweets, Candy
Paani	Water
Dahi	Yogurt, Curd

Common Nepali dishes

Daal bhaat tarkaari	Lentil soup, white rice and curried vegetables
Dahi chiura	Curd with beaten rice
Momo	Steamed dumplings filled with meat and/or vegetables
Pakora	Vegetables dipped in chickpea-flour batter, deep fried
Samosa	Curried vegetables in fried pastry triangles
Sekuwa	Spicy, marinated meat kebab
Taareko maachhaa	Fried fish

Common Newari dishes

Chataamari	Rice-flour pizza, usually topped with minced buff
Choyila	Buff cubes fried with spices and greens
Kachila	Paté of minced raw buff meat mixed with ginger and oil
Kwati	Soup made with sprouted beans
Momocha	Small meat-filled steamed dumplings
Pancha kol	Curry made with five vegetables
Woh	Fried lentil-flour patties served plain (mai woh) or topped with minced buff (la woh) or egg (khen woh)

Common Tibetan dishes

Kothe	Fried meat or veg dumplings (momo)
Thukpa	Soup containing pasta, meat and vegetables
Tsampa	Toasted barley flour

Vegetables (Tarkaari or Saabji)

Bhanta	Aubergine(eggplant)
Simi	Beans
Gaajar	Carrot
Kaauli	Cauliflower
Chaana	Chickpeas
Dhaniyaa	Coriander (Cilantro)
Makai	Corn
Lasun	Garlic
Daal	Lentils
Chyaau	Mushroom
Pyaaj	Onion
Kerau, Matar	Peas
Alu	Potato
Pharsi	Pumpkin
Mulaa	Radish (daikon)
Palungo, Saag	Spinach, Chard, Greens
Golbheda	Tomato

Meat (maasu)

Raangaako maasu	Buffalo ("Buff")
Kukhuraako maasu	Chicken
Khasiko maasu	Goat
Bungurko maasu	Pork

Fruit (phalphul) and nuts

Syaau	Apple
Keraa	Banana
Nariwal	Coconut
Nibuwaa	Lemon
Kagati	Lime
Aaph	Mango
Suntalaa	Orange, Mandarin
Badaam (Mampale near India)	Peanut
Kismis	Raisin
Ukhu	Sugar cane

Key food phrases

A Alikati	A little
Dherai	A lot
Aarko	Another
Bil dinus!	Bill, please!
Mitho	Delicious
Pugchha!	Enough!

Malaai pugyo!	I'm full!	Sahakaari	Vegetarian
Aru	More	Ma maasu khaanaa	I don't eat meat
...dinus	Please give me ...		

A glossary of Nepali, Newari and Tibetan terms

Avalokiteshwara the bodhisattva of compassion (also known as Chenrezig)

Avatar bodily incarnation of a deity

Baahun Nepali term for the Brahman (priestly) caste

Baba holy man

Bagh tiger

Bahal (or Baha) buildings and quadrangle of a former Buddhist Newar monastery (a few are still active)

Bahil (or Bahi) Newari term for Buddhist monastery

Bajra see vajra

Bajra Yogini (or Vajra Jogini) female tantric counterpart to Bhairab

Bakshish not a bribe, but a tip in advance; alms

Ban forest

Bar banyan (fig) tree

Barahi (or Varahi) Vishnu incarnated as a boar

Bazaar commercial area or street – not necessarily a covered market

Beni confluence of rivers

Betel see paan

Bhaat cooked rice; food

Bhairab terrifying tantric form of Shiva

Bhajan hymn, hymn-singing

Bhanjyang a pass (Nepali)

Bharat India

Bhatti simple tavern, usually selling food as well as alcohol

Bhojanalaya Nepali restaurant

Bhot Tibet

Bhotiya highland peoples of Tibetan ancestry (pejorative)

Bideshi foreigner (or **gora** – "whitey")

Bidi cheap rolled-leaf cigarette

Bihar (or Mahabihar) Buddhist monastery (Sanskrit)

Bodhisattva in Mahayana Buddhism, one who forgoes nirvana until all other beings have attained enlightenment

Brahma the Hindu creator god, one of the Hindu "trinity"

Brahman member of the Hindu priestly caste (baahun in Nepali); metaphysical term meaning the universal soul

Chaitya small Buddhist monument, often with images of the Buddha at the four cardinal points

Charash hashish

Chautaara resting platform beside a trail with trees (ber and/or pipal figs) for shade

Chhang (or Chhyang) home-made beer brewed from rice or other grains

Chhetri member of the Hindu ruling or warrior caste

Chilam vertical clay pipe for smoking tobacco or ganja

Cholo traditional half-length woman's blouse

Chorten another name for a chaitya in high mountain areas

Chowk intersection/crossroads, square or courtyard (pronounced "choke")

Chulo clay stove

Daada (or Danda) ridge, often used to signify a range of connected hilltops

Damaru two-sided drum

Danphe Nepal's national bird, a pheasant with brilliant plumage

Daura Suruwal traditional dress of hill men: wraparound shirt and jodhpur-like trousers

Devi see Mahadevi

Dewal (also **Deval**, **Degu**) stepped temple platform; temple with prominent steps

Dhaara communal water tap or tank

Dhaba Indian-style fast-food restaurant

Dhaka colourful hand-loomed material made in the Nepalese hills

Dhami shaman; the word is often used interchangeably with jhankri, or even as dhami jhankri

Dharma religion (especially Buddhist); correct behaviour

Dharmsala rest house for pilgrims

Dhoka gate

Dhoti Indian-style loincloth

Dhyani Buddhas meditating figures representing the five aspects of Buddha nature

Doko conical cane basket carried by means of a headstrap

Dorje Tibetan word for vajra

Dun low-lying valleys just north of the Terai (sometimes called inner Terai, or bhitri madesh – "inner plains")

Durbar palace; royal court

Durga demon-slaying goddess

Dyochhen private "home" of a Newari deity

Dzopkio sturdy yak-cattle crossbreed; the female is called a dzum

Gaaine wandering minstrel of the western hills (ghandarba is now the preferred term)

Gaida (or **gainda**) rhinoceros

Gajur brass or gold finial at the peak of a temple

Ganesh elephant-headed god of beginnings and remover of obstacles

Ganja cannabis, marijuana

Garud Vishnu's man-bird carrier

Gaun village

Ghandarva traditional musician

Ghanta a bell, usually rung at temples as a sort of "amen"

Ghat riverside platform for worship and cremations; any waterside locality

Ghazal crooning, poetic, sentimental form of Indian music

Gidda vulture; Nepali slang for Israeli

Gompa Buddhist monastery (Tibetan)

Goonda hooligan, thug

Gupha cave

Gurkhas Nepali soldiers who serve in special regiments in the British and Indian armies

Guthi Newari benevolent association that handles funeral arrangements, temple maintenance, festivals, etc

Hanuman valiant monkey king in the Ramayana

Hatti elephant

Himal massif or mountain range with permanent snow

HMG His Majesty's Government As was

Jaand (or **Jaar**) Nepali word for chhang

Jaatra festival

Janai sacred thread worn over left shoulder by high-caste (Baahun and Chhetri) Hindu men

Jhankri shaman, or medicine man, of the hills

Jyapu member of the Newari farming caste

Kali the mother goddess in her most terrifying form

Karma the soul's accumulated merit, determining its next rebirth

Kata white scarf given to lamas by visitors

Khat a litter or platform on which a deity is carried during a festival

Khola stream or river

Khukuri curved knife carried by most Nepali hill men

Kora circumambulation or pilgrimage around a Buddhist monument

Kot fort (pronounced "coat")

Krishna one of Vishnu's avatars, a hero of the Mahabharat

Kumari a girl worshipped as the living incarnation of Durga

Kund pond, water tank

La pass (Tibetan)

Lakh 100,000

Lakshmi consort of Vishnu, goddess of wealth

Lali Guraas tree rhododendron

Lama Tibetan Buddhist priest or high-ranking monk

Lek mountain range without permanent snow

Linga (or **Lingam**) the phallic symbol of Shiva, commonly the centrepiece of temples and sometimes occurring in groups in the open

Lokeshwar see Avalokiteshwara

Lokta traditional Nepali paper made from the bark of an indigenous shrub

Lungi brightly coloured wrap skirt worn by hill women

Machaan watchtower used by Terai farmers to ward off wild animals

Machhendranath rain-bringing deity of the Kathmandu Valley; also known as Karunamaya or Bunga Dyo

Mahabharat (or **Mahabharata**) Hindu epic featuring Krishna and containing the Bhagavad Gita

Mahabharat Lek highest range of the Himalayan foothills

Mahadev "Great God", an epithet for Shiva

Mahadevi the mother goddess

Mahayana form of Buddhism followed in Nepal, Tibet and East Asia; follows deities, saints and teachers

Mahout elephant handler

Mai common name for any local protector goddess

Mandala mystical diagram, meditation tool

Mandap pavilion

Mandir temple

Mani stone stone inscribed with the mantra Om mani padme hum

Mantra religious incantation

Maobaadi Maoist

Masaala spice; any mixture (thus masaala films, with their mixture of drama, singing, comedy, etc)

Math Hindu priest's home

Mela religious fair or gathering

Nadi river

Nag snake deity or spirit, believed to have rain-bringing powers

Nagar city

Nak female yak

Namaste polite word of greeting

Nandi Shiva's mount, a bull

Narayan common name for Vishnu

Nath "Lord"

Nirvana in Buddhism, enlightenment and release from the cycle of rebirth

Om Mani Padme Hum the mantra of Avalokiteshwara, roughly translating as "Hail to the jewel in the lotus"

Paan mildly addictive mixture of areca nut and lime paste, wrapped in a leaf and chewed, producing blood-red spit

Padma Sambhava alias Guru Rinpoche, the eighth-century saint who brought Buddhism to Tibet

Pahaad hill, or the area of Nepal also known as the Middle Hills; hence pahaadi, hill person

Panchaayat council or assembly, the basis for Nepal's pre-democratic government

Pandit Hindu priest

Parbat mountain

Parbati (or **Parvati**) Shiva's consort

Pashmina Nepali equivalent of cashmere

Pati open shelter erected as a public resting place

Phanit elephant driver

Phedi foot (of a hill, pass, etc)

Pipal holy fig (*ficus religiosa*); also known as bodhi, the tree under which Buddha attained enlightenment

Pokhari pond, usually man-made

Poubha Newari-style scroll painting

Prasad food consecrated after being offered to a deity

Puja an act of worship

Pujari Hindu priest or caretaker of a particular temple

Pul bridge

Raksi distilled spirit

Ram (or **Rama**) mortal avatar of Vishnu, hero of the Ramayana

Ramayana popular Hindu epic in which Sita, princess of Janakpur, is rescued by Ram and Hanuman

Rath chariot used in religious processions

Rinpoche "precious jewel": title given to revered lamas

Rudraksha furrowed brown seeds, prized by Shaivas

Sadhu Hindu ascetic or holy man

Sahib honorific term given to male foreigners, pronounced "sahb"; women are called memsahib

Sajha cooperative

Sal tall tree of the Terai and lower hills, valued for its timber

Sanyasin (or **Sunyasan**) Hindu who has renounced the world, usually in old age

Sarangi Nepali four-stringed violin

Saraswati Hindu goddess of learning and the arts

Sati (or **Suttee**) practice of Hindu widows throwing themselves on their husbands' funeral pyres

Sattal public rest house

Shaiva member of the cult of Shiva (pronounced "Shaib")

Shakti in Hindu tantra, the female principle that empowers the male; the mother goddess in this capacity

Shaligram fossil-bearing stones found in the Kali Gandaki River, revered by Vaishnavas

Sherpa man from one of Nepal's highland ethnic groups, originally; sometimes (incorrectly) used by foreigners to mean any Nepali guide or climber A woman is a **Sherpani**

Shikra (or **Shikhara**) Indian-style temple, shaped like a square bullet

Shiva "the destroyer", one of the Hindu "trinity" – a god of many guises

Shivalaya one-storey Shiva shrine containing a linga

Shradha prescribed rites performed after a death

Shri an honorific prefix

Sindur red mark on the parting of married women

Sirdar Nepali trek leader

Sita Ram's wife, princess of Janakpur, heroine of the Ramayana

STOL "Short Takeoff And Landing" (read "hair-raising") landing strip

Stupa large dome-shaped Buddhist monument, usually said to contain holy relics

Tal (or **Taal**) lake

Tantra esoteric path to enlightenment, a major influence on Nepali Hinduism and Buddhism

Tara Buddhist goddess; female aspect of Buddha nature

Tashi Delek Tibetan for welcome, namaste

Tempo three-wheeled scooter; also called autoriksha, tuk-tuk

Thangka Buddhist scroll painting

Tika auspicious mark made of rice, abhir powder and curd, placed on the forehead during puja or festivals or before making a journey

Tol neighbourhood

Tola traditional unit of weight (115g); precious metals are sold by the tola, as is hashish

Topi traditional Nepali brimless hat, either black (called Bhadgaonle) or multicoloured (dhaka)

Torana elaborate wooden carving, or metal shield, above a temple door

Torma dough offerings made by Buddhist monks

Trisul the trident, a symbol of Shiva

Tudikhel parade ground

Tulku reincarnation of a late great teacher in the Tibetan Buddhist tradition

Vaishnava follower of the cult of Vishnu (pronounced "Baishnab")

Vajra sceptre-like symbol of tantric power (pronounced "bajra")

Vajracharya Buddhist Newari priest

Vajrayana "Thunderbolt Way": tantric Buddhism

Vedas the oldest Hindu scriptures (pronounced "Bed" by Nepalis); hence Vedic gods

Vipassana ancient and austere Buddhist meditation practice

Vishnu "the preserver", member of the Hindu "trinity", worshipped in ten main incarnations (pronounced "Bishnu")

Yangsi reincarnated successor of a Tibetan lama

Yoni symbol of the female genitalia, usually carved into the base of a linga

Stay In Touch!

Subscribe to Rough Guides' FREE newsletter

News, travel issues, music reviews, readers' letters and the latest dispatches from authors on the road. If you would like to receive roughnews, please send us your name and address:

UK and Rest of World: Rough Guides, 80 Strand, London, WC2R 0RL, UK
North America: Rough Guides, 4th Floor, 345 Hudson St,
New York NY10014, USA
or email: newslettersubs@roughguides.co.uk

Small print and
Index

A Rough Guide to Rough Guides

Published in 1982, the first Rough Guide – to Greece – was a student scheme that became a publishing phenomenon. Mark Ellingham, a recent graduate in English from Bristol University, had been travelling in Greece the previous summer and couldn't find the right guidebook. With a small group of friends he wrote his own guide, combining a highly contemporary, journalistic style with a thoroughly practical approach to travellers' needs.

The immediate success of the book spawned a series that rapidly covered dozens of destinations. And, in addition to impecunious backpackers, Rough Guides soon acquired a much broader and older readership that relished the guides' wit and inquisitiveness as much as their enthusiastic, critical approach and value-for-money ethos.

These days, Rough Guides include recommendations from shoestring to luxury and cover more than 200 destinations around the globe, including almost every country in the Americas and Europe, more than half of Africa and most of Asia and Australasia. Our ever-growing team of authors and photographers is spread all over the world, particularly in Europe, the USA and Australia.

In the early 1990s, Rough Guides branched out of travel, with the publication of Rough Guides to World Music, Classical Music and the Internet. All three have become benchmark titles in their fields, spearheading the publication of a wide range of books under the Rough Guide name.

Including the travel series, Rough Guides now number more than 350 titles, covering: phrasebooks, waterproof maps, music guides from Opera to Heavy Metal, reference works as diverse as Conspiracy Theories and Shakespeare, and popular culture books from iPods to Poker. Rough Guides also produce a series of more than 120 World Music CDs in partnership with World Music Network.

Visit www.roughguides.com to see our latest publications.

Rough Guide travel images are available for commercial licensing at www.roughguidespictures.com

Rough Guide credits

Text editor: Emma Gibbs, Helen Ochyra & James Smart
Layout: Sachin Tanwar
Cartography: Maxine Repath & Jasbir Sandhu
Picture editor: Mark Thomas
Production: Rebecca Short
Proofreader: Stewart Wild
Cover design: Chloë Roberts
Photographer: Tim Draper
Editorial: Ruth Blackmore, Andy Turner, Keith Drew, Edward Aves, Alice Park, Lucy White, Jo Kirby, Natasha Foges, Róisín Cameron, Emma Traynor, Kathryn Lane, Christina Valhouli, Monica Woods, Mani Ramaswamy, Harry Wilson, Lucy Cowie, Amanda Howard, Lara Kavanagh, Alison Roberts, Joe Staines, Peter Buckley, Matthew Milton, Tracy Hopkins, Ruth Tidball; **Delhi** Madhavi Singh, Karen D'Souza, Lubna Shaheen
Design & Pictures: **London** Scott Stickland, Dan May, Diana Jarvis, Nicole Newman, Sarah Cummins, Emily Taylor; **Delhi** Umesh Aggarwal, Ajay Verma, Jessica Subramanian, Ankur Guha, Pradeep Thapliyal, Anita Singh, Nikhil Agarwal, Sachin Gupta
Production: Vicky Baldwin

Cartography: **London** Ed Wright, Katie Lloyd-Jones; **Delhi** Rajesh Chhibber, Ashutosh Bharti, Rajesh Mishra, Animesh Pathak, Karobi Gogoi, Alakananda Bhattacharya, Swati Handoo, Deshpal Dabas
Online: **London** George Atwell, Faye Hellon, Jeanette Angell, Fergus Day, Justine Bright, Clare Bryson, Aine Fearon, Adrian Low, Ezgi Celebi, Amber Bloomfield; **Delhi** Amit Verma, Rahul Kumar, Narender Kumar, Ravi Yadav, Debojit Borah, Rakesh Kumar, Ganesh Sharma, Shisir Basumatari
Marketing & Publicity: **London** Liz Statham, Niki Hanmer, Louise Maher, Jess Carter, Vanessa Godden, Vivienne Watton, Anna Paynton, Rachel Sprackett, Libby Jellie, Laura Vipond, Vanessa McDonald; **New York** Katy Ball, Judi Powers, Nancy Lambert; **Delhi** Ragini Govind
Manager India: Punita Singh
Reference Director: Andrew Lockett
Operations Manager: Helen Phillips
PA to Publishing Director: Nicola Henderson
Publishing Director: Martin Dunford
Commercial Manager: Gino Magnotta
Managing Director: John Duhigg

Publishing information

This sixth edition published October 2009 by
Rough Guides Ltd,
80 Strand, London WC2R 0RL
14 Local Shopping Centre, Panchsheel Park, New Delhi 110017, India
Distributed by the Penguin Group
Penguin Books Ltd,
80 Strand, London WC2R 0RL
Penguin Group (USA)
375 Hudson Street, NY 10014, USA
Penguin Group (Australia)
250 Camberwell Road, Camberwell, Victoria 3124, Australia
Penguin Group (Canada)
195 Harry Walker Parkway N, Newmarket, ON, L3Y 7B3 Canada
Penguin Group (NZ)
67 Apollo Drive, Mairangi Bay, Auckland 1310, New Zealand
Cover concept by Peter Dyer.

Typeset in Bembo and Helvetica to an original design by Henry Iles.
Printed in Singapore
© David Reed & James McConnachie 2009
No part of this book may be reproduced in any form without permission from the publisher except for the quotation of brief passages in reviews.
496pp includes index
A catalogue record for this book is available from the British Library
ISBN: 978-1-84836-138-6
The publishers and authors have done their best to ensure the accuracy and currency of all the information in **The Rough Guide to Nepal**, however, they can accept no responsibility for any loss, injury, or inconvenience sustained by any traveller as a result of information or advice contained in the guide.

1 3 5 7 9 8 6 4 2

Help us update

We've gone to a lot of effort to ensure that the sixth edition of **The Rough Guide to Nepal** is accurate and up-to-date. However, things change – places get "discovered", opening hours are notoriously fickle, restaurants and rooms raise prices or lower standards. If you feel we've got it wrong or left something out, we'd like to know, and if you can remember the address, the price, the hours, the phone number, so much the better.

Please send your comments with the subject line "**Rough Guide Nepal Update**" to ©mail @roughguides.com. We'll credit all contributions and send a copy of the next edition (or any other Rough Guide if you prefer) for the very best emails.
Have your questions answered and tell others about your trip at
® community.roughguides.com

ROUGH GUIDES

SMALL PRINT

Acknowledgements

James would especially like to thank: David Reed, the original author of this guide; Arnaud Galent, Emily Haslam-Jones and Shafik Meghji, for all their work on the road; Keith Drew, Emma Gibbs, Maxine Repath and Jasbir Sandhu, Mark Thomas and especially James Smart, at Rough Guides; Tim Draper, for his fine photography; David Allardice and Peter Stewart, for their invaluable rafting and biking expertise; Ramesh Chaudhary, for his excellent researches and trekking expertise; BK Shrestha and family, for advice and friendship in Kathmandu; and Alice and Florence McConnachie, for holding the fort.

Shafik would like to thank the many locals and travellers who helped out along the way. A special *dhanyabaad* must go to: James McConnachie, Emily Haslam-Jones and Arnaud Galent for their help, recommendations and company; James Smart and Helen Ochyra for their support and advice; Narbikram Thapa from Oxfam; Sushila Subba and family for their help and hospitality; DB Gurung from KEEP; Sunil Sharma from the Nepal Tourism Board; Pankaj Lama from Wayfarers; Paul Stevens from SNV; Sam Voolstra and all the staff at the *Last Resort*; Yogesh Adhikari from River Bank Inn for his invaluable help in Chitwan; Santosh Pokhrel and everyone at *Forest Hideaway*, without whom the Bardia section would not have been the same; Sophia K Tamot from Care International; Mads

Mathiasen for his insider's tour of Lazimpath; Rameshwar Nepal from Amnesty International Nepal; Cait Grant for her bungy stories and astrology insights; and Jean, Nizar and Nina Meghji for their love and support.

The authors would also like to thank: Lekha Nath Bhandari (Ample Travels), Anish Bhatta, Steve Berry, Helen Cawley (Tengboche Development Project), Wendy Cue, Keith Curtis, Binod Dhungel, Dr Jim Duff (International Porter Protection Group), Tulsi Ghimire, D.B. Gurung (KEEP Nepal), Steve Harbert (Mountain Kingdoms), Michael Hutt, Tek Khakurel, Tashi Lama, Rhicha Maharjan (Pilgrim's Book House), Tracy Martin, Sharmila Mulepati (Pagoda Guesthouse), Ganga Nepali (Nirvana Treks), Khagendra Nepali, Jitendra Raut, Dadi Ram Sapkota, Sharad Singh, Tinus Smits, Rabi Sthapit, "The Three Sisters", Mahendra Thapa, Sam Voolstra and Jennifer White.

Emily would like to thank: Adams Travels in Pokhara who helped on the fine checking of some details, The 3 Sisters and their wonderful staff (in Pokhara, too) for their information on trek routes, and my dear friend Isabelle Onians who put us in touch with James in the first place to make the whole thing possible. And, of course, to the great work and dedication of the other writers, Shaf and James and my beloved Arnaud.

Readers' letters

Thanks to all the readers who have taken the time to write in with comments and suggestions (and apologies if we've inadvertently omitted or misspelt anyone's name):

Lucía Álvarez de Toledo, Dagmar Ananou, Prakash Basel, William Batten, Rebecca Bell and David Williams, Nigel Bellamy, Scott Berry, Kerry Bowler, Pat Douglas, Ulrike von Duering, Heiner Engellandt, Ursula Fleckenstein-Lukas, Isla Glaister, Dr. Winfried van Gool, Jane Hollowell, Tony Jones, Emyr Kerfoot, Melanie Loake, Claire Martin, Dan McTiernan and Johanna Jalonen, Melinda McCall, Bob and Linda Miller, Pascale Newcombe, Marcus Andrew Norman, Susan Phillips, Jason Pilley and Yuka Mizuno, Angela Pitt, Kiersten Rowland, Mary Ryan, Sonja Schuffert, Nita Shah, Graham Tillotson, Nick Trautmann, Duncan Warne, Darna Weinstein, Jayne Wise.

Photo credits

All photos © Rough Guides except the following:

Things not to miss
09 Shivaratri festival © Robert Harding/Alamy
11 Dashain festival © Morten Svenningsen/Alamy

Pace of change colour section
Remote high altitude airstrip, Luka © Herman du Plessis/Getty Images
Truck on snowy mountain road © Imagebroker/Alamy

People of Nepal colour section
Rana Tharu peoples in traditional dress © Bruno Morandi/Getty Images

Black and whites
p.322 Border gate in Birgunj © Fredrich Stark/Alamy
p.406 Mountain biking in the Pokhara Valley © O.Weidemann/Commencal

Index

Map entries are in colour.

C

INDEX

INDEX

Map symbols

maps are listed in the full index using coloured text

-----	International boundary		★	Bus stop
----	Chapter boundary		◆	Point of interest
- - - -	National Park boundary		☀	Viewpoint
=====	Major road		♦	Museum
===	Minor road		⚑	Golf course
▬▬▬	Steps		■	Tower
▬•▬•▬	Railway		⊙	Statue
———	Unpaved road		⊤	Fountain
- - - - -	Path		⊠	Gate
———	Waterway		E	Embassy
———	Wall		⋀	Campsite
———	Ridge line		⊞	Hospital
⁙⁙⁙⁙⁙⁙	Hill		ⓘ	Information office
‿‿	Pass		⊠	Post office
⌂	Cave		◉	Accommodation
▲	Mountain peak		■	Restaurant
⌁	Mountain range		•—•	Cable car
⌁⌁⌁	Cliffs		▬	Building
✈	International airport		▦	Park/forest
✗	Domestic airport/airstrip		▢	Beach